THE
Backgrounds
OF
Shakespeare's Plays

KARL J. HOLZKNECHT

New York University

AMERICAN BOOK COMPANY

New York   Cincinnati   Chicago   Boston   Atlanta   Dallas   San Francisco

Holzknecht: THE BACKGROUNDS OF SHAKESPEARE'S PLAYS

PREFACE

As its title implies, *The Backgrounds of Shakespeare's Plays* is concerned with both the playwright's art and what lies behind it—the social, literary, theatrical, and philosophical antecedents which determine to a marked degree the modern reader's appreciation, understanding, and even prejudices about Shakespeare. This book is not an attempt to pluck out the heart of Shakespeare's mystery; more modestly it is merely a combination biography and critical handbook to Shakespeare's dramatic work, written for the student and the general reader who wants to know as well as to appreciate. It aspires to be simply a factual and an imaginative guide on a great adventure. The early chapters are concerned with William Shakespeare as an Elizabethan playwright, writing Elizabethan plays, for production in the Elizabethan manner, by Elizabethan actors, in an Elizabethan playhouse, before an Elizabethan audience. The later chapters, by tracing Shakespeare's after-fame, attempt to show how his plays have become something more as each succeeding age has accepted his works as contemporary and left the mark of its appreciation as a kind of patina around them.

A glance at the analytical table of contents will reveal an approach which is both historical and critical. What we really know about Shakespeare's life is here separated from what we merely surmise and is thus freed from the incrustation of speculation and ingenious deduction with which even the best biographies of the dramatist are inflated. The stirring age which produced Shakespeare is described in some of its more important social and cultural aspects, with especial emphasis upon the playwright's relation to them. Several chapters are concerned with the dramatic and theatrical traditions Shakespeare accepted and shared with his contemporaries; the conditions, social and professional, under which his work was first produced; and the importance of the Elizabethan stage, company, and audience to the playwright. The language Shakespeare used is discussed as a living, plastic medium, colored by the life, the thought, and the culture of his age. A chapter on

·[iii]·

Shakespeare's reading is concerned with something beyond mere source identification; it deals primarily with Shakespeare's use of his source materials, his perception of dramatic values in old stories, and his originality in developing what he appropriated. Another series of chapters treats both general aspects of Shakespeare's dramatic technique and his conceptions of the several arts of comedy, history, and tragedy, the great categories into which, since the publication of the First Folio, his plays have been divided. Finally, a chapter on how Shakespeare got into print introduces a series of discussions of Shakespeare's reputation—among the critics, on the stage, and in pictorial art.

Of necessity the book must deal with antiquarian and technical matters, yet it seeks to present such lore not for itself alone but in terms of the significance it has for Shakespeare's art. Always the author has sought an answer to the students' thoroughly justified question, "So what?"

Written and rewritten over a period of years, these chapters have been thoroughly tried out before being finally set down. They were thought out originally as lectures and discussions, and in consequence they retain much of the informal style of the classroom. But this book is not merely a new synthesis of what was well-known before; it is based upon long and careful first-hand study as well. Yet, in the nature of the case the author has placed the whole literature of Elizabethan scholarship under tribute, and his obligations are so great and so varied that it is impossible to acknowledge them individually save in the inadequate manner of footnote and bibliography. His greatest debt, however, is to the late Professor Homer A. Watt, the colleague and friend who was once to have been a collaborator. Much of what is best here was threshed out with him, in talk, in the classroom, over the desk.

Karl J. Holzknecht

CONTENTS

LIST OF ILLUSTRATIONS

"The procession of Shakespeare's characters, which was intended at Stratford-upon-Avon, and was obliged to be declined on account of the wetness of the weather, was to have been as represented on the copper-plate annexed."

I

SHAKESPEARE'S LIFE IN FACT

AND TRADITION

Did these bones cost no more the breeding, but to play at
loggats with 'em? Mine ache to think on't.
—*Hamlet*, V, i, 99–101.

THE SCANTINESS OF BIOGRAPHICAL MATERIAL ABOUT WILliam Shakespeare has never ceased to distress his worshippers. Men desire to know so much, and actually know so little, about the intimate doings of the dramatist that every scrap of record or of gossip concerning him has become priceless. Every modern facility for prying into the affairs of the dead has been utilized to reveal Shakespeare to us, and, where fact has remained hidden, conjecture has promptly filled the gap. "Shakespeare cannot be permitted to bewail his outcast state, but we must straight sniff a peccadillo," sighed Dr. Furness. Amazing fancies, like "the old fond paradoxes to make fools laugh i' the alehouse," have been spun by the mystery lovers, and the doubters have been sceptical about his very existence. As a result, the Shakespearean myth is of such a growth that its counterpart can scarcely be found elsewhere in literature, even around blind Homer himself.

Yet the paucity of fact about Shakespeare need not constitute a mystery unless we choose to make the mystery ourselves. To Shakespeare's daily companions, it may even have appeared that he lived a dull and commonplace existence. He never killed his man in a duel as did Ben Jonson, faced charges of sensational atheism as did Marlowe and Kyd, or lived in jeopardy of losing his ears as did Marston and Chapman. Shakespeare seems to have quietly lived a busy life and kept out of trouble—and, incidentally, out of the records. Nowadays, of course, a man of Shakespeare's eminence would be severely publicized. In any age, "what the great do, the less will prattle of," but, compared to the moderns, the Elizabethans seem to have been singularly incurious about details upon which posterity has set most store. No clipping bureaus filled huge scrapbooks with materials for future historians of Sir Philip Sidney, Lady Mary Pembroke, Sir Francis Drake, or Queen Bess herself. Few self-seeking publicists told indiscreet tales about them, and no writers of memoirs waited impatiently at their death-beds for the opportunity to begin. And much less would there have been any deliberate collection of materials about the life of a mere player and playmaker.

Nor can we attribute the slimness of fact about Shakespeare to any lack of contemporary appreciation. Biography, as we know it today, simply had not come into existence in Shakespeare's time. To be sure, meagre beginnings can be traced in the centuries preceding and following Shakespeare, but these beginnings are far from scholarly biography. The seventeenth-century compendia of *Lives*, in all of which Shakespeare has a place, seem to modern eyes mere uncritical obituary eulogies with a few facts and dates casually thrown in. Regrettably, *The Lives of All the Poets*, which Shakespeare's contemporary, Thomas Heywood, projected about 1614, was never finished. Even if he was a literary hack, Heywood presumably had a proper biographical interest, and he knew many of the dramatists personally. It was not until a century and a half later, when James Boswell undertook his life of Dr. Johnson, that a memorable and unique personality was snatched from the jaws of time, and indifference to biographical interest was dispelled. But there was no Boswell for Shakespeare nor any of his fellow Elizabethans.

Yet, when all is said, it is easy to exaggerate unduly the scantiness of the record regarding Shakespeare and the fact that a century elapsed before a biographer undertook the task of reconstructing and examining his life. Actually, we know more about William Shakespeare than about any other man of his time similarly situated, and he was no more neglected than his contemporaries. The birth-dates of many of Shakespeare's fellows are known only by conjecture; little can be discovered about their educations; and the facts of their careers must be guessed by the dates of their publications and by a few scattered allusions. Writing the life of John Dryden, Dr. Johnson opens with words that are equally applicable to Shakespeare:

> His contemporaries, however they reverenced his genius, left his life unwritten; and nothing therefore can be known beyond what casual mention and uncertain tradition have supplied.

In view of these circumstances, Shakespeare's career may be said to have enjoyed some advantages. Facts about him, particularly as they relate to a man of no great social standing born nearly four centuries ago, are quite as abundant as we have any reason to expect, and, moreover, they are quite precise. Supplementing these facts is a fairly large body of tradition, dealing with comparatively trivial matters and much more interesting for a study of myth-making than illuminating as biography.

Every outline of Shakespeare's life should distinguish sharply between two kinds of material: (a) what is known to be true and can be verified by the records, and (b) what may, could, or should be true—the incrustations of tradition, conjecture, and inference which surround the facts. Several centuries of tireless theorizing and effort to make a little yield a great deal have resulted in such a welter of confident assumption that the student often does not know where to begin to disentangle solid truth from the ingenious suppositions with which Shakespeare's biography has become inflated. Unverified gossip and surmise, repeated often enough and sufficiently embroidered with plausibility, soon acquire both the charm and the certainty of truth. An attempt has been made in the following outline, by pointing to the ultimate source of each bit of information, to sort out the mass of material into what is really known about Shakespeare and what is traditional or merely speculative. Only a few of the more specific references to performances have been included; those in the Revels Accounts and in the *Diary* of Dr. Simon Forman have been omitted because of questioned authenticity.

Most of the records, documents, and allusions here tabulated are obtainable in complete form in B. Roland Lewis, *The Shakespeare Documents, Facsimiles, Transliterations, Translations, and Commentary*, 2 volumes, Stanford University Press (1941), and in Sir Edmund K. Chambers, *William Shakespeare, a Study of Facts and Problems*, 2 volumes, Oxford (1930). Many are reprinted in J. O. Halliwell-Phillipps, *Outlines of the Life of Shakespeare*, revised edition, London (1887), and in Pierce Butler, *Materials for the Life of Shakespeare*, Chapel Hill (1930). They are calendared in D. H. Lambert, *Shakespeare Documents*, London (1904). An excellent study of the whole background of Shakespearean biography and a scrutiny of fact and fancy about the dramatist is John S. Smart's *Shakespeare Truth and Tradition*, London (1928). Two interpretative biographies may be considered standard: Sir Sidney Lee's *A Life of William Shakespeare* (originally published in 1898 and finally revised in 1925), and Joseph Quincy Adams's *A Life of William Shakespeare*, Boston and New York (1932). Sir Walter Raleigh's *Shakespeare* (English Men of Letters Series, 1907), and R. M. Alden's *Shakespeare* (Master Spirits of Literature Series, 1922), are studies of the plays as well as biographies.

THE FACTS ABOUT SHAKESPEARE[1]

1564 April 26 Baptism, "Gulielmus *filius* Johannes Shakespere" (*Stratford Parish Register*).

There is no record of William Shakespeare's actual birthday; all that can be inferred from the baptismal record and the inscription on Shakespeare's Stratford monument, that he died on April 23, 1616, "*anno ætatis* 53" (in

[1] All dates given are New Style.

the fifty-third year of his age), is that he was born not earlier than April 24, 1563, or later than April 23, 1564. April 23, 1564, is the conjectural date usually accepted. Neither is the exact place of the poet's birth known. Shakespeare's father had a house in Greenhill Street and two in Henley Street in Stratford, but it is not known in which of his houses he was living in 1564. It was not until the famous Jubilee Celebration in 1769 that the curiosity of tourists demanded the precise location of a birthroom. The selection of the present shrine in Henley Street—which was indeed one of John Shakespeare's properties in Stratford—was largely conjectural.

Some facts about the poet's family may be gleaned from the Stratford archives. William Shakespeare's father, John, was not a native of Stratford, but a "whyttawer" (tanner) and glover from Snitterfield, who came to Stratford some time before 1532. He also dealt in farm products and wool, held considerable property in Stratford, and had been, successively, ale-taster, burgess, constable, affeeror (a minor official who decided the fine to be imposed upon malefactors who had been convicted of a fault for which the statutes did not prescribe an express penalty), and chamberlain of Stratford. (For the tradition that he was also a butcher, see below, p. 22.) He became alderman, 1565; high bailiff, 1568; and chief alderman, 1571. During his administration as bailiff, players visited Stratford and received a reward from the Corporation. About 1557, John Shakespeare had married Mary Arden, daughter of Robert Arden, a wealthy "gentleman of worship" from Wilmecote. William was their third child; two sisters, Joan and Margaret, died in infancy. Other children born to the Shakespeares were Gilbert, 1566; a second Joan, 1569; Anne, 1571 (died 1579); Richard, 1574; and Edmund, 1580. There are no records of William Shakespeare's education (see below, p. 22).

> 1582 November 27 License to marry issued to "Willelmum Shaxpere *et* Annam Whateley *de* Temple Grafton" (*Episcopal Register, Diocese of Worcester*).
>
> 1582 November 28 Marriage bond of sureties for "Willm Shagspere" and "Anne Hathwey of Stratford" signed by Fulk Sandells and John Richardson, farmers of Stratford, that there is no "lawful let or impediment by reason of any precontract, consanguinity, affinity, or by any other lawful means whatsoever . . . William and Anne to be married together with once asking of the banns of matrimony" (*Episcopal Register, Diocese of Worcester*).

More has been written about William Shakespeare's marriage than about any other known event in his career, both by those who are not displeased to view him treading "the primrose path of dalliance" in youth and by those who feel it important to represent him as of a "pure and unstain'd prime." The most careful study of the documents in the light of contemporaneous custom and procedure is J. W. Gray's *Shakespeare's Marriage* (1905). So far as records go, the chief crux is lack of agreement in the documents as to the name of the bride. Some biographers believe that two William Shakespeares are here involved (Lee, *op. cit.*). Others see only a scribal error, explained by the fact that on the same day the clerk who wrote the entry had been taking testimony in the consistory court in a case involving a man named Whateley (Gray, *op. cit.* and Adams, *op. cit.*). "Hathaway" is the name given by Nicholas Rowe in 1709 before the records were discovered.

Evidence to enable us to reconstruct the circumstances of the marriage is likewise lacking. No record of its solemnization has been found, either at Stratford or elsewhere; the records of Temple Grafton are lost for this period. The posting of the bond and the record at Stratford of Susanna's baptism six months afterward have given support to the contention that the marriage was irregular. The bond itself was not unusual. Between Advent and Epiphany (December 2 and January 13, 1582–3) no banns of matrimony could be asked. But the consistory court had the power to license dispensations upon the filing of a sworn allegation, the payment of a fee, and the posting by the bridegroom of a bond as surety that the marriage was legal. Shakespeare was a minor, and, hence, ineligible as a guarantor. The absence of his father's name from the records is no basis for assumption that John Shakespeare disapproved of the marriage. Who were Sandells and Richardson —grim defenders of Anne's honor or just genial assistants to a romance? We do not know. The further stipulation of the bond, that "the said William Shakespeare do not proceed to solemnization of marriage with the said Anne Hathaway without the consent of her friends," suggests friendliness. They may have been family representatives; they also appear as supervisor and witness, respectively, to the will of Richard Hathaway, the bride's father, who died in 1581.

As to the happiness or unhappiness of Shakespeare's married life, there is not a shred of evidence. Passages from the plays and poems may be invoked as proof both ways (see A. H. Tolman, "Shakespeare's Supposed References to His Marriage," in *Falstaff and Other Shakespearean Topics*, 1925). According to her epitaph, Anne Hathaway was eight years older than Shakespeare, and, hence, a woman of twenty-six and he a youth of eighteen at their marriage. This fact and the bequest to her of "my second best bed with the furniture"—added only at the revision of Shakespeare's will—have been made much of by biographers. No special provision for her needed to be made; she was entitled to a widow's share. The most relevant fact is that Shakespeare bought New Place as early as 1597, and, after his career in London, returned to Stratford. A man who had not taken family responsibilities seriously in a small town could not have done that.

1583 May 26 Baptism of "Susanna, daughter to William Shakespeare" (*Stratford Parish Register*).

The birth of Susanna also troubles the biographers. Seen in the light of what is known of Elizabethan betrothal and marriage customs, however, there need be no discredit to the couple. Formal engagements, made before witnesses, were commonly considered a legally valid marriage without religious ceremony. Shakespeare's marriage bond mentions "precontract" as a lawful impediment to marriage. Situations in two of Shakespeare's plays involve similar unions. The marriage of Posthumus and Imogen was apparently only a hand-fasting, considered holy by the lovers and the rest of the court, but unrecognized by the jilted Cloten as a formal marriage in keeping with their social rank (*Cymbeline*, II, iii, 118 ff.). Compare the "true contract" of Claudio and Julietta and the Angelo-Mariana situation in *Measure for Measure* (I, ii, 149 ff. and IV, ii, 72 ff.). Custom, however, was changing (cf. *The Tempest*, IV, i, 14 ff.).

1585 February 2 Baptism of "Hamnet and Judith, son and daughter to William Shakespeare" (*Stratford Parish Register*).

The suggestion that the godparents were Hamnet and Judith Sadler, bakers in the High Street, Stratford, is probable. Hamnet Sadler was also a legatee and a witness in Shakespeare's will.

1592 Reference in Robert Greene's *A Groatsworth of Wit* to "an upstart crow, beautified with our feathers, that with his *tiger's heart wrapped in a player's hide*, supposes he is as well able to bombast out a blank verse as the best of you: and being an absolute *Johannes factotum*, is in his own conceit the only Shake-scene in the country."

This passage is frequently misinterpreted because quoted out of context. Brought to an early grave by riotous living, Robert Greene (1558?–92) on his death bed addressed to the gentlemen of his acquaintance "that spend their wits in making plays" one section of his *A Groatsworth of Wit Bought with a Million of Repentance*. In it he wished them "a better exercise and wisdom to prevent his extremities," and warned them against "those burs ... those puppets ... that spake from our mouths, those antics garnished in our colours" (i. e., the players who get all the glory and the profit from the labor of authors). In this tirade against the parasitic profession of acting, Greene mentions the "upstart crow." The "tiger's heart" phrase parodies a line in *3 Henry VI*. Too frequently the whole passage has been interpreted as a personal charge of plagiarism by Greene against Shakespeare. Yet, in context, such phrases as "beautified with our feathers," "bombast out a blank verse," and "Shake-scene" seem clear references to the actor rather than the writer. Moreover, granting that *Henry VI* was a revision of old plays in which Greene may have had a hand, he was a century or more ahead of his time if he were sensitive about such adaptation. Rather is the resentment that of a university man who saw mere nobodies without training succeeding in the new profession. (Compare *The Return from Parnassus*, Part II, III, iii.)

Later in the same year, Henry Chettle, Greene's literary executor, upon whom much of the blame for Greene's tirade fell, made handsome apology in his *Kind-Harts Dream* to one "whom at that time I did not so much spare, as since I wish I had . . . that I did not, I am as sorry, as if the original fault had been my fault, because my self have seen his demeanor no less civil than he excellent in the quality he professes: Besides, divers of worship have reported his uprightness of dealing, which argues his honesty, and his facetious grace in writing that approves his art." Although Shakespeare's name is nowhere mentioned in either book, the incident has generally been accepted as a reference to him.

Exactly when Shakespeare came to London is not known, but, if these allusions are actually to him, the actor-dramatist had made his way by 1592.

> 1593   *Venus and Adonis* published with a dedication, signed by the author, "to the Right Honorable Henry Wriothesley, Earl of Southampton and Baron of Titchfield."

The first certain record of Shakespeare in London concerns, not a theatrical career, but a bid for literary distinction. Shakespeare called the poem "the first heir of my invention," probably because stage-plays were not yet considered literature. During 1592–3, the London theatres were closed because of the plague. Shakespeare, who had doubtless been tinkering with plays, may well have taken the opportunity his enforced leisure provided to find out if he really could write. The book was registered in the Stationers' Register on April 19 and was printed by Richard Field, formerly of Stratford. Ten editions of *Venus* were issued during Shakespeare's lifetime, and six others before 1640, when his non-dramatic poems were collected into one volume.

> 1594   *The Rape of Lucrece* published, likewise with a signed dedication to the Earl of Southampton.

This is the "graver labour" promised in the dedication to *Venus and Adonis* the preceding year. The book was registered on May 9 and was also printed by Richard Field. Six editions of *Lucrece* were issued during Shakespeare's lifetime, and two others before 1640.

> 1594   December 28   Performance of "a Comedy of Errors (like to *Plautus* his Menechmus)" at Gray's Inn "by the players" (Gesta Grayorum).

The *Gesta Grayorum* is a mock-serious account of the doings at Gray's Inn when the Prince of Purpoole, Arch-Duke of Stapulia and Bernardia (i. e., Staple Inn and Barnard's Inn) received an embassy from the Inner Temple.

There is nothing but the title to identify the play performed on this occasion with Shakespeare's *The Comedy of Errors*. The Lord Chamberlain's Men, to which Shakespeare was now attached, appear to have been playing before the Queen on that night (see below), but a court payment to the Lord Admiral's Men for December 28 was also made. Sir Edmund Chambers suggests an error (*The Elizabethan Stage*, IV, 56).

> 1595   March 15   Payment of £20 to "William Kempe, William Shakespeare, and Richard Burbage, servants to the Lord Chamberlain . . . for two several comedies or interludes shewed . . . before her Majesty in Christmas time last past, viz., upon St. Stephen's Day and Innocents' Day" (December 26 and 28, 1594, at Greenwich) (*Record Office, Pipe Office, Declared Accounts*).

By 1594, therefore, Shakespeare must have acquired some reputation as an actor. Kempe was a celebrated comedian and Burbage the greatest tragic actor of the time. After 1595, court payments to the Chamberlain's Men became frequent. They were usually made to John Heminge (see E. K. Chambers, *The Elizabethan Stage*, IV, 164 ff.).

What theatrical company Shakespeare first joined is not exactly known; the title-pages of the earliest of Shakespeare's plays to be printed mention their having been acted by the Earl of Derby's (otherwise known as Lord Strange's), the Earl of Sussex's, or the Earl of Pembroke's Men, but the evidence is not decisive. The Lord Chamberlain's Men, to which Shakespeare certainly belonged from 1594 on, was reorganized after the plague of 1593 from remnants of other companies, to one or more of which Shakespeare may have at some time belonged.

> 1596   Shakespeare assessed 13*s*. 4*d*. on property valued at £5 in the parish of St. Helen's Bishopsgate; on November 15, 1597, when the second installment of this tax was to be paid, his name was entered among the defaulters. On October 1, 1598, he was again assessed, but in the same year his name is found in the list of those who have no goods or chattels, lands or tenements within the limits of the parish of St. Helen's. Further information, dated October 6, 1599, and October 6, 1600, refers to his residence in Surrey or among those under the jurisdiction of the Bishop of Winchester, i. e., residents of the Bankside in the Liberty of the Clink (*Record Office, Subsidy Rolls*).

The inference is that some time before October, 1596, Shakespeare had a residence in the parish of St. Helen's, Bishopsgate, and that by October, 1599, he had moved to the Liberty of the Clink on the Bankside. In 1796, Edmund Malone, the noted Shakespearean scholar, referred to a document in his possession which led him to assume that Shakespeare continued to live in Southwark until 1608. Unfortunately, the *Life* in which he promised to produce it was left incomplete, and James Boswell, his literary executor, failed to print the record. The Belott-Mountjoy testimony, however, makes Malone's conjecture improbable (see below, p. 17). The documents concerning the tax assessment have been reproduced in facsimile and the facts summarized by M. S. Giuseppi, *Transactions of the London and Middlesex Archeological Society* (1925).

> 1596 August 11 Burial of "Hamnet, *filius* William Shakespeare" (*Stratford Parish Register*).
>
> 1596 October 20 Grant of arms to John Shakespeare in consideration of the faithful and valiant service rendered by his antecedants to Henry VII: "Gold, on a bend sables, a spear of the first steeled argent. And for his crest or cognizance a falcon his wings displayed argent standing on a wreath of his colours: supporting a speare gold steeled as aforesaid set upon a helmet with mantles and tassles as . . . doth more plainly appear depicted in this margin" (*College of Arms MSS.*).

In the margin appears a trick of the coat and crest with the note "*non sanz droict*," which has usually been taken as the motto. There is no evidence that Shakespeare or his family used this motto. Another note indicates that application for arms had been made as early as 1576. "This John showeth a pattern hereof under Clarent Cooke's hand-paper, xx years past." Although it is Shakespeare's father who properly makes it, the application for a coat of arms is usually interpreted as Shakespeare's effort to better his social position and make it more nearly accord with his growing wealth.

> 1596 November 29 William Wayte craves sureties of the peace against William Shakespeare, Francis Langley (owner of the Swan Theatre), Dorothy Soer, wife of John Soer, and Anne Lee, for fear of death (*Public Record Office*).

Wayte was the stepson of William Gardiner, justice of the peace on the Bankside. The writ involving Shakespeare was but the culmination of old trouble between Gardiner and Langley. See J. L. Hotson, *Shakespeare vs Shallow* (1931), where the suggestion is made that Gardiner and Wayte are the prototypes of Shallow and Slender in *The Merry Wives of Windsor*.

> 1597 May 4 Purchased New Place and an acre of ground in Stratford from William Underhill for £60. From that time, Shakespeare described himself as "William Shakespeare of Stratford-upon-Avon, in the county of Warwick, gentleman" (*Birthplace Museum, Wheler MSS.; and Public Record Office*).

This purchase is the first of a series of investments made by Shakespeare of the profits of his profession. It is significant evidence also of the close touch he maintained with Stratford. New Place was built some time after 1483 by Sir Hugh Clopton, who also built the Guild Chapel and the Clopton Bridge at Stratford. He became Lord Mayor of London in 1491. In his will (1496), he refers to the building as "my great house in Stratford-upon-Avon." It is first called "the New Place" in a document of 1532 and described by the antiquary Leland (*c.* 1540) in his *Itinerary* as a "pretty house of brick and timber." In the year following Shakespeare's purchase, 1598, there is an entry in the Stratford Chamberlain's accounts: "pd to Mr. Shakespeare for one load of stone . . . x*d.*" Although it is impossible to identify which Master Shakespeare is meant, the poet or his father, the assumption has usually been that William Shakespeare, after repairing New Place, was disposing of surplus materials. That New Place was a good house may be inferred from the fact that as late as 1643 it was selected as the lodging of Queen Henrietta Maria when she visited the town. Only the foundations now remain; the building was torn down as the result of a quarrel with the Corporation by the Reverend Francis Gastrell in 1759.

Of some interest in connection with the purchase of New Place is the advice which the ghost of the highwayman, Gamaliel Ratsey, gave to a strolling player to go to London "and when thou feelst thy purse well lined, buy thee some place of Lordship in the country, that growing weary of playing, thy money may there bring thee to dignity and reputation." (*Ratsey's Ghost, c.* 1605.)

1598   Shakespeare's name appeared for the first time on published plays: *Richard II* (Q₂ and Q₃), *Richard III* (Q₂), and *Love's Labor's Lost* (Q₁).

1598   Described by Francis Meres in *Palladis Tamia* as the most excellent in both comedy and tragedy for the stage, mentioned as among the best lyric poets and "the most passionate among us to bewail and bemoan the perplexities of Love," and praised for his "mellifluous and honey-tongued" lines, "his sugared Sonnets among his private friends," and his "fine filed phrase." Meres named twelve plays: "for Comedy . . . his *Gentlemen of Verona*, his *Errors*, his *Love's Labor's Lost*, his *Love's Labor's Won*, his *Midsummer Night's Dream*, and his *Merchant of Venice*: for Tragedy his *Richard the 2*, *Richard the 3*, *Henry the 4*, *King John*, *Titus Andronicus*, and his *Romeo and Juliet*."

Francis Meres (1565–1647), a graduate of Pembroke College, Cambridge, became a rector and a schoolmaster. His *Palladis Tamia, Wit's Treasury* (1598), contains a comparison between the accomplishments in the arts of the Greeks, Romans, and Italians, and of contemporary Englishmen. The book was re-issued in 1634 as a schoolbook. Meres was not a writer of importance, and he probably was not intimately acquainted with the London theatres. *Love's Labor's Won* may be either a lost play or an alternate title to an extant one, more probably the latter.

1598   January 24   Letter of Abraham Sturley to his brother-in-law, Richard Quiney of Stratford, mentions that "our countryman, Mr. Shakespeare, is willing to disburse some money upon some odd yardland or other at Shottery or near about us" and adds that his informant, Quiney's father, "thinketh it a very fit pattern to move him to deal in the matter of our tithes . . . we think it a fair mark to shoot at, and not unpossible to hit. It obtained would advance him indeed, and would do us much good" (*Stratford Archives*).

Evidently Shakespeare was considered a man of substance in Stratford. However, he did not immediately negotiate for the Stratford tithes (see below, p. 15).

> 1598   February 4   Listed as the owner of ten quarters (about eighty bushels) of malt and corn in Stratford (*Stratford Archives*).

Because of a dearth of grain resulting from several bad seasons, 1594, 1595, 1596, and from the consequent engrossing of grain to insure high prices, there was much poverty and discontent. The Privy Council attempted to remedy these conditions by requiring that local constables obtain lists of grain holdings on the basis of which to regulate trade. Shakespeare's holdings were not large. He had apparently invested in grain, and of the six holders listed from his ward only two had more than he.

> 1598   Before September 20   Acted in Ben Jonson's *Every Man in His Humour*.

Shakespeare's name heads an actor list appended to the text of the play in the folio of Jonson's *Works* (1616). A contemporary letter, dated September 20, 1598, alludes to the play as new (see Chambers, *The Elizabethan Stage*, III, 359).

> 1598   October 25   Richard Quiney, in London on private business and on affairs of the Stratford Corporation, writes to Shakespeare from the Bell in Carter Lane to borrow £30. "You shall friend me much in helping me out of all the debts I owe in London, I thank God, and much quiet my mind which would not be indebted. . . . You shall neither lose credit nor money by me, the Lord willing" (*Birthplace Museum, Wheler MSS.*).

This letter is further evidence that Shakespeare maintained his Stratford connections. The fact that the letter is found in Quiney's own correspondence suggests that it was never delivered. There are three other letters in the Quiney correspondence alluding to this transaction or to another expectation of money from Shakespeare for investment (see E. I. Fripp, *Master Richard Quiney*, 1924). Quiney's son, Thomas, married Shakespeare's younger daughter (see below, p. 20).

> 1599   November 17–1600, March 24   Confirmation of the grant of arms to John Shakespeare and permission given to him and his posterity to impale their arms with the arms of Arden (*College of Arms MSS.*).

The exact date is omitted; the year is 42 Elizabeth (1599 O.S.).

1599   "*The Passionate Pilgrim*, by W. Shakespeare," published by William Jaggard.

By 1599, Shakespeare's name as author was deemed sufficient to guarantee the success of a book. Only five of the twenty poems making up this piratical collection are Shakespeare's. Two are Sonnets 138 and 144; the other three are the poetic missives from *Love's Labor's Lost*, IV, ii and iii. Several are known to have been written by Richard Barnefield, Bartholomew Griffin, and Christopher Marlowe. As to the rest, there is no clue to authorship. (For the tradition that Shakespeare was angry about the deception, see below, p. 28.)

> 1599   Before May 16   Erection of the Globe Theatre on the Bankside, Shakespeare holding a tenth share.

When James Burbage's lease to the Holywell property on which the Theatre was built expired in 1597, his landlord, Giles Alleyn, deferred renewing the lease in order that he might seize the building for himself. When his intention became evident, Burbage's heirs took steps to thwart him. On the night of December 28, 1598, Alleyn being absent in the country, they appeared with an armed confederacy, including Peter Street, a carpenter, and twelve workmen, tore down the Theatre, carried the timbers to the Bankside, and erected the Globe on ground leased from Nicholas Brend. The lease, formally signed on February 20, 1599, dated from December 25, 1598, and was to run thirty-one years. To finance the venture, a syndicate was formed: Richard and Cuthbert Burbage, the sons of James, to hold one moiety; and five of their fellows, William Shakespeare, Augustine Phillips, Thomas Pope, John Heminge, and Will Kempe, the other moiety. Each moiety was subject to an annual ground rent of £7 5s. The details of the financing are not known. On May 16, 1599, an inventory of Brend's properties described the new playhouse as "*una domo de nove edificata . . . in occupacione Willielmi Shakespeare et aliorum.*" (For further details, see J. Q. Adams, *Shakespearean Playhouses*, Boston [1917], pp. 234 ff., and E. K. Chambers, *The Elizabethan Stage*, II, 414 ff.)

> 1599   September 21   Thomas Platter, a Swiss visitor to London, "crossed the water and there in the house with the thatched roof [the Globe?] witnessed an excellent performance of the tragedy of the first Emperor Julius Caesar with a cast of some fifteen people" (Thomas Platter's Travels in England, 1599, *translated by Clare Williams, London* [1937], *p. 166*).

> 1600   March 6   Performance of a play on Sir John Oldcastle (i. e., *1 Henry IV*) by the Lord Chamberlain's players at a feast (probably at Hunsdon House, Blackfriars) to entertain Ludovic Vereiken, ambassador from the Spanish Low Countries (*Letter from Rowland White to Sir Rob-*

ert Sidney, under date of March 8, 1600, Letters and Memorials of State [Sidney Papers], *ed. Arthur Collins [1746], II, 175).*

1600   August 23   Shakespeare is first mentioned by name in the Stationers' Register in connection with *Much Ado* and *2 Henry IV.*

Registry in the books of the Stationers' Company was the Elizabethan equivalent of copyright, protecting not the author, however, but the printer.

1601   February 7   Performance at the Globe by the Chamberlain's Men of a "play of the deposing and killing of King Richard the Second" (*testimony of Augustine Phillips, one of the company, Sir Gelly Meyricke, and others at the trial of the Earl of Essex for treason, February 17–18, 1601*).

Phillips also testified that the play, which was old, was especially requested by Meyricke and other Essex supporters and that the company was paid "xl*s*. more than their ordinary for it." Apparently it was hoped that the play would in some manner induce support for Essex's fatal rebellion the next day. The players, however, seem to have been judged innocent; they were performing at court soon after.

1601   March 25   Mention in the will of Thomas Whittington, husbandman of Shottery, of "40*s*. that is in the hand of Anne Shakespeare, wife unto Mr. William Shakespeare, and is due debt unto me" (*Worcester Probate Register*).

Whittington directs Shakespeare to pay it, the sum to be given to the poor of Stratford. The date of the loan is unascertainable. "Thomas Whittington my shepherd" had been mentioned in the will of Richard Hathaway, of Shottery, who died in 1581.

1601   September 8   Burial of "Mr. Johannes Shakespeare," the poet's father (*Stratford Parish Register*).

1602   February 2   "A play called *Twelve Night, or What You Will,* much like the *Comedy of Errors* or *Menæchmi* in Plautus" was performed at a feast in the Middle Temple (*Diary of John Manningham, student in the Middle Temple*).

Manningham adds a brief synopsis of the Malvolio plot.

1602   May 1   Bought from William and John Combe 107 acres of land in Old Stratford for £320 (*Birthplace Museum*).

This property was freehold land and with it went the right to common pasturage. No messuage was included in the purchase. The land already had tenants, but whether they continued to occupy it after Shakespeare's purchase is not known. The poet was represented in the transaction by his brother, Gilbert. The "fine" completing the purchase mentions both 107 acres of land and 20 acres of pasture and is dated 1610. Whether or not the

£100 mentioned in this second transaction was an additional payment is not known.

> 1602 September 28 Bought from Walter Getley the copyhold of a cottage and about a quarter of an acre of land in Walker Street, Stratford, back of New Place (*Court Roll of Rowington Manor*).

The annual rent was two shillings and sixpence. Walker Street was also known as Chapel Lane and Dead Lane.

> 1603 Autumn or winter Acted in Ben Jonson's *Sejanus* (*Note appended to the text of the play in Jonson's* Works, *1616*).

The absence of Shakespeare's name from later actor lists in the Jonson folio has been taken as evidence that he retired from acting after 1603.

> 1603 May 17 and 19 Patent of King James I to "Lawrence Fletcher, William Shakespeare, Richard Burbage, Augustine Phillips, John Heminge, Henry Condell, William Sly, Robert Armin, Richard Cowley, and the rest of their associates freely to use and exercise the art and faculty of playing comedies, tragedies, histories, interludes, morals, pastorals, stageplays . . . for the recreation of our loving subjects as for our solace and pleasure when we shall think good to see them" (*Public Record Office, Patent Rolls*).

From this time the Shakespearean company is called the King's Men.

> 1604 Revival of *Love's Labor's Lost* before the Queen at the Earl of Southampton's house (*Hatfield MSS., Letter of Sir Walter Cope to Robert Cecil, Lord Craborne*).

No date is given; the manuscript is endorsed 1604.

> 1604 February 8 The King gave Burbage £30 as a "free gift" for "the maintenance and relief of himself and the rest of his company being prohibited to represent any plays publicly" because of the plague (*Public Record Office*).

> 1604 March Grant to the King's players of four yards of red cloth for a cloak and a quarter of a yard of crimson velvet for the capes "against his Majesty's . . . royal proceeding through the City of London." Shakespeare's name heads the list of players (*Record Office, Lord Chamberlain's Books*).

The actors' names appear among the Grooms of the Chamber (see Ernest Law, *Shakespeare as a Groom of the Chamber*, 1910).

> 1604 July Sued Philip Rogers, Stratford apothecary, to collect a debt of 35s. 10d. for malt supplied him (*Birthplace Museum, Wheler MSS.*).

> 1604 August 9–27 Shakespeare and eleven other members of the King's company of players, as Grooms of the Chamber, took up their resi-

dence at Somerset House to entertain an Ambassador Extraordinary from Spain. Allowed £21 12s. "for waiting and attending" (see Law, op. cit.).

1605   May 4   Will of Augustine Phillips bequeaths "to my Fellow William Shakespeare a thirty shillings piece in gold," to buy a memorial ring (Probate Court Calendar).

1605   July 24   Conveyance to Shakespeare from Ralph Huband of Ippesley of the moiety of an unexpired lease of the corn and hay tithes of Old Stratford, Welcombe, and Bishopton, together with a moiety of the wool, lamb, and other small tithes of the whole parish of Stratford-upon-Avon, for £440 (Birthplace Museum, Wheler MSS.).

Tithes were originally an annual tax of one-tenth of the increase arising from the land and stock (or its equivalent) payable to the clergy of the parish. There were two classes of tithes: great or predial tithes, those arising immediately from the produce of the land—hay, grain, wood, etc.—and small tithes, those arising from live stock—calves, lambs, pigs, wool, dairy products, eggs, etc. Because of the difficulty in collecting them, in practice tithes were usually farmed out or leased. Those in which Shakespeare acquired an interest had originally appertained to the College of Stratford (dissolved in 1546), and had passed to the town at its incorporation by charter in 1553. However, a lease made in 1543 to William Barker for ninety-two years was still in force, and the subject is further complicated by the fact that the tithes covered by the lease were in several parcels. The parcel of tithes in which Shakespeare purchased an interest was subject to two annual rent charges, one payable to John Barker (heir to William) who reserved it to himself when he assigned the lease in 1580 to John Huband (who willed it to Ralph), and the other payable to the Corporation of Stratford, to which the tithes would come at the expiration of the lease. Shakespeare's share of the first rent charge was fixed at £5, of the second at £17. The annual value of his moiety was estimated in 1611 at about £60, making the net return on his investment about £38 a year.

Shakespeare, therefore, was not the only tithe-owner in Stratford, nor even the principal one. The Combes held an equal moiety in the same parcel, one Richard Lane held a larger parcel, and the rest were distributed among various owners. Shakespeare's interest was about one-fifth. Naturally, with such a complicated leasing and sub-leasing, legal difficulties were inevitable. In 1611, Lane, Shakespeare, and others drew up a bill of complaint that all of the owners of the tithes were not paying their share of the annual rents reserved by the heirs of John Barker, so that "your orators, Richard Lane and William Shakespeare, and some few others . . . are wholly, and against all equity and good conscience, usually driven to pay the same for the preservation of their estates." They ask that the whole matter be clarified.

1607   June 5   Susanna, aged twenty-four, daughter of William Shakespeare, married to Dr. John Hall, "renowned in the healing art" (*Stratford Parish Register*).

1607–08   Performances on board the East India Company's ship *Dragon* of *Hamlet* (September 5, 1607, and March 31, 1608) and *Richard II* (September 30, 1607) by the ship's company, "which I permit to keep my people from idleness and unlawful games or sleep" (*"Journal" of Captain William Keeling of the* Dragon, *in T. Rundall,* Narratives of Voyages towards the North-West, *Hakluyt Society, 1849*).

1608   February 21   Baptism of Elizabeth, daughter of the Halls (*Stratford Parish Register*).

Elizabeth Hall was the only grandchild Shakespeare knew.

1608   August 9   Shakespeare became a housekeeper of the Blackfriars Theatre with a seventh share.

Other housekeepers were Richard Burbage, Cuthbert Burbage, Henry Evans, John Heminge, Henry Condell, and William Sly. The Blackfriars building was one inherited by Richard Burbage from his father, who had hoped to open it as a "public" playhouse. The Privy Council had forbidden such use of the building, but some time between 1597 and 1600 it had been opened as a "private" house. It was leased to Henry Evans and was used by his troupe of child-actors. In 1608, Evans surrendered his lease, and the newly organized syndicate re-leased the theatre for twenty-one years at the old annual rental of £40, each member binding himself to pay £5 14s. 4d. a year. (For further details, see Adams, *Shakespearean Playhouses*, Boston [1917], pp. 223 ff.)

1608   September 9   Burial of Mary Shakespeare, widow (*Stratford Parish Register*).

Mary Shakespeare was the poet's mother.

1608   October 19   Baptism of William, son of Henry Walker, mercer and Alderman of Stratford.

In his will Shakespeare bequeathed "to my godson William Walker, xxs. in gold." The inference is that the dramatist, in Stratford during the illness and death of his mother and for some time after, stood sponsor at the christening of the son of a friend.

1609   Publication of the Sonnets with a dedication to "Mr. W. H., the onlie begetter," signed "T. T."

This dedication is the most famous in English literature, but speculation regarding the identity of "Mr. W. H." has too frequently ignored the fact that the dedication was signed "T. T.," the initials of the publisher, Thomas Thorpe, and not by Shakespeare. The edition was probably unauthorized.

The date of composition is unknown. The sonnet vogue lasted from about 1592 to the end of the century, and Meres (see above, p. 10) had mentioned the circulation of Shakespeare's "sugared Sonnets among his private friends." An interesting association is the note in the account of the "household stuff" of Edward Alleyn, the player, of "a book, Shakesper Sonnettes, 5d."

> 1608   December 17–June 7, 1609   Lawsuit in Stratford against a debtor, John Addenbrooke, for £6. Shakespeare won the case, Addenbrooke absconded, and Shakespeare sued Thomas Horneby, Addenbrooke's security (*Stratford Archives*).

> 1611   September 11   Shakespeare's name appears on a list of Stratford contributors "towards the charge of prosecuting the bill in Parliament for the better repair of the highways and amending divers defects in the statutes already made" (*Stratford Archives*).

The frequent connection of Shakespeare with municipal affairs in Stratford during the second decade of the seventeenth century has given considerable support to the tradition that he retired there at the close of his life. The retirement was probably gradual.

> 1611   October 5   Inventory of goods of Robert Johnson of Stratford mentions "a lease of a barn that he holdeth of Mr. Shakespeare, £20."

Except for Shakespeare's will, this is the only record during the dramatist's lifetime of the Henley Street property acquired by his father.

> 1612   May 11–June 19   Shakespeare appeared as a witness in the suit of Stephen Belott versus Christopher Mountjoy, a Huguenot tire-maker, or manufacturer of women's headdresses, of London, to recover dowry promised to Belott on his marriage to Mountjoy's daughter, Mary (*Public Record Office, Court of Requests*).

Shakespeare is described as of Stratford-upon-Avon, gentleman, of the age of forty-eight or thereabouts. Other witnesses testified that Mountjoy had urged Shakespeare to act as matchmaker between his promising apprentice and his daughter. Shakespeare himself testified that he had lodged with the Mountjoy family at the corner of Silver and Mugwell Streets, Cripplegate, for several years prior to 1604, and signed a deposition that the defendant had authorized him to promise Belott a marriage portion, but could not remember the amount. The suit had its origin in Stephen's setting up shop for himself, old Mountjoy's refusal to pay, and his dissipations, which caused Belott to fear for his wife's inheritance and to petition for a court injunction against Mountjoy. The case was referred to the elders of the French church for arbitration. They awarded Belott twenty nobles which Mountjoy had not paid a year later (see C. W. Wallace, "Shakespeare and His London Associates," *University of Nebraska Studies*, X, 1910).

1613   March 10   Bought with "William Johnson, citizen and vintner of London, John Jackson, and John Heminge of London, gentlemen," from Henry Walker, "citizen and minstrel of London," a house, shop, and yard in Blackfriars for £140—£80 cash and £60 in mortgages. Spoken of as "William Shakespeare of Stratford-upon-Avon in the county of Warwick, gentleman" (*Guildhall Library, Folger Shakespeare Library, and British Museum*).

John Heminge was, doubtless, Shakespeare's fellow, the actor Heminge; William Johnson, on investigation, seems to have been none other than mine host of the Mermaid Tavern, Bread Street, Cheapside, with which only romantic tradition has until recently associated Shakespeare (see J. L. Hotson, "Shakespeare and Mine Host of the Mermaid," *Atlantic Monthly*, June, 1933). Of John Jackson nothing is known.

Other documents completing this transaction or dealing with litigation concerning it are dated March 11, 1613, April 26, 1615, May 5, 1615, and May 22, 1615.

1613   March 31   Payment of 44*s.* "to Mr. Shakespeare in gold" for some unspecified service about Francis Manners, Lord Rutland's impresa (i. e., an emblem and motto for a shield). A similar sum was paid to Richard Burbage for painting it (*Rutland MS.*).

1613   May 20   Payment of £93 6*s.* 8*d.* to John Heminge upon the Council's warrant, "for presenting before the Prince's Highness, the lady Elizabeth, and the Prince Palatine Elector, fourteen several plays," including *Much Ado, The Tempest, The Winter's Tale, Sir John Falstaff, The Moor of Venice,* and *Cæsar's Tragedy.* Also, on the same date, there is a payment to Heminge of £40, "and by way of his Majesty's reward," £20, "for presenting six several plays," including *The Hotspur* (i. e., *1 Henry IV*), and *Benedicte and Betteris* (i. e., *Much Ado*) (*Chamber Accounts, Bodl. Rawlinson MS.*).

These plays were performed as part of the festivities attending the betrothal and wedding of King James's daughter, the Princess Elizabeth, and Frederick, the Elector Palatine. Other plays mentioned by title are by Beaumont and Fletcher and by Jonson.

1613   June 29   The Globe playhouse burned to the ground during a performance of *Henry VIII.* Ordnance, discharged "in way of triumph," caused the thatch roof to ignite, and the building was destroyed within two hours. It was rebuilt the next year at a cost of £1400.

There are several contemporary accounts of the disaster, including gossipy letters by Thomas Lorkin and Sir Henry Wotton, a ballad, and a brief allusion in *An Execration upon Vulcan* by Ben Jonson.

1614   "Item for one quart of sack and one quart of claret wine given to a preacher at the New Place, xx*d.*" (*Stratford Archives, Chamberlain's Accounts*).

Shakespeare was evidently entertaining a distinguished visitor. Such a gift from the Corporation was a common courtesy.

1614   January 28   Mentioned as a legatee (£5) in John Combe's will (*Probate Court Calendar*).

1614   October 28   Secured from Combe's heir, William Replingham, a deed of indemnity against personal loss in the value of the tithes if the Welcombe common fields were enclosed. Shakespeare did not support the protest against such enclosure (*Birthplace Museum, Wheler MSS.*).

Land in the Middle Ages was of two classes: *freehold*, that owned outright by individuals, and *common*, that belonging to a community and apportioned to those who wished to cultivate it. Freehold land was enclosed and divided into fields; common land or "champion" lay open and unfenced. Everybody's cattle grazed in the common pasture, and those who cultivated the arable portions owned in common the necessary agricultural implements. Moreover, to insure a fair distribution of fertile and unfertile land, the arable sections were divided by "balks" of unploughed turf into half-acre strips, so that a holder who found himself in possession of ten acres in a field would have these ten acres cut into twenty half-acre strips, no two of which would be adjacent to each other. It is easily seen that in some respects this system would be wasteful and unprofitable, yet it appears to have been the original method of English agriculture, and more than half of England was still so cultivated until the eighteenth century.

By Shakespeare's time the disadvantages of the common-field system had become apparent, and here and there the wiser and more progressive farmers began to agitate for enclosure and farming in "several." When all the holders of the common fields agreed, the land could be divided up, each man's plot enclosed by a fence or hedge, and so virtually pass into private ownership. Enclosure of the common fields was one of the marked economic revolutions of the sixteenth century.

In Stratford, William Replingham and the Combes were the leaders in the agitation; but there was plenty of opposition. As a landowner who also enjoyed common-pasture privileges, and especially as a tithe-owner, Shakespeare was naturally interested in the effect such enclosure might have. The numerous references in the *Diary* (1614–15) of Thomas Greene, his cousin, to Shakespeare's concern in the matter make clear that he at least had doubts. Having safeguarded his own interest by the agreement with Replingham, Shakespeare apparently was content to remain neutral. The controversy dragged on for years after his death.

1614   November 17   "My cousin Shakespeare coming to town [London] I went to see him how he did" (*Diary of Thomas Greene, Stratford Archives*).

The relationship of Shakespeare and Thomas Greene, lawyer and Town Clerk of Stratford, is obscure. For a time he lived at New Place (*c.* 1609), and was now in London on Stratford business concerning the proposed enclosure of the common fields. Shakespeare was accompanied by his son-in-law, Dr. Hall.

> 1616 February 10 Marriage of Judith Shakespeare, aged thirty-two, to Thomas Quiney in Lent without license (*Stratford Parish Register*). Failing to appear before an ecclesiastical court when summoned, they were excommunicated (*Worcester Consistory Court*).

Thomas Quiney, son of Richard Quiney, was a vintner at the Cage in Stratford and Chamberlain of the Corporation. His later career shows that he was none too steady. Traces of the marriage may be seen in the revision of Shakespeare's will. Adams's suggestion (*Life*, p. 459) that Shakespeare disapproved of the match and lacked confidence in his son-in-law is a conjecture from the nature of the bequests.

> 1616 March 25 Shakespeare revised and signed his will. Among other bequests are: "to my fellows John Heminge, Richard Burbage, and Henry Condell, xxvj*s.* viij*d.* a piece to buy them rings," and "unto my wife my second best bed with the furniture" (*the will is preserved at Somerset House*).

Other persons mentioned in the will are Susanna and John Hall (Shakespeare's daughter and son-in-law), Judith (his daughter), Elizabeth Hall (his granddaughter), Joan Hart (his sister) and her three sons, William Walker (his godson), Thomas Combe, Thomas Russell, Francis Collins, Hamnet Sadler, William Reynolds, and Anthony and John Nash, all citizens of Stratford. John and Susanna Hall were appointed executors, and the witnesses were Francis Collins, Julius Shaw, John Robinson, Hamnet Sadler, and Robert Whattcott. The date on which the will was originally drawn up is not known.

> 1616 April 25 Burial of "Will Shakespeare, gent." (*Stratford Parish Register*).

The monument, which was erected before 1623, gives the date of the poet's death as April 23 and his age as fifty-three. It bears an inscription:

> *Iudicio Pylium, genio Socratem, arte Maronem:*
> *Terra tegit, populus mæret, Olympus habet.*
>
> Stay, Passenger, why goest thou by so fast?
> Read, if thou canst, whom envious Death hath placed
> Within this monument, Shakespeare, with whom
> Quick Nature died, whose name doth deck this tomb
> Far more than cost, sith all that he hath writ
> Leaves living art but page to serve his wit.

Nearby on the chancel floor, on a gravestone which itself bears no name, is another epitaph, usually identified as Shakespeare's:

> Good friend, for Jesus sake forbear
> To dig the dust enclosed here.
> Blest be the man that spares these stones,
> And curst be he that moves my bones.

For the tradition that Shakespeare wrote these lines himself, see below, p. 30.

Before the publication of the First Folio in 1623, sixteen of Shakespeare's plays had been published in forty-five editions, thirty-two of which bore the author's name on the title-page: *Titus Andronicus* (1594, 1600, 1611); *Richard II* (1597, 1598 [2], 1608, 1615); *Richard III* (1597, 1598, 1602, 1605, 1612, 1622); *Romeo and Juliet* (1597, 1599, 1609, and another without date); *1 Henry IV* (1598, 1599, 1604, 1608, 1613, 1622); *Love's Labor's Lost* (1598); *A Midsummer Night's Dream* (1600, 1619); *The Merchant of Venice* (1600, 1619); *2 Henry IV* (1600); *Much Ado about Nothing* (1600); *Henry V* (1600, 1602, 1619); *The Merry Wives of Windsor* (1602, 1619); *Hamlet* (1603, 1604–05, 1611, and another without date); *King Lear* (1608, 1619); *Troilus and Cressida* (1609 [2]); and *Othello* (1622).

During the dramatist's lifetime the following plays, not included in the First Folio, were published as by W. or William Shakespeare: *The London Prodigal* (1605); *A Yorkshire Tragedy* (1608); *Pericles* (1609); *The First Part of Sir John Oldcastle* (1619). The following were published with the initials W. S.: *Locrine* (1595); *Thomas, Lord Cromwell* (1602); and *The Puritan, or The Widow of Watling Street* (1607). Apparently Shakespeare's name had publicity value. All six of these plays were reprinted in the second issue of the Third Folio (1664). Shakespeare could have had nothing to do with *Sir John Oldcastle*, which is known to have been written by Michael Drayton and others (see below, p. 361).

Before 1616 there are more than two hundred allusions to Shakespeare and his works; nearly a hundred authors quote or parody lines from his plays or poems, occasionally mentioning Shakespeare's name. The works most frequently quoted or alluded to are: *Venus and Adonis*, 34 times; *Hamlet*, 29 times; *Henry IV* (both parts), 29 times; *Lucrece*, 18 times; *Richard III*, 16 times; *Romeo and Juliet*, 15 times. The character, Falstaff, is referred to 14 times (see F. J. Furnivall and J. Munro, *The Shakspere Allusion Books*, 2 volumes [1909]; reprinted, 1932).

TRADITIONS CONCERNING THE MAN AND HIS WORK

Tradition concerning Shakespeare has come down in three main streams. That from Stratford is richest in what is of importance to a biographer; that from Oxford is concerned solely with the Davenants; and that from London deals mainly with Shakespeare's career in the theatre and his relations with his contemporaries. No tradition has the validity of a document; much of that concerning Shakespeare is valueless, but some of it seems probable enough and is not inconsistent with other evidence.

Education and Apprenticeship

That William Shakespeare attended "at a Free School" (Rowe, *Life*, 1709). Nicholas Rowe (1674–1719), barrister, successful dramatist, poet laureate to Queen Anne, and friend of Addison and Pope, was Shakespeare's first editor and biographer. Rowe's *Life* was a part of the prefatory essay to his edition of Shakespeare, and can hardly be said to be the work of a diligent scholar. Rowe consulted few records and did not trouble to make a journey to Stratford to find out what might have been preserved there. Instead, he was content to gather such traditions as were circulating in London, especially from Thomas Betterton, the distinguished Restoration actor who made a "journey into Warwickshire on purpose to gather up what remains he could of a name for which he had so great a veneration." But in the eighteenth century there was doubt that even Betterton had made such a journey. Nevertheless, Rowe's biography sufficed for more than three-quarters of a century and was reproduced in edition after edition of Shakespeare's works.

Regarding Shakespeare's education, Rowe does not state whether the free school was at Stratford or elsewhere, but he does add that the boy was withdrawn from school by his father's straitened circumstances. There are no records of the Stratford Grammar School for this period.

> That his "father was a butcher, and I have been told heretofore by some of the neighbors, that when he was a boy he exercised his father's trade, but when he killed a calf, he would do it in a high style, and make a speech" (Aubrey, *Brief Lives*, 1681).

John Aubrey (1626–97), the antiquary—"a shiftless person, roving and magotty-headed"—collected biographical notes which were used later by Anthony à Wood in his *Athenæ Oxoniensis* (1691-2). As regards Shakespeare, Aubrey's chief informant, in addition to "some of the neighbors," was William Beeston, a Restoration actor and son of Christopher Beeston, a member of the Shakespearean company in 1598. Aubrey, however, permitted Beeston to die without exhaustively pumping him for information. The *Brief Lives* exist in a disordered manuscript in the Bodleian Library, Oxford; they were arranged and published by A. Clark in 1898. (For a statement contradictory to the above, also by Aubrey, see below, p. 24.) Shakespeare's father is known to have been a glover; numerous attempts have been made to reconcile this trade with that of butcher. He could hardly have been both.

That John Shakespeare took his son into "his own employment" (Rowe, 1709).

Departure from Stratford

"The clerk that showed me this church is above 80 years old; he says that this Shakespeare was formerly in this town bound apprentice to a butcher; but that he run from his master to London, and there was rec'd into the playhouse as a serviture, and by this means had an opportunity to be what he afterwards proved" ("Mr. Dowdall," Letter addressed to "Mr. Southwell" from Butler's Marston, Warwickshire, 1693).

Already, before the end of the seventeenth century, the inquisitiveness of tourists about the distinguished Stratfordian was evidently being satisfied in the usual way.

That he was "much given to all unluckiness in stealing venison and rabbits particularly from Sir [———] Lucy who had him oft whipt and sometimes imprisoned and at last made him fly his native country to his great advancement. But his revenge was so great that he is his Justice Clodpate and calls him a great man and that in allusion to his name bore three louses rampant for his arms" (additions of Richard Davies [died 1708] to a manuscript written by William Fulman and now at Corpus Christi College, Oxford).

That he fell into ill company, "some that made a frequent practice of deer-stealing . . . more than once . . . robbing a park that belonged to Sir Thomas Lucy of Charlecote, near Stratford. For this he was prosecuted by that gentleman, as he thought somewhat too severely; and in order to revenge that ill-usage, he made a ballad upon him . . . [and] was obliged to leave his business and family in Warwickshire, for some time, and shelter himself in London" (Rowe, 1709).

That "at Stratford, the family maintain . . . [he] stole Sir Thomas Lucy's buck to celebrate his wedding-day, and for that purpose only" (Sir Richard Phillips, *The Monthly Magazine, or British Register*, 1818).

That Shakespeare owed his release from Lucy's persecution "at last to the Queen's kindness" (*Biographia Britannica*, 1763).

That he was released from Lucy's persecution by Robert, Earl of Leicester (S. W. Fullom, *History of William Shakespeare*, 1862).

That the park was Fulbrook and not Charlecote. "Within this park is now standing, on a spot called Daisy Hill, a farm-house, which was anciently the keeper's lodge. To this lodge it is reported our Shakespeare was conveyed, and there confined at the time of the charge" (Samuel Ireland, *Picturesque Views on the Warwickshire Avon*, 1795).

The poaching tradition comes down in two independent streams—from Nicholas Rowe and from Richard Davies—though both probably were tapping the same vein for which William Oldys said Betterton was responsible. William Fulman (1632–88), a scholar of Corpus Christi College, Oxford, became a clergyman of Maisey-Hampton, Gloucestershire. He himself had little to say of Shakespeare, but his papers passed to Richard Davies (died 1708), rector of Sapperton, Gloucestershire, and later Archdeacon of Coventry, about whom little is certainly known, save that he made additions to Fulman's notes before they passed to Corpus Christi College. Davies confused Shakespeare's Justice Shallow with Clodpate in Shadwell's *Epsom Wells.*

William Oldys (1696–1761) made many notes on English authors as interlineations and marginalia in printed books. A *Life of Shakespeare* which Oldys had engaged to furnish a bookseller "with ten years of the life of Shakespeare unknown to the biographers and commentators," and for which he is known to have collected materials, is now lost. Some of the notes, however, were accessible to George Steevens, who quoted them in his *Works of Shakespeare* (1788).

The popularity of the poaching tradition accounts for its later embroidery. The change of the name of Lucy's park from Charlecote to Fulbrook is perhaps due to eighteenth-century knowledge that not in Sir Thomas's time, nor indeed until the time of his grandson in 1618, was there an impaled deerpark at Charlecote. Moreover, there is little similarity between Shallow, "this same starved Justice . . . like a man made after dinner of a cheese paring . . . this genius of famine . . . this Vice's dagger . . . become a squire," boasting of "the wildness of his youth and the feats he hath done about Turnbull Street," and the real Thomas Lucy, a conspicuous servant of the crown, who, about the time this incident is supposed to have taken place, was receiving the commendations of the Privy Council for his services in providing troops for Ireland. Nor is it likely that Shakespeare would have nursed his wrath and kept it warm for ten or fifteen years before taking his simple revenge. Part of the ballad was quoted by Oldys and all of it by Jordan in Malone's *Variorum*, Vol. II.

That "though as Ben Jonson says of him that he had but little Latin and less Greek, he understood Latin pretty well, for he had been in his younger years a schoolmaster in the country" (Aubrey, 1681).

A marginal note reads: "from Mr. ⸺ Beeston." The passage alluded to is to be found in Jonson's elegy prefixed to the First Folio, 1623: "thou hadst small Latin, and less Greek." This tradition has recently been revived by Adams (*Life*, p. 92) as the most plausible explanation of Shakespeare's "lost years."

Early Life in London

That "this William being inclined naturally to poetry and acting, came to London I guess about eighteen and was an actor at one of the playhouses and did act exceedingly well. Now B. Jonson was never a good actor, but an excellent instructor" (Aubrey, 1681).

That he was "received into the company then in being, at first in a very mean rank; but his admirable wit, and his natural turn of it to the stage, soon distinguished him, if not as an extraordinary actor, yet as an excellent writer" (Rowe, 1709).

That when Shakespeare first came from the country to the playhouse he was not admitted to act, but held horses during the performance; "by his dexterity and care he soon got a good deal of business in this way, and was personally known to most of the quality that frequented the house, insomuch that, being obliged . . . to train up boys to assist him, it became long afterwards a usual way among them to recommend themselves by saying that they were Shakespeare's boys" (Sir William Davenant, from a "MS. note in the University Library, Edinburgh," c. 1748, printed by Halliwell-Phillipps. Repeated by Robert Shiels, *Lives of the Poets*, 1753; Johnson, *Works of Shakespeare*, 1765; and *Lives of the Poets*, 1779).

Since some of Oldys's notes are said to have passed to the compilers of these *Lives*, it is possible that Oldys is really the source of this tradition. All it tells is that the eighteenth century had quite as naïve a belief that genius would out as has the twentieth.

That Shakespeare owed his rise in the theatre to his accidentally holding the horse of a gentleman at the door (Sir Richard Phillips, *The Monthly Magazine, or British Register*, 1818).

"There is a stage tradition that his first office in the theatre was that of call-boy, or prompter's attendant, whose employment it is to give performers notice to be ready to enter" (Malone, *Supplement*, 1790).

This statement does not appear in Malone's revision of his material for the *Variorum*.

That "from an actor of plays he became a composer" (William Fulman, before 1688).

His Acting

That he was "a much better poet than player" (*Historia Histrionica*, 1699).

That he "did act exceedingly well" (Aubrey, 1681).

That he played "kingly parts in sport, and would have been a king among the meaner sort" (John Davies of Hereford, *The Scourge of Folly*, 1620).

That "the top of his performance was the ghost in his own *Hamlet*" (Rowe, 1709).

That one of Shakespeare's younger brothers, who lived to a good old age, had in his younger days come to London and seen Shakespeare act in some of his plays. "All that could be recollected from him of his brother Will . . . was the faint, general, and almost lost ideas he had of having seen him act a part in one of his own comedies wherein being to personate a decrepit old man, he wore a long beard, and appeared so weak and drooping and unable to walk, that he was forced to be supported and carried by another person to a table, at which he was seated among some company, who were eating, and one of them sung a song" (Oldys, in Steevens, *Works of William Shakespeare*, 1778).

The part is that of Adam in *As You Like It*, II, vii. Unfortunately, none of Shakespeare's brothers survived him.

> "*The Tragedy of Hamlet:* Hamlet being performed by Mr. Betterton, Sir William [Davenant] (having seen Mr. Taylor of the Blackfriars company act it, who being instructed by the author, Mr. Shakespeare) taught Mr. Betterton in every particle of it" (Downes, *Roscius Anglicanus*, 1708).

> "*King Henry the 8th:* The part of the king was so right and justly done by Mr. Betterton, he being instructed in it by Sir William, who had it from old Mr. Lowin, that had his instructions from Mr. Shakespeare himself" (*ibid.*).

John Downes was a prompter in the London theatres of the Restoration, including the Lincoln's Inn Fields Theatre which housed Davenant's company. If his statements are true, there is an unbroken stage tradition in the case of two Shakespearean roles, one of them an important one. Shakespeare may have instructed Lowin, who joined the King's Men in 1603, but hardly Taylor, who was not a member before 1619.

The Plays and Poems

(1) *The Merry Wives of Windsor:*

> That *The Merry Wives* was written at Queen Elizabeth's command, "and by her direction, and she was so eager to see it acted that she commanded it to be finished in fourteen days, and was afterwards, as tradition tells us, very well pleased at the representation" (John Dennis, *The Comical Gallant, or The Amours of Sir John Falstaff*, 1702).

> That she "commanded Shakespeare to write the comedy of *The Merry Wives* and to write it in ten days time, so eager was she for the wicked diversion" (John Dennis, *The Person of Quality's Answer to Mr. Collier's Letter*, 1704).

John Dennis (1657–1734) was a Cambridge graduate, a dramatist, and a critic. His *Comical Gallant* was an adaptation of *The Merry Wives*, and the letter referred to was Jeremy Collier's *Dissuasive from the Playhouse*, 1703, one of several works by that author on the "immorality and profaneness" of the stage.

> "The fairies in the fifth act [of *The Merry Wives*] makes a handsome compliment to the Queen in her palace of Windsor, who had obliged him to write a play of Sir John Falstaff in love, and which I am very well assured he performed in a fortnight" (Charles Gildon, "Remarks on the Plays of Shakespeare," in *The Works of Mr. William Shakespeare, Volume the Seventh*, 1710).

Charles Gildon (1665–1724) was a dramatist and bookseller's hack pilloried in Pope's *Dunciad*. The volume in which his remarks appear contains Shakespeare's poems and was a supplement to the Rowe edition issued by another publisher.

> That "old Mr. Bowman the player reported from Sir William Bishop that some part of Sir John Falstaff's character was drawn from a townsman of Stratford, who either faithlessly broke a contract, or spitefully refused to part with some land for a valuable consideration adjoining to Shakespeare's in or near that town" (Oldys, in Steevens, *Works of William Shakespeare*, 1778).

John Bowman was an actor in Betterton's company. Sir William Bishop (died 1700) lived in Bridgetown, a part of Stratford.

(2) *Henry IV:*

> That the historical person with which Shakespeare "undertook to play a buffoon was not Falstaff, but Sir John Oldcastle, and that offense being worthily taken by personages descended from his title . . . the poet was put to make an ignorant shift of abusing Sir John Falstophe, a man not inferior of virtue, though not so famous in piety as the other" (Richard James, *Epistle* to Sir Harry Bourchier, c. 1625).

This fact was mentioned by others in the seventeenth century and is corroborated by bibliographical evidence in the quarto and folio texts of *1 Henry IV*. Richard James was librarian to Sir Robert Cotton. He has confused Falstaff with Fastolf.

(3) *Hamlet:*

> That "he writ the scene of the ghost in *Hamlet* at his house which bordered on the charnel house and churchyard" (Gildon, *Lives and Characters of the English Dramatic Poets*, 1698).

> *Hamlet*, I, iv, "I have been assured he wrote in a charnel house in the midst of the night" (Gildon, "Remarks on the Plays of Shakespeare," *loc. cit.*, 1710).

> That Shakespeare "received but five pounds for his *Hamlet*" (Oldys, as quoted by Malone, *Supplementary Observations*, 1780).

(4) *Romeo and Juliet:*

> That Shakespeare himself said he was forced to kill his Mercutio "in the third act to prevent being killed by him" (Dryden, Appendix to *The Conquest of Granada*, Part II, 1672).

(5) *Much Ado about Nothing:*

> "The humour of . . . the constable in *A Midsummer Night's Dream* he happened to take at Grendon in Bucks which is the road from London to Stratford, and there was living that constable about 1642 when I first came to Oxon. Mr. Joseph Howe is of that parish and knew him" (Aubrey, 1681).

In the margin Aubrey adds: "I think it was midsummer night that he happened to lie there." There is, of course, no constable in *A Midsummer Night's*

Dream; Aubrey must have been thinking, if at all, of *Love's Labor's Lost, Measure for Measure,* or *Much Ado.*

(6) *Titus Andronicus:*

"I have been told by some anciently conversant with the stage, that it [*Titus Andronicus*] was not originally his, but brought by a private author to be acted, and he only gave some master touches to one or two of the principal parts or characters" (Edward Ravenscroft, *Titus Andronicus, or The Rape of Lavinia,* 1678, an adaptation of Shakespeare's play).

This is the only tradition concerning the authenticity of any Shakespearean play.

(7) *Othello:*

"I'm assur'd from very good hands that the person that acted Iago was in much esteem for a comedian, which made Shakespeare put several words and expressions into his part (perhaps not so agreeable to his character) to make the audience laugh" (Charles Gildon, *Reflections on Rymer's Short View of Tragedy,* 1694).

(8) *The Passionate Pilgrim:*

That Shakespeare was "much offended" at William Jaggard, the stationer, who "altogether unknown to him, presumed to make so bold with his name" as to put it on *The Passionate Pilgrim,* of which he was not the sole author, and that to do himself right he published in his own name the poems stolen (Thomas Heywood, *An Apology for Actors,* 1612).

Personalia

(1) The Davenants:

That "he was wont to go to his native country once a year" . . . and "did commonly in his journey lie at [the house of John Davenant, vintner] in Oxon: where he was exceedingly respected" (Aubrey, 1681).

That Shakespeare was the godfather of William Davenant. "In all probability he got him" (Thomas Hearne, *Diary,* 1709).

This remark is elaborated by Hearne, Pope, Oldys, and others in the early eighteenth century upon the basis of an anecdote (without names) found in the works of Taylor the Water Poet.

That "Sir William [Davenant] would sometimes when he was pleasant over a glass of wine with his most intimate friends, e. g., Sam: Butler (author of *Hudibras*) etc., say that it seemed to him that he writ with the very spirit that Shakespeare, and was [*seemed* is written in interlinearily] contented enough to be thought his son." He would then tell them a story "in which way his mother had a very light report" (Aubrey, 1681).

Such was the vanity of Charles II's poet laureate! The doubt cast upon the scandal by that word *seemed* may be Anthony à Wood's, himself a resident of Oxford. In his account of Davenant, for which he used Aubrey's notes, though he elaborated somewhat upon the contrast between the sober, melancholic husband and the handsome, witty wife, "in which she was imitated by none of her children but by this William," Wood omits even the slightest allusion to scandal. It is not unlikely that the story got its start in much the way suggested by Hearne's preposterous parenthesis to the godfather tradition, quoted above. Thomas Hearne (1678–1735), like Wood, was famous as a historical antiquary who had made a lifelong study of Oxford antiquities. However the notion arose that William Davenant was more than a poetical child of Shakespeare, eighteenth-century London repeated this tale in its fullest form and accepted it as a story fostered by Davenant himself.

(2) Ben Jonson:

> That Shakespeare was responsible for getting Jonson's first play presented (Rowe, 1709).

> That Shakespeare was godfather to one of Ben Jonson's children, and, after considering for a great while what should be the fittest gift to bestow upon his godchild, said he resolved to "give him a dozen good latten spoons, and thou shalt translate them" (Sir Nicholas L'Estrange, *Merry Passages and Jests*, Harl. MS. 6395, n. d., and alluded to elsewhere).

Sir Nicholas L'Estrange (1629–55) was a collector of anecdotes who gave as authority for this story a "Mr. Dun" (Donne? or Duncombe?). *Latten*, here punned upon, was a kind of alloy formerly used for tableware and church utensils.

> That "many were the wit-combats betwixt him and Ben. Jonson, which two I behold like a Spanish great galleon and an English man of war; Master Jonson . . . built far higher in learning, solid but slow . . . Shakespeare . . . lesser in bulk, but lighter in sailing" (Thomas Fuller, *Worthies of England*, 1662).

> That Shakespeare wrote an epitaph on Ben Jonson (manuscript notes compiled by Nicholas Burgh, *c.* 1650 [Bodl. Ashm., 38] and by Thomas Plume (1630–74), Archdeacon of Rochester, *c.* 1657 [Plume MS. 25, at Maldon, Essex]).

The deep-seated tradition about enmity between Jonson and Shakespeare must have grown from very puny seed. All that disturbs the serenity is the allusion in *The Return from Parnassus* (*c.* 1600–02) to a "purge" Shakespeare gave Jonson "that made him bewray his credit" (III, iii); Jonson's criticism of Shakespeare's unrestrained facility in writing, and his reply to the players' praise of Shakespeare for never having "blotted out line"— "would he had blotted a thousand!" (*Timber*, 1641); and the remarks Jonson passed in his cups to Drummond about Shakespeare's having lacked art (*Notes of Conversations with Ben Jonson Made by William Drummond of Hawthornden*, January, 1619). But these detractions are negatived by Jonson's fine elegy, *To the Memory of My Beloved the Author, Mr. William Shakespeare, and What He Hath Left Us,* which was prefixed to the first collected edition of Shakespeare's plays (1623), and by Jonson's statement—also in *Timber*—that "I lov'd the man and do honor his memory on this side idolatry, as much as any."

(3) Closing Years:

> That "he frequented the plays all his younger time, but in his elder days lived at Stratford and supplied the stage with two plays every year, and for that had an allowance so large, that he spent at the rate of a £1000 a year, as I have heard" (John Ward, *Diary,* 1661–3).

John Ward (1629–81), as vicar of Holy Trinity Church, Stratford, from 1662 to 1681, had an excellent opportunity to collect biographical tradition about Shakespeare, but, unfortunately, he did not make the most of it. When he first arrived, Shakespeare's daughter, Judith Quiney, was still alive, and in his *Diary* Ward made a note: "a letter to my brother to see Mrs. Quiney." Judith, however, was buried on February 9, 1662. Other relatives of Shakespeare were also living in Stratford. Ward knew that Elizabeth Hall, Shakespeare's granddaughter, now married to Sir John Barnard, was living at Abington, Northants, but he apparently did not go to see her. Yet, as vicar of the church in which Shakespeare was buried, he seems to have been expected to know something about the dramatist. "Remember," he wrote, "to peruse Shakespeare's plays and be versed in them, that I may not be ignorant in that matter." The record quoted above, so far as it concerns Shakespeare's relations with his company, is not what from other sources is known to have been Elizabethan theatrical practice. The financial detail, obviously a folk calculation, is absurdly high. Ward's *Diary,* as a whole, is notoriously uncritical. Extracts were published by Charles Severn in the Camden Society publications, 1839.

> That his last days were spent "in ease, retirement, and the conversation of his friends" (Rowe, 1709).
>
> That "Shakespeare, Drayton, and Ben Jonson had a merry meeting, and it seems drank too hard, for Shakespeare died of a fever there contracted" (John Ward, *Diary*).
>
> That "he died a papist" (Davies's additions to Fulman's MS.).
>
> That he composed his own epitaph (Dowdall, 1693) to prevent his bones being removed to the bone-house (William Hall, Letter to Edward Thwaites, 1694).

Hall, a graduate of Queen's College, Oxford, adds these details to an account of a visit to Stratford which included a pilgrimage to the church "to visit the ashes of the great Shakespeare."

(4) Miscellaneous:

> That "he was a glover's son—Sir John Mennis saw once his old father in his shop—a merry cheek'd old man—that said—Will was a good honest fellow, but he durst have cracked a jest with him at any time" (MS. notes compiled *c.* 1657 by Thomas Plume, Archdeacon of Rochester, and now at Maldon, Essex).

This anecdote is the nearest thing to contemporary reminiscence that has been preserved. The only known Sir John Mennis, however, was born in Kent in 1599 and could not have remembered John Shakespeare, who died in 1601. His brother, Sir Matthew, born *c.* 1593, might have remembered him.

> That Shakespeare once preceded Richard Burbage to an assignation with a citizeness who admired Burbage, excusing the trick with the word that William the Conqueror was before Richard the Third (John Manningham, *Diary*, March 13, 1602).

This is the only contemporary anecdote.

> That Shakespeare "was not a company keeper, lived in Shoreditch, wouldn't be debauched, and if invited to, writ he was in pain" (Aubrey, 1681).

> That "he was, indeed, honest, and of an open, and free nature" (Jonson, *Timber*, 1641).

> That "he was a handsome well-shaped man: very good company, and of a very ready and pleasant smooth wit" (Aubrey, 1681).

> That his genius inclined "him to festivity, yet he could (when so disposed), be solemn and serious, as appears by his tragedies" (Fuller, *Worthies*, 1662).

> That the players "scarce received from him a blot in his papers" (Heminge and Condell, Preface to the First Folio, 1623, and Jonson, *Timber*, 1641).

> That Shakespeare "received great and uncommon marks of favor and friendship from the Earl of Southampton, who at one time gave him a thousand pounds to enable him to go through with a purchase he heard he had a mind to" (Rowe, 1709).

The gift seems unreasonably large when one considers the comparatively modest sums Shakespeare spent on even his most ambitious real-estate purchases.

> That James I "was pleased with his own hand to write an amicable letter to Mr. Shakespeare, which tho now lost, remained long in the hands of Sir William Davenant" (advertisement in *A Collection of Poems . . . by William Shakespeare, c.* 1709).

An ever alert conjecture has, of course, suggested its very subject: thanks to the poet for his complimentary notices of the Stuart dynasty in *Macbeth* and elsewhere.

That Fulke Greville desired to be "known to posterity under no other no-
tions than of Shakespeare's and Ben Jonson's Master, Chancellor Eger-
ton's Patron, Bishop Overal's Lord, and Sir Philip Sidney's Friend" (David
Lloyd, *Statesmen and Favourites of England*, 1665).

The basis of this statement is perhaps Greville's famous epitaph: "Servant to
Queen Elizabeth, Councellor to King James, Friend to Sir Philip Sidney."

That Shakespeare slept one night under a crab-tree at Bidford after a bout
with the Bidford sippers (Letter in *The British Magazine*, 1762, elaborated by John Jordan some time between 1770 and 1790).

Jordan is known to have conducted visitors through Stratford and to have
corresponded with Edmund Malone.

That Shakespeare wrote facetious verses on the name of John Combe (*A Relation of a Short Survey of Twenty-six Counties . . . by a Captain, a
Lieutenant, and an Ancient . . . 1634*).

The epigram is frequently quoted in the seventeenth and eighteenth centuries, and by 1740 it is stated that Shakespeare also wrote one on Tom
Combe, brother to John. More significant than the tradition of a paltry
satirical epitaph is the fact that, as early as 1634, Stratford was becoming a
shrine for pilgrims.

Portraits

Only two of the numerous portraits of Shakespeare can be regarded as in
any sense authentic: the half-length statue by Gerard Janssen on the monument in Holy Trinity Church, Stratford, and the copper-plate engraving by
Martin Droeshout for the First Folio edition of Shakespeare's plays, 1623.
Neither is a life portrait, but both were executed within six or seven years of
the poet's death, and both must have had the approval of Shakespeare's relatives, friends, or fellow workers. Other portraits professing to be Shakespeare's (including the "Flower Portrait," inscribed "1609" and called the
"Droeshout Original," in the Memorial Library at Stratford) have been rejected either as derivatives from the two accepted originals or as otherwise
unauthentic (see M. H. Spielmann, "Shakespeare's Portraiture," in *Studies in
the First Folio Written for the Shakespeare Association*, 1924).

SUGGESTED REFERENCES

For bibliography pertaining to this chapter, see p. 3.

2

SHAKESPEARE'S ENGLAND

How many goodly creatures are there here!
How beauteous mankind is! O brave new world,
That has such people in't!
                    —*The Tempest*, V, i, 182 ff.

The fear of external dangers causeth forces at home to be more united; it is to all sorts a kind of bridle, it maketh virtuous minds watchful, it holdeth contrary dispositions in suspense, and it settleth those wits on work in better things which would else be employed on worse.
                    —Richard Hooker, *Of the Laws of Ecclesiastical Polity,*
                    Dedication to Book V (1597).

THE NATURE OF OUR NATION IS FREE, STOUT, HAULT, PROD-igal of life and blood," remarked Sir Thomas Smith, Queen Elizabeth's ambassador to France and Secretary of State (*De Republica Anglorum* [1583], Book II, ch. 24). No formula will explain the Elizabethan Englishman, but many times in these pages the words of this scholar-statesman will come to mind.

THE SPIRIT OF TUDOR ENGLAND

The age that produced Shakespeare was an era of change and restlessness. Everywhere—in religion, in philosophy, in politics, in science, in literature—new ideas were springing into life and coming into conflict with the established order of things. It is possible to paint a brutal picture of Renaissance England by telling nothing that is not true. And by the same selective method it is just as possible to idealize the period as possessing all human virtues. Equally striking are the age's search for the "knowledge of causes and secret motions of things" and its adolescent flippancy and swaggering; its newly awakened sense of a world to be won and its love of glittering toys; its spirit of adventure and its warlike turmoil; its wonder at natural phenomena and its superstition; its concern for the souls of men and its mockery of holy things; its lusty enjoyment of the whole of life and its depravity and moral blunt-

·[33]·

ness; the luxurious ostentation of its apparel and the filth and squalor of its streets; its humanism and its bigotry; its common sense and its sentimentality; its idealism and its shamelessness; the sweetness of its songs and the coarseness of its jests.

The curious, almost grandiose, spirit of the Elizabethan age is eloquently summed up by Marlowe's Tamburlaine:

> Nature that fram'd us of four elements,
> Warring within our breasts for regiment,
> Doth teach us all to have aspiring minds.
> Our souls, whose faculties can comprehend
> The wondrous architecture of the world
> And measure every wand'ring planet's course,
> Still climbing after knowledge infinite,
> And always moving as the restless spheres,
> Wills us to wear ourselves and never rest,
> Until we reach the ripest fruit of all.
> (Part I, II, vi, 869 ff.)

For Tamburlaine "that perfect bliss and sole felicity" was an earthly crown; for others it was some other ideal. No Elizabethan would have thought Francis Bacon sophomoric for writing to his uncle, while yet an undergraduate, that he had taken all knowledge as his province. Similarly, Shakespeare's versatility and breadth of interest were but the full expression of the age in which he lived.

The age which produced Shakespeare was itself the product of several generations of preparation. The English Renaissance was something much more complex than the revival of Greek and Roman culture, important as that was, and it did not at once attain its full flowering. A whole series of events and discoveries, coming together at the end of the fifteenth century, transformed and compromised, if it did not actually sweep away, many of the institutions and the habits of mind that we call medieval. The gradual break-up of feudalism, the challenge to the authority and the unity of the medieval church, the discovery of gunpowder and the consequent revolution and democratization of warfare, the discovery of the mariner's compass and the possibility of safely navigating the limitless ocean, the production of paper and the invention of printing, and later, before the sixteenth century was half over, the Copernican system of astronomy which formulated a new center of the universe—all of these new conceptions had a profound effect upon human thought and became the foundations for intellectual, moral, social, and economic changes which quickly made themselves felt.

In Italy, in France, and in Germany, the Renaissance had developed gradually over several centuries and with a characteristic emphasis in each nation; in England, the insular position of the country and the conservative nature of the English people made its reception more tardy and, at the same time, less cataclysmic. Medieval England may be said to have come to an inglorious end with the fifteenth-century Wars of the Roses. These wars were followed by the unsettling experiences of the Protestant Reformation—itself an aspect of the reawakening—which prevented any early flowering of the Renaissance proper. Modern England was born in the Puritan Revolution which, politically as well as religiously, was an aftermath of the reforming zeal. The age of Elizabeth, therefore, was a kind of lull between two storms, glorious while it lasted and even more glorious in retrospect.

Both the Renaissance and the Reformation had been anticipated in England by more than a century. The poetry of Chaucer is more akin to Elizabethan poetry than it is to medieval; Wycliffe's preaching and the Lollard movement were spiritually similar to the activities of the Tudor reformers; even the national spirit had burst into flame for a moment under Edward III and the Black Prince, but had subsided. Now in the reign of the great queen, England entered upon an intellectual development abreast of the Continent. The humanistic spirit, eagerly interested in all the glorious, infinite capabilities of the individual, was abroad.

> What a piece of work is a man! How noble in reason! How infinite in faculty! In form and moving how express and admirable! In action how like an angel! In apprehension how like a god! The beauty of the world! The paragon of animals! (*Hamlet*, II, ii, 315 ff.)

The greatest literary example of the humanistic spirit is Shakespeare's Hamlet, the ideal, well-rounded prince of the Renaissance, possessed of "the courtier's, soldier's, scholar's, eye, tongue, sword."

EXPANSION AND OPPORTUNITY

For England in the sixteenth century the world had suddenly expanded. With the discovery of the new continents beyond the sea, the geographical center of the world shifted from the Mediterranean to the Atlantic. From being a comparatively unimportant island kingdom, lying at the northern edge of Christendom, Britain became a great power through her shipping. The sea was no longer merely an insulating barrier against unwelcome foreign influences, serving, as Shakespeare put it, "as a moat defensive to a house against the envy of less happier lands" (*Richard II*, II, i, 48). The sea became the great highway, and the Elizabethan sea-dogs, encouraged by their sovereign, went everywhere. Sir Francis Drake, Sir Humphrey Gilbert, Sir Walter Raleigh, Martin Frobisher, Sir John Hawkins, Sir Richard Grenville, Sir Hugh Willoughby, Richard Chancellor, Anthony Jenkinson, John Davis, Henry Hudson, William Baffin—many of them important in the history of our own country—are only a few of the daring English explorers or merchants whose deeds fired the imaginations of Shakespeare and his contemporaries.

The "Homer of these Elizabethan Odysseys" was Richard Hakluyt, who never went to sea in his life, but whose *Principal Navigations, Voyages, Traffics, and Discoveries of the English Nation* (1589), dedicated to Sir Francis Walsingham, Elizabeth's Secretary of State, is filled with pride at the heroic exploits of his countrymen:

> it cannot be denied, but as in all former ages they have been men full of activity, stirrers abroad and searchers of the remote parts of the world, so in this most famous and fearless government of her Most Excellent Majesty, through the special assistance and blessing of God, in search of the most opposite corners and quarters of the world, and to speak plainly in compassing the vast globe of the earth more than once have excelled all the nations and people of the earth. For which of the kings of this land before her Majesty had their banners ever seen in the Caspian Sea? Which of them hath ever dealt with the Emperor of Persia, as her Majesty hath done, and obtained for her merchant large and loving privileges? Whoever saw before this regiment an English ligier [resident ambassador] in the stately porch of the Grand Signior at Constantinople? Whoever found English consuls and agents at Tripolis in Syria, at Aleppo, at Babylon, at Balsara, and, which is more, whoever heard of Englishmen at Goa before now? What English ships did heretofore ever anchor in the mighty river of Plate? Pass and repass the unpassable (in former opinion) Strait of Magellan, range along the coast of Chile, Peru, and all the backside of Nova Hispania, further than any Christian ever passed, traverse the mighty breadth of the South Sea, land upon the Luzones in despite of the enemy, enter into alliance, amity, and traffic with the Princes of the Moluccaes and the Isle of Java, double the famous Cape of Bona Speranza, arrive at the Isle of Santa Helena, and, last of all, return most richly laden with the commodities of China, as the subjects of this now flourishing monarchy have done?

To be sure, the motive of much of this pioneering was greed of gain rather than the more lofty spirit of adventure. But Elizabethan England produced "stirrers abroad" whose insatiable curiosity sent them not only to Italy—the Mecca of all Elizabethan Englishmen—but, alone and on foot, far into unknown parts beyond. Fynes Moryson (1566–1630), for example, visited France, the Low Countries, Germany, Denmark, Poland, Switzerland, and Italy in 1591–5, and later the Holy Land and Constantinople, returning home to write a lengthy account of his travels in his *Itinerary* (1617). More famous was Thomas Coryat (1577–1617), who journeyed through France to Venice and back via Switzerland, Germany, and Holland, and published a gossipy account of his experiences in his *Crudities Hastily Gobbled Up* (1611). Later he ventured even further, and in the year of Shakespeare's death, Sir Thomas Roe, the English ambassador to the Great Mogul, wrote to Lord Pembroke from India on February 14, 1616, about Coryat's arrival in that distant land:

> He came hither afoot, hath past by Constantinople, Jerusalem, Bethlehem, Damascus, and briefly through all the Turk's territory, seen every post and pillar, observed every tomb, visited the monuments of Troy, Persia, and this king's dominion, all afoot, with most unwearied legs, and is now for Samarcand

in Tartarya to kiss Tamerlane's tomb, from thence to Susa, and to Prester Jhac in Ethiopia, where he will see the hill Amara, all afoot, and so foot it to Odcombe [his birthplace]. His notes are already too great for portage, some left at Aleppo, some at Hispan—enough to make any stationer an alderman that shall but serve the printer with paper.[1]

"Home keeping youth have ever homely wits," exclaims Valentine (*The Two Gentlemen of Verona*, I, i, 2), and the winds of Elizabethan England scattered young men

> through the world
> To seek their fortune farther than at home
> Where small experience grows.
> (*The Taming of the Shrew*, I, ii, 48 ff.)

Some influential fathers

> Put forth their sons to seek preferment out:
> Some to the wars, to try their fortune there;
> Some to discover islands far away.
> Some to the studious universities.
> (*The Two Gentlemen of Verona*, I, iii, 7 ff.)

In humbler rural circles, boys merely felt the strong attraction of London. Petruchio, the gentlemen of Verona, and William Shakespeare of Stratford were typical Elizabethan youths and brothers under their skins.

"Players," said Hamlet, "are the abstracts and brief chronicles of the time." The theatres of Shakespeare's London reflect this interest in the marvels of the great world, not only in the conventional Italian and other foreign settings of their plays, but also in their foreign themes, such as Marlowe's *Tamburlaine* (*c.* 1587), and in their glorification of the English traveler, such as Heywood's *Four Prentices of London* (1594) and Day and Rowley's *Travels of the Three English Brothers* (1607). The Elizabethan audience was willing and ready to love its heroes—as Desdemona did her Moor—for the dangers they had passed. Shakespeare's interest in faraway places was one he shared with his contemporaries. Even if it cannot be shown that he himself ever traveled, in London he had many opportunities to hear travelers' tales. He knew of Prester John, the fabulous Emperor of Abyssinia (*Much Ado about Nothing*); of Lapland sorcerers (*The Comedy of Errors*); of the Dutchman's reputation for polar exploration (*Twelfth Night*);

> And of the Cannibals that each other eat,
> The Anthropophagi and men whose heads
> Do grow beneath their shoulders
> (*Othello*, I, iii, 143 ff.);

of "the still vex'd Bermoothes," and of "mountaineers dewlapp'd like bulls" (*The Tempest*). His "deboshed fish," Caliban, was created partly from his

[1] *The Embassy of Sir Thomas Roe to India, 1615–19, as Narrated in his Journal and Correspondence*, ed. Sir William Foster, Oxford (1926), p. 83 n.

imagination and partly from tales he had heard or read of the aboriginals and the strange monsters seen by English seamen. "Were I in England now," exclaims Trinculo,

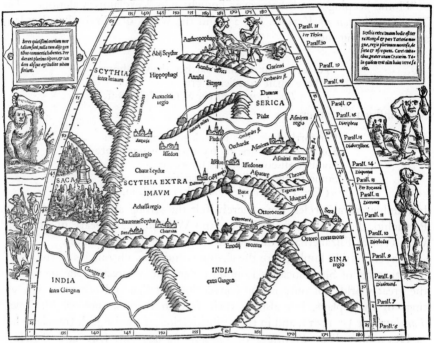

"Anthropophagi and men whose heads do grow beneath their shoulders" (From Claudius Ptolemaeus' *Geographia Universalis*, Basle, 1540)

as once I was—and had but this fish painted, not a holiday fool there but would give a piece of silver. There would this monster make a man; any strange beast there makes a man. When they will not give a doit to relieve a lame beggar, they will lay out ten to see a dead Indian. (*The Tempest*, II, ii, 28 ff.)

Michael Drayton had glorified colonization in his *Ode to the Virginian Voyage* (1605); Jonson, Chapman, and Marston had satirized it in *Eastward Ho* (1605); and there were some still provincial enough to laugh at travelers and bid them "See England First." To most Elizabethan Englishmen, their own country was still the most interesting in the world.

The bogus or "affectate" adventurer was also common enough.

He chooseth rather to be counted a spy than not a politician . . . rather to tell lies than not wonders . . . his discourse sounds big, but means nothing. . . . He disdains all things above his reach and preferreth all countries before his own. (Sir Thomas Overbury, *Characters, or Witty Descriptions of . . . Sundry Persons,* 1614.)

Such a person is that man of "a thousand aims," Sir Politic Would-Be, in Ben Jonson's *Volpone* (1606), whose "adventures [should be] put i' the Book of Voyages." In *Every Man out of His Humour* (1599) there is Shift, bragging of his exploits with his sword on foreign fields, and Puntarvolo, "over-Englishing his travels." The latter is also a ridiculous gambler in accident insurance—what Shakespeare calls a "putter-out of five for one" (*The Tempest,* III, iii, 48). "I do intend . . . to travel," says Puntarvolo in one of his expansive moments,

and because I will not altogether go upon expense, I am determined to put forth some five thousand pound, to be paid me five for one, upon the return of myself, my wife, and my dog from the Turk's court in Constantinople. If all or either of us miscarry in the journey, 'tis gone; if we be successful, why, there will be five and twenty thousand pound to entertain time withal. (II, i; cf. IV, iv.)

Such rascals and such fools haunted the London taverns and gambling dens, regaling the inexperienced with tales of wonders they had never seen:

"Did young gentlemen, as well as I, know the pleasure and profit of travel, they would not keep them at home within their native continent, but visit the world and win more wisdom in traveling two or three years than all the wealth their ancestors left them to possess. Ah, the sweet sight of ladies, the strange wonders in cities, and the divers manners of men and their conditions were able to ravish a young gentleman's senses with the surfeit of content, and what is a thousand pound spent to the obtaining of those pleasures?" All these novelties doth this pipned bragout boast on, when his only travel hath been to look on a fair day from Dover Cliffs to Calais. ("Cuthbert Coneycatcher," *The Defence of Coneycatching,* 1592.)

Valued at so high a rate, foreign experience "oftentimes [made] many to wander from themselves as well as from their country," as James Howell put it in his *Instructions for Foreign Travel* (1642):

and to bring back less wit than they carried forth. . . . They strive to degenerate as much as they can from Englishmen, and all their talk is still foreign . . . magnifying other nations.

The melancholy Jaques is a Shakespearean example of this type of traveler. "I fear you have sold your own lands," says Rosalind,

to see other men's. . . . Look you lisp and wear strange suits, disable all the benefits of your own country, be out of love with your nativity, and almost chide God for making you that countenance you are, or I will scarce think you have swam in a gondola." (*As You Like It,* IV, i, 22 ff.)

The most notorious of these affected fools, of course, was the Italianate Englishman. As early as 1570, Roger Ascham had not minced words in his excoriation of young gentlemen who traveled in Italy and brought back with them only her vanities and vices. He quotes an Italian proverb, *Englese italianato è un diavolo incarnato* ("an Englishman Italianate is a devil incarnate"), and adds:

> If some yet do not well understand what is an Englishman Italianated, I will plainly tell him. He, that by living and traveling in Italy, bringeth home into England out of Italy the religion, the learning, the policy, the experience, the manners of Italy. That is to say, for religion papistry or worse; for learning less commonly than they carried out with them; for policy a factious heart, a discoursing head, a mind to meddle in all men's matters; for experience plenty of new mischiefs never known in England before; for manners variety of vanities, and change of filthy living. These be the enchantments of Circes, brought out of Italy to mar men's manners in England. (*The Schoolmaster.*)

Ascham then girds at the "fond books, of late translated out of Italian into English"—like William Painter's *The Palace of Pleasure* (1566–7), though he specifically mentions none by name—which in the next generation were to serve Shakespeare and his fellows as source books for their plays. But even Shakespeare alludes to the

> Report of fashions in proud Italy,
> Whose manners still our tardy, apish nation
> Limps after in base imitation.
> (*Richard II*, II, i, 21–23.)

Whatever the abuses of travel in Shakespeare's day, the rising merchant class was quick to see the value of travel in broadening mental horizons, and Francis Bacon's essay *Of Travel* (1597) expresses the common-sense view. As a consequence, there was a great advance in commerce and manufacture, and a rapid growth of towns and seaports; colonies were planted; wealth increased; and the standards of comfort were improved. The Muscovy Company for trade with Russia was founded as early as 1595, and the famous East India Company dates from 1600. Later, these trading organizations were to lay their holdings, like foundling children, on the national doorstep. Thus, the Elizabethan age saw the beginnings of the far-flung British Empire upon which the sun never sets. Privateering also attained almost the dignity of a profession in Elizabethan times. All of the famous sea-dogs from Drake down played the dangerous game of "singeing the King of Spain's beard" by preying upon Spanish treasure-ships coming from the New World, and the queen gladly took a share of the booty. As has frequently been pointed out, St. George slew the dragon and rescued the fair lady, but he was also careful to appropriate the dragon's hoard.

For nearly thirty years, Philip II put up with piracy of his shipping, raiding of his colonies, and open assistance to his rebels before he determined to protect his monopoly in the New World. After 1588, of course, when God's wind and the English scattered the Invincible Armada, trade could be carried on without unnecessary risk. Shakespeare's age was a time in which men could grow rich, rapidly and sensationally, and Elizabethan England exhibited all the aggressiveness and social climbing which attend sudden affluence and the rise of a commercial class.

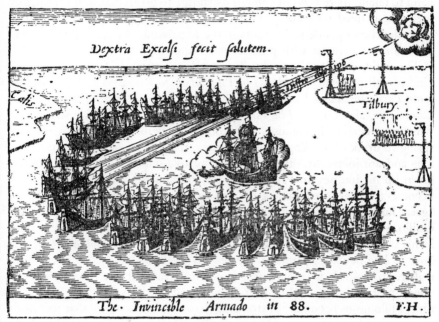

Dextra Excelfi fecit falutem.

The · Invincible Armado in 88.   F·H·

(From George Carleton's *A Fruitfull Remembrance of God's Mercie,* . . . Fourth Edition, 1630)

In his essay *Of Seditions and Troubles,* Francis Bacon named three factors that speedily bring a state to necessity—"the multiplying of nobility and other degrees of quality . . . an overgrown clergy, for they bring nothing to the stock, and in like manner when more are bred scholars than preferments can take off." All three, in varying degrees, presented minor problems to Tudor and Stuart England, but, to the student of Elizabethan literature, the last mentioned is of particular interest. Brilliant young men of all classes found their way to Oxford and Cambridge, and, while even a tradesman's son had a good chance of advancement in church or state, more left the universities than could possibly satisfy their ambitions. Often educated beyond their stations or accustomed to a life that rendered them incapable of ordinary occupations or unwilling to try them, such men naturally made straight for London, where competition was keen. Some drifted into the theatres to act or to "pen a part," others turned to pamphleteering and hackwriting for the booksellers; some became journalists in an age that, as yet, had no real place for them; some lived a wild bohemian life and depended upon their wits; most of them simply disappeared. In its attitude toward the scholar, Elizabethan England was still largely medieval. Though some nobles, like Leicester, Sidney, and later Southampton, were always ready to give a helping hand to talent, there was not enough patronage to go around, and Elizabethan literature is filled with complaints about the lack of encouragement. Moreover, the rise of gentlemen authors in the Renaissance was regarded by some as unfair competition with professional authorship.

The entire problem is vividly illustrated in a trilogy of satirical plays—a kind of college revue—entitled *The Pilgrimage to Parnassus* and *The Return from Parnassus*, Parts I and II, which were produced at St. John's College, Cambridge, about 1600. *The Pilgrimage* is an allegory of university life, in which the idealists, Philomusus and Studioso, hopefully approach the Muses' spring to drink of learning. In *The Return*, the pair set out to earn their livings and are joined by others on the way to London. Ingenioso, who had given up his journey to Parnassus in disillusionment and burned his books, becomes a writer of pamphlets, only to be rewarded with two groats by the "great lump of drowsy earth" who is his Mæcenas. He finds a new patron in Gullio, a vainglorious courtier who admires amorous poetry and is absorbed in his own sonneteering. Luxurio, who has learned little at college besides how to live beyond his means, escapes his creditors and becomes a ballad-maker. Studioso finds employment as a private tutor at five marks a year, in which post he is expected to wait at table and work in the fields at harvest time. Philomusus becomes a sexton and clerk, using "the voice that was made to pronounce a poet or an orator . . . like a bellman in the inquisition of a strayed beast." At the end of the play all are dismissed—Studioso because he offends his pupil by insisting that he do some work, Philomusus because he is too proud to whip dogs out of church, and Ingenioso because he forgets himself and speaks the truth to his patron. In Part II of *The Return*, which is subtitled *The Scourge of Simony*, the scholars see a coveted post go to Immerito and are reduced to trying quack medicine, acting, and fiddling for a livelihood. At last, in utter discouragement, they turn simple shepherds. The trilogy of plays is a satirical, pathetically realistic picture of what may be taken as the typical lives of the so-called "university wits" of the late 1580's —Marlowe, Greene, Peele, Nashe, Kyd, and Lodge—who embarked upon careers as professional men of letters and played an important part in the development of Elizabethan literature.

Yet, regarded as a whole, the age of Elizabeth was an age of opportunity. Old feudal barriers and rigid class distinctions had broken down, and upstart, capable families, like the Cecils, rose to incredible positions of authority where they earned the envy and the hatred of the older nobility. Social advancement of the kind Malvolio contemplated (*Twelfth Night*, II, v) was not unheard of: "There is example for't. The lady of the Strachey married the yeoman of the wardrobe." Even the feudal honor of knighthood could be obtained, not only by military service to the sovereign, but by financial assistance in times of peace. Both Richard Gresham (knighted 1537) and his brother John (knighted 1541), the founder of the Muscovy Company, lent money to their sovereigns and became Lords Mayor of London; and Thomas (knighted 1559), Richard's son and the founder of the Royal Exchange, was the trusted financial agent of the crown. Shakespeare's London was full of potential or at least hopeful Dick Whittingtons.

"It is very hard to know who is noble, who is worshipful, who is a gentleman, who is not," wrote a cantankerous old Puritan, Philip Stubbes, in 1583, when Shakespeare was nineteen:

> for you shall have those which are neither of the nobility, gentility, nor yeomanry . . . go daily in silks, velvets, satins, damasks, taffetas, and such like, notwithstanding that they be both base by birth, mean by estate, and servile by calling. This is a great confusion and a general disorder, God be merciful unto us! (*The Anatomy of Abuses.*)

More sensible persons, however, like William Harrison, the author of *A Description of England* prefixed to Holinshed's *Chronicles* (1577, 1587), showed only mild amusement or unconcern at the social climber:

> No man hath hurt by it but himself, who peradventure will go in wider buskins than his legs will bear, or as our proverb saith, now and then will bear a bigger sail than his boat is able to sustain.

That there is more to Stubbes's complaint than the sour nature of the Puritanical mind is made clear by frequent proclamations about "excess of apparel" in the reigns of Mary, Elizabeth, and James, summarizing the statutes concerning dress. One of 1574 is typical. Beginning in good Tudor fashion with an expression of grave concern over the importation of

> such superfluities of silks, cloths of gold, silver, and other such vain devices of so great cost for the quantity thereof as of necessity the moneys and treasure of the realm is and must be yearly conveyed out of the same to answer the said excess,

the document goes on to mention

> particularly the wasting and undoing of a great number of young gentlemen, otherwise serviceable, and others seeking by show of apparel to be esteemed as gentlemen, who allured by the vain show of those things do not only consume themselves, their goods and lands which their parents left unto them, but also run into such debts and shifts as they cannot live out of danger of laws.

Then follow three pages of detailed prohibitions, like the following:

MEN'S APPAREL

None shall wear in his apparel any:

Silk of the color of purple, cloth of gold tissued, nor fur of sables } but only the { King, Queen, King's { Mother, Children, Brethren and Sisters, Uncles and Aunts, } and except } Dukes, Marquesses, and Earls, who may wear the same in doublets, jerkins, linings. . . .

Cloth of { gold, silver, tinseled satin, } Silk, or cloth mixed or embroidered with any gold or silver, } except { all degrees above Viscounts. . . .

Woolen cloth made out of the realm. . . . Velvet, crimson or scarlet, Furs, black jenets, lucernes, Embroidery or tailor's work having gold or silver or pearl therein } except { Dukes, Marquesses, Earls, Viscounts, Barons. . . .

Satin, damask, silk chamlet, or taffeta, in gown, coat, hose, or uppermost garments. Fur, whereof the kind groweth not within the Queen's dominions . . . } except { the degrees and persons above mentioned, and men that may dispend £100 by the year, and so valued in the subsidy book. . . .

Hat, bonnet, girdle, scabbards of swords, daggers, etc., shoes and pantofles of velvet } except { the degrees and persons above named, and the son and heir apparent of a knight. . . .

Spurs, swords, rapiers, daggers, skaynes, wood-knives, or hangers, buckles of girdles, } { gilt, silvered, or damasked } except { Knights' and barons' sons, and other of higher degree or place.

WOMEN'S APPAREL

{ Cloth of gold, tissue, fur of sables } except { Duchesses, Marquesses, and Countesses, in their gowns, kirtles, partlets, and sleeves. . . .

{ Enamelled { Chains, Buttons, Igletts, Borders, } except { The degrees before mentioned. . . .

{ Velvet, tufted taffeta, Satin, or any gold or silver in their petticoats } except { Wives of Barons, Knights of the order . . . Gentlewomen of the privy chamber. . . .

{ Damask, taffeta, or other silk in their petticoats } except { Knights' daughters, and such as . . . shall not wear a garde of any silk upon their petticoats. . . .

Obviously, the old distinctions of feudal days were no longer recognizable by dress, and the repetition of the proclamations is in itself evidence that the luxury-loving *nouveaux riches* were hard to control. The players, as we shall see, were probably among the worst offenders.

Shakespeare's age, however, still believed in degree as the sound traditional basis of a well-ordered commonwealth. The discourse which the dramatist put into the mouth of Ulysses sums up the political creed of the average, prosperous, middle-class Englishman of his day:

> The heavens themselves, the planets, and this centre [i. e., the earth]
> Observe degree, priority, and place . . .
> And therefore is the glorious planet Sol
> In noble eminence enthron'd and sphered
> Amidst the other. . . . But when the planets
> In evil mixture to disorder wander,
> What plagues and what portents! What hunting!
> What raging of the sea! . . . O, when degree is shak'd,
> Which is the ladder of all high designs,
> Then enterprise is sick! How could communities,
> Degrees in schools, and brotherhoods in cities,
> Peaceful commerce from dividable shores,
> The primogenitive and due of birth,
> Prerogative of age, crowns, sceptres, laurels,
> But by degree, stand in authentic place?
> Take but degree away, untune that string,
> And hark what discord follows!
> (*Troilus and Cressida*, I, iii, 85 ff.)

SOVEREIGN AND PEOPLE

Opinions have differed regarding the queen who gave her name to the epoch. Like the age in which she lived, Elizabeth was a paradox. Vain, fickle, evasive, she could, nevertheless, on occasion be coldly calculating. Lord Burghley, her treasurer, and Sir Francis Walsingham, her Secretary of State, were her right hand and her left, but she was no mere figurehead of a queen. Almost masculine in mind and temperament, she could, when it served her purpose, be as unreasonably, provocatively feminine as the most capricious of her maids of honor. The center of a courtly adulation that has become a legend, she permitted none of her favorites to encroach upon her royal prerogatives. Her court was overrun by place-seekers, but it became the focus for her people. A "handsome and well-compacted person," "bold and plausible of tongue," might in the beginning be sure of her favor. It took something more substantial, however, to win her lasting regard. The favor she bestowed upon Sidney and Raleigh was merited favor, but she gave neither an important office; she never quite committed herself to Leicester; Christopher Hatton may have attracted her attention first by his dashing figure and his accomplished dancing, but he waited twenty-three years for the chancelorship; and she never trusted Essex, a reluctance for which time has been her vindication. She had many suitors, and scandals about her were not infrequent, yet Elizabeth kept her head and no man lost his over her as they did over her great rival, Mary Queen of Scots. Fond of ceremony and ritual, she was, unlike her sister Mary, devoid of a religious temperament, and, fortunately for her day, she valued uniformity in religion, not as a safeguard against heresy, but as a guarantee of unity in the state and of royal supremacy. Sir Robert Naunton's remark, that "she ruled much by faction and parties which herself both made, upheld, and weakened, as her own great judgement advised" (*Fragmenta Regalia*, 1653), tells a great deal, but it does not explain Elizabeth. She was both a Bullen and a Tudor. James, her successor, was squalid by contrast and "the greatest fool in Christendom."

When Elizabeth came to the throne in 1558, "mere English" as she boasted, she was a brilliant, accomplished princess of twenty-five, gifted, like her father, with a genius for kingship and for society, and she quickly became a kind of incarnation of the glory of England. "She was of beauty very fair," wrote William Camden,

> and worthy of a crown, of modest gravity, excellent wit, royal mind, happy memory, and indefatigable study of learning, insomuch as before she was seventeen years of age, she understood well the Latin, French, and Italian tongues, and was indifferently well seen in the Greek. Neither did she neglect music, so far forth as might beseem a princess, being able to sing and play on the lute prettily and sweetly . . . insomuch as she was even a miracle for her learning amongst the princes of her time. (*Annals, or History of the Most Renowned and Victorious Princess Elizabeth*, 3rd edition, 1635.)

Elizabeth loved pomp and display; everything she did was studied for effect, and, when Time robbed her of her early grace and charm, she managed with the aid of a false wig and cosmetics to maintain to the end a shriveled resemblance of what she once had been. "Her mind was of time like the gentle air that cometh from the westerly point in a summer's morn," wrote Sir John Harington,

> 'twas sweet and refreshing to all around her. Her speech did win all affections, and her subjects did try to show all love to her commands, for she would say her state did require her to command what she knew her people would willingly do from their own love to her. . . . Again, she could put forth such alterations when obedience was lacking, as left no doubtings whose daughter she was. (Letter to Robert Markham [1606], in *The Letters and Epigrams of Sir John Harington*, ed. N. E. McClure [1930], p. 122.)

Like James, her successor, she believed in the divine right of kings, but Elizabeth loved and trusted her people. In return, she inspired in them a passionate personal loyalty which, more than anything else, explains her greatness. "My mortal foe," she wrote to Sir Edward Stafford, her special ambassador negotiating the French marriage in 1580 which proved unpopular, "can wish me no greater loss than England's hate; neither should death be less welcome unto me than such mishap betide me" (*The Letters of Queen Elizabeth*, ed. G. B. Harrison [1935], p. 141).

Even today one comes upon expressions of this popular devotion to Elizabeth in the most unexpected places and in the humblest forms. In the Pierpont Morgan Library, in a copy of Cicero's *De Amicitia*, printed by William Caxton in 1481, there is a marginal note, written by a reader apropos of nothing at all in the text: "god preserve our noble Quene Elyzabeth from the false trechery which is wrought." In the Victoria and Albert Museum, there is an oak beam from an Elizabethan house in Radnorshire on which is carved as part of the decorative design: "God Save our Queen." In an Oxford college, in a *Cæsar* that belonged to a Westminster school boy about the time of the Spanish Armada, there is this simple couplet:

> The rose is red, the leaves are green
> God save Elizabeth, our noble queen.[2]

In the Huntington Library copy of Robert Laneham's *Letter*, concerning the princely pleasures at Kenilworth Castle (1575), there are the congratulatory lines written in a small but beautiful hand:

> While that oour neighbooure reams (alas) vprore dooth rend asunder
> In mirth amoong the subiects that her maiesty ar vnder
> She (thanks to God) leads pleasaunt dais: let spite and mallis wunder.

In Richard (?) Puttenham's *Art of English Poesy* (1589), as an illustration of *tapinosis*, or the use of base words that disgrace the matter described, there is an anecdote of one Sergeant Bendlowes:

> when in progress time coming to salute the Queen in Huntingdonshire, he said to her coachman, "Stay thy cart, good fellow, stay thy cart, that I may speak to the Queen," whereat her Majesty laughed as she had been tickled

and gave him her hand to kiss. On every occasion Elizabeth showed herself a friendly monarch.

Her answer in 1559 to a deputation from the Commons, troubled by the question of the succession and urging her to marry, is characteristic both in its evasion and in its deliberate popular appeal:

> "Yea, to satisfy you, I have already joined myself in marriage to an husband, namely, the Kingdom of England. And behold," said she, "which I marvel ye have forgotten, the pledge of this my wedlock and marriage with my kingdom." And therewith she stretched forth her finger and showed the ring of gold

[2] A. M. Bell, "An Elizabethan Schoolboy and His Book," in G. L. Apperson, *Gleanings After Time* (1907), pp. 144 ff.

wherewith at her coronation she had in a set form of words solemnly given herself in marriage to her kingdom. Here, having made a pause, "And do not," saith she, "upbraid me with miserable lack of children; for every one of you, and as many as are Englishmen, are children and kinsmen to me, of whom if God deprive me not, which God forbid, I cannot without injury be accounted barren." (William Camden, *Annals*.)

Vexing as was the question of the succession, Elizabeth alone seems to have realized fully that to recognize any of the rival claims would, in her own phrase, have been to spread a winding sheet before her eyes. There was no obvious heir, and civil war between the various claimants seemed inevitable. In *King John*, Faulconbridge's soliloquy over the body of Prince Arthur expressed a parallel foreboding:

> Now for the bare-pick'd bone of majesty
> Doth dogged War bristle his angry crest
> And snarleth in the gentle eyes of Peace.
> Now powers from home and discontents at home
> Meet in one line; and vast confusion waits,
> As doth a raven on a sick-fallen beast,
> The imminent decay of wrested pomp. (IV, iii, 148 ff.)

For years Elizabeth literally stood between her people and the double disaster of civil war and invasion from abroad, dangers which were not wholly dispelled even by the execution of Mary Queen of Scots and the defeat of the Spanish Armada. Through difficult problems—religious, social, economic, and international—she steered a steady keel, gave her nation a strong stable government, and—in spite of the threat of Spain, her active aid to the Netherlands, the perennial troubles in Ireland, and the Jesuit scares at home—Elizabeth brought England peace. Her voice was that of a united people. "To report her death," wrote Thomas Dekker,

> . . . took away hearts from millions, for having brought up, even under her wing, a nation that was almost begotten and born under her, that never shouted any other *ave* than for her name, never saw the face of any prince but herself; never understood what that strange outlandish word *change* signified. . . . She was the courtiers' treasure . . . the lawyers' sword of justice . . . the merchants' patroness . . . the citizens' mother . . . the shepherds' goddess. . . . Only the soldier . . . swore . . . that now was the hour come to bestir his stumps . . . but my *Signior Soldado* was deceived, the tragedy went not forward. (*The Wonderful Year 1603*.)

When Shakespeare came to London, Elizabeth had already been more than thirty years on the throne. She had long before become the subject of legend, and her work, for the most part, was over. Shakespeare, too, was much less sycophantic than the average Elizabethan poet. But into *A Midsummer Night's Dream*, one of his early plays, he did insert for her ear an allusion to "a fair vestal throned by the west" that was designed more to awaken

memories than to flatter an old lady of sixty-five. At her death he wrote no
elegy, and some have read in *England's Mourning Garment* (1603) a rebuke
for his failure to do so:

> Nor doth the silver tongu'd Melicert
> Drop from his honied muse one sable tear
> To mourn her death that graced his desert.

But later, in *Henry VIII*, when the aged queen had been dead for a decade,
when an unpopular foreign king was on the throne, and men could look
back and see more calmly, he paid her a beautiful tribute. It is in the form of
a prophecy, spoken at her baptism by Archbishop Cranmer, who holds the
baby princess in his arms:

> This royal infant—Heaven still move about her!—
> Though in her cradle, yet now promises
> Upon this land a thousand thousand blessings,
> Which time shall bring to ripeness. She shall be—
> But few now living can behold that goodness—
> A pattern to all princes living with her
> And all that shall succeed. Saba was never
> More covetous of wisdom and fair virtue
> Than this pure soul shall be. All princely graces
> That mould up such a mighty piece as this is,
> With all the virtues that attend the good,
> Shall still be doubled on her. Truth shall nurse her,
> Holy and heavenly thoughts still counsel her.
> She shall be lov'd and fear'd. Her own shall bless her;
> Her foes shake like a field of beaten corn
> And hang their heads with sorrow. Good grows with her.
> In her days every man shall eat in safety,
> Under his own vine, what he plants, and sing
> The merry songs of peace to all his neighbours. (V, v, 18 ff.)

These lines are a disinterested summary of what Elizabeth meant to her
people.

It is no small wonder, then, that in the new century under James men
should have looked back with nostalgia to the age of Elizabeth as to a merry
England, which had never had any existence outside their imaginations.
Times were changing, and the change that was coming over England was
hastened and rendered more visible by the passing of the last of the Tudors.
The sixteenth century had been an age of expansion and an eager, enthusiastic *outlook;* in the seventeenth the process was reversed. Colonization continued, but its motive was not adventure; it was dissatisfaction with things at
home. The foreign danger was past, but civil differences, political and religious, had taken its place, and the parties which were soon to clash on the
battlefield were formulating their differences and organizing their forces. At

the accession of James, while there was the beginning of friction, England was still a strong and a united nation. A tactful, intelligent king might have exercised a moderating influence upon faction. But James did not know the value of compromise. A foreigner, he outraged the nation by indiscriminately dubbing knights "with unhatched rapier and on carpet consideration"; he replenished his treasury by creating the title of baronet and selling the honor for what he could get; he imposed duties without consulting Parliament; he ignored the growing opposition to the free exercise of royal power; and he threw the weight of his influence upon the side of the episcopal party. Absolutism practiced by a Tudor was one thing; when it was professed by a Stuart who spoke with a burr, it became quite another. Elizabeth's ecclesiastical policy was political, but James's blunt enunciation, "no bishop, no king," antagonized the extreme Protestants, with the result that the Puritans allied themselves with the constitutional opposition. The Gunpowder Plot of 1605 aroused the new king's witch-hunting zeal against the Catholics. The mutual understanding and trust between ruler and ruled that had characterized the Tudor sovereigns was destroyed.

Moreover, what had been mere exuberant gaiety in the reign of Elizabeth became heartless frivolity in the reign of James, and comparisons were inevitable. A homely old poet wrote a ballad on *The Old Courtier of the Queen's*, contrasting the degenerate new days with the days of old in terms that crabbed age has always used of youth. Sir John Harington, the old queen's godson, who was hardly an unprejudiced witness, contrasted the pleasures of James's court with those of former times:

> but ne'er did I see such lack of good order, discretion, and sobriety, as I have now done. I have passed much time in seeing the royal sports of hunting and hawking, where the manners were such as made me devise the beasts were pursuing the sober creation, and not men in quest of exercise or food. I will now, in good sooth, declare to you, who will not blab, that the gunpowder fright is got out of all our heads, and we are going on, hereabouts, as if the devil was contriving every man should blow up himself, by wild riot, excess, and devastation of time and temperance. (Letter to Secretary Barlow, July, 1606, *op. cit.*, p. 118.)

Whatever else was true, there had been nothing squalid about a Tudor.

Naturally, the theatres of Shakespeare's day reflected the differences between the two reigns. The drama of the 1590's is filled with patriotism, national pride, or "matter for a May morning." Just as the deeds of the English explorers thrilled their contemporaries, so the chroniclers supplied the playwrights with materials that fed the pride in England's past. "That island of England breeds very valiant creatures," says Rambures in Shakespeare's *Henry V*,

> their mastiffs are of unmatchable courage. . . . And the men do sympathize with the mastiffs in robustious and rough coming on, leaving their wits with their

wives; and then, give them great meals of beef and iron and steel, they will eat like wolves and fight like devils. (III, vii, 150 ff.)

Such passages, directed at the groundling in the Elizabethan playhouses, gave him a kinship with the glory of his age and made him stand a little straighter, as did the bluff, sturdy, thoroughly English heroes, like Talbot, Faulconbridge, and Henry V. And John of Gaunt's lyrical description of England,

> This royal throne of kings, this sceptr'd isle . . .
> This other Eden, demi-paradise (*Richard II*, II, i, 40 ff.)

—the most magnificent lines ever written about any nation—was an appeal to something higher. As we shall see (below, pp. 294 ff.), the patriotic character of the history plays and their appeals for unity and loyalty had a special meaning for the original audiences at a time when England was threatened from abroad and in danger of factions at home. And the joyousness of Shakespeare's comedies belongs to the spirit of Elizabethan times.

In the reign of James, something heavier and graver began to be discernible. The joyous confidence of the sixteenth century was passing away and was replaced by a spirit akin to recklessness. The historical drama, glorifying the English, declined and was replaced by satire and the drama of intrigue. "The play[er]s do not forbear to present upon their stage the whole course of the present time, not sparing either king, state, or religion," wrote Samuel Calvert to Ralph Winwood, March 28, 1605.[3] "Consider, for pity's sake, what must be the state and condition of a prince," wrote the French Ambassador Beaumont, with exaggerated pessimism,

whom the preachers publicly from the pulpit assail, whom the comedians of the metropolis bring upon the stage, whose wife attends these representations in order to enjoy the laugh against her husband, whom the parliament braves and defies, and who is universally hated by the whole people. (F. von Raumer, *History of the Sixteenth and Seventeenth Centuries, Illustrated by Original Documents* [1835], II, 206-07.)

It is too much to suggest that Shakespeare's late plays reflect the spirit of the new age, but the sharp contrasts in some of them, like *Measure for Measure*, *Troilus and Cressida*, and *King Lear*—conceived in the cynical mood of the melancholy Jaques—may not be altogether unconnected with it. "The time is out of joint." Shakespeare's broad humanity and understanding of human problems were still present, but something was dead, and it was never again revived for long in the English drama.

COUNTRY LIFE AND TOWN LIFE

Although, as Hamlet remarked, the purpose and the end of playing is to show "the very age and body of the time his form and pressure," Shakespeare

---

[3] *Memorials of Affairs of State in the Reigns of Queen Elizabeth and King James I*, ed. Edmund Sawyer (1723), II, 54.

was so universal an artist that the value of his plays as social documents is certainly secondary. In this respect, Shakespeare differed from his contemporaries Dekker and Jonson, for example, in whose pages one finds so faithful a picture of the men and the manners of the day that one can extract from them little "characters" of Elizabethan types or precise scenes from Elizabethan life. Seldom in Shakespeare's plays does one come upon a scene that causes one instinctively to exclaim, "How Elizabethan!" rather than, "How true!" It is not that Shakespeare was unable to be specifically realistic or concrete in his descriptions; it is rather that he rose above immediacy and contemporaneousness and attained to universal truth. In Jonson's phrase, he was "not of an age, but for all time."

Yet, throughout, the background of life in Shakespeare's plays is Elizabethan life. The social order, the manners and customs, the human realities that Shakespeare knew intimately were Elizabethan. The student who wishes to know Shakespeare's people and their thoughts, to realize to the full their behavior and their relationships with one another, to understand their mental attitudes and their reactions to circumstance, to appreciate the vividness of their imagery and their allusions, cannot afford to overlook the life of Shakespeare's age. Enough has already been said to make clear that the tempo of Elizabethan life differed considerably from ours today and that Elizabethan values were not our values. The same is true of more humble everyday realities of food and drink, dress and decoration, houses and furniture, fields and villages, sports and pastimes. To be sure, Shakespeare's plays are set in ancient Rome, medieval Britain, and the cities of Italy, but they were written for a popular audience. In his theatre, neither the dramatist nor his hearers troubled much about the differences between court life in the days of Cymbeline and in the days of Richard II, between living in Elizabethan Windsor and on the seacoast of Bohemia.

Thus, Posthumus in *Cymbeline* is a "gentleman of the bedchamber" to a king who was "knighted" by Augustus Cæsar, Malvolio of Illyria is an Elizabethan steward, and Autolycus a decayed courtier who had once worn "three-pile." Hamlet receives the "tragedians of the city," Navarre and his courtiers entertain their ladies with a mumming of Muscovites, and Whitsuntide pastorals are performed in Italy. The cry of the London apprentices of "Clubs, bills, and partisans!" goes up in Verona streets, Claudius of Denmark has a guard of Switzers, and the "witches" Macbeth and Banquo meet on the heath may be the Fates, but they are garbed like the "secret, black, and midnight hags" of which King James lived in mortal dread. Clocks strike in ancient Rome and in ancient Britain; Snug the joiner, Flute the bellows-mender, and Snout the tinker ply their trades in Athens; a Warwickshire sheep-shearing takes place in Bohemia; and Cleopatra invites Charmian to a game of billiards. Claudio sends his betrothed a present of scented gloves, and Imogen's bedchamber is hung with tapestry of silk and silver. Falstaff thinks Mrs. Ford would look well in a semi-circled farthingale; Cleopatra bids her maids "cut her lace"; Doll Tearsheet accuses Ancient Pistol of tearing "a poor whore's ruff in a bawdy-house"; Romeo wears French slops (wide, loose breeches); in a wood near Athens there is a nine men's morris (court laid out in squares for a game, not unlike hopscotch, played with nine "men," i. e., pebbles or discs); Perdita picks English garden flowers in Bohemia; and Coriolanus speaks of the Roman mob as "Hob and Dick." The

Macbeth and Banquo Meeting the Weird Sisters   (From Holinshed's *Chronicles of England, Scotland, and Ireland,* 1577)

names of the characters and the allusions to specific localities in these plays are of the time and place, but the details of the life are recognizably Elizabethan.

Especially is this true of the social rank of Shakespeare's characters. Of his heroines, Olivia is a countess of rank to marry the ruler of Illyria; Portia of Belmont is an heiress; Hero the daughter of a governor; Julia and Sylvia ladies of position. Their witty, sharp-tongued attendants—Maria, Nerissa, Margaret, Ursula, and Lucetta—are not *maids* in the sense in which we use the term today; they are waiting-gentlewomen—maids of honor, if you please, but not servant girls. They have the same social standing as Anne Bullen, who in *Henry VIII* is a knight's daughter and a waiting-gentlewoman to Queen Katherine. Even if Sir Toby does call Maria "my niece's chambermaid," he does not mean what the Elizabethans meant by "chamberer." Socially, whatever else one may think, Maria is a suitable match for Olivia's jolly kinsman.

Likewise, Emilia, who helps Desdemona to undress, looks after her "nightly wearing," and even makes her bed, does no more than the waiting-gentle-women at court were accustomed to doing. She is, moreover, the wife of an officer second only to the husband of the lady she serves. Similarly, Shake-speare's young men—Valentine and Proteus, Claudio and Benedick, Bassanio and Gratiano, Romeo, Mercutio, and Benvolio—these gay young blades are fashioned after the young noblemen of Elizabeth's and James's court. Except as they may serve for comic purposes or provide an Arcadian background for courtly living, there is little in detail about the lower classes in Eliza-bethan literature.

The England in which Shakespeare lived was still a comparatively small place, essentially rural, and self-supporting. Its population was only four or five millions, and London was the only city of size in the kingdom. It was a land of "fertile fields of corn and verdant pastures," of orchards and gardens, dotted here and there with towns and villages. Most of the land was still unenclosed, but the old medieval system of cultivation in common was giv-ing way to modern methods. Times were changing even in the country, and William Harrison, writing the *Description of England* which served as a preface to Holinshed's *Chronicles* (1577, 1587), made the following observa-tion:

> There are old men yet dwelling in the village where I remain which have noted three things to be marvellously altered in England within their sound remem-brance. . . . One is the multitude of chimneys lately erected, whereas in their young days there were not above two or three, if so many, in most uplandish towns of the realm . . . but each one made his fire against a reredos in the hall, where he dined and dressed his meat. The second is the great, although not gen-eral, amendment of lodging; for, said they, our fathers, yea and we ourselves also, have lain full oft upon straw pallets, on rough mats covered only with a sheet, under coverlets made of dogswain or hopharlots (I use their own terms), and a good round log under their heads instead of a bolster or pillow. . . . The third thing they tell of is the exchange of vessel, as of treen [wooden] platters into pewter, and wooden spoons into silver or tin.

Foreign visitors also frequently noticed the unusual house furnishings, the walls hung with tapestry or painted cloths—"the story of the Prodigal or the German hunting in waterwork "(*2 Henry IV*, II, i, 158), the glass in the win-dows, and the excellence and variety of the fare. Indeed, as an Elizabethan gentleman of means, Gremio is hardly boasting when he describes his posses-sions:

> My house within the city
> Is richly furnished with plate and gold;
> Basins and ewers to lave her dainty hands;
> My hangings all of Tyrian tapestry;
> In ivory coffers I have stuff'd my crowns,
> In cypress chests my arras counterpoints,

Costly apparel, tents, and canopies,
Fine linen, Turkey cushions boss'd with pearl,
Valance of Venice gold in needlework,
Pewter and brass and all things that belongs
To house or housekeeping. Then, at my farm
I have a hundred milch-kine to the pail,
Six score fat oxen standing in my stall,
And all things answerable to this portion.
(*The Taming of the Shrew*, II, i, 348 ff.)

In town or country, Elizabethan houses were an improvement upon those of an earlier generation, though William Harrison did lament the luxury of oak in building and the consequent decline of "oaken men." The average house was still constructed of timber, and, except for the showy residences of the purse-proud, outwardly plain and simple (as English houses have always been), but rich and comfortable within. "Houses are built to live in, not to look on," wrote Francis Bacon, "therefore let use be preferred before uniformity, except where both may be had. Leave the goodly fabrics of houses, for beauty only, to the enchanted palaces of the poets, who build them with small cost" (*Of Building*, 1597). Falstaff calls Justice Shallow's house in Gloucestershire "a goodly dwelling and a rich" (*2 Henry IV*, V, iii, 7), and the phrase serves well to describe the typical Elizabethan house of the better sort. Usually, in the towns, houses were built with high gables and overhanging storeys, elaborately carved timbers, and a multiplicity of square, leaded windows. But, when space permitted, they commonly had an **E** or **H** shape with forecourts and gardens and a plenitude of light and air.

Hospitality was the virtue of the English most frequently noticed by foreign visitors in Shakespeare's time, especially in the country, and Elizabethan literature contains many attractive pictures of the host and his guests. In the seventeenth century, when, according to one writer, "pride, Puritans, coaches, and covetousness" brought on the decay of hospitality, one could only look back with praise for the older type of country gentleman who practiced it. Such a man

loved three things, an open cellar, a full hall, and a sweating cook; he always provided for three dinners, one for himself, another for his servants, the third for the poor. . . . Lusty able men, well maintained, were his delight, with whom he could be familiar; his tenants knew when they saw him, for he kept the old fashion, good, commendable, plain." (Donald Lupton, *London and the Country Carbonaded*, 1632.)

Whatever shortcomings Justice Shallow may have had, in his Cotswold house he practiced the old-fashioned hospitality. Sir John Falstaff is not permitted to go back to London without having at least a snack:

By cock and pie, sir, you shall not away tonight. . . . Excuses shall not be admitted; there is no excuse shall serve; you shall not be excused.

So Davy is dispatched to William cook:

> Some pidgeons, Davy, a couple of short-legg'd hens, a joint of mutton, and any
> pretty little tiny kickshaws, tell William cook.

And, when the feast is over, Shallow must still provide refreshment:

> Nay, you shall see my orchard, where, in an arbour, we shall eat a last year's
> pippin of mine own graffing, with a dish of caraways, and so forth. (*2 Henry
> IV*, V, i and ii.)

In a somewhat lower walk of life, prosperous country folk, like Perdita's
foster-father, were not far behind in their provision of good cheer:

> Fie, daughter! When my old wife lived, upon
> This day she was both pantler, butler, cook,
> Both dame and servant; welcomed all, served all;
> Would sing her song and dance her turn; now here,
> At upper end o' the table, now i' the middle;
> On his shoulder, and his; her face o' fire
> With labour, and the thing she took to quench it
> She would to each one sip.
> (*The Winter's Tale*, IV, iv, 55 ff.)

Like the old shepherd's wife, like the "queen of curds and cream," the lady
of an Elizabethan country household was in entire charge of her establishment, supervised the dairy work and the baking and the brewing, managed
her kitchen and the pantry and the linen closet, and kept good discipline
among her servants.

A kind of spiritual nostalgia for the simplicity of the country is frequently
expressed in Elizabethan literature, and the pastoral, in its various forms, is
peculiarly a Renaissance variety of the literature of escape. Poor harassed
Henry VI, waiting on a hill for the battle to be over, dwells longingly upon
the peace and quiet of the shepherd's existence:

> O God! methinks it were a happy life
> To be no better than a homely swain. . . .
> So many hours must I tend my flock,
> So many hours must I take my rest. . . .
> So many days my ewes have been with young,
> So many weeks ere the poor fools will ean,
> So many years ere I shall shear the fleece:
> So minutes, hours, days, months, and years,
> Pass'd over to the end they were created,
> Would bring white hairs unto a quiet grave.
> (*3 Henry VI*, II, v, 21 ff.)

As Shakespeare was well aware, the reality was somewhat different from
the ideal picture. He introduced into *As You Like It* an amusing debate upon
court life and country life between Touchstone the clown and Corin the

Arcadian shepherd. Into the same play he placed his yokels William and Audrey—the latter a blood relative to Touchstone's old love, Jane Smile, the washer-wench milkmaid with the pretty, chapped hands. Shakespeare knew what the country was like "when icicles hang by the wall . . . when blood is nipp'd and ways be foul . . . and Marion's nose looks red and raw" (*Love's Labor's Lost*, V, ii, 922 ff.).

Englishmen have always lived as much as possible out of doors, and the sports and pastimes of Shakespeare's day were essentially rural: hunting, hawking, angling, archery, bowling, riding, bull- and bear-baiting, and dancing around the Maypole or on the village green. A welcome diversion from the humdrum of daily chores in the country came at fair-time, harvest-home, or sheep-shearing, when jollity was mixed with labor, or a peddler and his pack made his appearance. Shakespeare's merry mountebank Autolycus is a portrait from life:

> He hath songs for man or woman, of all sizes; no milliner can so fit his customers with gloves. . . . He hath ribbons of all the colours i' the rainbow; points more than all the lawyers in Bohemia can learnedly handle, though they come to him by the gross; inkles, caddisses, cambrics, lawns—why, he sings 'em over as they were gods or goddesses; you would think a smock were a she-angel, he so chants to the sleeve-hand and the work about the square on't. (*The Winter's Tale*, IV, iv, 191 ff.)

And with his ballads in print o' life, about monsters and murders and strange events, the peddler brought his customers a glimpse of the world outside.

A bit of tawdry peddler's finery is harmless enough, but it brings to mind what seems to have almost a national vice in Shakespeare's day. "The English are . . . lovers of show," wrote Paul Hentzner in 1598, and the moralists of the time frequently took their countrymen to task for their extravagance and their inconstancy in setting and following fashions.

> One touch of nature makes the whole world kin
> That all with one consent praise new-born gawds.
> (*Troilus and Cressida*, III, iii, 174 ff.)

Men sold their acres to buy fine suits, citizens' wives dressed in silks and fine velvets, and all classes reveled it

> as bravely as the best,
> With silken coats and caps and golden rings,
> With ruffs and cuffs and farthingales and things;
> With scarfs and fans and double change of bravery,
> With amber bracelets, beads, and all this knavery.
> (*The Taming of the Shrew*, IV, iii, 54 ff.)

But it was the changeableness of the English, even more than their extravagance, that worried the reformers; "nothing is more constant in England than inconstancy of attire," wrote William Harrison. And many complained that, in a day when fashions were national, the English chose what pleased them from the ends of the earth. "How oddly he is suited!" exclaims Portia of Faulconbridge, the young baron of England, who typically knows neither Latin, French, nor Italian. "I think he bought his doublet in Italy, his round hose in France, his bonnet in Germany, and his behaviour everywhere" (*The Merchant of Venice*, I, ii, 78 ff.).

SHAKESPEARE'S LONDON

London has always been "that adamant which draweth unto it all the other parts of the land," but never before the days of Elizabeth had it taken such a hold upon the English imagination. London had become the permanent abode of the government and the Privy Council; it was the center of England's wealth and commerce, and of all the stir and energy of the time. According to John Lyly, it was

> a place both for the beauty of building, infinite riches, variety of all things, that excelleth all the cities in the world, insomuch that it may be called the storehouse and mart of all Europe. (*Euphues and His England*, 1580.)

It was rapidly becoming what it has remained, the greatest port of the world. Ships from distant places were always riding on the river, and the city was filled with men who had sailed with Drake and Frobisher, Gilbert, Hawkins, and Grenville, men who were familiar with the world and full of stories of adventure. It was still a small place, hardly a mile square, and inhabited by between two and three hundred thousand souls. But an Elizabethan who did not live in London lived in the country; there was no other choice.

The London that Shakespeare knew was what is today called the City, bounded on the south by the Thames and still surrounded, except on the riverside, by the old city wall which was pierced by Aldgate, Bishopsgate, Moorgate, Cripplegate, Aldersgate, Newgate, and Ludgate. But it was already spreading beyond its fortified limits, and both north of the walls and south of the river, suburbs were growing up. These outlying districts had a double reputation in Shakespeare's day. On the one hand, they were the sites of the airy, quiet homes of noblemen and the gentry, with gardens and orchards attached; on the other, especially to the south, they were sections of disrepute. On the Bankside and in the whole unruly district of Southwark were the brothels, the bull- and the bear-baiting rings, several theatres, and no fewer than five jails. But, for Elizabethan London, the fields were never far away; flower gardens, open spaces, and woods were everywhere, and many of the sections of modern London, like Stepney, Hackney, Hoxton, Islington, Highgate, Hampstead, and Chelsea, were country villages. Even in a city like London it was possible to resort to open places, and Shakespeare's love of gardens, flowers, and the countryside is not the least of his attractions.

The main thoroughfare of Elizabethan London was the Thames, and the river from the Tower to Westminster was the most important physical feature of the metropolis. It was a gay and lively stream, as well as a busy one; few cities had such a length of riverfront. Like Cleopatra on the Cydnus, Elizabeth might occasionally be seen in her brightly decked, gilded barge of state; the Archbishop of Canterbury, the Lord Mayor, and each of the City Guilds had barges; most of the great houses along the river's banks had their private landing stairs with boats attached; and there were innumerable craft of all sorts for hire, with the watermen offering to carry one "eastward ho!" or "westward ho!" Occasionally, too, the Thames was the scene of colorful water pageants and civic ceremonies, even state funerals. Withal, it must have been a beautiful place; almost all of the foreign visitors to London mentioned it, usually commenting upon the swans that floated upon the waters in many places. The banks were lined with palaces, like Baynard's Castle and the Savoy; the residences of noblemen, like Shrewsbury House, Somerset House, Leicester House, Durham House, or York House; or gardens, like those of the Temple, where the adherents of the houses of York and Lancaster had plucked roses (*1 Henry VI*, II, iv). To the east lay the Tower, at once a royal palace, a prison, a zoo where lions were kept, an armory, the mint, a treasury for keeping the crown jewels, and the archives in which court records were preserved. Shakespeare referred to the Tower more frequently than to any other London building, almost always with an allusion to the unfounded tradition that it had been built by Julius Cæsar (*Richard II*, V, i, 2; *Richard III*, III, i, 69). Here were the settings of many scenes in his history plays, and Shakespeare must have been familiar with the whole of London's waterfront.

Other London landmarks Shakespeare knew equally well, and he alluded to them frequently. The glory of London was London Bridge, a structure of twenty arches, erected, according to tradition, upon woolpacks, and in the form of a continuous street, like the Rialto in Venice or the Ponte Vecchio in Florence. It was the only thoroughfare north and south. On it were shops and "splendid, handsome, and well built houses," and, at either end, gate towers, on the southern one of which were displayed on pikes the heads of those executed as traitors—a grave warning to all who entered the town. Dominating the city was old St. Paul's, the largest and most magnificent cathedral in England. In Shakespeare's day, unhappily, it was devoted to many irreverent purposes. In its middle aisle, commonly called Duke Humphrey's Walk from the tomb of Humphrey of Gloucester, the wits and gossips of the town congregated. Here lawyers and business men waited for their clients; here serving men set up their bills for service; here rogues of all sorts gathered:

> What damnable bargains of unmerciful brokery and of unmeasurable usury are there clapped up? What swearing is there, yea, what swaggering, what facing and out-facing? What shuffling, what shouldering, what jostling, what jeering, what biting of thumbs to beget quarrels, what holding up of fingers to remember drunken meetings, what braving with feathers? . . . Yea, foot by foot and elbow by elbow, shall you see walking the knight, the gull, the gallant, the upstart, the gentleman, the clown, the captain, the apple-squire, the lawyer, the usurer, the citizen, the bankerout, the scholar, the beggar, the doctor, the idiot, the ruffian, the cheater, the puritan, the cut-throat. (Thomas Dekker, *The Dead Term*, 1608.)

Falstaff bought Bardolph in Paul's (*2 Henry IV*, I, ii, 57), and a "Paul's Man," of which Ben Jonson's Captain Bobadil is the best literary example, was a recognized type of disreputable hanger-on.

As in most medieval cities, so in old London, each street and district had its peculiar reputation. The printers were beginning to use Fleet Street, but it was still the show place of the town, famous for its taverns, its side-shows, and its "motions" (puppet-shows). Paul's Churchyard was the headquarters of the book-trade, and Cheapside was the principal commercial street, while Goldsmith's Row, a line of about ten houses in Cheapside, was known as the "Beauty of London." Bucklersbury was given over to grocers and apothecaries; Eastcheap to butchers' and cookshops; Thames Street, Fish Street Hill, and Friday Street to the fishmongers; while Ironmongers Lane, Hosiers Lane, Bread Street, Milk Street, The Poultry, Bowyers Street, and Fletcher Lane even today commemorate ancient trades. "What can there be," asked Lyly's Euphues, "in any place under the heavens that is not in this noble city either to be bought or borrowed?"

Elizabethan London was a crowded, noisy city; it was full of crime and sin; its narrow streets were most insanitary. But it was undeniably picturesque, and it must have been like wine in the blood of the young lad who came from Stratford to seek his fortune. Shakespeare's book, it has often been said, is a translation of human life into terms of dramatic poetry. The characters who sat for his universal human portrait—the ladies and gentlemen, the fools, the sots, and the rogues—were Elizabethan men and women, studied from the life around him. The garments in which they posed were the doublets and ruffs and farthingales of Elizabethan England. The colorful, lively background for the picture Shakespeare created was the rich, varied life of the Renaissance. Even some of the activities in which they engaged were Elizabethan. But Shakespeare's creatures are not of an age; they are for all time. The thoughts they think, the elations and the sorrows they feel, the visions they see, and the dreams they dream belong to the world and to human life as a whole.

SUGGESTED REFERENCES

BLACK, J. B. *The Reign of Elizabeth, 1558–1603.* Oxford, Clarendon Press, 1936. The Oxford History of England, VIII.

BOYD, MORRISON COMEGYS. *Elizabethan Music and Musical Criticism.* Philadelphia, University of Pennsylvania Press, 1940.

BYRNE, M. ST. CLARE. *Elizabethan Life in Town and Country.* London, Methuen, 1925; revised edition, 1934.

An account of the daily life of ordinary men and women in Shakespeare's time.

CAWLEY, R. R. *The Voyagers and Elizabethan Drama.* MLA Monograph. Boston and New York, Heath, 1938.

DAVIS, WILLIAM STEARNS. *Life in Elizabethan Days: A Picture of a Typical English Community at the End of the Sixteenth Century.* New York, Harper, 1930.

An account of an imaginary Elizabethan family.

FURNIVALL, F. J. (ed.). *William Harrison's Description of England in Shakspere's Youth.* New Shakespere Society Publication, 1877–8.

The best contemporary account, originally published as a Preface to Holinshed's *Chronicles.* The notes contain additional material from other sources.

HARRISON, G. B. (ed.). *England in Shakespeare's Day.* London, Methuen, 1928.

Social history in anthology form.

HOWARD, CLARE. *English Travellers of the Renaissance.* New York, Lane, 1914.

JUDGES, A. V. (ed.). *The Elizabethan Underworld: A Collection of Tudor and Early Stuart Tracts and Ballads Telling of the Lives and Misdoings of Vagabonds, Thieves, Rogues and Cozeners.* London, Routledge, 1930.

MADDEN, D. H. *The Diary of Master William Silence: A Study of Shakespeare and Elizabethan Sport.* London, Longman's, Green, 1897.

An imaginary diary of a hunting and hawking expedition.

SALZMAN, L. F. *England in Tudor Times: An Account of Its Social Life and Industries.* London, Batsford, 1926.

A bird's-eye view of England in the sixteenth century.

——. *Shakespeare's England: An Account of the Life and Manners of His Age* (2 vols.). Oxford, Clarendon Press, 1916.

An excellent work in thirty chapters, each written by an authority, examining every phase of Elizabethan life with special attention to Shakespeare's plays.

SHEAVYN, PHOEBE. *The Literary Profession in the Elizabethan Age.* Manchester University Press, 1909.

STOW, JOHN. *A Survey of London* (2 vols.). Edited by C. L. Kingsford. Oxford, Clarendon Press, 1908.

The best account of Shakespeare's London, originally published in 1598. There is also an edition in the Everyman Library.

SUGDEN, E. H. *A Topographical Dictionary to the Works of Shakespeare and His Fellow Dramatists.* Manchester University Press, 1925.

A dictionary of place names in the works of Shakespeare and other Elizabethan playwrights, together with a map of Elizabethan London and a reprint of several contemporary maps.

WILSON, JOHN DOVER (comp.). *Life in Shakespeare's England: A Book of Elizabethan Prose.* Cambridge University Press, 1911.

Social history in anthology form.

WITHINGTON, LOTHROP (ed.). *Elizabethan England.* London, Walter Scott, Ltd., 1889.

A popular abridgement of *William Harrison's Description of England in Shakspere's Youth.*

3

THE DRAMA BEFORE

SHAKESPEARE

. . . Tragedy, comedy, history, pastoral, pastoral-comical, historical-pastoral, tragical-historical, tragical-comical-historical-pastoral, scene individable, or poem unlimited; Seneca cannot be too heavy, nor Plautus too light.   —*Hamlet*, II, ii, 415 ff.

ALTHOUGH TODAY SHAKESPEARE SEEMS TRULY TO HAVE been "not of an age, but for all time," the student should bear in mind that his work was part and parcel of the Elizabethan drama. Shakespeare's studies of character and emotion do indeed emphasize constants in human nature, but, in both their limitations and their qualities of greatness, his plays belong essentially to the age in which he wrote. The plots he dramatized were taken from the same histories and story collections that provided quarry for his fellow-playwrights. His choice of subject and theme was as much determined as was theirs by theatrical demand; his treatment of his materials and his dramatic technique, in the last analysis, were no different from theirs; and he probably shared their tastes in more respects than has sometimes been supposed. As one of the most popular playwrights of his day, Shakespeare cannot be thought of as an isolated, aloof figure with ideals and theories that were magnificently indifferent to those of his contemporaries and the audiences for which they catered. Hence, to understand Shakespeare's art, some attention must be given to the dramatic traditions of the age in which he worked and to the accepted practices and conventions by which he and his fellow-dramatists were conditioned.

In Shakespeare's day, the drama was essentially a fresh and a new art. Playing, to be sure, is as old as time, but, when Shakespeare was born in 1564, there were in England no permanent theatres; professional acting was still indistinguishable from minstrelsy and mere vagabondage; and, indeed, drama that had freed itself from moral, educational, or controversial bias might almost be said to have been non-existent. Not until Elizabeth had been on the throne for more than a quarter of a century, providing England with the security of a long reign and a stable government, did the arts begin to flourish in her kingdom, and a vigorous national drama become possible. Yet both the drama and the theatre that Shakespeare knew had their roots deep in the past and could never have been what they became except for centuries of medieval preparation.

THE MIRACLE PLAYS

The drama of medieval Europe, like that of ancient Greece, was originally not entertainment at all but religion. Its basis was the symbolic nature of Christian worship—itself dramatic in tendency—and primitive drama developed out of the desire of the clergy to present more realistically and impressively to their congregations the salient facts of the Bible story upon which their theology was founded. On special occasions in very early times there developed certain antiphonal elaborations of the liturgy which, at first, were only musical, but which, as early as the ninth and the tenth centuries, were fitted with words and called *tropes*. The two great festivals of the church—Christmas, commemorating the birth of a Savior, and Easter, commemorating His death and resurrection—became, appropriately, the principal *nuclei*, first for little dramatic scenes and later for whole cycles of "miracle" or "mystery" plays[1] which depicted the Bible story from the Creation to the Last Judgment.

In its earliest form, the drama had no separate existence, but was closely attached to the church service. Allusion to one of the first of the Easter tropes, that in the *Concordia Regularis Monachorum* drawn up by Ethelwold, bishop of Winchester, during the reign of King Edgar (959-75), will make its dramatic nature clear:

> While the third lesson is being chanted, let four brethren vest themselves. Let one of these, vested in an alb, enter as though to take part in the service, and let him approach the sepulchre without attracting attention and sit there quietly with a palm in his hand. While the third respond is chanted, let the remaining three follow, and let them all, vested in copes, bearing in their hands thuribles with incense, and stepping delicately as those who seek something, approach the sepulchre. These things are done in imitation of the angel sitting in the monument, and the women with spices coming to anoint the body of Jesus. When therefore he who sits there beholds the three approach him like

[1] The terms "miracle" and "mystery," here used to denote plays based upon the Bible narrative, are not always used alike by writers on the early drama. In France, whence both terms were borrowed by English students, *mystère* refers to the Scriptural drama, while *miracle* usually means a play based upon the legend of some saint or upon a miracle wrought by some holy person or sacred relic. The medieval English names for these dramas are "Whitsuntide plays," "Corpus Christi plays," or just "pageants."

folk lost and seeking something, let him begin in a dulcet voice of medium pitch to sing *Quem quæritis* [Whom seekest thou]? And when he has sung it to the end, let the three reply in unison *Ihesu Nazarenum* [Jesus of Nazareth]. So he, *Non est hic, surrexit sicut prædixerat. Ite, nuntiate quia surrexit a mortuis* [He is not here, He has arisen as He predicted. Go, announce that He has arisen from the dead]. At the word of bidding let those three turn to the choir and say *Alleluia! resurrexit Dominus*. (E. K. Chambers, *The Medieval Stage*, II, 14.) There is, then, the pantomime of showing the grave clothes and placing them upon the altar; the choir sings the anthem *Surrexit Dominus de sepulchro*; and, as the hymn *Te Deum laudamus* is begun, all the bells chime out together.

Here, brief though it is, are all the essentials of a drama: mimetic action, impersonation, dialogue, setting, costume, and properties. Similarly, at Christmas, there developed a little scene in which the shepherds sought the crib and conversed with angels and the Virgin Mary.

From these simple, natural, but impressive, extensions of the symbolic rites which marked special holidays, the medieval drama began to evolve. At Easter, an element of excitement was introduced in the race of Peter and John to the empty tomb (eleventh or twelfth century); sometimes Mary Magdalen lingered behind, met the risen Christ, and mistook Him for a gardener; sometimes, before visiting the tomb, the Maries bought spices from an *unguentarius*, who became the first comic character on the medieval "stage." At Christmas, there was a similar development. The shepherds saw the star which heralded the birth of a Savior; the Magi brought rich gifts and placed them beside the rustic presents of the shepherds; later a raging Herod became the first villain on the "stage"; the mothers lamented the slaughter of the innocents; and, as a kind of prologue to the Christmas story, a procession of Old Testament prophets foretold the coming of the Christ. In the beginning, the text of these little scenes adhered as closely as possible to the words of the Scripture; later there was freer dramatic handling. Soon, too, the vernacular began to replace Latin (thirteenth century); lay actors were added to the cast of clerics; and chanting gave way to spoken dialogue.

At the same time, some difference of opinion as to the spiritual value of these elaborations arose among the clergy. It had long before been necessary to separate these scenes from the church service, and, as more and more episodes were added and the spectators grew more numerous and enthusiastic, performances were held outside the church as well as within, and in some places the clergy were forbidden to take part. The drama, however, had found a place in the hearts of the people, and sponsorship of this edifying entertainment gradually passed from the clergy to the semi-religious craft-guilds (the medieval counterparts of trade-unions and fraternal organizations), which were among the most powerful social forces in the Middle Ages. The guilds produced plays in or near their halls to honor their patron saints or to celebrate some religious festival, like that of Pentecost or Corpus Christi, both of which come in the late spring. Occasionally, in England at least, the civic corporations assumed control and assigned to the various guilds the episodes from the Bible story for which each was responsible. Under such circumstances, the religious drama became tremendously elaborate.

From England there have been preserved the major parts of at least four great cycles of miracle plays, i. e., series of religious dramas played by the guilds of some one town: (1) that cycle performed at York, consisting of forty-eight plays; (2) the Wakefield or Towneley cycle, so called because the manuscript was long preserved at Towneley Hall in Yorkshire, consisting of thirty-two plays; (3) *Ludus Coventriæ*, consisting of forty-two plays, but probably not performed at Coventry; (4) and the Chester cycle, consisting of twenty-four plays. All exist in fifteenth-century manuscripts. In addition, there are fragments of cycles from Coventry, Norwich, Newcastle, Dublin, and other localities, some of which cannot be definitely placed. No less than a hundred and twenty-seven towns in England are known, at one time or another, to have supported miracle plays.[2] The miracle play has survived as a type in the Oberammergau Passion Play and in such an experiment as *The Green Pastures* (1929) by Marc Connelly and George Kaufman, which also interpreted a faith in terms of those who held it.

In subject matter, in mood, in treatment, and in general technique, the English miracle cycles exhibit the greatest freedom and variety. The themes were always biblical and the purpose, achieved with varying degrees of skill and piety, was always to vivify the entire Bible story from the Creation to the Last Judgment. In setting, the plays ranged from Heaven to Earth and even to Hell Mouth itself. Some are pedestrian and dull, depicting only well-known biblical characters; in others—notably the Towneley cycle—the effort to achieve realism and the broadest human appeal led to the development of characters to whom neither Scripture nor legend had ascribed any individuality, like the shepherds who watched their flocks, the Pharisees, and the soldiers who guarded the tomb; or which the Bible had merely mentioned or not alluded to at all, like Cain's servant boy, Noah's wife, the detractors of the Virgin, and the lover of the woman taken in adultery. The authors of these dramas translated the remote Bible story into the simple understandable terms of everyday life and varied the sublime narrative with little scenes of realism. Thus, Noah's spouse is scornful of her pious husband for building a boat on dry land and refuses to enter the ark; Isaac pathetically begs his father to spare his mother's tears by withholding from her the news of his untimely death; the roguish Mak's trick of hiding a sheep he has stolen in a baby's cradle is a topsy-turvy parody of the nativity theme; Joseph is repre-

---

[2] E. K. Chambers, *The Medieval Stage*, II, 329–30.

sented as the suspicious, aged husband of a young wife; a uxorious Pontius
Pilate dallies with his wife in open court and is rebuked for it by his beadle;
the despair of Judas is followed by a scene in which a squire is cheated of his
title-deeds to Calvary; the soldiers who set up the cross wrangle and quarrel
over their work. In general, there was a good deal of camaraderie between
actors and audience. Ironically, what had begun as an instrument of devotion
and instruction became in the fourteenth century primarily a spectacle for
the wonder and the mirth of the crowd.

SIGNIFICANCE OF THE MIRACLE PLAYS FOR THE ELIZABETHAN DRAMA

What is the significance of this development to Shakespeare and the Elizabethan drama? In England, from the very beginning, there had grown a free,
hearty, live drama which expressed the mentality of the folk, was unrestrained by any false sense of dignity, realistically mirrored familiar life even
when it told an old, old story, and permitted the serious and the sublime to
rub shoulders with the gross, the homely, and the grotesque. In this dramatic
past the great, firm taproot of the Elizabethan drama was embedded, and no
amount of theorizing about the pseudo-classical unities could wither it. In
the drama of Shakespeare and his contemporaries, as in the medieval drama,
the most vital element was its contact with wholesome everyday life. Audiences looked upon a story as something that had happened and could be
re-experienced as if it were contemporary with themselves. Hence, for Shakespeare's audiences, there was no incongruity in the Elizabethan character of
the Roman crowds in *Julius Cæsar* or *Coriolanus*, in the homely English
rusticity of the old countryman in *Antony and Cleopatra*, or in Duke
Theseus celebrating his wedding by ordering his Elizabethan master of the
revels to stir up the Athenian youths to merriments in the production of
amateur plays. Similarly, the episodic treatment of the long stories that had
to be told in the history plays was not unconventional, nor were the drunken
porter who appeared in *Macbeth*, Peter and the musicians in *Romeo and
Juliet,* the grave-diggers in *Hamlet,* or the sword-play, the wrestling, the
singing, dancing, and romping that characterizes both Shakespeare's comedies and tragedies. All of it was as old as the miracle cycles, and it could
give offense to none but those whose tastes were artificially refined. It was
natively English.

After the Reformation, and long before Shakespeare's time, miracle plays
had begun to decline. But, in some rural districts of England, they survived
until the seventeenth century, and there is every reason to believe that Shakespeare and most of the Elizabethans were familiar with them. Shakespeare's
allusions to them are not frequent and are confined to stock figures and
devices that were popular, like Hamlet's description of the actor who "o'er-
does Termagant" and "out-herods Herod" (III, ii, 14–15). The latter char-

acter, now a symbol of general wickedness, is also used to describe Falstaff when Mrs. Page exclaims: "What a Herod of Jewry is this?" (*The Merry Wives of Windsor*, II, i, 20); another thread to the miracle cycles is the boy who refers to Ancient Pistol as "this roaring devil in the old play" (*Henry V*, IV, iv, 75). Similarly, Celia's remark that Orlando's hair is "something browner than Judas's (*As You Like It*, III, iv, 7) may also refer to conventions of make-up from the miracle plays. But in no sense were these allusions literary; they were intended to recall to the audience visual memories of the old cycles. Shakespeare also referred to the dramatic associations of Whitsuntide (*The Two Gentlemen of Verona*, IV, iv, 164 ff.; *Henry V*, IV, iv, 25 ff.; *The Winter's Tale*, IV, iv, 134 ff.).

But the miracle-play tradition influenced the Elizabethan drama in yet another way—staging. Obviously, one cannot speak of the medieval "theatre" because none existed; there were only temporary, seasonal makeshifts. At first, the church itself was the theatre, and a medieval cathedral was a vast collection of pictorial symbols. Here, carved in wood or stone, was the Rood, flanked by Our Lady and St. John; there on canvas was the Nativity, the Trial before Pilate, the Ascension into Heaven. Hence, just as the liturgy had proved fruitful of religious drama, so the church itself was readily adaptable as a setting for these scenes. Some object or section of the building could symbolize a manger, the pastures around Bethlehem, the Garden of Gethsemane, or the Tomb. Later, this use of the church as theatre on special occasions influenced church architecture, and permanent structures representing the Christmas crib or the Easter sepulchre came into existence. But, permanent or temporary, the position of such properties was determined by the structure of the church. Hence, from the beginning, there arose the convention of an intimate theatre and of placing all the scenes of the action before the audience at once, the actors merely moving to the spot appropriate for the action of the immediate episode. This tradition of symbolical settings and multiple staging, with some elaboration and complexity, lasted in the innyards and the early theatres until Shakespeare's time and beyond.

When the drama was removed from the church to the cathedral close or the market place, the same principles of staging obtained. The whole sequence of necessary settings were arranged within the open space available. Some properties had to be built, but existing facilities were adapted to use whenever possible. The church itself could stand for Heaven, and the drama of the Last Judgment be enacted before the great West Door under the tympanum, which usually represented the Judgment Seat with carved figures of the saved and the damned to the right hand and the left. Plans for such arrangements of localities have been preserved at Lucerne, Donaueschingen, and Valenciennes, but not in England.

Stationary settings do not appear to have been common in England, and

Ludus Coventriæ is the only one of the existing cycles that suggests the use of a single stage. Instead, the guilds preferred to produce their plays on *pageants* or movable floats which were, in effect, separate settings on wheels, suitable for the various episodes making up the cycle. These pageants moved through the town from one designated performance station to the next, and a theatrical performance under such circumstances became a succession of scenes which were repeated at various stations. The audience alone remained stationary. The theatrical principles involved in the use of pageants, however,

A Medieval Pageant   (From Chambers' *Book of Days,* 1863)

were not essentially different from those of the stationary multiple setting. In both cases there was a localized area for acting and an unlocalized area outside it, and in neither case was the line which separated the two sharply drawn. Just as the actor could step out of the stationary set, so he could step out of a localized area on the pageant, or off the pageant altogether. "Here Herod rages in the pageant and in the street also," reads a stage direction in the Coventry *Shearmen and Tailors' Play*, and, again, "the three kings speak in the street." A herald clatters down a medieval lane and mounts the pageant, and the devils at the Last Judgment snatch at the spectators gathered round. This convention of intimacy also continued into Shakespeare's time. In his theatre, as we shall see, the line between the real world and that of make-believe was vaguely drawn, and his platform stage, surrounded on three sides by spectators, was not unlike the unlocalized area around the pageant-wagon.

THE MORALITY PLAYS AND THEIR INFLUENCE

Not all of the traditions influencing the Elizabethan plays were as old as those that sprang from the religious drama; other medieval plays, somewhat more secular in nature, contributed to the stream. While the miracle cycles were still at their height, there developed in the fifteenth century in England, as elsewhere in Europe, another type of drama called the morality play. The morality was a single play complete in itself rather than one episode in a long series. It was less biblical than the average miracle play, but sometimes more religious; it represented another variety of didacticism—the allegorized dramatic sermon. Unlike the miracle play, the morality was less concerned with the Bible than with ethical doctrine and the spiritual conflict between good and evil in the soul of man. To make this conflict vivid, the morality play depicted on the stage abstract virtues and vices and exhorted men to right living by parable or example. Occasionally, however, morality elements found their way into the miracle cycles. Devils, of course, are common to both types, but in *Ludus Coventriæ* a character called Contemplacio serves as a kind of chorus and expositor for the drama, Mors as "God's messenger" calls for King Herod, and the Four Daughters of God appear as Veritas, Misericordia, Justicia, and Pax. In the Digby *Mary Magdalene*, Mundus and the Seven Deadly Sins are represented, and Mary herself is wooed by Curiosity. But such blends of the two types of drama are rare. Occasionally, too, since the moralities were acted by strolling entertainers as well as by amateurs, they often contained elements from popular minstrelsy, like singing, acrobatics, and dancing.

At their best, the moral plays are represented by *The Summoning of Everyman* (fifteenth century), which with *Pride of Life* (fifteenth century), the earliest in England, is a kind of dramatized Dance of Death with universal significance. Less effective is *The Castle of Perseverance* (fifteenth century), which represents the soul of Mankind alternately won over to evil and to good, beleaguered by the forces of the World, the Flesh, and the Devil, overthrown by Death, and finally tried before God with Justice and Truth as accusers and Mercy and Peace as advocates.

Unhappily, not all of the moralities are as impressive as these. Many are portentously dull because little variety of plot or situation was possible. The pre-Reformation moralities, like those already named, *Mankind* (fifteenth century), and *Mundus et Infans* (printed 1522), are broadly religious; those produced after the Reformation are more restricted in theme. Some are doctrinal, like *The Interlude of Youth* (early sixteenth century) or *Respublica* (1553), both Catholic; or like R. Wever's *Lusty Juventus*, or *Mind, Will, and Understanding*, both early sixteenth century and both Protestant. Some treat of the temptations of youth, like *Hickscorner* (*c.* 1530), *Nice Wanton* (*c.* 1553), *The Disobedient Child* (*c.* 1560), or W. Wager's *The Longer Thou Livest, the More Fool Thou Art* (*c.* 1559), which is described as "a mirror very necessary for youth, and specially for such as are to come to dignity and promotion." Some are political, like John Skelton's *Magnificence* (1516), which represents only one class of society, or Sir David Lyndesay's *Satire of the Three Estates* (1540), which treats of all classes. Others are merely pedagogical debates, like Henry Medwall's *Nature* (before 1500), John Rastell's *The Nature of the Four Elements* (1517), or John Redford's *Wit and Science* (1540).

But, for all that, the moralities represented an advance over the miracle dramas. They placed the emphasis upon a dramatic conflict; they often treated the tragic aspect of death as retribution, not only for the sins of Adam, but also as the nemesis of particular sinners; and the stories they told, as well as the dialogue, were invented for this purpose. Moreover, in their efforts to overcome the anemia of so much moral abstraction, the moralities admitted much realistic farcical material and developed some especially popular elements borrowed from the miracle plays—the Devil and his active agent of evil, the Vice. Dressed usually in a fool's outfit and armed with a wooden sword, the Vice had many aliases—Iniquity, Fraud, Ambidexter, Folly, Haphazard, Vanity—and became a satirical sport- and mischief-maker who contributed much to the Elizabethan stage rogue and fool.

Although the moralities had lost their popularity by the time Shakespeare began to write, Elizabethan audiences were familiar with them, and all Elizabethan drama has its roots in these early plays as well as in the miracle cycles. Morality elements also appear in many true comedies and tragedies. Both Good and Bad Angels and the Seven Deadly Sins survive in Marlowe's *Dr. Faustus*, and the character of the tragic conflict in this play is constantly reminiscent of the moralities. Characteristic devices from the type also appear in George Gascoigne's *The Glass of Government*, Robert Greene's

Friar Bacon and Friar Bungay, Lodge and Greene's *A Looking Glass for London*, and even the plays of Jonson. Abstractions and moral types are found occasionally in the *dramatis personæ* of other plays. The morality was revived on both stage and screen as recently as Lynn Root's *Cabin in the Sky* (1940).

Shakespeare, likewise, felt the influence, and his allusions to the morality plays are frequent. Thus, Hamlet describes his uncle as "a very Vice of kings . . . a king of shreds and patches" (III, iv, 98 ff.), in reference to the motley garb that frequently distinguished the Vice. Feste the clown mentions the Vice's dagger of lath and his antics in trying to pare the Devil's talons (*Twelfth Night*, IV, ii, 134). Falstaff refers to Justice Shallow as a "Vice's dagger" now become a squire (*2 Henry IV*, III, ii, 343); Luciana begs Antipholus of Syracuse to "apparel Vice like Virtue's harbinger" (*The Comedy of Errors*, III, ii, 12); Escalus interrupts the wrangle between Elbow the constable and Pompey the clown by asking "which is the wiser here, Justice or Iniquity?" (*Measure for Measure*, II, i, 180); and Cassio in remorse refers to his breach of discipline in morality terms: "It hath pleased the devil Drunkenness to give place to the devil Wrath" (*Othello*, II, iii, 297), in allusion to the Deadly Sins who were the seducers of innocence in the old plays. There is similar mention of Envy and Luxury in *Troilus and Cressida* (II, iii, 23 and V, ii, 55). Many of the tag-names of Shakespeare's characters seem to be in the tradition of the morality, like Touchstone, Benvolio, Malvolio, Shallow, Ariel, though the device was also common in classical comedy. Jaques's Seven Ages of Man speech (*As You Like It*, II, vii, 139 ff.) recalls the morality, and allusion to Good and Bad Angels are frequent (*The Comedy of Errors*, IV, iii, 20; *1 Henry IV*, III, iii, 199; *2 Henry IV*, I, ii, 186 and II, iv, 362; *Measure for Measure*, II, iv, 16; *Macbeth*, I, vii, 19; *Othello*, V, ii, 208; *King Lear*, III, vi, 34; and Sonnet 144).

Of greater significance are the scenes and characters which Shakespeare obviously conceived of according to the familiar morality formula. Launcelot Gobbo's debate with himself about running away from Shylock is cast into the form of the old conflict between Good and Evil: " 'Budge,' says the fiend. 'Budge not,' says my conscience" (*The Merchant of Venice*, II, ii, 1 ff.). The mind of Dromio of Syracuse seems also to be running on old tussles between Man, the World, the Flesh, and the Devil as he fetches the purse of angels from "Mistress Redemption" to release his master from the jailer and aids him in fleeing from "Mistress Satan" the courtesan (*The Comedy of Errors*, IV, ii and iii). The drunken porter in *Macbeth* who imagines he is porter at Hell Gate is likewise in the morality tradition. Even more important are several characters in Shakespeare that have morality functions. Falstaff, for example, is "that revered Vice, that grey Iniquity, that Father Ruffian, that Vanity in years" in the *Henry IV* plays (Part 1, II, iv, 499), and he is occasionally referred to as a misleader of youth (*1 Henry IV*, II, iv, 509; *2 Henry IV*, I, ii, 185). The embodiment of worldliness and sensuality—glutton, lecher, braggart, sluggard, and coward—Falstaff is all of the Seven Deadly Sins rolled into one, and, characteristically, he threatens to run Prince Hal out of the kingdom with a dagger of lath (*1 Henry IV*, II, iv, 151). Richard III, on the other hand, represents the sinister side of the Vice as he mutters aside:

> Thus, like the formal Vice, Iniquity,
> I moralize two meanings in one word. (III, i, 82.)

Finally, in Feste and Autolycus, the very mischievous spirit of the Vice is incarnate. Feste's torment of Malvolio (*Twelfth Night*, IV, ii) is in the morality vein, and Autolycus even points to his kinship as he comes from the sheep-shearing: "Ha, ha! What a fool Honesty is! And Trust, his sworn brother, a very simple gentleman!" (*The Winter's Tale*, IV, iv, 605 ff.). A reference to medieval dramatic tradition often illuminates Shakespeare.

THE TUDOR INTERLUDE

The transition from medieval drama, with its secondary interests of didacticism and morality, to modern comedy and tragedy, without ulterior motives, was brought about largely by two means: (a) the development of the *interlude*, and (b) the humanistic influence of classical dramatic literature.

The term *interlude* is not capable of any sharp definition. Papers in a lawsuit involving John Rastell, the printer (*c.* 1530), seem to discriminate between "stage plays in summer and interludes in winter." Perhaps, for contemporaries, brevity and indoor performance before a small audience were all that distinguished the interlude from other plays. Certainly, throughout the sixteenth century, *interlude* is almost synonymous with *play*. Some scholars have argued that the term refers to the intervals of banquets during which these plays were performed; some insist that the word means merely a dialogue between two persons; others believe that it is the equivalent of *pastime* or *amusement*. Some stress the aristocratic character of the new type; others observe its similarity to the homely farce—like the antics of Noah's wife or the sheep-stealing of Mak that had enlivened the earlier drama. Judging by the plays to which the name was applied, however, elements of all kinds went into the type—farce, social satire, abstractions suggestive of the moral play. Some interludes are entirely devoid of didactic purpose or symbolic technique; others are little more than morality plays. But all interludes are short, witty, simple, and easy to present; the actors who participated were few in number—usually four men and a boy—and the setting nothing more elaborate than a cleared space before the fire or a dais at one end of a hall.

The first English play of this type is *Fulgens and Lucres* (*c.* 1496) by Henry Medwall, chaplain to Cardinal Morton, who based his play upon a humanistic tale that had been printed by William Caxton in 1481. Actually, *Fulgens and Lucres* is a treatise on true nobility illustrated in a contest between a pleasure-loving patrician named Publius Cornelius and a high-principled commoner named Gaius Flaminius for the hand of the beautiful Lucrece, daughter of Fulgens, a Roman Senator. But the use of a comic underplot, featuring Jone the maid and the servants of the two suitors in a burlesque of the main theme, is an anticipation of a technique that is almost Shakespearean. And the straddling purpose of the play is frankly acknowledged by the last speaker, who explains that it was produced:

> Not only to make folk mirth and game,
> But that such as be gentlemen of name
> May be somewhat moved
> By this example for to eschew
> The way of vice and favor virtue.
> For sin is to be reproved
> More in them, for the degree,
> Than in other persons such as be
> Of poor kin and birth.

It is "merry John Heywood" (1497?–1580?), a distant relative of Sir Thomas More, the grandfather of John Donne the poet, and a privileged wit and musician in Henry VIII's household, who raised the interlude to the dignity of an independent artistic form. His *Merry Play between John the Husband, Tib His Wife, and Sir John the Priest* is a vivacious farce with not a trace of edification and with characters and situations that are reminiscent of the *fabliaux* or of stories by Boccaccio or Chaucer. His *Four PP* is a satire on women in a contest between a Pardoner, a Peddler, a Palmer, and a "Poticary" to determine which can tell the biggest lie. His *Play of the Weather* presents various occupational types petitioning different kinds of weather from Jupiter and the decision that results. Altogether, between 1520 and 1540, Heywood is thought to have written six plays; the others attributed to him are *A Play of Love*, *The Pardoner and the Friar*, and *A Dialogue concerning Witty and Witless*. His importance in the history of the English drama is that he recognized diversion alone as sufficient justification for a play and thus set the artistic spirit free.

Plays in both the Medwall and the Heywood traditions may be found in the sixteenth century. Of the former, a typical example is *Gentleness and Nobility: a Dialogue between the Merchant, the Knight, and the Plowman, disputing who is a very Gentleman* (*c.* 1527), a skillful dialogue which has sometimes been attributed to Heywood. Of the latter, a homely village farce called *Tom Tyler and His Wife* (*c.* 1560) is a fair example. But, before the possibilities of the interlude could be fully developed, other influences became operative on English drama which called the attention away from the short one- or two-act play. What English drama needed, however, it is not likely that it could at this time have evolved of itself. English drama lacked restraint, refinement, and a sense of form and structure. It had not as yet recognized clearly the line of cleavage between comedy and tragedy. It required something that would increase the narrow resources of the morality and the interlude and give them a broader human application. It needed new plot- and character-types that would replace or considerably individualize the old ethical abstractions of the native drama. It lacked the intellectuality that would transform mere buffoonery into wit. And these needs were supplied, not from critical theory, but from the example of the drama of ancient Rome.

NATIVE AND FOREIGN ELEMENTS IN COMEDY AND TRAGEDY

An interest in Latin comedy was an inevitable result of humanism, and the plays of both Terence and Plautus were early in high repute in both court and academic circles. "A goodly comedy of Plautus" was performed at a state entertainment of Henry VIII in 1520, and the boys of Paul's School were producing the plays of both Latin writers as early as 1527–8. Before long, the reading and acting of Latin dramas were part of the curriculum of most Tudor schools. Imitations of favorite plays were also occasionally produced both as academic exercises and as entertainment, and, as a consequence, English comedy, in the words of Stephen Gosson, soon "smelt of Plautus." One of the earliest of these Plautine adaptations is *Ralph Roister Doister*, composed some time between 1534 and 1553 by Nicholas Udall, who was, successively, head master of Eton and Westminster, the editor of *Flowers of Latin Speaking Selected and Gathered out of Terence* (1535), and later producer of plays before Queen Mary. *Ralph Roister Doister* is a characteristic graft of classical comedy upon English. Its plot is elaborate but well constructed; its hero is a boastful coward in pursuit of a wealthy widow. The former is a Latin character-type, but the latter is English. In his characterization and the rough-and-tumble scenes he devised, Udall was thoroughly English rather than classical. Similarly, *Gammer Gurton's Needle*, written by "Mr. S." some time around 1552–3, is wholly native in the village life it represents, but plainly patterned on a Plautine model. Other comedies, like *Jack Juggler* (*c.* 1555), which translates an episode from the legend of Amphitryon and Alcmena into terms of contemporary life; *Thersites* (*c.* 1537), a burlesque of the braggart-soldier theme; or *Misogonus* (*c.* 1560), which centers around a rascally wastrel, all to a greater or lesser extent have been Anglicized and are quite as much in the native as in the foreign tradition. Shakespeare's *Comedy of Errors*, which was based upon Plautus's *Menæchmi*, is a similar adaptation of a classical plot to the familiar terms of the Elizabethan theatre.

More subtle, and at the same time more easily absorbed, was the classical influence that came to English comedy by way of Italy. Here the Latin plots and character-types had already been partly adapted to the conditions of sixteenth-century life. Typical examples of such Italianate comedy are *The Bugbears* (1561), a racy play of romantic love, trickery, and intrigue, and George Gascoigne's *Supposes*, based upon Ariosto's *Gli Suppositi* and acted at Gray's Inn in 1566. *Supposes* later became the sub-plot featuring the wooing of Bianca in Shakespeare's *Taming of the Shrew*. Soon Italian story collections were to supply the Elizabethan dramatists with plenty of material for romantic plots.

More will be said of these influences later in a discussion of Shakespeare's comedy (see below, pp. 270 ff.), for, directly or indirectly, the Elizabethans owed a great deal to Plautus and Terence. Thence they obtained the patterned plots they found so serviceable—the separated and reunited families, the background of war or disaster, the clandestine love affairs, the disguise, and the mistaken identity. Thence they learned to construct the ludicrous situations, the intrigues, the amusing mix-ups, the comic wrangles, and similar devices that served the stage for generations. Thence, too, came the stock character-types, often bearing tag-names: the prosperous merchant, like Baptista Minola; a "proper stripling and an amorous," like Lucentio; the braggart cowards, like Don Armado, Pistol, and Falstaff; the clever roguish servants, like Launcelot Gobbo and the Dromios; the friar confessors, like Laurence and Francis; the sorcerers, burlesqued in Pinch and glorified in Prospero; the innkeepers, like Mine Host of the Garter; the soubrettes, like Lucetta, Nerissa, and Maria; the doctors, the pedants, and the clerks, like Caius, Holofernes, and Sir Nathaniel. Hamlet is alluding to these conventionalized figures as he prepares to welcome the players to Elsinore:

> He that plays the king shall be welcome; his Majesty shall have tribute of me; the adventurous knight shall use his foil and target; the lover shall not sigh gratis; the humorous man shall end his part in peace; the clown shall make those laugh whose lungs are tickle o' the sere; and the lady shall say her mind freely, or the blank verse shall halt for't. (II, ii, 332 ff.)

Often, to be sure, classical comedy merely reinforced the native English tendency toward broad humor and riotous farce. But from it the English dramatist learned to articulate plots and draw character; it multiplied his resources and led to the development of technical devices that might otherwise have remained unsought and unknown.

If early Elizabethan comedy represents an amalgam of native and foreign elements, tragedy on the English stage had similar beginnings. Episodes in both the miracle and the morality plays had familiarized audiences with human suffering on the stage, but it is only the latter which left a lasting influence upon serious drama. To be sure, the sacrificial death of a Savior and His suffering at the hands of those He came to save were of the essence of great tragedy. But the spectacle offered little opportunity for the spectator to identify himself with the Hero or to feel in His passion pain which human beings might as readily deserve. Moreover, on the whole, the epic theme of the miracle cycles had been the happy one of the fulfillment of God's promise to redeem erring man, and the climax of this drama—the Resurrection and the victory over suffering and death—nullified to a great extent whatever tragic pity and fear the Crucifixion had aroused. But if the miracle plays had little meaning in terms of worldly tragedy, the morality plays approached more closely the spirit of human tragedy. Their hero was neither Savior nor saint, but simply Man, placed in a world of moral stress and strain; they shifted attention from God's saving mercy to His avenging justice. Nevertheless, the moral play could not resist mixing "mirth with care"; it seldom gave a tragic emphasis to its moralizing.

It is in the non-dramatic stories of the falls of princes and of capricious Fortune and her wheel that one must seek the most important tragic legacy of the Middle Ages. Such collections of tragedies as Boccaccio's *De Casibus Virorum Illustrium*, Chaucer's *Monk's Tale*, or Lydgate's *Falls of Princes*, were ample reminders of the mutability of fortune and the dangers of trusting too implicitly in worldly happiness or prosperity (see below, pp. 323 ff.). These stories, which were drawn mainly from classical history, were, in the nature of the case, not of the people, as the early drama had been, but they did attract large audiences of readers. Then they attracted imitators and eventually supplied the tragic dramatists with materials for plots. Many well-known Elizabethan tragic stories, like those of Appius and Virginia or Antony and Cleopatra, find their place in these books of the falls of illustrious men and women.

Early sixteenth-century audiences, as was natural, showed a marked preference for humor on the stage. It is not surprising that more than thirty years of Elizabeth's reign were to pass before a widespread popular interest in serious drama could develop, nor that, for a time, the early tragedians wrote for a limited audience of scholarly enthusiasts and established traditions of classical drama which were wholly independent of the popular stage. Only in the last decade of the sixteenth century, when playwrights sought native subjects, did tragedy become at once popular and artistic.

The ultimate models of Elizabethan tragedy were the plays of the Latin philosopher-dramatist, Seneca the Younger (4 B.C.–65 A.D.). The ten rhetorical tragedies attributed to him, of which *Medea*, *Agamemnon*, and *Thyestes* are typical, were literary exercises fashioned after the manner of late Greek tragedy—several are little more than paraphrases of Euripides—and probably not intended for stage representation. As in many of the medieval *De Casibus* stories, crime and its retribution is the burden of each of Seneca's plays, and his themes were among the most sensational ones of incest, adultery, unnatural murder, and revenge in the whole of classical mythology. Nine of the ten have a revenge motive. Each exhibits a hero in conflict with one or more opponents; principal characters usually appear with a friend as confidant; and prominence is given to supernatural visitants—furies, deities, and ghosts. In style, the Senecan drama is characterized by artifice, rhetoric, and sententiousness. The action is slow and divided into five acts; much of these dramas, especially the scenes of horror, is presented through long declamatory speeches by messengers instead of shown on the stage. There are elaborate analyses of moods, passions, and forebodings, and choruses interpreting the action are frequent. Most of these characteristics the English playwrights sedulously imitated, but some of them, as extraneous to the action, tend to disappear as the dramatists gained in skill. Seneca left his mark deep upon English dramatic technique.

English Senecan drama may be divided into two main classes: (a) the more or less academic imitations written either as closet drama or for production before a cultivated audience at the Inns of Court, the universities, or Whitehall, and (b) the less pure imitations designed for the popular stage.

In the former category belongs the first English tragedy, *Gorboduc, or Ferrex and Porrex*, which was first acted by members of the Inner Temple during the Christmas revels in January, 1562, and later before Queen Elizabeth at Whitehall. Its authors were two lawyers, Thomas Norton and Thomas Sackville, the latter of whom had an important part in the writing of *The Mirror for Magistrates* (first published in 1559), a collection of stories of the falls of princes which was to open to the tragedian the inexhaustible well of British history and legend. The subject of *Gorboduc* is English and deals with the dissension, murder, and civil war that grow out of the division of the kingdom between the king's two sons. But, except for its disregard of the unities, the model of the play is Senecan. *Gorboduc* was followed by *Jocasta* (1566), written by George Gascoigne and others; *Gismond of Salerne* (1567–8), founded upon a tale in Boccaccio's *Decameron* by R. Wilmot; *The Misfortunes of Arthur* (1587), based upon the conflict of Mordred and King Arthur by Thomas Hughes—all were produced first at one of the Inns of Court and later before the queen. The universities also followed the taste for Roman tragedy. At Oxford, such plays as Nicholas Grimald's *Christus Redivivus* (1543) and William Gager's *Ulysses Redux* (1580), and, at Cambridge, John Christopherson's *Jephthes* (1546), Thomas Watson's *Absalon* (1563, now lost), and Thomas Legge's *Richardus Tertius* (1579), cast biblical story, classical legend, and national history into classical moulds. To the same general category belong the literary dramas of the coterie surrounding the Countess of Pembroke, like Thomas Kyd's translation of *Cornélie* (1593) by the French Senecan Robert Garnier, Samuel Daniel's *Cleopatra* (1593) and *Philotas* (1604), and Fulk Greville's *Alaham* (1600) and *Mustapha* (1603–08). *Seneca His Ten Tragedies, Translated into English*, by Jasper Heywood, John Studley, Thomas Newton, and others, was published in 1581, and, though hardly something to be played, yet, as Thomas Nashe put it,

> English Seneca read by candlelight yields many good sentences, as "Blood is a beggar," and so forth; and if you entreat him fair in a frosty morning, he will afford you whole *Hamlets*, I should say handfuls, of tragical speeches. (Preface to Robert Greene's *Menaphon*, 1589.)

Nashe is alluding to an early play, now lost, upon which Shakespeare's great tragedy may have been based.

At the same time, classical tragedy, somewhat impassioned and diluted with morality elements and farce, seems to have won at least the temporary favor of a more popular audience in such crude productions as *The Tragical Comedy of Damon and Pithias* (*c.* 1565) by R. Edwards; *A New Interlude of Vice containing the History of Horestes, with the Cruel Revengement of His Father's Death upon His Own Natural Mother* (1567) by John Pickering; *A Lamentable Tragedy mixed full of Pleasant Mirth, containing the Life of Cambyses, King of Persia* (*c.* 1567) by Thomas Preston; and *A New Tragical Comedy of Appius and Virginia* (1567), an adaptation of Chaucer's *Physician's Tale* by R. B.—plays which Shakespeare was soon to parody. Bottom expresses his admiration for "Ercles vein, a tyrant's vein . . . a part to tear a cat in" (*A Midsummer Night's Dream*, I, ii, 31 ff.), and Falstaff in the burlesque interview between the king and Prince Hal does it "in King Cambyses vein" (*1 Henry IV*, II, iv, 425). Some of the classical moralities seem to have been written originally for schools; some were even performed at court; some were passed on to the public stage. But they are an interesting blend of the drama of the Inns of Court and of Whitehall with the vigorous native entertainment of the innyards which preserved the infant drama from the double danger of classical frigidity, on the one hand, and mere buffoonery and lack of dignity, on the other.

It was Thomas Kyd (1558–94) who, more than anyone else, popularized Senecan tragedy on the public stage. The son of a scrivener, Kyd attended the Merchant Tailors' School, drifted into literature, and became the author of the most popular play of his generation. His *Spanish Tragedy* (*c.* 1589) is a play in which romantic intrigue, blood, and revenge mingle to produce good theatrical melodrama in the story of the vengeance of a father for his son. Much besides the central theme of the play is Senecan—its rant and bombast, its use of both chorus and vengeful ghost, its sensationalism—but

The Spanish Tragedy ventured upon one important departure from the strict Senecan decorum. With the true instinct of the dramatist for action, Kyd produced his murders on the stage instead of merely reporting them, and so established a tradition that took a long while for good taste to restrain. What else Kyd wrote, besides his translation of Garnier's *Cornélie*, is not known. He and Marlowe shared the same work table for a time. Perhaps he was the author of the original *Hamlet* which was on the boards in 1594. Certainly, Kyd set the fashion which made Shakespeare's *Titus Andronicus* and *Hamlet* possible and contributed elements of *Richard III*, *Julius Cæsar*, and *Macbeth*.

THE DRAMA OF THE COURT

Still another stream of refined entertainment flowed into the mighty river of the Elizabethan drama, that of the court. All of the Tudor sovereigns had a remarkable gust for the outward forms of medieval chivalry, for color and splendor and pomp. Elizabeth, in particular, loved ceremony, and she never rode through the London streets or rowed on the river without being attended by all sorts of pageantry. When, in the summer months, she went "on progress," accompanied by her court, to visit one of the universities or her nobles at their country seats, she received a homage that would have satisfied the vanity of any sovereign. The citizens of the various towns through which she passed outdid one another in their loyal welcome to their queen; the streets were decorated and there were frequent pauses for music, elaborate addresses, and various kinds of folk revelry. At the castle of her host, further tribute of every conceivable kind would be paid. The accounts of Elizabeth's progresses contain numerous descriptions of entertainments offered her, and in all of them the dramatic element was in some form present.[3]

"The Princely Pleasures at Kenilworth," when the queen was feted for three weeks by the Earl of Leicester in 1575, are the best known, and they are typical. A giant porter, representing Hercules, welcomed the queen as she approached the gate of the castle; the Lady of the Lake attended by nymphs next greeted her; as she came from hunting, a Savage Man, clad in ivy, engaged with Echo in a poetic dialogue full of studied compliments; Sylvanus, god of the Woods, bade her a gracious farewell; and Deep Desire spoke verse out of a holly-bush and sang a song. By day there were feats of agility, mock fights, a bride-ale, and a Hock-tide play; at night there were masques in the hall and fireworks and water sports on the lake. The devisers of these confections were several: George Gascoigne, leading poet of his day; William Hunnis, master of her Majesty's Chapel; Master Badger, beadle of the University of Oxford; and Richard Mulcaster, master of the Merchant

---

[3] For contemporary accounts of these splendors, see John Nichols, *The Progresses and Public Processions of Queen Elizabeth*, 3 volumes (1788–1821).

Tailors' School. Three years later, when Leicester again entertained Eliza-beth at Wanstead House, Sir Philip Sidney composed a lively little pastoral called *The Lady of May*. As she walked in the garden, the queen was met by a beautiful lady courted by a hunter and a shepherd. Out of this situation a play developed, decorated with songs and rustic music, and at the end her Majesty was called upon to act as arbiter between the lovers. The principal ingredient of these entertainments, it will be seen, were classic myth, allegory, pastoralism, and folklore.

In the court calendar at Whitehall, Richmond, Hampton Court, or Green-wich, several specific seasons were set apart for revelry, sometimes dramatic in character. Accession Day (November 17), Christmas, New Year's, Twelfth Night, Candlemas, and Shrovetide were habitually celebrated at court by "pastimes," "feats of agility and tumbling," "fighting at barriers," mummings and maskings, dances, and "inventions," arranged by the Office of the Revels. Further, no visitation of princes, reception of ambassadors, or similar ceremonial was complete without some sort of dramatic or symbolical entertainment. Records of these functions are fairly complete,[4] and from the plays named some impression at least may be gained of courtly taste. There are some moralities, like *Wit and Will* (1567), *Truth, Faithfulness, and Mercy* (1574), and *A Game at Cards* (1582); an occasional biblical play, like *Sapientia Solomonis* (1565); a few classical comedies, like *Miles Gloriosus* and *Heautontimorumenos* (1565); Italian stories, like *Gismond of Salerne* (1566), *The Three Sisters of Mantua* (1578), and *Ariodante and Genevra* (1583); an occasional pastoral, like *Phyllida and Corin* (1584); and others of doubtful character, like *The King of Scots* (on the Darnley murder?), *As Plain as Can Be, Jack and Jill, Six Fools* (all 1567), and *The Cruelty of a Stepmother* (1578). But by far the largest number had a classical theme: *Orestes* (1567), *Ajax and Ulysses* (1572), *Iphigenia* (1571), *Perseus and Andromeda* (1572), *Philemon and Philecia* (1574), *Scipio Africanus* (1580), *Pompey* (1581), and *Agamemnon and Ulysses* (1584), to name only a few at random. Hence, in matters of dramatic taste, the Elizabethan court seems to have set the fashion for little that was new, except in classical learning and refinement.

The actors of these plays were, from the beginning, either the professional adult companies patronized by Elizabethan noblemen (see below, pp. 101–2), or boys from schools like Westminster or Merchant Tailors', or from one of the royal choirs, like the Children of her Majesty's Chapel, St. Paul's Cathe-dral, or Windsor Chapel. Occasionally, the adult troupes and the boys' com-

---

[4] See Albert Feuillerat, *Documents Relating to the Office of the Revels in the Time of Queen Elizabeth* (1908); Mary Susan Steele, *Plays and Masques at Court during the Reigns of Elizabeth, James, and Charles* (1926); and E. K. Chambers, "A Court Calendar," in *The Elizabethan Stage*, IV, 75 ff.

panies seem to have co-operated for a performance. More will be said later concerning the boys' companies (see below, pp. 102–3). Originally, playing was only a part of the boys' academic training, but their popularity at court soon brought about their development into professional companies, and, during the sixties, seventies, and eighties of the sixteenth century, they attracted a group of master playwrights to write for them.

Of the dramatists who wrote especially for the limited audience of the court, the most important was John Lyly (1554–1606). Educated at both Oxford and Cambridge, Lyly sprang into instant fame in 1579 at the publication of his mannered courtly romance called *Euphues, the Anatomy of Wit.* Thereafter, he seems to have devoted himself to the effort of acquiring a place at court, only to be disappointed in his hopes. To this end, during the decade of the 1580's, he wrote for Paul's boys a series of court comedies on classical and mythological themes. His *Sappho and Phao* (*c.* 1584) dramatizes a legend that Venus endowed the ferryman Phao with extraordinary beauty only to have Sappho—here not the poetess, but Queen of Syracuse—fall in love with him and become her rival. *Campaspe* (*c.* 1584) tells of the rivalry in love between Alexander the Great and a poor painter, Apelles, for the beautiful Theban prisoner of the conqueror. *Galathea* (before 1588) is a mythological pastoral which introduces two girls disguised in boys' clothing who fall in love and are saved from disappointment when Venus miraculously changes the sex of one of them. There is a parallel plot of Diana and her nymphs, among whom Cupid has insinuated himself to the annoyance of the goddess. *Endymion* (*c.* 1588) tells the story of the shepherd lad who venerated the goddess Cynthia and left unrequited the love of Tellus the earth goddess, and who is punished by being cast into a deep sleep from which nothing can awaken him except the chaste kiss of Cynthia. *Midas* (*c.* 1589) and *Love's Metamorphosis* (*c.* 1589) are both stories taken from Ovid; *Mother Bombie* (*c.* 1587), with a tangle of love intrigues, has some resemblance to Latin and Italian comedy, while in *The Woman in the Moon* (*c.* 1590), the only one of his plays which is written in verse, Lyly elaborated the classical story of Pandora and her gifts from the gods.

Lyly's purpose, according to the prologue to *Sappho and Phao,* was to awaken "soft smiling, not loud laughing," and it is as the originator of cultured comedy that Lyly is important. Many of his comic devices—contrasts, intrigues, disguise, substitution—are borrowed from Latin and Italian comedy, as are his fondness for stock character-types—the crafty servant, the love-sick youth, the whimsical old man, the braggart, and the page. But the "new English" which he wrote, even if it was artificial and precious, was something unknown before in the English drama; he put songs and lyricism to new uses, and, in general, rendered his comedy less gross and amateurish than did the writers for the public stage. His habit of running variations on a theme and setting off high comedy with low and daintiness with grotesqueness, in the manner of the court masque, doubtless had some effect upon the technique of Shakespeare. There is hardly a play of Lyly's, also, that is not filled with flattery of the queen.

Lyly wrote only for the court, but it was George Peele (*c.* 1537–96) who took the drama of the court to the common theatres. The son of a clerk at Christ's Hospital, who was himself a maker of pageants, Peele, like Lyly, was an Oxford man. During his stay at the university he distinguished himself by his poetry and his wit, and, after his coming to London, he was for a time a rival of Lyly at court. His *Arraignment of Paris* (*c.* 1584) is, if anything, even more flattering to the queen than the plays of Lyly. Ate, the goddess of Discord, throws the golden apple among the goddesses, and the shepherd Paris pronounces judgment. Juno, however, is dissatisfied and summons Paris before her to vindicate his sentence. At the end, a nymph of Diana describes Eliza; the characters speak directly to the queen, who was in the audience; all the goddesses yield to her, because she equals Juno in majesty, Minerva in wisdom, Venus in beauty, and Diana in virtue; and they deliver the golden apple to

> the noble phoenix of our age,
> Our fair Eliza, our Zabeta fair.

The play is garlanded with songs and lyrics, dumb-shows, and processions. Another such play by Peele, called *The Hunting of Cupid* (*c.* 1591), is known only from fragments copied out by Drummond of Hawthornden about 1609, but it seems to have been written in very much the same style.

Having tried at court, Peele turned to the public stage. A roisterer and a spendthrift, he may even have become a professional actor as well as a playwright who attempted everything likely to prove popular. *The Battle of Alcazar* (*c.* 1589), attributed to him, is a drama of blood; *Edward I* (*c.* 1593), a crude chronicle play; *David and Bethsabe* (*c.* 1594), a biblical drama; *The Old Wives' Tale* (*c.* 1591–4), a burlesque of the absurdities of old romance. So varied were his talents that Peele's hand has been sought in nearly every anonymous play of the period.

Once the court manner was popularized on the public stage, its influence is traceable upon most of the later dramatists. Of Shakespeare's plays only three—*Love's Labor's Lost, A Midsummer Night's Dream,* and *The Tempest* —bear the marks of having been written originally, not for the public theatre, but for a more limited audience. All three are lyrical and poetic rather than strictly dramatic; in each a courtly story is treated in the mock-serious vein that would be suitable for a courtly revel; in each is a contrast of courtly and rustic social groups and of minor plot burlesquing main plot, and each is filled with songs. Even the subject matter of *Love's*

Labor's Lost seems lifted from a royal progress. There is a princely embassage, a series of courtly flirtations, masking and mumming, deer-hunting that is celebrated in verse by a village poet, and a *Pageant of the Nine Worthies* presented by yokel actors. *A Midsummer Night's Dream* contains a description of a mermaid on a dolphin's back, with stars shooting wildly from their spheres while Cupid takes aim at a fair vestal throned by the west who passes on in maiden meditation fancy-free (II, i, 158 ff.)—all reminiscent of the water-shows and fireworks and mythological pageantry that graced many a royal tour. Finally, in *The Tempest*, written in the time of James, when court entertainment reached even greater extravagance and ingenuity than in the reign of Elizabeth, there is, in addition to other court elements, a formal betrothal masque presented by spirits for the delectation of a pair of betrothed lovers (IV, i, 60 ff.). Other of Shakespeare's plays are known to have been presented at court, and, according to tradition, *The Merry Wives of Windsor* was written so that Queen Elizabeth might see Falstaff in love (see above, p. 26).

THE DRAMA OF THE PUBLIC THEATRES

Simultaneously with the more or less academic Senecan vogue, the nationalistic spirit of Elizabethan England, as well as classical example, suggested to playwrights a new field of stirring subject matter, the glories and the vicissitudes of England's past. The chronicle play that developed was only one form of an extensive and varied literature which expressed the national spirit, but it was the most striking, and Shakespeare became its greatest exponent. More will be said later about the backgrounds of Shakespeare's histories and of his technique in this form of drama (see below, p. 220). It is sufficient here to allude merely to its popularity. Folk plays of St. George and Robin Hood had come into existence in the Middle Ages; Bishop Bale had combined historical matter with that of a polemical morality in *King Johan* (c. 1547); and the Senecan vogue, as we have seen, had produced several historical dramas in both English and Latin. But it was the patriotic fervor of the 1580's that made possible the discovery for the public stage of many good stories. Between the days of the Spanish Armada and the close of Elizabeth's reign, approximately one play in every five had at least a background of English history. Centering about the personality of a king or some other national hero either historical or legendary, such plays were often little more than a succession of scenes filled with glamorous personages and vigorous action, and, in their dramatization, classical and other foreign models were of scant service. In its more primitive form, the chronicle history was a thoroughly native product.

Shakespeare had numerous affiliations with these history plays. His earliest writing, there is reason to believe, was in refurbishing older histories to produce the *Henry VI* trilogy, and more than half of his plays have historical subjects, some of them treated by earlier dramatists. One of the most popular of the early chronicle plays was *The Famous Victories of Henry V* (*c.* 1580), a crude dramatization of legends about the wild Prince Hal. It set the style for combining matter from the chronicles with comic scenes drawn from everyday life and became the basis for Shakespeare's *Henry IV*. Others with considerable Shakespearean significance are *The Tragedy of Locrine* (*c.* 1591) and the anonymous *Life and Death of Lord Cromwell* (before 1602), both once attributed to Shakespeare; *The Life and Death of Jack Straw* (before 1593) and *The Tragedy of Thomas of Woodstock* (1592–5), both treating events in the reign of Richard II; and *The Chronicle History of King Leir* (1594), which was later reworked by Shakespeare in *King Lear*. Still other examples will be mentioned among the works of Shakespeare's contemporaries.

The work of Christopher Marlowe (1564–93), more than that of any other playwright, vindicated the independence of this new English drama from rigid classical influences. Without humor himself, Marlowe called his audiences away

> From jigging veins of rhyming mother wits
> And such conceits as clownage keeps in pay,

and led them

> to the stately tent of war
> Where you shall hear the Scythian Tamburlaine
> Threat'ning the world with high astounding terms.

He applied the loose, episodic method of the chronicle play to the purposes of tragedy. It was Marlowe's "mighty line" of blank verse and his "high astounding terms" that gave to serious drama both a stateliness and a passion that it had not known before.

The son of a Canterbury cobbler, Marlowe was only two months older than Shakespeare. He had the advantages of a good education at King's School in his native place and at Cambridge, matured rapidly, became a secret agent for the crown, came to London, and had his life snuffed out before Shakespeare had hardly begun. But in his short career he wrote six plays—*Tamburlaine* (in two parts and ten acts, *c.* 1587), *Dr. Faustus* (*c.* 1588), *The Jew of Malta* (*c.* 1589), *Edward II* (*c.* 1592), *Dido, Queen of Carthage* (1593), and *The Massacre at Paris* (1593)—as well as translations of Lucan and Ovid, and an unfinished poem, *Hero and Leander*.

More of a poet than a playwright, Marlowe gave to his plays something of his own rebellious spirit as well as the restless striving of the Renaissance. He built his dramas around a central superman hero—conqueror, scholar, villain, seeker of wealth or power, as the case might be—who dwarfs all other characters in the play and falls, not because of any flaw in his own character, but because he seeks the unattainable and is faced by fateful forces that are bigger than he is. Only in *Edward II*, which many consider his masterpiece, is there anything like a true dramatic conflict in the clash of wills between the king and his barons. His other plays are a mere succession of scenes, studded by passages of magnificent poetry, and animating the simple philosophy that characterized the medieval *Falls of Princes* and the stories of Fortune and her wheel:

> Base Fortune, now I see that in thy wheel
> There is a point to which when men aspire
> They tumble headlong down. That point I touched,
> And seeing there was no place to mount higher,
> Why should I grieve at my declining fall? (*Edward II*, 2627 ff.)

But to experience the whole of life and to penetrate to its inner depths as Shakespeare did, Marlowe was temperamentally incapable.

Yet the influence of Marlowe upon Shakespeare's early work is unmistakable. Aside from his burlesque of the fustian manner in the jargon of Ancient Pistol, one occasionally finds in Shakespeare a Marlowesque conception, a reminder of Marlowe's fire and rhetoric, or an echo of his phraseology or his "mighty line." Aaron the Moor in *Titus Andronicus* is a villain in the Marlowe tradition; so is the dominating Richard III, but Shakespeare's king represents more subtle characterization than anything in Marlowe. Shylock and his daughter Jessica are obvious imitations of Barabas and Abigail in *The Jew of Malta*, but Shakespeare's Jew is more poignantly human than Marlowe's. Shakespeare's *Richard II*, like Marlowe's *Edward II*, centers around a weak monarch, ruled by unworthy favorites, and in the end deposed and slain. There is even the same curious shift of sympathy in favor of the hero in the closing acts of both plays. Sir Hugh Evans makes confused quotation of Marlowe's lyric "Come live with me and be my love," in *The Merry Wives of Windsor* (III, i, 15–27), and in the same play horses are stolen by impostors who "set spurs and away, like three German devils, three Doctor Faustuses" (IV, v, 170–1). Shylock's lament, "My daughter! O my ducats! O my daughter!" (*The Merchant of Venice*, II, viii, 15), is clearly reminiscent of Barabas's cry:

> O my girl!
> My gold! my fortune! my felicity! . . .
> O girl! O gold! O my bliss! (*The Jew of Malta*, 689 ff.)

and Richard II's apostrophe to the looking glass:

> Is this the face which fac'd so many follies,
> That was outfac'd by Bolingbroke (IV, i, 281 ff.)

suggests that Shakespeare had not forgotten the famous lines in *Dr. Faustus:*

> Was this the face that launched a thousand ships
> And burned the topless towers of Ilium? (1328-9.)

(Cf. *Troilus and Cressida,* II, ii, 80–1.) Numerous other parallels might be cited. If, as there is reason to believe, Shakespeare first joined the Pembroke company, for which Marlowe was writing, it is possible that he received his first training in playwriting from this greatest of his predecessors. It is not without significance that Shakespeare's only direct reference to a contemporary author should have been to Marlowe. In *As You Like It,* Phebe quotes a line from the unfinished *Hero and Leander:*

> Dead shepherd, now I find thy saw of might,
> "Who ever loved that loved not at first sight?" (III, v, 80–1.)

Marlowe is but one of a group of "university wits" already alluded to, including John Lyly, George Peele, Robert Greene, Thomas Lodge, and Thomas Nashe, who together are the most significant of Shakespeare's predecessors. Their fortunes were various; some, like Lyly, wrote only for the court; others only for the public stage. Some, like Peele, tried everything; some, like Nashe, wrote only a play or two and turned to pamphleteering and fiction. In *The Return from Parnassus,* Will Kempe the comedian is made to say: "Few of the university pen plays well; they smell too much of that writer Ovid, and that writer Metamorphoses, and talk too much of Proserpina and Jupiter" (Part II, III, iii, 18 ff.). Yet the theatres needed these scholars and exploited their talents; they were Shakespeare's school masters in the art of playwriting. Of this group, Greene and Lodge were representative, and together they did much to establish on the stage the type of romantic comedy that Shakespeare took up in *The Two Gentlemen of Verona* and developed later in *Much Ado about Nothing* and *Twelfth Night.* Each also was the author of a novel that Shakespeare was to dramatize.

Robert Greene (1558–92) was a Norwich man, a master of arts of both Oxford and Cambridge, a traveler in Spain and Italy, an actor, and a born journalist in an age that had no newspapers. If one may believe even half of what he confesses in his autobiographical pamphlets, or what his contemporaries wrote about him, Greene's life was that of a witty bohemian who meant well but who performed badly, a series of reckless dissipations punctuated by periods of the most poignant repentance. Nearly forty publications are associated with his name, but his dramatic output was small, and to him a great deal of dubious and anonymous work has been ascribed. The plays that are certainly his all seem to have been inspired by the fashion of the moment. With Lodge he collaborated on *A Looking Glass for London* (*c.* 1590), which is in the tradition of the morality play. His *Alphonsus of*

Aragon (*c.* 1587) and *Orlando Furioso* (*c.* 1591) are imitations, perhaps burlesques, of the new heroical high-flown style of Marlowe's *Tamburlaine*. His *Friar Bacon and Friar Bungay* (*c.* 1589) is thought by some to have been written to rival *Dr. Faustus*, though the date of neither play is known. His *History of James IV of Scotland* (*c.* 1591) is not, as its title suggests, a chronicle play, but an adaptation of an Italian *novella* which introduces Oberon, King of the Fairies, to the English stage. Only *George a Greene, the Pinner of Wakefield* (1590), which has been attributed to him, is a comedy of simple English life. Perhaps his greatest distinction has come from his supposed attack upon the young Shakespeare (see above, pp. 6–7) and the fact that he wrote a pastoral romance called *Pandosto, or The History of Dorastus and Fawnia* (1588) which Shakespeare much later put on the stage as *The Winter's Tale.*

Thomas Lodge (1558?–1625) is a much more shadowy figure in the English drama than Robert Greene, and seems to have become a respectable physician who was ashamed of his youthful connection with the theatre. The son of a Lord Mayor of London, Lodge was educated at Oxford and at Lincoln's Inn, abandoned law for literature, became a freebooter and a voyager to distant places, and whiled away the time at sea by writing lyrics and pastoral romances, the best of which, *Rosalynde: Euphues Golden Legacy* (1590), became the source of Shakespeare's *As You Like It.* His career as a dramatist began early, but only two plays can certainly be identified as his: *A Looking Glass for London*, which has already been mentioned, and *The Wounds of Civil War . . . in the True Tragedies of Marius and Scilla* (*c.* 1588), the latter a somewhat tame imitation of Marlowe, which, nevertheless, has the distinction of introducing the work of Plutarch to the English stage. By 1589, Lodge expressed in *Scylla's Metamorphosis* his determination:

> To write no more of that whence shame doth grow,
> Or tie my pen to penny knaves' delight,
> But live with fame, and so for fame to write.

Lodge's later history is curious. He gave up his imaginative writing altogether, became a convert to Roman Catholicism, took a medical degree, and published only laborious treatises and translations.

The names of these and lesser dramatists or the titles of their plays are mentioned in the *Diary* or account book of Philip Henslowe, owner of several Elizabethan playhouses (see below, pp. 106–7). Writing for Henslowe's theatres were not only such minor contemporaries of Shakespeare as Anthony Munday (*c.* 1553–1633), Henry Chettle (*c.* 1560–1607), Michael Drayton (*c.* 1563–1631), Henry Porter (*fl.* 1596–7), and William Haughton (*c.* 1575–1605), but also such important playwrights as George Chapman (*c.* 1560–1634), the translator of Homer and the author of satirical comedies and revenge plays; Ben Jonson (1572–1637), the founder of the comedy of humors; Thomas Dekker (c. 1572–c. 1632), pamphleteer and dramatist of London life; and Thomas Heywood (c. 1570–1641), whose output was various—London comedy, classical legend, chronicle play, romance, domestic tragedy. Later playwrights were Thomas Middleton (c. 1570–1627), John Marston (c. 1575–1634), John Webster (?–1634?), Francis Beaumont (1584–1616), John Fletcher (1579–1625), and Philip Massinger (1583–1640). Most of these dramatists worked, not singly, but in collaboration, and only a fraction of their plays has survived.

Thus, by Shakespeare's time, the traditions of a vigorous popular drama were firmly established. Its range was that of Elizabethan life itself, from the glitter of the court to the life of rural England and the bustle and merriment of London. Shakespeare accepted it and tried his hand at nearly everything that was known to the contemporary stage. Before him lay the example of classical experiment, the allegorical court drama of Lyly, the realism and the humor of Greene, the fire and passion of Marlowe, the chronicle histories, the romantic world of Italian story—in short, an infinite variety of dramatic art that is unparalleled anywhere. He led the way to no new dramatic form that was untried before, and he experimented with no new subject matter. Instead, he perfected what he found, expanded it into a universal picture of human life, and, through his imagination, his poetic gifts, and his broad outlook, explored the nobility and the failings of which men and women are capable.

SUGGESTED REFERENCES

BASKERVILL, CHARLES READ. *The Elizabethan Jig and Related Song Drama.* University of Chicago Press, 1929.

BASKERVILL, CHARLES READ, HELTZEL, VIRGIL B., *and* NETHERCOT, ARTHUR H. (eds.). *Elizabethan and Stuart Plays.* New York, Holt, 1934.
    A good collection of forty-two plays from Udall to Shirley.

BOAS, FREDERICK S. *Shakspere and His Predecessors.* New York, Scribner, 1896.
    Shakespeare's debt to the work of the earlier Elizabethans.

———. *University Drama in the Tudor Age.* Oxford, Clarendon Press, 1914.

———. *An Introduction to Tudor Drama.* Oxford, Clarendon Press, 1933.
    A brief account of the dramatic conditions which had their flowering in Shakespeare's plays.

BOND, R. WARWICK (ed.). *Early Plays from the Italian: Supposes, The Bugbears, Misogonus.* Oxford, Clarendon Press, 1911.

CHAMBERS, E. K. *The Medieval Stage* (2 vols.). Oxford, Clarendon Press, 1903.

An account of medieval minstrelsy, folk drama, religious drama, and the interlude, with appendixes of documents.

CREIZENACH, WILHELM. *The English Drama in the Age of Shakespeare.* Translated from *Geschichte des neueren Dramas.* London, Sidgwick and Jackson, 1916.

CUNLIFFE, J. W. (ed.). *Early English Classical Tragedies: Gorboduc, Jocasta, Gismond of Salerne, The Misfortunes of Arthur.* Oxford, Clarendon Press, 1912.

GATCH, KATHARINE HAYNES. "Shakespeare's Allusions to the Older Drama," *Philological Quarterly,* VII (1928), pp. 27–44.

GREEN, A. WIGFALL. *The Inns of Court and Early English Drama.* New Haven, Yale University Press, 1931.

GREG, W. W. *Pastoral Poetry and Pastoral Drama.* London, A. H. Bullen, 1906.

——— (comp.). *A Bibliography of the English Printed Drama to the Restoration,* London, Bibliographical Society, 1939.

A definitive list of which only the first volume has appeared.

HARBAGE, ALFRED. *Annals of English Drama: 975–1700. An Analytical Record of All Plays, Extant or Lost, Chronologically Arranged and Indexed by Authors, Titles, Dramatic Companies, etc.* Philadelphia, University of Pennsylvania Press, 1940.

MACKENZIE, W. R. *The English Moralities from the Point of View of Allegory.* New York, Ginn, 1914.

PARROTT, THOMAS MARC *and* BALL, ROBERT HAMILTON. *A Short View of Elizabethan Drama, together with Some Account of Its Principal Playwrights and the Conditions under which It Was Produced.* New York, Scribner, 1943.

An excellent, brief account of the rise, development, and decline of the English drama from its beginnings in the liturgy of the Church to its sudden end with the closing of the theatres in 1642.

POLLARD, ALFRED W. (ed.). *English Miracle Plays, Moralities, and Interludes. Specimens of the Pre-Elizabethan Drama.* Revised edition, Oxford, Clarendon Press, 1923.

SCHELLING, FELIX E. *Elizabethan Drama, 1558–1642. A History of the Drama in England from the Accession of Queen Elizabeth to the Closing of the Theaters, to which is prefixed a résumé of the earlier drama from its beginnings* (2 vols.). Boston and New York, Houghton, 1908.

STEELE, M. S. *Plays and Masques at Court during the Reigns of Elizabeth, James, and Charles.* New Haven, Yale University Press, 1926.

THOMPSON, E. N. S. *The English Moral Plays.* New Haven, Yale University Press, 1910.

WELSFORD, ENID. *The Court Masque: A Study in the Relationship between Poetry and the Revels*. Cambridge University Press, 1927.

YOUNG, KARL. *The Drama of the Medieval Church* (2 vols.). Oxford, Clarendon Press, 1933.

A collection of the dramatic texts used by the medieval Church as a part of public worship, together with a discussion.

ELIZABETHAN THEATRICAL

COMPANIES

England affords those glorious vagabonds,
That carried erst their fardels on their backs,
Coursers to ride on through the gazing streets,
Sooping it in their glaring satin suits,
And pages to attend their masterships.
—*The Return from Parnassus*, Part II, V, i.

For the law of writ and the liberty, these are the only men.
—*Hamlet*, II, ii, 420.

ONE OF THE MOST PUZZLING CIRCUMSTANCES TO THE NEW student of the Elizabethan drama is the curious inconsistency in attitude which the age adopted toward the drama and the stage. Accustomed to hearing the Elizabethan period lauded as the golden age of English drama and its people, royal and common alike, praised for their whole-hearted patronage of the theatre, the student is a little bewildered, not only by severe criticism of the drama as a legitimate form of art and entertainment, but more especially by a social stigma placed upon the actor. In book after book, players and playwrights are referred to as "priests of Belial," "caterpillars of the commonwealth," or at best as "a very superfluous sort of men who should be wholly stayed and forbidden." In the statutes "common players" are coupled with "rogues, vagabonds, and sturdy beggars." Acting, it is apparent, did not always occupy the respectable position it now holds both as an art and as a profession. In Shakespeare's time, the theatre was only beginning to grow in dignity and repute. A brief review of the rise of professional playing will serve to make the Elizabethan attitude clearer.

THE ANCESTRY OF PROFESSIONAL PLAYING

The Elizabethan professional actor was the lineal descendant of two medieval ancestors, the one amateur, the other professional. The more reputable of the two was the amateur, including the guild actor in miracle play, saint's play, or morality, and later the actor in academic plays at schools, the universities, and the Inns of Court. These amateur antecedents of the Elizabethan players were tradesmen or students who merely acted in their spare time or on special occasions in plays the ultimate purpose of which was edification rather than pure amusement, and they were not dependent for their livelihood upon their histrionic talents. On the professional side stood the medieval minstrel, himself a descendant from that degenerate offspring of the Roman theatre, the *mime*. Traveling in small bands, minstrels were versatile entertainers—jugglers, tumblers, animal trainers, acrobats, and sleight-of-hand artists—who knew how to amuse crowds gathered in taverns as well as in baronial halls or monasteries. When, in the early fifteenth century, dramatic entertainment proved popular, the more enterprising minstrel troupes added to their other tricks a few plays. Like the modern mountebank and his "medicine-show," these strollers lived by their wits, and their reputation with the authorities was deservedly bad. They picked the pockets of their awed spectators, they pilfered from the farms they passed, they robbed orchards, and, when they reached the next town or fair they disposed of the pigs and lambs and produce they had stolen. Hence, as a matter of course, the itinerant minstrel of the Middle Ages inherited and passed on to his Elizabethan descendants, the players, something of the brand of *infamia* which Roman law had accorded the mime.

Touring entertainers performed wherever they could find room—in public squares, on street corners, in barns, or in the yards of inns. The medieval carriers' inns were especially suited to dramatic performances. Since these ready-made, makeshift theatres continued in use even in Shakespeare's day and left their mark upon both the structure and the conduct of the first permanent playhouses, it will not be amiss to stop for a moment to describe them. Some of these ancient inns, like the New Inn in Gloucester, are still standing in England. They consisted of galleried buildings erected around a large open court which was entered from the street through an archway. On the ground floor were the offices, the public rooms, and the stables— today the garage—and an outside stairway led to the galleries of the upper floors on which were the rooms rented to guests. When the players arranged with an innkeeper to use his innyard, a few barrels or trestles could be put into position to support a temporary stage at one end of the court, a curtain, if needed, could be hung from the gallery above, and the stables would serve admirably as dressing rooms. The crowd, admitted through the archway, could be accommodated with standing room in the yard about the stage, while the more opulent could arrange with the innkeeper for a seat in comfort in the galleries overhead.

One of the earliest English moralities, *Mankind* (fifteenth century), was acted by strolling players, and the text, as we have it, gives us an amusing glimpse of an innyard production. Originally, *Mankind* seems to have been as serious a drama as *Everyman*, showing how Mankind might be saved by Mercy from the machinations of the World, the Flesh, and the Devil. However, in its extant form, the ethical theme of the play is almost obscured by the broad humor which was obviously written in with an innyard audience in mind. In her opening speech, Mercy addresses the two classes of innyard auditor as

O ye souerns that sytt, & ye brothern that stonde ryghte wppe.

The actors push through the crowd with such remarks as

Make rom, sers, for we have be longe!

Make space! for Cokkes body sakyrde, make space!

Avante, knavys! lett me go by!

Out of my wey, sers, for drede of fyghtynge!

And, at the proper moment, when the Devil is about to put in his "abhomynabull" appearance, provision is made for a collection:

Now gostly to ower purpos, worschypfull souerence,
We intende to gather mony, if it plesse yower neclygence. . . .
He [i. e., the Devil] ys a worschypfull man, sers, sauynge yower reuerens;
He louyth no grotes nor pens or to-pens,
Gyf ws red reyallys [royals, i. e., gold coins] yf ye wyll se hys abhomynabull presens.

The speaker is interrupted by Nowadays:

Not so! Ye that mow not pay the ton, pay the tother.
At the goode-man of this house [i. e., the innkeeper] fyrst we wyll assay.
God blysse yow, master! Ye say us yll, yet ye will not sey nay.

Mankind reveals a good deal about the intimate innyard theatres and the camaraderie between actors and audience, as well as some of the rowdier aspects of early popular performances.

To return to the minstrel, the lot of the early strolling entertainer was hard, not only because he was often a rascal and because his plays were boisterous and coarse, but also because he was unattached. Medieval society saw the individual only as a member of a class with some reputable personage or organization responsible for him. In the state there was the feudal system with its carefully graded classes, each person owing allegiance to some suzerain, lay or ecclesiastical. In the church, too, there were ranks and orders, and in industry and trade, the guilds or corporations. A wandering player was a masterless man with no place in the social scheme, an unproductive outcast and a potential menace because he was responsible to no one. Medieval minstrels made their adjustment to this condition in several ways. They imitated the trades and organized guilds by regulating their calling, or they became retainers of some powerful lord. The social responsibilities of medieval noblemen were tremendous, and among their household retainers were usually four or five minstrels whose duty it was to furnish entertainment for their masters and their courts—songs, feats of agility, and, later, plays. If such troupes traveled, as they frequently did, they were dressed in their lord's livery and toured under his protection. Out of these retainers in baronial households grew the superior type of actors who, in time, developed into the Elizabethan dramatic companies.

Thus, by the end of the fifteenth century, there had emerged the two well-marked types of professional theatrical entertainer that were to continue into Elizabethan times. On the one hand, there were the unattached strollers, catering to whatever audience they could find; on the other, the more respectable nobleman's servants, catering to their lords and their friends. Henry Bourchier, Earl of Essex, and Richard, Duke of Gloucester, had troupes of players as early as 1482; Arthur, Prince of Wales, had his company in 1498, and Prince Henry, afterward Henry VIII, by 1506. Before 1500, the earls of Northumberland, Oxford, Derby, and Shrewsbury all had players. When, like the "tragedians of the city" referred to in *Hamlet,* these retainers traveled, they went under their lords' names and were usually not obliged to earn a precarious living wholly by passing the hat before whatever audience they could collect. When they visited a town, they presented themselves to the mayor and the corporation, produced their lord's letter of recommendation, and asked formal permission to play. If the mayor and his aldermen approved, the players found a suitable playing place—a hall or the yard of a reputable inn—and proved their quality by performing before the better class of citizen. If the mayor disapproved and still wished to show no disrespect to a powerful patron, the town council might offer them "an angel towards their dinner" or some other inducement to "rid the town" without playing. The civic rewards for itinerant playing must, in many cases, have been discouraging enough unless they included the privilege of taking an admission price from spectators. The medieval custom of paying by refreshments survived into the seventeenth century, and, as late as the year of Shakespeare's death, the Prince's players at Coventry were rewarded with seventeen-pence worth of refined sugar (a quarter of a pound) and a quart of sack (J. T. Murray, *The English Dramatic Companies,* II, 249).

One account of such a local play has especial interest because its author,

R. Willis, was born in the same year as Shakespeare, and in Gloucester, which is not far from Stratford.

In the city of Gloucester the manner is (as I think it is in other like corporations) that when players of interludes come to town they first attend the Mayor to inform him what nobleman's servants they are and so to get license for their public playing; and if the Mayor like the actors or would show respect to their lord and master, he appoints them to play their first play before himself and the aldermen and common council of the city, and that is called the Mayor's Play where every one that will comes in without money, the Mayor giving the players a reward as he thinks fit to show respect unto them. At such a play my father took me with him and made me stand between his legs as he sat upon one of the benches where we saw and heard very well. The play was called *The Cradle of Security,* wherein was personated a king or some great prince, with his courtiers of several kinds, amongst which three ladies were in special grace with him, and they keeping him in delights and pleasures, drew him from his graver counsellors, hearing of sermons, and listening to good counsel and admonitions, that in the end they got him to lie down in a cradle upon the stage, where these three ladies joining in a sweet song rocked him asleep that he snorted again; and in the meantime closely conveyed under the clothes wherewithal he was covered, a vizard like a swine's snout upon his face, with three wire chains fastened thereunto, the other end whereof being holden severally by those three ladies, who fall to singing again, and then discovered his face that the spectators might see how they had transformed him, going on with their singing; whilst all this was acting there came forth of another door at the farthest end of the stage two old men, the one in blue with a sergeant at arms, his mace on his shoulder, the other in red with a drawn sword in his hand, and leaning with the other hand upon the other's shoulder, and so they two went along in a soft pace around about by the skirt of the stage, till at last they came to the cradle, when all the court was in greatest jollity, and then the foremost old man with his mace struck a fearful blow upon the cradle, whereat all the courtiers, with the three ladies and the vizard, all vanished, and the desolate prince starting up barefaced and finding himself thus sent for to judgment, made a lamentable complaint of his miserable case, and so was carried away by wicked spirits. This prince did personate in the moral the wicked of the world, the three ladies, Pride, Covetousness, and Luxury; the two old men, the end of the world and the Last Judgment. This sight took such impression in me that when I came towards man's estate it was as fresh in my memory as if I had seen it newly acted. (*Mount Tabor,* 1639.)

The boy Shakespeare may very well have attended similar impressive performances, for, during the time that his father was High Bailiff of Stratford, players visited the town on several occasions, each time receiving a reward from the city treasury.

THE LEGAL STATUS OF PLAYERS

Unattached rovers, however, were more numerous than these patronized bands. The coarseness of their plays and the disorders attending performances brought reproach upon the whole new profession and the secular drama that was developing. Moreover, it became more and more difficult to distinguish between reasonably honest players and "ruffians and evil-disposed persons." One of the most trying problems in Tudor England was that of "masterless men." The break-up of feudal households at the Wars of the Roses, the return of unattached soldiers from the wars, and the dissolution of the monasteries cast upon the roads hordes of retainers, beggars, and destitute persons who had, in times past, lived upon the institutions that were no more. Stringent laws, therefore, were enacted to control them and to provide severe punishment for those "having not land or master, nor using any lawful merchandise, craft, or mystery, whereby he or she might get his or her living" (1572). "And for the full expressing what person or persons shall be intended within this branch to be rogues, vagabonds, and sturdy beggars," this statute of 1572 is typical. It includes not only "all jugglers, peddlers, and petty chapmen," but also

all fencers, bearwards, common players in interludes, and minstrels, not belonging to any baron of this realm or towards any other honorable personage of greater degree . . . which shall wander abroad and have not license of two justices of the peace at the least.

Although, strictly speaking, this law could apply only to unattached or wandering players, actually it was a reproach to all. "They forget they are in the statute, the rascals," sneers the truculent Tucca in Ben Jonson's *The Poetaster*, which satirized the "common stages"; "they are blazon'd there; there they are trick'd, they and their pedigrees; they need no other heralds, iwiss." He is alluding, perhaps, to the efforts of some actors, like Shakespeare, who sought to improve their social conditions by purchasing lands and coats of arms that they might write themselves "gentlemen." "Methinks, if nothing else . . . the very reading of the public edicts should fright thee from commerce with them" (I, ii). Some critics, like old Stephen Gosson, himself a convert from playwriting, did grudgingly admit that "it is well known that some of them are sober, discreet, properly learned, honest householders, and citizens well thought on among their neighbors at home." But, as late as the year of Shakespeare's death, T. G. made no discrimination when he wrote in *Rich Cabinet:*

Player is afraid of the statute, for if he have no better supportation than his profession, he is neither admitted in public, nor if he be a roamer dares justify himself in private, being a flat rogue by the statute.[1]

[1] The statute of 1572 concerning rogues was renewed from time to time in almost the same terms, and became one of the chief supports of the opponents of the drama. The power of protection exercised by noblemen was largely curtailed in 1604 when barons of the realm were deprived of the power to "free and discharge the said persons . . . from the pains and punishments of the said statute." (E. K. Chambers, *The Elizabethan Stage*, IV, 337.)

Even Shakespeare felt the stigma and exclaimed against Fortune:

> That did not better for my life provide
> Than public means which public manners breeds.
> Thence comes it that my name receives a brand,
> And almost thence my nature is subdu'd
> To what it works in, like the dyer's hand.
> (Sonnet 111: cf. Sonnet 110.)

Hence, in Elizabethan times as in the Middle Ages, outside of the professions, like theology, law, or medicine, there was no place in the social scheme for the economically unproductive. Players, and literary men as well, could exist safely only if they secured patronage to protect them. At worst, in Shakespeare's day a man who elected to become an actor was professionally liable to arrest; at best, he might better be working as a true man ought to do and remain an amateur. "It hath not been used or thought meet heretofore," answered the Corporation of London to the petition of "her Majesty's poor players" in 1584, when Shakespeare was twenty, "that players have or should make their living in the art of playing, but men for their living using other honest and lawful arts, or retained in honest services."

PATRONAGE OF ACTORS

Under such circumstances, the solution which the Elizabethan players sought was the logical one. In social structure, Elizabethan England was still in many respects essentially medieval, and even the severest of the statutes held out a hope in retention by a baron of the realm. Accordingly, in 1572, when the statute concerning retainers was revived, the players of the Earl of Leicester sought to strengthen the informal relationship which, up to that time, had existed between themselves and their lord. Headed by James Burbage, a man who became famous in the annals of the theatre, they asked Leicester to retain them not merely as liveried retainers but

> as your household servants and daily waiters, not that we mean to crave any
> further stipend or benefit at your lordship's hands but our liveries as we have
> had, and also your honor's license to certify that we are your household servants
> when we shall have occasion to travel amongst our friends as we do usually once
> a year, and as other noblemen's players do and have done in time past, whereby
> we may enjoy our faculty in your lordship's name as we have done heretofore.
> (E. K. Chambers, *The Elizabethan Stage*, II, 86.)

Theirs was the final step in the evolution of the companies that had long been kept by noblemen for their own entertainment. The relationship between actors and patron, described in their petition, remained the same until the closing of the theatres.

Since it is so important, this relationship may be more closely examined.

Technically, the players became members of the Earl of Leicester's household, with all the privileges of servants, but without pay. Theoretically, their patron was responsible for them. Actually, especially in the case of the larger Elizabethan companies, the obligations of the lord were little more than nominal. The actors' dependence was legal rather than economic. The baron was not expected to provide for his company's subsistence; he merely allowed it the use of his name, permitted its members to wear his livery and badge, furnished them with his "certificate" or letter of recommendation, and became, in a way, answerable for their conduct. Sometimes, too, as a courtesy, he took an active interest in obtaining for his men the privilege of playing in various places as they traveled, by writing letters in their behalf to mayors and other officials in order to insure local protection. One of these letters, preserved among the *Henslowe Papers*, is typical.

> Sir:
> I am given to understand that you have forbidden the company of players that call themselves mine the exercise of their plays. I pray you to forbear any such course against them, and, seeing they have my license, to suffer them to continue the use of their plays; and until you receive other signification from me of them, to afford them your favor and assistance. And so I bid you heartily farewell. From Hampton Court the xiijth of October, 1604.
>
> Your loving friend,
Lenox.
>
> To all Mayors, Justices of Peace, Sheriffs, Bailiffs, Constables, and all other his Highness' Officers and loving subjects to whom it shall or may in any wise appertain. (*Henslowe Papers*, ed. W. W. Greg [1907], p. 62.)

There were numerous ways in which the name and the influence of a powerful noble could smooth the path for his men or help them when they got into undeserved difficulty.

On the other hand, there were reciprocal responsibilities and courtesies on the part of the company. Since they valued their lord's protection, it behooved patronized players to conduct themselves in such a manner as to uphold the dignity of their lord and not bring his name into disrepute. Not only did this require honest behavior and conformity to statutes regulating public safety and decency, at least to the satisfaction of mayors and other magistrates, but it made necessary as well a repertory of respectable plays. On the whole, the system probably had a wholesome effect upon the drama. In addition, a noble's own company was expected to "exercise their quality" by supplying entertainment on festival occasions as required. The petition of Leicester's Men, it will be clear, did not in any sense suggest a departure from a system which had evolved among the minstrels, and which, as regards players, was already fairly well established by the opening of the Tudor period. However, it did mean that, with the growing popularity of players, the practice became more widespread and less economic in nature. As the new profession gained recognition, although not entirely independent of court patronage, it was mainly reliant upon popular favor.

This system of patronage, like any other devised by man, was open to abuses of all kinds. *Ratsey's Ghost,* a pamphlet of 1605, describes the tactics of a company somewhat hampered by the limited power of its patron. "For being far off, for their more countenance they would pretend to be protected by such an honorable man, denying their lord and master, and coming within ten or twenty miles of him again, they would shroud themselves under their own lord's favor." Bogus companies, too, frequently imposed upon the authorities, especially in the provinces. In 1584, when the Queen's Men petitioned for the privilege of playing in London that they might rehearse for their service before her Majesty, the Council pointed out that the year before, when such discrimination had been made, "all the places of playing were filled with men calling themselves the Queen's players." A troupe calling itself the Master of the Revels' Men imposed upon Leicester, Ludlow, and Bath in 1583-4, and, as late as 1616, Norwich entertained four of these make-believe companies, two calling themselves the Queen's, one the King's Revels', and another the Prince Palatine's. Moreover, some organizations deliberately forged, bought, or stole licenses, and several London companies even sent special troupes made up of "extras" to tour the provinces with duplicate licenses.

STROLLING PLAYERS

An amusing picture of the lowest sort of Elizabethan company in an old play called *Histrio-Mastix, or The Player Whipt* (1599) makes clearer yet that the objections to actors were not wholly imaginary or prejudicial. By tracing the fortunes of a theatrical troupe through the cycle of Peace, Plenty, Pride, Envy, War, Poverty, and Peace again, it satirizes patronage—not only the fashionable patronage of players, but the humbler form of mere playgoing as well. A group of tippling mechanicals—Incle, a peddler; Belch, a beard-maker; and Gut, a fiddle-string maker—decide that "trades serve no turns" and set about forming a company of actors, "for we can all sing and say, and so, with practice, soon may learn to play." They engage Post-hast, a poetaster, to write for them, call in a scrivener to bind them "for running away," and decide to become Sir Oliver Owlet's men—"there was never a better man to players"—and to take as their badge "the owl i' th' ivybush." Then they solicit the support of Master Bougle to furnish them with apparel, and forthwith advertise a play in the market place. Invited to perform before a lord, they name their repertory: "*Mother Gurton's Needle* (a tragedy), *The Devil and Dives* (a comedy), *A Russet Coat and a Beggar's Purse* (a pastoral), and *The Widow's Apron Strings* (a nocturnal)." The instability

of the average theatrical troupe is lampooned in the song they sing as prologue to their play:

> Besides we that travel, with pumps full of gravel,
>   Made all of such running leather,
> That once in a week, new masters we seek,
>   And never can hold together.

They begin their play on the theme of *Troilus and Cressida*, but soon mix
with it "a roaring devil with the Vice on his back and Iniquity in one hand
and Juventus in the other." The lord breaks off the performance in the middle
as "lame stuff," but, nevertheless, like a true gentleman, gives them forty
pence and sends them on their way. Flushed by success, they try to get
Chrisoganus, a scholar, to write for them, but he asks ten pounds a play. "The
company's hard of hearing o' that side," and they retain Post-hast, leaving
Chrisoganus to lament an age when every scrivener's boy, every apprentice,
and every ballad-monger writes and pleases the vulgar taste. In the end, the
troupe falls upon evil days. War breaks out, and they are all pressed as
soldiers. When they return, they find living so hard that they resolve to go
back to work again.

Another such picture occurs in Middleton's *The Mayor of Queenborough*
(V, i), a play difficult to date, where Simon, a pompous tanner now become
mayor, is fleeced by a troupe of rascals who pretend to be players. An
itinerant company interviews his Honor and desires leave to act in the town
hall. Simon, who in his apprentice days had been a follower of the drama,
feels all his old enthusiasm return as they prove their quality before him by
performing a play called *The Cheater and the Clown*. Simon's pretty taste
for buffoonery is so outraged by the actor who plays the clown that he at
last takes off his mayor's robes and essays the role himself. Then the rogues
throw meal in his face, take his purse and silver spoons, and flee. The clerk
who restores Simon's dignity informs him that they are really not players at
all, but "only take the name of country comedians to abuse simple people
with a printed play or two, which they bought at Canterbury for sixpence,
and what is worse, they speak but what they list of it, and fribble out the
rest."

Both of these scenes are satires upon the element, doubtless large in the
Elizabethan theatrical world, which had no ability, but was attracted to the
theatre by prospects of gain and an unfettered life of dissipation. Fortunately
for the drama, not all were of this sort, and the excellence of the London
organizations has by now amply justified an easily abused system.

ADULT AND CHILDREN'S COMPANIES

This is not the place for a detailed history of the Elizabethan theatrical
companies. It will suffice to mention some of the more famous. The most

important of all was the Lord Chamberlain's company to which Shakespeare was attached. It was organized in 1594 from the remnants of older companies, was patronized by two Lords Chamberlain,[2] and became the King's Men in 1603 at the accession of James I. Its star actors were Will Kempe in comedy, until he left the company in 1599, and Richard Burbage, son of James Burbage, in tragedy. Next in fame were the Lord Admiral's Men, also reorganized in 1594, and the principal rivals of the Shakespearean company. Under the new monarch they became first Prince Henry's Men and, at his death in 1612, the Men of the Palsgrave, or the Elector Palatine, then in England wooing the Princess Elizabeth. Their principal actor was Edward Alleyn, who had created the heroes in Marlowe's plays.

In addition to these two, there were numerous other companies, some of which were very short-lived, and some of which confined their activities entirely to the country and never came to London at all. The earls of Sussex sponsored one of the most long-lived of Elizabethan theatrical troupes. It lasted through the lives of three earls. The earls of Oxford and of Essex were among the first to patronize actors, but their Elizabethan companies were of minor importance. Queen Elizabeth also had a company which was very famous while its principal comedian, Richard Tarleton, was alive, but, after his death about 1588, it declined rapidly and was just a provincial troupe during practically the whole of Shakespeare's career in London. In Elizabethan times the earls of Arundel, Hertford, Derby, Pembroke, and Worcester all patronized actors, the latter's troupe becoming the Queen's Men under the new Stuart dynasty.

As early as 1578, a Privy Council order limited the number of London companies to six. During most of Shakespeare's career, the Lord Chamberlain's and the Lord Admiral's Men enjoyed a virtual monopoly, a fact which received official recognition by the Privy Council in a letter to the Master of the Revels and the Justices of the Peace of Middlesex and Surrey, dated February 19, 1598. Occasionally, ambitious rival companies challenged these licenses. After 1603, however, the supremacy of the King's Men was undisputed. As time went on, the privilege of retaining actors was gradually more and more restricted to a higher rank of nobleman, until finally, at the accession of James, the patronage of theatrical companies was practically limited to the royal family.

Besides these professional companies which were composed, as we shall see, largely of adults, there were in London in Shakespeare's time several semi-professional companies composed entirely of boy actors, such as the Children of St. Paul's School and the Children of Queen Elizabeth's Chapel. They

[2] For a few months, from July 22, 1596, until March 17, 1597, when Sir George Carey, Lord Hunsdon, succeeded his father as Lord Chamberlain, the company was known as Lord Hunsdon's Men.

acted, not in public theatres, but in so-called "private" theatres, and at one time, when they engaged in a satirical war with the "common stages," they achieved such popularity that they quite eclipsed the Chamberlain's and Admiral's companies. Shakespeare alludes to them in *Hamlet:*

> There is, sir, an aery of children, little eyases, that cry out on the top of question, and are most tyrannically clapp'd for 't. These are now the fashion, and so berattle the common stages—so they call them—that many wearing rapiers are afraid of goose-quills and dare scarce come thither. (II, ii, 354 ff.)

These boys were expert actors and commanded the talents of some of the best Elizabethan dramatists. John Lyly wrote his amusing court dramas for them, as did Ben Jonson and George Chapman. Originally, they were members of choral schools, in training as singers in the royal choirs. By virtue of a warrant, the masters of these singing schools were permitted to "take up" or impress boys with good voices wherever they found them. Playing was probably at first only a part of their academic exercises, but their popularity soon suggested to their masters the possibility of making acting and not singing their principal concern.

The operation and practices of these schools are made known to us by a famous Star Chamber case. In 1600, Nathaniel Giles, Henry Evans, James Robinson, and others from the Chapel Royal impressed the wrong boy. They took up Thomas Clifton, only son and heir of Henry Clifton, a gentleman of Norfolk, "to exercise the base trade of a mercenary interlude player to his utter loss of time, ruin, and disparagement." Clifton protested, but got no satisfaction, and then quietly set about investigating and exposing a serious abuse of power. Apprentices and school boys, he charged, were kidnapped, nominally for the chapel choirs, but actually for service in the theatres for profit, and he cited a number of specific cases, among them "Nathan Field, a scholar of a grammar school in London . . . and Salmon Pavey, apprentice to one Peerce." These he asserted were children "no way able or fit for singing, nor by any the said confederates endeavored to be taught to sing, but by them . . . abusively employed . . . only in plays and interludes." The affair caused a shake-up from which the children's companies never recovered. The boy actor Field, the son of a Puritan preacher, later joined the King's Men and became a professional actor and dramatist. Salmon, or rather Salathiel, Pavey was famous for his acting of old men. When he died, aged thirteen, Ben Jonson wrote his epitaph:

> Years he number'd scarce thirteen
> When Fates turn'd cruel,
> Yet three fill'd zodiacs had he been
> The stage's jewel.
> And did act—what now we moan—
> Old men so duly

As sooth the Parcæ thought him one
He play'd so truly.

(Epigram 120.)

THE PROFESSIONAL ORGANIZATION OF AN ELIZABETHAN COMPANY

It must not be supposed that the average Elizabethan theatrical company was a haphazard aggregation of unstable individuals. A London company of Shakespeare's time was an established business organization working under laws and customs as definite as those which govern a company today. Just as the players had sought protection in the medieval system of patronage, so the organization within the individual companies—not of the Elizabethan theatrical profession as a whole—resembled that of the medieval trade-guild. At the top of the scale in the guild were the *masters,* who were the heads of their crafts or trades; beneath them, the *freemen* or *journeymen,* i. e., potential masters, who had completed their training and attained sufficient maturity, but who had not as yet qualified as masters; and, at the bottom, the *apprentices,* or learners.

A similar classification prevailed in the Elizabethan theatrical company. At the head, roughly corresponding to the masters of the guild, were the *members* of the licensed or patent company, usually from nine to twelve in number. These were the leading actors who controlled the company and were the *sharers* in its financial gains. The members, of course, could not unaided carry on all the work of the company; attached to the Elizabethan actor troupes were various persons whose activities are separately organized today. In each company there were two other classes: the *hired men* and the *apprentices.* The hired men in a theatrical company corresponded roughly to the freemen or journeymen of the guild, except that not all of them were actors. Here, in addition to minor players, were the "musicians and other attendants," the stage hands, the "gatherers" (i. e., collectors of admissions), the "bookholder" (i. e., the prompter or stage manager), and, more important than these, the poets who made the plays. All of these were hired and received for their services, not a share in the takings, but a fixed wage, usually from four to six shillings a week. A playwright received a stipulated sum for each play. Wages in Elizabethan times were fairly well standardized by law, and journeymen actors or hirelings received the normal wages of journeymen. The apprentices were boys, bound not to the company as a whole, but to individual members, who were responsible for their training and support. These boys were not menials, but the pupils and prospective successors to their masters.

The English actors of Shakespeare's time were the most excellent in Europe. If the conditions under which they worked were not always conducive to highly finished art, they required at least a high degree of efficiency and versatility. Judging from the records of the companies that acted at the Rose, it is clear that there were no long runs of popular plays as at present; programs were changed daily; from fifteen to thirty pieces were produced in a season; and the average life of a play was from six to twenty performances, often scattered over several months. Revivals of old favorites were not infrequent, but few new offerings lasted more than a year. Playing, it will be seen, might be attractively profitable, but it was also an arduous profession. The actor's training, therefore, had to be of the best. Johannes Rhenanus, a German visitor to London about 1610, wrote as follows:

> So far as actors are concerned, they, as I noticed in England, are daily instructed, as it were in a school, so that even the most eminent actors have to allow themselves to be instructed by the dramatists, which arrangement gives life and ornament to a well-written play, so that it is no wonder that the English players—I speak of the skilled ones—surpass and have the advantage of others. (Preface to *Speculum Aistheticum* [1613], reprinted in W. Creizenach, *Die Schauspiele der englischen Komödianten* [n. d.], p. 328.)

Under the system of apprenticeship this training began early, was conducted in the hard school of experience, and produced a versatility which is found today, if at all, only in the most stable repertory company. There were no actresses on the Elizabethan stage, and all of the roles in Shakespeare's plays were originally written to be acted by companies composed of men and boys. When the apprentices had acquired sufficient experience, the acting of women's parts was entrusted to them because of their suitability in voice and complexion and build. Elizabethan law was fairly specific in its apprenticeship requirements, but whether the dramatic companies observed them, there are no direct instances of proof. In all probability they did. At least seven years of training were required, and a lad had to be at least twenty-four years old before his apprenticeship was terminated. But boys who expected to become actors must have begun their training early, certainly long before their voices changed. Some, we know, were experienced "actresses" at thirteen; Salathiel Pavey, mentioned above, began acting in a boys' company at ten. Ten to thirteen seems to have been the usual age at which the actor's apprenticeship began, and it was probably over before he reached the traditional age of twenty-four, perhaps when the boy outgrew his usefulness as an actor of women's parts. If a young actor was promising, some effort would be made to retain him. He might become a hireling. If there was room, he might be taken into the company. In the Shakespearean company, promotion was usually from apprentice to member of the company, rarely through the intermediate stage of hired man. Some, of course, left the theatre altogether; others found employment in other companies.

These three classes, then—members of the company, hired men, and apprentices—constituted the professional organization and were much the same for all companies.

FINANCIAL ARRANGEMENTS

The various troupes, however, differed from one another in the arrangement of financial details. So long as the actors traveled in the provinces, their stock of furnishings was necessarily limited, and they acted, as we have seen, in makeshift accommodations, such as halls or innyards. When the London companies settled down in permanent theatres, however, conditions changed, and a new class of theatrical personage came into existence. He was the *housekeeper*, i. e., the financier, who owned and controlled the theatre building and from whom the company rented the playhouse. In the innyard theatres he was the innkeeper, and, as might be expected, certain customs which had arisen in innyard playing survived when the new permanent theatres were built. In the innyards there had been two admission fees, one for entrance to the yard and another for a place of vantage in one of the galleries, the innkeeper retaining as his share the gallery receipts. When the permanent theatres were built, the companies merely adapted the innyard customs. The troupe secured the playhouse from the housekeeper, just as it had secured the yard from the innkeeper, giving him a share of the gallery receipts, usually half, and retaining as its share the other half and all of the general admissions.

The housekeeper, however, had other functions than those merely of landlord. Theatrical folk were, as a rule, notoriously impecunious and commonly bad managers. Acting in a permanent theatre required costly furnishings, costumes, and properties. If the players had insufficient capital to furnish their own supplies, they were obliged to make arrangements with someone, usually the theatre-owner, either to rent these things or to purchase them out of their share of the receipts. A theatre-owner was quite likely to have accumulated considerable stock. If a company was reduced to bankruptcy while playing at his house, he might have to take its property to satisfy his debt. But a shrewd housekeeper found the possession of stock an advantage in another way. If the company finally paid for the furnishings, then they legally belonged to the troupe. A good manager, therefore, would use every device to have the stock declared forfeit in order to get it back to sell again. This kind of swindle seems to have become a regular system at several of the Elizabethan theatres.

The most famous of all of the Elizabethan theatre-owners was Philip Henslowe, the "Banker of the Bankside." He was not an actor, but a shrewd business man who early perceived that large gains could be realized from "show business," and he reaped a rich harvest from the labors of the players. As a young man, Henslowe had tried various businesses—dyeing, starch-making, dealing in wood. He came to the theatre by way of pawnbroking and moneylending. In association with the famous actor, Edward Alleyn, he built and controlled several of the London theatres, the Rose, the Fortune, and the Hope. His *Diary*, or account book, none too carefully kept, is a source of much detailed information about the workings of the Elizabethan theatre. Henslowe recorded the daily receipts from plays during the acting season, his expenditures for materials and costumes, his payments to playwrights for supplying or remodeling plays, his loans to actors and dramatists, and the numerous occasions on which he bailed them out of jail. Henslowe dealt with the players on much his own terms, and they were not easy. The "articles of oppression against Mr. Henslowe," drawn up by the discomfited actors in 1615 and preserved by him with apparent relish, throw considerable light upon the business arrangements of the average Elizabethan company. They mention not only devious dealing in regard to stock for which the players hoped to pay, but also "bonds for his stock," i. e., security against depreciation and dishonesty, and "our security for playing with him," i. e., protection against loss if the theatre stood empty, "so that he hath in his hands, bonds of ours to the value of £5000 and his stock too, which he denies to deliver and threatens to oppress us with." Henslowe's methods can best be understood from his own words: "Should these fellows come out of my debt, I should have no rule with them." (*Henslowe Papers*, ed. W. W. Greg [1907], pp. 89 ff.)

The Shakespearean company seems to have been the first to try a superior method of financial organization.[3] When the Globe was opened in 1599, a syndicate, in which the members of the company were represented, was substituted for the individual owner and financier. The actors themselves, not an outsider, were the owners of the theatre and the controllers of the furnishings. This syndicate, consisting of Richard and Cuthbert Burbage and five of their associates, became the housekeepers of the Globe. The Burbage brothers supplied most of the building materials and, as joint tenants, held five shares; the five actors—William Shakespeare, Augustine Phillips, Thomas Pope, John Heminge, and Will Kempe—invested in the venture, and, as joint tenants, held the other five. Each group bore half of the housekeeping expenses, and each shared equally in the profits. The actual effect of this interlocking partnership between theatre-owners and actors was to create another class in the organization of the company, the highest class and the goal of every man's ambition. Just as the apprentice looked forward to becoming some day a member of the company he served, so the member looked forward to having his merit recognized by being granted the opportunity of investing in the theatre to which he was attached. Hamlet, no doubt, is alluding to the recog-

---

[3] There is some evidence that the Globe organization was not an absolute innovation; the Curtain seems also to have been so controlled, but no details are known.

nition of talent in Shakespeare's own theatre, when, in jubilation at the success of the "dozen or sixteen lines" which he had inserted into *The Murder of Gonzago*, he asks Horatio:

> Would not this, sir, and a forest of feathers . . . with two Provincial roses on my razed shoes [i. e., a striking actor's costume], get me a fellowship in a cry of players, sir? (*Hamlet*, III, iii, 286 ff.)

There can be no doubt that this system was one of the great advantages of the Shakespearean company. Essentially, it promoted stability. It prevented the troupe from shifting from one playhouse to another. It prevented haggling, bickering, and discontent. One member of the company simply became financial manager. It is excellent testimony of the efficiency of the scheme, as well as of the character of the man, that John Heminge was manager of the Shakespearean troupe for more than a quarter of a century without leaving the trace of any dissatisfaction. Moreover, such an organization guaranteed an excellent company. Only the best became housekeepers, and, like all profit-sharing schemes, it tended to elicit from each member his fullest energies and to stimulate everyone by providing the actors a future to which they could look forward. But, above all, it promoted a close personal relationship which, more than any legal arrangements, insured the success of the organization. Many of these men were associated from their apprentice days, and the remembrance of an actor's "fellows" in will after will makes clear that they considered themselves not merely business associates, but comrades. They were a team of actors rather than a mere company.

SHAKESPEARE'S INCOME

A word should perhaps be said here about Shakespeare's income. It will be clear that it was drawn from three sources. As a poet, Shakespeare was a hired man in his company, receiving either a fixed wage or a stipulated sum for each play he produced. In addition, at the close of his career, when the custom was becoming prevalent, he may even have enjoyed an occasional benefit. As an actor, he was a sharer with his fellow-actors, and as a housekeeper in both the Globe and Blackfriars, a sharer in the profits incident to running the theatres. Also, he had the revenue from his real-estate investments in both Stratford and London. It is hardly possible to estimate precisely what his earnings were, but scholars have suggested a sum between £200 and £350 a year, equivalent to from eight to ten times that amount today. Other Elizabethan men of the theatre, like Richard Burbage, Thomas Pope, Augustine Phillips, John Heminge, and Henry Condell, all appear to have been men of substance when they died. More fortunate than any was Edward Alleyn, who was able to retire from the stage before he was forty and, in 1614, to spend £10,000 in the purchase of Dulwich Manor and in founding there the

College of God's Gift, which is still in existence. Part of its original endowment was a freehold to the Fortune Theatre. Thereafter, Alleyn spent some £1700 a year upon his household and his philanthropies, married as his second wife Constance, daughter of John Donne, dean of St. Paul's, and, in 1624, was desirous of "some further dignity," perhaps a knighthood. Shakespeare, more modestly, was content with a good house and a coat of arms. The London theatres of Shakespeare's time, it will be seen, offered men of the proper talent opportunities of the kind which Hollywood extends today.

OPPOSITION TO PLAYS AND PLAYERS

As Londoners flocked in ever larger numbers to the innyards to see plays, and as the actors consequently increased in number and opulence, two forces of opposition, Puritanism and civic authority, were aroused. Their reasons for hostility differed, but they were alike in their zeal. When, in the course of time, Puritans became City aldermen, the combined animosity was sufficient to drive playing out of London into the suburbs and finally to prohibit it altogether.

The Puritans opposed the stage on grounds of morality. To them the drama was idolatrous, ungodly, and popish. Hence, it was contrary to Holy Writ and destructive of religion. Playwrights and poets were "caterpillars of the commonwealth," playhouses "Satan's synagogues" and "seminaries of impiety," and plays "the Devil's own recreation to mock at holy things." "Theft and whoredom, pride and prodigality, villainy and blasphemy, these three couples of hellhounds never cease barking there, and bite many." "The argument of tragedies," wrote Stephen Gosson in *Plays Confuted in Five Actions* (1582),

is wrath, cruelty, incest, injury, murder either violent by sword or voluntary by poison . . . the groundwork of comedies is love, cozenage, flattery, bawdry, sly conveyance of whoredom.

"If you will learn," thundered the preacher John Northbrooke,

how to be false and deceive your husbands, or husbands their wives, how to play the harlots, to obtain one's love, how to ravish, how to beguile, how to betray, to flatter, lie, swear, forswear, how to allure to whoredom, how to murder, how to poison, how to disobey and rebel against princes, to consume treasures prodigally, to move to lusts, to ransack and spoil cities and towns, to be idle, to blaspheme, to sing filthy songs of love, to speak filthily, to be proud, how to mock, scoff, and deride any nation . . . shall not you learn, then, at such interludes how to practice them? (*A Treatise Wherein Dicing, Dancing, Vain Plays Are Reproved*, 1577.)

Hence, to the moralist, plays were an Augean stable "impossible to be cleansed before they be carried out of England with a stiff stream." This is not the place for a detailed account of the warfare. Enough has been said to show that it was both unreasonable and violent. Moreover, what answer can be given to the impassioned question of the preacher John Stockwood: "Will not a filthy play, with the blast of a trumpet, sooner call thither a thousand than an hour's tolling of a bell bring to a sermon a hundred?" Elizabethan clergymen dealt long and earnestly with refractory man only in the end to sigh sadly: "Many can tarry at a vain play two or three hours, when as they will not abide scarce one hour at a sermon." Occasionally, the Puritans tolerated a popular evil by requiring the players to contribute heavily to the poor of the parish in which they played. Elizabethan consciences were quite as easily lulled to sleep as those of the twentieth century, British and American, by hospital sweepstakes and milk-fund boxing bouts. But the Puritan's opposition was unremitting.[4]

The civic authorities, on the other hand, had no more love for the actors than had the divines, and from a not too remotely related cause. "The politic state and government of this city," exclaimed one Lord Mayor, "by no one thing is so greatly annoyed and disquieted as by players and plays, and the disorders which follow thereupon." Plays were both an idle pastime whereby apprentices, servants, and the younger sort generally were "drawn or provoked to vain expense, loss of time or corruption of manners," and the convenient occasions for the meeting of loose characters of all sorts: "all vagrant persons and masterless men that hang about the city, thieves, horse-stealers, whoremongers, cozeners, coney-catching persons, practicers of treason, and such like," as another Lord Mayor characterized them. The opportunity afforded such persons for evil were apparently not overlooked, and the fact lent much color to the denunciations of the Puritans. Moreover, since the proprietors of the inns where plays were given made a large share of their profits from the sale of beer, ale, and liquor to theatre crowds, theatrical performances were frequently attended by drunkenness, rowdyism, bloodshed, and general disorder. Turbulent apprentices and other factions frequently met by appointment at plays for the purpose of starting riots or breaking jails. The note of the City Recorder to Lord Burghley, therefore, is humorously full of meaning: "Upon Whitsunday, by reason no plays were the same day, all the city was quiet."

The civic authorities also kept an eye on the theatre for political reasons. Current gossip of all sorts gave flavor and sparkle to Elizabethan plays, just as it does to much of our entertainment today, and, while this is all very well so long as it remains innocent, it could be an unpleasant scourge if misdirected. From earliest times, however, plays had been used as polemical

---

[4] For an amusing caricature of the Puritan opponent of the drama and his arguments, see Zeal-of-the-Land Busy, who tries to break up a puppet-show and matches wits with one of the "actors" in Ben Jonson's *Bartholomew Fair*, V, iii.

weapons, and an age like the Elizabethan, seething with controversy, offered many opportunities to the satirist. "We do understand that certain players that use to recite their plays at the Curtain in Moorfields," wrote the Privy Council on May 10, 1601,

> do represent upon the stage in their interludes the persons of some gentlemen of good desert and quality that are yet alive under obscure manner, but yet in such sort as all hearers may take notice both of the matter and the persons that are meant thereby. (E. K. Chambers, *The Elizabethan Stage*, IV, 332.)

Elizabethan plays could be incredibly audacious.

Above all, in the hot summer months when the plague threatened, gatherings of "great multitudes of the basest sort of people" were a menace to public health. Moreover, the logic of the argument that "the cause of the plague is sin, and the cause of sin is plays" appealed to many. In time of epidemic, of course, playing was prohibited, but the actors whose living was denied them were hard to control, and often the sickness got a full start before plays could be suppressed.

The attempts of the Lord Mayor and his aldermen to regulate the players was often made most difficult because all of the troupes of standing were protected and encouraged by patrons high in authority. Sometimes the actors gained in their behalf the polite intervention of some baron whose request could not lightly be ignored by the Common Council; more frequently, since the difficulties affected all companies, they had the support of the Privy Council, representing the Crown and the nobility in general. The conflict of authority between the Privy and the Common councils over actors and acting was long and notable. The crisis, however, was reached early. In 1573, a strongly Puritanical Lord Mayor, Sir James Hawes, began to place more and more obstacles in the way of actors. The players appealed to the Privy Council, and several indignant letters were exchanged between the two boards. Finally, the queen herself took a hand and openly sided with the players. On May 10, 1574, she issued to James Burbage and the Earl of Leicester's company the first royal patent, licensing them to play "as well for the recreation of our loving subjects as for our solace and pleasure when we shall think good to see them," and authorizing them to act "as well within our City of London and liberties of the same as also within the liberties and freedom of any our cities, towns, boroughs, etc., whatsoever as without the same, throughout our realm of England." Moreover, she charged all magistrates:

> as ye tender our pleasure to permit and suffer them herein without any your lets, hindrance, or molestation . . . any act, statute, proclamation, or commandment heretofore made, or hereafter to be made, to the contrary notwithstanding. (*Ibid.*, II, 87–8.)

This direct challenge, however, did not check the Lord Mayor and the aldermen. Without defying the patent openly, they set about nullifying it in another way. On December 6, 1574, the Common Council of London passed a remarkable ordinance. In good Tudor fashion it solemnly called to mind:

> sundry great disorders and inconveniences . . . to this city by the inordinate haunting of great multitudes of people, specially youth, to plays, interludes, and shows, namely occasion of frays and quarrels, evil practices of incontinancy in great inns having chambers and secret places adjoining to their open stages and galleries, inveigling and alluring of maids, specially orphans and good citizens' children under age, to privy and unmeet contracts, the publishing of unchaste, uncomely, and unshamefast speeches and doings, withdrawing of the Queen's Majesty's subjects from divine service on Sundays and holidays, at which times such plays were chiefly used, unthrifty waste of the money of the poor and fond persons, sundry robberies by picking and cutting of purses, uttering of popular, busy, and seditious matters, and many other corruptions of youth and other enormities, besides that also sundry slaughters and maimings of the Queen's subjects have happened by ruins of scaffolds, frames, and stages, and by engines, weapons, and powder used in plays,

as well as dangers of the plague. Having covered everything, the Common Council then decreed:

> that no innkeeper, tavernkeeper, nor other person whatsoever within the liberties of this city shall openly show or play, nor cause or suffer to be openly showed or played, within the house, yard, or any other place . . . any play, interlude, comedy, tragedy, matter, or show, which shall not be first perused and allowed. . . . And that no person shall suffer any plays . . . to be . . . showed . . . but only such persons and in such places as . . . shall be . . . permitted and allowed by the Lord Mayor and aldermen. (*Ibid.*, IV, 273 ff.)

THE ERECTION OF PERMANENT PLAYHOUSES, PUBLIC AND PRIVATE

Such an order, of course, did not prohibit plays; it merely established censorship by the Common Council. But its effect must have been far-reaching. It placed responsibility upon the innkeepers, and, by making them wary, struck at their old partnership with the players. It must have made evident to James Burbage and other actors that plays were not only unwelcome in London, but also that prohibition of them altogether was the ultimate event toward which the edict was but a first step. The ordinance, however, had an important effect which had not been anticipated. It led to the erection of the first permanent playhouse. Just outside the City jurisdiction, but close enough to attract London holiday crowds, lay the dissolved priory of Holywell in Finsbury Fields, Shoreditch. In 1576, acting, not for his company, but as a private speculator, James Burbage, a carpenter as well as an actor, leased the site for twenty-one years and built upon it a house in which performances could be held without interference. He called his structure simply the Theatre.

The effects of Burbage's act cannot be overestimated. It immediately systematized the players' irregular calling and changed the whole course of the English drama. Previously, both actors and audiences had been content with primitive, temporary, theatrical makeshifts in innyards and halls, and it is not unlikely that they would have continued so had not external pressure been applied. The wisdom of Burbage's investment was quickly apparent to other business men. Unable to finance the entire venture himself, Burbage borrowed what he could and interested his brother-in-law, John Brayne, in the scheme. Brayne was a prosperous grocer, who became so enthusiastic over the prospect of huge gains that he not only sold his house and entire stock, but even pawned his and his wife's clothes to provide capital. Within a year, too, the Theatre had a rival. The Curtain, so named because it occupied the Curtain estate, was erected a few rods away.

These two playhouses were sufficient for a decade. Meanwhile, another pleasure district, the Bankside in Southwark, was proving more convenient and attractive than the fields north of the City. Here, just across the Thames from London, in the disreputable section of the stews and the bull- and bear-baiting pits, most of the new theatres were erected: the Rose (*c.* 1587), the Swan (*c.* 1595), the Globe (1599), and the Hope (1613). Only the Fortune (1600) and the Red Bull (1605) were built in the fields, and then somewhat to the west of the sites of the old Theatre and Curtain. Thus, the theatre districts of Shakespeare's London were two: Finsbury Fields and the section north of the City, and the Bankside, across the river in Surrey. In addition to these public theatres, there were within London several "private" playhouses, like Blackfriars, also owned by the Burbage family and, after 1608, the winter house of the Shakespearean company, Whitefriars (*c.* 1605), and others whose existence was more ephemeral. They were built upon the sites of dissolved monasteries within the City, "liberties" over which the Crown and not the Lord Mayor had jurisdiction. The name "private theatre" had its origin in a legal deception; the Act of 1574 had made exception in the case of plays

> showed in the private house, dwelling, or lodging of any nobleman, citizen, or gentleman . . . for the festivity of any marriage, assembly of friends, or other-like cause without public or common collection of money of the auditory or beholders thereof.

These "private" playhouses, though they differed in structure, in facilities, and in clientele from their "public" rivals, were open to all classes. Usually, however, they were occupied by the children's companies and, as time went on, attracted dramatists who were gentlemen or who were socially better connected than those writing for the "common stages."

SUGGESTED REFERENCES

BALDWIN, THOMAS WHITFIELD. *The Organization and Personnel of the Shakespearean Company.* Princeton University Press, 1927.

A study of the laws and customs governing the organization of an Elizabethan company, with special reference to the Shakespearean troupe.

GILDERSLEEVE, VIRGINIA C. *Government Regulation of the Elizabethan Drama.* New York, Columbia University Press, 1908.

GREG, W. W. (ed.). *Henslowe's Diary* (2 vols.). London, A. H. Bullen, 1904–08.

—— (ed.). *Henslowe Papers, Being Documents Supplementary to Henslowe's Diary.* London, A. H. Bullen, 1907.

HILLEBRAND, H. N. *The Child Actors: A Chapter in Elizabethan Stage History.* University of Illinois Studies, 1926.

An account of the boys' companies.

MURRAY, JOHN TUCKER. *English Dramatic Companies, 1558–1642* (2 vols.). London, Constable, 1910.

A history of both the London and the provincial companies and their performances.

NUNGEZER, EDWIN. *A Dictionary of Actors and Other Persons Associated with the Public Representation of Plays in England before 1642.* New Haven, Yale University Press, 1929.

A *Who's Who* of the early theatre.

SHARPE, ROBERT BOIES. *The Real War of the Theaters: Shakespeare's Fellows in Rivalry with the Admiral's Men, 1594–1603.* MLA Monograph. Boston and New York, Heath, 1935.

THOMPSON, E. N. S. *The Controversy between the Puritans and the Stage.* New York, Holt, 1903.

THE ELIZABETHAN PUBLIC

PLAYHOUSE

Can this cockpit hold
The vasty fields of France? Or may we cram
Within this wooden O the very casques
That did affright the air at Agincourt?
—*Henry V,* Prologue to Act I.

Unfortunately, no description of burbage's the-atre has been preserved, but this playhouse served as a model for other structures, and of these a few facts have come down to us. This information, however, is so meagre that any reconstruction of a typical Elizabethan stage must be largely conjectural. A few drawings, two builder's contracts—those of the Fortune and the Hope—almost devoid of detail, and a few allusions in contemporary books are all that remain. Yet the general physical features of Shakespeare's theatre are well known, and they are quite unlike those of the theatres of today. When we go to a modern playhouse, we sit before a magnified peep-show surrounded by an ornate proscenium arch which can be closed off by a front curtain. The figures who move and speak across the footlights live out their lives on a different plane from ours, and paint, canvas, and artificial light do what they can to drug our senses into the illusion that all is real. The Elizabethan stage made use of none of these. The first essential to an understanding of the conditions under which Shakespeare's plays were originally produced is that one free his mind of all preconceptions derived from the modern picture-frame stage. Imagine a doughnut-shaped, amphitheatric structure of galleries surrounding an open court into the middle of which juts a platform, and you have the essentials of Shakespeare's playhouse.

ESSENTIAL PHYSICAL FEATURES

Obviously, the general design of the Elizabethan theatre was shaped by the popular entertainments from which the English drama had sprung. Its characteristics are traceable with little deviation to the makeshifts of the innyards in which the actors had been accustomed to play. A permanent platform merely replaced the boards stretched across a few barrels in the innyard, and a suitably appointed tiring-house took the place of the stables that had once served as dressing rooms. In general, all of the arrangements were a little more convenient and handsome because they were built with the players and their needs in mind. But that is all; the early public playhouse differed in no other essential way from the innyards. In both, acting took place in the afternoon by natural light. In the new theatres, as in the innyards, seats were available (at extra cost) in the galleries, in the "gentlemen's rooms," or on the stage itself, but part of the audience still stood in the pit. The actor in the fifteenth-century innyard play *Mankind* who addressed his auditory as

> ye souerns that sytt, & ye brothern that stonde ryghte wppe

would have been quite at home in the Theatre or the Globe. Not during the Shakespearean era did the advantages of comfort for all contribute to the alteration of the playhouse's architectural design. Moreover, the inns continued to be used even after the permanent theatres were built. The Bell in Gracechurch Street was used by the Queen's Men at least until the death of Tarleton (*c.* 1588); both the Bull in Bishopsgate and the Cross Keys in Gracechurch Street were still in use as late as 1594, the latter serving as the winter house for the Shakespearean company after 1608; and the Boar's Head in Whitechapel was preferred to the Rose by the Oxford-Worcester company in 1602 and used by Prince Charles's Men in 1608 (see E. K. Chambers, *The Elizabethan Stage*, II, 379 ff.).

Although they retained the same essential features, the permanent Elizabethan theatres varied as much in shape, size, and facilities as do our theatres today. The usual shape, if we may judge from the representations on the pictorial maps of old London, was either polygonal or round. Only the Fortune was set square, a shape which apparently proved disadvantageous, for, after the fire of 1621, the Fortune was rebuilt in the old circular shape. As to size, Elizabethan playhouses were certainly not small. According to the builder's contract, the Fortune, "like unto the Globe" in other respects, was 80 feet in outside dimension and 55 feet inside, thus having galleries 12½ feet deep. In height, the three galleries were 12, 11, and 9 feet, making the entire building, with allowance of a few feet for foundation, thickness of floors, roof, tower, and the like, about 40 or 45 feet in height, or about half the theatre's over-all width. The representations on the old maps which show

Interior of the Swan Theatre
(From a drawing made by Johan de Witt, *c.* 1595)

them to have been towers are obviously distorted.[1] Various estimates, both contemporary and modern, have been made of the capacities of the Elizabethan theatres, the figures ranging between 1300 and 3000 spectators each.[2] In size, Elizabethan theatres must have compared favorably with the early nineteenth-century Covent Garden and Drury Lane (see below, p. 424). As to the material of which they were constructed, a contemporary description of the Swan says that that theatre was erected of flint stones (probably only stucco); the second Fortune, built after the fire of 1621, was of brick. The contracts for the earlier Fortune and the Hope, as well as the lawsuit documents about the Theatre, mention no materials save "good and sufficient oaken timber" and plaster. The Globe, built in part from the old timbers of the Theatre, was probably of similar construction. The Fortune and the Hope had tiled roofs; others were thatched, like the first Globe, which, at its burning in 1613, left the poor King's Men with little but the piles, "and wit since to cover it with tiles" (Ben Jonson, *An Execration upon Vulcan*, written in 1625 when his own library burned).

The "private" and court theatres, of course, bore no resemblance to the innyards out of which the public theatre evolved. At Whitehall, Richmond, Hampton Court, Greenwich, or Windsor, at the Inns of Court, as well as at Blackfriars, plays were staged in a great hall in which a special platform had been constructed at one end. The spectators sat on tiers of seats around the walls or on the stage itself, the queen on a tapestried dais put up in the middle of the hall or on the stage. The air was perfumed, and candles and torches made the hall as bright as day. Elaborate scenic equipment and splendid costume were the rule. Consequently, production problems at court and at Blackfriars were in some respects different from those at the public theatres.[3] Since Blackfriars was used as a winter theatre by the King's Men after 1608, some of Shakespeare's later plays can best be understood by reference to this more pretentious method of production. But it is the public theatres, where Shakespeare and his fellow-dramatists developed their talents, that are our

[1] No dimensions are given for the Globe. But a recent deduction, based upon contemporaneous material, Elizabethan building methods, and standard Elizabethan timber lengths, suggests that the Globe was octagonal in shape within and without, that it was 84 feet from outside wall to outside wall and 58 feet across the yard, that its galleries, like those of the Fortune, were 12½ feet deep and 12, 11, and 9 feet in height, and that, making allowance for foundation and thickness of floors, it was about 34 or 35 feet high at the eavesline. Its stage, again like that of the Fortune, was 43 feet in greatest width, but was probably bluntly wedge-shaped, measuring 25 feet on a side. See John Cranford Adams, *The Globe Playhouse* (1942), pp. 19 ff.

[2] Johan de Witt, who made the drawing of the Swan reproduced on p. 117, estimated its capacity at 3000. Modern estimates tend to reduce this somewhat as an average figure. See Alfred Harbage, *Shakespeare's Audience* (1941), pp. 19 ff., and John Cranford Adams, *op. cit.*, pp. 87 ff.

[3] See J. Isaacs, *Production and Stage-management at the Blackfriars Theatre*, Shakespeare Association Pamphlet (1933).

main concern. In the public theatres more simple and primitive conditions prevailed, uninfluenced by the court or the classical theatres.

Although Fynes Moryson, the English traveler, stated that the London theatres "are more remarkable for the number and for the capacity than for the building," it must not be supposed that the Elizabethan public playhouses were squalid. Rather were they among the sights of London. "Our players are not as the players beyond sea," boasted Thomas Nashe,

> a sort of squirting bawdy comedians that have whores and common courtesans to play women's parts, and forbear no immodest speech or unchaste action that may procure laughter, but our scene is more stately furnished than ever it was in the time of Roscius, our representations honourable, and full of gallant resolution, not consisting like theirs of Pantaloon, a whore, and a zany, but of emperors, kings, and princes, whose true tragedies . . . they do vaunt. (*Pierce Penniless*, 1592.)

Foreign visitors to London were almost invariably impressed by the playhouses as a phenomenon quite unknown elsewhere. Another English traveler, Thomas Coryat, found Venetian theatres in 1608 "very beggarly and base in comparison of our stately playhouses in England, neither can their actors compare with us in apparel, shows, and music." Preachers inveighed in vain against the "gorgeous playing place erected in the fields," and the "sumptuous Theatre houses a continual monument of London's prodigality and folly." Even so unemotional a person as William Harrison found it an evident token of a wicked time "when players wax so rich that they can build such houses."

STAGES FOR THE ACTION

To the student of the drama, however, it is the stage, rather than mere externals, which is most important. Shakespeare's stage was not a gigantic alcove which could be cut off completely from the audience by a curtain as can our modern stage, nor was it a single entity at all. Instead, his main stage was a platform, rectangular or bluntly wedge-shaped, to which there were at least two annexes—an inner stage, built directly back of the platform and separated from it, when not in use, by a traverse curtain of tapestry or painted cloth; and an upper stage, on the level of the second gallery, also fitted with a curtain. Occasionally, though rarely, action even took place on a still higher level (see below). Sheltering the platform from sun and rain, and serving as well to decrease undesired echoings of sound, was a shed or overhanging storey called the "shadow" or the "heavens," which sometimes was painted with a moon and stars to simulate a bit of sky. Above was the "hut" from which, as in the modern American ball park, a flag was flown to convey to pleasure-seekers beyond the Thames that a performance would be held that afternoon. From the hut, too, at short intervals before the entry of the Prologue, a trumpeter blew three short blasts on a trumpet as a signal that the play was about to begin. Many theatrical effects also had their origin in the hut. Ordnance was set off there and thunder simulated by "rolled bullet" or "tempestuous drum." There were the windlass and other apparatus for lowering the "creaking throne" that pleased the boys in Marlowe's *Dr. Faustus*, and the cradle of flowers with Cupid in *Tancred and Gismunda*, the cloud with Jupiter in *Cymbeline*, and—"if you can conveniently"—the chair for drawing Venus aloft in Greene's *Alphonsus*.

The main scene of action in the Elizabethan theatre was the platform surrounded on three sides by spectators, some of whom sat on stools on the very boards themselves. In the Fortune Theatre this platform was forty-three feet across and projected into the middle of the pit. The stage of the Globe was similar. Here on the platform were enacted those scenes, so frequent in the old drama, which require a neutral background, or which have been vaguely localized by later editors as taking place in a street, a public place, a garden, or the hall of a castle. Scenes out of doors are much more numerous in Elizabethan plays than scenes within doors. Little in the way of scenery or properties could be supplied on the open platform beyond what the actors could conveniently carry on themselves, or what was already built into the theatre. The Elizabethans simply utilized the composite façade of the tiring-house as a permanent and highly adaptive background for their plays. The walls easily gave the illusion of the front of a house, and the tapestry hangings of an interior. In Cartwright's *The Ordinary*, for instance, a maid admits a caller into the house and bids him amuse himself by tracing the "pretty stories in the hangings" until she acquaints her mistress with his presence.

Entrance to the platform was gained by two doors from the tiring-house placed obliquely on either side of the stage. These doors were constantly in the mind of the practical dramatist as he visualized the action on his stage. "Enter a Fairy at one door and Robin Goodfellow at another" wrote Shakespeare in a scene which modern editors set in "a wood near Athens" (*A Midsummer Night's Dream*, II, i). On a field of battle "Enter Lucius, Iachimo, and the Roman army at one door and the Briton army at another" (*Cymbeline*, V, ii); "Canidius marcheth with his land army one way over the stage; and Taurus, the lieutenant of Cæsar, the other way" (*Antony and Cleopatra*, III, x). As he wrote these directions, Shakespeare was thinking of the way the scenes would be staged in the Elizabethan theatre. If these directions seem whimsical to the modern reader, it is because, unlike Shakespeare, he is not keeping in mind the physical conditions of the Elizabethan stage. A good many Elizabethan scenes, moreover, are laid outside the doors of houses—settings readily suggested by the doors of the tiring-house.

Occasionally, the space below the platform, known usually as the "cellarage" or as "hell" (perhaps traditionally from similar localities used in the miracle plays), was also used in stage production (Adams, *op. cit.*, pp. 123 ff.). Somewhere in the floor were one or more trapdoors to serve as the pit in *Titus Andronicus*, the grave of Ophelia in *Hamlet*, and the means of appearance and disappearance for the witches in *Macbeth* (*ibid.*, pp. 113, 209, 219). From the cellarage the majesty of buried Denmark proposed the oath to Hamlet's companions (I, v).

The principal annex to the platform was the inner stage, which, with its curtain, corresponds closely to the whole stage of the modern theatre. Its size is conjectural, but a recent estimate that it was 23 feet wide, between 7 and 8 feet deep, and 12 feet high is reasonable (*ibid.*, pp. 172–3). The inner stage was more remote than the platform, but, taking into account the modern theatre's orchestra pit, footlights, and apron, probably no more so than the stage of today, and, in a daylight amphitheatre, it would not be dark. With its curtain, the inner alcove could be used precisely like our modern stage; however, the Elizabethan producer usually did not use it in that way.

(1) The traverse curtain itself might serve as a scenical contrivance or a locality for the action. It served for the bed hangings through which Juliet fell after drinking the sleeping potion (*Romeo and Juliet*, IV, iv). It was the arras which concealed the executioners who came to blind Arthur (*King John*, IV, i), or which concealed Polonius and the King when they overhear Hamlet's interview with Ophelia (*Hamlet*, III, i; cf. II, ii, 163). Through this curtain Hamlet pursued the spectre of his father (I, iv).

(2) The curtains and the inner stage were sometimes used to "discover" (i. e., reveal) characters on the stage. Prospero "discovers" Ferdinand and Miranda at chess in his cell (*The Tempest*, V, i, 171); Portia bids Nerissa "draw aside the curtains" to reveal the caskets (*The Merchant of Venice*, II, vii) and has her close them again when each suitor has made his choice. Paulina draws the curtains to reveal Hermione standing as a statue in the chapel of her house (*The Winter's Tale*, V, iii). Frequently, the drawing of the curtain is described by the practical playwright in terms of entry: "Enter Duke and Senators set at a table with lights and attendants" (*Othello*, I, iii); "Enter Queen and her women, as at work" (*Henry VIII*, III, i); and "Enter Imogen, in her bed" (*Cymbeline*, II, ii). These directions merely mean that the scene opened in the modern manner with the drawing of the curtains. Although the device of discovery is frequently used in Shakespeare, there are very few scenes in his plays which both begin and end in the picture-stage manner with the opening and closing of the curtains. One is *Cymbeline* II, ii, which opens with Imogen in bed reading and closes with Iachimo's exit into the trunk.

(3) Most commonly, the inner stage was employed to indicate a small recess, especially one requiring properties, such as a study, a tent, an arbor, a cell, or a shop. At various times it was a study for Dr. Faustus (I, i), Claudio's

prison (*Measure for Measure*, IV, iii), Belarius's or Timon's cave (*Cymbeline*, III, v and *Timon of Athens*, IV, iii and V, i), the Princess of France's pavilion (*Love's Labor's Lost*, V, ii), Friar Laurence's cell (*Romeo and Juliet*, II, vi), Juliet's tomb (*ibid.*, V, iii), or a council chamber in the Tower (*Richard III*, III, iv). It was the closet into which Simple is thrust (*The Merry Wives*, I, iv), and the arbor in which Benedick and later Beatrice each overhears the gossip of their friends (*Much Ado*, II, iii and III, i). Half opened, it was Achilles's or Chalcas's tent (*Troilus and Cressida*, III, iii and V, ii), or poor Tom's hovel (*King Lear*, III, iv). In Dekker's *The Roaring Girl* the inner stage was divided to accommodate side by side "a potecary's shop . . . a feather shop [and] . . . a sempster's shop." Always, in such scenes, the inner stage was not thought of as existing alone, but rather as an annex to the platform.

(4) The back wall of the inner stage was also hung with tapestry which could, on occasion, be alluded to or employed in the action. Thus, Imogen's bedchamber (*Cymbeline*, II, ii), says Iachimo, was hung

> With tapestry of silk and silver; the story
> Proud Cleopatra, when she met her Roman,
> And Cydnus swell'd above the banks. (II, iv, 69 ff.)

Queen Gertrude's chamber must have had a similar hanging behind which Polonius could hide and be stabbed (*Hamlet*, III, iv). So had Hostess Quickly's tavern (*1 Henry IV*, II, iv) and Ford's house (*The Merry Wives*, III, iii), for Falstaff tries at least to hide his bulk behind the arras in each of these places. It was into the inner stage—"into the shadow of these trees," represented perhaps on the tapestry hangings—that the queen retires to overhear the gardeners in *Richard II* (III, iv). Here in the inner stage could be hung any localizing backdrops, if the public playhouses of Shakespeare's day made use of any painted scenery, as did the court theatres. Among the possessions of the Admiral's Men in 1598 were two objects described as "the city of Rome" and "the cloth of the Sun and Moon," which sound like such backgrounds.

(5) Since drawing the curtain always had the effect of expanding the acting area of the platform, the two stages were frequently thrown together for greater impressiveness and convenience in presentation. While the audience sat on the outer platform, the inner stage was used for the play in *Hamlet* (III, i), the production of Pyramus and Thisbe in *A Midsummer Night's Dream* (V, i), or the pageant of the Nine Worthies in *Love's Labor's Lost* (V, ii). Richard II sits in the inner stage when the outer represents the lists at Coventry (*Richard II*, I, iii). The inner stage was the repository of the caskets in *The Merchant of Venice* (III, ii) and the bar of justice at Antonio's trial (IV, i). But there were some less simple uses of the double stage. Two

extraordinary examples in Shakespeare are ghost scenes. In *Cymbeline* (V, iv) the platform represents the interior of the prison in which Posthumus lies asleep, and the inner stage represents his vision. The apparitions appear from the arras hangings to solemn music, and out of the "heavens" above "Jupiter descends in thunder and lightning, sitting on an eagle" to throw a thunderbolt. Then the ghosts vanish—by going through the curtain again. More interesting still is *Richard III*, V, iii. Here the platform represents Bosworth Field with Richard encamped on one side and Richmond on the other. While they sleep, both see the same vision; ghosts appear on the inner stage portending evil to Richard and good to Richmond. Thus, by the simple convention of shortening the distance between the two opponents, their contrasting moods on the eve of battle are presented simultaneously.

The uses of the upper stage, of course, were less numerous than those of the inner stage, but this area must have been a resourceful place of action, for the frequency of scenes requiring an elevation is a notable characteristic of the old drama as compared with the new. Generally speaking, the upper stage of Shakespeare's theatre was employed for any scenes "above" or "aloft." From its uses, however, it is apparent that the upper stage was really four stages: (1) a narrow balcony in the middle jutting over the inner stage below; (2) a curtained alcove directly over the study and an architectural duplicate of it; and (3 and 4) a pair of bay windows flanking the alcove.

The narrow balcony, or *terras*, as it was sometimes called, was probably three or four feet wide and frequently represented the wall of a city or castle on which the citizens come to parley with besiegers beneath. Thus, it was the wall of Angiers (*King John*, II, i), or Harfleur (*Henry V*, III, iii), or Orleans (*1 Henry VI*, I, iv), or Corioli (*Coriolanus*, I, iv), or Athens (*Timon of Athens*, V, iv), or Flint Castle (*Richard II*, III, iii). It was the castle wall from which Prince Arthur leaps to his death in *King John* (IV, iii). But here also was the pulpit in the Roman forum from which Brutus and Antony deliver their orations to the citizens (*Julius Cæsar*, III, ii), and the hill near Philippi which Pindarus ascends to view the fight (*ibid.*, V, iii).

The inner curtained alcove usually served as a "chamber" and here, possibly, rather than on the floor below, was Juliet's (*Romeo and Juliet*, IV, iii), Gertrude's (*Hamlet*, III, iv), Desdemona's (*Othello*, V, iii), and Imogen's bedroom (*Cymbeline*, II, ii), or the private room of the Boar's Head Tavern (*2 Henry IV*, II, iv). Like the inner stage below, this upper alcove was hung with tapestry and could be used for similar scenes. Occasionally, the use of the upper annex gave the audience an opportunity to watch two scenes at once. "I'll dine *above* with you today," says Adriana to Antipholus of Syracuse (*The Comedy of Errors*, II, ii, 215), and the amusement of the following scene is conceivably heightened by the possibility that the diners, oblivious of the turmoil at the door, were plainly visible to the audience.

When an upper window was required, one of the tiring-house windows above the oblique doors was brought into use and not the whole upper stage. Here was a suitable place for Juliet, in the so-called "balcony scene," when Romeo below in Capulet's garden exclaims,

> But soft, what light through yonder window breaks?
> It is the east, and Juliet is the sun. (II, ii, 2 ff.)

She leans out of this bay casement as Romeo descends his ladder of cords (III, v). Indeed, the stage direction in the first quarto edition of this play (1597) reads: "Enter Romeo and Juliet at the window." Here, too, Silvia hears the serenade of Thurio and Proteus (*The Two Gentlemen*, IV, ii); from this upper window Brabantio thrusts his head in answer to Roderigo's alarm (*Othello*, I, i), and Jessica tosses the jewels of Shylock to Lorenzo waiting under the penthouse (i. e., jutty) below (*The Merchant of Venice*, II, vi). Here, too, was Malvolio's prison (*Twelfth Night*, IV, ii), which "hath baywindows transparent as barricadoes, and the clerestories toward the south-north are as lustrous as ebony." Here, too, at one of the bay windows was Cleopatra's monument to which the wounded Antony was heaved aloft (*Antony and Cleopatra*, IV, xv). Apparently, when they were not needed in the action, the rooms above the tiring-house, like the platform itself, were made a source of revenue by being equipped for the use of lords who had fine satin to display. Later they were abandoned to an inferior type of play-goer.

Occasionally, the space above the stage on the level of the third spectator gallery could be utilized for scenes requiring special elevation "on the top." Such scenes are rare in Shakespeare. From a height, Joan of Arc gives the signal for the attack upon Rouen:

> The burning torch in yonder turret stands. (*1 Henry VI*, III, ii, 30.)

Another such scene occurs in *The Tempest* (III, iii). Alonso, Sebastian, Antonio, Gonzalo, and the rest are on the platform. The stage direction reads:

> Solemn and strange music; and Prospero on the top invisible [i. e., to the actors, but not to the audience]. Enter several strange shapes bringing in a banquet . . . and inviting the King, etc., to eat.

Then, in a moment, to thunder and lightning, Ariel enters, like a harpy descending from the "heavens." He claps his wings over the table, and, "with a quaint device," the banquet disappears. He delivers his message of vengeance and "vanishes in thunder," as the shapes reappear and, to soft music, carry out the table.

Hence, it will be seen that Shakespeare's theatre was a far more resourceful place than one might at first suppose. Instead of being confined for all of his effects to a single boxlike stage, the Elizabethan producer had at his disposal at least four settings: (1) the main platform (with the curtains closed), (2) the platform and the inner stage together (with the curtains open), (3) the platform and the upper stage together (with the lower curtains closed), and (4) the platform, inner stage, and upper stage together. He could, in addition, employ both the cellarage and the "top." Architecturally, his stage supplied him with built-in sets for balcony and window scenes which have to be especially constructed in the modern theatre, and he could use his main stage with or without an annex while the inner curtained area was being made ready for playing with properties.

PRODUCTION PROBLEMS ON THE ELIZABETHAN STAGE

Obviously, one of the chief production problems in the Shakespearean theatre was that of locality and change of place. The Elizabethan drama was most informal in this respect; the stage could be anywhere because specifically it was nowhere. "You shall have Asia of the one side, and Afric of the other," complained Sir Philip Sidney in his *Defence of Poesie* (c. 1580),

> and so many other under-kingdoms that the player, when he cometh in must ever begin with telling where he is, or else the tale will not be conceived. Now ye shall have three ladies walk to gather flowers, and then we must believe the stage to be a garden. By and by we hear news of a shipwreck in the same place, and then we are to blame if we accept it not for a rock. Upon the back of that comes out a hideous monster with fire and smoke, and then the miserable beholders are bound to take it for a cave. While in the meantime two armies fly in, represented with four swords and bucklers, and then what hard heart will not receive it for a pitched field?

The answer is "not one"—in Sidney's time or Shakespeare's or our own. "He that can take the stage at one time for the palace of the Ptolemies," wrote Dr. Johnson, "can take it in half an hour for the promontory of Actium." In any theatrical production, it is simply an audience's willingness to accept the conventions of situation and character and to believe that the boards of the theatre are wherever the author says they are that makes playing possible at all.

Obviously, too, on Shakespeare's stage more had to be explained by the dialogue than in the modern theatre. An audience today has so much done for it that it hardly needs to use its imagination at all, though, one must admit, the problems of locality and time are not yet wholly solved. Today costume, painted canvas, and electrical effects indicate time and place, but, to make assurance double sure, our spectators are equipped beforehand with programs which are explicit on many points, even to the relationships of the characters. Shakespeare's theatre got along without such aids because time and place were given less emphasis. The exact setting of each scene usually mattered little; what happened and what was said were of more importance than precisely where and when. When such information was important it could be conveyed directly and gracefully in the dialogue. The Elizabethan audience had no more difficulty in following than do we when we listen to a play on the radio.

For example, when Viola asks the seamen, "What country, friends, is this?" and is told, "Illyria," Illyria it is to everyone who hears her. An audience hearing Celia and Rosalind prepare to join the exiles in Arden and seeing them again disguised and travel worn, hardly needs Rosalind's sigh, "Well, this is the Forest of Arden," to know that they are there. Often, necessary information about place was given naturally and casually without having attention called directly to it. Description sometimes did the trick, especially if a few properties were used. A throne symbolized a presence chamber, an altar with candles a chapel, a table and a few benches a tavern. Such properties, of course, were placed in the inner stage. The stage doors helped to localize the action in *The Comedy of Errors,* especially in III, i, where they represented the entrances to the houses of Antipholus of Ephesus and the Courtesan. Even characters themselves might serve as localizing properties. In *Twelfth Night,* neither Orsino nor Olivia leaves home until the final scene when Orsino appears at Olivia's house. The early theatres seem to have used locality boards, like the pennons bearing place names which are sometimes seen in old tapestries. "Who is it," demands Sidney again, "that seeing Thebes written over a great door doth believe it is Thebes?" The answer is again "no one." But the willing spectator can make believe that it is Thebes or the seacoast of Bohemia, not because the trickery of the stage produces any genuine resemblance, but because he pretends it is so.

Changes of locality in the Elizabethan theatre illustrate better than anything else the magic flexibility of the stage and its difference from our own. *Henry V* opens with a conversation between the Archbishop of Canterbury and the Bishop of Ely in what modern editors have properly called "an antechamber in the King's palace." They remember a four o'clock appointment when the king will receive the French ambassador, and they hurry out. The next scene in modern editions is laid in "the presence chamber" with King Henry on his throne surrounded by his court. He calls for the ecclesiastics, and in a moment they reappear. In Shakespeare's theatre, the action of these two scenes was continuous. The moment the churchmen in Scene i left the platform, the curtain between it and the inner stage was drawn, revealing the king and his courtiers, and the whole took on the locality of the inner stage. Another interesting shift occurs in *Romeo and Juliet* (I, iv and v). Romeo and the revelers appear on the platform which represents the street in front of Capulet's house, discuss their plans for the evening, and listen to Mercutio's Queen Mab foolery. In conclusion, Romeo shouts, "On, lusty gentlemen," the drum beats, and the stage direction in the First Folio reads, "They march about the stage. Enter serving men with napkins." Modern editors begin a new scene. What happened on Shakespeare's stage was that the band moved through one of the doors—the door of Capulet's house—and walked "about the stage" in back. The instant that the platform was thus cleared, the curtains of the inner stage were drawn, and what had a moment before been a street became part of the hall in which serving men were setting out a banquet. In a few minutes the maskers entered again by a door at the back, and the ball was on. A similar shift occurs when Cæsar meets Artimedorus in the street and invites him to "come to the Capitol" (*Julius Cæsar*, III, i). The curtains were merely drawn, and the change of location had taken place. Modern editors do not divide this scene; somewhat paradoxically they describe it as "before the Capitol" and add a stage direction at line 12, "Cæsar goes up to the Senate-house, the rest following." The First Folio text omits both the locality note and the direction; they are not needed.

Sometimes a change of locality was indicated simply by an actor's exit and his immediate reappearance. Hamlet willingly follows the ghost from the stage and presently reappears demanding, "Where wilt thou lead me? Speak, I'll go no further." Everyone seeing him knows that he and the ghost have gone to "another part of the platform." How unimportant locality sometimes was may be observed from a scene in *Othello* (IV, ii). This scene opens in what is a private room in Othello's castle with conversation between the Moor and Emilia, who are joined soon by Desdemona; it closes in conversation between Iago and Roderigo, which more properly would take place in the street. In *King Lear*, II, ii–iv, the stage is actually two places at once. Kent is put into the stocks and falls asleep on the stage. Edgar, disguised as poor Tom, appears and soliloquizes about his life as a fugitive; as he goes out, Lear and his Fool enter to discover Kent in the stocks. Actuality has been sacrificed to dramatic effect; Kent in the stocks is simply an incongruous property that is not needed for Scene iii, and poor Tom and the audience oblige by taking no notice of him. Space was sometimes gained when armies marched about the stage in procession; distances were often traversed with no more ado than in Greene's *George a Greene*. "Darest thou walk to the town's end with me?" demands Jenkin of the shoemaker with whom he is picking a quarrel. The latter promptly puts down his tools, and they walk to the front of the platform. "Now we are at the town's end, what say you now?" Only on the vaudeville stage can one find a parallel in the modern theatre. It is all a matter of how much make-believe an audience is willing to contribute. Such informality, however, made for rapid and continuous action in the Elizabethan theatre, and for multiplicity of scenes.

The passage of time also presented a production problem which was just as easily solved in a theatre without lighting effects. "There is no clock in the forest," says Rosalind, and one might add anywhere else in Shakespeare, because the poet carries his own watch to refer to when he wishes. Whenever it matters, a few allusions to the hour are all that is necessary, as in *A Midsummer Night's Dream* (III, ii, 5, 61, 177, 187, 355, 379–80, etc.); *Julius Cæsar* (II, i, 3, 45, 78, 192, 221, etc.); or *Cymbeline* (II, ii, 3, 51), the last mentioned a short scene which begins "near midnight" and ends with the clock striking three. The transition from night to day is completed by opening the next scene with a dawn-song, "Hark, hark, the lark." Other examples of the striking clock to indicate the hour or the passage of time occur in *The Merry Wives*, III, ii, 46; *Twelfth Night*, III, i, 141; *Julius Cæsar*, II, i, 192. Occasionally, time is indicated by an allusion to the setting of the sun or moon (e. g., *The Two Gentlemen*, V, i, 1; *3 Henry VI*, II, i, 21–2; *Richard III*, V, iii, 19; *A Midsummer Night's Dream*, II, i, 60; *The Merchant of Venice*, V, i, 1; *Macbeth*, II, i, 2). If it is necessary to create the illusion of night in the daylight, description can help to produce the atmosphere and a few torches aid the audience in their make-believe. Brutus's ability to read a letter at night requires a special explanation (*Julius Cæsar*, II, i, 44–5), and characters frequently are unable to recognize one another in the "dark" (*King John*, V, vi, 1, 17; *The Merchant of Venice*, II, vi, 60; *Julius Cæsar*, II, i, 74, 89).

A single scene from *Macbeth* (II, i) will serve to illustrate how an Elizabethan playwright could rely upon a convention for dramatic effect. Banquo and Fleance enter with torches and talk a little about the lateness of the hour. Macbeth, lighted by a servant with a torch, joins them, and there is some conversation about the entertainment of the king and the prophecies of the Weird Sisters, after which Banquo and Fleance retire. The stage is set. Macbeth dismisses his man:

> Go, bid thy mistress when my drink is ready
> She strike upon the bell.

It is the signal agreed upon for the murder of Duncan. Left in the "dark," Macbeth immediately becomes prey to his mental agitation and sees before him the air-drawn dagger.

Clearly, time and place had no existence for an Elizabethan playwright, except as they were dramatically significant. Only rarely can a modern dramatist set his play "once upon a time, and in a certain place." It was always possible in Shakespeare's theatre. Hence, it is not surprising that Shakespeare's plays today need little doctoring for radio production—they are ready equipped with verbal scenery and light effects, verbal changes of locale, and verbal time indications.

COSTUME ON THE ELIZABETHAN STAGE

The Elizabethan actor atoned for any lack of elaborate scenery by rich costume. From very early times, players were notorious for their extravagant finery.

> I thought verily by your apparel
> That ye had been a player,

says one of the characters to another in Medwall's *Fulgens and Lucres* (*c.* 1496), one of the earliest secular plays:

> There is so much nice array
> Amongst these gallants nowaday
> That a man shall not lightly
> Know a player from another man.

In Shakespeare's time, allusions to the actors' fine clothes are frequent. The very hirelings, wrote Stephen Gosson, "jet under gentlemen's noses in suits

Doctor Faustus Conjuring   (From the 1628 edition of Marlowe's play)

The Lamentable and Tragical History of Titus Andronicus (From the Roxburghe Ballads, early seventeenth century)

of silk," and Robert Greene in *A Quip for an Upstart Courtier* (1592) introduces an "applesquire," who is a player, dressed in a

> moire cloth gown . . . faced down before with grey coney, and laid thick on the sleeves with lace, which he quaintly bore up to show his white taffeta hose and black silk stockings. A huge ruff about his neck wrapped in his great head like a wicker cage, a little hat with brims like the wings of a doublet, wherein he wore a jewel of glass, as broad as a chancery seal.

Theatrical companies had their common stock of costumes to which they constantly added new finery. Henslowe, as pawnbroker, doubtless replenished his stock from the wardrobes of spendthrifts, who, having laid out their acres for fine clothes, "brought them next week," as Donne wrote, "to the theatre to sell." Players sometimes acquired fine apparel in other ways. "The actors are most expensively and elaborately costumed," wrote Thomas Platter, a Swiss visitor to London in 1599,

> for it is the English usage for eminent lords or knights at their decease to bequeath and leave almost the best of their clothes to their serving men, which it is unseemly for the latter to wear, so that they offer them then for sale for a small sum to the actors. (*Thomas Platter's Travels in England, 1599*, translated by Clare Williams, London [1937], p. 167.)

Henslowe's and Alleyn's accounts amply attest the splendor of the stage wardrobe and the importance attached to it by the company. Their inventories are rich in such finery as "a scarlet cloak with two broad gold laces,

The Lamentable and Tragical History of Titus Andronicus (From the
Roxburghe Ballads, early seventeenth century)

with gold buttons of the same down the sides," "a short velvet cap cloak embroidered with gold and gold spangles," "a purple satin welted with velvet
and silver twist," "the black velvet gown with white fur," "a crimson robe
striped with gold, faced with ermine," "a gilt leather coat," and "a blue
taffeta suit, laid with silver lace." There were jerkins and doublets of flame,
ginger, green, black, red, and carnation velvet or satin, French hose of "blue
velvet embroidered with gold," Venetians of "purple velvet cut in diamonds
laced and spangled," of "green striped satin," and of "carnation satin . . .
laid with gold lace," and women's gowns of "white satin . . . laid with
white lace," "changeable taffeta," and "cloth of gold."[4] Henslowe also employed two tailors to make up costumes as needed from materials bought in
quantity; payments to the "little tailor" are frequent and sometimes conside.-
able in amount.

Such a wardrobe was costly. Alleyn paid £20 10s. 6d. for a "black velvet
cloak with sleeves embroidered all with silver and gold"; a "doublet and hose
of seawater green satin" cost £3; and Henslowe paid £6 13s. for a "woman's
gown of black velvet for the play of A Woman Killed with Kindness," but
paid the dramatist, Thomas Heywood, only £3 in full for the play itself. The
full significance of this extravagance is appreciated when one remembers
that Shakespeare bought a good house in Stratford for only £60; that a pig
was worth only 6d., a chicken 3d., and a barrel of small beer 4s. 4d.; that

[4] *Henslowe Papers*, ed. W. W. Greg (1907), pp. 52 ff.

sheep varied in price from 6s. to 11s., eggs from 2s. to 6s. 4d. the hundred, and butter from 3s. to 5s. the dozen pounds. Is it a wonder, therefore, that the Elizabethan player wished to display his finery in the tavern to his friends, and that, to prevent unnecessary wear and tear upon the company's stock, Henslowe levied a fine upon anyone who wore his costume outside the theatre?

For, rich though it was, equipment on the Elizabethan stage was essentially that of the day, with little attempt at historical accuracy. The unclassical Romans in *Coriolanus* carry pikes, cannon are alluded to in *King John*, Brutus turns down a leaf in the book he is reading and puts it into his doublet pocket, the Athenians in *A Midsummer Night's Dream* talk of cloaks and hats and ribboned pumps and of being sent into a nunnery. A sensitiveness to what we recognize as anachronisms is a sophistication of the modern audience. A Cleopatra whose ruff and farthingale made us think of Mary Queen of Scots, and a Cæsar or an Antony in doublet and hose would make a modern audience laugh. Yet costume not very different from this was prevalent on the stage until the nineteenth century, and we still expect to see a medieval Hamlet in garments that fit him no better. As W. S. Gilbert said of him in *Rosencrantz and Guildenstern:*

> Strange to say, whate'er his tongue may be,
> Whether he's dark or flaxen—English—French—
> Though we're in Denmark, A. D. ten-six-two—
> He always dresses as King James the First!

While it is true that on Shakespeare's stage doublet and hose or ruff and farthingale clothe alike the inhabitants of Windsor and Rome and Illyria, some pains were taken to distinguish peculiar types by peculiar dress. Malcolm apparently recognizes Ross as his countryman by his dress (*Macbeth*, IV, iii, 160), Posthumus refers to his "Italian weeds" (*Cymbeline*, V, i, 23), Shylock alludes to his Jewish gaberdine (*The Merchant of Venice*, I, iii, 113), Navarre and his followers masquerade as Muscovites (*Love's Labor's Lost*, V, ii, 121), ladies appear as Amazons in *Timon of Athens* (I, ii, 137), and the Puck recognizes the quarreling lovers by the "weeds of Athens" they have on (*A Midsummer Night's Dream*, II, i, 266 and ii, 71; III, ii, 349). National peculiarities also appear among the costumes of Henslowe's inventories. There were "two Danes' suits," "the suit of motley for the Scotchman," "one Moor's coat," "four Turks' heads," and "old Mahammet's head." The last mentioned probably refer, not to the heads themselves, but to such "Turkish bonnets" as are alluded to in *Soliman and Perseda*.

Distinctions of trade or profession were also made by dress. Tradesmen wearing holiday garb appear in *Julius Cæsar* (I, i, 8); mariners appear in *The Tempest* (I, i, 54); "sunburned sicklemen of August weary," "properly habited," dance with nymphs in the same play (IV, i, 134); and mummers "habited like shepherds" attend a masque at Cardinal Wolsey's (*Henry VIII*, I, iv, 64). Arthur disguises himself as a ship-boy (*King John*, IV, iii, 4), and Helena dresses as a pilgrim (*All's Well*, III, v, 32); Portia and Nerissa dress as lawyer and clerk (*The Merchant of Venice*, IV, i, 118, 168); Titus appears as a cook (*Titus Andronicus*, V, iii, 26); and the Courtesan in the "habit of a light wench" (*The Comedy of Errors*, IV, iii, 52). Blue coats and tawny coats identify the serving men of Gloucester and of Winchester (*1 Henry VI*, I, iii). Henslowe also had many habiliments to symbolize callings: a "friar's gown of gray," a "cardinal's gown," a "doctor's gown," a "senator's gown," "priests' coats," "white shepherd's coats," "antic's coats," "torchbearers' suits," "soldiers' coats," "janissary's gowns," a "pedant's trousers," a "fool's coat, cap, and bauble," and even "knaves' suits." Kings on all occasions wore the crowns which identified them, even in bed (*3 Henry VI*, IV, iii, 48, and *2 Henry IV*, IV, v, 5).

In addition, other distinctions were frequently indicated by costume. Titus Andronicus is offered "this palliament of white and spotless hue," a candidate's robe (*Titus Andronicus*, I, i, 182), and Coriolanus wears similar dress which is described as "a gown of humility" (II, iii). "Wailing robes" are referred to in *1 Henry VI* (I, i, 86), "mourning gowns" in *2 Henry VI* (II, iv, 161), and "riding robes" in *King John* (I, i, 217), while dancers make themselves "all men of hair" in *The Winter's Tale* (IV, iv, 331 ff.). Austria wears a lion's skin in *King John* (II, i, 136). In *As You Like It*, when the Duke and his followers appear "like foresters" or "outlaws" (II, i and vii), they apparently wear some artificial courtly version of rustic garb, perhaps not unlike the "swain's wearing" adopted by Prince Florizel (*The Winter's Tale*, IV, v, 9), who changes with Autolycus and causes that rascal to be mistaken for a courtier.

Allegorical and supernatural beings likewise wore a distinctive dress on Shakespeare's stage. "Rumor, painted full of tongues," speaks the Induction to *2 Henry IV*. "Time" appears as chorus in *The Winter's Tale*, and, when Ariel entered first as a water-nymph and then as a harpy, his garments must have suggested his form (*The Tempest*, I, ii and III, iii). Romeo dresses as a pilgrim to symbolize his worship at the shrine of Love (*Romeo and Juliet*, I, v, 95 ff.), and the typical lover's disarray is described in *As You Like It* (III, ii, 392) and *The Two Gentlemen* (II, i, 18). It was a particularly amusing idea to dress Nobody in the play *Nobody and Somebody* in breeches reaching to his neck so that "no body" was visible when he appeared, and Somebody in a doublet which reached to the ankles. Henslowe's accounts also mention such symbolical dress as a "fairy's gown of buckrum," a "pair of giant's hose," "coats for giants," a "witch's gown," a "hood for a witch," a "devil's suit and spirit's," a "ghost's suit," and a "ghost's bodice." Stage directions "enter like a ghost," refer, no doubt, to some such conventional costume. By far the most interesting of these symbolical garments is the "robe for to go invisible," for which, with a "gown for Nembia," Henslowe paid the ridiculously reasonable price of £3 10s. Both Prospero and Oberon had duplicates of this costume. Henslowe's accounts frequently mention other special garments identified either with some specific character or with a play: "Tamburlaine's coat with copper lace" and "breeches of crimson velvet," "Harry the V's velvet gown" and "satin doublet laid with gold lace," "Juno's coat," "Dido's robe," "Eve's bodice," "the white satin doublet for Phæton," "the suit for Neptune," "Iris's head [i. e., headdress] and rainbow," "the green coats for Robin Hood," and "the green gown for Marion."

Nobody and Somebody
(From the play of that title, 1606)

Shakespeare occasionally used costume as a means of characterization or of indicating a change in a character. Most familiar, of course, are Hamlet's "nighted color" (*Hamlet*, I, ii, 68) and Malvolio's cross-gartering (*Twelfth Night*, III, iv). But there are also other instances. Thus, Parolles in *All's Well* is described as " a snipt-taffeta fellow," "a red-tailed bumble-bee," and "that jackanapes with scarfs" (IV, v, 2 and 5; III, v, 88). He garters up his arms and makes hose of his sleeves (II, iii, 264-5)—why, "the soul of this man is in his clothes" (II, v, 48). Falstaff, too, must have rigged out the little page, given to him by Prince Hal, in an astonishing livery to provoke Hal's remark: "A' had him from me Christian; and look, if the fat villain have not transformed him ape" (*2 Henry IV*, II, ii, 75). Then there is Benedick. One mark of Don Pedro's success as a matchmaker is Benedick's adoption of dress which he had condemned as foppish before, and the fact that "he looks younger than he did, by the loss of a beard. —— Nay, a' rubs himself with civet; can you smell him out by that?" (*Much Ado*, III, ii, 31 ff.).

Finally, one must not forget the animals, for, while real live beasts were frequently actors on the Elizabethan stage, the artificial variety were still more dependable. Launce's dog (*The Two Gentlemen*, II, iii and III, iv), the dog which accompanies Moon (*A Midsummer Night's Dream*, V, i), and the bear that pursued the unhappy Antigonus (*The Winter's Tale*, III, iii) were doubtless live, but that "fearful wild fowl," the lion (*A Midsummer Night's Dream*, III, i and V, i) was not. *A Midsummer Night's Dream* also requires an ass's head for Bully Bottom. Henslowe's inventories again supply specific information about what equipment players at his theatre had: "i lion"

Tamora Pleading for Her Sons Going to Execution
(From a drawing attributed to Henry Peachum, dated 1595)

and "i black dog," "i lion's skin," "ii lions' heads," "i bear's skin," "i snake," "Cerberus' iii heads," "i bear's head," "i bull's head," "i dragon in *Faustus*," and several "firedrakes' suits."

Hence, even in Shakespeare's time, at least some attempt was made to mount a play with distinctive costume. Theatrical attire was already becoming conventionalized, and, while Elizabethan garments clothed the unimportant characters, it is not improbable that the costume of the principal actors may have symbolized the remoteness of time and place for the entire play. Indeed, the first illustration to Shakespeare (1595?), probably inspired by a performance in the theatre, bears out this supposition. It represents a scene from *Titus Andronicus* in which Tamora, an ordinary tragedy queen, is shown pleading for her sons who are being led to execution. The minor characters wear a nondescript contemporary garb, but Titus gives a classical flavor to the whole by appearing in what at least passes for a Roman toga.

PLATFORM-STAGE SPECTACLE

Elizabethan drama, therefore, was more than just an appeal to the ear; it was an appeal to the eye as well, for spectacle of a special sort was possible on the platform stage. The glitter of rich costumes, the kaleidoscopic pageantry of the numerous processions, the enthralling sword-play, the dumb-shows, the appearances of witches and ghosts, the descent of gods and goddesses, awed the gaping groundling of Shakespeare's day just as similar effects delight his counterpart today. "For the eye," wrote the outraged Stephen Gosson in *Plays Confuted in Five Actions* (1582),

> beside the beauty of the houses and the stages, he sendeth in garish apparel, masques, vaulting, tumbling, dancing of jigs, galliards, morrises, hobby-horses, showing of juggling casts; nothing forgot that might serve to set out the matter with pomp, or ravish the beholders with variety of pleasure.

So, Tamburlaine appears in a king-drawn chariot (*2 Tamburlaine*) and Pluto in a devil-drawn car (Heywood's *The Silver Age*), a burning town is shown in *2 Tamburlaine*, fireworks explode when Dr. Faustus is carried off by the devil, and in Greene's *Friar Bacon and Friar Bungay* there is not only a brazen head that speaks, but also a monster that spits fire all the time he is on the stage. Examples are to be found in Shakespeare's plays as well. Some have already been alluded to. Both *Love's Labor's Lost* and *A Midsummer Night's Dream* end in amateur theatricals; there are "urchin-shows" and "living drolleries" in *The Tempest* (II, ii and II, iii); Prospero puts on a masque with allegorical figures representing Juno, Iris, and Ceres, followed by an anti-masque of reapers and nymphs; there are also masques in *Love's Labor's Lost* (V, ii), *Timon of Athens* (I, ii), and *Henry VIII* (I, iv). There is a supper dance in *Romeo and Juliet* (I, v) and *Much Ado* (II, i). In *The Winter's Tale* there is a dance of shepherds and shepherdesses, followed by a dance of satyrs "which the wenches say is a gallimaufry of gambols because they are not in it" (IV, iv). In *As You Like It* there is a wrestling match (I, ii), and there are visualized dreams in *Richard III* (V, ii), *Cymbeline* (V, iv), and *Henry VIII* (IV, ii). There is the show of kings in *Macbeth* (IV, i). *Henry VIII* also has a coronation (IV, i), and this play, to quote a letter by Sir Henry Wotton (1613), with its "extraordinary circumstances of pomp and majesty . . . the Knights of the Order, with their Georges and Garter, the Guards with their embroidered coats and the like," seems to have been especially famous for display. The stage directions are more full and more specific than those of any other Shakespearean play.

MUSIC ON THE ELIZABETHAN STAGE

For the achievement of these and similar effects, playing frequently called to its aid the sister art of music. "Some little amusement," wrote Orazio

THE

HONORABLE
HISTORIE OF
FRIER *BACON*, AND
FRIER BONGAY.

As it was lately plaid by the Prince *Palatine* his Seruants.

Made by *Robert Greene*, Master of Arts.

Time is.   *Time was.*

Time is past.

LONDON,
Printed by ELIZABETH ALLDE dwelling
neere Christ-Church. 16,0.

The Brazen Head That Speaks   (Title-page of Robert Greene's *Friar Bacon and Friar Bungay*, edition of 1630)

Busino, a Venetian visitor to London in 1617, "may be derived from gazing at the very costly dresses of the actors and from the various interludes of instrumental music and dancing and singing." The Admiral's Men, playing at the Rose in 1598, had among their stock: "iii trumpets and a drum, and a treble viol, a bass viol, a bandore, a zither," "i chime of bells," "iii timbrels," and "i sackbut." Even the casual reader of Shakespeare is impressed not only by the numerous "Sennets," "Tuckets," "Flourishes," and "Alarums," that accompany "drum and trumpet" histories, but also the numerous incidental songs in other plays as well. The tradition was one inherited from the miracle plays, but, during Shakespeare's day, musical elements in the drama, both instrumental and vocal, increased in amount and were a featured offering at the private theatres, like Blackfriars. Processions like those in *Henry VIII* were always conducted to the music of trumpets or hautboys. "Hautboys and torches" accompany Duncan to Dunsinane (*Macbeth*, I, vi). "Blackamoors with music" accompany the Muscovite masquers in *Love's Labor's Lost* (V, ii), masquers with a drum attend Leonato's feast in *Much Ado* (II, i) and Capulet's ball in *Romeo and Juliet* (I, iv), loud hautboys' music accompanies the dance of the Amazons in *Timon of Athens* (I, ii), and Thurio, Cloten, and Cassio all go serenading with musicians (*The Two Gentlemen*, IV, ii; *Cymbeline*, II, iii; *Othello*, III, i). Funeral processions, too, like those in *Titus Andronicus*, *Hamlet*, *King Lear*, and *Coriolanus*, were made to dead marches, usually with drums alone.

Since music is emotional in its appeal, the Elizabethan playwright used it sometimes to create or enhance effects that were otherwise difficult. Shakespeare created the sentimental mood of *Twelfth Night* by having Duke Orsino, as the play opens, call for instrumental music as the "food of love"; he adds music to the romance of Portia's moonlit garden (*The Merchant of Venice*, V, i), and increases the tension by having Portia call for music while Bassanio contemplates the caskets (III, ii). Supernatural effects, too, were produced or enhanced by the use of music. "Music of the hautboys as under the stage," heard by the soldiers in *Antony and Cleopatra*, means to them that the god Hercules, Antony's guiding spirit, will accompany him no more (IV, iii). Ariel's music, coming from nowhere, helps to create the atmosphere of enchantment in *The Tempest*. In the same play, solemn and strange music is played as the weird shapes spread the banquet. Sad and solemn music accompanies the visions in *Cymbeline* and *Henry VIII*, and soft music introduces mythological beings like Iris and Ceres in *The Tempest* and Hymen in *As You Like It*. Physicians sometimes use the softening influence of sweet sound as a restorative. Both Thaisa (*Pericles*, III, ii) and Lear (V, iii) are aroused from coma by music. Shakespeare did not have anyone die to slow music, as did Marlowe; the nearest he came to melodramatic effect is when Hermione descends from her pedestal to an appropriate musical accompaniment (*The Winter's Tale*, V, iii). For Shakespeare's use of vocal music, see below, pp. 262 ff.

STAGE PROPERTIES

As to properties, a complete list of the objects needed for the production of Shakespeare would be formidable. One recalls the tomb in *Romeo and Juliet* which must be wrenched open with a crow-bar, the box-tree which conceals the conspirators in *Twelfth Night* while Malvolio reads the letter, the witches' cauldron in *Macbeth*, the stocks in *King Lear*, the clothes-line of glistening apparel in *The Tempest*, the three caskets in *The Merchant of Venice*, the human heads in many a gruesome tragedy, Yorick's skull in *Hamlet*, and the scaling ladders in *1 Henry VI*. There must even have been practical trees, or at least a tapestry curtain representing them, in *As You Like It* for Orlando to hang his verses on, red and white rose bushes in *1 Henry VI*, and a hawthorn brake in *A Midsummer Night's Dream*. Unfortunately, we do not have the property list of the Globe, but there was once a list, now lost, of what the Admiral's Men had on hand at the Rose in 1598.[5] This list makes evident that the Elizabethan showman not only used such simple essentials as lances, targets, foils, clubs, and harmless leathern hatchets, but also allowed himself such frills as Cupid's bow and quiver, Mercury's wings and caduceus, and the Golden Fleece for Jason. There is even a nice distinction between the crowns in the company's possession: "iii Imperial crowns, i plain crown, i crown with a sun, i ghost's crown." In addition, the actors had in stock "i rock, i cage, i tomb, i bedstead, ii moss banks, i wooden canopy, i little altar, ii coffins, and i cauldron for the Jew" [i. e., *The Jew of Malta*]. More elaborate properties are also listed: "i Hell mouth, i pair of stairs for Phæton, Phæton's chariot, Phæton's limbs, ii steeples, i beacon, i hobby-horse, i great horse with his legs" [i. e., for a Troy play]. Even "i bay tree," "Tantalus's tree," and a "tree of golden apples" for *Old Fortunatus* are mentioned. The Elizabethan stage was far from bare of properties.

Generally speaking, however, properties on the Shakespearean stage were intended to symbolize rather than fully to realize a scene, as is most often the case in the modern theatre. A bedstead made clear that the setting was a chamber, a table and some benches that it was a tavern, a throne and canopy that it was a court-room. Nothing was merely imagined if it could conveniently be shown. However, if the Elizabethan producer had difficulty "expressing a sea," as Thomas Heywood put it in *The Fair Maid of the West*, has the modern scenic artist yet been able to make his illusions perfect?

REALISM ON THE ELIZABETHAN STAGE

The mention in Henslowe's account book of the "scaffold and bar for the play of Biron," the "frame for the heading of Black Jone," and the "pulleys

[5] *Henslowe Papers*, ed. W. W. Greg (1907), pp. 113 ff.

and workmanship for to hang Absalom" quite properly brings up the subject of Elizabethan stage realism. Just how was the misfortune of David's unhappy son represented to the awed gaze of the Elizabethan groundling? What was the nature of the "quaint device" by which the banquet in *The Tempest* is made to vanish? How was the illusion of reality thrown over the numerous killings and maimings with critical spectators standing close about, if not actually sitting on the stage itself? We can only guess. Elizabethan actors, blending with their art the accomplishments of acrobats and sleight-of-hand tricksters, apparently had no difficulty. In one of the plays of Jakob Ayrer, the Nuremberg dramatist who was much influenced by the English comedians who visited Germany in the late sixteenth century, rain is produced on the stage in this ingenious manner:

> He stands under the tree, and it rains. The waterworks are so arranged that from above water is poured into a hanging sieve from a dish that has a string on it, so that when John [Posset, the clown] conveniently pulls the string, the water falls on John and makes him rather wet. (*Comedia von König in Cypern.*)

Admitting their ingenuity, it is also true that the Elizabethans probably went further in the realism of their thrillers than even the modern movie. *The Spanish Tragedy* requires an arbor with the body of a murdered man swinging from it. Scenes of bloodshed must have been particularly revolting. In the old *Cambises*, when Smirdis is killed and Cruelty cries:

> Even now I strike his body to wound,
> Behold now his blood springs out on the ground,

the stage direction reads: "a little bladder of vinegar prickt." In the case of another blood-and-thunder play we have even more gruesome details. According to the "plat" or stage summary for George Peele's *The Battle of Alcazar*, among the properties required are "3 vials of blood and a sheep's gather" [i. e., the lungs, heart, and liver]. In the dumb-show Furies bring in three characters for judgment and torture by devils, and presumably one of these organs is plucked from each of the unhappy trio, the vials of blood completing the gory scene. Could actualism ask for more?

The number of such scenes in Shakespeare, even in *Titus Andronicus* and *Hamlet*, is not excessively large, but a study of some of Shakespeare's plays reveals problems of the theatre that are highly complex. Think of the ingenuity required of the producer by a single play like *The Tempest*. Or think of *A Midsummer Night's Dream* or *King Lear*, both of which have frequently been dismissed as unproducible. Yet Shakespeare and his stage managers knew how to manipulate the resources of the Elizabethan stage to produce them. It is well to bear this fact in mind before assuming that theatrical conventions which are different from ours were merely crude and primitive. Some of these plays, to be sure, may have been produced at court or in the private theatres where elaborate stage machinery, artificial lighting, and painted scenery were in use. But even so, to the Elizabethan actor must still go a great deal of the praise, for the skill required of him was of no mean order. When Edgar, for example, becomes poor Tom, he must change his voice from what it naturally is as Edgar; he must change it again and speak dialect when he pretends to be the peasant who finds Gloucester at the foot of Dover Cliff (IV, vi), and he must change it back again each time he speaks outside of his assumed roles in an aside or a soliloquy. He must literally climb a hill with his voice (IV, vi), with it give shape and dimension to the cliffs

The Murder of Horatio   (From the 1633 edition of *The Spanish Tragedy*)

of Dover, and with it, at the same time, turn Gloucester from despair to patience. But there is little in the stage directions to tell him specifically how to accomplish these changes.

STAGE DIRECTIONS

Compared with the plays of Galsworthy, Shaw, Barrie, or Granville-Barker, Elizabethan plays seem woefully lacking in stage directions. Shakespeare and his fellow-dramatists did not always write a note to direct the actor to "suit the action to the word." They expected him to understand the action implied by the dialogue. When Boyet hurries in "with mirth in his face" and declares that he is "stabbed with laughter," he must act so (*Love's Labor's Lost*, V, ii, 79–80). Olivia (*Twelfth Night*, I, v) makes such "good view" of Cæsario that her eyes seem to have "lost her tongue" and she speaks in "starts distractedly"—but her behavior is not described until two scenes after (II, ii). In *3 Henry VI* (III, iii), Queen Margaret, the Earl of Warwick, and King Lewis all receive letters which have the same import, and the dialogue of the onlookers makes clear their different reactions as they read:

> I like it well that our fair Queen and mistress
> Smiles at her news, while Warwick frowns at his . . .
> Nay, mark how Lewis stamps as he were nettled.

When Biron says of "honey-tongued" Boyet,

> The stairs as he treads on them kiss his feet,

the very walk of the actor in the role is described (*Love's Labor's Lost*, V, ii, 330). All too frequently in modern productions these hints to the player are ignored.

Most of the Elizabethan dramatists were also actors who could visualize their material on the stage. No better evidence of Shakespeare's genius as a man of the theatre can be found than just these directions to the actor. To take a classic example from *Macbeth* (V, iii), Shakespeare never forgot for an instant that, though other thoughts are uppermost in his mind, a tired, harassed, desperate man is girding on his harness for his last fight:

> *Give me mine armour.*
> How does your patient, doctor? . . .
> Throw physic to the dogs; I'll none of it.—
> *Come, put mine armour on. Give me my staff.*
> *Seyton, send out.*—Doctor, the thanes fly from me.—
> *Come, sir, dispatch.*—If thou could'st, doctor, cast
> The water of my land, find her disease,
> And purge it to a sound and pristine health,
> I would applaud thee to the very echo,
> That should applaud again.—*Pull 't off, I say.*—
> What rhubarb, senna, or what purgative drug,
> Would scour these English hence? Hear'st thou of them? . . .
> *Bring it after me.*
> I will not be afraid of death and bane,
> Till Birnam forest come to Dunsinane.

Here, in this broken speech, addressed to several people, is excellent theatre, excellent drama, and excellent psychology at the same time. The audience of the twentieth century has for some time been in reaction against the star-system which permitted a distinguished actor to dwarf all parts but his own. But, in the theatre and in modern pictures, it has also become accustomed to the development of theatrical art as independent of the art of the playwright. Today the arts of both the actor and the producer have ceased to be merely interpretative; they are creative. In Shakespeare's day the claims of neither were dangerous. A theatrical production in Shakespeare's playhouse was essentially a co-operative effort rather than a composite of several arts.

Such, then, were the conditions under which all of Shakespeare's comedies, histories, and tragedies were produced. This was the only theatre he knew, and study of Shakespeare's plays reveals that he knew it thoroughly and used its limitations as conveniences, just as he would have accepted the modern stage were he writing today. In his theatre he counted himself a king of infinite space, though to modern eyes he seems bounded by a nutshell. When he does chafe at limitations, as in the choruses of *Henry V*, he is thinking of the inadequacy of any stage to do justice to so great a theme:

> O for a Muse of fire, that would ascend
> The brightest heaven of invention,
> A kingdom for a stage, princes to act,
> And monarchs to behold the swelling scene! . . .
>   But pardon, gentles all,
> The flat unraised spirits that have dared
> On this unworthy scaffold to bring forth
> So great an object. Can this cockpit hold
> The vasty fields of France? Or may we cram
> Within this wooden O the very casques
> That did affright the air at Agincourt?

Of course not. Shakespeare's appeal—"piece out our imperfections with your thoughts"—is the unvoiced appeal of every striver for stage realism. Literal-mindedness was as much an obstacle in Shakespeare's day as in our own. It is also misleading—and unfair—to speak unimaginatively of the trickery of Elizabethan staging, for no one, even in the realistic theatre of today, thinks of stage devices as real. They are merely symbolic aids to the imagination.

The problems which vexed Peter Quince, when he attempted to present *Pyramus and Thisbe*, are still perplexing the modern producer. There is not only that matter of the lion among ladies, but also two more difficult effects—bringing the wall and moonlight into a chamber. "You can never bring in a wall." And what would happen to the actor's profession if one insisted upon the objection raised by Sir Nathaniel about the Nine Worthies: "Where shall you find men worthy enough to present them?" Like Nathaniel himself, all actors are—"alas, you see how 'tis—a little o'erparted." It is, of course, absurd to insist that the theatrical conditions which obtained in Shakespeare's time were perfect for the production of plays. But for the Elizabethan drama they were satisfactory, and they determined, as nothing else did, the entire character of that drama.

SUGGESTED REFERENCES

ADAMS, JOHN CRANFORD. *The Globe Playhouse: Its Design and Equipment.* Cambridge, Harvard University Press, 1942.

ADAMS, JOSEPH QUINCY. *Shakespearean Playhouses: A History of English Theatres from the Beginnings to the Restoration.* Boston and New York, Houghton, 1917.

BENTLEY, GERALD E. *The Jacobean and Caroline Stage: Dramatic Companies and Players* (2 vols.). Oxford, Clarendon Press, 1941.
A companion volume to Chambers, *The Elizabethan Stage.*

CAMPBELL, LILY B. *Scenes and Machines on the English Stage during the Renaissance.* Cambridge University Press, 1923.

CHAMBERS, E. K. *The Elizabethan Stage* (4 vols.). Oxford, Clarendon Press, 1923.
An account of the court, the control of the stage, the companies of actors, plays, and playwrights, with appendixes which reprint documents and allusions to theatrical matters.

COWLING, GEORGE H. *Music on the Shakespearian Stage.* Cambridge University Press, 1913.
The part played by music in an Elizabethan production.

GRAVES, THORNTON SHIRLEY. *The Court and London Theaters during the Reign of Queen Elizabeth.* Menasha, Banta, 1913.

LAWRENCE, WILLIAM J. *The Elizabethan Playhouse and Other Studies* (2 vols.). Stratford-on-Avon, The Shakespeare Press, Series I, 1912; Series II, 1913.

———. *The Physical Conditions of the Elizabethan Public Playhouse.* Cambridge, Harvard University Press, 1927.

———. *Pre-Restoration Stage Studies.* Cambridge, Harvard University Press, 1927.

———. *Those Nut-cracking Elizabethans: Studies in the Early Theatre and Drama.* London, The Argonaut Press, 1935.

MOORE, JOHN ROBERT. "The Songs of the Public Theaters in the Time of Shakespeare," *Journal of English and Germanic Philology,* XXVIII (1929), pp. 166–202.

POEL, WILLIAM. *Shakespeare in the Theatre.* London, Sidgwick and Jackson, 1913.

REYNOLDS, GEORGE F. "Some Principles of Elizabethan Staging," *Modern Philology,* April 1905 (pp. 1–34), June 1905 (pp. 1–29). *The Staging of Elizabethan Plays at the Red Bull Theater, 1605–1625.* MLA Monograph. New York, Heath, 1940.

RHODES, R. CROMPTON. *The Stagery of Shakespeare.* Birmingham, Cornish Brothers, 1922.

A Series of Papers on Shakespeare and the Theatre . . . by Members of the
Shakespeare Association. London, Humphrey Milford, Oxford University Press, 1927.
Among the papers are the following:
F. S. Boas, "The Play within the Play."
M. St. Clare Byrne, "Shakespeare's Audience."
G. H. Cowling, "Shakespeare and the Elizabethan Stage."
W. W. Greg, "Edward Alleyn."
C. M. Haines, "The Development of Shakespeare's Stagecraft."
G. B. Harrison, "Shakespeare's Actors."
J. Isaacs, "Shakespeare as Man of the Theatre."
Richmond Noble, "Shakespeare's Songs and Stage."

THORNDIKE, ASHLEY H. *Shakespeare's Theatre.* New York, Macmillan, 1916.
WRIGHT, LOUIS B. "Animal Actors on the English Stage before 1642," *Publications of the Modern Language Association,* XLII (1927), pp. 656–69.
————. "Juggling Tricks and Conjuring on the English Stage before 1642," *Modern Philology,* XXIV (1927), pp. 269–84.
————. "Stage Duelling in the Elizabethan Theatre," *Modern Language Review,* XXII (1927), pp. 265–75.
————. "Variety Entertainment by Elizabethan Strolling Players," *Journal of English and Germanic Philology,* XXVI (1927), pp. 294–303.
————. "Elizabethan Sea Drama and Its Staging," *Anglia,* LI (1927), pp. 104–19.
————. "Extraneous Song in Elizabethan Drama after the Advent of Shakespeare," *Studies in Philology,* XXIV (1927), pp. 261–74.
————. "Variety Show Clownery on the Pre-Restoration Stage," *Anglia,* LII (1928), pp. 51–68.
————. "Vaudeville Dancing and Acrobatics in Elizabethan Plays," *Englische Studien,* LXIII (1928), pp. 59–76.
————. "Madmen as Vaudeville Performers on the Elizabethan Stage," *Journal of English and Germanic Philology,* XXX (1931), pp. 48–54.

6

THE INFLUENCE OF
THEATRICAL CONDITIONS
ON SHAKESPEARE

And almost thence my nature is subdu'd
To what it works in, like the dyer's hand.
—Sonnet 111.

Eternal conditions of theatre and acting deter-
mine to a high degree the nature of the drama of any age. Only in our own
generation was it possible to mount the revue, which was wholly an effect of
electricity, carpentry, and spectacle; the movie scenario is essentially different from the drama intended for the ordinary stage; and the introduction
of the talking picture imposed a whole set of new conventions. Three centuries have made a tremendous difference in the theatre. Not only did the
platform give way to the picture-frame stage (which is, in turn, beginning
to give way), but also the very meaning of the word *play* suffered a change.
Elizabethan stage conventions left their mark deep upon the structure, the
acting, and the very style of the drama, and their effect upon Shakespeare
deserves more than passing attention.

A word of caution, however, is not out of place. In describing Shakespeare's
theatre, it is usual to speak in general terms of Elizabethan stage technique as
if it were the same in all theatres and remained unchanged throughout the
whole Elizabethan period. Actually, the art of the theatre, as such, was comparatively new, and, like all new arts, its early development must have been
rapid. Changes in technique between 1576 and, say, 1600 must have been
comparable to the development of the art of the moving picture in our own
time. What might have been a stage problem in the old Theatre would no

·[146]·

doubt have been solved less crudely in the Globe, and differences in production between the public theatres and the private houses, like Blackfriars, were even greater. As the manner of presentation evolved, so did the manner of writing plays; a court drama would differ in some essential ways from one originally designed for the common stages. Yet the influence of certain general features of the Elizabethan playhouse can be recognized.

THE PLATFORM STAGE

Of the physical features of Shakespeare's theatre, the most important in its effect upon the drama was the platform stage. Essentially, it made for greater intimacy between actors and audience than does the modern stage. The implications of that fact are important indeed. A platform surrounded on at least three sides by spectators does not permit detachment or remoteness of action, any more than did the medieval pageant wagon or the innyard stage (see above, pp. 68–70 and 93–94). In most theatres today, one of the basic conventions is the tacit understanding that the players may live out their stage lives as if no audience was present. Audience and actors are separated by footlights and orchestra pit, and in no serious play can the player take his audience into his confidence and speak directly to it. On Shakespeare's stage, there was no reason why he should not do that very thing, especially if it were essential that there be perfect understanding from the start. Hence, at the Globe, both the soliloquy and the aside were natural—the one explained to the whole audience something it must know to avoid misunderstanding later; the other honored some individual on the side lines with a confidence. Indeed, in one play, Robert Yarington's *Two Lamentable Tragedies* (*c.* 1601), asides are labeled "to the people." Falstaff talks to the spectators as naturally as to his fellow-players, Richard and Iago lay open their bold black hearts before the audience, and soul-sick Hamlet questions, "To be or not to be?"

In comedy, this informality seems natural enough, and there are numerous allusions in the early drama to extempore clowning, like Tarleton's rhyming on his flat nose and his retorts to an audience during a performance (*Shakespeare Jest Books*, II, 224). Hamlet, it will be recalled, girds at fools who "speak more than is set down for them." But the evolution of the Elizabethan soliloquy from the clumsy exposition of the miracle play and the intimate by-play of the interlude make the convention perfectly clear. On his platform the Elizabethan actor could not ignore his audience; he kept it in on the secret all of the time. Moreover, the line between the world of make-believe and the world of reality was much more vague on the Elizabethan stage than it is upon the modern. To the Elizabethan dramatist and the Elizabethan actor, the platform represented only a convenient, neutral area upon which could be presented that portion of the action that was essential for the audience to see. They constantly kept in mind the world backstage and the continuity of which their scenes were only a part.

How far the Elizabethans considered the soliloquy an exercise in elocution, as well as necessary exposition and character revelation, will probably never be known with certainty. The contact established with the audience, when the actor stepped to the skirt of the stage and spoke into the individual ears of his hearers, almost certainly threw such passages into theatrical relief and gave them a peculiar emphasis. Yet one of the bases for Charles Lamb's contention that Shakespeare's plays "are less calculated for performance than those of almost any other dramatist whatever" was these very soliloquies:

> Why, nine parts in ten of what Hamlet does are transactions between himself and his moral sense. . . . How can they be represented by a gesticulating actor who comes and mouths them out before an audience, making four hundred people his confidants at once! (*On the Tragedies of Shakespeare.*)

To Shakespeare and his fellows such a point of view would have been incomprehensible.

On the other hand, in his lectures, Coleridge pointed out as one of Shakespeare's excellences as a dramatist the fact that in his plays he gives us almost always "expectation in preference to surprise." From the beginning, the audience enjoys the superiority of full knowledge that there are two Dromios and two Antipholuses while watching the ludicrous mistakes to which those ignorant of the fact are prone. We know who Ganymede, Cesario, and Master Brook are, and we watch expectantly for the players likewise to penetrate their disguises. We know thoroughly the villainy of Iago and must suffer in silence while he deceives a noble nature and brings it to ruin. This distinction of Shakespeare, however, is but the result of his acceptance of the conventions of his theatre. If an Elizabethan actor could not ignore his audience, neither could an Elizabethan dramatist. When, in the Restoration period, the platform stage became first an apron and then gradually shrank to make room for the boxlike stage which we know today, a loss of intimacy resulted between actor and audience that is now almost complete.

A second effect of the platform concerns acting and was no less important. In the modern theatre, considerable emphasis is laid upon pantomime and stage business. It is not only necessary to hear *what* a character says, but *how* he says it. On the Elizabethan stage this was less true. No minor stage business is possible on a platform; the action had to be simple and essential, but, in all cases, it was of less importance than the dialogue: "Words above action; matter above words." Attention was concentrated upon the actor, boldly defined against a simple background, and upon the rapid delivery of his lines.[1]

[1] It has been estimated that the Elizabethan actor's rate of speech was twenty lines of blank verse a minute. See Alfred Hart, "The Time Allotted for Representation of Elizabethan and Jacobean Plays," *Review of English Studies*, VIII (October, 1932), 395 ff.

It has been frequently said that the Elizabethan audience came more to *hear* a play than to *see* one, that it liked to hear verse declaimed, and that at the theatre it got its poetry without taking the trouble to read it. Perhaps Ben Jonson was alluding merely to an unattained ideal when he caused his actor to declaim in the Prologue to *The Staple of News* (1625):

> For your own sakes, not his, he [the poet] bade me say,
> Would you were come to hear, not see a play.
> Though we his actors must provide for those
> Who are our guests here, in the way of shows,
> The maker hath not so; he'd have you wise,
> Much rather by your ears, than in your eyes.

Certainly, the Elizabethan drama, as a whole, was a rhetorical drama rather than a spectacular one, and Shakespeare's plays are laden with soliloquies and addresses. The Elizabethans sometimes expressed emotion, not by action, but by words. To many moderns they seem exquisite poets rather than play-makers. On the other hand, an Elizabethan play had a poetic appeal to the ear which many modern plays lack, and mere words on the Renaissance stage had a force which they were soon to lose.

In technique, Elizabethan acting was probably more "stagey" and animated than is acting now. The acoustics of a building open to the sky are poor, and the Theatre or the Globe doubtless made necessary a vigorous rather than a shaded enunciation of rhythmic verse. There is evidence that actions were to some extent stylized. Recipients of bad news threw themselves on the ground, like Romeo, "taking the measure of an unmade grave" (*Romeo and Juliet*, III, iii, 70); persons in frenzy or despair, like Elizabeth (*Richard III*, II, ii), Cassandra (*Troilus and Cressida*, II, ii), and Constance (*King John*, III, iv), appear with their hair "about their ears"; lovers all sighed; and a man who was melancholic or in trouble, like Brutus, "suddenly rose and walked about, musing and sighing, with his arms across" (*Julius Cæsar*, II, i, 239–40). In the old play *King Leir*, Regan

> knits her brow, and bites her lips
> And stamps and makes a dumb show of disdain.

No doubt this cultivated artificiality led to a certain amount of rant. The "o'erwrested seeming" of the strutting player

> whose conceit
> Lies in his hamstring, and doth think it rich
> To hear the wooden dialogue and sound
> 'Twixt his stretched footing and the scaffoldage
> (*Troilus and Cressida*, I, iii, 153 ff.)

was probably common enough on the Elizabethan stage. Bully Bottom, of course, prefers a "part to tear a cat in, to make all split." So does Ancient

Pistol. Even Hamlet liked rant in moderation when he commends a play as "caviare to the general" and asks for a passionate speech from it—Æneas's tale to Dido (II, ii). Such a request in the modern theatre would not be productive of the best results. It is eloquent testimony, however, of what was Elizabethan good taste.

Yet Hamlet's advice to the players clearly shows that the ideal was not violence, but simplicity and truth in the portrayal of character and emotion.

> Speak the speech, I pray you, as I pronounced it to you, trippingly on the tongue; but if you mouth it, as many of your players do, I had as lief the town-crier spoke my lines. Nor do not saw the air too much . . . but use all gently. . . . O, it offends me to the soul to hear a robustious, periwig-pated fellow tear a passion to tatters, to very rags. . . . Be not too tame neither, but let your own discretion be your tutor. Suit the action to the word, the word to the action . . . o'erstep not the modesty of nature." (III, ii, 1 ff.)

Here is William Shakespeare instructing the boys in the green-room. There were other attempts than Shakespeare's to tone down the ranting actor. Ben Jonson even used the term "over-act" in *The Staple of News* to censure a player "who having got the habit of it will be monstrous still in spite of counsel." Such caution was doubly needful on the Elizabethan platform stage.

It would be easy to cite from Shakespeare and his contemporaries passages that are a temptation to such acting. A wholesome balance will perhaps be preserved if we turn aside a moment for an example or two of delicacy and restraint. One of the most notable occurs in *Macbeth* (IV, iii). When Macduff is told how his castle has been surprised and his wife and babes savagely slaughtered, he is too deeply moved to speak. He merely pulls his hat down over his face and is silent, and Malcolm is frightened:

> Merciful heaven!
> What, man! Ne'er pull your hat upon your brows;
> Give sorrow words; the grief that does not speak
> Whispers the o'er-fraught heart and bids it break.

Another similar situation occurs in *Coriolanus* (V, iii) just after Volumnia has finished her long plea to her son to spare the city of Rome. The stage direction in the First Folio reads: "Holds her by the hand, silent"; then, Coriolanus's welling emotions break forth with:

> O, Mother, Mother,
> What have you done?

Shakespeare knew how much more effective at times was silence than a spate of words.

THE ABSENCE OF A FRONT CURTAIN

If the platform without changeable scenery affected style and action, the absence of a front curtain left an even deeper mark upon the work of Shakespeare and his fellows. It has been frequently noted that Shakespeare did not use the beginnings and the ends of acts as does a modern dramatist. The playwright today usually begins vigorously *in medias res* and drops his curtain to arrest the action suddenly upon a telling situation. Shakespeare did not do that. Almost all of his scenes open with entrances and close with exits. His stage is always cleared when the action is finished, and his acts sometimes outrun the climax. To say that it was impossible for Shakespeare to find his actors on the stage or to leave them there is not strictly true. As we have seen, the curtain to the inner stage could be used in every respect as the modern curtain is used. But the fact remains that Shakespeare, as a rule, did not use it that way.

His first scenes, however, are almost always vigorous and arresting. *The Tempest* opens with thunder and lightning and the commotion attending a storm at sea; *Othello* with an altercation between Roderigo and Iago, begun off-stage; *Romeo and Juliet* with the braggadocio of Gregory and Sampson, spoiling for a fight; and *Hamlet* under such tense circumstances that a seasoned soldier in his agitation so far forgets himself as to challenge the guard instead of waiting to be challenged. *Twelfth Night* opens with music, and *Coriolanus*, *Julius Cæsar*, *Macbeth*, and *Titus Andronicus* all begin with noise and excitement.

The reason for a vigorous beginning is to be found in the physical conditions of the Elizabethan playhouse. In the modern theatre, the house lights dim; as the curtain rises, a hush comes over the audience and its attention is focused upon a bright stage. In Shakespeare's open-air amphitheatre, something else had to startle the boisterous playgoers into attention. Nuts, card-playing, and bottle-ale must be forgotten. The Prologue helped a little, but the first few lines of a play could be counted upon as lost anyway. The playwright, therefore, used them to create an atmosphere and to arouse interest. Once he obtained it, he could go on and unfold his story. It will be observed that, in the modern theatre, the star usually does not come on until the audience has settled itself and a few late-comers have taken their seats. The strong beginnings of Shakespeare's plays and the slow take-offs of his stories are just as readily traceable to his theatre and its public.

The lack of a front curtain had its most marked effect at the ends of acts. The platform had to be cleared, and, in a tragedy, some disposition made of the dead bodies. In *Hamlet* on the modern stage, the curtain usually falls as Hamlet expires in the arms of Horatio, the rest of the scene being cut. The dead—Hamlet, Claudius, Gertrude, and Laertes—can get up and walk off, and the star appear in a moment to take a bow. Not so at Shakespeare's Globe. That last scene with its fencing match had to be held out in front on the open platform, and the dead had to be disposed of in some way. Years ago, when Forbes-Robertson revived the funeral procession at the close of *Hamlet*, the scene was praised as theatrically impressive. And so it is, invariably, when the play is uncut. Less effective is the dead march at the end of *King Lear*. At the end of *Othello*, all that was necessary to hide the dead bodies was to draw the bed-curtains, i. e., those of the inner stage. All of these scenes were shaped by the physical restrictions of the Elizabethan theatre. So, too, in comedies, the retreat of the actors from the stage is covered by a song-epilogue, as in *Love's Labor's Lost* or *Twelfth Night*, or brought about gracefully by the whole company participating in a dance, as in *Much Ado*. Sometimes there is some other sort of epilogue. The ends of these acts merely illustrate what good use Shakespeare made of his limitations.

The necessity of clearing the stage is not always so gracefully met. When Hamlet lugs out the body of Polonius, the action to many readers is repulsive and wholly unworthy of his refined, sensitive nature. On the modern stage the scene would not be necessary. Other examples of the expedient are equally gruesome. Cornwall orders the servant he has slain to be thrown on a dunghill (*King Lear*, III, vii); Hector is dragged out to be tied to the tail of Achilles's horse (*Troilus and Cressida*, V, viii); the murderer of Clarence drags out his body to drown it in the malmsey butt (*Richard III*, I, iv). On the other hand, Falstaff's carrying out Hotspur is simply ludicrous, as it was intended to be, and the universal resurrection at the end of *Pyramus and Thisbe* only adds to the merriment (*A Midsummer Night's Dream*, V, i).

One other important effect of the absence of a front curtain was that it made "pictures" or *tableaux* impossible on the Elizabethan stage. The drama of the last century went in more heavily for such effects than does the theatre of today, but the device is familiar to every playgoer. On Shakespeare's platform it was difficult to compose statuesque groups that would show well from all sides. When spectacle was desired, it was obtained by pageantry or procession.

THE ABSENCE OF PAINTED SCENERY

However important in effect the absence of elaborate scenery, light effects, and similar theatrical trumpery may have been for Elizabethan drama, the lack, as we have seen, did not come from lack of knowledge. At the court, where Italian influence was strongest, movable scenery for plays and masques had been in use for years. In the Revels Accounts are numerous payments for "drawing the city and temple of Jerusalem and painting towers," "canvas to cover divers towns and houses and clouds and other devices," "canvas for a monster," "apt houses made of canvas, framed, fashioned, and painted accordingly," "timber for the rock . . . and for other frames for players' houses," "counterfeiting thunder and lightning," "holly, ivy, fir poles, and moss for the rock in a play," "long boards for the steer of a cloud," "pulleys for the clouds and curtains," "double girts to hang the sun in the cloud," "sponges for snowballs," and "provision and carriage of trees and other things to the court for a wilderness in a play."[2] At Oxford in 1605, there were greater wonders still. The students entertained their king at a play for which the stage-set was

> a false wall fair painted and adorned with stately pillars, which pillars could turn about; by reason whereof, with the aid of other painted cloths their stage did vary three times in the acting of one tragedy. (*Progresses, Processions, and Festivities of James I,* ed. John Nichols [1828], I, 538.)

Later, the architectural ingenuity of Inigo Jones contrived other marvels. One may be sure that, had the practicability of movable scenery for the public stage been demonstrated, the Elizabethan showmen would have adopted it. As is, such devices simply do not belong in an amphitheatre. They are useful only when the scene does not shift rapidly or when the theatre has the modern box-stage.

Instead, the public theatres gained their pictorial effects with the aid of the poet. To a large extent, we owe the exquisite descriptions in Shakespeare's plays to the conditions of his stage. What modern scenic artist can surpass the setting for Lorenzo and Jessica's honeymooning?

> How sweet the moonlight sleeps upon this bank!
> Here will we sit and let the sounds of music
> Creep in our ears. Soft stillness and the night
> Become the touches of sweet harmony.
> Sit, Jessica. Look how the floor of heaven
> Is thick inlaid with patens of bright gold.
> There's not the smallest orb which thou behold'st
> But in his motion like an angel sings,
> Still quiring to the young-ey'd cherubins.
> Such harmony is in immortal souls;
> But, whilst this muddy vesture of decay
> Doth grossly close it in, we cannot hear it.
> Come, ho, and wake Diana with a hymn;
> With sweetest touches pierce your mistress' ear
> And draw her home with music.
> (*The Merchant of Venice,* V, i, 54 ff.)

But if we read these lines only as the work of a descriptive poet substituting for the scene-painter and the electrician, we miss half their beauty. They are the work of an artist in dramatic effects as well. How appropriate a setting

---

[2] *Documents Relating to the Office of the Revels in the Time of Queen Elizabeth,* ed. Albert Feuillerat, Louvain (1908).

they provide for the happy, successful homecoming of Portia and for her words about a good deed in a naughty world! And what contrast their peace and harmony present to the bitter anguish of Antonio's trial!

There are many other instances of such dramatic scene-painting in Shakespeare. Duncan's and Banquo's famous description of Macbeth's stronghold is another:

> This castle hath a pleasant seat; the air
> Nimbly and sweetly recommends itself
> Unto our gentle senses. . . .
>
>   This guest of summer,
> The temple-haunting martlet, does approve,
> By his loved mansionry, that the heaven's breath
> Smells wooingly here. No jutty, frieze,
> Buttress, nor coign of vantage, but this bird
> Hath made his pendent bed and procreant cradle.
> Where they most breed and haunt, I have observed,
> The air is delicate.
>
>   *(Macbeth,* I, vi, 1 ff.)

How masterly does this peaceful setting where birds build their nests contrast with the treachery within! What canvas setting could so dramatically have portrayed the vast difference between things as they seem and things as they sometimes are? Shakespeare the dramatist is inseparable from Shakespeare the poet.

Shakespeare also occasionally attempted to produce other stage effects by means of his pen. In his open daylight theatre, he created the illusion of darkness during the conspiracy in *Julius Cæsar.* Just a few lines give the setting of the pale, threatening dawn before Shrewsbury (*1 Henry IV,* V, i, 1 ff.); of enchanted yellow sands in *The Tempest* (I, i, 376 ff.); of the storm-torn heath in *King Lear* (III, i ff.); and of the romantic moonlit orchard for love-making in *Romeo and Juliet* (II, ii, 1 ff.). With a few words, he created the breaking day and singing birds at the parting of the same lovers, or, in *Much Ado* (III, i), the orchard and the

>   pleached bower
> Where honey-suckles ripened by the sun,
> Forbid the sun to enter.

Descriptive lines such as these, resulting in great part from the needs of Shakespeare's theatre, are art of the highest kind.

Moreover, there can be little doubt that Shakespeare's stage was not only responsible for the vagueness of place and the rapidity of action so characteristic of Elizabethan drama, but that it also encouraged romantic, far-away scenes. No local color was possible or necessary on the platform; one could wander where one's fancy led him. How superficial was the local color of the average Elizabethan play is illustrated by Jonson's *Every Man in His Humour*. As originally written, the play had the conventional Italian setting and Italian *dramatis personæ*. But all that was needed to convert it into a comedy of English life was to remove it to London and change the names of the characters and places. In Shakespeare's plays, a remote setting is of no greater importance. What is there of Italy in *Romeo and Juliet* or *The Merchant of Venice*, of classical Athens in *Timon* or *A Midsummer Night's Dream*, except what one is willing to read into them? Alter a few words, change the names of the characters, and the setting is anywhere.

One recalls with amusement the scrupulous care of the early nineteenth-century actor, Charles Kean, that every detail in his elaborate mountings for Shakespeare should be accurate. When he put on *The Winter's Tale* in 1856, his preparations would have done credit to any research department in Hollywood. Observing that the pivot of the plot around which the story revolves is the appeal to the oracle at Delphi, he chose as the proper time for his production the period when Syracuse had developed from a mere Doric colony into a rival in splendor of Athens itself. *Tableaux vivants* presented the private and public life of the ancient Greeks. Instead of a dance of the twelve rustics "who have made themselves all men of hair," there was a dance in honor of Bacchus, as more in keeping with the season in which a classical sheep-shearing would take place. "Time, as Chorus" was replaced by Chronon, the ancient representative of Time, set in "an allegorical tableau of Luna and the Stars (personified) sinking before the Car of Phœbus." In the interests of chronological consistency, modern Bohemia gave way to ancient Bithynia, which was metrically suitable and gave opportunity for marked contrast in costume between Greek and Phrygian dress. The background was decorated with "vegetation peculiar to Bithynia," adopted from the private drawings of George Scharf, Esq., F. S. A., "taken on the spot." What *would* William Shakespeare have thought of such a truly awe-inspiring production? (See illustration p. 455.)

THE INFLUENCE OF THE COMPANY

The physical stage was not the only force that moulded Shakespearean drama; the Elizabethan player left his mark as well. Most important was the absence of women actors, a lack which can be seen in almost every play. To-day we wonder how boys could interpret a Juliet, a Rosalind, a Portia, or a Cleopatra; but Shakespeare's contemporaries, with less faith in feminine capability, wondered how women could possibly do as well. Thomas Coryat, the traveler, mentioned having seen actresses in Venice, but found English boys preferable. As we have seen, these boy actors were not untrained amateurs, but the apprentices or understudies of their masters, and as carefully trained as any actress today. To do what the lord asks in the Induction to *The Taming of the Shrew* requires no mean skill:

> Sirrah, go you to Barthol'mew my page,
> And see him dress'd in all suits like a lady.
> That done, conduct him to the drunkard's chamber;
> And call him madam, do him obeisance.
> Tell him from me, as he will win my love,
> He bear himself with honorable action,
> Such as he hath observ'd in noble ladies
> Unto their lords, by them accomplished;
> Such duty to the drunkard let him do
> With soft low tongue and lowly courtesy. . . .
> And then with kind embracements, tempting kisses,
> And with declining head into his bosom,
> Bid him shed tears, as being overjoy'd
> To see her noble lord restor'd to health. . . .
> And if the boy have not a woman's gift
> To rain a shower of commanded tears,
> An onion will do well for such a shift. . . .
> I know the boy will well usurp the grace,
> Voice, gait, and action of a gentlewoman.
>
> (i, 105 ff.)[a]

A boy's period of usefulness as an actress, of course, was limited by the breaking of his voice. Hence, Hamlet's greeting to one of the players is meaningless when, on the modern stage, it is addressed to a girl:

What, my young lady and mistress! By'r lady, your ladyship is nearer to heaven than when I saw you last, by the altitude of a chopine. Pray God, your voice, like a piece of uncurrent gold, be not cracked within the ring. (II, ii, 444 ff.)

The prince is playfully referring to a boy whose growth he feared would soon render him unfit for women's roles. There are numerous other allusions to the convention in Shakespeare's work. Flute, the bellows-mender's apprentice in *A Midsummer Night's Dream*, objects to playing Thisbe because he

---

[a] Compare Ben Jonson's tribute to Dick Robinson:

> There's Dickey Robinson,
> A very pretty fellow, and comes often
> To a gentleman's chamber, a friend of mine. We had
> The merriest supper of it there, one night,
> The gentleman's landlady invited him
> To a gossip's feast. Now he, sir, brought Dick Robinson,
> Dressed like a lawyer's wife, amongst them all;
> I lent him clothes.—But to see him behave it,
> And lay the law, and carve and drink unto them,
> And then talk bawdy, and send frolics! O,
> It would have burst your buttons, or not left you
> A seam.   (*The Devil Is an Ass*, II, iii.)

has a beard coming (I, ii, 49 ff.); Cleopatra envisions that odious day when her story will be put on the stage by the "quick comedians" and "some squeaking Cleopatra boy [her] greatness i' the posture of a whore" (V, ii, 219 ff.). Sometimes the situation created is quite whimsical, as when the boy who plays Julia in *The Two Gentlemen*, disguised as a boy once more, mentions his selection to play a woman's part in a Pentecost play (IV, iv, 163 ff.), or when the actor who is Rosalind speaks the Epilogue to *As You Like It* half in character and half out. Whatever else may be true, it is at least pleasant to reflect that playgoers of Shakespeare's age were spared the ordeal of elderly Rosalinds, Juliets, and Violas. In another age, when the custom had degenerated, Thomas Jordan could write:

> Our women are defective, and so siz'd
> You'd think they were some of the Guard disguis'd.
> For (to speak truth) men act, that are between
> Forty and fifty, wenches of fifteen;
> With bone so large, and nerve so incompliant,
> When you call "Desdemona," enter Giant.[4]

The time was ripe for women to come to the stage.

The necessity of using boys in women's roles seriously affected the Elizabethan dramatist. Excellent mimics they may be, but boys cannot be expected to enter into emotions that are alien to their experiences or their natures. A boy's interpretation of feminine roles, therefore, might be convincing as far as it went, but it would be objective on the whole and lacking in the fuller, more subtle emotional qualities that a girl would bring to the same roles. Shakespeare's writing was doubtless affected to a marked degree by this fact. One is struck immediately by the few feminine characters in the average Elizabethan play. Generally speaking, too, Elizabethan heroines seem simple and uncomplicated as compared with the men. Even Shakespeare's finest heroines run to conventional types—the sentimental, like Viola or Julia; the pathetic, like Desdemona, Imogen, or Ophelia; the witty, like Maria, Portia, or Rosalind. Only in the case of the strong woman, like Cleopatra and Lady Macbeth, are they drawn on a scale comparable to that of the men.

The frequency with which these characters adopt male attire impresses even the casual reader. Julia in *The Two Gentlemen* follows her false Proteus as a page. Viola in *Twelfth Night* serves Orsino. Portia and Nerissa impersonate a lawyer and his clerk, and Jessica elopes disguised as a boy. Rosalind becomes Ganymede and Imogen becomes Fidele. In some cases, Shakespeare's sources furnish the reason; in others the expedient may be traced to the tradition of classical comedy. But not in all. On the modern stage, even a girl has difficulty managing full Elizabethan skirts. Could it be that the Elizabethan

[4] *A Prologue to Introduce the First Woman that Came to Act in the Tragedy Call'd the Moor of Venice* (1660).

dramatist made dramatic capital of the conventions of his stage by allowing his boys to masquerade as themselves so that they could devote their attentions wholly to their parts and lend greater realism to their playing? It has been pointed out that the chief examples of such disguise in Shakespeare are found in plays that may be dated within a few years of one another, and that there was perhaps a boy in the Shakespearean company who was a good actress, but who simply could not be happy in farthingales.

Be that as it may, it is perfectly certain that Shakespeare wrote without one of the principal stocks in trade of the modern producer. He could put no reliance upon "feminine charm" to carry his plays. The modern playgoer is all too familiar with the actress who has little to commend her save looks, vivacity, and the ability to wear clothes. But the convention of the boy actors affected more than the cast. Love in Shakespeare, it has been noticed, is a healthy, normal, matter-of-fact emotion, something to be reverenced, feared, mocked at, as the case may be. But there are no "vamps" among Shakespeare's women, few coquettes, and no neurasthenics. As the late Harley Granville-Barker observed, Shakespeare had to be constantly careful to demand nothing of his boy actresses that might be unseemly or ridiculous and so destroy the effect he was trying to produce. On the coarser side, scenes which feature Doll Tearsheet and Mistress Overdone are checked and kept from going too far; on the sentimental side, though Constance mourns over little Arthur, Lady Macduff is shown with her little son, and Hermione and her maids amuse Mamillius, there is in Shakespeare's plays no mother crooning over a babe in arms.

Love scenes, especially, are tactfully managed. The young fleshly love of Romeo and Juliet is beautifully idealized. The lovers are seldom alone for any length of time, except in that most famous of all love-scenes, the "balcony scene," and then they are kept from all contact with each other. Juliet is at her casement window, and Romeo is in the garden below. A more significant example is *Antony and Cleopatra*. Here is a tragedy of sex without a single scene of passion. The voluptuousness of Cleopatra is by no means unemphasized, but it is reflected in talk about her when she is out of sight. Philo and Enobarbus are not at all mealy-mouthed in their descriptions of her (I, i; II, ii), but the squeaking boy who played the role was not required to act accordingly. The lovers have only half a dozen scenes together in the entire play, and most of them are scenes of chiding rather than of love. Only when the play has plunged toward tragedy and Antony's infatuation for Cleopatra has been lost in something deeper, are they shown in each other's arms. But the scene is Cleopatra's monument, and they are chaperoned by Death. One has but to consider a Cleopatra created to the advantage of a modern actress to appreciate Shakespeare's lack. Summing up the demands made of the modern actress playing Cleopatra, Granville-Barker concluded:

Shakespeare . . . has left no blank spaces for her to fill with her charm. He asks instead for a self-forgetful clarity of perception, and for a sensitive, spirited, athletic beauty of speech and conduct, which will leave prettiness and its lures at a loss, and the crudities of more Circean appeal looking very crude indeed. (*Prefaces to Shakespeare*, First Series [1927], pp. xxvii ff.)

Elizabethan actors, however, conditioned the dramatists in even a larger and more vital way. All of Shakespeare's plays were composed for one particular group of actors who constituted the company to which he belonged, and at every stage of his work he had to bear that company in mind. Only occasionally, as in the case of *Love's Labor's Lost, A Midsummer Night's Dream, The Merry Wives of Windsor*, and *The Tempest*, does he seem to have been writing for an unusual company, and in these cases it was probably his own troupe augmented by a troupe of boy actors. Nowadays, as a dramatist writes, he has in mind at most only a few special players, perhaps only the star, for whom he is designing roles. He does not usually know beforehand who will act the parts he is creating. A special company is engaged for every new play, and the producer selects his performers from a number of unemployed actors and actresses. In Shakespeare's time, the only reputable actors, like the playwrights, were attached to one or another of the existing companies in London. The poet, therefore, composed his plays with a full knowledge of just what talent his troupe afforded.

Indeed, in both the quarto and folio texts of *Much Ado*, the names of the actors Kempe and Cowley appear instead of those of the characters Dogberry and Verges (IV, ii); in the second quarto of *Romeo and Juliet* the name of Will Kempe is found instead of Peter (IV, v). Whether or not Shakespeare himself was responsible for the substitution in these cases, there can be no doubt that he frequently thought of his *dramatis personæ*, not only as characters in a story, but as parts which were to be fitted to particular actors as well.

In fact, Professor T. W. Baldwin, who has most recently studied the personnel of the Shakespearean company, is so deeply impressed by its influence upon Shakespeare's playwriting that he believes his work can be divided into definite periods solely upon a knowledge of the talents of the leading actors who made up the company, and that the type of play changed as the type of actors in the company changed. It cannot be accidental, he writes,[5] that the four periods into which Shakespeare's work is conventionally divided correspond to four major reorganizations in the company. His first period was predominantly one of comedy, not a surprising circumstance when one remembers who were the principal actors at the time: Will Kempe, the famous clown; Thomas Pope, also famous as a comedian and probably in

[5] *The Organization and Personnel of the Shakespearean Company*, Princeton (1927), pp. 310 ff.

roles of the *miles gloriosus* type, like Falstaff; Augustine Phillips, a musician with some comic tendencies; and John Heminge, who probably performed whimsically humorous characters. The natural tendency of this company would be to comedy. During the greater part of the second period, 1595–1600, the former membership remained intact, with some significant additions. In 1594, Shakespeare himself, whose natural bent, Professor Baldwin believes, was toward the serious, was admitted as a member. So was Richard Burbage, who became the famous tragedian. Other new members were Henry Condell, who performed a dignified line, and William Sly, who essayed the fiery juvenile lead, with a touch of comedy. Hence, there was a tendency to a more serious type of play, still prevailingly comic, but to high comedy, not low. The third period was predominantly serious. Burbage and Shakespeare were the controlling forces in the company. Kempe, who had withdrawn in 1599, was succeeded by Robert Armin, whose specialty was satirical court jesters, not slapstick clowns. Pope also became inactive, and Augustine Phillips died. An important addition, John Lowin, was famous for his gruff soldier parts. In 1608, another change of direction was reflected in Shakespeare's work. The company took over Blackfriars, the stronghold of one of the children's companies, and with it two of the principal actors of the boys' company, William Ostler and John Underwood, who had by this time grown to manhood. The manager of the company that formerly occupied Blackfriars was trying to keep his troupe together. Therefore, it became necessary for the Shakespearean company to exert itself to retain the Blackfriars clientele by providing the dramatic fare with which the "little eyases" drew their select audience—music, both instrumental and vocal, dancing, masque elements, tragicomedy, and romance.

Whether or not the company in every case had so radical an influence upon the dramatist, certainly the writer or adaptor had to take into account, not only the actors' capabilities, but their physical qualities as well, and to refrain from introducing into a part anything that was unsuited to the player taking it. It has been pointed out that Shakespeare's heroines show an important variation, not necessarily because Shakespeare was interested in a particular type of woman at a particular time, but because there was an apprentice in the company whose natural expression was that type of woman. A not very reliable tradition says that "the person that acted Iago was in much esteem for a comedian which made Shakespeare put several words and expressions into his part (perhaps not so agreeable to his character) to make the audience laugh." Also, the presence of the singing actor in the plays of a particular period in Shakespeare's career—Balthazar in *Much Ado*, Amiens in *As You Like It*, Feste in *Twelfth Night*, and the Fool in *King Lear*—is not so much evidence of especial sunniness in the dramatist's outlook upon life, as of the fact that, just then, there was in the company a player with a good singing voice, perhaps Jack Wilson, who, we know, took the role of Balthazar.

The necessity of finding parts for popular actors may account for several scenes in Shakespeare, such as those featuring Peter and the musicians in *Romeo and Juliet*, the drunken porter in *Macbeth*, and the grave-diggers in *Hamlet*. Charles Cowden Clarke says of the scene in *Romeo and Juliet* that it was the poet's intention "to show how grief and gaiety, pathos and absurdity, sorrow and jesting, elbow each other in life's crowd." And De Quincey's essay *On the Knocking at the Gate in Macbeth* is famous:

> When the deed is done, when the work of darkness is perfect . . . the knocking at the gate is heard, and it makes known audibly that the reaction has commenced; the human has made its reflux upon the fiendish: the pulses of life are beginning to beat again.

These and other scenes have found favor in the eyes of critics and audiences alike. But, in introducing his very human clowns, Shakespeare was probably just making dramatic capital of necessity.

The recurrence of certain physical types in Shakespeare's plays suggests that the adaptation of play to company extended to personal details of stature, build, and temperament. Very noticeable is a physical contrast in heroines running through several plays, the one a short vivacious brunette, the other a tall statuesque blonde. In *A Midsummer Night's Dream*, this disparate pair is represented by Hermia and Helena. Little Hermia is spoken of as an "Ethiope" and a "tawny Tartar," and she is very sensitive about her size. "Though she be but little, she is fierce . . . she was a vixen when she went to school," warns Helena, and Lysander does not improve her temper by calling her "you dwarf, you minimus . . . you bead, you acorn." She turns upon the tall Helena who has slightingly called her "puppet" in the lovers' quarrel:

> Puppet? Why so? Ay, that way goes the game.
> Now I perceive that she hath made compare
> Between our statures; she hath urged her height;
> And with her personage, her tall personage,
> Her height, forsooth, she hath prevail'd with him.
> And are you grown so high in his esteem,
> Because I am so dwarfish and so low?
> How low am I, thou painted May-pole? Speak!
> How low am I? I am not yet so low
> But that my nails can reach unto thine eyes.
>   (III, ii, 289 ff.)

A similar contrast is found in *Love's Labor's Lost* between the "amber-colour'd raven," Katherine, whose beauty is somewhat marred by smallpox (V, ii, 45), and Rosaline, "a whitely wanton, with a velvet brow, with two pitch-balls stuck in her face for eyes" (III, i, 198–9). Another comparable pair, with a variation as to disposition, appears later in *Much Ado* and in *As You Like It*. In the former play, Beatrice is tall and vivacious, while Hero, "Leonato's short daughter," is "too low for a high praise, too brown for a fair praise, and too little for a great praise" (I, i, 173 ff.). In the latter, Rosalind is "more than common tall," while Celia is "low and browner than her brother." Other feminine contrasts probably existed in Shakespeare's theatre between Julia and Silvia in *The Two Gentlemen*, Nerissa, "the little scrubbed boy," and Portia in *The Merchant of Venice*, and Maria and Viola in *Twelfth Night*. Maria's size and lively officiousness are distinctly emphasized. She is "the little villain," "the youngest wren of nine," and, ironically or teasingly, Olivia's "giant," or "Penthesilia," for she was no Amazon. Yet a New York producer, not many years ago, assigned the part to a plump matronly lady who had been excellent as Juliet's nurse, and, though he cut other parts of the play, retained these allusions to Maria's physique without sensing their absurdity.

Among distinct male parts, there is that of the tall, lean man with a thin face. He is the "saffron-faced" Pinch, the conjuring school master in *The Comedy of Errors*, "a hungry, lean-faced, villain; a mere anatomy . . . a needy, hollow-eyed, sharp-looking wretch; a living dead man," who administers to the supposedly mad Antipholus. He is Don Armado in *Love's Labor's Lost* and Prince Hal in *1 Henry IV*. "You starveling," cries Falstaff, "you elf-skin, you dried neat's tongue. . . . O for breath to utter what is like thee! You tailor's-yard, you sheath, you bow-case, you vile standing-tuck" (II, iv, 270 ff.). In Part II of the same play, this actor probably doubled in the role of the "half-faced fellow, Shadow," one of Falstaff's recruits. "Give me this man," exclaims that doughty captain, "he presents no mark to the enemy; the foe may with as great aim level at the edge of a penknife" (III, ii, 283 ff.). Later in the play, it is not impossible that he also took the part of one of the beadles, that "filthy famish'd correctioner," that "thin thing," that "starved blood-hound," "goodman Death, goodman Bones" (V, iv, 23 ff.). In his youth, too, Justice Shallow was just such a walking shadow, "the very genius of famine." "You might have thrust him and all his apparel into an eel-skin" (III, ii, 325 ff.). Falstaff, "saw'd into quantities," would make "four dozen of such bearded hermits' staves" as he (V, i, 70 ff.). The same actor, perhaps, is the "half-faced" Robert Faulconbridge in *King John* (I, i, 92 ff.); he reappears in *Julius Cæsar* as "spare Cassius" with the "lean and hungry look" (I, ii, 194 ff.) and in *Twelfth Night* as that "thin-fac'd knave," Sir Andrew Aguecheek, who is "as tall a man as any's in Illyria" and whose hair "hangs like flax on a distaff" (I, iii, 20, 108). In *The Merry Wives* he is Slender, who "hath but a little whey face, with a little yellow beard, a Cain-colour'd beard" (I, iv, 22).

Apart from the merely physical likenesses, there are other family resemblances among Shakespeare's characters that suggest the influence of his company of actors. There is a likeness among the early clowns—Dromio, Costard, Bully Bottom, Launcelot Gobbo, Launce—and later among the court jesters—Touchstone, Feste, Lear's Fool, and Trinculo. There is the coarse woman, like Juliet's nurse, Mrs. Quickly, and Mrs. Overdone. There is the cheeky little page-boy, like Moth in *Love's Labor's Lost*, or the lad who attends Falstaff (*2 Henry IV*). This boy transfers his services to Pistol in *Henry V*, and, having grown a little older, is Robin in *The Merry Wives*. There is also the fat man addicted to sack, like Falstaff and Sir Toby Belch; and the affected water-fly, usually acting the dull foolish lover, like Thurio in *The Two Gentlemen*, Monsieur Le Beau in *As You Like It*, Malvolio in *Twelfth Night*, Osric in *Hamlet*, and Roderigo in *Othello*. In addition, but no less distinct, there are those dashing secondary roles, like Faulconbridge, Hotspur, Richmond, Mercutio, and Cassio; heavy parts, like Don John in *Much Ado*, Edmund in *Lear*, Iago in *Othello*, the usurping duke in *As You Like It*, and the king in *Hamlet*; and those of dignified old men, like Ægeon in *The Comedy of Errors*, Friar Laurence in *Romeo and Juliet*, Brabantio in *Othello*, Duncan in *Macbeth*, the Chief Justice in *2 Henry IV*, the duke in *Measure for Measure*, and Gonzalo in *The Tempest*. All of these character-types, in some measure, may bear the marks of actors in Shakespeare's company.

SOME ADVANTAGES OF THE ELIZABETHAN STAGE

Thus far, we have considered only those influences of Elizabethan theatrical conditions which were in the nature of limitations upon the dramatist. But Shakespeare's stage had some advantages; it provided a maximum of liberty for both the playwright and the player. Something has already been said about the effect of Shakespeare's flexible stage upon the structure of Elizabethan plays and the way in which it simplified the problem of setting. In choice of theme, too, the Elizabethan stage afforded the playwright opportunities which the modern dramatist is denied. Drama to the Elizabethans was a narrative art, a story put into action and told rather than fully realized. The plots of Elizabethan plays are often not dramatic in the modern sense, because the play is rather just a history, a novel, or a tale told in dialogue. The author could begin at the beginning and tell his story in all its details as does the novelist. One can readily see how little difference there is in narrative method by comparing one of Shakespeare's plays with the novel or tale from which it was derived. *Pericles, As You Like It, The Winter's Tale* —to name only a few—are not constructed in the conventional way approved by the modern dramatist. The continuity of performance on the Elizabethan stage, and the ease with which in presentation one scene could blend into another without long waits for shifting scenery, encouraged a continuity in the Elizabethan drama that is matched in modern times only by the moving picture. Shakespeare's technique in telling a story is, in some respects, not unlike that of the cinema. How effective these plays can be has been demonstrated again and again by producers who have recaptured the Elizabethan tempo and presented them as a succession of scenes.

The history plays, particularly, are often loose in construction. They are frequently episodic without any dominating conflict, a series of dramatic situations clustered about some central figure. The *Henry VI* plays were, to a large extent, constructed in this fashion. The story to be told was a long one. The dramatist, therefore, simply measured off five acts of it and called it a play. The *Henry IV* plays are more centralized, but not altogether unlike the earlier ones. Shakespeare, however, improved his structure as time went on. With his interest in people, he came to consider history plays as little different from ordinary tragedies and constructed them around a central dominating character, as in *King John, Richard II, Richard III,* and *Henry V.* Successive stages in this development may be noticed in the plays mentioned.

Other plays reveal the same looseness of structure. The average Elizabethan comedy was more like a vaudeville show than a well-made play. "Player hath many times many excellent qualities," wrote T. G. in *The Rich Cabinet* (1616), "as dancing, activity, music, song, elocution, ability of body, memory, vigilancy, skill of weapon, pregnancy of wit, and such like." We have already mentioned Elizabethan stage spectacle, but there was variety entertainment as well. Two-man sets, practical jokes, horse-play, and general buffoonery are frequently found, even in Shakespeare. And there are the acrobatics, the elaborate duels, and the use of trained animals. Dromio is beaten, Tybalt fights "by the book of arithmetic," Orlando wrestles with the duke's champion, and Launce talks to his dog. Trinculo is attracted by the idea of taking Caliban to England and exhibiting him as a strange fish, and, in Jasper Mayne's *The City Match,* a foolish lout is made drunk and actually exhibited as a monster in a side-show.

Some of these tricks belong to a tradition as old as that of the roaring devils of the religious drama. All were sure-fire entertainment, and Shakespeare's public applauded, just as the public applauds the same stuff today. Sir William Davenant, adopting a superior air to all this in the Prologue to *The Unfortunate Lovers* (1638), speaks of the "good easy judging souls" of the past age,

> with what delight
> They would expect a jig, or target fight,
> A furious tale of Troy, which they ne'er thought
> Was weakly written so 'twere strongly fought.

Shakespeare called the same kind of play a show of "fool and fight" (Prologue to *Henry VIII*). It was begot of his intimate stage and the tastes of his audience. Shakespeare's contemporaries used song, dance, and other stage tricks with varying degrees of skill; he himself usually made them serve some dramatic purpose when he could. If not, they went in anyway, sometimes with as little relevance or logic as similar elements have in a modern "talkie" or musical comedy.

To say, of course, that all of these characteristics we have been discussing were wholly traceable to stage conditions and stage customs would be untrue. Where the art begot the convention or the convention the art cannot always be determined. But that, in the theatre of the Elizabethan time, there existed a whole code of conventions cannot be denied, and their influence upon the drama was profound. It is likewise untrue to say that, with new conventions, it is wholly impossible to produce Elizabethan plays. In our theatre we do not, of course, see Shakespeare's plays as they were intended to be produced. In the necessary modification—mangling sometimes—to make them fit the picture-frame stage, we see a compromise. Only rarely do we find an effort made to adapt the stage to the play, and not the play to the stage. In addition, Shakespeare's stage greatly contributed to his plays as works of literature. "It is a noble and just advantage," wrote Ben Jonson about court masques in the Preface to *The Masque of Hymen* (1606):

> that the things subjected to understanding have of those which are objected to sense; that the one sort are but momentary, and merely taking; the other impressing, and lasting: else the glory of all these solemnities had perished like a blaze, and gone out, in the beholders' eyes. So short-lived are the bodies of all things in comparison of their souls. And though bodies oftimes have the ill luck to be sensually preferred, they find afterwards the good fortune (when souls live) to be utterly forgotten.

In conclusion, it must not be inferred that a lack of knowledge of the theatrical conditions of Shakespeare's day excludes one permanently from the soul of Shakespeare's dramas. It is comparatively unimportant to an appreciation of what is vital in the work of Shakespeare who was "not of an age, but for all time." We cannot turn Elizabethan to see and hear his plays. But enough has been said to demonstrate that such knowledge is a wonderful aid to a proper comprehension, and, in some cases, the only means of understanding him. Shakespeare was an Elizabethan playwright, writing his plays to be performed by Elizabethan actors in an Elizabethan theatre before an Elizabethan audience. By now he has become much more. But the understanding of that fact is the beginning of wisdom where a study of Shakespeare is concerned.

When, in 1623, Heminge and Condell gathered between the covers of one book the plays they thought should belong to the corpus of "Master William

Shakespeare's Comedies, Histories, and Tragedies," their labor of love made posterity eternally grateful. But it also laid the foundation for future misconceptions. The demand which gave rise to the publication of the First Folio was for Shakespeare's plays as reading matter. They came to be regarded as literature and less and less as pieces for the stage. Libraries became their abode, and the claim of the theatre was secondary. In the eighteenth century, when Shakespeare's works required an editor, theatrical conventions had changed. His editors have been poets, antiquarians, bibliographers, or critics who knew books and not the theatre. The commentators on his works have eulogized him as poet, philosopher, moralist, botanist, lawyer, and expert on mental diseases. Too frequently have they forgotten that what has become great literature for us was, for the author and his contemporaries, only words to be mouthed by actors on a stage.

SUGGESTED REFERENCES

BOAS, GUY. "The Influence of the Boy Actor on Shakespeare's Plays," *The Contemporary Review*, CLV (1937), pp. 69–77.

BRADBROOK, M. C. *Elizabethan Stage Conditions: A Study of Their Place in the Interpretation of Shakespeare's Plays.* Cambridge University Press, 1932.

DAVIES, WILLIAM ROBERTSON. *Shakespeare's Boy Actors.* London, Dent, 1939.

GRANVILLE-BARKER, HARLEY. *Prefaces to Shakespeare* (5 vols.). London, Sidgwick and Jackson, 1927–47.

A series of studies of individual plays by an experienced practical man of the theatre. The plays treated are: (I) *Love's Labor's Lost, Julius Cæsar, King Lear;* (II) *Romeo and Juliet, The Merchant of Venice, Antony and Cleopatra, Cymbeline;* (III) *Hamlet;* (IV) *Othello, Macbeth, Coriolanus.* Also published in two volumes, Princeton University Press, 1946–47.

HALE, E. E., JR. "The Influence of Theatrical Conditions on Shakespeare," *Modern Philology,* I (1904), pp. 171 ff.

HARBAGE, ALFRED. "Elizabethan Acting," *Publications of the Modern Language Association,* LIV (1939), pp. 685–708.

7

SHAKESPEARE'S AUDIENCE

How is't possible to suffice
So many ears, so many eyes?
Some in wit, and some in shows
Take delight, and some in clothes.
Some for mirth they chiefly come,
Some for passion,—for both some;
Some for lascivious meetings, that's their arrant;
Some to detract, and ignorance their warrant.
How is't possible to please
Opinion toss'd in such wild seas?
—Thomas Middleton, *No Wit, No Help Like a Woman's* (1613)

As we have seen, elizabethan critical opinion was, on the whole, unreasonably prejudiced against both plays and players. Even playgoers did not escape censure and disparagement:

> Now the common haunters are for the most part the lewdest persons in the land, apt for pilfery, perjury, forgery, or other rogueries, the very scum, rascality, and baggage of the people, thieves, cutpurses, shifters, cozeners; briefly an unclean generation and spawn of vipers. Must not here be a good rule, where is such a brood of Hell-bred creatures? For a play is like a sink in a town, whereunto all the filth doth run, or a bile in the body that draweth all the ill humors unto it. (Henry Crosse, *Virtue's Commonwealth, or The Highway to Honour,* 1603.)

THE COMPOSITION OF THE ELIZABETHAN AUDIENCE

But through such biased opinions, however, one fact about the Elizabethan audience stands out most clearly. Whether or not you frequented the theatre in Shakespeare's day depended in no way upon your condition in life, for the Elizabethan playhouse was one of the most democratic of institutions. "The place," said Thomas Dekker in his *Gull's Hornbook* (1609),

> is so free in entertainment, allowing a stool as well to the farmer's son as to your Templar, that your stinkard has the self-same liberty to be there in his tobacco fumes which your sweet courtier hath; and that your carman and tinker claim

as strong a voice in their suffrage and sit to give judgment on the play's life and death as well as the proudest Momus among the tribe of critic.

Ben Jonson, too, alluded to the diversity of folk that filled the theatres. "The wise and many-headed bench," he wrote, "that sits upon the life and death of plays, is

> Compos'd of gamester, captain, knight, knight's man,
> Lady or pucelle, that wears mask or fan,
> Velvet or taffeta cap, rank'd in the dark,
> With the shop's foreman, or some such brave spark,
> That may judge for his sixpence.
> (Commendatory Verses to Fletcher's
> *The Faithful Shepherdess,* 1608-10.)

Playhouses varied in their appeal; they flourished and declined in popularity, gained unsavory reputations, or became known for a particular type of offering or style of acting. Toward the close of Shakespeare's career, the Red Bull seems to have become the resort of the rougher element; the Theatre and the Curtain declined when the new Bankside houses drew audiences to Southwark; the Admiral's Men were characterized by the vigorous, melodramatic acting of Edward Alleyn in the *Hieronimo, Tamburlaine,* and *Faustus* plays that suited him. What Hamlet condemned as "inexplicable dumb show and noise" quite conceivably satisfied a Rose audience. The actors at the Red Bull and the Fortune were described as "terrible tear-throats." Private theatres, like Blackfriars and Paul's, may have attracted a more refined type of playgoer. The author of *Jack Drum's Entertainment* (1600), a Paul's School play, rejoiced in the opportunity of commending his audience:

> I like the audience that frequenteth here
> With much applause. A man shall not be choked
> With the stench of garlic, nor be pasted
> To the barmy jacket of a beer brewer.

At this distance in time, however, most of the differences have been leveled down. The average Elizabethan audience ranged from noblemen, like the young Earl of Southampton, who were daily frequenters of playhouses, to the rabble of apprentices and cutpurses, who cracked nuts and fought for bitten apples in the pit. In Middleton and Dekker's *The Roaring Girl* (*c.* 1610), a Fortune play, Sir Alexander walks to the front of the stage and shows his friends his magnificent house:

> Stories of men and women, mix'd together,
> Fair ones with foul, like sunshine in wet weather. (I, i.)

It is a fair summary of the average theatre audience. But what the ratio was in the Elizabethan theatre of "squint-eyed groundlings" to gentle folk, men to women, citizens to noblemen, one clique to another, we shall probably never really know. Whether Shakespeare's company catered to the same or to a different clientele from that served by rival companies is also at the present time a subject for speculation, not certain knowledge. There cannot have been a great difference. Shakespeare's audience was a cross-section of the London population of his day. A popular playwright, as Ben Jonson knew, had to concoct something for everyone, dramatic cates which would

> Be fit for ladies; some for lords, knights, 'squires;
> Some for your waiting wench and city wires;
> Some for your men and daughters of Whitefriars.
> (Prologue to *Epicœne*, 1609.)

THEATRE-TYPES

When all is said, detailed information about the Elizabethan playgoers and their playgoing habits is rather scanty. Two main sources of information furnish matter for study: (1) in contemporary literature, there are some sketches of various theatre-types of Shakespeare's day, mainly biased or satirical, and, hence, not very satisfactory witnesses, and (2) there are the inferences about the tastes and psychological make-up of the audience to be drawn from the plays which Shakespeare and his fellow-dramatists placed before it. Taken together, these data tell us a great deal.

"Your gallant, your courtier, and your captain," said Thomas Dekker, "had wont to be [the players'] soundest paymasters." In Henry Fitzgeffrey's *Third Book of Humours* (1617),[1] there is a whole gallery of such theatre-types. The playhouse is Blackfriars, but its patrons cannot have differed greatly from the pleasure-seekers who filled the Globe, the Rose, and the Swan. In any case, with Fitzgeffrey's book in hand, we can take our places early, and at the risk of being made "adder-deaf with pippin cry" and choked with this new Indian pastime, tobacco "drinking," watch an audience assemble.

There is a braggart, Captain Martio, who, if you give him half an opportunity, will recount his marvelous feats and tell you

> How many men a soldier ought to slay
> For a lieutenantship,

or, like Touchstone, read a lecture on the etiquette of picking a fight—when

> Quarrels are mortal, when seconds may come in.

He may boast

> how in fury, crossed,
> For a false reckoning once he slew his host

[1] In *Certain Elegies, Done by Sundry Excellent Wits, with Satires and Epigrams*, reprinted at the Beldornic Press . . . (1843).

or—who should know better?—

> teach you how ye might
> Be counted valiant and never fight.

Next comes the traveler, Sir Iland Hunt, an equally favored butt for Elizabethan satire, who has brought home as a curio a fragment of Jacob's ladder and can tell of stranger things "than Pliny or Herodotus e'er writ of." Then comes a "Cheapside dame," and after her a man of fashion who, like Portia's English suitor, has purchased his garments from the ends of the earth:

> His boot speaks Spanish to his Scottish spurs,
> His suit cut Frenchly, round bestuck with burs;
> Pure Holland is his shirt, which proudly fair,
> Seems to out-face his doublet everywhere. . . .
> What country May-game might we this suppose?
> Sure, one would think a Roman by his nose.
> No! In his habit better understand,
> He is of England by his yellow band.

Next arrive two creatures who are adequately described, one as a "woman of the masculine gender," the other as a "plumed dandebrat," "a lady's shuttle-cock," "a musk-ball milksop":

> This is the puppet which the ladies all
> Send for of purpose and solicit so
> To dance with them.

Following them comes a "misshapen prodigal" with his whole year's revenues upon his back, and with him a "spruce coxcomb,"

> yon affecting ass,
> That never walks without his looking glass
> In a tobacco box or dial [watch] set
> That he may privately confer with it
> How his band jumpeth with his Piccadilly,
> Whether his band strings balance equally,
> Which way his feather wags, and, to say truth,
> What words in utterance best become his mouth.

He even diets to keep his school-boy figure, wears a whalebone bodice, and is best at home in a dancing school. Finally, in Fitzgeffrey's audience are the crabbed playwright himself and his arch-enemy, the truculent critic.

It is unfair, of course, to accept these caricatures as portraits of Elizabethan playgoers. But, if one makes allowance for the shafts of satire, one can perceive the diverse individuals who were attracted to the playhouses and whom the Elizabethan dramatist strove to please. So universal are they that one can recognize their counterparts—male and female—in audiences today. Add to Fitzgeffrey's Blackfriars audience a sprinkling of respectable citizens—an element which grew larger as time went on—a few more women, some students from the Inns of Court, some rowdy apprentices and "understanding men" crowding around the stage, and you have a fair cross-section of the public-theatre audience that filled the Globe. One must not fail, also, to include a fair proportion of the "judicious"—never a conspicuous element in any theatre crowd—but important enough "to outweigh a whole theatre of others." Orazio Busino, chaplain of the Venetian embassy, wrote that the best treat, when he visited the Fortune in 1617, was

> to see such a crowd of nobility so very well arrayed that they looked like so many princes, listening as silently and soberly as possible. These theatres are frequented by a number of respectable and handsome ladies, who come freely and seat themselves among the men without the slightest hesitation. ("Diaries and Despatches of the Venetian Embassy at the Court of King James I in the Years 1617, 1618," translated by Rawdon Brown, in *The Quarterly Review*, CII, 416.)

Busino then described the joke that his Excellency and the Secretary played upon him by placing him in a bevy of fair, but masked, young women, one of whom tried to converse with him in a language he did not understand. These were probably courtesans, but in the group which Busino described there must have been a few persons of breeding and taste. It is too easy to overemphasize the boorish element in the Elizabethan audience and to forget that the public theatres were not a little dependent upon the cultured element of London.[2]

THEATRE BEHAVIOR

How did this miscellaneous crowd behave itself in the playhouse? Enough has already been said to justify the assumption that occasionally some of it was none too tractable. Since seats in the Elizabethan theatres were not as a rule reserved, the zealous playgoers came early and beguiled the time with talk, smoking, card-playing, reading the pamphlets that were hawked about, cracking nuts, eating pippins, or drinking bottle-ale. In *The Unfortunate Lovers* (1638), Sir William Davenant flattered his own audiences by referring to those of twenty years before, who

> to the Theatre would come
> Ere they had din'd to take up the best room;
> There sit on benches, not adorn'd with mats,
> And graciously did vail [lift] their high-crown'd hats
> To every half-dress'd player, as he still
> Through th' hangings peep'd to see how th' house did fill.

By the time the play began this audience was already tired, and the least decorous part of it remained standing during the performance. The peculiar psychology of such a crowd in an open-air theatre must be appreciated.

[2] See J. D. Wilson, *The Elizabethan Shakespeare*, a British Academy Lecture (1929).

Here was an audience eager and alive, quick to accept the fun of "fool and fight," and to distinguish vice from virtue, but not too patient of dullness or of excess subtlety.

Prices of admission to Elizabethan playhouses varied from a penny to as much as half a crown. In 1599, Thomas Platter, a Swiss traveler, described the custom of admission to the theatres:

The playhouses are so constructed that . . . everyone has a good view. There are different galleries and places, however, where the seating is better and more comfortable and therefore more expensive. For whoever cares to stand below only pays one English penny, but if he wishes to sit he enters by another door and pays another penny, but if he desires to sit in the most comfortable seats which are cushioned, where he not only sees everything well, but can also be seen, then he pays yet another English penny at another door. (*Thomas Platter's Travels in England, 1599*, translated by Clare Williams, London [1937], p. 167.)

Once inside the theatre, according to Stephen Gosson, it was

the fashion of youths to go first into the yard and to carry their eye through every gallery, then like unto ravens where they spy the carrion thither they fly, and press as near to the fairest as they can. (*Plays Confuted in Five Actions*, 1582.)

You shall see such heaving and shoving, such itching and shouldering to sit by the women, such care for their garments that they be not trod on . . . such pillows to their backs that they take no hurt . . . such giving them pippins to pass the time . . . such toying, such smiling, such winking, and such manning them home . . . that it is a right comedy to mark their behavior. (*The School of Abuse*, 1579.)

Making allowance for a biased mind, one can read in Gosson's description at least this fact, that in the Elizabethan playhouse there were other things to interest the audience if the play did not.

"Player is much out of countenance," wrote T. G., "if fools do not laugh at them, boys clap their hands, peasants ope their throats, and the rude rascal rabble cry, 'Excellent, Excellent'" (*The Rich Cabinet Furnished with Variety of Descriptions*, 1616). But such approval was probably not so easily obtained as in the modern theatre. The satirical advice which Dekker gave in his *Gull's Hornbook* on "How a Gallant Should Behave Himself in a Playhouse," is a classic and our only full-length account of theatre behavior, even though the gallant is hardly representative of the average theatregoer of the time. Whether in a public or a private playhouse, "our feathered Estridge," advised Dekker, should make his way, not to the gentlemen's rooms where nowadays much new satin is damned and smothered to death in darkness, but to the "very rushes where the comedy is to dance, yea, under the state of Cambises himself." By sitting on the stage, "a conspicuous eminence is gotten, by which means the best and most essential parts of a gallant (good clothes, a proportionable leg, white hand, a Persian lock, and a tolerable beard) are perfectly revealed." Before the play begins, Dekker suggested, the young gallant should fall to cards, and, to impress the ragamuffins who stand about gaping, just at the third sounding, throw the torn cards about the stage as if he had lost. If he has a grudge against the author, or merely wishes to show his eminence as a critic, he should laugh aloud "in the midst of the most serious and saddest scene of the terriblest tragedy," or "rise with a screwed and discontented face" and walk out, not quietly, but saluting all of his acquaintance as he goes. If it should rain and you are obliged to remain or spoil a fine suit, then, added Dekker,

> turn plain ape, take up a rush and tickle the earnest ears of your fellow gallants to make other fools fall a laughing, mew at passionate speeches, blare at merry, find fault with the music . . . whistle at songs.

The gull, Dekker made clear, belonged to no single social class; he might be "a fool or a justice of peace, a cuckold, or a captain, a Lord Mayor's son, or a dawcock, a knave, or an under-sheriff." If he ever really existed at all, he formed only a small portion of the average audience. But he was certainly not the least conspicuous. Dekker does not permit us to believe that the "opposed rascality" in the Elizabethan audience suffered such fools gladly. They hooted, mewed, and hissed; they spat and threw dirt, especially when, to attract the maximum of attention, the gallant played his favorite trick of waiting to take his place until the play began. This would only add to the general commotion. Be that as it may, there is ample reason to believe that an Elizabethan playhouse was a much more rowdy place than most theatres today. Seeking for a figure to make vivid his description of a "troublous noise" with confused shouts and cries, Edmund Spenser said it was "such as the troubled theatres oftimes annoys." "I have known . . . at Shrove-tide," wrote Edmund Gayeton, reminiscing about the "good old days,"

> when the players have been appointed, notwithstanding their bills to the con-trary, to act what the major part of the company had a mind to, sometimes *Tamerlane*, sometimes *Jugurth*, sometimes the *Jew of Malta*, and sometimes parts of all these, and at last, none of the three taking, they were forc'd to un-dress and put off their tragic habits and conclude the day with the merry milk-maids. And unless this were done, and the popular humor satisfied, as sometimes it so fortun'd, that the players were refractory, the benches, the tiles, the laths, the stones, oranges, apples, nuts, flew about most liberally, as there were me-chanics of all professions who fell everyone to his own trade. (*Pleasant Notes upon Don Quixote*, 1654.)

The claque, too, was not unknown. Sometimes those "whose hands are as hard as battledores with clapping" were hired to lead the applause, and, if surmise is correct, no less a person than Jonson, who felt keenly the lack of popular success, made use of them. In *Satiromastix* (1602), Dekker had his Horace (usually thought of as a caricature of Jonson) assert:

> I can bring, and that they quake at, a prepar'd troupe of gallants, who for my sake shall distaste every unsalted line in their fly-blown comedies. (410 ff.)

The audience as a whole, however, must have taken its drama with more respect. "The people generally," says Valentine of the public theatres of Utopia in Jonson's *The Case Is Altered* (before 1609), "are very acceptive, and apt to applaud any meritable work." But he lunges hard at "two sorts of persons that most commonly are infectious to a whole auditory":

> one is the rude barbarous crew, a people that have no brains, and yet grounded judgments; these will hiss anything that mounts above their grounded capacities. But the other . . . a few capricious gallants . . . have taken such a habit of dislike in all things, that they will approve nothing, be it never so conceited or elaborate, but sit dispersed, making faces, and spitting, wagging their upright ears, and cry, "Filthy! Filthy!" . . . to turn the good aspects of all that shall sit near them from that they behold.
>
> But the sport is at a new play, to observe the sway and variety of opinion that passeth it. A man shall have such a confused mixture of judgment, poured out in the throng there, as ridiculous as laughter itself. One says he likes not the writing, another likes not the plot, another not the playing. And sometimes a fellow that comes not there past once in five years, at a parliament time or so, will be as deep mired in censuring as the best. . . . The rankest stinkard of them all will take upon him as peremptory, as if he had writ himself *in artibus magister*. (II, iv.)

One probably did not have to travel far from Jonson's London to know what the author was alluding to. In the Induction to *Bartholomew Fair* (1614), Jonson even had the bookholder and a scrivener draw up articles of agreement between the author and the spectators at the Hope, where the play was first performed:

> Imprimis. It is covenanted and agreed [that] . . . the said spectators and hearers . . . remain in the places their money or friends have put them in, with patience, for the space of two hours and a half, and somewhat more. . . .
>
> It is further agreed that every person here have his or their free-will of censure, to like or dislike at their own charge. . . . It shall be lawful for any man to judge his sixpen'worth, his twelve-pen'worth, so to his eighteen pence, two shillings, half a crown, to the value of his place; provided always his place get not above his wit . . . .

One wonders who, besides the arrogant author, was pleased with stuff like this. It matters little whether these remarks of Jonson's justify any conclusions about what an Elizabethan playwright had to contend with from those who were not of the "judicious." There are some, even in the modern audience, who do not know what to think of a new play until they see the reviews the next morning. Any spectator who buys amusement has the right to say whether he likes it or not. Obviously, by Shakespeare's time, an audience was no longer awed by its entertainment. That it was also receptive of excellence when it was offered is likewise clear, and Shakespeare's popularity speaks well for his Elizabethan auditory.

TASTES OF THE ELIZABETHAN AUDIENCE

What of the psychology and the tastes of the frequenters of Shakespeare's Globe? It is Beaumont and Fletcher's *The Knight of the Burning Pestle*, itself an example of the intimacy between actors and audiences, that presents the average London playgoer. A grocer, his wife, and his apprentice are the important characters, and the emphasis is placed not so much upon eccentricities of deportment, as upon their likes in drama and their demands upon the playwright who would please them. By 1611, when *The Knight of the Burning Pestle* came to the boards, dramatic and theatrical fashions were beginning to change. The stage-keeper of Master Tarleton's time who recommended rough practical jokes was now thought an ass, and "he that will swear *Jeronimo* [i. e., *The Spanish Tragedy*] and *Andronicus* are the best plays yet," Jonson's *Bartholomew Fair* (1614) assures us, "shall pass unexcepted here as a man whose judgment shows it is constant and hath stood still these five and twenty or thirty years." It was, after all, not a very long while before William Cartwright could compare Fletcher with Shakespeare and call the former more refined. In *The Knight of the Burning Pestle*, it is the old type of auditor, as well as bourgeois taste in drama, which are made sport of. The portraits are satirical, but so subtle that little allowance need be made to infer from them what the Shakespearean playgoer liked.

An audience is assembled in a London theatre to see a play called *The London Merchant*. The Prologue has come forward to describe the piece, but is interrupted by a grocer, a member of the civic corporation and freeman of the city, who has attended plays there these seven years. He has grown tired of the constant girds at citizens. "Why could not you be contented," he demands, "as well as others, with *The Legend of Withington*, or *The Life and Death of Sir Thomas Gresham, with the Building of the Royal Exchange*, or *The Story of Queen Eleanor, with the Rearing of London Bridge upon Woolsacks?*" He'll have them present "something notably in honor of the commons of the City." He'll have a citizen, and of his own trade, too, do admirable things. And so, in spite of the embarrassment of the Prologue, he bids his wife and their apprentice Ralph to join him on the stage and help him devise a plot for Ralph in the hero's role. The wife is not a frequenter of plays. "I was ne'er at one of these plays, as they say, before, but I should have seen *Jane Shore* once, and my husband hath promised me, any time this twelvemonth, to carry me to *The Bold Beauchamps*, but in truth he did not." However, all three know what they like. They delight in stories like that of Sir Dagonet, who was also a grocer's apprentice, *Palmerin of England*, and *Amadis of Gaul*. The grocer's favorite plays are *The Four Prentices of London*, *Jeronimo*, *Mucedorus*, and *The Travels of the Three English Brothers*. Ralph, called upon to speak a "huffing part" to prove his abilities as an actor, thunders out a speech of Hotspur's from Shakespeare's *1 Henry IV*:

> By Heaven, methinks it were an easy leap
> To pluck bright Honour from the pale-faced moon.

In short, they like romance of the extravagant kind, national and civic history, and emotional tragedy.

Into their drama, then, which centers around a runaway apprentice and his rivals for the love of his master's daughter, Ralph, with a burning pestle emblazoned on his shield, stalks like another Quixote. The citizen and his wife care little for congruity or logic; they would see brave deeds. Their interest is in the story, and, like children, they have a tremendous ability to make believe. "Let him kill a lion with a pestle," is the citizeness' first thought when they are asked what Ralph shall do. The apprentice, too, loves the well-spoken, courteous days when all ladies were at least "right beauteous," if not actually "distressed damsels" as well, when forests and heaths were "deserts," and all horses "palfreys." He reads pages from *Palmerin of England* and shuts up his grocery shop to enter the world of fancy with these words:

> But what brave spirit could be content to sit in his shop, with a flappet of wood and a blue apron before him, selling mithradatum . . . to visited [i. e., plague-stricken] houses, that might pursue feats of arms, and through his noble achievements, procure such a famous history to be written of his heroic prowess.

What is more, his master and mistress approve heartily: "Well said, Ralph, some more of those words, Ralph." They caution him not to strain himself too much at first, but soon he is in the midst of so romantic a knight-errantry that the Prologue again and again begs them not to forget the plot. The honest grocer's retort is significant: "Plot me no plots. . . . I care not what become on't." Romance reaches its climax in the demand of the citizen to "let the Sophy of Persia come and christen him a child," and his wife's substitute suggestion:

> Let Ralph travel over great hills, and let him be very weary, and come to the King of Cracovia's house, covered with black velvet; and there let the king's daughter stand in her window, all in beaten gold, combing her golden locks with a comb of ivory: and let her spy Ralph, and fall in love with him, and come down to him, and carry him into her father's house, and then let Ralph talk with her.

Hollywood could do no better.

The sympathy of these folk is given to the hero from the beginning, and they never desert him. They enjoy the fighting, lay wagers on their favorites, and shout encouragement to them: "Break's pate, Ralph," "fetch him o'er the hip, boy," "cut him in the leg, boy, cut him in the legs." They are easily prejudiced, they judge by appearances, and they frequently give their sympathy to the wrong characters. When he whom they mistake for the villain is successful, they call upon the gentlemen around them to see justice done and the king's peace kept: "If there is any law in England, I'll make some of them smart for't!" When their Ralph is himself overthrown on his first encounter, they are quick to perceive what is wrong. His adversary must have taken unfair advantage:

> As sure as we are here, he is enchanted; he could no more have stood in Ralph's hand than I can in my lord mayor's. I'll have a ring to discover all enchantments, and Ralph shall beat him yet: be no more vexed, for it shall be so.

And his good mistress gives Ralph some sugar candy to console him.

Music and noise especially delight the pair. Ralph's is a stately part; he must have shawms (i. e., wind instruments). Accordingly, the grocer gives two shillings to have the Southwark waits (i. e., musicians in the employ of the town) play solemn music to accompany his brave deeds. They love violins and drums and trumpets to accompany battles. They dispute among themselves as to which is the better tune, *Baloo* or *Lachrymæ*. The old reprobate Merrythought is an immediate favorite with them simply because he sings. Dancing at the ends of acts also fascinates them, though it has no place in the play, and the citizeness tips a little boy with twopence for dancing *Fading* for her. She had originally asked for a tumbling- and a fire-eating act, but the lad can only do trick dancing.

In these ways and in many others, these folk frequently blend their make-believe world and the real one. A modern audience rarely forgets that what it is watching is, after all, a play. This burlesque grocer and his wife constantly confuse the two worlds. She interrupts the action to advise a remedy for the chilblains and the cold in the head of which one of the travelers complains:

> Faith, and those chilblains are a foul trouble. Mistress Merrythought, when your youth comes home, let him rub all the soles of his feet . . . with a mouse skin, or, if none of your people can catch a mouse, when he goes to bed, let him roll his feet in the warm embers, and, I warrant you, he shall be well.

When Mistress Merrythought scolds her wayward son for running away from his master, the grocer's wife hastens to set her right:

> No, indeed, Mistress Merrythought, though he be a notable gallows, yet I'll assure you his master did turn him away, even in this place; 'twas i' faith, within this half-hour, about his daughter; my husband was by.

They both apply to themselves the maxims of the play. When someone remarks: "Never trust a tailor that does not sing at his work; his mind is of nothing but filching," the good wife remembers Godfrey, her tailor, who never sings, and who used fourteen yards of material to make a gown when she'll be sworn Mistress Pennistone had one made with twelve. The poor lady trembles like an aspen leaf with vexation and terror and is soothed in her husband's arms. Further to relieve her distress, he goes out for a pot of beer for her, and she drinks the health of the gentlemen around. Even in playland, the honest grocer calls his boy aside and slips money into his hand to make sure that Ralph is beholden to no one, pays his score at the tavern, and does the right thing about tipping the household at Cracovia. And both are proud of their hero when he prefers Susan the cobbler's maid in Milk Street to a foreign princess. They are wholeheartedly orthodox and conservative in manners and morals.

The end of this absurd affair has no more logic than its beginning. An offering must be laid on the altars of patriotism and civic pride. Ralph has been long enough on adventures. He is brought back on May Day morning to speak upon a conduit "with all his scarfs about him, and his feathers and his rings and his knacks." For the credit of the Strand he is to dance a morris, and then the good wife thinks of the "bravest thing for him to do."

> I would have thee call all the youths together in battle-ray, with drums, and guns, and flags, and march to Mile End in pompous fashion, and there exhort your soldiers to be merry and wise, and to keep their beards from burning, Ralph, and then skirmish, and let your flags fly and cry, "Kill, kill, kill!" My husband shall lend you his jerkin, Ralph, and there's a scarf.

Finally, for no reason at all, and in a comedy, too, Ralph is to come in and die. These good folk must enjoy some pathos. Accordingly, Ralph enters with a forked arrow through his head, and, in a speech that parodies the opening lines of the Ghost of Andrea in *The Spanish Tragedy*, gives a long summary of his virtues, commends his soul to Grocer's Hall, and piteously expires.

The Knight of the Burning Pestle, therefore, is valuable, if burlesque, evidence of what the average patrons of the old playhouses, like the Globe, expected when they went to a play. Corroborated by the Elizabethan plays themselves, it justifies drawing some inferences about public taste and making some speculations about the influence of this taste upon Shakespeare.

THE CREDIT SIDE OF THE LEDGER

First of all, it will be evident that the Elizabethan playgoer, like our modern movie audience, came to the theatre primarily for amusement. He was not interested in moral or sociological problems. He wanted a story—old, patched, or borrowed, he cared not—so long as there was plenty happening and something to make him concerned with how it would end.

> If a child could be born in a play, and grow up to a man, in the first scene, before he went off the stage; and then after that come forth a squire, and be made a knight: and that knight to travel between the acts, and do wonders in the Holy Land and elsewhere; kill Paynims, wild boars, dun cows, and other monsters; beget him a reputation and marry an emperor's daughter for his mistress: convert her father's country; and at last come home lame . . . these miracles would please, I assure you . . . for there be of the people that will expect miracles. (Jonson, *The Magnetic Lady* [1632], I, i.)

If an auditor had heard the yarn before, so much the better; he would be more able to follow it and know what was coming. In character he demanded only people who were not too subtle to recognize and understand, and he expected a hero with whom he could sympathize. If he cared to, it was the privilege of the dramatist to introduce any nice distinction in character, so long as he did not interfere with the tale or complicate the virtues of the hero. Hence, all of Shakespeare's plays have well-defined plots—usually two or three—sometimes illogically resolved, but all presenting a hero or a heroine on the horns of a dilemma, like Hamlet, Othello, Lear, or Imogen. Part of the interest for the Elizabethan playgoer logically grew out of how the plot would be resolved, though seldom was there any surprise. Setting mattered little, so long as it was romantic; the Elizabethans were not punctilious about geography or history. The author of *The Four Prentices of London* (Prologue, 1615), shifting his scene to Jerusalem, appealed with confidence to his audience: "Had ye not rather, for novelty's sake, see Jerusalem ye never saw, than London that ye see hourly?"

That Shakespeare was more interested in his people than in his plots is further evidence that he understood his auditory well. Sometimes, when he had a particularly illogical story, such as *Much Ado*, by slightly tarnishing the figures of his main plot, and by making his minor characters more attractive, he could use a tale of pathos and potential tragedy for high comedy. Certainly, Shakespeare was only rarely concerned with a problem, as is so often the modern dramatist. It is interesting to reflect that those plays of Shakespeare's which deal with problems, like *All's Well*, *Measure for Measure*, *Troilus and Cressida*, and *Cymbeline*, are the least appealing on the stage. The Elizabethan audience did not see in *Hamlet* the social problem of whether or not blood revenge is justifiable. That was a code to which they subscribed no more than we do. The interest for them—as for us—lay rather in an attractive character facing a situation to which he is temperamentally unsuited. Moreover, the modern critic who reads into *Othello* the problem of intermarriage between different races, like the theme treated by Eugene O'Neill in *All God's Chillun*, reckons without the play and without the Elizabethan audience. One of the marks of Shakespeare's greatness is that he did not turn his plays into mere ethical or social propositions; as T. S. Eliot has it, "He was occupied with turning human actions into poetry" (*Shakespeare and the Stoicism of Seneca*, Shakespeare Association Lecture, 1927). In Shakespeare's plays, the interest lies rather in character and incident; in Bernard Shaw's, in the problem expounded in the preface. Yet, as has been pointed out, Shaw failed to gain a popular following until he wrote *Saint Joan*, which has both an appealing heroine and plenty of action. Audiences, perhaps, have not changed greatly in three hundred years, for how many of those who were moved by *Saint Joan* cared anything about Shaw's thesis or even understood it?

As to themes the Elizabethan preferred, a glance at Shakespeare's plays confirms the testimony of Beaumont and Fletcher. Like a large part of the modern audience, the Elizabethans hungered for romance, no matter how extravagant. They had an infinite capacity for make-believe. In the lands of their fancies, they could reach seacoasts of Bohemia and tropical forests of Arden where palms and lionesses and green and gilded snakes exist side by side with brambles and hawthorn bushes, and where the sole enemy is winter and rough weather. The very title *As You Like It* is a gracious bow to the audience. Here are an attractive hero and heroine—he, honest, brave, strong, generous, mistreated; she, witty, self-reliant, and lovable—who live in Arden where disguises are impenetrable, where wars are averted by sudden conversions, where love at first sight is the expected thing, and where anything can happen. *Twelfth Night, or What You Will* is similar. Not in this world, but only in Illyria, can a girl disguised as a page produce such complexities. *The Comedy of Errors, Pericles, The Winter's Tale, Cymbeline*, and *The Tempest* are possible only in the glorious world of romance.

If an Elizabethan dramatist was given a free hand in his themes, he was, however, held strictly to account in other ways. Varied settings in time and place did not permit varied manners in plays. Manners had to conform to the code. The Elizabethans demanded realistic conceptions in their romantic theatre. Hence, Shakespeare's anachronisms did not exist for his contemporaries, and are noticed by us only when we look for them. Theseus celebrates his wedding as an Elizabethan noble whose master of the revels stirs up the Athenian youth to merriments and prepares a play for entertainment, and the mobs of ancient Rome behave exactly like London crowds. The dwellers in far-off places are all presented as Elizabethans and would not have been understood if they were not. But in other ways, too, behavior had to be that with which the audience was socially and morally familiar. The situations might be far-fetched, but the character's behavior in them had to be realistic. Studying the plays with other than Elizabethan eyes, we are sometimes in danger of misreading Shakespeare. *The Two Gentlemen of Verona*, read as a love story, goes to pieces when Valentine turns to the repentant Proteus with the words: "All that is mine in Silvia I give thee." Read as an exemplification of the Renaissance code of friendship, however, the play has meaning, and Valentine retains his nobility. In the modern theatre world, when love and friendship come into conflict, love is expected to be the stronger of the two bonds. Shakespeare's audience had precisely the opposite ideal.

An example of another kind may be found in the unbelievable matrimonial arrangements of some of the plays. Readers of Shakespeare are sometimes puzzled that such a prize as Portia should be awarded to a spendthrift fortune-hunter like Bassanio, that so devoted a soul as Julia is bestowed upon so changeable a fellow as Proteus, or that the rejected Mariana of the moated grange is matched with the "outward sainted Angelo." A modern audience is amused when Fabian, as spokesman for the conspirators, confesses the joke on Malvolio:

> Maria writ
> The letter at Sir Toby's great importance,
> In recompense whereof he hath married her.
> (*Twelfth Night*, V, i, 370 ff.)

Toby is no prize. The solution to the question is perhaps to be found in the Elizabethan attitude toward marriage. In the plays it approved, as in life, the Elizabethan audience was loath to see the charm of an attractive heroine "withering on a virgin thorn." It was satisfied only when all the roses were gathered—by good up-standing men, if that could be; if not, by such as there were. Shakespeare's audiences were simple, conventional, practical folk, even in the playhouse, and the dramatist's acceptance of the "Jack shall have Jill" pattern for his comedies is evidence of his recognition of that fact.

In structure, too, a satisfactory chain of events, not logic, was the rule, even in Shakespeare. The titles of the old quartos show how variety attracted Elizabethan spectators:

The Tragedy of King Richard the Third. Containing his Treacherous Plots against his brother Clarence, the pitiful murder of his innocent nephews, his tyrannical usurpation, with the whole course of his detested life and most deserved death. (Quarto 1, 1597.)

The Most Excellent History of the Merchant of Venice. With the extreme cruelty of Shylock the Jew towards the said merchant, in cutting a just pound of his flesh, and the obtaining of Portia by the choice of three chests. (Quarto 1, 1600.)

A Most Pleasant and Excellent Conceited Comedy of Sir John Falstaff and the Merry Wives of Windsor, intermixed with sundry variable and pleasing humors of Sir Hugh the Welsh knight, Justice Shallow, and his wise cousin M. Slender. With the swaggering vein of Ancient Pistol and Corporal Nym. (Quarto 1, 1602.)

These synopses make clear what Shakespeare's audiences liked. In 1602, one Richard Vennar hoaxed an audience by inviting it to the Swan to see a play called *England's Joy*, said to contain the following delicacies: the civil wars from the time of Edward III to the end of Queen Mary's reign, the coronation of England's Joy, Queen Elizabeth,

> her throne attended with Peace, Plenty, and Civil Policy. A Sacred Prelate standing at her right hand, betokening the Serenity of the Gospel; at her left hand Justice; and at her feet War, with a scarlet robe of peace upon his armor, a wreath of bays about his temples, and a branch of palm in his hand.

Then three Furies, representing Dissension, Famine, and Bloodshed, were to be thrown into Hell; the envy of Spain with the attendant plots of Lopez and the Jesuits, the Irish rebellion, and the final triumph over the Spanish Armada were to be presented; and twelve gentlemen were to fight at barriers. The show was to close with a pageant of the Nine Worthies, the coronation of the Queen by Angels with an imperial crown,

> garnished with the sun, moon, and stars. And so with music both with voice and instruments she is taken up into heaven, when presently appears a throng of blessed souls, and beneath under the stage set forth with strange fireworks, divers black and damned souls, wonderfully described in their several torments.

Having packed the house, Vennar showed his audience "a fair pair of heels" and absconded with the money. When variety was necessary to draw the crowds, what could be duller than a single plot in a play?

It is evident, also, that an Elizabethan play supplied more than is thought proper to demand of a play today. Shakespeare's audience was not homogeneous, yet prince and peasant, side by side, were pleased by the same dramatic fare. Some in that assembly expected philosophical speculation, some wanted rough-and-tumble comedy, some liked music and dancing, some loved a good knockabout fight with plenty of sword-play, some made sure that the play had a clown in it before they paid the admission price, many were incapable of enjoying anything but inexplicable dumb-shows and noise, and some were for a jig or a tale of bawdry or they slept. In the modern theatre, separate types of entertainment cater to this variety of tastes. *Hamlet* and *Romeo and Juliet* supplied them all. An Elizabethan play had to present something for everybody. To appropriate what Anthony Scolaker said of a perfect epistle:

> It should be like never-too-well read *Arcadia*, where the prose and verse . . . are like his mistress's eyes . . . or to come home to the vulgar's element, like friendly Shakespeare's tragedies, where the comedian rides when the tragedian stands on tip-toe; faith, it should please all, like Prince Hamlet. (*Diaphantus, or The Passions of Love*, 1604.)

That Shakespeare's audience still possessed a simple childlike power to "play-like" and a willingness to co-operate with the poet and the actors in the theatre is also evident. That it was more able than a modern audience to picture specifically and concretely a background suggested by poetic description may be doubted. The Elizabethans got what everyone gets from Shakespeare in the theatre—an atmosphere. That was all it needed. Can one say that they appreciated in the playhouse the full beauty of Shakespeare's lyricism as does the modern reader in his study? The Elizabethan audience certainly must have listened with a great deal more patience to long expository description or moralizing than will an audience today; it also seems to have expected the kind of summary of what it had seen take place that Friar Laurence gives at the end of *Romeo and Juliet*.

THE DEBIT SIDE OF THE LEDGER

What has thus far been said about the influence of Shakespeare's audience on his plays has been entered, generally speaking, on the credit side of the ledger. But there are other affairs in which the audience had a hand, and not always for the better. Some years ago, the late poet-laureate Robert Bridges voiced his indignation at elements in Shakespeare's plays which he found incompatible with Shakespeare's gentility of mind.[3] He could not account in any other way for the bad jokes, the frequent indelicacy and obscenity, except on the supposition that the poet was writing down to his audience. He also believed that sometimes Shakespeare not only curried favor by such questionable measures, but actually took advantage of the stupidity and moral bluntness of his audience. Holding such a view, Dr. Bridges was naturally indignant with "those wretched beings who can never be forgiven their share in preventing the greatest poet and dramatist of the world from being the best artist." It is doubtful if every student of Shakespeare will share Dr. Bridges's nice sensitiveness. Indelicacy, brutality, and cheapness there are in Shakespeare, and, as has often been pointed out, in the Bible as well. But fixing the blame is not simple. Was the audience alone the scapegrace, and Shakespeare so far above the rest of his contemporaries that he winced each time he inserted the necessary spice?

The obscenity is least easy to condone; as Dr. Bridges points out, it sullies some of Shakespeare's brightest pages. But it is always well to ask the poet's intent and to perceive into whose mouth such expressions are put. The unsentimental Mercutio is one of the most lovable of Shakespeare's creations, but he is also one of the freest in speech. The foul mouth of Juliet's nurse is excellent characterization. Falstaff's portrait would be a shadow were

[3] *The Influence of the Audience on Shakespeare's Drama*, Volume I of *Collected Essays, Papers, etc.*, Oxford (1927). The essay was originally printed in Volume X of the *Stratford Town Shakespeare* (1907).

he made delicate. Expressions objectionable in themselves are often dramatically appropriate. Even when they are used for their own sakes, seldom will it be found that Shakespeare meant them in any way save as a harmless jest. Squeamishness in matters of this kind can be overdone, and it doubtless made some difference that the "actresses" who spoke or heard the gross phrases in his theatre were really boys in disguise.

Much has been made, too, of scenes of brutality and physical horror, and most of the blame for these scenes laid at the door of the audience which originally approved them. The crimes in *Titus Andronicus, Hamlet, Macbeth*, and *King Lear* have frequently been totaled and displayed either as the sins of the gentlest of dramatists, or as proof that those who came to his playhouse had iron nerves and took a bloodthirsty joy in realistic horror. Horror, of course, is the stock in trade of the tragic dramatist; Shakespeare found it in his sources, and to deny him the fullest use of it would be to cripple him seriously. It was essential to his plots. To be sure, as we have seen, the Elizabethans perhaps went a little further than we do today and were perhaps a little blunter in their sensibilities. But even our melodrama goes quite far enough. Employ upon contemporary drama—or popular detective fiction—the method that has sometimes been applied in criticizing Shakespeare's plays, and some undeservedly hard deductions could be made about the modern playgoer or reader.

Other shortcomings are less serious. Shakespeare's audience liked drum and trumpet history, sword-play and alarms, and he gave it *Henry V*. It liked clowns and fools, and he created Costard, Launcelot Gobbo, Feste, Touchstone, and the Fool in *King Lear*. It expected mirth even in tragedy, and he put the grave-diggers into *Hamlet*, the porter into *Macbeth*, and the old countryman into *Antony and Cleopatra*. It liked to gape at monsters, and he created Caliban. It liked music, both soft and noisy, and he inserted songs into his plays. But, judging by the frequency of such scenes, there is the possibility that Shakespeare liked them, too. He probably enjoyed verbal trifling also. "To see this age," exclaims Feste. "A sentence is but a cheveril glove to a good wit. How quickly the wrong side may be turn'd outward!" Is one wholly mistaken if he detects here something of the dramatist's own admiration for his fool?

To have great art, it has often been remarked, it is necessary first to have a great audience. It is especially true in the theatre, for the drama reflects rather than prophesies; it is based upon the sentiment of the present, not upon that of the future. Less than the other arts is the drama ahead of its time; a successful play is never "caviare to the general." Hence, any attempt to understand Shakespeare's work with any degree of fullness cannot omit a study also of his audience, with which very properly the study of any play might begin. The spectators at the time of Shakespeare's youth made possible *The*

Spanish Tragedy, Doctor Faustus, The Comedy of Errors, and *Henry IV;* those of his maturity approved of *As You Like It, Hamlet, A Woman Killed with Kindness,* and *Every Man in His Humour.* The audience of the post-Shakespearean period applauded *The Maid's Tragedy* and *The Broken Heart;* that of the Restoration *The Conquest of Granada* and *The Man of Mode;* and that of the eighteenth century *The Beggar's Opera,* the pantomime, and *The History of George Barnwell.* The stamp of the audience is unmistakable upon most popular plays; it accounts to a large extent for both the virtues and the defects of the Elizabethan drama. Nor need it be a reproach to say that Shakespeare wrote to please his audience. Time has been his vindication.

SUGGESTED REFERENCES

BENNETT, H. S.   *Shakespeare's Audience.* Annual Shakespeare Lecture of the British Academy, 1944.

BRADLEY, A. C.   "Shakespeare's Theatre and Audience," in *Oxford Lectures on Poetry.* London, Macmillan, 1909.

BRIDGES, ROBERT.   *The Influence of the Audience on Shakespeare's Drama.* Oxford, Clarendon Press, 1927.
    Originally published in the *Stratford Town Shakespeare,* 1907.

BYRNE, M. ST. CLARE.   "Shakespeare's Audience," in *A Series of Papers on Shakespeare and the Theatre* . . . by Members of the Shakespeare Association. London, Humphrey Milford, Oxford University Press, 1927.

HARBAGE, ALFRED.   *Shakespeare's Audience.* New York, Columbia University Press, 1941.
    An interpretation of the evidence as to the size, social composition, behavior, and the esthetic and intellectual capacity of Shakespeare's audience.

SISSON, CHARLES J.   *Le Goût public et le théâtre Elizabéthain jusqu'à la mort de Shakespeare.* Dijon, Imprimerie Darantière, 1922.
    A discussion of public taste in the Elizabethan theatre.

8

SHAKESPEARE'S ENGLISH

To see this age! A sentence is but a cheveril glove to a good wit. How
quickly the wrong side may be turned outward!
—*Twelfth Night*, III, i, 12–14.

Taffeta phrases, silken terms precise,
  Three-piled hyperboles, spruce affectation,
Figures pedantical.
—*Love's Labor's Lost*, V, ii, 406 ff.

To GET A MEANING FROM SHAKESPEARE IS USUALLY SIMPLE
enough, but to get *the* meaning is sometimes quite another matter. The reason
lies in the fact that the difference between Elizabethan and modern English
is greater than is ordinarily supposed. For three centuries, critics and editors
emphasizing the universality of Shakespeare have done all in their power to
disguise the real nature of the language used by that Elizabethan author who
is most read by the average lover of books. His uncertain, irregular spelling
and punctuation have been modernized, his archaic grammar has been made
to conform as much as possible to modern standards, and his text has come
to have a distinctly familiar look. Yet, for all that, Shakespeare's English is in
some ways closer to Chaucer's than it is to ours. The student, therefore,
should become familiar with some of the characteristics of the language
Shakespeare used and begin to cultivate that alertness which is essential to
appreciating the richness and the subtlety of Elizabethan English. Shakespeare is the master of the image-making, sense-stimulating word; it is too
easy to think, with Dryden, of his diction as merely "pestered with figurative expressions."

A PLASTIC MEDIUM

The most impressive qualities of the vernacular in Shakespeare's service
are freshness and flexibility. His English was a living speech that was only

beginning to submit to the taming influences of printing. In Shakespeare's day, there were no grammars, dictionaries, or accepted conventions of diction, as in Latin, and very few literary models. Spelling and pronunciation were chaotic, meanings were yet plastic, and the language was feeling its way to a standard syntax. It was still growing, delighting in novelties, being particularly hospitable to foreign words, and freely forming new compounds. For literary purposes, English was still a new language. Chaucer, to be sure, had made it his medium, but his contemporary Gower sought to make immortality triply sure by writing books in French and Latin as well as English. Even Francis Bacon, Shakespeare's contemporary, held his native tongue so much in distrust that he wrote his serious philosophical works in Latin, the respectable language of scholars, and committed to English only the jottings and notes he called *Essays*. Compared with Chaucer's English, Shakespeare's had, of course, attained a certain amount of uniformity, but an Elizabethan author of talent could still mould his plastic medium as he liked.

COINAGE OF WORDS

Never has there been another age of riotous individualism in English like the Renaissance. Language was made fresh as it was needed, and the native store enriched by the adoption of words from Latin, Greek, Italian, Spanish, and French. The humanists of the early sixteenth century who sought to use their native tongue as a literary medium were confronted by a dearth of English words to express their meanings and had to resort to clumsy, ear-offending compounds. There was no other way than to adopt a Latin vocabulary. By Shakespeare's time, appropriation of language from foreign sources had become the practice. A few critics, like Sir Philip Sidney, understood that English was a mingled language and praised its suppleness. Many others, like Thomas Wilson, Roger Ascham, George Gascoigne, or Sir John Cheke, preached discretion, or gravely warned the enthusiasts that if English were ever borrowing and never paying it would in time be bankrupt. Even E. K., commending Spenser's *Shepherd's Calendar* to Gabriel Harvey (1579), called English "a gallimaufrey or hodge-podge of all speeches." But they could do little to dampen the linguistic zeal. Sir Nathaniel and Holofernes were not the only ones who had been at a great feast of languages and stolen the scraps (*Love's Labor's Lost*, V, i, 39).

Some of the innovators were astonished at their own daring in handling this verbal wealth. In his *Art of English Poesie* (1589), Richard(?) Puttenham made public apology for some of the inventions of which he had been guilty, justifying himself by saying that there were no English equivalents. Among them are *scientific, idiom, method, methodical, function, refine, compendious, prolix, figurative, inveigle, impression, numerous, metrical, penetrate, penetrable, indignity, savage, obscure, delineation, dimension.* He was especially dubious about *audacious, fecundity, egregious, compatible* (Book III, ch. iv). A modern reader has difficulty in believing that these words were ever dangerous neologisms. Other writers had their penance forced upon them. With loving care, Thomas Nashe culled from the works of Gabriel Harvey some flowers of "over-racked absonism" and exposed them in *Strange News* (1592). Among his objections, *conscious, ingenuity, jovial, valorous, rascality, artificiality, fantasticality, incendiary, addicted, perfunctory, idea, abyss, exaggerations, amnesty, amicable, extensively employed, notoriety, negotiations,* and *mechanician* have all survived as useful words. When Harvey replied in *Pierce's Supererogation* (1593), he pilloried from Nashe's vocabulary such innocents as *sacrilegiously contaminated, decrepit capacity, finicality, disputative, declamatory styles, infringement, destitute, indictment, ratifying, eligible.* Even so thorough a Latinist as Ben Jonson thought that the classics could intrude too far. In his *Poetaster* (1601), he produced Crispinus, a caricature of John Marston, and, by the ungentle method of an emetic, made him disgorge a whole vocabulary into a basin. *Retrograde, reciprocal, defunct, clumsy, spurious, puffy, inflate, ventosity, furibund, strenuous, conscious, damp, clutched* are among the words which Time has robbed, not only of all offense, but of all freshness as well.

Along with the rest of the word-creators, Shakespeare went full swing. With the aid of the great historical *New English Dictionary*, it is possible to make lists of his innovations. In a little pamphlet on *Shakespeare's English* (1928), Professor George Gordon of Oxford has made very vivid the debt of ordinary speech to Shakespeare:

> So far as history can yet tell us, he was the first of our writers to speak of 'cudgelling one's brain,' 'falling to blows,' 'breathing' a word, and 'breathing' one's last. It is in Shakespeare, on this same testimony, that firearms and debts were possibly first 'discharged,' persons 'humoured,' letters 'directed,' and unkindness 'buried'; there also for the first time men 'bury' their faces in their cloaks. The stirring people of his plays 'drink healths' and 'pledges,' say 'done!' to a bargain, 'lay odds' and play 'the ten,' 'grovel' or 'hedge,' are 'spiritless' and stare on 'vacancy,' or 'reel' along the street: all, possibly, for the first time in print. On the same reckoning they were the first public characters to call the world 'dull,' to speak of the 'acts' of a play, to find speeches 'flowery' and plain faces 'homely,' to be 'fond' of each other, to 'wear their hearts on their sleeves,' to have 'balmy slumbers,' and lie on the 'lush' grass. No earlier writer is yet known to have spoken of a man's toes 'looking through' his shoes, of the 'makings' of a thing, of an 'abrupt' answer; of 'men of note' and of sending a 'note'; of 'the minute' drawing on; of 'backing' a horse; of things that 'beggared' all description; of 'catching' a person up, or 'catching' a meaning or a cold; of painting from 'the life'; of being 'bright and cheerful,' or of being 'sick' of a thing; of 'sealing' one's lips; of 'returning' thanks, or a present, or an answer; of 'getting' information, or 'getting' an ailment; of 'getting clear' of debt, or of a ship, or 'getting' aboard, or back, or off, or on ('Get on thy boots'). For the first time, also, we have literary authority to call a vehicle a 'conveyance,' a

ship's crew a 'company,' anything that happens an 'event' [whence his coinage 'eventful'], and a road a 'road.'

All of these words or meanings are so common that it is hard to conceive of a time when they did not exist.

Reading for the *N. E. D.* was necessarily selective, and, in the case of single words, there must always linger a doubt whether Shakespeare or another was the actual inventor. About terse expressive phrases, however, there can be no question. Many of the following fit our tongues so nicely that we have almost forgotten that they were originally quotations from Shakespeare: *flaming youth, the primrose path, to the manner born, the glass of fashion, hoist with his own petard, something rotten in the state of Denmark, it smells to heaven, the dog will have his day, my mind's eye, there's the rub, this mortal coil, yeoman's service, by indirections find directions out, method in his madness, brevity is the soul of wit, as easy as lying, the whips and scorns of time, more matter and less art, the witching hour, neither a borrower nor a lender be* (all from *Hamlet*); *to chronicle small beer, the green-eyed monster, pomp and circumstance, who steals my purse steals trash, a round unvarnished tale, a foregone conclusion* [i. e., a previous experience], *not wisely but too well, the seamy side* (*Othello*); *Greek to me, an itching palm, master spirits, a dish fit for the gods, a lean and hungry look, masters of their fates, the dogs of war* (*Julius Cæsar*); *give the Devil his due, tell truth and shame the Devil, come betwixt the wind and his nobility, hearts of gold, the better part of valor is discretion, take mine ease at mine inn, a coward by instinct* (*1 Henry IV*); *he has eaten me out of house and home, the weaker vessel* (*2 Henry IV*); *make assurance double sure, the crack of doom, the milk of human kindness, a sorry sight, the wine of life, applaud to the very echo, coign of vantage, vaulting ambition* (*Macbeth*); *merry as the day is long, fear and trembling, good men and true, a valiant trencher man* (*Much Ado*); *too much of a good thing, laid on with a trowel, this working day world, much virtue in 'if,' an ill-favored thing but mine own* (*As You Like It*); *what's in a name, the public haunt of men, a fool's paradise, the pink of courtesy, Fortune's fool* (*Romeo and Juliet*); *paint the lily, elbow room, cold comfort* (*King John*); *every inch a king, more sinned against than sinning, the wheel has come full circle* (*King Lear*); *flutter the dove cotes, die by inches* (*Coriolanus*); *my salad days, infinite variety, I wish you joy o' the worm* (*Antony and Cleopatra*); *single blessedness* [originally the Divine blessing accorded a life of celibacy], *a lion among ladies* (*A Midsummer Night's Dream*); *make a virtue of necessity, a woman's reason* (*The Two Gentlemen*); *as good luck would have it, the long and the short of it, throw cold water on it, the world's mine oyster* (*The Merry Wives*); *like Patience on a monument, a carpet knight* (*Twelfth Night*); *out of the question* (*Love's Labor's Lost*); *halcyon days* (*1 Henry VI*); *the main chance* (*2*

Henry VI); the worm will turn, a nine days' wonder (3 Henry VI); a harm-less necessary cat, it's a wise father who knows his own child, a Daniel come to judgment, my own flesh and blood, hold a candle to (The Merchant of Venice); a spotless reputation, a tower of strength (Richard III); household words (Henry V); something in the wind (The Comedy of Errors); poor, but honest (All's Well); one touch of nature (Troilus and Cressida); let the world slide (The Taming of the Shrew); misery acquaints a man with strange bedfellows, such stuff as dreams are made on (The Tempest); a snapper up of unconsidered trifles (The Winter's Tale). Even such a restricted list leaves a profound impression of the unobtrusive wealth contributed to the English language by this single artist. Only from the Bible could a similar collection be compiled.

Besides these rich new phrases, many audacious compounds rolled from Shakespeare's mind and pen, like *proud-pied* April, a *furnace-burning* heart, *wind-changing* Warwick, a *heaven-kissing* hill, *swart-complexioned* night, a *glass-faced* flatterer, a *mortal-breathing* saint, the *always-wind-obeying* deep, the *all-seeing* sun, *plough-torn* leas, *neighbor-stained* steel, a *lack-lustre* eye, *saint-seducing* gold, a *still-soliciting* eye, *eagle-winged* pride, *rival-hating* envy, *lean-look'd* prophets, the *ne'er-lust-wearied* Antony, *plume-pluck'd* Richard, *crafty-sick* Northumberland, the *nook-shotten* isle of Albion, a *fool-born* jest, *thief-stolen* brothers, some *carry-tale*, some *mumble-news*, some *trencher-knight*, or *wall-eyed* wrath, and *cat-a-mountain* looks. The list of more homely expressions is endless: *all-knowing, bare-ribb'd, after-eye, over-eye, here-approach, hence-going, new-apparell'd, new-killed, night-shriek, out-sweeten, out-tongue, over-awe, quick-answer'd, sea-change, sea-sorrow, sun-bright, well-wished.* The vituperative value of this freedom can be appreciated by hearing Kent speak but part of his mind regarding Oswald:

A knave, a rascal, an eater of broken meats; a base, proud, shallow, beggarly, three-suited, hundred-pound, filthy, worsted-stocking knave; a lily-livered, action-taking knave, a whoreson, glass-gazing, super-serviceable, finical rogue; one-trunk-inheriting slave. (*King Lear*, II, ii, 15 ff.; cf. *Troilus and Cressida*, V, i, 29 ff. and *1 Henry IV*, II, iv, 69 ff.)

"The fool hath planted in his memory an army of good words!"

This linguistic ferment of the Renaissance, of course, produced a heady drink which was responsible for all kinds of extravagance and affectations. It fostered not only new expressions and what Ben Jonson called "foot and half-foot words," but a high style as well:

> Taffeta phrases, silken terms precise,
> Three-pil'd hyperboles, spruce affectation,
> Figures pedantical. (*Love's Labor's Lost*, V, ii, 406 ff.)

"These summer flies," cries Biron, "have blown me full of maggot ostentation; I do forswear them," and he promises to conduct his wooing with "russet yeas and honest kersey nos." But, immediately, he falls back into fantastic speech. "Bear with me," he begs Rosaline, "I am sick; I'll leave it by degrees." What had been a necessity in the days of Sir Thomas More had, by Shakespeare's time, become a game. "How every fool can play upon the word!" exclaims Lorenzo. "I think the best grace of wit will shortly turn into silence, and discourse grow commendable in none only but parrots" (*The Merchant of Venice*, III, v, 48). It would be surprising if Shakespeare had escaped the infection of this linguistic virus. But he was conscious of its absurdities as well. "Can sick men play so nicely with their names?" asks King Richard when John of Gaunt puns extensively about the effects of time and care upon him. *Love's Labor's Lost* is a burlesque of all the current fads in language. Throughout the plays, even individual words are singled out for satire. Hamlet has his joke with *imponed* and *carriages*, which he picks up from Osric (V, ii, 161 ff.); Feste refuses to say "out of your *element*" because "the word is over-worn" (*Twelfth Night*, III, i, 65), and, when Sebastian bids him *vent* his folly elsewhere, is sure he picked the word up from some great man (IV, i, 12). And there is that 'leven pence farthing difference between *remuneration* and *guerdon* (*Love's Labor's Lost*, III, i, 137 ff.).

By no means did all of these Elizabethan coinages survive. Rejects, like chips, are strewn about everywhere. Puttenham had been quite guilty of such monstrosities as *assubtiling*, *numerosity*, and *harmonical;* Harvey of *canicular*, *entelechy*, *mentery*, and *addoulce;* Nashe of *absonism*, *carminist*, *providatory*, *corrigidore*, *gimpando*, a *dromidote ergonist*, *horrisonant*, and *sillogistry;* and Marston of *glibbery*, *snotteries*, *turgidous*, *oblatrant*, *prorumped*, and *obstupefact*. It is not possible to match these lists with another from Shakespeare, but he has some splendid failures which one might wish could have survived. There is a distinct loss in *smilet*, 'a little smile' (*King Lear*, IV, iii, 21); *summer's tanlings*, 'sun-tanned children' (*Cymbeline*, IV, iv, 29); *o'eroffice*, 'lord over' (*Hamlet*, V, i, 87); *convive*, 'feast together' (*Troilus and Cressida*, IV, v, 272); *dispunge*, 'squeeze out' (*Antony and Cleopatra*, IV, ix, 13); *stelled*, 'starry' (*King Lear*, III, vii, 61); *argentine*, 'silver bright' (*Pericles*, V, i, 251); *congree*, 'agree together' (*Henry V*, I, ii, 182); *disproperty*, 'take away' (*Coriolanus*, II, i, 264); *discandy*, 'melt' (*Antony and Cleopatra*, IV, xii, 22); *razorable*, applicable to a youth ready to be shaved (*The Tempest*, II, i, 250); and *forgetive*, applied by Falstaff to the action of sack in the brain (*2 Henry IV*, IV, iii, 107). There are others, like *wealsman*, 'statesman' (*Coriolanus*, II, i, 60); *birthdom*, 'native place' (*Macbeth*, IV, iii, 4); *fineless* or *confineless*, 'infinite' (*Othello*, III, iii, 173; *Macbeth*, IV, iii, 55); *implorator*, 'solicitor' (*Hamlet*, I, iii, 129); *solicity*, 'courtship' (*Cymbeline*,

II, iii, 52); *pensived*, 'saddened' (*A Lover's Complaint*, 219); *oathable*, 'capable of taking an oath' (*Timon of Athens*, IV, iii, 136)—all of which have given way to other words doubtfully their betters.

CHANGES IN PRONUNCIATION

These words, new or old, would sound amusingly queer to us today could we attend an Elizabethan theatre, for modern standard pronunciation was still slowly evolving in Shakespeare's time. The pronunciation of a past age is a difficult subject to study because the look of a word in print gives little indication of its quality on the tongue. But there are a few clues, like rhyme, metre, and erratic spelling, that aid the phonetician. Shakespeare, for example, rhymes *one* with *loan; was* with *grass; are* with *care; were* with *hear; convert* with *art; love* with *prove; break* with *speak; have* with *grave; dumb* with *tomb; tongue* with *wrong; last* with *taste; cost* and *lost* with *boast; there* with *dear; death* with *bequeath; sweat* with *heat; blest* and *jest* with *beast; feature* with *nature; blood* with *stood, good,* and *wood; heard* with *ward* and *regard; field, yield,* and *shield* with *gild* and *kill'd; sorry* with *glory; great* with *eat; crab* with *bob; bless* with *peace; coward* with *toward;* and *water* with *flatter.* Few of these, if any, are eye-rhymes, even if it is sometimes difficult to determine the actual quality of the vowel. However, the possibility of rhymes like *should* and *cool'd, swine* and *groin,* and *voice* and *juice* tells even more.

Sometimes the old spelling of the quartos and folios, whether Shakespeare's or his printers', furnishes corroborative or additional evidence as to how the words sounded. We find *sedule* (schedule), *fadom* (fathom), *philome* (film), *stockens* (stockings), *ortagriphie* (orthography), *spaches* (speeches), *spake* (speak), *wary* (weary), *venter* (venture), *conster* (construe), *creadulous* (credulous), *reaks* (recks), *leasure* (leisure), *divell* (devil), *stauk* (stalk), *byle* (boil), *cusnage* (cozenage), *berrord* (bearward), *doone* (done), *hudwincke* (hoodwink), *gardon* (guerdon), *wrastler* (wrestler), *marchant* (merchant), *marmaide* (mermaid), *wrenching* (rinsing), *Fraunce, graund, auncient,* and *slaunder, totters* (tatters), *ottomie* (atomy), *souldier* (soldier), *ougly* (ugly), *boudge* (budge), *seely* (silly), and *spleet* (split).

Metre, on the other hand, gives information, not about sound, but about stress. Shakespeare seems to have accented some words differently from us, thus: *as·pect', can·on'ize, char·ac'ter, com'plete, com·merce', con·fis'cate, en'gi·ner, noth·ing', op·por'tune, per'spec·tive, rev·e'nue, sep·ul'chre, tri·umph'.* He sometimes made dissyllables of words like *fear, dear, fire, hour, where, tears;* trisyllables of words like *action, question, soldier, carriage, business, statue, ocean, conscience, creature,* and quadrisyllables of *perfection, ambition, promotion,* and *confusion.* He could even introduce an extra syllable into *ent(e)rance, rememb(e)rance, Eng(e)land, wrest(e)ler,* and

Hen(e)*ry* without offense. There was, of course, much less uniformity in sixteenth-century pronunciation than there is now, and Shakespeare himself appears to have accepted the possibility of two enunciations of the same word.

Changes which tended to make pronunciation what we now consider normal were taking place in Elizabethan times, but they were probably looked upon as affectations by many of Shakespeare's contemporaries. When the news-crammed Le Beau hurried in to Rosalind and Celia and said, "Fair princess, you have lost much good sport," he must have pronounced his last word "spawt" in a manner often affected today. "Sport?" [spot], queries Rosalind. "Of what colour?" [i. e., (a) kind, (b) hue] (*As You Like It*, I, ii, 106). In *Love's Labor's Lost*, the pedant Holofernes is horrified by "such rackers of orthography" as Don Armado who says:

> *dout*, fine, when he should say *doubt; det*, when he should pronounce *debt,—* *d, e, b, t*, not *d, e, t*. He clepeth a calf, *cauf*; half, *hauf;* neighbour vocatur *nebour; neigh* abbreviated *ne*. This is abhominable, which he would call *abbominable;* it insinuateth me of insanie. (V, i, 22 ff.)

In this speech, it is the modern pronunciation that is found objectionable.

As might be expected, there are many cases in Shakespeare where Elizabethan pronunciation affects the meaning. A passage from Cassius's tirade against Cæsar:

> When could they say (till now) that talk'd of Rome,
> That her wide walks encompass'd but one man?
> Now is it Rome indeed, and room enough,
> When there is in it but one only man
> (*Julius Cæsar*, I, ii, 154 ff.)

becomes significant the moment one realizes the rhyme of *Rome* and *room*. Yet the rhyme of *Rome* and *roam* was also possible (*1 Henry VI*, III, i, 51). Similarly, Shakespeare's verbal play on *ship* and *sheep* (*The Comedy of Errors*, IV, i, 93–4), *on* and *one* (*The Two Gentlemen*, II, i, 2), *lac'd* and *lost* (*ibid.*, I, i, 102), *kin* and *kind* (*Hamlet*, I, ii, 65), *made* and *mad* (*Twelfth Night*, III, iv, 59), *wode* and *wood* (*A Midsummer Night's Dream*, II, i, 192), *ass* and *ace* (*ibid.*, V, i, 311–12), *lief* and *live* (*Julius Cæsar*, I, ii, 95), *dolour* and *dollar* (*The Tempest*, II, i, 19), *mood* and *mud* (*All's Well*, V, ii, 5), *body, beauty,* and *booty* (*1 Henry IV*, I, ii, 28), *ache* and *H* (*Much Ado*, III, iv, 56) are less far-fetched than they appear to the modern reader. To get the full effect of Romeo's "What says my *conceal'd* lady to our *cancell'd* love?" (*Romeo and Juliet*, III, iii, 97–8), involves on most tongues today both false accent and false quality. A difference of pronunciation also explains Falstaff's retort to Poins's demand for the reason of his flight at Gadshill: "Give you a *reason* on compulsion? If *reasons* [raisons] were as plenty as blackberries, I would give no man a reason upon compulsion, I" (*1 Henry IV*, II, iv, 266 ff.).

Occasionally, to modern eyes the meaning appears obscure indeed. "I would I had bestowed that time in the tongues that I have in fencing, dancing, and bear-baiting," sighs Sir Andrew Aguecheek, and Sir Toby replies, "Then hadst thou had an excellent head of hair." "Would that have mended my hair?" asks the astonished Andrew. "Past question," replies Toby, "for thou seest it will not curl by nature" (*Twelfth Night*, I, iii, 97 ff.). The obscurity vanishes immediately when one perceives the pun upon *tongues*, 'languages,' and *tongs*, 'curling irons.' So, too, Beatrice's comment upon the sulking Claudio, who is "neither sad, nor sick, nor merry, nor well; but civil count, civil as an orange, and something of that jealous complexion," is full of meaning when one remembers that oranges came to England from Seville and were bitter (*Much Ado*, II, i, 303 ff.). Something like modern Cockney pronunciation is suggested in Jaques's "the 'why' is plain as way to parish church" (*As You Like It*, II, vii, 52).

Likewise, some lines that appear to be eye-puns to us instead of ear-puns, like Gratiano's taunt to Shylock:

Not on thy *sole*, but on thy *soul*, harsh Jew,
Thou mak'st thy knife keen (*The Merchant of Venice*, IV, i, 122–3),

were perhaps more easily intelligible to an Elizabethan audience than to a modern because of a subtle dissimilarity in pronunciation now lost.

NATIVE AND FOREIGN WORDS

The shifting values of words themselves, however, are more important than differences of sound. All of Shakespeare's words look just like words in common use today, and, if he knows only modern English, the reader may be misled by appearances. For example, a line from *Troilus and Cressida* is so well known that it has become a proverb: "One touch of nature makes the whole world kin" (III, iii, 175). But it is not the glowing declaration of the brotherhood of man which it appears to modern eyes when examined out of context. The "touch of nature" Shakespeare meant was a weakness rather than a fellow feeling of another sort. *Jealousy* is another example. In Shakespeare's time, it still had its general meaning of 'suspicion' or 'apprehension of evil' rather than its more narrow modern sense of 'fear of rivalry in matters of love.' *Ecstasy* and *rapture* for Shakespeare had no poetic associations; the one was synonymous with 'madness,' and the other meant a 'fit.' *Natural*, as an adjective, was coming to have our modern meaning, but, as a noun, it was applicable alike to a fool, an idiot, or a half-wit, thus giving point to Mercutio's description of "this drivelling love . . . like a great *natural*, that runs lolling up and down" (*Romeo and Juliet*, II, iv, 96). *Honesty* meant 'honor,' or, when applied to a woman, 'chastity'; to *take a hint* was to seize an opportunity, not to act upon a covert suggestion; a man's *neaf* was his fist; *weeds* for the Elizabethans were just clothes; a *treacher* was a traitor (*King Lear*, I, ii, 133); Salisbury's "tears of soft *remorse*" at the death of Prince Arthur were not the result of conscience, but of pity (*King John*, IV, iii, 50); *suggest* meant 'tempt,' *still* meant 'always,' and to be *stuffed* was to have a cold (*Much Ado*, III, iv, 64).

Occasionally, modernization of spelling has erased some of the meaning. "He wears *cruel* garters," is the Fool's comment upon Kent in the stocks (*King Lear*, II, iv, 7). His wit would be better appreciated if the spelling *crewel*, meaning 'embroidered,' of the quarto edition had been preserved. Sometimes the conditions of Elizabethan life color the most vivid figures of speech. Thus, in the touching scene with Brutus, Portia asks:

> Dwell I but in the suburbs
> Of your good pleasure? If it be no more,
> Portia is Brutus' harlot, not his wife. (*Julius Cæsar*, II, i, 285 ff.)

Shakespeare is thinking, not of Rome, but of his own London and the disreputable districts across the Thames.

As a whole, Shakespeare's English is nearer to its sources than is English today, and his words, whether native ones or foreign derivatives, are nearer the root meanings than at present. Thus, *starve*, like its root, Anglo-Saxon *steorfan* and German *sterben*, may mean simply 'to die.' *Atone* retains its original sense of 'reconcile' [literally, to make *at one*]. *Doom* means 'judgment' as in *Doomsday*. *Meat* is 'food,' and "the funeral baked meats" of *Hamlet* (I, ii, 180) 'pastry.' *Gossip*, as a noun, is a 'crony' or a 'familiar'; *sadness* is but 'seriousness,' and *quick*, 'alive.' *Shrewd*, meaning 'sharp,' is more frequently used to describe a woman's tongue than a man's wits; *wit* refers to the mind generally; to *lie* in a city is to 'dwell' there; to *tell* is to 'count'; and to *owe* often means to 'own.' *Let* usually has its modern legal sense of 'hinder,' as in Hamlet's "Unhand me, gentlemen. . . . I'll make a ghost of him that *lets* me" (I, iv, 85). *Learn* has both its modern meaning and the sense of 'teach,' as in Desdemona's words to her father:

> My life and education both do *learn* me
> How to respect you. (*Othello*, I, iii, 183–4.)

Poor Tom's "Mice and rats, and such small deer" (*King Lear*, III, iv, 144), preserves an obsolescent meaning for 'animals.' Compare "When night dogs run, all sorts of deer are chas'd" (*The Merry Wives*, V, v, 252). To *like* may be used in its modern sense to express a preference, but it also has its old meaning of to 'please.' Thus, Diomed says to Cressida, "I do not *like* this fooling," and the surly Thersites mutters, "Nor I, by Pluto; but that that *likes* not you, pleases me best" (*Troilus and Cressida*, V, ii, 101). Likewise, *brave*, which is frequently applied to attire, has its original Italian meaning of 'splendid,' or at least a sense of general approbation: "That's my *brave* spirit" (cf. German *brav*, 'good').

Words derived from Latin also retain more of their original meaning than at present. Thus, Bolingbroke and Mowbray *appeal* [accuse] each other of treason (*Richard II*, I, i, 27); Warwick is *advertis'd* [informed] of the Queen's approach (*3 Henry VI*, II, i, 116); and Henry V at Harfleur that his army is *address'd* [ready] for the march to Calais (*Henry V*, III, iii, 58). So, too, *prevent* in Shakespeare often has its original meaning of 'go before' or 'anticipate'; *reduce* of 'bring back'; *credit* of 'believe'; *repeal* of 'call back'; *expect* of 'wait for'; *provoke* of 'call forth'; *abuse* of 'deceive'; *peruse* of 'examine thoroughly'; *prove* of 'test'; and *invest* of 'clothe.' *Envy* means 'malice'; a *fact* is a 'deed,' often a 'crime'; *accident* is but a 'happening'; to be *desperate* is to be 'without hope'; an *aspersion* is but a 'sprinkling'; *important* letters are 'urgent' ones; an *argument* is but a 'subject for discussion'; *passion* is any 'strong emotion,' particularly of 'suffering'; *competitors* are 'partners' and not 'rivals'; and *success* but a 'result,' either good or bad. Rosalind threatens Touchstone with being whipped for *taxation* [censure] (*As You Like It*, I, ii, 91); Bassanio discovers "fair Portia's counterfeit [portrait]" in the leaden casket (*The Merchant of Venice*, III, ii, 116); Oberon describes Helena of Athens as "all *fancy* sick [love-sick] and pale of *cheer* [face]" (*A Midsummer Night's Dream*, III, ii, 96); warlike Harry will "assume the *port* [bearing] of Mars" (*Henry V*, Prologue); Hermia and Helena, "like two *artificial* [skillful] gods" with their needles created both one flower on a piece of embroidery (*A Midsummer Night's Dream*, III, ii, 203); Horatio swears he could not have believed in the ghost "without the *sensible* [perceived by the senses] and true avouch" of his own eyes (*Hamlet*, I, i, 57); things rank and gross in nature possess Denmark *merely* [completely] (*ibid.*, I, ii, 137); Hamlet bids the players "o'erstep not the *modesty* [moderation] of nature" (III, ii, 21); Banquo questions the witches to learn whether they are "*fantastical* [creations of the imagination] or that which outwardly they show" (*Macbeth*, I, iii, 53); and Lady Macbeth, reading the letter from her husband, reflects upon those qualities of character which impede him

> from the golden round
> Which Fate and *metaphysical* [supernatural] aid doth seem
> To have thee crown'd withal. (I, v, 29–31.)

In each case, the italicized word had a meaning in Shakespeare's time which was closer to the Latin root meaning than at present. How literally Latin much of the Elizabethan vocabulary actually was can be perceived from the following passage from Prospero's speech to Miranda in *The Tempest* (I, ii, 26 ff.):

> The direful *spectacle* [sight] of the wrack, which touch'd
> The very *virtue* [essence] of *compassion* [pity] in thee,
> I have with such *provision* [foresight] in mine art
> So safely ordered, that there is no soul—
> No, not so much *perdition* [loss] as an hair
> Betid to any creature in the vessel
> Which thou heard'st cry, which thou saw'st sink.

Not to recognize these original meanings is, of course, to fail to appreciate the niceties of expression of an Elizabethan writer.

Occasionally, the difference between Shakespeare's meaning and ours lies in the fact that the modern meaning represents a figurative use, whereas the earlier meaning does not. *Bombast*, now altogether metaphorical, presents a pretty illustration, because Shakespeare used it in both its literal and its figurative sense. The word is derived from the Latin *bombax* and referred to a kind of padding which puffed out gentlemen's trousers in Shakespeare's time. Therefore, it is appropriately used by Prince Hal to describe Falstaff: "my sweet creature of *bombast*" (*1 Henry IV*, II, iv, 359). But it also had its modern sense in the description of how Othello evaded Iago's mediators

> with a *bombast* circumstance,
> Horribly stuff'd with epithets of war. (*Othello*, I, i, 13.)

To *haggle*, at present, usually implies a wrangling over prices; in Shakespeare's day, its meaning was to 'hack':

> Suffolk first died, and York, all *haggled* over,
> Comes to him. (*Henry V*, IV, vi, 11.)

Horatio, explaining the effect of cock-crow upon ghost-walking, speaks of the "*extravagant* and *erring* spirit" hying to his confines, indicating, not a spirit who lives beyond his means or makes mistakes, but one who merely wanders out of bounds (*Hamlet*, I, i, 154). Our modern meanings of both of these words are figurative. Likewise, Macbeth's words to Banquo's ghost: "Thou hast no *speculation* [sight] in those eyes" (*Macbeth*, III, iv, 95), represent the Latin meaning, while our word *speculation* represents a figurative application.

Another interesting result of Elizabethan Latinity may be seen not only in the use of Latin words to replace native ones, but also in the use of native words as the precise equivalents of borrowed ones. Thus, Prospero works his high charms that his enemies are "all *knit up* [perplexed: Latin *per* + *plectere*, 'to knit'] in their distractions" (*The Tempest*, III, iii, 89); Adriana, the ridiculously jealous wife of Antipholus of Ephesus, is "*press'd down* [depressed] with conceit [worry]" (*The Comedy of Errors*, IV, ii, 65); Romeo hurries to his "*ghostly* [spiritual] father's cell" (*Romeo and Juliet*, II, ii, 189); and Brutus bids Cassius "*chew* [ruminate] upon this" as he gives evidence of being moved by his friend's blandishments (*Julius Cæsar*, I, ii, 171). Prince Hal, standing beside his father's death-bed, washes "with *kindly* [natural] tears his gentle cheeks" (*2 Henry IV*, IV, v, 84). The friar in *Measure for Measure* (III, ii, 153) justifies the absent duke by begging that he be "but testimonied in his own *bringings forth* [productions]." Rosalind promises to produce Orlando's beloved if he really is as much enamored as his gesture "*cries it out* [proclaims it]" (*As You Like It*, V, ii, 69). Cymbeline, pleased at Posthumus's forgiveness of Iachimo, learns his "*freeness* [liberality] of a son-in-law," and pardons all his prisoners (*Cymbeline*, V, v, 421). Beatrice, at the repudiation of her innocent cousin Hero, exclaims: "What, *bear her in hand* [maintain her hopes] until they came to take hands" (*Much Ado*, IV, i, 304–05). Other examples are *bears down* [oppresses] (*The Merchant of Venice*, V, i, 214), and *put you o'er* [refer] (*King John*, I, i, 62). All of these phrases are literal translations of the Latin derivatives we should use more naturally in their places today.

Still another effect of Elizabethan familiarity with Latin was the possibility of bilingual puns. "Ovidius Naso was the man," exclaims the pedant in *Love's Labor's Lost* (IV, ii, 127), "and why indeed Naso, but for the smelling out the odoriferous flowers of fancy." The allusion to Latin *nasus*, 'nose,' is only too obvious. Similarly, Touchstone talks over the head of the ridiculous goat-girl Audrey, but not over that of the Elizabethan auditor, when he explains: "I am here with thee, and thy goats, as the most *capricious* [Latin *caper*; hence, goatlike, lascivious] poet, honest Ovid, was among the *Goths* [pronounced *goates*]" (*As You Like It*, III, iii, 7). Another double pun upon the same Latin word occurs in *Twelfth Night*, I, iii, 129. The spindly Sir Andrew is showing Sir Toby how he can dance: "Faith, I can cut a *caper*." And Toby adds significantly, "And I can cut the *mutton* to't." Here *caper* sauce probably suggested *mutton*, which was also Elizabethan slang for 'prostitute'; but it is possible, too, that the *capers* of young goats produced the connection through Latin. Similar, but involving Italian, is another pun in the same play. Hearing that Dick surgeon is drunk, Sir Toby calls him a rogue and a *passy measures pavin*. The epithet is a tipsy corruption of *passamezzo pavana*, a slow and stately dance with eight bars to each "strain" of music. It was suggested by Feste's remark that Dick's eyes are "*set at eight* i' the morning" (V, i, 205–07). When such associations could be expected in the public theatre, it is not likely that Shakespeare's Latin—or Italian either —remained small for long.

DEPRECIATION AND ELEVATION

Words, of course, have their ups and downs, and many of the changes in meaning from Shakespeare's day to this represent either a depreciation or an improvement in meaning. Like the word *occupy*, "which was an excellent good word before it was ill-sorted" (*2 Henry IV*, II, iv, 161), many of the expressions Shakespeare used have since been ruined by their associations. The verb *blubber*, which is now applied to bubbly weeping of spoiled children, in Shakespeare's time still meant to cry hard, and was suitable for describing the paroxysms of grief in which the nurse left Juliet (*Romeo and Juliet*, III, iii, 87). But it was already slipping. When Falstaff, setting out for the wars, calls once more to take leave of Doll Tearsheet, the stage direction reads: "She comes *blubbered*" (*2 Henry IV*, II, iv, 421). The word *imp* originally meant merely 'child' or 'offspring'; but puerile mischief alone is not responsible for its decline, as its associations in "the Devil and his imps" will witness. Shakespeare, however, could still use the word in its noblest sense and speak of young Prince Hal as "a royal *imp* of fame" (*2 Henry IV*, V, v, 46), or apply it playfully to Moth who was about to present Great Hercules in the pageant of the Nine Worthies (*Love's Labor's Lost*, V, ii, 592). Cleopatra's "pretty *worm* of Nilus" is still a snake (*Antony and Cleopatra*, V, ii, 243); a *bug* is not a harmless insect, but a 'bugbear' (*The Winter's Tale*, III, ii, 93); *noise* may refer to music in the air (*Antony and Cleopatra*, IV, iii, 13 ff.; *The Tempest*, III, ii, 136); *sullen* still means 'solemn' without suggestion of ill-humor; *silly* women are merely 'helpless'; and *silly sooth* is the 'simple truth.' To *wink* in Shakespeare means to close both eyes and keep them closed, not to blink playfully with one. Hence, Valentine's remark to his rival Thurio: "Upon a homely object Love can *wink*" (*The Two Gentlemen*, II, iv, 98), acted upon in the modern sense might have a very different effect from the one intended. Kent speaks of *horrid* [Latin *horridus*, 'bristly,' i. e., hair-raising] thunder on the heath (*King Lear*, III, ii, 46), and *naughty* had for Shakespeare's time no connotation of triviality. *Naughty* meant literally 'good for nothing,' as in "thou *naughty* varlet" (*Much Ado*, IV, ii, 74), and "So shines a good deed in a *naughty* world" (*The Merchant of Venice*, V, i, 91). Yet its modern significance was already beginning to appear: "You smile and mock me," says Cressida coyly, "as if I meant *naughtily*" (*Troilus and Cressida*, IV, ii, 38).

Numerous other words in Shakespeare's vocabulary have later histories that are sad witnesses of human frailty. The tendency to procrastinate is reflected in words of time. Both *presently* and *by and by* in Shakespeare, as a rule, have their original meaning of 'immediately.' "Come, answer not, but to it *presently*," orders the impatient Julia as Lucetta prepares her disguise (*The Two Gentlemen*, II, vii, 89). But they are already slowing down. "I come *anon*," says Juliet, lingering with Romeo, "*by and by*, I come" (*Romeo and Juliet*, II, ii, 150). *Soon*, too, had lost its original precision, and in such phrases as "*soon* at night," "*soon* at five o'clock," had acquired the sense of 'about.'

Other words illustrate other human failings. *Lewd*, 'ignorant,' and *vulgar*, 'pertaining to the common people,' still retain in Shakespeare their original meanings, but the implication of contempt was already creeping in. Reference is made to a "*vulgar* comment" in *The Comedy of Errors* (III, i, 100), and the meanings 'common,' 'low,' and 'mean' are frequent. Into *cunning*, applied to cooks and school masters as well as to witches with the original meaning 'skillful,' the sense of crookedness and trickery was only just filtering. Likewise, when Richard of Gloucester expresses his contempt for the pleasures of the piping times of peace and his determination to play the *villain* (*Richard III*, I, i, 30), he means merely that he will be 'boorish.' Shakespeare could apply *smug* to a bridegroom (*King Lear*, IV, vi, 202) meaning only that he was neatly and bravely attired. *Officious* is used merely as 'zealous in duty' without the implication of meddlesomeness, *censure* is 'judgment' rather than 'fault-finding,' and *plausible* still has its root meaning of 'praiseworthy' rather than 'specious.' A *libertine* was but one who followed his own inclinations, and *lust*, like German *lust*, sometimes still retained for Shakespeare a general meaning of 'pleasure' or 'delight.' *Wench*, originally just 'girl' before it was applied, like *maid*, to servants, was still unstained:

> The tongues of mocking *wenches* are as keen
> As is the razor's edge, invisible. (*Love's Labor's Lost*, V, ii, 256–7.)

Wanton, too, implied nothing more than playfulness or irresponsibility. "I would have thee gone," says Juliet to Romeo:

> And yet no farther than a *wanton's* bird
> That lets it hop a little from his hand . . .
> And with a silken thread plucks it back again.
> (*Romeo and Juliet*, II, ii, 178 ff.)

An adjective use occurs in *King Lear* (IV, i, 38):

> As flies to *wanton* boys are we to th' gods,
> They kill us for their sport.

Happily, it is possible to place beside these modern degenerates a few words that have grown in vigor since Shakespeare's time. A good example is *nice*. Today, aside from its vaguely commendatory sense, the word is so anemic as to have hardly any meaning at all. Originally, about Chaucer's time, it came into English through French, from Latin *nescius*, 'ignorant' or 'foolish.' By Shakespeare's day, the meaning had narrowed to 'foolishly particular' or 'prudish.' The lady beloved of Silvia's father is *"nice and coy"* (*The Two Gentlemen*, III, i, 82); Rosaline, inviting the gentlemen to dance, says "we'll be not *nice;* take hands" (*Love's Labor's Lost*, V, ii, 219); and Benvolio bids Tybalt "bethink how *nice* [trivial] the quarrel is" (*Romeo and Juliet*, III, i, 159). The sense of 'precise' is already coming in, but *nice* does not have in Shakespeare its modern colloquial meaning. *Fond* is another word that has shown improvement through the ages. Shakespeare uses it in its general meaning of 'foolish.' "How *fondly* dost thou reason," says Adriana to the wrong Antipholus (*The Comedy of Errors*, IV, ii, 57), and Lear speaks of himself as a "very foolish *fond* old man" (*King Lear*, IV, vii, 60). So, too, *vulgar fame* is but 'common talk,' *emulation,* 'jealous contention,' rather than the striving toward an ideal, a *tom-boy,* now applied to a young hoyden, is a 'strumpet,' and luxury means 'lust' or 'bestiality,' a sense it has today exchanged for 'splendor' or 'extravagance.' *Fellow* and *companion,* now words of repute, were in Shakespeare's time still words of contempt. "Turn Melancholy forth to funerals," says Theseus apropos of his wedding, "the pale *companion* is not of our pomp" (*A Midsummer Night's Dream*, I, i, 16). *Modern* for Shakespeare may mean 'according to pattern' or 'moderate,' as well as 'fashionable,' or 'up to date.' Hence, "violent sorrow seems a *modern* ecstasy" (*Macbeth*, IV, iii, 170); the empty overdone grief of Juliet's family is a *"modern* lamentation" (*Romeo and Juliet*, III, ii, 120); and the Justice in Jaques's Seven Ages of Man is "full of wise saws [proverbs] and *modern* instances [outworn examples]" (*As You Like It*, II, vii, 156). Of course, the number of words that succeeded in becoming elevated is less than that of those which deteriorated through the centuries.

SHAKESPEARE'S VOCABULARY AND ELIZABETHAN CULTURE

Besides these changes in value, there are other effects of time upon language which are just as important to the reader of Shakespeare. Words express the thought and the civilization of an age, and there are many expressions in Shakespeare, now obsolete, that are rich in the color of Elizabethan culture. Ancient scientific theories and superstitions, which have now been abandoned, like the Plinian and medieval unnatural natural history, yield many puzzling allusions. There are not only mentions of the well-known myths, like the swan-song (*Othello*, V, ii, 247), the transformation of horse-hairs into snakes (*Antony and Cleopatra*, I, ii, 200), and the madding shrieks of the mandrake root (*Romeo and Juliet*, IV, iii, 47), but more attractive ones still. Juliet's "death-darting eye of *cockatrice*" (*Romeo and Juliet*, III, ii, 47) and Polixenes's plea:

> Make me not sighted like the *basilisk;*
> I have look'd on thousands who have sped the better
> By my regard, but kill'd none so (*The Winter's Tale*, I, ii, 388 ff.)

are allusions to the mythical reptile, hatched from a cock's egg, the very look of which could kill (cf. *Twelfth Night*, III, iv, 215). The myth arising from the chameleon's small interest in food gives point to Speed's assurance to his love-sick master: "Though the chameleon Love can feed on the air, I am one that am nourish'd by my victuals, and would fain have meat" (*The Two Gentlemen*, II, i, 178; cf. *Hamlet*, III, ii, 98). The fabulous toadstone furnishes the banished duke in Arden with a figure for his praise of the sweet uses of adversity:

> Which, like the toad, ugly and venomous,
> Wears yet a precious jewel in his head. (*As You Like It*, II, i, 13.)

The belief, probably begot of its feeding habits, that the pelican nourished its young on its own life-blood, yields the phrase, "the kind life-rendering pelican" in *Hamlet* (IV, v, 146), and the allusion to the rapacious daughters of King Lear as "those pelican daughters" (III, iv, 77). The old supposition that ferns produced invisible seed capable of communicating invisibility to anyone who possessed it is also alluded to (*1 Henry IV*, II, i, 96). None of these allusions was obscure to Shakespeare's audiences; they were part of Elizabethan lore.

Occasionally, however, an allusion seems much more recondite. Regan's remark to her doting father:

> I profess
> Myself an enemy to all other joys
> Which the most *precious square of sense* possesses;
> And find I am alone felicitate
> In your dear Highness' love (*King Lear*, I, i, 74 ff.)

puzzled scholars for centuries. On the assumption that the text must be corrupt, numerous attempts were made to emend the italicized phrase—*precious spirit, precious sphere, spacious sphere, precious treasure, precious shape*, and so on. At length, a Shakespearean scholar read a popular scientific treatise of the Middle Ages which made all clear. Bartholomeus Anglicus in his book *Of the Properties of Things* divides the soul into three parts: (a) the vegetable soul, which consists of the three virtues of self-sustainment, growth, and reproduction, "like to a triangle in Geometry"; (b) the sensible soul,

> like to a quadrangle square and four cornered. For in a quadrangle is a line drawn from one corner to another corner, afore it maketh two triangles; and the soul sensible maketh two triangles of virtues. For wherever the soul sensible is, there is also the soul vegetabilis;

and (c) the rational soul, which is likened to a circle, the most perfect of figures. It is to the sensible soul that Regan alludes.[1]

[1] Edward Dowden, "Elizabethan Psychology," in *Essays Modern and Elizabethan*, London (1910).

Similarly, an examination of the old science of physiology serves to explain some other passages. Queen Margaret's references to blood-consuming or blood-drinking sighs (*2 Henry VI*, III, ii, 61 and 63) and Oberon's description of love-sick Helena, pale of cheer "with sighs of love, that costs the fresh blood dear" (*A Midsummer Night's Dream*, III, ii, 97), are allusions to the popular notion that every sigh caused the heart to lose a drop of blood. So, too, Sir Toby's conviction of Sir Andrew's cowardice: "if he were open'd and you find so much blood in his liver as will clog the foot of a flea, I'll eat the rest of the anatomy" (*Twelfth Night*, III, ii, 66), is but one of many references to the liver as the seat, not only of love and the violent passions, but of courage as well. The adjectives *pale-livered, lily-livered, milk-livered* occur frequently.

The theory that one's physical and mental qualities were determined by the *disposition* in the body of the four humors—blood, phlegm, choler, and melancholy—is also often found. Don Armado, ordinarily not a model of common sense, when afflicted by "the black oppressing humor," very wisely takes a walk in the park as a cure (*Love's Labor's Lost*, I, i, 235). *Choleric* is used many times for 'angry' or 'irascible,' and Hostess Quickly, notorious for her misapplications of words, bids the excitable Dr. Caius "be not so *phlegmatic*" when he discovers Simple in his closet (*The Merry Wives*, I, iv, 79). *Sanguine* is the only one of these adjectives that Shakespeare does not use figuratively; it has always a literal meaning, as when Falstaff is called a "*sanguine* [red-faced] coward" (*1 Henry IV*, II, iv, 268). The word *humor* itself has a variety of meanings in Shakespeare, and its fashionable vogue with his contemporaries is frequently ridiculed, notably in Corporal Nym, who has become famous for "there's the humor of it." All of this physiological vocabulary is still good English, even though the theory which gave it birth has been abandoned. But Shakespeare's usage is nearer the original significance than ours.

Astrology also yielded frequent allusions to the music of the spheres or the influence of the stars upon human destiny or character. Romeo and Juliet are "star-crossed lovers," and Don John's birth under Saturn (*Much Ado*, I, iii, 12) itself goes a long way toward explaining his evil nature. But there are other allusions as well. When Prince Hal finds Falstaff dandling Doll Tearsheet on his knee, his amazement is expressed in astronomical terms: "Saturn and Venus this year in conjunction? What says the almanac to that?" (*2 Henry IV*, II, iv, 286). Even more amusing is an allusion in *Twelfth Night*, when thin-faced Sir Andrew and rotund Sir Toby set about some revels and the anemic Andrew begins to dance. His confession a moment before that he feared his beef-eating spoiled his wit is too much for Sir Toby, who demands: "Were we not born under Taurus?" Olivia's suitor, however, detects a false allusion: "Taurus? That's sides and heart." "No, sir," says Sir Toby, "it is legs and thighs" (I, iii, 147 ff.). Both are wrong; Taurus, much more appropriately to these topers, governed neck and throat. And the Elizabethan audience knew it.

TECHNICAL TERMS

Many Elizabethan technical terms naturally found their way into Shakespeare's text. The abundance of musical terms especially is most remarkable; by no other author are they used so frequently. The words are often not our words, which are Italian and a later importation. But, even if they sound strange to us, we may be sure that they were familiar enough to Shakespeare's auditors, whose love of music has already been commented upon. Most of the instruments are now archaic, like the *dulcimer* and the *psaltery* (both stringed); the *recorder*, a kind of flute; the *sackbut*, a kind of harpsichord; the *viol de gamba*, a bass viol; or the *hautboy* [oboe]. The musical instruments of the English Bible, it will be seen, are Elizabethan rather than Hebrew. The names of songs, likewise, are quite as unfamiliar to a modern reader. There are *plain-songs* [simple melodies] and *catches* [part-songs], *descants* [accompaniments], and *airs* [melodies], *madrigals* [elaborate part-songs], and *dumps*, "so dull and weary." The terminology is stranger still: notes are *crotchets*, the keys of an instrument are the *jacks*, discords are *jars*, soft music is *still music*, a part-song is *broken music*, refrains or burdens are called *holdings*, and a concert is a *consort*. Only before an audience familiar with music would it be possible for Julia and Lucetta to enjoy such an extended musical metaphor as this over a letter from Proteus:

Jul.	Some love of yours hath writ to you in rhyme.
Luc.	That I might sing it, madam, to a *tune*.
	Give me a note; your ladyship can *set*.
Jul.	As little by such toys as may be possible.
	Best *sing* it to the *tune* of "*Light o' Love.*"
Luc.	It is too *heavy* for so *light* a *tune*.
Jul.	*Heavy?* Belike it hath some *burden* then?
Luc.	Ay, and *melodious* were it, would you *sing* it.
Jul.	And why not you?
Luc.	I cannot *reach* so *high*.
Jul.	Let's see your *song*. How now minion!
Luc.	Keep *tune* there still, so you will *sing* it out.
	And yet methinks I do not like this *tune*.
Jul.	You do not?
Luc.	No, madam, it is too *sharp*.
Jul.	You, minion, are too saucy.
Luc.	Nay, now you are too *flat*,
	And mar the *concord* with too harsh a *descant*.
	There wanteth but a *mean* to fill your *song*.
Jul.	The *mean* is drown'd with your unruly *bass*.

(*The Two Gentlemen*, I, ii, 79 ff.)

Shakespeare frequently used musical terms in a figurative as well as literal sense. Mercutio describes the Italianate fencer Tybalt with: "He fights as you sing *pricksong* [a song written down]; keeps time, distance, and proportion; rests me his *minim rest* [a short rest], one, two, and the third in your bosom" (*Romeo and Juliet*, II, iv, 21 ff.). "See if thou canst find Sneak's noise [i. e., band of musicians]," bids Hostess Quickly's drawer. "Mistress Tearsheet would fain hear some music" (*2 Henry IV*, II, iv, 13 ff.). Frequently, musical terms are the basis of puns. "Come," says bluff Prince Hal very prettily to the French princess, "your answer in *broken music*, for thy voice is music and thy English broken" (*Henry V*, V, ii, 263 ff.). Quite beautiful is Juliet's description of the lark whose song announces the dawn which separates her from Romeo:

> Some say the lark makes sweet *division* [melodic runs];
> This doth not so, for she divideth us.
> (*Romeo and Juliet*, III, v, 29–30; cf. *King Lear*, I, ii, 149.)

Dancing terms, too, fill Shakespeare's pages and furnish him with figures of speech. There is the French *brawl* which Don Armado mistakes for quarreling in French, the stately *galliard*, the lively *coranto*, the *canary*, and the *jig*. With all of these the Elizabethan audience was as familiar as we are with waltzes, tangos, or rhumbas. "Wooing, wedding, and repenting," says Beatrice cynically,

> is as a Scotch jig . . . and full as fantastical; the wedding, mannerly-modest, as a measure, full of state and ancientry; and then comes repentance and, with his bad legs, falls into the cinque pace [pronounced *sink apace*] faster and faster, till he sink into his grave. (*Much Ado*, II, i, 76 ff.)

Hunting, hawking, archery, fencing, jousting, and other enthusiasms which Shakespeare shared with his contemporaries are referred to in his pages. Falconry gave the famous allusion to the troupe of boy actors as an "*aery* [nest, i. e., training school] of children, little *eyases* [hawks]" in *Hamlet* (II, ii, 354), Viola's description of a court fool who must

> like the *haggard* [wild, intractable hawk], *check* at every feather
> That comes before his eye (*Twelfth Night*, III, i, 71–2),

and Othello's heart-broken resolution about Desdemona, even if he did not act upon it:

> If I do prove her *haggard* [irreclaimable],
> Though that her jesses [thongs] were my dear heart-strings,
> I'ld *whistle her off* and let her *down the wind* [release her and give her
> freedom]
> To prey at fortune. (*Othello*, III, iii, 260 ff.)

Petruchio punningly speaks of Katharina the Shrew as if she were a hawk he was taming:

> My *falcon* [female hawk] now is *sharp* [hungry], and passing empty,
> And till she *stoop* [(a) yield, (b) turn upon her prey], she must not be full gorg'd,
> For then she never looks upon her *lure* [apparatus used to recall a hawk].
> Another way I have to *man* [tame] my *haggard*,
> To make her come, and know her keeper's call:
> That is to *watch* her [keep her awake], as we *watch* these kites,
> That *bate* [(a) flutter impatiently, (b) bait, feed], and beat, and will not be obedient.
>
> (*The Taming of the Shrew*, IV, i, 193 ff.)

Anticipating Romeo's coming, Juliet, too, thinks of herself as an untamed, agitated falcon:

> Come, civil night. . . .
> *Hood* my *unmanned* blood, *bating* in my cheeks.
> (*Romeo and Juliet*, III, ii, 10–14.)

Northumberland alludes to the practice of grafting new feathers in the wing of an injured hawk when he bids his loyal friends join with him to "*imp* out our drooping country's broken wing" (*Richard II*, II, i, 292). Macbeth is thinking of another practice, that of sewing shut the eyes of a hawk in training, as he waits impatiently for the night so that he might get up courage to kill Banquo and Fleance:

> Come, *seeling* Night,
> *Scarf up the tender eye* of pitiful Day.
> (*Macbeth*, III, ii, 46–7.)

An amusing compound, typically Shakespearean, is *woman-tyred*, 'henpecked,' in allusion to the practice of giving a hawk a leg or a wing of a pullet at which to pluck (*The Winter's Tale*, II, iii, 74). Hunting furnished the reference to Malvolio as a cur that is good at *faults* [breaks in the trail] and to a constable as a "hound that *runs counter* [follows a trail in the direction opposite to that which the game has taken, with a pun upon counter, 'debtors' prison'] and yet *draws dryfoot* [follows a scent] well" (*The Comedy of Errors*, IV, ii, 39).

Benedick is thinking of the lists when he replies to the twitting of Claudio: "Sir, I shall meet your wit *in the career*, an you charge it against me. I pray you choose another subject." Claudio maintains the figure: "Nay, then, give him another *staff*; this last was *broke cross*" (*Much Ado*, V, i, 135 ff.). Concerning archery, there are frequent allusions to *flights, bird-bolts, butts,* and *butt-shafts,* as well as to more technical matters (cf. *Much Ado*, I, i, 40).

In the same way, devotees of other Elizabethan amusements, now obsolete, found particularly vivid Shakespeare's many allusions to popular games. Thus, bowling supplies the metaphor for Faulconbridge's famous outburst against Commodity:

> the *bias* of the world,—
> The world who of itself is *peised* well,
> Made to run even upon even ground,

until this "vile-drawing *bias*" deflects its course,

> Makes it take head from all indifferency,
> From all direction, purpose, course, intent,

like a badly weighted bowl (*King John*, II, i, 574 ff.). No such figure would be possible today because too few persons are frequenters of bowling greens. Similarly, primero, a popular card game in Shakespeare's time, gave him a very useful phrase *to set up one's rest*, i. e., 'to hazard one's all' or 'to be determined.' Thus, Launcelot Gobbo, somewhat paradoxically, has "*set up his rest* to run away" (*The Merchant of Venice*, II, ii, 110), and Dromio jovially describes the constable as one "that *sets up his rest* to do more exploits with his mace than a morris pike" (*The Comedy of Errors*, IV, iii, 27), while the irresistible pun upon *rest*, 'repose,' at Juliet's tomb yields one of Romeo's most moving speeches:

> O, here
> Will I *set up my everlasting rest*,
> And shake the yoke of inauspicious stars
> From this world-wearied flesh. (*Romeo and Juliet*, V, iii, 109 ff.)

The names of Elizabethan coins give point to some of Shakespeare's puns. When the Chief Justice upbraids Falstaff with misleading young Hal: "You follow the young prince up and down, like his ill angel," the fat knight adroitly interprets "ill angel" as Lucifer, the angel of light, and also as the gold coin, worth six shillings and eight pence, which would not pass if it fell below the legal weight. "Not so, my lord," he replies, "your ill angel is light. But I hope he that looks upon me will take me without weighing" (*2 Henry IV*, I, ii, 186 ff.). At another time, the old rascal is not above thinking of the "legion of *angels*" that are at the bidding of Mrs. Ford (*The Merry Wives*, I, iii, 60; cf. *The Comedy of Errors*, IV, iii, 41). When Prince Hal dismisses the *noble*man who has been sent as a messenger from the court with the words: "Give him as much as will make him a *royal* man, and send him back again" (*1 Henry IV*, II, iv, 317 ff.), he is punning upon the names of two gold coins, *noble* and *royal*, which differed in value by ten groats. Touchstone's reply to weary Celia's plea that he bear with her is an allusion to the markings of the copper coins every member of Shakespeare's audience had in his pockets. "For my part, I had rather bear with you than bear you; yet I should bear no cross if I did bear you, for I think you have no money in your purse" (*As You Like It*, II, iv, 11 ff.). It is to the spare profile of Queen

Elizabethan Coins

GOLD

Sovereign

Ryal

Angel

SILVER

Groat

Sixpence

Threepence

(From R. Ruding: *Annals of the Coinage of Great Britain*, 1840)

Elizabeth with the Tudor rose back of the head that the bastard Faulconbridge is referring when he says that if he were as thin as his brother, then

> in mine ear I durst not stick a rose
> Lest men should say, "Look, where three-farthings goes!"
> (*King John*, I, i, 142–3.)

A similar design, without the rose, distinguished the "half-faced groat."
Other coins, like the *crown*, which Shakespeare uses to express large sums,
the *mark*, the *tester* or *testrel* (sixpence, stamped with a head), are frequently
mentioned, as well as various coins of foreign mintage, like the *cruzado*, the
denier, the *doit*, the *dollar*, the *ducat*, the *guilder*, the *quart d'ecu*, and the
chequin.

The legal terminology which Shakespeare used so glibly is another plentiful source of difficulty to his readers, some of whom, indeed, have looked
upon it as evidence that Shakespeare had more than an ordinary acquaintance
with the law and may even have been apprenticed to a solicitor. Macbeth resolves to "make *assurance double sure*, and take a *bond* of Fate" (*Macbeth*,
IV, i, 83–4), and the poet thinks of the time

> When to the *sessions* of sweet silent thought,
> I *summon* up remembrance of things past. (Sonnet 30.)

But other Elizabethan dramatists used law terms quite as freely as Shakespeare, who, investigation has shown, was not always accurate in his employment of them. It does not take a profound knowledge of law either to write
or to comprehend Hamlet's conglomeration of technicalities as he muses over
what might be a lawyer's skull:

> Where be his *quiddeties* now, his *quillets*, his *cases*, his *tenures*, and his *tricks?*
> . . . This fellow might be in's time a great buyer of land, with his *statutes*,
> his *recognizances*, his *fines*, his *double vouchers*, his *recoveries*. Is this the fine
> [end] of his *fines*, and the *recovery* of his *recoveries*, to have his fine pate full
> of fine dirt? (*Hamlet*, V, i, 107 ff.)

Whether or not the average London playgoer of Shakespeare's time was
better acquainted with current legal phraseology than his modern counterpart, either could appreciate the point of these allusions. The lingo, however,
is Elizabethan and not modern.

Heraldry also contributes its quota to Shakespeare's technical vocabulary,
and some of his most vigorous figures of speech are heraldic. One recalls
immediately the image of

> The rugged Pyrrhus, he whose *sable* arms,
> Black as his purpose . . .
> Hath now this dread and black complexion smear'd
> With *heraldry* more dismal. Head to foot
> Now is he total *gules*, horridly *trick'd*
> With blood of fathers, mothers, daughters, sons. (*Hamlet*, II, ii, 474 ff.)

Like most Elizabethan writers, Shakespeare repeatedly employed heraldic similes and metaphors, often punningly, as when Beatrice jests at Benedick's expense: "If he have wit enough to keep himself warm, let him bear it for a *difference* [i. e., a distinction which marks the arms of younger branches of a family] between himself and his horse" (*Much Ado*, I, i, 69 ff.; cf. Ophelia's "You must wear your rue with a *difference*," *Hamlet*, IV, v, 182). *Blazon, quarter, field, coat, shield,* and *crest* also occur frequently—simply, not technically—as in the description of Hermia and Helena:

> with two seeming bodies, but one heart;
> Two of *the first,* like coats in heraldry,
> Due but to one and crowned with one *crest.*
> (*A Midsummer Night's Dream,* III, ii, 212 ff.)

To many of Shakespeare's modern readers, his technical vocabulary may at first seem difficult and remote, but it is not, therefore, necessary to suppose Shakespeare in any way more learned in all these matters than many of his contemporaries. An observant man, he perceived the poetical relations of things and easily picked up about him the live words he needed to express these relations.

DIALECT, COLLOQUIALISM, AND SLANG

Besides these technical terms, which belong to a specialized vocabulary, now obsolete, there is another class of words in Shakespeare which gives trouble to the modern reader. It represents dialect, colloquialisms, or slang rather than standard English, and is pithy and flavorful rather than pretty. *Aroint,* the word used in putting witches to rout; *ballow,* a 'cudgel'; *buss,* to 'kiss'; *pother* and *pudder,* a 'disturbance'; *fardel,* a 'bundle'; *sprag,* 'active'; *tar,* to 'incite'; *cling,* to 'pinch,' 'shrivel'; *blood-boltered,* 'clotted'; *gleek,* to 'abuse'; *fettle,* to 'make ready'; *minnick,* 'mimic'; *squinny,* 'squint'; *quat,* 'pimple'; and *keel,* 'cool,' used to describe the stirring of greasy Joan, are all examples of homely village speech.

Sometimes such expressions are snares to the feet of the unwary interpreter. The old shepherd's first question on finding little Perdita: "A boy or a *child,* I wonder?" was not meant as a pointed distinction from which the actor can raise a laugh. Shakespeare merely used the word *child* as it is still used in the Midlands of England to mean 'girl.' There is also at least one instance in which Shakespeare used a dialectal word for subtle characterization. When the player declaims Æneas's tale to Dido before Hamlet and comes to the description of the aged Hecuba: "But who, O who, had seen the *mobled* queen"—he is interrupted by the sensitive young prince who detects the intrusion of the homely word instead of the appropriate poetic one: "The *mobled* queen?" Polonius, however, who is no judge in such matters and cannot be expected to appreciate Hamlet's dubiety, immediately approves:

"That's good; *'mobled* [muffled] queen' is good" (*Hamlet*, II, ii, 525 ff.). A point may be missed by the student who ignores the values of Elizabethan words.

Other expressions are colloquialisms or slang. Hamlet's reference to Polonius as a *fishmonger* [i. e., a pander] (*Hamlet*, II, ii, 173) may have some significance for his remarks to Ophelia later (III, i, 122 ff.). Juliet's nurse calls old Capulet a *cotquean*, 'old woman,' as he putters about the kitchen preparing for the wedding feast; Coriolanus's small son is just a *crack*, 'pert youngster'; Malvolio is made the "most notorious *geck* and *gull* that e'er invention play'd on"; to the Tribunes, Menenius's defense of Coriolanus is *clean kam*, 'all wrong.' Even "Ethiopes of their sweet complexion *crack* [boast]." *Bully* and *bully-rook* are terms of familiarity; *chinks* is money; a toper is appropriately called a *malt-worm*, a *toss-pot*, or a *malmsey-nose*; to be *fap* is to be maudlin drunk; a *fresh-fish* is a novice; and a *guinea-hen* is a strumpet. In addition, there is a fair-sized list of canting terms. Lesser linen drying on a hedge sets Autolycus's *pugging* [thieving] tooth on edge (*The Winter's Tale*, IV, iii, 7); a *prig* is a thief; a *bung*, a pickpocket; a *setter*, a decoy in a robbery; *coney-catching* rascals are fleecers; and a *crack-hemp* is a gallows-bird.

ELIZABETHAN USAGE

Just as there are peculiarities of meaning in Elizabethan words, so too there are peculiarities of usage and syntax. Measured by modern standards, Shakespeare's English often appears unconventional and ungrammatical, but it must not be supposed, therefore, that it is abnormal or that it represents lack of cultivation. It is merely representative of the best usage of his day. Whereas good usage now is bookish and scholarly, in Shakespeare's time standard English was closer to colloquial speech than is our writing today.

One of the most noticeable of Elizabethan licenses, and one closely akin to the coinage of new words, is the freedom with which one part of speech is used for another. Nouns are frequently made from verbs without at all altering their form. Claudius does not doubt that the "*hatch* and the *disclose*" of Hamlet's melancholy will be some danger (*Hamlet*, III, ii, 174); "besides *commends* and courteous breath," Bassanio sends rich gifts before him to Belmont (*The Merchant of Venice*, II, ix, 90); Portia commits the "husbandry and *manage*" of her house into Lorenzo's hands (*ibid.*, III, iv, 25); and Hermia is angry with Helena because "she hath made *compare* between our statures" (*A Midsummer Night's Dream*, III, ii, 290). Nouns are also formed from adjectives: "a sudden *pale*" usurps Venus's cheek (*Venus and Adonis*, 589), and Hamlet commends a play that was "caviare to the *general*" (*Hamlet*, II, ii, 457); often nouns are formed from adverbs, as in "the dark *backward* and abysm of Time" (*The Tempest*, I, ii, 50), "I was an *inward* of his" (*Measure for Measure*, III, ii, 138), or France's words to Cordelia, "Thou losest *here*, a better *where* to find" (*King Lear*, I, i, 264). Moreover, pronouns are used precisely as if they were common nouns: "Mantua's law is death to any *he* that utters" mortal drugs (*Romeo and Juliet*, V, i, 66), and Orlando carves verses on every tree in Arden to "the fair, the chaste, and unexpressive *she*" (*As You Like It*, III, ii, 10).

Similarly, verbs are formed from nouns and other parts of speech. "Still *virginalling* upon his palm?" queries Leontes as he watches Hermione and Polixenes exchange courtesies (*The Winter's Tale*, I, ii, 125). Posthumus thinks the oracle promising an end of his miseries "such stuff as madmen *tongue*, and *brain* not" (*Cymbeline*, V, iv, 147); Antony is filled with bitterness when the hearts that *spaniel'd* him at heels now "discandy, melt their sweets" on blossoming Cæsar (*Antony and Cleopatra*, IV, xii, 21); Claudius draws a figure from the "harlot's cheek *beautied* with plastering art" (*Hamlet*, III, i, 51); Henry IV will keep no "tell-tale to his memory that may repeat and *history* his loss" (*2 Henry IV*, IV, i, 203); and Cleopatra in imagination sees the time when scald rhymers will *ballad* her and Antony out of tune:

> The quick comedians
> Extemporally will *stage* us. . . . And I shall see
> Some squeaking Cleopatra *boy* my greatness
> I' the posture of a whore. (*Antony and Cleopatra*, V, ii, 215 ff.)

Occasionally, an intensive *it*, as object, is brought in to aid the noun in becoming a verb. Thus, "Lord Angelo *dukes it* well" (*Measure for Measure*, III, ii, 100), or "Shall sweet Bianca practice how to *bride it?*" (*The Taming of the Shrew*, III, ii, 253).

Adjectives, too, are made to do noun service:

> My master loves her dearly;
> And I, poor monster, *fond* as much on him
> (*Twelfth Night*, II, ii, 34–5),

says Cesario (Viola) after her first embassy to Olivia; "poor Andromache *shrills* her dolour forth" (*Troilus and Cressida*, V, iii, 84); and usury "*happies* those that pay the willing loan" (Sonnet 6). In the same way, adjectives are formed from other parts of speech. Ophelia thinks of the honey of Hamlet's "*music* vows" (*Hamlet*, III, i, 164); Hamlet speaks of the "*region* kites" and of being a "rogue and *peasant* slave" (*ibid.*, II, ii, 576); Oswald raises the house "with loud and *coward* cries" (*King Lear*, II, iv, 43); the Poet speaks of "this *beneath* world" (*Timon of Athens*, I, i, 44); there is the mention of the "fine point of *seldom* pleasure" (Sonnet 52); and Juliet gave Paris "what *becomed* love" she might (*Romeo and Juliet*, IV, ii, 26). "He *childed* as I *fathered*" (*King Lear*, III, vi, 117), is Edgar's exclamation as he makes comparison between Lear's unnatural daughters and his own (as he supposes) unnatural father. Adjectives are also used as adverbs. Shakespeare could speak of growing *instant* old (*Hamlet*, I, v, 94), of a sentiment being *noble* spoken (*Antony and Cleopatra*, II, ii, 98), of telling a person *plain* (*The Taming of the Shrew*, II, i, 171); he could even say, "*Sure*, he'll come" (*The Merry Wives of Windsor*, IV, iv, 77), a usage especially singled out as a vulgarism today. Even nouns occasionally take on adverbial functions: Coriolanus is "*vengeance* proud" (*Coriolanus*, II, ii, 6). To be sure, the use of one part of speech for another is in no wise different from usage sanctioned today, but the freedom was greater in Shakespeare's time than it is now.

Another peculiarity of Elizabethan usage, illustrated in Shakespeare, was the irregularity in the inflection of pronouns. Whereas, today, there is uncertainty in only a few instances, particularly regarding *who* and *whom*, in Shakespeare's day the confusion was much greater. The use of the nominative for the objective form is quite common: "You have seen Cassio and *she* together" (*Othello*, IV, ii, 3); "Pray you, *who* does the wolf love?" (*Coriolanus*, II, i, 8); "*who* t'advance and *who* to trash" (*The Tempest*, I, ii, 80–1); "He is in love, with *who?*" (*Much Ado*, I, i, 214). Shakespeare even used "between you and *I*" on one occasion (*The Merchant of Venice*, III, ii, 321). The use of the accusative form for the nominative is less frequent, but by no means unknown: "Blossom, speed *thee* well" (*The Winter's Tale*, III, iii, 46); "Is she as tall as *me?*" (*Antony and Cleopatra*, III, iii, 14); "That's *me*, I warrant you" (*Twelfth Night*, II, v, 87).

But it was the possessive case that was most troublesome. In the general absence of inflections, no Elizabethan seemed quite sure what to do with a genitive. Generally, the old case ending was retained; occasionally, it was dropped without a trace because it was clumsy, as in "my uncle Clarence angry ghost" (*Richard III*, III, i, 144). Sometimes the expression is made clumsier still by the introduction of *his*, as in: "the count *his* gallies" (*Twelfth Night*, III, iii, 26), a form which, by ellipsis, gradually became the practical equivalent of the old case ending. But the indefinite pronoun *it* was most bewildering. *His*, the historically correct form, seemed hardly proper since it was also the masculine possessive, and *its* had not yet established itself. Hence, Shakespeare frequently allowed the possessive of *it* to stand uninflected. The bitter Constance cries to little Arthur:

> go to *it* grandma, child!
> Give grandam kingdom, and *it* grandam will
> Give it a plum, a cherry, and a fig.
> (*King John*, II, i, 160–3.)

Another interesting passage is from *King Lear*. "You know, nuncle," says the Fool, "the hedge-sparrow fed the cuckoo so long, that it had *it* head bit off by *it* young" (I, iv, 236–8). Yet Shakespeare's use of *its*, on occasion, as in

The Winter's Tale (I, ii, 151–2): "How sometimes Nature will betray *its* folly, *its* tenderness," is an indication that the modern form was beginning to establish itself. The omission of the relative pronoun altogether was more widespread than in modern English, as in Isabella's: "I have a brother is condemned to die" (*Measure for Measure*, II, ii, 34), or Green's: "Besides, our nearness to the king in love is near the hate of those love not the king" (*Richard II*, II, ii, 127–8).

But what is perhaps more interesting to the general reader of Shakespeare than these matters of grammar are certain uses of the possessive and dative of pronouns. When Hamlet says to Horatio:

> There are more things in heaven and earth, Horatio,
> Than are dreamt of in *your* philosophy (Q₂ *Hamlet*, I, v, 166–7),

he is not emphasizing pointedly the shortcomings of his friend, as many actors do, but of philosophy generally. Shakespeare merely used a colloquial possessive where we should use no word at all. The case is precisely the same in Hamlet's dissertation upon grave-worms: "*Your* worm is *your* only emperor for diet. . . . *Your* fat king and *your* lean beggar is but variable service" (*ibid.*, IV, iii, 22 ff.), or in Lepidus's tipsy explanation of the origin of Egyptian reptiles: "*Your* serpent of Egypt is bred now of *your* mud by the operation of *your* sun; so is *your* crocodile" (*Antony and Cleopatra*, II, vii, 29–30). The ethical dative, too, is allowed to stand alone without the preposition required by modern usage. "John lays *you* plots," warns Pandolph (*King John*, III, iv, 146), instead of "lays plots *for you*"; and Borachio says of Margaret, "She leans *me* out at her mistress' chamber-window" [i. e., leans out *to me*] (*Much Ado*, III, iii, 156). Shakespeare was well aware of the absurdity to which these expressions on occasion led, and he made comic capital of it, as when Petruchio bids his man Grumio, "Knock *me* here," "rap *me* here," "knock *me* soundly," at the door to Hortensio's house. The dull fellow takes his meaning literally and begins looking over the audience: "Whom should I knock? Is there any man has rebus'd your worship?" and then, thinking he perceives the meaning, "Knock you here, sir! Why, sir, what am I, sir, that I should knock you here, sir?" (*The Taming of the Shrew*, I, ii, 5 ff.).

Another peculiarity is the use to which adjectives are sometimes put. Those ordinarily having an active sense are employed passively, and those of passive form have an active meaning. Thus, Juliet addresses Friar Laurence as "O *comfortable* friar" (*Romeo and Juliet*, V, iii, 148), instead of *comforting;* Benedick is described as a man who hath a *contemptible* [i. e., a contemptuous] spirit (*Much Ado*, II, iii, 187); warriors, like lions, do rush upon "their *hungry* prey" [i. e., that for which they are hungry] (*1 Henry VI*, I, ii, 28); Desdemona asks what *ignorant* sin she had committed (*Othello*,

IV, ii, 70); and heaven's cherubim are horsed upon the "*sightless* [invisible] couriers of the air" (*Macbeth*, I, vii, 23). Sometimes those adjectives properly expressing effect in modern English signify cause as Shakespeare used them. Thus, Adam is "oppressed with two *weak* evils, age and hunger" (*As You Like It*, II, vii, 132), the older Hamlet's death was caused by a "*leperous* distilment" [i. e., one causing leprosy] (*Hamlet*, I, v, 64), and Cæsar perceives that he is in "*negligent* danger" [i. e., danger caused by neglect] (*Antony and Cleopatra*, III, vi, 81).

Just as there is irregularity of other kinds, so there is irregularity of agreement in number. Many of these divergencies from modern standard English have been subjected to emendation by editors, but, in the original texts, Shakespeare speaks of a "team of horse" (*The Two Gentlemen*, III, i, 265), "twenty mile" (*The Merry Wives*, III, ii, 33), and even "these kind of knaves" (*King Lear*, II, ii, 107) and "these set kind of fools" (*Twelfth Night*, I, v, 95). In the case of subject and verb, plurals and compounds often draw singular verbs. Thus, "hanging and wiving goes by destiny" (*The Merchant of Venice*, II, ix, 83), "my old bones aches" (*The Tempest*, III, iii, 2), "Banquo and his Fleance lives" (*Macbeth*, III, ii, 37), "here comes the townsmen on procession" (*2 Henry VI*, II, i, 68), and "these high wild hills and rough uneven ways draws out our miles, and makes them wearisome" (*Richard II*, II, iii, 4–5). But there are instances when a singular subject is assigned a plural verb: "the voice of all the gods make heaven drowsy" (*Love's Labor's Lost*, IV, iii, 344–5), and "the silken tackle, swell with the touches of those flower-soft hands" (*Antony and Cleopatra*, II, ii, 214–5). The relation of pronoun and antecedent is particularly uncertain. "God send every one their heart's desire," says Margaret (*Much Ado*, III, iv, 61), and Venus and Adonis are represented "each leaning on their elbows and their hips" (*Venus and Adonis*, 44). In Shakespeare's day, these grammatical relationships had not yet been standardized.

Verbs, too, have their peculiarities. The subjunctive mood was more widely used in Shakespeare's time than it is now, appearing not only in conditional and other subordinate clauses, but also in independent clauses expressing possibility, desire, or command, thus:

> *Live* Roderigo,
> He calls me to a restitution. (*Othello*, V, i, 14.)

> She *were* an excellent wife for Benedick. (*Much Ado*, II, i, 366.)

> In thy vats our cares *be* drown'd,
> With thy grapes our hairs *be* crown'd.
> (*Antony and Cleopatra*, II, vii, 122–3.)

Further, as in foreign languages, the auxiliary *to be* is employed with verbs of motion: "His lordship *is* walk'd forth into the orchard" (*2 Henry IV*, I, i, 4); "the king himself *is* rode to view their battle" (*Henry V*, IV, iii, 2); "Don Pedro *is* approached" (*Much Ado*, I, i, 95); and "my cousin William *is* become a good scholar" (*2 Henry IV*, III, ii, 11). Intransitive verbs are also readily transformed into transitive ones: "The common executioner . . . *falls* not the axe upon the humbled neck, but first begs pardon" (*As You Like It*, III, v, 3-5), and every tedious stride Bolingbroke makes will but *remember* him what a deal of world he *wanders* from the jewels that he loves (*Richard II*, I, iii, 269).

Prepositions were also less restricted in Elizabethan than in modern English. Nowadays, there is uncertainty in only a few instances, such as 'averse *to*,' 'averse *from*'; 'compare *to*,' 'compare *with*'; 'different *to*,' 'different *from*,' 'different *than*.' In Shakespeare's day, there were fewer fetishes about such little words. Shakespeare could think *upon* or *on* a thing rather than *about* it, and he could make preparation *against* an event. His heart could burn *for* anger and his face be red *for* shame, instead of *from* or *with*, and an unperfect actor in his theatre might *with* his fear be put *besides* his part (Sonnet 23). He could know a thing *at* heart, have power *upon* rather than *over* another, speak the truth *by* his associates instead of *about* them, or have a quarrel *to* them (*Much Ado*, II, i, 243). He could trust *by* leisure him that mocked him once (*Titus Andronicus*, I, i, 301), and even have poor Antigonus torn to pieces *with* a bear (*The Winter's Tale*, V, ii, 69)—all because he lived in the kingdom of a fair vestal throned *by* the west (*A Midsummer Night's Dream*, II, i, 158). Some of these idioms recall Latin or German idioms, but, to modern eyes, it almost appears that any preposition would serve as well as another if it happened to come first to Shakespeare's hand. This freedom in the use of prepositions is seen also in several Elizabethan locutions which occur frequently. One is very near to the Latin dative of advantage or disadvantage: "I have a king here *to* my flatterer" (*Richard II*, IV, i, 306); "he's a yeoman that has a gentleman *to* his son" (*King Lear*, III, vi, 13); and "Destiny . . . that hath *to* instrument this lower world" (*The Tempest*, III, iii, 54). Today we should need *as* or *for* to express the meaning. Another example of the use of prepositions is the genitive of characteristic, illustrated by "thieves of mercy" [i. e., merciful thieves] (*Hamlet*, IV, vi, 21); "your state of honour" [honorable state] (*Macbeth*, IV, ii, 66); "men of sin" [sinful men] (*The Tempest*, III, iii, 53); "god of power" [powerful god] (*ibid.*, I, ii, 10); "brow of youth" [youthful brow] (*King Lear*, I, iv, 306); and "mind of love" [loving mind] (*The Merchant of Venice*, II, viii, 42).

IDIOM AND SYNTAX

Two extremely interesting idiomatic survivals into Shakespeare's time from earlier speech deserve especial attention here because they were stumbling blocks to Shakespeare's early editors, who were sticklers for grammatical convention and ignorant of historical English. They are the double comparative or superlative and the double negative. When Alexander Pope set about preparing Shakespeare's text for his edition in 1725, he altered many of the lines to conform to eighteenth-century usage. The double comparative and superlative had disappeared. He altered *more fitter* to *more fitting, more corrupter* to *far corrupter*, and Antony's splendid, "this was the *most unkindest* cut of all," to "this, this was the unkindest cut of all." Pope was not the only editor who supposed these constructions to have been errors. One finds in Shakespeare *more better, more fairer, more mightier, more proudlier, worser, most worst, most best, most boldest, most worthiest,* as well as *chiefest, perfectest,* and *extremest.* They are merely emphatic. Similarly, the double negative for emphasis is a native, natural English construction. In Anglo-Saxon it is very common, and everyone will recall Chaucer's quadruple negative in his description of the Knight, who

> never yet no vileynye ne sayde,
> In al his lyf, unto no manner wight.

In Shakespeare's time, the sophistry that two negatives make a positive had not yet been appropriated from Latin. "First he *denied* you had in him *no* right," reports the conscientious Luciana to her jealous sister (*The Comedy of Errors*, IV, ii, 7); and Trinculo and Stephano warn Caliban, "We'll *not* run, Monsieur Monster. *Nor* go *neither*" (*The Tempest*, III, ii, 21-2). However, it is not only Shakespeare's illiterates who use the double negative. Mercutio "will *not* budge for *no* man's pleasure" (*Romeo and Juliet*, III, i, 58), and Richard II asks the loyal groom who visits him in prison how he comes there

> Where *no* man *never* comes but that sad dog
> That brings me food to make misfortune live?
> (*Richard II*, V, v, 70-1.)

Besides these differences in usage between Shakespeare's English and our own, there are a few peculiarities of Elizabethan syntax to which the reader must become accustomed. Shakespeare's word order is not always that which is usual today; at first sight, his sentences often appear chaotic. He writes "dear my lord" for "my dear lord" (*Julius Cæsar*, II, i, 255), and "sweet my mother" instead of "my sweet mother" (*Romeo and Juliet*, III, v, 200). He speaks of "so new a fashion'd robe" (*King John*, IV, ii, 27), of "thou little better thing than earth" (*Richard II*, III, iv, 78), of "our suffering country under a hand accursed" (*Macbeth*, III, vi, 48-9), of "too hard a keeping oath" (*Love's Labor's Lost*, I, i, 65), of Orlando's "poor a thousand crowns" (*As You Like It*, I, i, 3), of "what a candy deal of courtesy" (*1 Henry IV*, I, iii, 251), and of "that whiter skin of hers than snow" (*Othello*, V, ii, 4).

"Tongue-tied our queen, speak you," bids Leontes, when we should say, "Our tongue-tied [i. e., silent] queen" (*The Winter's Tale*, I, ii, 27); and Hamlet is sure that

> Foul deeds will rise,
> Though all the earth o'erwhelm them, to men's eyes.
> (*Hamlet*, I, ii, 257-8.)

Finally, the freedom of Elizabethan language, as well as the colloquialism of the dramatic form, made it possible for Shakespeare to be more elliptical than we can. Shakespeare occasionally omitted terminations or whole words which modern usage requires to be included. Sometimes a simple objective case is used where today we should require both a personal and a relative pronoun, as in the following instances:

> *Him* [i. e., he whom] I accuse
> The city ports by this hath enter'd. (*Coriolanus*, V, vi, 5-6.)

> *Who* [i. e., he who] does i' the wars more than his captain can
> Becomes his captain's captain. (*Antony and Cleopatra*, III, i, 22-3.)

Elizabethan convention accounts for the suffixes *-ly* and *-est* used on only one word in a series when today they are required by all of the words:

> Good gentlemen, look fresh and merrily. (*Julius Cæsar*, II, i, 221.)

> The generous and gravest citizens. (*Measure for Measure*, IV, vi, 13.)

But the ease of dramatic speech accounts for most of the omissions of whole words:

> I bleed, sir; but not kill'd. (*Othello*, V, ii, 288.)

> They call him Doricles; and boasts himself
> To have a worthy feeding. (*The Winter's Tale*, IV, iv, 168-9.)

> I am in blood
> Stepp'd in so far that, should I wade no more,
> Returning were as tedious as go o'er. (*Macbeth*, III, iv, 136 ff.)

Ruff and doublet and farthingale were the ordinary costume of Shakespeare's time, but no one would seriously adopt them for modern street wear, and only the most quixotic enthusiast would suggest that we adopt the language which went with them for ordinary use today. Yet a survey such as this makes it easy to understand why the vigor and the richness of Shakespeare's English remains an inspiration to all who have a sense of style. Not since Shakespeare's day has language been so readily adaptable to the concrete, picturesque expression of feeling or thought. There is no better conclusion to a discussion of Elizabethan English than the splendid prophecy of its future which Richard Mulcaster penned in his *Elementary* (1582), when Shakespeare was just growing into manhood:

It is very manifest that the tongue itself hath matter enough in itself to furnish out an art and that the same mean which hath been used in the reducing of other tongues to their right will serve this of ours both for generality of precept and certainty of ground. . . . Whatsoever shall become of the English state, the English tongue cannot prove fairer than it is at this day, if it may please our learned sort to esteem so of it and to bestow their travail upon such a subject, so capable of ornament, so proper to themselves, and the more to be honored because it is our own. . . . This prerogative and liberty which the people hath to use both speech and pen at will is the cause, and yet not blamed therefor, why the English writers be now finer than they were some hundred years ago.

SUGGESTED REFERENCES

ABBOTT, E. A. *Shakespearian Grammar: An Attempt to Illustrate Some of the Differences between Elizabethan and Modern English.* London, Macmillan, 1869.

BARTLETT, JOHN (comp.). *A New and Complete Concordance or Verbal Index to Words, Phrases, and Passages, in the Dramatic Works of Shakespeare.* New York, Macmillan, 1894.

EKWALL, EILERT. *Shakespeare's Vocabulary, Its Etymological Elements.* Upsala University Press, 1903.

FRANZ, WILHELM. *Shakespeare-Grammatik* (3rd edition). Heidelberg, Carl Winter, 1924.

GORDON, GEORGE. *Shakespeare's English.* Society for Pure English Tract, xxix. Oxford, 1928.
  A brief study, with Shakespearean examples, of the Elizabethan freedom of making language as it was needed.

ONIONS, C. T. *The Oxford Shakespeare Glossary.* Oxford, Clarendon Press, 1911; revised edition, 1919.
  A fresh analysis of Shakespeare's vocabulary in the light of results published in the *New English Dictionary.*

SCHMIDT, ALEXANDER. *Shakespeare-Lexicon. A Complete Dictionary of All the English Words, Phrases, and Constructions in the Works of the Poet* (2 vols.). Revised and enlarged by Gregor Sarrazin. Berlin, Georg Reimer, 1902.

WILLCOCK, G. D. *Shakespeare as Critic of Language.* Shakespeare Association Lecture, 1934.

WILSON, F. P. *Shakespeare and the Diction of Common Life.* British Academy Lecture. Oxford, 1941.
  The contribution of homely diction to Shakespeare's vocabulary.

9

THE SOURCES OF

SHAKESPEARE'S PLAYS

For out of olde feldes, as men seyth,
  Cometh al this newe corn from yer to yere,
And out of olde bokes, in good feyth,
  Cometh al this newe science that men lere.
    —Chaucer, *Parlement of Foules.*

THE NEW STUDENT OF THE EARLY DRAMA IS OFTEN
shocked to learn that few of the Elizabethan dramatists troubled to invent
their own plots, and that Shakespeare, the greatest creator of them all, preferred to retell old stories which were familiar to his audiences. We know
the exact source of most of Shakespeare's plays. In some cases, it is difficult
to determine just which of several extant versions of an old tale he used,
but it is the exceptional play, of which *Love's Labor's Lost* and *The Tempest*
are the only examples, for which no satisfactory literary original has been
found. Moreover, all of the books Shakespeare used were popular in his day.
Beyond occasionally giving his stories a conventional Italian setting and
assigning Italian names to the characters, he made no attempt to disguise his
borrowing.

ELIZABETHAN "PLAGIARISM"

If, at first, this fact seems to deprive Shakespeare of some of his greatness,
one need only be reminded that Elizabethan values are not our values and
that modern conceptions of literary property belong to an age in which
literature has a competitive commercial value. Today, when an author
dramatizes or otherwise adapts the work of another, he does so with the

·[220]·

consent, often the collaboration, of the original author. The debt is acknowledged on the title-page or in the theatre program, and the two creators share in the royalties. The Elizabethans had a somewhat different standard. Stories, ideas, even phrases, were regarded as common literary property which anyone could translate or adapt. Consequently, Shakespeare's contemporaries set less store upon inventive originality than we do. Instead of searching futilely for novelty, their purpose was reinterpretation, transformation, re-expression of old things in the spirit of their own day and of their own individualities—in short, what we should call "creative imitation." A new treatment of an old subject merely became an open rival of the original.

Thus, John Lyly took a large part of his letter on education in *Euphues* (1579) from Plutarch, but gave it new significance in the development of his ideal Renaissance hero. Thomas Dekker's *Bellman of London* (1608) was borrowed wholesale from John Awdeley's *Fraternity of Vagabonds* (1561) and Thomas Harmon's *Caveat for Common Cursitors* (1566), but Dekker is immeasurably the racier author. Ben Jonson's famous song *To Celia*—"Drink to me only with thine eyes"—was taken, without formal acknowledgment, almost literally from the Greek of Philostratus, and his *Timber, or Discoveries Made upon Men and Matter* (1641) were observations "as they flow'd out of his daily readings." Dryden's defense of Jonson is equally applicable to Shakespeare:

> he has done his robberies so openly that we may see that he fears not to be taxed by any law. He invades authors like a monarch, and what would be theft in other poets is only victory in him. (*An Essay of Dramatic Poetry*, 1668.)

Hence, just as the Latin writers of the days of Plautus and Terence regarded an adaptation from the Greek as a new work, so the poets and dramatists of Shakespeare's day—like the 'Omer of Kipling's poem—thought nothing of taking what they might require—themes, plots, even stylistic ornament—from their predecessors. They regarded all earlier literature as an inexhaustible mine from which to dig treasure. The age was not deceived, nor was there any intent to deceive it. The sources were by no means obscure, but no formal acknowledgment was expected, and no man's monopoly was violated. Even Robert Greene's famous denunciation in his *A Groatsworth of Wit* (1592) of the "upstart crow beautified with our feathers" can hardly be interpreted as a direct charge of plagiarism against Shakespeare. As we have seen above (pp. 6–7), it was probably only a warning to his fellow playwrights that the new professional actors were parasites who, by mouthing their lines on the stage, would get all the gain and the glory from playwriting.

To be sure, there were some objections in Shakespeare's day to this practice of wholesale appropriation of other men's work. Joseph Hall, the satirist, lunges hard at the "plagiary[1] sonnet-wrights" who

> filch whole pages at a clap, for need,
> From honest Petrarch, clad in English weed.
> (*Virgidemiarum*, "Satires" [1598], Book IV,
> Satire ii, and Book VI, Satire i.)

Sir John Harington also has several amusing epigrams upon stealers of verses.[2] The objection, however, was generally not that plagiarism was dishonest, but rather that too frequently it was servile, uncritical, or secretive; it led to pedantry and affectation. It was what one did with what one appropriated that entitled one to claims of literary excellence. A quarryman is not a sculptor.[3] Or, as John Davies of Hereford put it:

> Old pictures well refreshed do seem as new,
> And none but artists know them to be old:
> Then they earn praise, as those that first them drew,
> Who made them, newly, their old beauty hold.
> (*Wit's Pilgrimage*, c. 1605–10.)[4]

Like the medieval author in his dependence upon authority, the Elizabethan poet sometimes preferred praise as a refresher of old beauty. Instead of looking directly at nature and into his own heart, he turned first to books and sought to give life to what he found there. Nowhere can one appreciate more fully the originality of Shakespeare than in a comparison of his works with their sources.

SHAKESPEARE'S READING

At the end of this chapter will be found a list of the principal sources of Shakespeare's plays, together with a brief indication of how, in each, the dramatist transformed his material. A careful examination of this list will produce several revelations: (a) Varied as Shakespeare's reading was, his acquaintance with books, even for his day, was not extraordinarily extensive. Others in his time—Daniel, Chapman, and Jonson, to name only a few— were much more widely read and took books much more seriously than did Shakespeare. Shakespeare may be called a "creative" reader rather than a scholar; he was apparently not familiar with what his age would have re-

---

[1] The *New English Dictionary* cites this as the first instance of the word in English. *Plagiarism* does not occur until 1621, *plagiarist* until 1674, and *plagiarize* until 1716. Even when they complained loudest, the English epigrammatists, one suspects, were merely conventional. Martial had made almost the same objections.

[2] Especially 112 and 149 in *The Letters and Epigrams of Sir John Harington*, ed. N. E. McClure (1930), pp. 191 and 206.

[3] Harington, Epigram 149.

[4] *The Complete Works of John Davies of Hereford*, ed. A. B. Grosart, II, h. 53.

THE

First and second

volumes of Chronicles,
comprising

1 The description and historie of England,
2 The description and historie of Ireland,
3 The description and historie of Scotland:

First collected and published by Raphaell
Holinshed, William Harrison,
and others:

Now newlie augmented and continued
(with manifold matters of singular
note and worthie memorie)
to the yeare 1586. by
Iohn Hooker *alias* Vowell Gent.
and others.

With conuenient tables at
the end of these
volumes.

Historiæ placeant nostrates ac peregrinæ

Title-page of Holinshed's *Chronicles*, Second Edition, 1586–7 garded as esoteric or strange lore. (b) Further, it will be apparent that there is no need to condone Shakespeare's borrowing merely on the ground that, by his genius, he easily transformed dross into living literature. Only rarely were the books that Shakespeare used inferior works. Today, some of his favorites, like the highly popular collections of *novelle* which had been brought to England from Italy, seem tiresomely artificial, sentimental, and tawdry. However, we cannot be sure that the Elizabethans thought of them in the same way. On the other hand, there are other books, like Holinshed's *Chronicles* or Plutarch's *Lives*, which were splendid reading in his time and have remained so to the present. They certainly did not need to borrow interest from the Shakespeare who dramatized them. (c) Finally, Shakespeare's adherence to his originals was far from slavish. Many of his plays— for example, *A Midsummer Night's Dream, The Merchant of Venice, King Lear, Cymbeline*—are really amalgams of diverse materials. There is hardly a play in which the dramatist did not modify his plot in some important way or enrich it greatly by his knowledge of the fundamental human significances of his theme.

The works from which Shakespeare fashioned his plays can be divided roughly into three main classes: (a) History and Biography, (b) Romantic Fiction in both prose and verse, and (c) the Older Drama. In addition, numerous other works, both ancient and modern, learned and popular, furnished hints which he turned to good purposes.

(a) In the first group belong such important works as *The Chronicles of England, Scotland, and Ireland*, compiled by Raphael Holinshed, himself like Shakespeare a Warwickshire man, out of the works of earlier historians. The book was first published in 1577 and again in an augmented edition in 1587. The second edition of Holinshed, and, doubtless, some of Holinshed's sources, including Edward Hall's *The Union of the Two Noble and Illustre Families of Lancaster and York* (1547), Shakespeare read with enthusiasm and knew well, for upon them he based not only his ten plays dealing with the reigns of English kings, but also *Macbeth, King Lear*, a story that had already been dramatized, and parts of *Cymbeline*. In addition, Shakespeare knew *The Mirror for Magistrates*, published in numerous editions from 1559 to 1610 and filled with "sad stories of the death of kings" and other illustrious men and women. Another outstanding book that also belongs in this group is *The Lives of the Noble Grecians and Romans, Compared together by that Grave, Learned Philosopher and Historiographer, Plutarch of Chæronea*, *c.* 75 A. D. One of the world's great books, Plutarch's *Lives* was particularly influential in the sixteenth century, when it was translated from Greek into Latin and most of the languages of Europe. It was in the noble English version of Sir Thomas North (1579), who worked from a French translation rather than from the original, that Plutarch reached Shakespeare. In this book

THE LIVES

OF THE NOBLE GRE-
CIANS AND ROMANES, COMPARED
together by that graue learned Philosopher and Historiogra-
pher, Plutarke of Chæronea:

Tranflated out of Greeke into French by IAMES AMYOT, Abbot of Bellozane,
Bishop of Auxerre, one of the Kings priuy counfel, and great Amner
of Fraunce, and out of French into Englishe, by
Thomas North.

Imprinted at London by Thomas Vautroullier dvvelling
in the Blacke Friers by Ludgate.
1 5 7 9.

Title-page of North's *Plutarch*, 1579

he found the materials for his Roman plays besides suggestions for several others. Hence, to the works of Holinshed and North, Shakespeare was indebted for nearly half of his dramas.

(b) To the second major class of material, that of Romantic Fiction, belong many stories, English and foreign, the pedigrees of which are much too long and complicated to recount here. Suffice it to say that, among the English writers, Shakespeare levied upon the best work of both his predecessors and his contemporaries. His *Troilus and Cressida*, for example, shows an acquaintance not only with Geoffrey Chaucer's version of this famous medieval love story, but, more particularly, with sixteenth-century modifications and continuations of the tale, especially as regards the character of the heroine. Chaucer's contemporary John Gower appears as Chorus in *Pericles*, and his presence as a character in that play is sufficient evidence that Shakespeare knew Gower's version of this famous old story of painful adventures in his *Confessio Amantis* (c. 1390), as well as the Elizabethan prose redactions of Lawrence Twine (1576, 1607) and George Wilkins (1608). For the immediate source of *Romeo and Juliet*, one need search no further than *The Tragical History of Romeus and Juliet*, a poem by Arthur Brooke (1562), which, in turn, was a redaction of a famous old story that appears in a number of forms in Italian. In Edmund Spenser's *Faerie Queene* (Book II, canto 10) he might have found one version of the Lear story as well as an episode (Book II, canto 4) that proved suggestive for *Much Ado about Nothing*, and from Sir Philip Sidney's *Arcadia* (1590) he derived the story of Gloucester and his sons to parallel that of Lear and his daughters. Shakespeare's debt to the contemporary novel, however, is greatest in *As You Like It* and *The Winter's Tale*. The former is a reworking of Thomas Lodge's pastoral romance, *Rosalynde: Euphues Golden Legacie* (1590), but conceived in the spirit of comedy instead of sentiment, while the latter represents a considerable modification of Robert Greene's *Pandosto: The Triumph of Time* (1588).

On the other hand, the stories of several of Shakespeare's plays, like that of Hamlet's *Mousetrap*, are "extant and writ in choice Italian," French, or Spanish. "Admirable and memorable histories" enjoyed great popularity in Elizabethan England, and several translations of these sensational stories were published, like William Painter's *Palace of Pleasure* (1566), Barnabie Riche's *Farewell to Military Profession* (1581), or George Whetstone's *Heptameron of Civil Discourses* (1582), each of which contains stories used by Shakespeare. The ultimate sources of these compilations were Boccaccio's *Decameron* (c. 1350), Cinthio's *Hecatommithi* (1565), Bandello's *Novelle* (1554), or some other foreign volume. The whole subject of the foreign sources from which Shakespeare drew is complicated by the question of what foreign languages the dramatist could have read. Upon that point scholars are not

THE
Painfull Aduentures

of *Pericles* Prince of
Tyre.

Being

The true Hiſtory of the Play of *Pericles*, as it was
lately preſented by the worthy and an-
cient Poet *Iohn Gower*.

Iohn   *Gower.*

At LONDON
Printed by T.P. *for* Nat: Butter,
1608.

John Gower as Presenter of *Pericles*
(Title-page of George Wilkins' novel)

in agreement. In an age nourished, as was the Elizabethan, upon Italian culture and eager for Italian stories in the theatre, it would be surprising if a popular playwright could not have conducted a search for profitable material in the original. Be that as it may, several of Shakespeare's plays, notably *Othello* and *Much Ado about Nothing*, derive from Italian stories by Cinthio or Bandello which were not translated into English when Shakespeare used them. In few of these stories are the characters more than types or shadows. Shakespeare's first task as an adapter was to develop them.

(c) Occasionally, Shakespeare found a story which attracted him in an old play that, for one reason or another, had outlived its usefulness on the stage. His *King John* is based, not directly upon Holinshed's *Chronicles* which, however, contributed some details, but upon an anonymous two-part drama called *The Troublesome Reign of King John*, printed in 1591 and republished during Shakespeare's lifetime as "written by W. Shakespeare." The historical plays featuring the madcap Prince Hal also owe something to *The Famous Victories of Henry the Fifth*, an old play popular about the time of the Spanish Armada. *The Tragedy of King Lear*, though an old story which exists in more than fifty versions, owes most to an anonymous tragicomedy called *The Chronicle History of King Leir and His Three Daughters*, published in 1605, but written *c.* 1594. *Hamlet* also appears to be a redaction of an old play which is now lost. Other plays, notably *Romeo and Juliet*, *The Taming of the Shrew*, *Henry VI*, *Richard III*, *Measure for Measure*, may, to a greater or lesser degree, be indebted to earlier dramas. For at least one of his plays, *The Comedy of Errors*, Shakespeare turned to the Latin drama and adapted to the Elizabethan stage the *Menæchmi* of Plautus.

(d) In addition to these three main classes of source materials, allusions in Shakespeare's plays make clear his knowledge of other authors. He knew the classics, from William Lyly's *Short Introduction of Grammar* (1574), in which, like William Page, he must have made his first acquaintance with the accidence, through those authors usually read in school, like Æsop, Mantuan, Cæsar, Cicero, and Pliny, to "sweet witty Ovid," whose *Metamorphoses* had an irresistible attraction for him. Indeed, Shakespeare seems to have been acquainted with all the great names of classical literature from Homer down —"Seneca cannot be too heavy, nor Plautus too light." Among French authors, he certainly knew both Rabelais and Montaigne and perhaps Belleforest and Boisteau's *Les Histoires tragiques* (1559, 1570), a translation of Bandello's *novelle*. But a study of Shakespeare's reading reveals him as a snapper up of all kinds of unconsidered literary trifles as well. Stories of "the anthropophagi and men whose heads do grow beneath their shoulders" with which Othello charmed Desdemona are found in Philemon Holland's translation of Pliny (1601). The devils with whom the feigned madman

Edgar communes in *King Lear* are enumerated in a tract against witchcraft by Samuel Harsnett (1603). Gonzalo's description of an ideal commonwealth comes from the *Essais* of Montaigne; in the same play, the famous passage beginning "Ye elves of brooks" was lifted from Ovid. Shakespeare was also acquainted with contemporary books of travel, like Richard Hakluyt's *Voyages* (1589, 1598–1600), which were filled with the wonders of the brave new worlds the Elizabethan sea-dogs were discovering. He knew the heroes of popular romance, like Robin Hood, King Arthur, Roland, Guy of Warwick, Bevis of Hampton, and the Squire of Low Degree. He knew folk tales of fairies, ghosts, and goblins. He knew old ballads, like *King Cophetua and the Beggar Maid* and *Jephthah, Judge of Israel*, and old songs like *Greensleeves, Heart's Ease, Light o' Love*, and *Heigh-ho for a Husband*. He knew the jest books of the day, like *The Hundred Merry Tales* and *The Book of Riddles*. And, above all, he knew his Bible well, including the Apocrypha, and *The Book of Common Prayer*.

SHAKESPEARE'S USE OF SOURCES

A more intimate examination of Shakespeare's use of his source material reveals, as nothing else can, the dramatist's methods and his craftsmanship. Everywhere one perceives the shaping spirit of his art—re-emphasizing events, creating or revitalizing characters, transmuting the language, rejecting this or adding that—to suit the needs of his theatre. Most of the originals Shakespeare used were written, not to be acted, but to be read. These stories, therefore, had to be retold in vivid dialogue and otherwise rendered dramatic. Some of the stock patterns one finds recurring in his plays were also in the original sources—the scenes of pastoral simplicity, the pairs of lovers involved in distressful adventure, the lost or kidnapped children, the girls disguised as boys. But, on the stage, Shakespeare had less leisure to tell a story; his episodes had to be related as causes and effects; his characters had to breathe and throb with life and be something more than the ornamental figures in a tapestry. Artificial as these situations were, his characters had to act real in them. Hence, he did not hesitate to condense, reproportion, rearrange, or expand his stories, reverse their conclusions, add episodes from other stories, or invent whatever seemed to him properly effective. Sometimes he introduced realism to contrast with romance, or a bit of clowning to dull the edge of grief. Sometimes he changed the mood of his story, turning sentimentality into sentiment, cynicism into wholesomeness, and immorality into virtuous behavior. Shakespeare was always unfettered. It cannot be said that mere respect for his sources very often checked his sense of dramatic effect. He read always with the eye of a dramatist interested in character expressing itself in action.

Thus, even in his histories or in his Roman plays, when he was presenting on the stage something that actually had happened once upon a time, Shakespeare was always a playwright rather than a historian. He frequently compressed events, occasionally altering their sequence, and he reinterpreted character. To arouse sympathy, little Arthur is represented, in *King John*, as a child and not as a youth who had already seen service in battle, as Holinshed had shown him, and Constance of Brittainy is depicted as a sorrowing widow, when she was really a virago, divorced from her second husband and married to a third. In *Richard II*, to give force to his rebukes of his misguided nephew, John of Gaunt is represented as the unselfish "time-honoured Lancaster," whereas, historically, he was only fifty-nine years old when he died. In *1 Henry IV*, to provide contrast and dramatic conflict, the irresponsible, fun-loving Hal is placed side by side with the young "Mars in swaddling clothes," Harry Hotspur of the North. These two are made the same age, though, historically, Hotspur was three years older than Hal's father. In the play, the careers of these young men are traced until they meet on the field of Shrewsbury and the impetuous Percy dies at the hands of the prince he scorned. Likewise, Hal's father, who was only thirty-six at the time, is represented as an aged monarch who must be rescued from his enemies by the son whose riots he deplored. Actually, as Shakespeare knew from Holinshed, the prince was only sixteen when he fought at Shrewsbury and was wounded, and he did not encounter Hotspur, who died by an unknown hand. In *Richard III*, not only is the character of the king blackened, but other changes are made as well. Richard's wooing of the Lady Anne is pure invention; Richmond's two invasions of 1483 and 1485 are combined into one; and Margaret of Anjou, the unhappy Lancastrian queen, is brought back to England from retirement in France to serve as a kind of chorus to the drama.

Similarly, though Shakespeare respected the language of North's *Plutarch* and followed his narrative more closely than was his custom with other writers, he nevertheless condensed and rearranged incidents to create an artificial rapidity of action or to suggest an inner connection between events. Thus, to touch upon only one play, in *Julius Cæsar* the triumph over Pompey's sons, which took place in October of 45 B. C., is combined with the celebration of the Feast of the Lupercal, which occurred in the following February. Cæsar's triumph, the fickle celebrants, the silencing of the tribunes, Cæsar's desire for an heir, the offer of the crown, and the hatching of the conspiracy are presented in the play to create the illusion of a sequence of causes and effects. The events of the Ides of March follow almost directly; the assassination of Cæsar is succeeded immediately by Antony's oration and the reversal of popular opinion; twenty months of rivalry and intrigue before the establishment of the Triumvirate are dismissed as irrelevant; two quarrels between Brutus and Cassius and two battles at Philippi are compressed into one. In history, the story told in *Julius Cæsar* covers a period of three years; in Shakespeare's play, it is all concentrated into five eventful days, which, while not consecutive, at least produce the effect of a close sequence. All of these events had to be co-ordinated from three biographies, those of Cæsar, Brutus, and Antony. Perhaps the touch that shows Shakespeare's dramatic power most clearly is his transformation into the ghost of Cæsar of "a wonderful strange and monstrous shape of a body coming towards him," which Brutus saw and spoke to on the eve of Philippi. The event and the conversation are the same. The identification of this apparition, however, brings to the audience the realization that not Cæsar's greatness in life, but his greatness even in death is the central theme of the tragedy, and that his vengeful spirit ranges abroad, turning the swords of the conspirators into "their own proper entrails."

Occasionally, Shakespeare's alterations of his sources were inspired by the need of reinterpreting foreign conditions or a foreign point of view in Elizabethan terms. Many of the events in the Roman plays, such as the crowd scenes, for example, are more like life in Elizabethan London than Rome; in *A Midsummer Night's Dream*, which is set in a very unclassical Athens, Duke Theseus stirs up the Athenian youths to merriments and sets about celebrating his wedding as if he were at the Elizabethan court, "with pomp, with triumph, and with revelling." The most interesting of the plays from this point of view, however, is *The Comedy of Errors*, which was based upon a classical source. Characters in Plautus's *Menæchmi*, like Peniculus the parasite, for which there was no counterpart in Elizabethan society, had to be replaced by an English equivalent—in this case by a servant, Dromio of Ephesus. Medicus, the ridiculous physician in Plautus's play, who is sent to attend the "madman," must be replaced by another "quack," more familiar to the Elizabethan audience, in Pinch, the hungry, lean-faced school-master who drives out evil spirits by conjurations in Latin. A love interest, always a necessity in an English comedy, must be supplied by substituting a sister of Adriana, who will also serve as an effective foil to the jealous wife, for the father to whom the lady complains in *Menæchmi*. But most important is the reshaping of the whole story according to the romantic pattern in which "all losses are restored and sorrows end." Unlike Plautus's version, the parents of the Antipholuses in Shakespeare's play are kept alive, an element of distress is introduced by opening the play with the arrest of Ægeon, and the story of family misfortune is utilized as a contrasting enveloping action to the farce, which is resolved at the close by contact with the serious action. Finally, the whole story is given a complete moral disinfection.

Shakespeare sometimes saw possibilities in a plot but found it desirable to reconceive it in an entirely different mood. Such a play is *As You Like It*, which, as far as plot goes, is little more than a dramatization of Thomas Lodge's

Rosalynde. Lodge's story, however, is a sentimental pastoral romance of the type popular in Elizabethan England between 1580 and 1590. It is written in euphuistic language and equipped with characters who, today, seem quite lifeless or unreal. Shakespeare accepted the general plot with all its conventionalities, including the life of Arcadian simplicity, the heroine's disguise as a boy, and the pastoral wooing, and adhered to it rather closely. The few changes he made were merely in the interests of dramatic economy. In the original, the exiled duke and the usurper are unrelated. Shakespeare made them brothers so that their story might parallel that of Orlando and Oliver. The banished ladies are presented as cousins, instead of merely friends, as in Lodge's story. Also, in the original, the usurper is killed in battle with the rightful duke; in Shakespeare, he is converted by an old religious man and retires from the world, thus producing no discord to mar the happy weddings at the end of the play.

But, if the plot-framework is nearly the same, there is a vast difference in spirit between the two works. Lodge's story is only pleasantly artificial; Shakespeare's is whimsically humorous. Lodge's Arden, like Shakespeare's, is inhabited by Arcadian natives as well as by courtiers in exile, but there is no suggestion, in his romance, of their social contrast, and no farcical children of the soil, like Audrey and William, to challenge the reality of the Dresden china rustics, Phebe and Silvius, and the courtly emulators of Robin Hood and his merry men. There is in Lodge's work no witty realist, like Touchstone, and no cynical railer, like Jacques. What is even more important, Lodge's heroine, with all her attractions, is but a shadow when compared with Shakespeare's natural, tender, fun-loving girl, blessed with a keen sense of absurdity and a healthy laughter that ripples around every sentimental convention in the play. Shakespeare developed his drama as a series of contrasting love affairs on differing social levels; he retained much of Lodge's lyricism, but, through Rosalind, Touchstone, and Jaques, he poked gentle fun at all the artificialities and pretenses that Lodge had taken seriously.

Sometimes, especially in a serious play, Shakespeare's new conception of the characters made it impossible for him to employ the episodes of the original story. An example of such a play is *Othello.* In Cinthio's *Hecatommithi,* he found a cheap, sordid tale, badly conceived and clumsily told. Its chief characters, except the heroine, who is called Disdemona, were unnamed, but here were the warlike Moor in the service of Venice, the virtuous lady who married him for his merits in spite of the opposition of her relatives, the intriguing *alfiero* of amiable outward appearance and his wife, the captain against whom the Moor's suspicions are aroused, and the captain's mistress. The plot—even to the episodes involving the handkerchief—is much the same as that of Shakespeare's tragedy, until the Moor and the ensign prepare his revenge upon Disdemona:

And discoursing together, if poison or the dagger would be best, and not liking either the one or the other, the ensign said, "A method has occurred to me that would satisfy you without creating the least suspicion. The house where you live is very old, and the ceiling of your chamber is broken in many places. Disdemona might be beaten to death with a stocking full of sand, and no marks of this would remain on the body: when she is dead we will pull down a part of the ceiling, and bruise your wife's head; then give out that a beam in falling has done this and killed her. If you follow my advice you will avoid all suspicion, and everyone will believe her death to have been accidental."

This savage advice pleased the Moor; and waiting for a convenient opportunity, he concealed the ensign one night in a closet that communicated with their chamber.

And, thus, at the hands of the villain, not of the husband who sacrifices her "else she'll betray more men," does the original Disdemona perish. The plan is successful, no suspicion falls upon the Moor, but he mourns for his dead wife, quarrels with the ensign, and cashiers him. Thereupon, the ensign denounces him to the captain (Cassio); the Moor is tried by the Senate, banished, and afterward slain by Disdemona's kinsmen. Only later, and for reasons entirely unrelated to these events, does Heaven overtake the villainous ensign, who is put to the torture and slain.

There is nothing in Cinthio's story about the Moor's early favoritism for Cassio and Iago's desire for his place, which, in Shakespeare's play, concentrates Iago's villainies and motivates his intrigues against Othello and Desdemona. In Cinthio, his motive is that, like Shakespeare's Roderigo, he lusts after Desdemona, is repulsed, and believes that Cassio enjoys her favors. But there is no Roderigo and no Brabantio in Cinthio's novel. Nor is there anything remotely suggesting Shakespeare's characterization, the headlong rush of the action, or the poetic beauty of the whole.

Similarly, the new mood in which Shakespeare conceived his stories, and the new emphasis he gave his characters, account for the happy ending he presented in *The Winter's Tale* and the tragic close which he alone believed was proper for *King Lear*. In Greene's *Pandosto*, the wife of the jealous king actually dies of a broken heart; when he first meets his lost daughter, Pandosto makes ardent love to her, and, unable to realize the new relation in which he must stand to Fawnia (Perdita), takes his own life at her marriage. Instead of a lesson in the evil effects of jealousy, *The Winter's Tale* is a romance in which sincere repentance rights all wrongs and the loves of the children cement once more the interrupted friendship of their fathers. But the mood of reconciliation is absent from *King Lear*. All of the versions before Shakespeare's restore the old king to his throne and give him a few happy years with his devoted daughter. Shakespeare's King Lear is an oak that is unable to bend. Adversity breaks him, and the madness and death of the "poor, infirm, weak, and despised old man" is the logical result of Shakespeare's new conception of the character and of the bitter fatalistic philosophy that surrounds the play.

Shakespeare's modifications of plot and character were not always wholly successful. Today, *Measure for Measure* is a puzzling, repulsive play, both because of its Elizabethan ethics and its characters. The original, as retold from Cinthio by George Whetstone, was much simpler. In his desire to emphasize Angelo's severity in applying a law against fornication to true lovers, like Claudio and Juliet, and to save his heroine, Isabella, from submitting to the dishonorable advances of the deputy, Shakespeare introduced a substitute in Mariana, the jilted betrothed of Angelo, a character not found in the original. The parallelism afforded by the Claudio-Juliet and Angelo-Mariana situations is attractive and very dramatic, but, at the same time, it produces an unlucky inconsistency in the character of Angelo. First portrayed as an austerely virtuous character who believed himself strong enough to withstand any temptation, Angelo is shown, after the beginning of Act III, to have been all along a blackguard and a hypocritical opportunist who had cast aside a devoted lady merely because she had lost her dowry. What is worse, all this was known by Duke Vincentio at the time he selected Angelo as his deputy to enforce the laws of Vienna. Structurally superior to its original, *Measure for Measure* is, nevertheless, one of Shakespeare's few artistic failures.

Often, it is what Shakespeare added, rather than what he merely appropriated or adapted, that reveals the hand of the master craftsman. Some of the most complicated of his plays, from the point of view of source identification, are probably the result of his bringing together a number of serviceable elements, each one necessitating some modification of the other. *A Midsummer Night's Dream*, for example, is an amalgamation of a common romantic story of parental opposition making difficult the course of true love, a heroic story drawn from Plutarch's *Lives*, an element from folklore, another from real life, and a mock-heroic episode that serves as a burlesque of the whole romantic theme. *The Merchant of Venice*, likewise, consists of at least three components—the "pound of flesh" story, the casket story, and the elopement theme—each of which has its origin in a different source. *King Lear*, as Shakespeare told it, consists of parallel stories of two fathers, the one with unfilial daughters, the other with an unfilial son. Each is derived from a separate source. Similarly, *The Two Gentlemen of Verona*, *The Taming of the Shrew*, *The Merry Wives of Windsor*, *Cymbeline*, and *Macbeth*, all represent a blending together of various story elements rather than the simpler adaptation of a single plot.

But Shakespeare also invented both characters and incidents. There is no Autolycus and no Paulina, for example, in the source for *The Winter's Tale*, no Malvolio, Sir Toby, Sir Andrew, Maria, Feste, or Fabian in that of

Twelfth Night, no Benedick, Beatrice, Dogberry, or Verges in that of *Much Ado*, no Fool in *King Lear*, and, as has been remarked above, no Roderigo or Brabantio in that of *Othello*, no Touchstone or Jaques in that of *As You Like It*, and only the shadow of Enobarbus in that of *Antony and Cleopatra*, or of Mercutio in that of *Romeo and Juliet*. These, and many more minor characters, like Launce and Speed, Launcelot Gobbo, Peter, Elbow and Pompey, Dorcas and Mopsa, as well as the episodes in which they take part, are originally Shakespeare's.

Perhaps the best illustration of how Shakespeare deliberately altered a plot by his creations is *Much Ado about Nothing*. In one of Bandello's novels, Shakespeare found a tear-soaked story from which he recreated Claudio and Hero—the characters in the main plot of a play noted for its brilliant comedy and character contrasts. As foils to these sentimental story-book lovers, he created an unsentimental pair in Benedick and Beatrice, whose "merry war" is an effective contrast to the darker nature of the main situation. Just as Don John conspires by villainous slander to wreck the happiness of Claudio and Hero and make them fall *out* of love with one another, so his genial brother, Don Pedro, to while away the time between the betrothal and the wedding, undertakes "one of Hercules' labors," and devises "honest slanders" with which to stain Benedick and Beatrice, and so to bring them "into a mountain of affection, th' one with th' other." Further, to resolve his serious conspiracy, Shakespeare brought it into contact with comedy by having the conspiracy discovered by the stupid watchmen under Dogberry and Verges; to bring about a declaration of love between Benedick and Beatrice, he brought his comic conspiracy into contact with the serious one. Not only is *Much Ado about Nothing* an excellent example of Shakespeare's contrast of romance and realism in comedy, but it is also the work of an artist who knew how to construct a plot.

Finally, as illustrations of how Shakespeare appropriated even the language of his original, on occasion, and transmuted it into his own characteristic blank verse, parallel passages may be cited from widely differing plays and widely differing sources. Compare the closing lines of the old *Troublesome Reign of King John* and its outworn polemical bias with those of Shakespeare's *King John*:

The Troublesome Reign:

> Let England live but true within itself,
> And all the world can never wrong her state.
> Lewis, thou shalt be bravely shipped to France,
> For never Frenchman got of English ground
> The twentieth part that thou hast conquered.
> Dauphin, thy hand; to Worcester we will march.
> Lords all, lay hands to bear your sovereign

> With obsequies of honor to his grave.
> If England's peers and people join in one,
> Nor Pope, nor France, nor Spain can do them wrong.

King John:

> This England never did, nor never shall,
> Lie at the proud foot of a conqueror
> But when it first did help to wound itself.
> Now these her princes are come home again,
> Come the three corners of the world in arms,
> And we shall shock them. Nought shall make us rue
> If England to itself do rest but true.

More striking still is Shakespeare's debt to the simple, fresh, vigorous prose of North's *Plutarch:*

The poop . . . was of gold, the sails of purple, and the oars of silver, which kept stroke in rowing after the sound of the music of flutes, hautboys, citherns, viols, and such other instruments as they played upon in the barge. And now for the person of herself: she was laid under a pavilion of cloth of gold of tissue, apparelled and attired like the goddess Venus, commonly drawn in picture; and hard by her, on either hand of her, pretty fair boys apparelled as painters do set forth god Cupid, with little fans in their hands, with the which they fanned wind upon her. Her ladies and gentlewomen also, the fairest of them, were apparelled like the nymphs Nereids (which are the mermaids of the waters) and like the Graces, some steering the helm, others tending the tackle and ropes of the barge, out of the which there came a wonderful passing sweet savour of perfumes, that perfumed the wharf's side, pestered with innumerable multitudes of people. (*Life of Marcus Antonius.*)

Antony and Cleopatra:

> The barge she sat in, *like a burnish'd throne,*
> *Burn'd on the water.* The poop was *beaten* gold;
> Purple the sails, and so perfumed that
> *The winds were love-sick with them.* The oars were silver,
> Which to the tune of flutes kept stroke, and made
> *The water which they beat to follow faster,*
> *As amorous of their strokes.* For her own person,
> *It beggar'd all description.* She did lie
> In her pavilion—cloth-of-gold of tissue—
> *O'er-picturing* that Venus where we see
> *The fancy outwork nature.* On each side her
> Stood pretty *dimpled* boys, like *smiling* Cupids,
> With *divers-colour'd* fans, whose wind did seem
> *To glow the delicate cheeks which they did cool,*
> *And what they undid did.* . . .
> Her gentlewomen, like the Nereides,
> So many mermaids, *tended her i' the eyes,*
> *And made their bends adornings.* At the helm
> A *seeming* mermaid steers. The *silken* tackle
> *Swell with the touches of those flower-soft hands*

That yarely frame the office. From the barge
A strange *invisible* perfume *hits the sense*
Of the adjacent wharfs. The city *cast*
Her people out upon her; and Antony,
Enthroned i' the market-place, did sit alone. . . .
(II, ii, 196 ff.)

For the idea and even some of the language, Shakespeare's debt to his source is great. But, in a passage like the above, the words which have been italicized render a striking description more effectively imaginative and poetic. They are Shakesepare's characteristic contribution.

THE PRINCIPAL SOURCES OF SHAKESPEARE'S PLAYS

Comedies

Love's Labor's Lost:

No literary source has been identified for this play. The names of the characters, however, suggest that it was topical; contemporary events, particularly court gossip and Anglo-French diplomatic relations, must have given the drama a great deal more point for an Elizabethan audience than for a modern. The name of Don Armado was obviously suggested by the late Spanish scare. In France, the Protestant Henri of Navarre was encountering much opposition to his claim to the throne. The Duc de Mayenne (Dumain) was chief of the League opposed to Henri; the Marshal de Biron, the Duc de Longeville, and the Duc de Mercade were Henri's principal supporters, while the Marquis de la Mothe was Henri's ambassador in England. In 1590, Elizabeth became Henri's ally, sending him both money and troops under the Earl of Essex. The embassage of the Princess of France may have been suggested by a visit in 1578 of Marguerite de Valois, who was a princess of France, to her estranged husband Henri of Navarre. Questions of dowry, involving territorial disputes in Aquitaine, were at issue; the princess was accompanied by a troop of ladies; and the couple were temporarily reconciled. The embassage, with its hunting episode and its masque, may also have been suggested by one of the numerous progresses of Queen Elizabeth. The vow to study doubtless had its origin in the intellectual affectations of Elizabethan courtiers, perhaps those around the Earl of Southampton or Sir Walter Raleigh. Hence, it is impossible not to look for court allegory in the play. The suggestion that so notorious a philanderer as Henri of Navarre should take a vow of celibacy is alone comic. The entire production must have been an Elizabethan equivalent of a modern satirical revue.

The Comedy of Errors:

Menæchmi, or The Twins, a Latin farce by Plautus, adapted to the Elizabethan comic formula and to Elizabethan social conditions, is the main source, direct or indirect. No translation of *Menæchmi* appeared until 1595. The parallelism of twin servants and twin masters, and the barring-out scene (III, i) were probably suggested by *Amphitruo,* also by Plautus. The framework of family misfortunes, alluded to only in the

Prologue to Plautus's play, may have been developed from *Apollonius of Tyre,* which was, however, only the prototype of the romance of distressful adventure common in medieval and Renaissance literature.

The Two Gentlemen of Verona:

The Proteus-Julia story of this play is most closely related to that of Felix and Felismena in Jorge de Montemayor's *Diana Enamorada,* a Spanish romance translated into English by Bartholomew Yonge about 1582, but not published until 1598. For the rest of the play, involving Valentine and Silvia, no satisfactory parallel has been found, but the conflict of love and friendship, together with the contrast of a loyal and a faithless friend, is common in Renaissance literature, notably in the story of *Titus and Gisippus,* which was translated from Boccaccio's *Decameron* by Sir Thomas Elyot in *The Gouvernour* (1531).

A Midsummer Night's Dream:

No single source has been identified for this play, but the various elements which compose it were well known. (a) The nucleus story of Theseus and Hippolyta is found in Chaucer's *Knight's Tale,* as well as in Plutarch's *Lives.* (b) The romantic main plot of the "course of true love" that does not run smooth follows a common Elizabethan dramatic formula. (c) The fairy element draws upon both folklore and early fairy literature. Oberon, the helpful King of Fairyland who is the friend of young lovers, is first found in the romance of *Huon of Bordeaux,* translated into English by Lord Berners in 1534 and reprinted in 1570 and 1601. (d) Finally, the "tragical comedy" of Pyramus and Thisbe is a *reductio ad absurdum* of a popular classical tale from Ovid's *Metamorphoses,* retold in Chaucer's *Legend of Good Women,* and elsewhere. Analogues to details in the action are numerous, but the unification of these diverse materials into a firmly knit plot is a peculiarly Shakespearean feat.

The Merchant of Venice:

The various stories which make up this play also come from scattered sources. (a) The bond or "pound of flesh" story is essentially a folk tale, possibly of Oriental origin, of which there were several English versions in prose and in ballad form in Shakespeare's time, and some of these may have contributed details to Shakespeare's play. The analogue nearest to Shakespeare's drama, however, is an Italian *novella* in Ser Giovanni Fiorentino's *Il Pecorone,* written *c.* 1378, but not published until 1554 and untranslated in Shakespeare's time. This story includes the lover and his older Venetian friend, a wooing episode (on a much less delicate plane) of a lady of Belmonte, the usurious Jew, the newly wedded wife disguised as a lawyer, and the stratagem of the ring begged as a fee. (b) The Casket theme, also of Oriental origin, was likewise well known in Italian and English, but the version most nearly like Shakespeare's, in the *Gesta Romanorum,* a popular collection of medieval sermon stories, shows a princess and not a suitor as the chooser. The same collection also contains a version of the "pound of flesh" story. That these two main themes had already been blended in an earlier drama is suggested by an allusion in Stephen Gosson's *School of Abuse* (1579) to a play called *The Jew*, which represented "the greediness of worldly choosers and the bloody mind of usurers." But it is lost. (c) The elopement theme (Lorenzo and Jessica) has also several analogues, the most interesting of which appears in Anthony Munday's novel, *Zelauto* (*c.* 1580), where it is combined with another bond story, and in the *novelle* of Massuccio di Salerno (1476).

The Taming of the Shrew:

The relation of *The Taming of the Shrew* to an earlier anonymous play, *A Pleasant Conceited History Called the Taming of A Shrew* (1594), is in dispute. Most scholars believe that it is the direct source of Shakespeare's play; others, that it represents a badly garbled version (see below, p. 355). All of the various plot elements are common to both *A Shrew* and *The Shrew*. The Induction, dealing with the transformed drunkard, is a folk tale which is at least as old as *The Arabian Nights*, and analogues are common. The theme of the shrewish wife is also widespread in popular literature, an Elizabethan example being *A Merry Jest of a Shrewd and Curst Wife Lapped in Morel's Skin for Her Good Behavior* (*c.* 1560). The sub-plot of romantic wooing bears a resemblance to Ariosto's *I Suppositi*, translated by George Gascoigne as *Supposes* (1566).

The Merry Wives of Windsor:

This farce, written, according to tradition, that Queen Elizabeth might see Falstaff in love (see above, p. 26), is a mosaic of popular comic devices. The jealous husband, the merry wife (usually not honest), and the lover concealed in household stuff, are commonplaces in Renaissance literature, English and Italian. The themes of the "tricker tricked" and the "boy-bride" derive ultimately from Plautus and Italian comedy. Although numerous analogues to the play exist, no single source can be identified. The legend of Herne the hunter was well known.

Much Ado about Nothing:

The main plot of malicious slander, involving Claudio and Hero, is adapted directly or indirectly from the sentimental tale of Don Timbreo and Fenecia in Bandello's *Novelle* (1554), itself a version of a very old story. Of this there was no translation into English when Shakespeare wrote his play. Some details of the deception episode, especially Margaret's impersonation of her mistress, may have been suggested by a similar story of Ariodante and Genevra in Ariosto's *Orlando Furioso*, translated by Sir John Harington (1591) and adapted by Edmund Spenser in *The Faerie Queene* (Book II, canto 4). No satisfactory literary source has been found for the contrasting parallel plot of "honest slander" involving Benedick and Beatrice, or for the low comedy of Dogberry and the Watch.

As You Like It:

The source of this play is Thomas Lodge's pastoral romance, *Rosalynde: Euphues Golden Legacie* (1590), conceived in a different spirit, with some significant additions and parallels.

Twelfth Night:

The sentimental main plot, involving Orsino, Olivia, Viola (Cesario), and Sebastian, is a loose adaptation of the tale of Apolonius and Silla retold from Bandello's *Novelle* by Barnabie Riche in his *Farewell to Military Profession* (1581). Bandello, in turn, based upon an Italian comedy called *Gl'Ingannati* (*The Deceived*) (1537), of which a Latin translation, entitled *Lælia* after the heroine, was performed at Queen's College, Cambridge, in 1590 and again in 1598. The "wooing by proxy" theme and the lady who falls in love with the disguised page have some similarity to the story of Felix and Felismena in Montemayor's *Diana*, which Shakespeare apparently used in *The Two Gentlemen of Verona*. For the comic plot involving Malvolio, Sir Andrew, Sir Toby, Maria, and Feste, no source is known. The characterization throughout is Shakespeare's.

All's Well that Ends Well:

The source of this play is the story of Giletta of Narbonne from Boccaccio's *Decameron* as retold by William Painter in *The Palace of Pleasure* (1566).

Measure for Measure:

The main source, considerably modified, is George Whetstone's play, *Promos and Cassandra* (before 1578), and a version in the form of a novel in the same author's *Heptameron of Civil Discourses* (1582), both based upon a story in Giraldi Cinthio's *Hecatommithi* (1565) and the same author's *Epitia*, a play. Shakespeare's principal modification is the creation of Mariana, which establishes certain parallel dramatic patterns and necessitates the introduction of the "substitute bride" theme, common in folkstories and already utilized in *All's Well*.

Pericles, Prince of Tyre:

This very old story, which is found in all European languages, was "gathered into English" in Shakespeare's day by Lawrence Twine in a prose novel, *The Pattern of Painful Adventures* (1576, reprinted in 1607). Earlier English versions appear in John Gower's *Confessio Amantis* (*c.* 1390), the *Gesta Romanorum*, and *Apollonius of Tyre*. A novel, called *The Painful Adventures of Pericles, Prince of Tyre*, by George Wilkins (1608), mentions the play and was probably written after it, though the relationship between the play and the novel is obscure. Shakespeare's principal sources seem to have been Twine and Gower.

Cymbeline:

The framework of legendary history in this play is freely adapted from Holinshed's *Chronicles;* the main plot of the separation and reunion of true lovers, like the story of Romeo and Juliet, is a common romantic theme; the wager story, which involves Posthumus, Imogen, and Iachimo, and is introduced as a complicating episode in the main plot, is a folk theme, derived directly or indirectly from the story of Bernabo of Genoa in Boccaccio's *Decameron*. Numerous analogues are extant. The kidnapped princes, the cruel stepmother, the wrongly accused wife, and the sleeping-draught, are commonplaces in romantic literature. Parts of the story have been traced to an old play, *The Rare Triumphs of Love and Fortune* (1582?), which also contains a cave occupied by a wronged courtier, a sleeping powder, and disguise in stolen apparel. To some scholars, the apparent death of Fidele and her burial by the lads for whom she has kept house seem referable to the folk tale of *Schneewitchen.* Shakespeare's contribution was his unification of these diverse stories and the characterization.

The Winter's Tale:

The main source of this play is a pastoral romance by Robert Greene entitled *Pandosto: The Triumph of Time, or The History of Dorastus and Fawnia* (1588, reprinted in 1607), but considerably modified to the extent of keeping the wronged queen alive, discarding the unpleasant incestuous attraction of the king to his new-found daughter, and preserving him from suicide at the end. The episode of the statue coming to life may have been suggested by the Pygmalion or the Alcestis myths, and the character of the rogue Autolycus by the coney-catching pamphlets also written by Robert Greene (1591-2).

The Tempest:

No satisfactory literary source is known for this play, but the character of the main story, and the existence of analogues to it in Italian, Spanish, German, and other literatures, suggest the possibility of a source which is now lost or has escaped detection. Travelers' tales and contemporary pamphlets, particularly two describing the wreck of a shipload of colonists on the Bermudas in 1609, may have contributed the background of the island in the sea and some of the details of the story. By October, 1610, one of the survivors, Sylvester Jourdan, wrote *A Discovery of the Bermudas, otherwise called the Isle of Devils.* Another, William Strachey, wrote a long letter entitled *A True Repertory of the Wrack and Redemption of Sir Thomas Gates, Knight; upon, and from, the Islands of the Bermudas* (dated July, 1610, but first printed in Purchas's *Pilgrims,* 1625), upon which the Council of Virginia based *A True Declaration of the Estate of the Colony in Virginia* (1610) to set fears at rest. Passages in the drama suggest a number of minor sources, notably Montaigne's *Essais,* translated by John Florio (1603), which seem to have suggested the character of Caliban and Gonzalo's description of an ideal commonwealth (II, i). Monsters and aboriginals are frequently described by Elizabethan voyagers to strange places. The supernatural element is likewise developed from a mere suggestion.

Histories

1, 2, and 3 Henry VI:

All three of these plays are probably revisions of earlier dramatic works which cannot now be clearly traced. The principal sources of the historical matter are Raphael Holinshed's *Chronicles of England, Scotland, and Ireland* in the second, enlarged, edition of 1587; and Edward Hall's *The Union of the Two Noble and Illustre Families of Lancaster and York*

(1547). Much of Part 1, including the interview between Talbot and the Countess of Auvergne (II, ii and iii), the scene in the Temple Gardens (II, iv), and the wooing of Margaret by Suffolk (V, iii), is fictitious. There is no unanimity of opinion among scholars as to the relation between *2* and *3 Henry VI* and two other plays covering the same material: *The First Part of the Contention betwixt the Two Famous Houses of York and Lancaster* (1594), and *The True Tragedy of Richard Duke of York* (1595). An edition of these plays, in 1619, bears Shakespeare's name on the title-page. Some hold that *The Contention* and *The True Tragedy* are crude, unrevised sources of *2* and *3 Henry VI*; others, that *2* and *3 Henry VI* are the originals as Shakespeare wrote them and that *The Contention* and *The True Tragedy* are piratically printed and mutilated copies (see below, p. 355).

Richard III:

Holinshed and Hall furnish the historical materials. Whether or not Shakespeare knew earlier versions of the story and worked directly from them cannot be determined. The chronicles, however, furnished only the outline for this play; the emphasis of the story, and the interrelations of persons and events, were original with Shakespeare. Richard's wooing of the Lady Anne (I, ii) is imaginary.

King John:

The principal source is *The Troublesome Reign of King John*, an anonymous two-part play printed in 1591 and republished in 1611 and in 1622 as "written by W. Shakespeare." Shakespeare followed the old drama fairly closely as regards events, but he omitted many episodes, and he modified and redirected considerably the strong nationalistic and Protestant bias of the earlier play.

Richard II:

The basis is again Holinshed; the characterization is largely Shakespeare's. The scene of the gardeners (III, iv) and the parting of Richard and his queen (V, i) are Shakespeare's invention.

1 and 2 Henry IV: }
Henry V: }

Holinshed's *Chronicles* furnish the historical material; a popular, crude play called *The Famous Victories of Henry the Fifth* (acted before 1588 and printed in 1594, though the earliest extant edition dates 1598), suggests several incidents and the possibilities of a realistic, comic sub-plot. Ancient Pistol's huffing speeches are frequently parodies of lines from plays, notably Marlowe's and Peele's, which were acted by rival companies.

Henry VIII:

Holinshed's *Chronicles* supply most of the material; the scenes dealing with Cranmer (V, i, ii, iii) are derived from Foxe's *Book of Martyrs* (1563). Wolsey's famous speech, "Had I but served my God with half the zeal I served my king," bears an interesting resemblance to a passage in Thomas Storer's *Life and Death of Thomas Wolsey, Cardinal* (1599).

Tragedies

Titus Andronicus:

This legend of an imaginary Roman emperor had some currency in Shakespeare's England, but the immediate source of his play, which was also the basis of a Dutch and two German versions, is lost. The revenge theme, involving the "horrid banquet," is Senecan; it occurs in the story of Atreus in Seneca's *Thyestes* and also in that of Philomela in Ovid's *Metamorphoses*, retold in several Elizabethan story collections. The sacrifice of the captive to appease the shades of the dead (I, i), which is the mainspring of the whole drama of vengeance, also occurs in Seneca's *Troades*. The story of Aaron the Moor has some similarity to a tale in Bandello's *Novelle* (1554), and Titus's slaying of Lavinia suggests the story of Virginius and his daughter.

Romeo and Juliet:

The direct source is *The Tragical History of Romeus and Juliet*, a poem by Arthur Brooke (1562), which, in turn, was a redaction of a famous story that appears in a number of forms in Italian. Shakespeare certainly knew the story in Painter's *Palace of Pleasure* (1566), a version derived via Boisteau and Belleforest's *Histoires tragiques* from Bandello. Brooke mentioned having seen the story "set forth on the stage," but the version, if it existed, is lost.

Julius Cæsar:

The material for this play is derived mainly from the *Lives* of Julius Cæsar, Marcus Brutus, and Marcus Antonius in Plutarch's *Lives of the Noble Grecians and Romans Compared* as translated into English by Sir Thomas North (1579) from the French version of Jacques Amyot (1559).

Hamlet, Prince of Denmark:

This tragedy is a redaction of an older lost play, conjecturally attributed to Thomas Kyd, which was based upon a legend retold in French in Boisteau and Belleforest's *Histoires tragiques* (1582), which, in turn, is derived from the *Historiæ Danicæ* of Saxo Grammaticus, a twelfth-century Danish historian. Belleforest was translated into English as *The History of Hamblet* in 1608. Saxo's story includes not only the main outlines of Shakespeare's play—fratricide, incest, usurpation, feigned madness, and the son's obligation to avenge the murder—but most of the minor elements as well—the fair maiden (Ophelia) with whom the king hopes to entangle the prince, a spying courtier (Polonius), the prince's friend and fellow-student (Horatio), and the agents of the king (Rosencrantz and Guildenstern). There is also the private interview of Hamlet with his mother, the journey to England, and the forged letter. The secret murder of the older Hamlet, the ghost, the play scene, and the death of the hero belong to the conventions of the Senecan tragedy of revenge. Whether Shakespeare or an earlier writer is responsible for these modifications of the original story, as well as for the parallel actions, involving Hamlet, Laertes, and Fortinbras, is not known.

Troilus and Cressida:

The basis of the love story, which constitutes only about one-third of this play, is Chaucer's narrative poem, *Troilus and Criseyde,* modified, however, as to Cressida's character, by sixteenth-century redactions and continuations of the tale. The background of the Trojan War and other details of the story, such as the duel between Hector and Ajax and the love of Achilles for Polyxena, are derived, probably, from John Lydgate's *Siege of Troy* (*c.* 1420), William Caxton's *Recuyell of the Histories of Troy* (1475), or Homer's *Iliad,* in the translation of George Chapman or Arthur Hall. The story of Troilus and Cressida, as well as that of the Trojan War, had been told many times in dramatic form, and there was already a stage tradition in Shakespeare's day.

Othello, the Moor of Venice:

The story of the Moor, his ensign, and his wife, Disdemona, appears in Giraldi Cinthio's *Hecatommithi* (1565). There was no English translation in Shakespeare's time.

King Lear:

The main plot of this tragedy is a free adaptation of an anonymous earlier play which has a happy ending and is called *The True Chronicle History of King Leir and His Three Daughters* (published in 1605, but written about 1594). Shakespeare seems to have been familiar also with the story as originally told in Geoffrey of Monmouth's and Holinshed's chronicles; in *The Mirror for Magistrates* (1574), an Elizabethan narrative of the falls of illustrious persons; in Spenser's *Faerie Queene* (Book II, canto 10), where the heroine is named Cordelia for the first time; and in Warner's *Albion's England* (1586), a popular historical poem. The parallel story of Gloucester and his sons is not in the old play nor in any other version, but is derived from the story of the unkind King of Paphlagonia in Book II, chapter 10 of Sidney's *Arcadia* (1590). Lear's madness, the tragic ending, and the character of the Fool are also Shakespeare's additions. The death of Cordelia may have been suggested by *The Mirror for Magistrates* or by Spenser's *Faerie Queene,* in both of which the nephews of that lady rebel against her and throw her into prison, where she dies by hanging.

Macbeth:

This tragedy derives from Holinshed's *Chronicles* and is a blend of two stories. Added to the account of Macbeth's usurpation are details borrowed from the story of King Duff and Donwald, which records a similar murder of a king by his thane, with the thane's wife as the evil counselor. Other details, like the king's troubled conscience, his hearing of voices, and his sleeplessness, seem to have come from the account of King Kenneth's murder of Malcolm Duff. The allusion to the touching for the king's evil (IV, iii) may have been suggested by Holinshed's account of Edward the Confessor.

Antony and Cleopatra:

The source, closely followed, is Plutarch's *Life of Marcus Antonius*, as translated by North.

Timon of Athens:

A brief story of Timon the man-hater appears incidentally in Plutarch's *Life of Marcus Antonius*, from which a free rendering in Painter's *Palace of Pleasure* is derived. There is reason to believe that certain details of the play, such as the faithful steward and the mock-banquet of warm water, came to Shakespeare from some intermediary source, possibly derived from Lucian's *Misanthropos*. The contrasting parallel plot is based upon Plutarch's *Life of Alcibiades*, which also refers to Timon.

Coriolanus:

The direct source is Plutarch's *Life of Coriolanus* in North's translation.

SUGGESTED REFERENCES

ANDERS, H. R. D. *Shakespeare's Books: A Dissertation on Shakespeare's Reading and the Immediate Sources of His Works.* Berlin, Georg Reimer, 1904.

BOSWELL-STONE, W. G. *Shakespeare's Holinshed: The Chronicle and Historical Plays Compared.* London, Chatto and Windus, 1896; revised edition, 1907.

A reprint of only those passages used by Shakespeare.

COLLIER, J. PAYNE *and* HAZLITT, W. CAREW (eds.). *Shakespeare's Library: A Collection of the Plays, Romances, Novels, Poems, and Histories Employed by Shakespeare in the Composition of His Works* (2nd edition, 6 vols.). London, Reeves and Turner, 1875.

HAZLITT, W. CAREW (ed.). *Fairy Tales, Legends, and Romances Illustrating Shakespeare and Other Early English Writers.* London, Reeves and Turner, 1875.

LATHAM, MINOR WHITE. *The Elizabethan Fairies: The Fairies of Folklore and the Fairies of Shakespeare.* New York, Columbia University Press, 1930.

NICOLL, ALLARDYCE and JOSEPHINE (eds.). *Holinshed's Chronicle as Used in Shakesepare's Plays.* Everyman Library. London, Dent, 1927.

A convenient volume based upon the text of Boswell-Stone, but without his notes.

NOBLE, RICHMOND. *Shakespeare's Biblical Knowledge, and Use of the Book of Common Prayer, as Exemplified in the Plays of the First Folio.* London S.P.C.K., 1935.

ROOT, ROBERT K. *Classical Mythology in Shakespeare.* New York, Holt, 1903.

The Shakespeare Classics, Being the Sources and Originals of Shakespeare's Plays. Prepared under the general editorship of Sir Israel Gollancz. London, Chatto and Windus, and Oxford University Press, 1907–26.

    1. *The Chronicle History of King Leir,* edited by Sir Sidney Lee (1909).

    2. *The Taming of A Shrew,* edited by F. S. Boas (1908).

  3–4. *Shakespeare's Plutarch* (2 vols.), edited by C. F. Tucker Brooke (1909).

    5. *Sources and Analogues of A Midsummer Night's Dream,* edited by Frank Sedgwick (1908).

    6. *Lodge's Rosalynde,* edited by W. W. Greg (1907).

    7. *Greene's Pandosto,* edited by P. G. Thomas (1907).

    8. *Brooke's Romeus and Juliet,* edited by J. J. Munro (1908).

    9. *The Troublesome Reign of King John,* edited by F. J. Furnivall and J. J. Munro (1908).

   10. *The Menæchmi: The Latin Text together with the Elizabethan Translation,* edited by W. H. D. Rouse (1912).

   11. *Rich's Apolonius and Silla,* edited by Morton Luce (1912).

   12. *The Sources of Hamlet,* edited with Essays on the Legend by Sir Israel Gollancz (1926).

WHITE, HAROLD OGDEN. *Plagiarism and Imitation during the English Renaissance: A Study in Critical Distinctions.* Cambridge, Harvard University Press, 1935.

SOME GENERAL ASPECTS

OF SHAKESPEARE'S

DRAMATIC ART

How hast thou purchased this experience? ——By my penny of observation.
—*Love's Labor's Lost*, III, i, 27–8.

THE INDUCTION TO "A WARNING FOR FAIR WOMEN" (1599) opens with the entrance at opposite doors of "History with drum and ensign" and "Tragedy in her one hand a whip, in the other hand a knife." Soon they are joined by Comedy, apparently playing on a fiddle. Tragedy is jealous of the popularity of her rivals and threatens to whip them from the stage. Though they make common cause against her, they at last good-naturedly permit themselves to be driven out with this reflection for the spectators:

> Then Tragedy kill them today with sorrow,
> We'll make them laugh with mirthful jests tomorrow.

Here, in these allegorical figures, "all three met at once," are symbolized the three major types of Elizabethan drama, in each of which Shakespeare was pre-eminent. For the innumerable minor variations, one must consult Polonius.

DRAMATIC CONVENTIONS

With all of these dramatic types, the Renaissance playwright, including Shakespeare, was conditioned in every important way by conventions imposed by the medium in which he worked, by the kind of theatre for which he wrote, by the company of actors which produced his plays, and by the audience he expected to attract. His choice of stories, as well as the manner

·[247]·

in which he told them, was often determined by current tastes in the theatre and by literary and theatrical traditions from the past. His style of writing and the scenic presentation of his dramas had to be suited to the flexible Elizabethan stage and the training of its actors, who knew how to speak verse and were accustomed to make the most of voice and suggestion. The characters he created and the motives which animate them often sprang from old familiar stories and well-worn stage practices. In dramatic technique, the Elizabethan playwright found as much that was taken for granted as does the modern playwright and scenario- or radio-script writer. Renaissance tradition and modern tradition, of course, are not the same. Shakespeare achieved his success as he would have to achieve it today, not so much by flaunting convention as by conforming to it and, at the same time, making the most of it. Mere rebellion in art can be an overrated virtue.

Some of these conventions and their influence upon Shakespeare have already been discussed in their proper places, and others will be discussed in the chapters on comedy, history, and tragedy which follow. There are a few others, however, which deserve consideration here because they are exemplified in all of Shakespeare's plays rather than in any particular dramatic type.

SHAKESPEARE'S CONCEPTION OF DRAMA

One of these is Shakespeare's attitude toward his dramatic material and, in effect, his entire conception of his calling. "If you were asked to point out the special features in which Shakespeare's plays are so transcendently excellent," wrote J. A. Froude,

> you would mention, perhaps, among others, this, that his stories are not put together, and his characters are not conceived, to illustrate any particular law or principle. They teach many lessons, but not any one prominent above another; and when we have drawn from them all the direct instruction which they contain, there remains still something unresolved—something which the artist gives, and which the philosopher cannot give.
>
> It is in this characteristic that we are accustomed to say Shakespeare's supreme *truth* lies. He represents real life. His dramas teach as life teaches—neither less nor more. He builds his fabrics as nature does, on right and wrong; but he does not struggle to make nature more sympathetic than she is. In the subtle interflow of good and evil—in the unmerited sufferings of innocence—in the seeming blindness with which justice, in attempting to assert itself, overwhelms innocent and guilty in a common ruin—Shakespeare is true to real experience. The mystery of life he leaves as he finds it; but, in his most tremendous positions, he is addressing rather the intellectual emotions than the understanding,—knowing well that the understanding in such things is at fault, and the sage as ignorant as a child. ("The Science of History" [1863], in *Short Studies on Great Subjects.*)

The final end of drama and the answer to the question as to why mankind takes pleasure in both comedy and tragedy must be left to the philosophers.

Since the time of Aristotle, the problem has been under discussion and, doubtless, it was the subject of talk at the Mermaid or the Devil or wherever one or two Elizabethan playwrights gathered together. The final satisfying answer is still being sought. Do we go to see *Hamlet* or *Othello* to have our "emotions sublimated," or for a "catharsis through pity and fear"? Do we enjoy *The Merry Wives* or *Twelfth Night* because we like to see Scorn's own image and give vent to repressions, whether our malice or our less polite emotions? Do we go to plays because, for a small price, we can enjoy suffering without being hurt, play with fire without being burned, or have a good laugh at some other fool's expense? Dancing is a good exercise, but few people dance for that reason. "Suppose we asked some queue-waiter," writes F. L. Lucas,

"Why are you standing two and a half hours in the rain to see this thing? Is it that you need your emotions purged?" . . . Or suppose we said: "I have not wept properly for three months, so tonight I shall relieve my pent-up feelings by going to *The Garden of Allah*"; should we expect to be taken seriously? (*Tragedy in Relation to Aristotle's "Poetics"* [1928], p. 28.)

Mr. Lucas, theorizing about tragedy, suggests that "the theatre is not a hospital." "Life is fascinating to watch, whatever it may be to experience." We go to the playhouse,

not in the least to get rid of emotions, but to have them more abundantly; to banquet, not to purge. Our lives are often dull; they are always brief in duration and confined in scope; but here, vicariously, even the being "whose dull morrow cometh and is as today is" can experience something more. (*Ibid.*, p. 54.)

We do not know whether or not Shakespeare ever stopped to formulate a theory of drama or subscribed to any of the philosophies that were being discussed around him. But we do have his plays, and, to judge from them, Froude's observation is sound. Shakespeare would have agreed with Aristotle that a play should be "a representation, an imitation" of life. He would probably have been content simply to let it go at that.

COMEDY, HISTORY, AND TRAGEDY

As we have seen, Shakespeare's audience liked a romantic story (above, pp. 178 ff.). Hence, his plays, whether comedy, history, or tragedy, always reveal interesting people involved in a more or less exciting action. They are not expositions of ideas, doctrines, or ethical theses—not propaganda, but literature.

More than any other literary form, the drama is direct in its imitation of life. The playwright must seem to draw his characters objectively; his creatures must each, more or less, have a philosophy of life and think and talk and act as men and women in life think and talk and act. So far as possible, we, as audience, must be permitted to judge them and their deeds as we judge real men and women, by what they say and do, and by what other people think about them. Much less than the novelist can the playwright himself intrude and tell us directly what to think. Occasionally, he may make one of his characters his spokesman, but in whatever he does the dramatist must be subtle. What has unfortunately been called Shakespeare's "impersonality" is nothing more than his superlative dramatic gift. Shakespeare was able to project himself into characters very unlike himself—obviously, he could not have been like all his creations—and to think and speak as a Romeo or a Hamlet, an Iago or a Brutus, an Imogen or a Cleopatra thought or spoke. Except in a general way, it is impossible to know what Shakespeare thought about anything; the disagreement among his critics as to his beliefs should make this clear, if nothing else did. Shakespeare was content to depict what he saw, the universal in terms of the particular.

What are the differences between the various Elizabethan types of drama? Differences of mood, largely. In the Middle Ages, when both the terms *comedy* and *tragedy* were applied in the vernacular to non-dramatic compositions, Dante could describe the distinction between the two forms:

Tragedy at the beginning is admirable and placid, but at the end or issue is foul and horrible . . . whereas comedy begins with sundry adverse conditions but ends happily.

He called his great work *The Divine Comedy* because

at the beginning it is horrible and foul, as being Hell; but at the close it is happy, desirable, and pleasing, as being Paradise. As regards the style of language, [it] is unstudied and lowly, as being in the vulgar tongue, in which even women-folk hold their talk. ("Letter to Can Grande della Scala," *Epistola* X, c. 1319.)

These formulæ, as we shall see below, were still traditionally significant for the Elizabethans.

Elizabethan tragedy is heroic and moving; it begins with the protagonist in happiness and prosperity, relates the steps in his fall, and ends with his death. Elizabethan comedy, on occasion, can be filled with misery and pathos, but it reverses the formula by beginning with things all wrong, or rapidly becoming so, and ending when "all losses are restored and sorrows end." Its aim is delight rather than laughter. Both comedy and tragedy are full of adventure; what happens belongs to the never-never Land of Storybook, though the people in the play act as if all were real. As to character, tragedy on the whole (certainly in roles of importance) confines itself to persons of dignity and position, though it does "mingle kings and clowns." In comedy there is a complete social range—kings and princes, courtiers and their ladies, burghers and their wives, Dresden-china pastoral figures, country wenches and village yokels, even goblins and sprites, the picturesque and the realistic side by side. But the differences between the two forms are not always great, and today it is occasionally possible for an Elizabethan play of one kind to be mistaken as the representative of another type. Of Shakespeare's dramas, *Cymbeline* was printed with the tragedies in the First Folio, and *Troilus and Cressida* between the histories and tragedies. Few critics know what to call the latter. These plays, however, are not typical.

What of history? History was largely an accidental form, closely akin to tragedy, the product of Elizabethan national sentiment and a dramatic vehicle for exercising and fostering patriotism.

THE MIXTURE OF SERIOUS AND COMIC

To attain truth to life, Shakespeare usually did not oversimplify, and he was not above artifice. As an artist, he knew the tricks of his trade. For example, most of Shakespeare's plays are mixed in mood; his comedies are usually touched with sorrow, and his tragedies include some episodes that provoke laughter. Literary and theatrical tradition, as we have seen, will account for this fact as readily as the poet's independent observation that, in the theatre of life, tears and smiles are strangely mingled. Stern classical theory, of course, preferred unity of mood, as well as unity of time, place, and action. But the craving for both sentiment and laughter is human. The miracle play and the morality, developing without the aid of classical models, relieved a serious narrative with "japes" of all sorts—horseplay, clownishness, or anything to get a laugh. In much the same way, medieval missals and other church-service books often carried an antidote for their own dullness in the comic illuminations of monkey-tricks in the margins. Certainly, from the beginning, the fusion of serious and comic was firmly established in romantic drama. Early Elizabethan plays, to Sir Philip Sidney's thinking, were

> neither right tragedies, nor right comedies . . . but [only a sort of] mongrel tragicomedy. (*The Defense of Poesie, c.* 1580.)

Even Shakespeare's day produced some strange bedfellows, sometimes matching "hornpipes and funerals."

Blame for the mixture is frequently heaped upon the Elizabethan stage clown and his popularity with the audience; indeed, the incongruous introduction of this profane funster is satirized in *The Pilgrimage to Parnassus*, where a clown is forcibly dragged in by a rope. But the juxtaposition of contrasting moods can be skillfully used when the playwright understands some of the higher possibilities of the device. "Comic relief" in Shakespeare's plays is not always introduced to give the audience a rest from grief; often it has the opposite effect of intensifying sorrow by throwing it into emotional relief. Thus, the inconsequential joking of Peter and the musicians in *Romeo and Juliet*, or the gossip of the grave-diggers in *Hamlet*, or the garrulity of the old countryman about the "pretty worm of Nilus" in *Antony and Cleopatra*, emphasize the emotional depths of the scenes they interrupt by the simple means of changing the emotional key. Events which are cataclysmic are about to occur, but, for aught that the man in the street knows, life is going on as usual. The normal and the abnormal are placed side by side, and the normal appears heartlessly indifferent.

Examples are various. Iago and Edmund almost combine the functions of villain and clown, but their witty cynicism is so realistic that they are all the more villains for it. Even better illustrations are Lear's Fool and the drunken porter in *Macbeth*. Here are types, traditionally associated with ribald fun, employed to augment tragedy. The bitter Fool is almost the spokesman of Lear's conscience, and the king's toleration of his blunt comments produces an exquisite pain, as if the old man were twisting a dagger that pierced his own heart. The sottish porter, who pretends to be the keeper of Hell Gate, speaks truer than he knows. As DeQuincey pointed out, the knocking at the gate—and the entrance of the porter—make us realize how far events have departed from normality,

and the re-establishment of the goings-on of the world in which we live, first makes us profoundly sensible of the awful parenthesis that has suspended them. (*On the Knocking at the Gate in Macbeth.*)

But the porter's function is even more dramatic. In order that the full effect of what they have done may be felt by Macbeth and his Lady, the murder must be discovered before they have succeeded in composing themselves. The killers have had time only to wash, but, from the very beginning, the audience must see that a little water cannot clear them of their deed.

Similarly, heartache in comedy only makes more great the joy of its removal. Ægeon's hard luck in *The Comedy of Errors* may have either of two ends; we have little doubt as to which it will be as we watch the play. But the misfortunes of Ægeon's family and the death-sentence which hangs over him form a dark framework for the bright, variegated colors of the farcical misfortunes in the mix-ups of the twins. So, too, the tragic blunders that have passed make all the more charming the idyllic life in sheepcote and cave in *The Winter's Tale* and *Cymbeline*. And Jaques's cynicism only serves to make more bright the romantic sunshine in the Forest of Arden. Shakespeare often used a contrasting action to frame or initiate another. Thus, as we have seen in *Much Ado* (p. 235, above), Don John's plot of villainous slander to wreck true love is balanced by Don Pedro's device of "honest slander" to produce it. The second plot has the same roots as the first and is resolved by it. The skillful playwright can frequently achieve unity out of disparity.

PARALLELISMS AND CONTRASTS OF PLOT

The foregoing suggests two of the most important devices by which Shakespeare guided his audiences without actually telling them what to think, namely, parallels and contrasts. Thus, in *Hamlet*, Polonius and his son Laertes are the aged and the youthful counterparts of one another—worldly wise, practical politicians, loving platitudes, and by indirections finding directions out. So, too, Gertrude and Ophelia, in various ways, illustrate the frailty that is woman. Hamlet's honest, unspectacular friend Horatio takes life as it comes and is

> not a pipe for Fortune's finger
> To sound what stop she please.

Rosencrantz and Guildenstern, however, are untrustworthy time-servers who seek to play upon the prince and pluck out the heart of his mystery. The prince himself, in his inky cloak and customary suit of solemn black, is a figure apart from the heartless court which, as it were, "with one auspicious and one dropping eye," has at least given tacit consent to mirth in funeral and dirge in marriage.

But, more important, Shakespeare developed his play as three parallel stories of sons who have lost their fathers—Hamlet, Fortinbras, and Laertes. Some time before his murder, the elder Hamlet, in response to a wager-challenge, has killed the elder Fortinbras in single combat and taken possession of some of his land. In Norway, as in Denmark, the throne has passed, not to the son of the dead king, but to his brother. When the drama opens, the young Prince Fortinbras, "of unimproved mettle hot and full," is quietly gathering an army, without his sovereign-uncle's knowledge, to take advantage of political changes in Denmark and retrieve the territory which had been forfeit. As audience, we are not expected to become excited over the justice or injustice of vengeance for death in a fair fight. We are merely to recognize, as Hamlet himself does, the similar position in which the two young princes stand, and the differences in their temperaments. After Hamlet has killed Polonius and Laertes has returned from Paris demanding satisfaction, Hamlet justly observes "by the image of my cause, I see the portraiture of his." It is the contrasts between these three characters which give significance to the parallelisms. The intelligent, sensitive Hamlet and the hot-headed Machiavellian Laertes perish on the same poisoned foil, leaving the kingdom to the cool-headed Norwegian, who has been a shrewder contriver than either. To drop the Fortinbras scenes from the play, as is frequently done in modern productions, is to destroy Shakespeare's dramatic plan.

Other plays, serious and comic, reveal the same technique. *King Lear* develops as two parallel stories which reinforce one another; Gloucester, another Lear, casts off his faithful son as Lear does Cordelia, and the unfilial sisters have a counterpart in the bastard Edmund. The effect is to render the theme of the play more universally applicable. Throughout, too, the parallel stories are closely interrelated; both Goneril and Regan are in love with Edmund, Gloucester is blinded because of his loyalty to Lear, Edgar in disguise attends the king on the heath and at last becomes the agent of justice. Likewise, the turmoil in Lear's mind parallels the physical storm on the heath, and the king's eventual resignation to what is (III, iv), is paralleled by Gloucester's (IV, i). Moreover, the alleged belief "that in their old age and declining years the father should be as ward to the son," which angers Gloucester against Edgar, is but an expression of the principle Lear has acted upon voluntarily. The parallelism assists the audience in achieving the proper perspective.

The same general structure often holds true for comedy. *As You Like It* tells the parallel stories of two pairs of contrasting brothers, as well as a series of love stories on different social levels. *The Tempest* is compact of conspiracies, both grim and comic. Its characters are presented in pairs—two servants of Prospero, Ariel and Caliban, the one representing the higher elements, the other the lower, and each seeking a different way to gain his freedom; the good and the bad pupils of the magician-duke, Miranda and Caliban, neither of whom has seen any other person of the opposite sex and both of whom are amazed at the "brave new world" that opens for them; two lovers of Miranda, log-bearing savage brute and log-bearing dream-prince. Each reinforces the belief, frequently expressed by Miranda, in the connection between beauty and goodness, ugliness and evil. Of like significance is the contrast between the two sorcerers, Sycorax and Prospero, workers in "black" magic and "white," and its implication that not power and learning alone, but character is of prime importance. Other examples are too numerous to mention.

Frequently, in both his lighter and his more serious plays, Shakespeare seems merely to be running variations on a theme. In several plays, there are different varieties of love, or attitudes toward it, notably in *The Merry Wives*, *A Midsummer Night's Dream*, and *Othello*. In *A Midsummer Night's Dream*, the range includes the stable, mature conjugal affection which has come into being after strife between Theseus and his Amazonian princess; the unstable, fitful, quarrel-producing romance of the young lovers; the childlike bickering and reconciliation of Oberon and Titania; and the mock-heroic love which is the theme of the ridiculous drama performed by the amateur actors. In addition, there are the various practical jokes, real and accidental, performed by the Puck, and the variations on the dream-motif. Titania's dotage seems but as a nightmare; Bottom's adventures are to him a vision so rare that he will get Peter Quince to write a ballad on them; and their perplexing experiences seem to the lovers, when they awake, "but as the fierce vexation of a dream." The Puck, as Epilogue, even suggests that we, the audience, consider the whole thing a dream—hence, the title of the play.

So, too, in tragedy, *Othello* is a drama of differing kinds of intrigues and jealousies and loves and deceptions. As the play opens, Iago the sharper is already involved in intrigue with Roderigo, on the theory that a fool and his money are soon parted. Iago the soldier, who knows his worth, seeks revenge upon Michael Cassio, who has unwittingly blocked his advancement, and upon the Moor for passing him over. His desire for Cassio's place is satisfied early, but, by that time, Iago has aroused forces that are not easily quelled, and he finds himself involved in a broader and deeper intrigue against both Cassio and Othello, an intrigue that involves the unoffending Desdemona. Iago's worldly cynicism permits him to believe in nothing; he is professionally jealous of Cassio, and he suspects both Cassio and the Moor with Emilia. He arouses in Othello the terrible suspicion of a trusting nature which is "not easily jealous, but, being wrought, perplexed in the extreme." Roderigo experiences the natural disappointments of the love-sick fool, and Bianca the unbecoming jealousy of the courtesan who has made the mistake of falling in love. By contrast, Desdemona and Cassio are marked by a complete absence of suspicion, and their very guilelessness is their undoing. In the same way, the attraction of opposites in Othello and Desdemona and the perfect tempered love they attain are placed against the intemperate passion which the characterless Roderigo nourishes for the belle of Venice who could never be for him, the vulgar misalliance of Cassio and Bianca, and the absence of anything that can be called love between Iago and Emilia. In addition, there are the philosophies of love expounded by both Emilia and Iago, who is not above lust for Desdemona. Further, *Othello* is a series of variations on the theme of deception and self-deception, developed from the remark of old Brabantio:

> Look to her, Moor, if thou hast eyes to see.
> She has deceived her father, and may thee. (I, iii, 293-4.)

To a lesser degree, *Macbeth* is also built around variations on the theme of treachery, a note first struck in the story of the thane of Cawdor in whom King Duncan had an absolute trust. Banquo and Macbeth are parallels; both receive the same stimulus, but one reacts in one way, the other in another. The misanthropy of Timon is matched by the misanthropy of Apemantus, and the story of Timon by that of Alcibiades. Sometimes, instead of developing in parallel, the actions are arranged in series or tandem. Thus, in *Julius Cæsar*, the conspiracy against Cæsar is followed by the revenge for his death, and, in *Titus Andronicus*, the ruthless vengeance of Tamora against

Titus is followed by the counter-revenge of Titus against the barbarian queen.

It has been suggested that this placing of one plot beside another may ultimately be traceable to the court masque, in which the dignified and dainty masque proper contrasted with the grotesque or comic antimasque. Whatever the origin of the device, Shakespeare found the pattern serviceable for dramatic effect. Seldom are the parallelisms and contrasts of plot in Shakespeare's sources; he invented them himself.

FOILS, OR CONTRASTS OF CHARACTER

In effect, by frequently presenting his characters in pairs, Shakespeare, like Prince Hamlet, bids us

> Look here, upon this picture, and on this,
> The counterfeit presentment of two brothers,

or friends or kings or servants, as the case may be. Black appears more black when it is placed beside white, and virtue always will

> show more goodly and attract more eyes
> Than that which hath no foil to set it off. (*1 Henry IV*, I, ii, 237–8.)

Sometimes Shakespeare's contrasts of character are simply physical—tall and short, fat and thin, blonde and brunette, young and old. We have already seen how these differences may reflect the physical characteristics of actors in his company (above, p. 161). This physical contrast in character is one source from which Shakespeare developed his comedy. Usually, however, physical contrast is accompanied by social, intellectual, or temperamental contrast as well. Thus, in *A Midsummer Night's Dream*, the "tawny Ethiope," little Hermia, "when she's angry . . . is keen and shrewd. She was a vixen when she went to school." The tall, blonde Helena, who is her foil, has "no gift at all in shrewishness" and is a "right maid for her cowardice." In *As You Like It*, the ill-favored Audrey not only looks different when placed beside a princess, like Celia, or a dainty Arcadian, like Phebe, but she also belongs to a lower social order and has a different sense of values. Love in court circles is one thing; when a goat-girl is involved in a triangle, the situation is absurdly different from what it is when the same thing happens to little Bo-peep, the Dresden-china shepherdess. Somehow, keeping sheep is poetic and keeping goats is not. In the same play, both Touchstone and Jaques are realists, but one is a genial fun-maker, the other a bitter railer.

Shakespeare was fond of the paradox of the wise fool and the foolish wit. He often placed side by side the wise man who acted foolishly and the fool who spoke wisely, notably Lear and his clear-eyed jester—"This is not altogether fool, my lord" (I, iv, 165).

There are, of course, endless variations to character contrast. In *Love's Labor's Lost*, the "tender juvenal" Moth is foil to the "tough senior" Don Armado, and not only sets him off physically, but also has about two intellectual heartbeats to his master's one. Costard's blunt way of putting things illuminates the overrefined writing of the Spaniard (I, i, 220 ff.). In *The Two Gentlemen*, Valentine follows after honor, Proteus after love,

> He leaves his friends to dignify them more;
> I leave myself, my friends, my all, for love. (I, i, 64–5.)

When the "squirrel" dog which Proteus sends to Silvia is stolen from poor Launce by the boys in the market place, Launce is obliged to sacrifice his own mutt Crab as a substitute. The serious, substantial Antonio is the friend of the gay spendthrift Bassanio; the merchant and the moneylender are at opposite poles; Portia is bound by her dead father's will, while Jessica flippantly casts aside everything her parent holds sacred. The jealous Ford is foil to the sensible Page; the "venom clamours" of Adriana are set off by her Patient Griselda sister Luciana; the strict, "outward sainted" Angelo, who is not so strong as he thinks he is, must judge the all too human Claudio. Cloten the boor, who is incapable of princely virtue, sets off Arviragus and Guiderius, the princelings who have been reared in the mountains; the manner in which Imogen receives Iachimo's slander of Posthumus is characteristically different from Posthumus's acceptance of Iachimo's slander of Imogen.

Incongruity, of course, is the very essence of comedy, but contrast of character can be just as useful a device in serious drama. The feverish impetuosity of Romeo and Juliet contrasts with the calm, cool wisdom of Romeo's "ghostly father," Friar Laurence, and the ideal union of the lovers with the grossness of the nurse and the ribaldry of Mercutio. A similar gulf is fixed between both of the young people and their parents. In *King Lear*, the fulsomeness of the hypocritical sisters sets off the honesty of Cordelia, who cannot heave her heart into her mouth and so must "love, and be silent." The honest, blunt Kent is matched by the honest Albany, Goneril's "mild husband," who is slow to wrath. Othello, the rough soldier who feels insecure socially, contrasts with the well-bred Cassio, who

> hath a person and a smooth dispose
> To be suspected, framed to make women false. (I, iii, 403–04.)

The generous dignity with which the Senate nominates Coriolanus consul by acclaim (II, ii) is followed by the ostentatious humility the unpolitic hero must put on before the plebeians will condescend to ratify the nomination (II, iii). They

> Must have their voices; neither will they bate
> One jot of ceremony.

Julius Cæsar is especially noteworthy in this connection. The conqueror who is "the noblest man that ever lived in the tide of times" (III, i, 256–7), and who "doth bestride the narrow world like a Colossus" (I, ii, 135–6), is shown on the stage as a braggart god whose feet are clay and who is afflicted with senile infirmities and superstitions. Shakespeare was not bungling or being inconsistent in his character drawing, nor was he playing Cæsar down, as some have thought. He was merely demonstrating that Cæsar's greatness was independent of petty considerations and that it was this greatness, even in death, against which Cassius and Brutus must contend. Brutus is shown with Portia (II, i, 234 ff.) and Cæsar with Calpurnia (II, ii, 1 ff.) in two of the most attractive of Shakespeare's intimate domestic scenes. That between Brutus and Portia is the more moving and poetic, but that between Cæsar and Calpurnia is more humorously lifelike, as the blustering, nervous Cæsar strives to save face before the superbly feminine strategy of the wife, half humoring, half wheedling her husband. The lean Cassius, who "thinks too much," and the sleek Antony, who "revels long o' nights," are, nevertheless, practical politicians who speak the same language. Together they contrast strikingly with the idealism of Brutus. The noble Brutus regrets bloodshed and will not permit a ruthless course (II, i, 154 ff.); the Triumvirs spare no one in their proscription lists:

> *Oct.* Your brother too must die; consent you, Lepidus?
> *Lep.* I do consent—
> *Oct.*   Prick him down, Antony.
> *Lep.* Upon condition Publius shall not live,
>   Who is your sister's son, Mark Antony. (IV, i, 2 ff.)

Shakespeare's histories are equally rich in such character contrasts; they are the dramatist's way of helping his audience form their own judgments.

OTHER CONVENTIONS OF DRAMATIC EXPOSITION

In addition to these devices of plot and character, there were other conventions which the dramatist used in keeping his audience fully informed and under control. Unless he begins *ab ovo*, a playwright usually has a great deal to explain to his hearers before he can unfold his story. The classical drama frequently used a prologue for initial exposition, but Shakespeare used the device sparingly. He secured attention, as we have seen, by opening in an arresting manner and then as quickly as possible giving the audience the information it required. Sometimes, as in *The Comedy of Errors*, Shakespeare began with a direct recital of past events; sometimes, as in *The Tempest*, he combined this method with another in which one character asks a second questions the answers to which both know—a clumsy artifice which Sheridan gaily parodied in *The Critic* (II, ii). Sometimes, less statically,

Shakespeare employed a series of conversations, as in *Hamlet* and *As You Like It*, or even a soliloquy, as in *Richard III*.

But, frequently, as the play progresses, various things have to be explained; characters have to be identified, events recapitulated, action prepared for, or details of time and place clarified. Such information Shakespeare managed to convey by various means—soliloquies, asides, chorus characters who comment upon the action or give direct testimony on their fellows, or simple and casual conversation. In the modern theatre, similar information may be printed in the program; Shakespeare had to convey much more by dialogue than does the playwright of today. There are very few surprise scenes in Shakespeare's dramas and few important details that are left unclear.

The soliloquy was an old convention in the Elizabethan drama, suited to the platform stage. But not all of Shakespeare's soliloquies are alike. Some are direct addresses to the audience, some reveal the character thinking aloud, others talking to himself. It is not always possible to distinguish one kind from another. Autolycus's identification of himself (*The Winter's Tale*, IV, iii, 1 ff.), Petruchio's plans for shrew-taming (*The Taming of the Shrew*, II, i, 169 ff.), or Iago's candid outline of his intrigues (*Othello*, especially II, iii, 342 ff.) seem clearly intended to be heard and not merely overheard. Many of Shakespeare's comic monologues are of this sort. On the other hand, Hamlet's "To be or not to be," Brutus's "It must be by his death," or Macbeth's "If it were done when 'tis done" suggest thinking; and day-dreams, like Henry VI's (*3 Henry VI*, II, v, 1 ff.), or Faulconbridge's (*King John*, I, i, 182 ff.), or Malvolio's (*Twelfth Night*, II, v, 27 ff.), suggest that the character is simply talking to himself. Like the aside, the soliloquy is an unrealistic technical device of which the world has again become more tolerant since the advent of stream-of-consciousness fiction.

Much more interesting is Shakespeare's use of certain characters whose function it is both to participate in the action and, somewhat in the manner of the Greek chorus, to serve as clear-eyed commentators upon it or upon their fellow-characters. Sometimes these characters are quite minor, like the citizens in *Richard III* (II, iii) or the officers who lay cushions in the Senate in *Coriolanus* (II, ii). Sometimes a play will contain several. In *Hamlet*, for instance, the task is divided between Hamlet himself, Horatio, the grave-diggers, and Fortinbras; in *King Lear* between Goneril and Regan (cf. especially I, i, 286 ff.), the soliloquizing Edmund, and the Fool. But, more often, there is a single character to whom we look for comment and guidance. He is Friar Laurence in *Romeo and Juliet*, Margaret in *Richard III*, Touchstone in *As You Like It*, Menenius in *Coriolanus*, and Enobarbus in *Antony and Cleopatra*. The last named is a particularly interesting example. Enobarbus looks to the past and describes for Mecænas and Agrippa the first meeting between Antony and the Egyptian queen (II, ii, 191 ff.); he comments upon present events, particularly Antony's infatuation (III, xiii, 31 ff.); and he prophesies the future. When the reconciliation of Antony and Octavius is sealed by Antony's marriage to Cæsar's sister, the two emperors seem forever knit together. But Enobarbus lets us know what to expect:

If I were bound to divine of this unity, I would not prophesy so. . . . [Antony] will to his Egyptian dish again. Then shall the sighs of Octavia blow up the fire in Cæsar; and . . . that which is the strength of their amity shall prove the immediate author of their variance. (II, vi, 124 ff.)

VERSE AND PROSE

Something must also be said of Shakespeare's literary medium and how he used it. When Shakespeare began his career as a playwright, he found blank verse already established as the conventional medium for both comedy and tragedy. Lyly, however, had written his court comedies in prose, and verse and prose were frequently mixed. Plays entirely in rhyme were out of fashion. About a quarter of Shakespeare's total output is in prose, and he is as great a prose-writer as he is a poet.

Normally, Shakespeare's medium is blank verse, i. e., iambic pentameter without rhyme. But there is considerable variation. As we shall see, Shakespeare's later verse is much more flexible than his earlier. In addition to this normal evolution in skill, however, Shakespeare frequently varied his verse patterns, perhaps even deliberately experimented with them, substituting trisyllabic or monosyllabic feet for the usual dissyllables, allowing the thought to dominate the form, freeing it from monotony, and suiting its cadences to changing dramatic mood. Generally speaking, all elevated and dignified or pompous and sentimental passages, or those uttered by persons of rank and breeding, are in metre. Comic and light parts, including dialect and broken English, are often in prose. Letters are also usually in prose, as are proclamations and similar documents. Persons of low station, fools and clowns, and those who lose their reason—like Ophelia, Lear, Lady Macbeth, Lepidus when he is drunk, and Othello in his fit—speak prose. Masters speaking to their servants use prose. The medium fits the context; the same person may speak prose sometimes and metre at others, according to his state of mind or the company he is in. Never is the medium mixed within the dialogue; all speak prose or all speak metre. But, within a scene, the mood may change, and there are frequent instances of scenes which begin in one medium and change, or even change back again. When the speech of one character shifts, however, that of the others also shifts (cf. *Much Ado*, I, i).

Rhyme is frequent and often difficult to explain. Most common are couplets, but more sustained rhymed passages occur occasionally. Certain uses are clear:

(a) Couplets or longer rhymed passages frequently mark the close of scenes or acts: cf. *The Merchant of Venice*, II, ix, 99–101; *Henry V*, III, iii, 42–3; *Measure for Measure*, III, ii, 275–96; *Hamlet*, I, ii, 257–8. *As You Like It*, III, iv, ends in a double couplet; *Pericles*, I, ii, in a five-line group rhyming *aabcc*.

(b) Couplets within scenes frequently serve as a cue for the entrance of another actor or for off-stage business, such as sound-effects: cf. *3 Henry VI*, III, iii, 42–3; *Troilus and Cressida*, I, i, 114–5; *Romeo and Juliet*, II, v, 16–17.

(c) Couplets sometimes mark a change of mood or thought, and are introduced even within a speech: cf. *3 Henry VI*, II, v, 19–20; *Twelfth Night*, I, i, 7–8; *Hamlet*, III, iv, 209–10; *The Merchant of Venice*, IV, i, 346–7.

(d) Couplets are sometimes used after prose as a forceful opening and to indicate a shift from one medium to the other: cf. *Julius Cæsar*, I, i, 37–8; *Measure for Measure*, III, ii, 196–9; *Othello*, II, i, 295–6.

(e) Rhyme sometimes serves to link closely one speech with its immediate predecessor: cf. *1 Henry VI*, I, iii, 52–3; IV, iii, 28–33; *Titus Andronicus*, V, i, 49–52; *Romeo and Juliet*, I, iii, 57–8; I, v, 76–7; IV, i, 18–21.

(f) Rhyme is sometimes used for speeches of excitement, passion, or high-flown sentiment: cf. *A Midsummer Night's Dream*, III, ii, 43 ff. and 122 ff.; *Richard II*, I, i, 41 ff. and elsewhere in this scene; *Macbeth*, III, iv, 69–70 and 99–100; IV, i, 94–101.

(g) Rhyme may throw into relief sententious observations, gnomic remarks, epigrams, flippancy, mockery, amusement, satire, and the like: cf. *Measure for Measure*, II, iv, 184–5; III, i, 275 ff.; *The Merry Wives*, II, ii, 215–6; *The Comedy of Errors*, II, i, 10 ff.; *Richard II*, I, i, 154 ff. and 200 ff.; IV, i, 322–5; *Troilus and Cressida*, IV, v, 30 ff.; *King John*, I, i, 142–3 and elsewhere in this scene; *Othello*, II, i, 130 ff. (Iago's epigram on women); *Romeo and Juliet*, II, iii (Friar Laurence's soliloquy on herbs and his interview with Romeo).

(h) Sustained rhyme sometimes is used to create a special mood of romance: cf. *A Midsummer Night's Dream*, I, i, 171 ff. and elsewhere in this play; *The Merchant of Venice*, III, ii, *passim* (the casket-scene); *Romeo and Juliet*, I, v, 95–108, where the lovers divide an English sonnet between them.

(i) Rhyme, or even a variant verse form, may be used to distinguish a character or a group of characters from the others. Trochaic or anapestic tetrameter, for example, is the fairy dialect in *A Midsummer Night's Dream;* the caustic wit of the bastard in *King John* is often couched in rhyme, as are the lamentations of the women in *Richard III*.

(j) In addition, there are other rhymed passages in various metres in Shakespeare, like the poetic missives in sonnet form in *Love's Labor's Lost;* the writings in the caskets in *The Merchant of Venice;* lyrics in several plays; songs, of course; as well as masques, prologues, epilogues, and choruses.

DRAMATIC SONG

Lord Macaulay once wrote, as the highest praise he could give Shakespeare,

that the great plays . . . would lose less by being deprived of all the passages which are commonly called fine . . . than those passages lose by being separated from the play. (*The Edinburgh Review*, June, 1831.)

This is particularly true of Shakespeare's songs, which have almost always been treated by composers and singers and actors alike as if they were without relation to their context and had been introduced merely to please public taste. Both Shakespeare and his Elizabethan audiences loved music, and, as we have seen (above, pp. 65 ff.) the tradition of singing and playing instruments on the stage was a very old one. Almost alone among his contemporaries, Shakespeare, however, succeeded in making his songs dramatic, and the more he gained in experience the more relevant did he make them to character or situation. To illustrate:

(a) Shakespeare sometimes used song to create an atmosphere or a background, like that of enchantment in *A Midsummer Night's Dream* or *The Tempest*, or of irresponsible sylvan Arcadianism in *As You Like It*. "Over hill, over dale" is our introduction to fairyland in *A Midsummer Night's Dream* (II, i); it is sung by Queen Titania's dainty little harbinger and sets the mood for what follows. In the same way, "Come unto these yellow sands" creates a setting in *The Tempest* (I, ii), and "Under the greenwood tree" (II, v), the ribald hunting song, "What shall he have that killed the deer" (IV, ii), and "It was a lover and his lass" (V, iii) set the mood for various scenes in *As You Like It*. Lady Mortimer's Welsh song (*1 Henry IV*, III, i) doubtless had the same dramatic purpose, though no words are given for it in the text. Two such songs of mood or atmosphere are drinking songs: "And let me the canakin clink" (*Othello*, II, iii) and "Come thou monarch of the vine" (*Antony and Cleopatra*, II, vii). The first is sung by Iago, in pretended good fellowship, as part of his subversion of Cassio's discipline; the second while the bacchanalians, including Antony and Octavius, the pillars of the world, join hands and dance, Lepidus having already been carried out.

(b) Sometimes Shakespeare used song for humorous effect. In *The Merry Wives*, the pretended fairies in Windsor Forest dance around Falstaff, pinching him and singing a "scornful rhyme," "Fie on sinful fantasy; fie on lust and luxury" (V, v). In *Twelfth Night*, "Come away, come away, death" (II, iv) is amusingly pat in fitting the mood, not of one, but of two self-conscious amorists, Orsino sighing for Olivia's love, and Viola desperate of Orsino's.

> Mark it, Cesario; it is old and plain.
> The spinsters and the knitters in the sun
> And the free maids that weave their thread with bones
> Do use to chant it. It is silly sooth.

Sometimes the humor arises out of disparity between the song and the singer or the audience for which it is sung. "O mistress mine" (*Twelfth Night*, II, iii), a song of youth and springtime wooing, is sung by Feste at request for Sir Toby, who is already fat and middle-aged, and Sir Andrew Aguecheek, who is both uninspired and uninspiring as a wooer. The song is humorously incongruous, as is that in praise of "Love, love, nothing but love" in *Troilus and Cressida* (III, i), sung, suitably enough, to Paris and Helen, but by that senile voluptuary Pandarus. Similarly absurd is the ribald ballad which Justice Silence sings in his cups (*2 Henry IV*, V, iii).

(c) Sometimes Shakespeare fitted a song with a contrast or a parody. Jaques, who can "suck melancholy out of a song as a weasel sucks eggs," adds a

realistic third stanza to "Under the greenwood tree." Queen Titania is put to
sleep by a dainty lullaby, "You spotted snakes" (*A Midsummer Night's
Dream*, II, ii), which charms away everything except that against which she
most needs protection. She is aroused from her slumbers by the braying of
Bottom, singing "The woosell cock so black of hue" (III, i), and exclaims:
"What angel wakes me from my flowery bed?" So, too, Ariel's song of free-
dom, "Where the bee sucks" (V, i), has a parallel in what has been called
Caliban's *Marseillaise*, "No more dams I'll make for fish" (II, ii).

(d) Two of Shakespeare's songs are serenades, "Who is Silvia?" (*The Two
Gentlemen*, IV, ii) and "Hark, hark, the lark" (*Cymbeline*, II, iii). Both are
sung by professionals "well-skilled in music," but on behalf of foolish bump-
kins whose love-suits are foredoomed to failure. And there may be humor in
the suggestion that, under the circumstances, both are a little overdone and
extravagant, even for serenades. Proteus has treacherously advised Thurio to
serenade Silvia:

> You must lay lime to tangle her desires
> By wailful sonnets [i. e., little songs], whose composed rhymes
> Should be full-fraught with serviceable vows. . . .
> Say that upon the altar of her beauty
> You sacrifice your tears, your sighs, your heart;
> Write till your ink be dry, and with your tears
> Moist it again. (*The Two Gentlemen*, III, ii, 68 ff.)

Thus encouraged, Thurio goes out to hire musicians to sing a song which,
presumably, he has himself composed:

> I have a sonnet that will serve the turn
> And give the onset to thy good advice. (*Ibid.*, 93–4.)

When the song is over, Thurio leaves Proteus to woo for him. But Silvia is
unmoved by the music:

> Think'st thou I am so shallow, so conceitless,
> To be seduced by thy flattery. (*Ibid.*, IV, ii, 93–4.)

Likewise, Cloten, having heard that music would "penetrate," has got the
best that money could buy, "a very excellent conceited thing," "a wonderful
sweet air, with admirable rich words to it," and a eunuch to sing the song.
"Hark, hark, the lark" is an *aubade*, or dawn-song, and the "judicious" in
Shakespeare's audience would not miss the humor of Cloten's choice, or its
failure.

(e) Song sometimes affords an effective means of entrance or exit for a
character. Thus, Autolycus's carefree spring-song, "When daffodils begin to
peer" (*The Winter's Tale*, IV, iii), is part of his soliloquy and reveals his
gay rascality quite as much as his confidences. Then, at the end of the scene,
after having made us accomplices during the fact to his robbery of a Good
Samaritan, the rogue swaggers out:

> Jog on, jog on, the foot-path way,
> And merrily hent the stile-a.

Similarly in character are his hawking songs as peddler at the sheep-shearing
(IV, iv). In *The Tempest*, Stephano, the drunken butler and a thorough land-

lubber, staggers in singing two incongruous sailors' songs, "I shall no more to sea" and "The master, the swabber, the boatswain, and I" (II, ii). Feste is forever singing snatches of popular songs, and, on one occasion, he makes an effective exit as he sings, "I am gone, sir, and anon, sir" (*Twelfth Night*, IV, ii).

(f) Sometimes song is used to clear the stage at the end of the play, or as a kind of epilogue, as in *Love's Labor's Lost,* where singers, symbolizing Spring and Winter, sing "When daisies pied" and "When icicles hang by the wall" (V, ii). Similar is the epithalamium and dance-song at the end of *A Midsummer Night's Dream* and Feste's singing of "When that I was and a little tiny boy" at the close of *Twelfth Night.*

(g) Most dramatic are the songs that either serve as a kind of chorus to the action or actually advance it. A good example is "Tell me where is fancy bred?" (*The Merchant of Venice*, III, ii). Bassanio's winning of Portia is not just luck. The lady, of course, knew the lucky casket, and she knew Bassanio, but she was bound by her father's will. Yet she is sufficiently feminine in siding with her heart—or perhaps it was Nerissa—in cheating just a little by giving the man she loved a hint in a song. Bassanio's musing over the caskets takes its cue from what he has just heard; so does the uncharacteristic choice of this fortune-hunter. Sometimes a song comments upon a dramatic situation. "Sigh no more, ladies" (*Much Ado*, II, iii) is a genial mockery of the cocksureness of the woman-hater Benedick, who is hiding; "Blow, blow thou winter wind" (*As You Like It*, II, vii) comments upon a specific instance of man's inhumanity to man; "Take, O take those lips away" (*Measure for Measure*, IV, i) and "Orpheus with his lute made trees" (*Henry VIII*, III, i) are alike in that they are sung to comfort deserted women. "Full fathom five" (*The Tempest*, I, ii) and "While you here do snoring lie" (*ibid.*, II, i) also belong to this group. Similarly, the popular, but ribald, love songs which Ophelia sings in her madness contrast with her earlier prudishness and parallel her sorrows sufficiently to accent her tragedy. The ballad snatches sung by Lear's Fool and Desdemona's "Willow Song" (*Othello*, IV, iii) have the same function. The grave-digger's song in *Hamlet* is not only humorously incongruous; it also emphasizes the indifference of ordinary living to tragedy which does not immediately concern it. Only two of Shakespeare's songs are elegies, "Fear no more the heat of the sun" (*Cymbeline*, IV, ii), which is spoken, not sung; and the epitaph which Claudio sings at the tomb of Hero (*Much Ado*, V, iii).

Unfortunately, little of the music to which these lyrics were originally sung has survived, and, except for the ballads Shakespeare merely appropriated, none that we can be sure was actually used in the first performances. Both the quartos and the folios are content to print the words of the songs and omit the music. A few settings, however—like Thomas Morley's for "O mistress mine" and "It was a lover and his lass," Robert Johnson's "Full fathom five" and "Where the bee sucks," or Dr. John Wilson's "Lawn as white as driven snow" and "Take, O take those lips away"—are contemporary, or nearly so. Modern settings are numerous.

SUGGESTED REFERENCES

ARNOLD, MORRIS L. *The Soliloquies of Shakespeare: A Study in Technic.* New York, Columbia University Press, 1911.
Aspects of Shakespeare. British Academy Lectures. Oxford, Clarendon Press, 1933.
　　A reprint of the following lectures:
　　　L. Abercrombie, "A Plea for the Liberty of Interpreting."
　　　E. K. Chambers, "The Disintegration of Shakespeare."
　　　H. Granville-Barker, "From Henry V to Hamlet."
　　　W. W. Greg, "Principles of Emendation in Shakespeare."
　　　E. Legouis, "The Bacchic Element in Shakespeare."
　　　A. W. Pollard, "The Foundations of Shakespeare's Text."
　　　C. F. E. Spurgeon, "Shakespeare's Iterative Imagery."
　　　A. H. Thorndike, "Shakespeare in America."
　　　J. D. Wilson, "The Elizabethan Shakespeare."
BAKER, GEORGE PIERCE. *The Development of Shakespeare as a Dramatist.* New York, Macmillan, 1907.
BETHELL, S. L. *Shakespeare and the Popular Dramatic Tradition.* London, P. S. King and Staples, 1944.
　　Convention and naturalism in Shakespeare, through a consideration of the popular theatre audience.
BRIDGE, SIR FREDERICK. *Shakespearean Music in the Plays and Early Operas.* London, Dent, 1923.
———. *Songs from Shakespeare: The Earliest Known Songs.* London and New York, n. d.
CHAMBERS, E. K. *Shakespeare: A Survey.* London, Sidgwick and Jackson, 1925.
EDWARDS, E. *A Book of Shakespeare Songs with Musical Settings by Various Composers.* New York, A. Schirmer, 1903.
ELLIS-FERMOR, UNA. *Some Recent Research in Shakespeare's Imagery.* A Shakespeare Association Paper. Oxford, 1937.
FLATTER, RICHARD. *Shakespeare's Producing Hand: A Study of His Marks of Expression to Be Found in the First Folio.* New York, Norton, 1948.
　　A study of Shakespeare as producer and actor on the theory that many of the irregularities of metre, line divisions, punctuation, and the like, which have been regarded as blunders or corruptions, are in reality Shakespeare's directions to his actors.
FREEBURG, V. O. *Disguise Plots in Elizabethan Drama: A Study in Stage Tradition.* New York, Columbia University Press, 1915.
FRIPP, EDGAR. *Shakespeare—Man and Artist* (2 vols.). Oxford, Clarendon Press, 1938.

HARBAGE, ALFRED. *As They Liked It: An Essay on Shakespeare and Morality.* New York, Macmillan, 1947.

A study of Shakespeare's creation of situations involving good and evil and his arousal of moral interests in his listeners—important reasons for Shakespeare's immense popularity in his own day and for his lasting reputation.

HARDY, T. MASKELL. *The Songs from Shakespeare's Plays, Set to the Old Tunes* (2 parts). London and Philadelphia, J. Curwen and Sons, n. d.

KREIDER, PAUL V. *Repetition in Shakespeare's Plays.* Princeton University Press, 1941.

MACKAIL, J. W. *The Approach to Shakespeare.* Oxford, Clarendon Press, 1930.

MATTHEWS, BRANDER. *Shakespeare as a Playwright.* New York, Scribner, 1913.

MEGROZ, R. L. *Shakespeare as a Letter Writer and Artist in Prose.* London, Wishart and Company, 1927.

NAYLOR, E. W. *Shakespeare and Music, with Illustrations from Music of the 16th and 17th Centuries.* London, Dent, 1896; revised edition, 1931.

NESS, FREDERIC W. *The Use of Rhyme in Shakespeare's Plays.* New Haven, Yale University Press, 1941.

NOBLE, RICHMOND. *Shakespeare's Use of Song, with the Text of the Principal Songs.* Oxford, Clarendon Press, 1923.

QUILLER-COUCH, SIR ARTHUR. *Shakespeare's Workmanship.* London, T. Fisher Unwin, 1918.

RIDLEY, M. R. *Shakespeare's Plays: A Commentary.* New York, Dutton, 1938.

SCHÜCKING, LEVIN LUDWIG. *Character Problems in Shakespeare's Plays: A Guide to a Better Understanding of the Dramatist.* New York, Holt, 1922.

Historical criticism.

SPENCER, HAZELTON. *The Art and Life of William Shakespeare.* New York, Harcourt Brace, 1940.

Chapters on Shakespeare's life, his medium, and his plays.

SPENCER, THEODORE. *Shakespeare and the Nature of Man.* New York, Macmillan, 1945.

A study of the meaning of Shakespeare's work in relation to the world of the Elizabethans with its mixture of medieval tradition and Renaissance thought.

SPRAGUE, ARTHUR COLBY. *Shakespeare and the Audience: A Study in the Technique of Exposition.* Cambridge, Harvard University Press, 1935.

SPURGEON, CAROLINE F. E. *Leading Motives in the Imagery of Shakespeare's Tragedies.* Shakespeare Association Lecture, 1930.

————. *Shakespeare's Iterative Imagery: (i) As Undersong, (ii) As Touch-stone in His Work.* British Academy Lecture, 1931.

————. *Shakespeare's Imagery and What It Tells Us.* London and New York, Macmillan, 1935.

A collection, assortment, and study of Shakespeare's poetic images and figures of speech, which is more valuable for the data accumulated than for the inferences drawn from them.

STOLL, ELMER EDGAR. *Shakespeare Studies: Historical and Comparative in Method.* New York, Macmillan, 1927.

————. *Art and Artifice in Shakespeare: A Study in Dramatic Contrast and Illusion.* Cambridge University Press, 1933.

Historical criticism which attempts to strip away sentimentalized and philosophized conceptions and to arrive at what Shakespeare meant in his own day.

TILLYARD, E. M. W. *Shakespeare's Last Plays.* London, Chatto and Windus, 1938.

A discussion of *Cymbeline, The Winter's Tale,* and *The Tempest.*

VINCENT, CHARLES. *Fifty Shakespearean Songs.* Boston and New York, Oliver Ditson Company, 1906.

SHAKESPEAREAN COMEDY

Dost thou think, because thou art virtuous, there shall be no more cakes and ale?
—*Twelfth Night*, II, iii, 123-4.

Frame your mind to mirth and merriment,
Which bars a thousand harms and lengthens life.
—*The Taming of the Shrew*, Induction, ii, 137-8.

Horace walpole's well-known sophistry that "life is a comedy to those who think, a tragedy to those who feel" has enjoyed the currency of most epigrammatic half-truths. A remark such as this implies that comedy, in Meredith's phrase, is "the fountain of sound sense," and a critical thing of the intellect, applying the corrective of laughter to the foibles of men. This is no doubt true of some forms of comedy—that of Greece and Rome, of Molière in France, of the Restoration in England, and much modern comedy as well. But the theory does not apply to Elizabethan comedy, as a whole, and few writers in Shakespeare's day, except Ben Jonson, would have understood it. "What a piece of work is a man!" exclaims the serious creature of feeling. "How infinite in faculty! . . . How like an angel! How like a god!" But the cynic echoes: "What a piece of work indeed! The gods are laughing on Olympus! For all his immortal longings, Man is finite; a beast, no more. He tumbles in the dust, he loses his hair, he grows fat and scant of breath." So the comedian jests at scars as though he never felt a wound, but, life being what it is, the poet knows that

> Our sincerest laughter
> With some pain is fraught,
> Our sweetest songs are those that tell of saddest thought.

Hence, English comedy, as a whole, has seldom tried to exclude serious emotions. It is too hard to know where thinking begins and feeling ends,

THE ELIZABETHAN CONCEPTION OF COMEDY

Obviously, it should be possible for a man to laugh in two ways—as the head laughs, and as the heart laughs. These opposite kinds of merriment can best be understood by what it is that provokes them. *Wit* has been described as the "swift play and flash of mind" of "Reason in its judgment seat." Its province is that of words and ideas; it surprises with its ingenuity, its unexpected twists, its comparisons, its paradoxes, its word-play, its epigrams. This is the laughter of the mind—clever, but sometimes as cruel as breaking butterflies. *Humor*, on the other hand, has been described as "thinking in fun, while feeling in earnest." It has a broader tolerance for human foibles; it has a more good-natured sense of the incongruities of life. It takes pride in no extraordinary perception; more objectively, it calls attention to what needs merely to be seen to be appreciated. It deals folly a smack, but in such a manner that we perceive that "there but for the grace of God, go I." This is the laughter of the heart.

The difference can be illustrated by comparing, for a moment, the comedy of Ben Jonson with that of Shakespeare. Jonson's comedy—or the Restoration comedy of manners, for that matter—was based upon the "humors" of men, i. e., their eccentricities, their affectations, their departures from normality, all exaggerated and underscored and tagged in the manner of the caricaturist so that they could not be overlooked. "My soul," says Jonson's spokesman Asper in the Induction to *Every Man out of His Humour*,

> Was never ground into such oily colors
> To flatter vice, and daub iniquity. . . .
> I'll strip the ragged follies of the time
> Naked as at their birth . . . and with a whip of steel,
> Print wounding lashes in their iron ribs.

Jonson's "humor" characters are almost all knaves, quacks, hypocrites, extravagants, or rogues, and their dupes—clever, some of them, or simply ridiculous—who are castigated by a remorseless justicer. Such comedy as Jonson's finds its natural prey in Folly; again in Meredith's phrase,

> it is with the springing delight of hawk over heron, hound over fox, that it gives her chase, never tiring, sure of having her, allowing her no rest. (*On the Idea of Comedy and the Uses of the Comic Spirit*, 1877.)

Shakespeare's comedy includes this intellectual satisfaction; he could, on occasion, wield the whip, savagely in *Troilus and Cressida* or on Sebastian and Antonio in *The Tempest;* less severely upon Malvolio, Parolles, or Lucio. But "Lord, what fools these mortals be!" which is the attitude of the Puck, that mirthful wanderer of the night, is not the prevailing one in Shakespeare's comedies. His characters, to be sure, can be very mocking and witty, occasionally at one another's expense, but Shakespeare, on the whole, was too sympathetic, too understanding, too tolerant, too much in touch with common humanity to administer the corrective. He was an indulgent parent; he loved life and his creatures too well to want to cure them of their foibles. When he went in search of folly, it was not to scourge it from the earth, but to enjoy it as a blessing. He may have carried the whip, but there was a twinkle in his eye. In short, instead of laughing with the brain alone, Shakespeare laughed with his whole being. Who was he to judge? He accepted what he found—Falstaff, larding the lean earth; that stupid jack Dogberry, enjoying his place in the sun; that "dear fool" Sir Andrew Aguecheek; or that pair of illiterate loiterers Launce and Speed. These were not created for mere derision; equally with Hamlet and Othello and Lear, they appeal to what is all too human in ourselves. We laugh *with* Shakespeare's creatures more frequently than *at* them. Hence, Shakespeare may be described as a poetic humorist rather than a writer of pure comedy.

The differences between Jonson and Shakespeare are, in part, individual temperamental differences, but not wholly so. Jonson's comedy was classical and thoroughbred in origin; Shakespeare's largely native and mongrel. The miracle plays and the moralities mixed buffoonery with pious didacticism, and the Tudor interlude, though it often included morality elements and was heavily serious and didactic at times, did eventually free the playwright to exploit broad laugh-producing tricks in dramatized satiric *fabliaux*, sometimes filled with coarse and indecorous fun. The native roots of English comedy were in humor rather than in wit, and Shakespeare followed this unacademic tradition.

The discovery by the English scholar-playwrights, just before Shakespeare was born, of classical models in Plautus and Terence acquainted the stage with conventions which may have been well worn, but which have remained sure-fire theatre to this day. Moreover, here was a comic drama completely separate from tragedy. The plots of Latin comedy were the patterned plots of trickery and sex-intrigue, mistaken identity and disguise, comic wrangles and ludicrous entanglements, practical jokes and deceits, occasionally with the theme of the recovery of long-lost children or parents or brothers providing a little sentiment and romance. The characters were stereotyped and often equipped with tag-names—love-sick youths, miserly fathers, jealous husbands, braggart soldiers, shameless courtesans, clever parasites, rascals, and slaves, outroguing one another. In short, here was farce and fun which reinforced the native English tendencies toward broad humor.

Soon, in the words of Stephen Gosson, English comedy "smelt of Plautus." At first, such adaptations, of which *Ralph Roister Doister* (1534–53) and *Gammer Gurton's Needle* (1552–3) are well-known examples, were confined to the academic stage. Later, they were transferred to the public theatre. The discovery of Italian comedy merely confirmed the influence of Latin. Stock characters of the *commedia dell' arte*, mentioned by Shakespeare and frequently exemplified in his plays, were the old "magnifico" (*Othello*, I, ii, 12), the "lean and slippered pantaloon" (*As You Like It*, II, vii, 158), a "proper stripling and an amorous" (*The Taming of the Shrew*, I, ii, 144), the zany (*Twelfth Night*, I, v, 96), "the pedant, the braggart, the hedge-priest, the fool, and the boy" (*Love's Labor's Lost*, V, ii, 245).

All that these ingredients of plot and character needed to produce good popular comedy was direction, restraint, a little ethical refinement, and infusion with the spirit of real life. To produce great comedy, poetry was also needed. Improvement was soon brought about by the Englishman's love of a good story. The best Elizabethan drama—serious or comic—is simply animated narrative. The sources in which the comic playwright sought his plots were precisely the same as those which yielded more serious drama: Boccaccio, Bandello, Cinthio, Painter, classical and medieval romance, pastoral literature, folk story, or, indirectly, contemporary adaptations of these. "I may boldly say it because I have seen it," wrote Stephen Gosson in alarm,

> that the *Palace of Pleasure*, the *Golden Ass*, the *Æthiopian History*, *Amadis of France*, the *Round Table*, bawdy comedies in Latin, French, Italian, and Spanish have been thoroughly ransacked to furnish the playhouses of London. (*Plays Confuted in Five Actions*, 1582.)

This was only the beginning. Add, as a further element of refinement, the masques and dramatic entertainments of a brilliant, pleasure-loving court.

But how can one grasp and analyze a conception which includes stories that differ as widely as *The Comedy of Errors* on the one hand and *Measure for Measure* on the other, with *A Midsummer Night's Dream*, *Twelfth Night*, and *The Winter's Tale* sandwiched in between? Here, surely, is a great range in mood and subject matter. Yet Shakespeare's comedies do have some common denominators. Unlike tragedy, comedy is less a matter of philosophy and rule than the employment of certain devices.

SHAKESPEARE'S ROMANTICISM

Ben Jonson's plays are frequently laid in the streets of London—Moorfields, Picthatch, Totten-court, the Devil Tavern, the Palace Stairs, the middle aisle of St. Paul's, or even the booths of Bartholomew Fair. Shakespeare seldom encumbered himself with actuality. Only one of his comedies, *The Merry Wives*, has a contemporary English setting; the rest are laid in past times and faraway places. We may roam as we please—through the streets of Ephesus, Milan, or Venice, about a garden at Belmont or in the sunlit Forest of Arden, along the golden sands of a desert island, or on the seacoasts of Illyria and Bohemia, even to Fairyland. All are regions in the realm of fancy.

What occurs in these locales is just as romantic as the settings themselves. The plot of a Shakespearean comedy is "as strange a maze as e'er men trod." The material of which it is composed is variegated, and there is usually an astonishing range of emotional appeal. No bourn is set between serious and comic; the romantic formula permits the separation and reunion of families; children are lost and found again, their identification depending upon a mole, a curious mantle, or some jewels lost with them. Misunderstandings, obsessions, and intrigues all but destroy happiness. There are shipwrecks, usurpations, imprisonment, and jeopardy of life. There are villainy and revenge and even death, as well as idyllic love, sweet content, witticisms, and clownage.

Thus, to illustrate from a single play, because of his groundless jealousy, Leontes in *The Winter's Tale* loses his life-long friend Polixenes; his honest counselor Camillo; his infant daughter Perdita, who is abandoned on a desert shore; and his faithful courtier Antigonus, who is shipwrecked and devoured by a bear while carrying out the king's orders. His heir Mamillius dies of grief, and, at the news, his matchless queen Hermione, apparently dead, is borne out of the court where she has been enduring the ignominy of a public trial for adultery. All this occurs within three acts. Then the whole tone changes. After sixteen years of penitence, Leontes's losses are all but completely restored when the foundling princess Perdita, now a shepherdess, and Florizel, the son of Polixenes, fall in love and elope to Sicilia. Laughter and joy are the by-products of a Shakespearean comedy; the chief interest is a romantic tale which may bring us near to tears and heartbreak before the final happy conclusion.

Not all of Shakespeare's comedies are alike; they reveal varying moods. There are robust farces, like *The Comedy of Errors, The Taming of the Shrew,* or *The Merry Wives;* there are masquelike plays, such as *Love's Labor's Lost, A Midsummer Night's Dream,* and *The Tempest,* which suggest that Shakespeare was writing for a court audience. There are comedies of wit and humor, like *The Two Gentlemen of Verona, The Merchant of Venice, Much Ado about Nothing, As You Like It,* and *Twelfth Night.* These are the so-called "sunny comedies." Then there are more serious pieces—*Measure for Measure, All's Well that Ends Well,* and *Troilus and Cressida,* which constitute the "darker comedies." Finally, there are the tragicomedies or "romances"—*Cymbeline, Pericles, The Winter's Tale,* and *The Tempest,* too. The sweep is from pure lyric poetry to slapstick, from the idyllic to earthy realism. But the romantic formula and the ingredients are much the same for all, even though the proportions vary.

"THE COURSE OF TRUE LOVE"

Love, which is seldom the subject of tragedies in Shakespeare, is universally the central interest in his comedies. Here the formula of initial distress working toward a final solution is adhered to. If the lovers are unmarried when the play opens, they either have not met or find some obstacles in the way of their love. "Ay me," sighs Lysander to Hermia,

>   for aught that I could ever read,
>   Could ever hear by tale or history,
>   The course of true love never did run smooth;
>   But, either it was different in blood—
> *Her.* O cross! Too high to be enthrall'd to low.
> *Lys.* Or else misgraffed in respect of years—
> *Her.* O spite! Too old to be engaged to young.
> *Lys.* Or else it stood upon the choice of friends—
> *Her.* O hell! To choose love by another's eyes.
> *Lys.* Or, if there were a sympathy in choice,
>   War, death, or sickness did lay siege to it,
>   Making it momentary as a sound,
>   Swift as a shadow, short as any dream.
>   (*A Midsummer Night's Dream*, I, i, 132 ff.)

Examples of the obstacles these lovers mention will occur to every reader of Shakespeare. One might add to them slanderous tongues, which nearly wreck love in *Much Ado;* the will of a dead parent, as in *The Merchant of Venice;* the misapplication of law, as in *Measure for Measure;* and rival interests, such as the vow to asceticism, in *Love's Labor's Lost,* the conflict of love and friendship in *The Two Gentlemen,* Olivia's mourning and Orsino's sentimentalism in *Twelfth Night,* or the independence of woman-hater and man-hater in *Much Ado.* In one play, the obstacle is only an unmarried sister. Katharina's wildcat disposition not only makes it unlikely that she will ever have a wooer, but also that Bianca will ever be married, unless their father relents in his determination to admit no suitor for the younger sister until the older has a husband (*The Taming of the Shrew*).

Sometimes the obstacles impeding the course of true love develop as the play advances and furnish some of the amusement. Both hero and heroine may have to contend with one or more rivals with varying support from parents or circumstance. Most of the girls have several suitors, and though it may frequently be fun for them—or us—the situation makes the heroes uneasy. Triangles are very common (*The Comedy of Errors, The Two Gentlemen, A Midsummer Night's Dream, Measure for Measure, The Winter's Tale*), and a "love chain" develops in *A Midsummer Night's Dream, Twelfth Night,* and *As You Like It,* in one case as the result of disguise. Viola outlines the entanglement in which she is involved:

>   How will this fadge? My master loves her [Olivia] dearly;
>   And I, poor monster, fond as much on him;
>   And she, mistaken, seems to dote on me.
>   What will become of this? As I am man,

> My state is desperate for my master's love;
> As I am woman—now alas the day!—
> What thriftless sighs shall poor Olivia breathe!
> O Time, thou must untangle this, not I;
> It is too hard a knot for me to untie!
> (*Twelfth Night*, II, ii, 34 ff.)

What can happen when love-in-idleness in the human heart is assisted by the juice of a magic flower called "love-in-idleness," which is squeezed by a mischievous sprite into sleeping eyes, may be seen in *A Midsummer Night's Dream.*

If the lovers are already married when the play opens, or marry soon after, the formula is much the same. Division and discord and jealousy threaten their harmony; sometimes happiness can be attained only after some seemingly impossible conditions have been fulfilled—like those which Bertram imposes upon Helena in *All's Well.*

The end which we can reckon upon, however, is in any case a bright future. Love has on its side right, resource, and the good graces of nature; love finds a way. If the lovers are single, then marriage is their happy lot:

> Jack shall have Jill;
> Nought shall go ill;
> The man shall have his mare again, and all shall be well.
> (*A Midsummer Night's Dream*, III, ii, 461 ff.)

Sweethearts parade to the altar as a single pair, if it cannot be helped; in greater numbers if possible. In more than one Shakespearean play it would appear that there was "another flood toward, and these couples are coming to the ark." After all, "can one desire too much of a good thing?" If the lovers are married, all misunderstandings are cleared up and faults forgiven.

THE HAPPY ENDING

The happy conclusion of a Shakespearean comedy is the operation of an ethical code which is neither sternly logical nor severe; one cannot concoct even a comic omelette without breaking a few eggs. In tragedy, "violent delights have violent ends," which take some tears in the performing; in comedy, the perplexities of love are both lawless and laughable. Circumstances alter cases. Love may be a mighty lord in Shakespeare's world, but such is our desire for happiness that we are willing to stretch law and order a little. Thus, in comedy, character is not consistently destiny, for, if it were, there are some who could scarce escape hanging. Folly, credulity, and error are not followed by their inexorable consequences, and mercy tempers justice (cf. especially *The Merchant of Venice* and *Measure for Measure*). Human frailty is forgiven. The mood of comedy is expressed by Prospero in *The Tempest:*

> Though with their high wrongs I am struck to the quick,
> Yet with my nobler reason 'gainst my fury
> Do I take part. The rarer action is
> In virtue than in vengeance. (V, i, 25 ff.)

Conceived in a severer mood, some of Shakespeare's comedies might have been tragedies, notably *Much Ado, Measure for Measure, Cymbeline, The Winter's Tale,* and even *The Tempest.* The latter might be called "The Revenge of Prospero," but the hero returns good for evil. In the realm of romance, however, when men do evil they do in some sort confess it, and sincere repentance rights most wrongs:

> The end men looked for cometh not,
> And a path there is where no man thought.

That is not to say that wickedness is not justly punished. Don John is apprehended, but his punishment shall be tomorrow and of the brave sort which the mirthful Benedick shall devise. Lucio must marry a punk, but she is the mother of his child. Falstaff, punished three times by the merry wives before he even begins to perceive that he is made an ass, joins the Fords and the Pages at a merry supper, to "laugh this sport o'er by a country fire" (*The Merry Wives,* V, v, 256).

Conversions are common and never open to question. The false Proteus, once he is found out, repents, and his friend Valentine is generous—to a fault. Demetrius's disposition is changed by magic; after a night in the forest around Athens he never does come to. Shylock yields only perforce and remains unchanged, as do Sebastian and Antonio. But Iachimo—the Iago of comedy— makes what restitution he can; so do Angelo, Leontes, Alonso, and Oliver. Duke Frederick puts on a religious life. Kate the Curst becomes a submissive wife, lecturing the other brides on their duties to their husbands. Benedick, who once challenged Cupid at the flight, becomes Benedick "the married man." Why? "When I said I would die a bachelor, I did not think I should live till I were married" (*Much Ado,* II, iii, 252). And his dear Lady Disdain yields only upon great persuasion, "and partly to save your life, for I was told you were in a consumption" (V, iv, 96). The laws of comedy are liberal laws.

THE MILIEU OF COMEDY

The society in which all of these events take place is an environment in which the comic spirit can flourish: in Meredith's phrase, "a cultivated society . . . wherein ideas are current and the perceptions quick," and where women are on an equal social footing with men. There is, of course, plenty of low comedy in Shakespeare, but, except in the farces, it is incidental. The main stories in his plays are about people of intelligence and taste and refinement.

The hero is usually possessed of the "May of youth and bloom of lusti-hood" (*Much Ado*, V, i, 76); he is at least virtuous and noble,

> His years but young, but his experience old,
> His head unmellowed, but his judgment ripe . . .
> He is complete in feature and in mind
> With all good grace to grace a gentleman.
> (*The Two Gentlemen*, II, iv, 69 ff.)

Usually, "he hath wit to make an ill shape good, and shape to win grace though he had no wit" (*Love's Labor's Lost*, II, i, 59–60). "He capers, he dances, he has eyes of youth, he writes verses, he speaks holiday, he smells April and May" (*The Merry Wives*, III, ii, 68 ff.). Sometimes, like Benedick, the hero of comedy may be "stuffed with all honourable virtues. . . . But for the stuffing—well, we are all mortal" (*Much Ado*, I, i, 57 ff.). Some of Shakespeare's leading men are "scambling, out-facing, fashion-monging boys" (*ibid.*, V, i, 94), quick-answered, saucy, and "as quarrelous as the weasel" (*Cymbeline*, III, iv, 162). Some, like Benedick again, may try to cut Cupid's bow-string, but there is none in Shakespeare's comedies that the little hangman dare not shoot at. Others, like Orsino, are sentimentalists, in love with love; some might answer to the title of "Count Comfect," or "Lord Lackbeard." One or two, like Proteus and Angelo, are frankly double-dealers. Some wear their faith but as the fashion of their hats. Some, like Petruchio and Bassanio, are looking for rich wives. Seldom are they worthy of the good women they marry.

Shakespeare's heroines are just as varied, but much more single-minded and constant than the men; only Cressida is an amorous weathercock. The most attractive, like Rosaline, Portia, and Rosalind, are lively golden funsters with keen senses of absurdities—girls whose "conceits have wings fleeter than arrows, bullets, wind, thought, swifter things" (*Love's Labor's Lost*, V, ii, 260). Occasionally, one, like Beatrice, may be framed temporarily of proud stuff, spelling her lover backward. Realists all, even the hardest have moments of tenderness, however; Beatrice's human sympathy—which, at the moment, she alone possesses—betrays her into letting the bars down to Benedick, and Rosalind's wit before her lover is often caressing when it is most playful. Usually, as in the cases of Portia and Ann Page, the future of these girls is secured by good dowries—"seven hundred pounds and possibilities is goot gifts." Some are sensible wives, like those of Windsor, merry, yet honest, too. Some are long-suffering ideal women who give their all for love, like Hermione and Imogen, and are quietly dignified in adversity and almost impossibly forgiving when it is over. Occasionally, like Julia, Shakespeare's heroines reveal these traits before marriage, sitting "like Patience on a monument, smiling at grief" (*Twelfth Night*, II, iv, 117–8). Viola, who thus de-scribes herself, may be wistful as Viola, but the tune changes when, as

Cesario, she burlesques love-messengers and tantalizes Olivia. Others, like the incomparable Perdita and Miranda, are wonder-children of nature in their frankness.

All of these women know that it is their destiny "to be overmastered with a piece of valiant dust" and that men will not be perfect "till God make [them] of some other metal than earth." They know perfectly that "men are April when they woo, December when they are wed" and that "with a good leg and a good foot . . . and money in his purse a man can win any woman in the world—if a' could get her good-will." Above all, they know their own minds and hearts, long before the young men.

Of course, both Jack and Jill fall in love quickly in Shakespearean comedy, and love at first sight is not uncommon. The heroes all, sooner or later, "will thrust their necks into the yoke and sigh away Sundays." Part of the fun comes from our privilege to watch how "all men in love are mortal in folly." Some, like Benedick, may "have some odd quirks and remnants of wit broken upon them"; some, dedicating their behaviors to love, are transformed—if not exactly into oysters, yet transformed—witness the wrestler Orlando hanging love-sick sonnets on Arden's trees. Only rarely are the girls made to appear as giddy, unless, like Olivia and Beatrice, they deserve it. What in man is jeered at by some such taunt as "flesh, flesh, how art thou fishified!" is merely charming in woman. Shakespeare's heroines keep their wits about them; they guide the plot. Sometimes they actually take the initiative; certainly, they conduct their own courtships on their own terms. And the men suspect it no more in these plays than they do in real life.

Occasionally, both to vex him and to give him confidence in his prowess, the hero must contend with a stupid rival who is his foil. This competitor is usually a well-landed, homely object, cowardly and quarrelsome, like Thurio or Slender or Sir Andrew Aguecheek, with a "little whey face" and a "Cain-colored beard"; sometimes he is even a knight "dubb'd with unhatch'd rapier and on carpet consideration." "Does he not hold up his head as it were, and strut in his gait?" Some of Shakespeare's best comedy is to be found in scenes featuring these fools. "I am not a-hungry! I thank you forsooth," protests Slender, who would rather be unmannerly than troublesome, when sweet Ann Page invites him in to dinner. He clears Simple out of the way:

"Go, sirrah, for all you are my man, go wait upon my cousin Shallow. A justice of peace sometime may be beholding to his friend for a man. I keep but three men and a boy yet, till my mother be dead. But what though? Yet I live like a poor gentleman born. . . . I'faith, I'll eat nothing. I thank you as though I did. . . . I had rather walk here. I thank you. . . . You are afraid if you see a bear loose, are you not? . . . That's meat and drink to me, now. I have seen Sackerson loose twenty times, and have taken him by the chain. But, I warrant you, the women so cried and shrieked at it, that it passed. But women, indeed, cannot abide 'em; they are very ill-favoured rough things. (*The Merry Wives,* I, i, 280 ff.)

It is a perfect asinine build-up, made doubly amusing by the gentle courtesy with which Ann accepts it.

The *dramatis personæ* of a Shakespearean comedy is composed of all sorts and conditions of men and women, ranging in rank from king and duke to light-fingered rogues of the road, drunken tinkers, and bellows-menders' apprentices. This divergency even includes the supernatural, from the wind-borne Ariel to Caliban, who is "a freckled whelp, hag-born . . . not hon-oured with a human shape." Usually, the characters belong to three social groups (or more, if the play treats of the supernatural). To the middle plane belong the lovers and their immediate friends and rivals. Above them are their superiors in influence or authority—their princes and their elders to whom they owe obedience and respect. Below them, for contrast, are the humbler orders—the justices, the citizens, the wenches, and the clowns. Thus, in *A Midsummer Night's Dream,* there are among the mortals (a) the court group around Duke Theseus and his betrothed, (b) the romantic courtly lovers, and (c) the city mechanicals and hard-handed men of Athens. In addition, there are ranks and orders of fairies around Oberon and Titania. In *As You Like It,* there are the court group, including the lovers; the Arcadian shepherds and shepherdess; and the real rustics, including the slat-ternly goat-girl and her yokel swain. Moreover, in both of these plays, a love affair of one sort or another is developed in each of these contrasting groups.

COMIC CHARACTER-TYPES

Many of the divergent characters in these groups fall readily into conven-tional stage types: the more or less genial princes and dukes, like Prospero or Theseus; the faithful old counselors, like Camillo or Gonzalo; the spiritual advisers, like Friar Francis. There are the old parents—sometimes strict, some-times indulgent—occupied with business and the making of profitable matches for their children. And, in contrast, there are the young men and women—meekly submissive or, more usually, careless of paternal feelings and purse. There is the resourceful or blundering servant attached to the hero, the *lena,* either maid or nurse, attached to the heroine. Both of these types are inclined to be realistically earthy and coarse. There is the co-educational "college of wit-crackers," consisting of ladies-in-waiting to the heroine and friends to the hero. There is the rough and homely, but kind-hearted, burgher, like Mine Host of the Garter, as well as the boors, the sots or the slatterns, and the types already mentioned as inherited from classical and Italian comedy. Shakespeare, however, had a lively sense of the variety of human nature. His figures are usually individualized, even when they conform to a general norm of family resemblance and, as is sometimes the case, have tag-names. Not all belonging to the same group are alike.

Some of these stereotypes, of course, were especially provocative of laughter on the Elizabethan stage. Chief among these was the fool or clown. "I would fain see the fool," says Gossip Tattle in Jonson's *The Staple of News*,

> the fool is the finest man in the company, they say, and has all the wit. He is the very justice o' peace of the play, and can commit whom he will, and what he will, error, absurdity, as the toy takes him, and no man say black is his eye, but laugh at him. . . . My husband, Timothy Tattle,—God rest his poor soul!—was wont to say there was no play without a fool or a devil in't.

Her point of view was common, and English clowns of Shakespeare's day were famous all over Europe.

One should distinguish, however, between ranks and orders of comedians. *Fool* and *clown* were both generic terms as the Elizabethans used them, but, generally speaking, *fool* is more properly restricted to the professional jester —like the "allowed fool" Feste, the roynish "motley-minded" Touchstone, that "pied ninny" Trinculo, or Lear's Fool—who was attached to courts and great households, wore a parti-colored livery with a coxcomb, and carried a bauble. The *clown*, on the other hand, is properly a rustic bumpkin, like "that unlettered small-knowing soul" Costard and his feminine counterpart Jaquennetta, or William and Audrey, or Bully Bottom and those "hempen home-spuns" with "unbreathed memories" who "never laboured in their minds" until they tried to produce a play. Usually, the clowns are dronish servants who are "huge-feeders," "snail-slow in profit" and sleepers by day, like Launce, Speed, and Launcelot Gobbo. Not all of them are stupid; some have a pretty wit, and the range is all the way from the "twice-sod simplicity" of Anthony Dull the constable to the chop-logic of the Dromios. Often they hunt in pairs—Launce and Speed, the two Dromios, Launcelot and his father, Curtis and Grumio, the two grave-diggers, Dogberry and Verges, Justice Shallow and Justice Silence, Trinculo and Stephano. Closely akin to these laugh-provokers, but yet a distinct type, is the clever rogue, best represented by Autolycus, that "snapper-up of unconsidered trifles."

The stage tricks of fool, clown, and rogue were pretty well stereotyped in Shakespeare's theatre, some of them dating back to classical comedy or the medieval drama. "What must I do?" asks the clown who has been drawn in with a cart-rope in *The Pilgrimage to Parnassus*. He receives this reply:

> Why, if thou canst but draw thy mouth awry, lay thy leg over thy staff, saw a piece of cheese asunder with thy dagger, lap up drink on the earth, I warrant thee they'll laugh mightily.

"I have laughed," says an admirer in Thomas Goffe's *The Careless Shepherdess* (*c*. 1629):

> Until I cried again to see what faces
> The rogue will make. O, it does me good
> To see him hold out's chin, hang down his hands,
> And twirl his bauble! There is never a part
> About him but breaks jests.
> I had rather hear him leap and laugh or cry,
> Than hear the gravest speech in all the play.
> I never saw Reade peeping through the curtain
> But ravishing joy entered into my heart.

So, in Shakespeare, these fun-makers engage in chop-logic with their social superiors; they stumble awkwardly about the stage and bump into people; they run away on errands before they learn what they are sent for; they come back again and again with new questions; they linger around after they have been dismissed; they spin out rambling and excited accounts of what they had heard, interrupting them with "said he" and "said I"; they simply cannot keep secrets; they fall readily to fisticuffs; they burst into comic tears. Frequently, they soliloquize, with a great deal of corroborative circumstance, as Launce does when he arranges his shoes, his hat, his walking-stick, and his dog around him to represent members of his sorrowing family, and demonstrates how he said farewell to each of them (*The Two Gentlemen*, II, iii). The large number of waistcoats which the grave-digger in *Hamlet* solemnly removes in many a modern production probably is a very old stage tradition.

On the whole, of course, the fool was productive of higher comedy than the clown; at its best, the professional wit of the jester is to be seen in *As You Like It*. Largely by parody or contrast, Touchstone "uses his folly like a stalking-horse, and under the presentation of that he shoots his wit" (V, iv, 111 ff.). His humor ripples over everything—courtiers' oaths, breaking ribs as sport for ladies, travelers' complaints, romantic love, the course of time, the irregularities of fortune, the shepherd's life, the courtier's life, rustic philosophy, pastoral innocence, the code of quarreling by the book, even the ill-favored wife of his choice. In the presence of anything false or specious, Shakespeare would rather have a fool to make him merry than experience to make him sad. He had real admiration for a good fool:

> He must observe the mood on whom he jests,
> The quality of persons, and the time,
> And, like the haggard, check at every feather
> That comes before his eye. This is a practice
> As full of labour as a wise man's art;
> For folly that he wisely shows is fit,
> But wise men, folly-fall'n, quite taint their wit.
> (*Twelfth Night*, III, i, 67 ff.)

Another comic type which was traditional on the Elizabethan stage was the *miles gloriosus* or the braggart soldier who intends more than he is able to do. Ancient Pistol, with his bombast and quotation of scraps from old blood-curdling plays, is Shakespeare's best example. But there is a good deal of the type in Falstaff, Sir Andrew Aguecheek, Cloten, and others. Frequently, this swaggerer is set off by a pert and cheeky page, like that "well-educated infant," that "sweet ounce of man's flesh," that "handful of wit," that "pigeon egg of discretion," that "most pathetical nit," Armado's "pretty knavish page" Moth. Another is the present Prince Hal gave Falstaff to set him off, a boy who is "fitter to be worn in [his master's] cap than to wait at [his] heels." Before him Falstaff walks "like a sow that hath overwhelm'd all her litter but one" (*2 Henry IV*, I, ii, 11).

Another source of delight was the foreigner, whose idiosyncrasies and broken English were fair game for the comedian. The earliest of these figures to appear in Shakespeare's plays is Don Adriano de Armado, that "refined traveller of Spain," in *Love's Labor's Lost:*

> A man in all the world's new fashion planted,
> That hath a mint of phrases in his brain;
> One who the music of his own vain tongue
> Doth ravish like enchanting harmony. (I, i, 165 ff.)

Armado is not so much a swashbuckler as a fop or a fantastic. "He is too picked, too affected, too odd, as it were, too peregrinate, as I may call it" (V, i, 14 ff.). Another is Dr. Caius in *The Merry Wives*, "abusing God's patience and the king's English." More good-natured is the treatment accorded the Welshmen—Captain Fluellen in *Henry V*, who is pedantic about the "disciplines of war," and Sir Hugh Evans, the school master in *The Merry Wives*, "one who makes fritters of English" with his "proverbs and his no-verbs." Even national characteristics are hit off, the Welsh fondness for cheese, leeks, and pippins, and the fiery quick temper of the Latin. Dr. Caius says that even Ford's frenzy "is not jealous in France" (III, iii, 184). Gallic effeminacy may be suggested in Le Beau, who talks with pursed lips as "pigeons feed their young" and can but answer "as wit and fortune will, or the Destinies decree" (*As You Like It*, I, ii, 100 ff.). It may even be that Don Armado wears the sixteenth-century equivalent of the continental dicky. He cannot take off his doublet before ladies to fight Costard because he wears no shirt (V, ii, 711 ff.).

Even more amusing to Shakespeare's spectators were certain affected types, such as the fop or "water-fly" and the self-conscious melancholic. Shakespeare's portrayals of this type are as near as he came to creating "humor" characters in the Jonson manner. Osric in *Hamlet*, displaying his court manners, is a good example, or that "damnable both-sides rogue" Parolles, in

All's Well. Sometimes the fop is an admiring disciple of the *miles gloriosus,* and, when he goes courting, we see him in Sir Andrew, Roderigo, or Slender. Best of the lot is that "old love-monger," "Cupid's grandfather," the subservient usher Boyet in *Love's Labor's Lost,* who exclaims when sent on a trivial errand, "Proud of employment, willingly I go" (II, i, 35).

> This fellow pecks up wit as pigeons pease,
> And utters it again when God doth please.
> He is wit's pedler, and retails his wares
> At wakes and wassails, meetings, markets, fairs. . . .
> This gallant pins the wenches on his sleeve;
> Had he been Adam, he had tempted Eve.
> A' can carve too, and lisp; why, this is he
> That kiss'd his hand away in courtesy;
> This is the ape of form, monsieur the nice,
> That when he plays at tables, chides the dice. . . .
>   The ladies call him sweet;
> The stairs, as he treads on them, kiss his feet. (V, ii, 315 ff.)

The melancholics in Shakespeare's plays range all the way from such "an affectioned ass" and kill-joy as Olivia's steward to the melancholy Prince Hamlet. Not all of the examples of the type are comic. Hamlet is not, but Romeo, "stabbed with a white wench's black eye," is comic, until he meets Juliet. So is that solemn "time-pleaser" and precisian Malvolio, who is "sick of self-love" and a hater of laughter. So is the melancholy Jaques, who moralizes every spectacle into a thousand similes and would cynically chastise sin. He is at his best when he proudly analyzes his exquisite state of mind:

> I have neither the scholar's melancholy, which is emulation; nor the musician's, which is fantastical; nor the courtier's, which is proud; nor the soldier's, which is ambitious; nor the lawyer's, which is politic; nor the lady's, which is nice; nor the lover's, which is all these; but it is a melancholy of mine own, compounded of many simples, extracted from many objects, and indeed the sundry contemplation of my travels. (*As You Like It,* IV, i, 10 ff.)

In addition, Shakespeare's audiences found amusement in certain occupational types. There is open season on constables and school masters in Elizabethan comedy, no less than in the modern movie. The minions of the law sleep on their beats, capture malefactors only by accident, bungle in their duty, and then attain a self-importance that nothing can ruffle. All are men "who are thought the most senseless and fit men for their office" (*Much Ado,* III, iii, 25). Anthony Dull is harmless enough: "he hath never fed of the dainties that are bred in a book; he hath not eat paper, as it were; he hath not drunk ink; his intellect is not replenished; he is only an animal" (*Love's Labor's Lost,* IV, ii, 25 ff.). So is Elbow in *Measure for Measure.* Dogberry, however, is the jack-in-office *in excelsis:*

I am a wise fellow, and, which is more, an officer, and, which is more, a house-holder; and, which is more, as pretty a piece of flesh as any is in Messina, and one that knows the law, go to; and a rich fellow enough, go to; and a fellow that hath had losses, and one that hath two gowns, and everything handsome about him. . . . O that I had been writ down an ass! (*Much Ado*, IV, ii, 81 ff.)

The two arts-men, Holofernes and Sir Nathaniel, in *Love's Labor's Lost*, are reminiscent of Dr. Johnson's acid remark about the elder Sheridan:

Why, Sir, Sherry is dull, naturally dull; but it must have taken him a great deal of pains to become what we now see him. Such an excess of stupidity, Sir, is not in Nature. (Boswell, *Life of Dr. Johnson*, under date of 1763.)

The sedulously acquired stupidity of pedant and hedge-priest balances the natural stupidity of constable and clown in Dull and Costard. To these must be added from *The Comedy of Errors*, the pedant-mountebank-conjurer Pinch; from *As You Like It*, Sir Oliver Martext; and from *Twelfth Night*, Dick surgeon, whose "eyes were set at eight i' the morning." The latter, how-ever, is only alluded to and does not appear on the stage. Besides the learned, we have in *The Merry Wives* the reluctant school boy William Page, who does not "remember in [his] prain," and the carefree student Lucentio in *The Taming of the Shrew*.

The trades and the lesser arts are also represented. Besides the mechanicals in *A Midsummer Night's Dream*, there is a timorous ladies' tailor in *The Taming of the Shrew* and among Falstaff's selectees in *2 Henry IV*. There are singers, forever protesting that they are out of voice and needing to be coaxed to perform, in *As You Like It* and *Much Ado*. A ballad-monger is portrayed to the life in Autolycus:

He hath songs for man or woman, of all sizes; no milliner can so fit his customers with gloves. He has the prettiest love-songs for maids, so without bawdry, which is strange; with such delicate burdens of dildos and fadings, "jump her and thump her"; and where some stretch-mouthed rascal would, as it were, mean mischief, and break a foul gap into the matter, he makes the maid to an-swer, "Whoop, do me no harm, good man"; puts him off, slights him, with "Whoop, do me no harm, good man." (*The Winter's Tale*, IV, iv, 191 ff.)

There are gluttons and topers, like Sir Toby and Falstaff, to whom "care's an enemy to life." Indeed, Falstaff seems to be the summation of all the deadly sins rolled into one and of all stage butts for laughter. Yet he is also a wit in his own right. There is the tapster Francis, with his "anon, anon, sir," in *1 Henry IV*, and the tapster-bawd Pompey Bum, whose "occupation does stink in some sort, sir; but yet, sir. . . . Truly, sir, I am a poor fellow that would live" (*Measure for Measure*, II, i). There is even a common hangman, glorying in the name Abhorson, who thinks his profession discredited when he is assigned the bawd as his assistant (*ibid.*, IV, ii).

HUMOR OF DIALOGUE

The Elizabethan audience apparently enjoyed the intellectual pleasure of following a jest that was bandied like a shuttlecock from mind to mind or depended upon a keen perception of words. Hence, some of the best scenes in Shakespeare are scenes of wit and repartee. Here again, Shakespeare employed conventional devices.

The monologue, which was a direct address to the audience, was an old fool's trick on the Elizabethan stage, but more than fools employ it in Shakespeare. Launce may talk over his sour-natured dog (*The Two Gentlemen*, IV, iv) or Trinculo the strange fish he has stumbled over (*The Tempest*, II, ii), but there are also Benedick's disquisition on love (*Much Ado*, II, iii), Autolycus's on honesty (*The Winter's Tale*, IV, iv, 605 ff.), and Falstaff's on his soldiers and on honor (*1 Henry IV*, IV, ii and V, i). Occasionally, the monologue becomes a duologue by the entrance of another character, as when Launcelot interrupts his debate about running away to try "confusions" with his blind, "true-begotten father" (*The Merchant of Venice*, II, ii), when the old shepherd's grumbling about boiled-brained youth is cut short by his son (*The Winter's Tale*, III, iii), or when Autolycus spies his natural prey, the clown (*ibid.*, IV, iii).

Duologue acts in the vaudeville manner frequently interrupt the action of a Shakespearean comedy. The most common variety is that between trained intelligence and mother-wit, i. e., between master and man—like the encounters of Antipholus of Syracuse and his Dromio (*The Comedy of Errors*, II, ii and III, ii) and Valentine and Speed (*The Two Gentlemen*, II, i); between mistress and maid—like those between Julia and Lucetta (*The Two Gentlemen*, I, ii), Portia and Nerissa (*The Merchant of Venice*, I, ii), or Beatrice and Margaret (*Much Ado*, III, iv). Often these dialogues amount to little more than feeding the wit the right questions or otherwise "administering occasion" to the wit, who may be either party. Variations occur when the master bandies words with a maid, as Benedick does with Margaret (*Much Ado*, V, ii), or the mistress with a male servant or a professional jester, as Jessica does with Launcelot (*The Merchant of Venice*, III, v), as Rosalind does with Touchstone (*As You Like It*), or as Olivia, Maria, and Viola all do with Feste (*Twelfth Night*). Sometimes the duologue occurs between two servants, Launce and Speed, or Grumio and Curtis; two philosophers, Corin and Touchstone; or teacher and pupil, Sir Hugh Evans and William Page. In each case, we have an amusing little act, indulged in for its own sake, and not materially to advance the story.

Of a higher order is the "skipping dialogue," the "wise-crack" interchange either between men and women or between persons of the same sex. It is here that the comic spirit finds its richest opportunities. The "merry war" of the sexes brightens many a Shakespearean comedy—Biron and Rosaline, Benedick and Beatrice, Petruchio and Katharina, Rosalind and Orlando (a contest that is a little one-sided here), and even Armado and Jaquennetta. One of the best of such scenes is the ball in *Much Ado about Nothing* (II, i, 90 ff.). Social banter between men is exemplified in most of the plays just alluded to, notably *Love's Labor's Lost* and *Much Ado*, in the flashing verbal duel between Romeo and Mercutio (II, iv, 38 ff.), or Falstaff's "quick answers" to the Chief Justice (*2 Henry IV*, I, ii). Such dialogue becomes even more like a fencing match when two girls participate, one of them disguised as a man, as in *The Two Gentlemen*, *As You Like It*, and *Twelfth Night*. "Now, by the salt wave of the Mediterranean," exclaims Don Armado as his page Moth finishes off Holofernes,

> a sweet touch, a quick venue of wit! Snip, snap, quick and home! It rejoiceth my intellect. True wit! (*Love's Labor's Lost*, V, i, 61 ff.)

Much of Shakespeare's audience thought likewise.

Some of Shakespeare's comic characters "are wont to speak plain and to the purpose," like honest men; with others, "their words are a very fantastical banquet, just so many strange dishes" (*Much Ado*, II, iii, 20 ff.). Some of these wit-snappers answer "you right painted cloth, from whence [others] have studied [their] questions" (*As You Like It*, III, ii, 290–1). Their witticisms are pure jest-book humor, like the repartee in *The Hundred Merry Tales* or in Tottel's *Book of Riddles*, which Slender wished he had by him when he called on Ann Page. But even the puns, the ingenuities with "tricksy words," the mispunctuation of the Prologue to *Pyramus and Thisbe*—even fellows, like Nym, who "fright English out of his wits" (*The Merry Wives*, II, i, 141–2)—are still much more amusing than some folk pretend. "We must speak by the card, or equivocation will undo us. . . . The age is grown so picked that the toe of the peasant comes so near the heel of the courtier, he galls his kibe" (*Hamlet*, V, i, 148 ff.).

On lower social levels, humor of language is to be found in malapropisms, which are a kind of farcical mistaken identity in words. Most of Shakespeare's yokels have blessed his pages with their matchless blunders. Dull reprehending the duke's own person (*Love's Labor's Lost*, I, i, 184); Costard welcoming the sour cup of prosperity; affliction may one day smile again (*ibid.*, 315 ff.); Launce receiving his proportion, like the Prodigious Son (*The Two Gentlemen*, II, iii, 3 ff.); Bottom aggravating his voice so that he will roar you as gently as any sucking dove or even a nightingale (*A Midsummer Night's Dream*, I, ii, 84 ff.), or pointing out that at the duke's Oak the amateurs may rehearse most obscenely and courageously (*ibid.*, 111); Dogberry charging the watch to comprehend all vagrom men (*Much Ado*, III, iii, 25); Hostess Quickly denying that Falstaff ever cried out against women or called them devils incarnate: "'A' could never abide carnation; 'twas a colour he never liked" (*Henry V*, II, iii, 36); Elbow accusing the notorious benefactors and protesting that the time is yet to come when his wife was ever respected with man, woman, or child (*Measure for Measure*, II, i, 177); Slender taking comfort in the reflection that if there is no great love at the beginning of the match proposed for him, yet Heaven may decrease it upon better acquaintance—"His meaning is good" (*The Merry Wives*, I, i, 254 ff.) —all are as good as Mrs. Malaprop's "allegory on the banks of the Nile" and as ingenious as the Mock-turtle's "reeling, writhing, and fainting in coils." These malapropisms are the product, not so much of mere illiteracy, as of stupid aspiration to artistry in language.

Occasionally, too, Shakespeare satirized affectations of speech. Rustic pre-occupation with proverbial platitude is hit off in Corin, as are Mine Host's pet phrase "bully rook" and Bardolph's "the humour of it." But the sport extends further. *Love's Labor's Lost* makes fun, not specifically of euphuism, but rather of the self-conscious courtly diction that euphuism represents. Armado's soliloquy on love is in the euphuistic vein (I, ii, 172 ff.), but Rosaline's wit seeks out all sorts of "taffeta phrases and three-piled hyperboles" (V, ii, 406 ff.). Holofernes's ode on the princess's hunting prowess, beginning "The preyful princes pierced and prick'd a pretty pleasing pricket," is a burlesque on excess alliteration, as well as all "forms, figures, shapes, objects, ideas, apprehensions, motions, revolutions . . . [which] are begot in the ventricle of memory, nourished in the womb of pia mater, and delivered upon the mellowing of occasion" (IV, ii, 58 ff.). The sonneteering of the courtiers is in

> the liver vein, which makes flesh a deity,
> A green goose a goddess, pure, pure idolatry. (IV, iii, 74-5.)

And Holofernes's dinner-table criticism may have been

> sharp and sententious; pleasant without scurrility, witty without affectation, audacious without impudency, learned without opinion, and strange without heresy (V, i, 3 ff.),

but it takes off pedantry and ostentation to the life.

Elsewhere, Shakespeare amused himself and his audience with some literary satire: *The Lamentable Comedy of Pyramus and Thisbe*, Falstaff's declamation in "King Cambyses' vein," Pistol's huffing play scraps, Autolycus's broadside ballads (*The Winter's Tale*, IV, iv), travelers' tales (*The Tempest*), pastoral conventions and Arcadian wooing (*As You Like It*), the habit of composing halting love-sonnets in spite of Providence (*Much Ado*), and the marks by which one can identify a lover (*As You Like It* and *Romeo and Juliet*). Shakespeare enjoyed turning the light of laughter upon anything that was overblown and pompous.

HUMOR OF PLOT AND SITUATION

In plot, also, Shakespeare employed with variation many tried devices, some of them almost as old as the theatre. These devices produce humor rather than wit, and chief among them are amusing predicaments or events which, in the Puck's phrase, "befall preposterously." Sometimes such scenes are roughhouse revelry, like those in Dame Quickly's tavern or Olivia's cellar. Some are frankly farce, as when Falstaff is carried out in a buckbasket under the jealous Ford's very nose and dumped—with the rest of the dirty linen—into the Thames. Concealing a lover in household ware—usually a tub or a chest—is common in the *fabliau*. Or the fun may grow out of a police-court scene in which a ridiculous officer, like Elbow, brings a clever rascal to justice. Titania's weaving a coronet of flowers for her asinine lover is farcical, but its absurdity is increased by the queen's disappointment in Bottom's conversation. She bids her attendants

> Tie up my love's tongue; bring him silently.
> (*A Midsummer Night's Dream*, III, i, 206.)

Apparently there are limits to infatuation and even to the efficacy of the magic blossom, love-in-idleness. Sometimes, however, such situations are much more subtle. The "students" in *Love's Labor's Lost* bind themselves by an oath that is too hard to keep. Navarre has overlooked the embassy of the princess. Instead of entertaining her in his palace, he has to make her comfortable in a pavilion in his park. In a thousand ways the votarists are forsworn. The girls have nothing to do—young blood simply does not obey an old decree. The situation is all the more absurd because the vow also applies to the animal Costard.

Variations of the ludicrous situation are endless: Thurio, Claudio, and Orsino wooing by proxy; that old goat Falstaff attempting, with mimeographed love letters, to translate the merry wives out of honesty into English; two faint-hearted rivals, like Cesario and Sir Andrew or Evans and Dr. Caius, brought to the verge of a duel; Merchant Minola possessed of one daughter who is a "commodity lay fretting by [him]" and another for whom suitors outbid one another; the transformed make-sport Benedick breaking off diplomatic relations with his prince and grimly challenging Claudio for killing a sweet and innocent lady. At its best, this device can be considerably more than mere farce.

Sometimes the comic device is mistaken identity, a laugh-provoker derived from Latin drama. The best examples involve the confusion of twins, as in *The Comedy of Errors* and *Twelfth Night;* in the latter, the deception is produced by disguise. Popularly, mistaken identity is often dismissed as merely improbable and artificial. But we are in the realm of light comedy;

identical twins do exist in real life, and the possibility of confusion on the stage taxes the credulity of no one who has ever seen a pair. In neither of these plays is the audience confused, because it enjoys the dramatist's complete confidence. A willingness to make-believe is little enough for him to demand in return, particularly when laughter is the reward.

Variations of mistaken identity are the "bed-trick" or "substitute bride" theme, derived from folk story and employed in both *Measure for Measure* and *All's Well;* inability to recognize a character in the dark or through a mask, as in *Much Ado;* and such mistakings as the deboshed monster Caliban worshipping Stephano, the brave god who bears celestial liquor.

One variety, disguise, may be thought of as artificial or premeditated confusion. The modern playgoer also thinks it too artificial; it is doubtful that such a thought ever occurred to the Elizabethans. Sir James Melville, genial ambassador of Mary Queen of Scots in 1564, told of Queen Elizabeth's curiosity about her Scottish cousin and added:

> I offered to convey her secretly to Scotland by post, clothed like a page; that under this disguise she might see the Queen, as James the Fifth had gone in disguise to France with his own ambassador, to see the Duke of Vendome's sister, who should have been his wife. Telling her, that her chamber might be kept in her absence as though she were sick; that none needed to be privy thereto, except my Lady Strafford and one of the grooms of her chamber. She appeared to like that kind of language, only answered it with a sigh, saying, alas, if I might do it thus. (*Memoirs of Sir James Melville of Halhill* [1683], folio 51.)

Realistic or not, Shakespeare used disguise in both serious drama and comedy. The expedient was partially suggested by his sources, in part by old stage tradition, in part by the composition of his acting company. Girls disguised as boys appear in at least five of the comedies, but, though they are caparisoned as men, seldom do they have a doublet and hose in their dispositions. The device in reverse, the "boy-bride" trick, was also used by Shakespeare at the end of *The Merry Wives,* when Dr. Caius and Slender are cozened and made to elope with great lubberly boys. Variations of disguise, when one person pretends to be another, are also frequent. Tranio changes places with his master, Lucentio becomes Cambio, the pedant is passed off as Lucentio's father and confronted by the man he is impersonating. Ford masquerades as the amorous Brook, feeding his jealousy and flattering Falstaff; Vincentio dresses as a friar to play Haroun-al-Rashid in the underworld of Vienna. There are veiled brides in *Much Ado.* The dramatist was well aware that such thin disguises would be accepted on the stage.

More fertile and more subtle is the device of the misplaced character, the fish out of water, the person out of his element or in the wrong environment. *As You Like It* is filled with examples. There are the exiled courtiers —all men of the metropolis—translating in the Forest of Arden the stubbornness of Fortune in as sweet a style as possible, playing Robin Hood, wearing what the well-dressed forester-outlaw wears, and generally being as rustic as vacationists on a dude-ranch. There is Touchstone, the only realist in the court, who still wears his motley in the forest and acts the clown among courtiers and the courtier among clowns. He is like Ovid among the Goths—"O knowledge ill-inhabited, worse than Jove in a thatched house" (III, iii, 10–11). There is Jaques the far-traveled, who is the disillusioned product of court life and becomes the only member of the court group who does not hurry back to town when the opportunity offers. There is William, who was born in the forest and proud of it, coming into contact with "society" for the first time and unable to compete. Other plays yield additional examples: Viola and Julia, the love-lorn "pages," who cannot promote their own love affairs because they are employed by their masters as envoys to other women; the Old Shepherd and his son, decked "in the blossoms of their good fortune" and standing on their prerogatives as "gentlemen born" (*The Winter's Tale*, V, ii, 134 ff.), or Trinculo and Stephano cast away on the desert island. At home, the jester would be ever witty and the butler professionally subservient and sober. On the island, Trinculo is viceroy and general yes-man to the tippling Stephano, who, among other oddities, sings a rough "fo'c'sle" song about the execrable Kate. A thorough landsman, Stephano in his element could only be an object of contempt to a true sailor.

Shakespeare's fondness for contrast has already been commented upon, and comparison is one of his most effective comic devices. Shakespeare sometimes thought out his comedy in terms of parallel scenes or parody. For example, the claims which Luce-Dowsabel, the foul kitchen vestal who is "a wondrous fat marriage," lays to Dromio of Syracuse is a *reductio ad absurdum* of the affair that has been developing above-stairs between his master and Adriana (*The Comedy of Errors*, III, ii). Likewise, Valentine and Proteus discuss their mistresses (*The Two Gentlemen*, II, iv) and a few moments later Launce and Speed discuss theirs (III, i). The idyllic wooing of Florizel and Perdita, with her charming favors of flowers, is interrupted and parodied by the clown's double entanglement with Mopsa and Dorcas:

> If I were not in love with Mopsa, thou shouldst take no money of me; but being enthralled as I am, it will also be the bondage of certain ribbons and gloves [usually an engagement present].
> *Mop.* I was promised them against the feast; but they come not too late now.
> *Dor.* He hath promised you more than that, or there be liars.
>   (*The Winter's Tale*, IV, iv, 233 ff.)

Another parody is the double rehearsal which Prince Hal and Falstaff hold in the tavern in preparation for the prince's coming interview with his father. "This chair shall be my state, this dagger my sceptre, and this cushion my crown" (*1 Henry IV*, II, iv, 415 ff.) (see illustration, p. 456).

As You Like It is full of examples of this device of parallelism. Touchstone's description of unrequited affection parodies Silvius's love-longing (II, iv, 46 ff.); the triangle involving Audrey, William, and Touchstone is a *reductio ad absurdum* of the love chain which develops in a better social circle; the verses which Orlando hangs on the trees are such that Touchstone can parody "eight years together, dinners and suppers and sleeping hours excepted"; Jaques's third stanza to "Under the greenwood tree" shows what Arcadian philosophy amounts to.

Practical jokes also regaled the Elizabethan playgoer. The transfiguration of Titania and Bottom and the lovers is by no means a lone example. Many have already been alluded to in other connections. The masked ladies exchange favors to confuse their lovers in *Love's Labor's Lost* (V, ii); Sly the tinker is transferred to a nobleman's bedroom; Malvolio is gulled into a nay-word by a dropped letter; Benedick and Beatrice are tricked into falling in love; Lucentio woos Bianca in a Latin lesson; Henry V has his joke with Williams; Autolycus finds the simple Bohemian sheep-shearing most profitable; wise-cracking audiences of courtiers try to put yokel players out of countenance in *Love's Labor's Lost* and *A Midsummer Night's Dream*. The Puck plays his mischievous pranks, and Prospero's urchin-shows mock the shipwrecked company with a banquet that disappears (*The Tempest*, III, iii). Occasionally, the "enginer [is] hoist with his own petard." Shylock's "merry bond" is legally impossible of collection, but his refusal to collect it also serves to convict him of plotting against Antonio's life. The farcical duel in *Twelfth Night* rebounds upon the heads of its perpetrators. It is the last straw that throws Sir Toby completely out of favor with his niece, and it results in bloody coxcombs when Toby and Andrew meet Sebastian. The "biter bitten" was a well-worn trick from Latin farce.

Audiences enjoy a good rough-and-tumble knockabout, and, from the time when the miracle plays showed Noah and his wife, wrangles, name-calling contests, "flytings," tall tales, and general raillery and fisticuffs have been laugh-provokers on the stage. None are dignified, but the "fair frays" between ladies and gentlemen represent the high-comedy use of the device. The bottom of the scale is far down. Examples are too numerous, but one may mention the disagreements of the lovers in *A Midsummer Night's Dream*, the railing of Shylock along the Rialto, the cudgeling of Pistol, the Gadshill robbery and its aftermath, the tavern Billingsgate of Doll Tearsheet, and the attempted arrest of Falstaff. "This sanguine coward, this bed-presser, this horseback-breaker, this huge hill of flesh," begins Prince Hal, only to be interrupted by Falstaff:

'Sblood, you starveling, you elf-skin, you dried neat's tongue, you bull's pizzle, you stock-fish! O for breath to utter what is like thee! (*1 Henry IV*, II, iv, 267 ff.)

Shakespeare was not above using the familiar stock situations and devices to which his audiences were accustomed.

SHAKESPEARE'S NORMALITY

Finally, in comedy as elsewhere, Shakespeare's attitude was always healthy and normal—what Coleridge called "keeping at all times on the high road of life." Nothing unnatural, pathological, or perverted appears in his comedies for the sake of getting a laugh from those whose "lungs are tickle o' the sere." "Shakespeare has no innocent adulteries," wrote Coleridge,

no interesting incests, no virtuous vice:—he never renders that amiable which religion and reason alike teach us to detest. . . . If he occasionally disgusts a keen sense of delicacy, he never injures the mind; he neither excites, nor flatters, passion, in order to degrade the subject of it; he does not use the faulty thing for a faulty purpose, nor carries on warfare against wickedness, through the medium of a morbid sympathy with the unfortunate. In Shakespeare vice never walks as in twilight. (*Lectures on Poetry, the Drama, and Shakespeare,* 1818.)

SUGGESTED REFERENCES

BUSBY, OLIVE MARY. *Studies in the Development of the Fool in the Elizabethan Drama.* London, Humphrey Milford, Oxford University Press, 1923.

CAMPBELL, OSCAR JAMES. *Shakespeare's Satire.* London and New York, Oxford University Press, 1943.
Shakespeare's relation to the satirical current of his day.

CHARLTON, H. B. *Shakespearian Comedy.* London and New York, Macmillan 1938.
A reprint of lectures given at the George Rylands Library, Manchester.

COULTER, CORNELIA. "The Plautine Tradition in Shakespeare," *Journal of English and Germanic Philology,* XIX (1920), pp. 68 ff.

DAVEY, SAMUEL. "The Fools, Jesters, and Comic Characters in Shakespeare," *Transactions of the Royal Society of Literature,* Second Series, XXIII (1902), pp. 129–61.

DOWDEN, EDWARD. "Shakespeare as a Comic Dramatist," in C. M. Gayley, *Representative English Comedies,* I, 635 ff. New York, Macmillan, 1903.

FORSYTHE, ROBERT S. "Comic Effects in Elizabethan Drama," *University of North Dakota Quarterly Journal,* XVII (1927), pp. 266–92.

GORDON, GEORGE. *Shakespearian Comedy and Other Studies.* Oxford University Press, 1944.
Essays on Shakespeare's conception of comedy, the world of the comedies, Shakespeare's women, Shakespeare's clowns, etc.

LAWRENCE, WILLIAM WITHERLE. *Shakespeare's Problem Comedies.* New York, Macmillan, 1931.

A study of Shakespeare's "darker comedies" in the light of medieval customs and literary traditions.

LEA, KATHLEEN MARY. *Italian Popular Comedy: A Study of the Commedia Dell' Arte, 1560–1620, with Special Reference to the English Stage* (2 vols.). Oxford, Clarendon Press, 1934.

PALMER, JOHN. *Comic Characters of Shakespeare.* London, Macmillan, 1946.
A study of Berowne, Touchstone, Shylock, Bottom, and Benedick and Beatrice.

PARROTT, THOMAS MARC. *Shakespearean Comedy.* New York, Oxford University Press, 1949.
An analysis of comedy as Shakespeare understood it and practiced the art in his plays.

THORNDIKE, ASHLEY H. *English Comedy.* New York, Macmillan, 1929.
There are two chapters on Shakespeare, pp. 95–139.

TILLYARD, E. M. W. *Shakespeare's Problem Plays.* University of Toronto Press, 1949.
An analysis of *Hamlet, Troilus and Cressida, All's Well,* and *Measure for Measure*

SHAKESPEARE'S HISTORY

PLAYS

This England never did, nor never shall,
Lie at the proud foot of a conqueror
But when it first did help to wound itself.
—*King John*, V, vii, 112–14.

For certainly there may no greater peril grow to a prince than to have a subject equally powerful to himself.
—Sir John Fortescue, *The Governance of England* (*c*. 1475).

AT LEAST THREE EMINENT ENGLISHMEN—THE DUKE OF Marlborough, Lord Chatham, and Robert Southey—have acknowledged that their principal acquaintance with English history was derived from the plays of Shakespeare. Without confessing it, most of us have also received lasting impressions of the Middle Ages—to say nothing of classical times—more frequently from Shakespeare than from the history books. Like life itself, Shakespeare's plays stir the blood; they present the mystery of human experience without plucking the heart out of it. "Let no man," said Coleridge, "blame his son for learning history from Shakespeare."

Of the thirty-seven plays usually attributed to Shakespeare, more than half are on historical themes. Some, like *King Lear* and *Cymbeline*, are free dramatizations of legends from Britain's past. Some, like the Roman tragedies, are classical biographies. Others, like *Hamlet* and *Macbeth*, treat of early medieval history, and still others, like *Love's Labor's Lost* and *Othello*, use contemporary happenings merely as added spice or a convenient background for an unhistorical story. All of these plays, of course, find their proper niches among the tragedies or comedies; it is for the ten dramas upon the reigns of historical English kings—ranging from King John to Henry VIII— that the category "histories" was reserved by the First Folio editors.

THE ELIZABETHAN CHRONICLE PLAY

The "history"—or chronicle play, as it was most frequently called—was entirely of English growth and a distinctly Elizabethan type. Nothing like it had appeared in the drama of any other country, and, though it had roots in the morality play, the folk festival, and the ballad, the history play owed little to any literary antecedents. Dramatically, it was a hybrid, constructed more or less loosely of elements containing both tragedy and comedy—an eye-filling pageant, a dramatic tapestry of rich colors of light and shade. In spirit, it was of the people and for the people, telling the Elizabethans what they wanted to hear about the English past. In short, it was one of the popular by-products of that tide of patriotic enthusiasm which united all England when the tight little island and its queen met the challenge of the Spanish Armada. In the chronicle play, the Elizabethan groundling basked in a reflected glory and rejoiced that he was an Englishman.

Something has already been said above (see pp. 35 ff.) of the spirit of Renaissance England and the growth of national consciousness. Throughout the Tudor period, industrious chroniclers, like William Caxton, Robert Fabyan, John Rastell, Edward Hall, John Foxe, Richard Grafton, John Stow, Raphael Holinshed—to name only a few who wrote in the national tongue—produced an unexampled bulk of historical writing, substantial food for the English patriot bent upon the discovery of his own country and its past. Most of these volumes were enormous tomes, even when their titles proclaimed them mere summaries. With varying eloquence, they celebrated the beauty of the island, the character of its people, and the exploits of its kings. They appealed to a wide circle of readers, and few failed of frequent reprinting. Two of these works—*The Chronicles of England, Scotland, and Ireland*, in its enlarged edition (1586-7), which was compiled by Raphael Holinshed and a corps of assistants, and Edward Hall's *The Union of the Two Noble and Illustre Families of Lancaster and York* (1548)—were Shakespeare's chief historical sources.

Moreover, most Elizabethan books of this sort were competently written. In the hands of the Tudor chronicler, history not only became literature, but also the cause and the inspiration of better literature by other men. Metrical chronicles and historical poems abound. Among them was *The Mirror for Magistrates* (see below, p. 326), which, in countless editions and expansions and supplements, related nearly a hundred tales of English

> princes of renown,
> That whilom sat on top of Fortune's wheel
> Now laid full low, like wretches whirled down
> Even with one frown, that stayed but with a smile.

There were Samuel Daniel's *The Civil Wars between the Two Houses of Lancaster and York* (1595, and expanded in 1609); William Warner's *Albion's England*, expanded to sixteen books in seven editions from 1586 to 1612; or the numerous works of Michael Drayton. Drayton's *Barons' Wars in the Reign of Edward the Second* was originally published in 1596 under a different title and rewritten in 1603; *England's Heroical Epistles*, a collection of imaginary letters in verse, went through seven editions before 1630; *Polyolbion, or A Choreographical Description of Great Britain* was reprinted three times from 1612 to 1622; and, not only did he compose the stirring *Ballad of Agincourt*, but he also wrote an ambitious epic on the subject as late as 1627.

The chronicle play, therefore, was only one of the popular literary by-products of Tudor nationalism. It has been estimated that, during the fifteen years that elapsed between the destruction of the Armada and the death of the great queen, some two hundred plays dealing with English history and biography were produced, representing at least a fifth of the total number on the boards. Their subjects ranged from the exploits of the earliest legendary rulers to events only a few months old. "Two days ago," wrote a correspondent to Sir Robert Sidney on October 26, 1599,

> the overthrow of Turnhout [taken January 24, 1598] was acted upon a stage and all our names used that were at it, especially Sir Fra. Veres; and he that played that part got a beard resembling his and a watchet satin doublet, with hose trimmed with silver lace. You was also introduced, killing, slaying, and overthrowing the Spaniards. (*Letters and Memorials of State* [*Sidney Papers*], ed. Arthur Collins [1746], II, 136.)

Some reigns, of course, like those of King John, Edward III, Henry V, Richard II, and Richard III, proved especially attractive, and the Wars of the Roses were of prime popularity.

The chronicle play was one of the most effective forms of patriotic writing. To enjoy it, a man did not need to trouble himself about reading. It was the unlettered man's epic. Hence, when in admiration Meercraft says to Fitzdotterel: "By my faith, you are cunning in the chronicle, sir," he gets an honest Elizabethan answer:

> No, I confess I have it from the playbooks,
> And I think they are more authentic.
> (Ben Jonson, *The Devil Is an Ass*, II, i.)

It is not surprising, therefore, that when the players were obliged to defend themselves against their Puritan critics, they pointed out the educational value of dramatic history:

> Plays have made the ignorant more apprehensive, taught the unlearned the knowledge of many famous histories, instructed such as cannot read in the

discovery of all our English chronicles; and what man have you now of that weak capacity that cannot discourse of any notable thing recorded even from William the Conqueror, nay from the landing of Brute, until this day. (Thomas Heywood, *Apology for Actors*, 1612.)

How would it have joyed brave Talbot (the terror of the French) to think that after he had lain two hundred years in his tomb, he should triumph again on the stage and have his bones new embalmed with the tears of ten thousand spectators at least (at several times), who in the tragedian that represents his person imagine they behold him fresh bleeding. (Thomas Nashe, *Pierce Penniless His Supplication to the Devil*, 1592.)

Shakespeare, too, had this instructional value of plays in mind when Cassius dips his hands in Cæsar's blood and exclaims:

> How many ages hence
> Shall this our lofty scene be acted over
> In states unborn and accents yet unknown!
> (*Julius Cæsar*, III, i, 111–13.)

THE POLITICAL PHILOSOPHY OF THE CHRONICLE PLAYS

But in an even broader and deeper sense, the Tudor chronicle and its off-spring were instructional. Among other things, the sixteenth century was an age of discipline and repose which had succeeded the unrest and the strife of the Hundred Years' War with France and the Civil Wars of the Roses. Under the capable Henry VII and his equally capable, if capricious, son, England had been made over. After a trying interlude during the brief reigns of Edward VI and Bloody Mary, the nation recovered self-respect at home and prestige abroad in the stable government of Elizabeth. In spite of social, political, and ecclesiastical change, of dissension between class and class, creed and creed, the old order and the new, England had become a new nation, inspired by a new spirit, and miraculously united in a great national crisis. For the Elizabethan chronicler, and through him for the historical dramatist, these facts were tremendously impressive. History became a political guide, a mirror in which those in high place or low might read lessons in how to conduct themselves before God and man. "There be examples found in histories convenient for every man privately in his degree," wrote the compilers of *An Epitome of Chronicles* (1559). In Grafton's *A Chronicle at Large and Mere History of the Affairs of England* (1569), Thomas N[orton?] summarized the value of history:

Kings may learn to depend upon God and acknowledge his governance in their protection: the nobility may read the true honor of their ancestors: the Ecclesiastical state may learn to abhor traitorous practices and indignities done against kings . . . high and low may shun rebellions by their dreadful effects, and beware how they attempt against right, how unable soever the person be that beareth it: we all may be warned to thank God for the most virtuous, wise, and peaceable government that we now enjoy in comparison of terrible times heretofore: each man may have a glass to see things past, whereby to judge justly of things present and wisely of things to come. . . . Men of elder honor may learn not to deface their forefathers' praise: the newer sort may seek to bring light and dignity to their houses: and finally all men, in seeing the course of God's doings, may learn to dread his judgments and love his providence: may see how good doings be defended, evil doings and wrongs revenged, blood with blood, violence with violence, injuries with miseries, and so grow into an affection to give to each matter his right judgment, to each superior his right duty, to each other that which justice or charity willeth. . . .

"And above all things," continued Thomas N.,

forget not to give God thanks for the Queen's majesty's most gracious reign, so far in comparison exceeding the times that here thou readest of. And beseech him long to preserve her, without or after whom there is great danger and small hope, and specially let every one endeavor for himself not to move God for our sins to call her home from us too hastily.

Hence, the uncertainty of succession to the crown and its possible consequences gave to genealogical history in the days of Elizabeth an interest which it is difficult for a modern reader to appreciate. The chronicles are filled with dynastic pedigrees. There are passages, even in Shakespeare's "histories"—for example, *2 Henry VI*, II, ii, 11 ff., and *Henry V*, I, ii, 32 ff.—that have for us today just about the interest of the "begat" chapters in the Old Testament. But to Shakespeare's audiences, they traced claims that had been written in blood, and who knew when similar strife might arise again? Some of the early chroniclers, let it be confessed, were not altogether disinterested; they were bent upon authenticating the claims of Henry VII and his heirs to the English throne. The Tudor claims were none too good, but there were no better. By the end of the century, the headsman's axe and the good stewardship of the Tudor sovereigns had rendered such efforts obsolete. But, because Queen Elizabeth had never married, the problem remained. It will be recalled that *Gorboduc* (1562), the first English tragedy, retold a legend from Holinshed as a warning of the dissensions and turmoil which follow dynastic uncertainty. What Shakespeare's contemporaries dreaded, even more than the threat of Spain, was a disputed succession and a consequent renewal of civil war which might expose the land to a foreign invasion. This double danger was not imaginary.

What mischief hath insurged in realms by intestine division, what depopulation hath ensued in countries by civil dissension, what detestable murder hath been committed in cities by separate factions, and what calamity hath ensued in famous regions by domestical discord and unnatural controversy, Rome hath felt, Italy can testify, France can bear witness, Beaume [Bohemia] can tell, Scotland may write, Denmark can show, and especially this noble realm of England can apparently declare and make demonstration. . . . And the Turk can

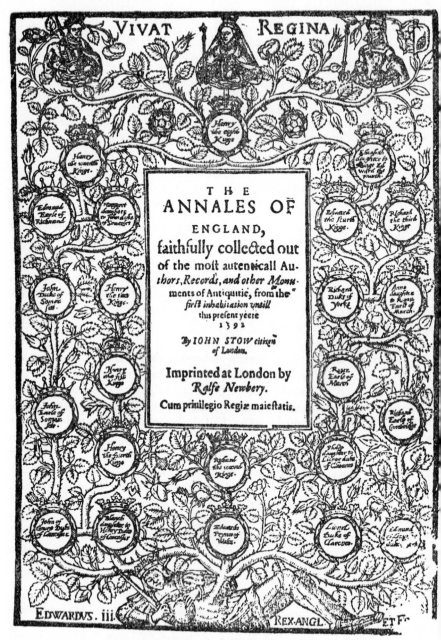

Genealogical Tree of Lancaster and York
(Title-page of John Stow's *Annales of England*, 1592)

bear good testimony which by the discord of Christian princes hath amplified greatly his seigniory and dominion.

Here in the opening sentences of Hall's chronicle is the central theme of Shakespeare's history plays. With the single exception of *Henry V*, all show England either suffering from "the intestine shock and furious close of civil butchery" and torn by intriguing factions, or threatened by foreign aggression. And, in *Henry V*, a great medieval hero-king leads a united nation against a great traditional enemy, France.

How much dynastic strife was in the minds of sixteenth-century Englishmen and how high were their hopes of good governance at the accession of Elizabeth may be seen, also, in the allegorical pageants with which they honored her coronation. According to Holinshed, as the new queen rode through the City from the Tower where, following custom, she had lodged on the eve of her coronation, the procession was stopped innumerable times in order that her Majesty might patiently hear the salutations recited by children in "costly apparel," inspect the elaborate settings against which they declaimed their verses, and listen to them interpret the allegory. Holinshed's account of these pageants occupies pages, but some passages of his description of the pageant in Gracechurch Street of "The Uniting of the Two Houses of Lancaster and York" are relevant here. A stage with an elaborate framework was erected from one side of the street to the other, and on it was constructed an animated family tree of the new sovereign

representing King Henry the Seventh . . . of the house of Lancaster . . . enclosed in a red rose . . . [and] Queen Elizabeth, being heir to the house of York enclosed with a white rose, each of them royally crowned and decently apparelled as apperтаineth to princes. . . . And these personages were so set that the one of them joined hands with the other with the ring of matrimony perceived on the finger. Out of which two roses sprang two branches gathered into one, which were directed upward to the second stage or degree, wherein was placed one representing the valiant and noble prince King Henry the Eight . . . and by him sat one representing the right worthy lady Queen Anne . . . mother to our most sovereign lady Queen Elizabeth . . . both apparelled with sceptres and diadems and other furniture due to the state of a king and queen. . . . From their seat also proceeded upwards one branch directed to the third and uppermost stage or degree, wherein likewise was planted a seat royal, in the which was set one representing the queen's most excellent majesty. . . . All the empty spaces thereof were furnished with sentences concerning unity, and the whole pageant garnished with red roses and white. And in the forefront . . . in a fair wreath, was written the name and title of the same, which was "The Uniting of the Two Houses of Lancaster and York." This pageant was grounded upon the queen's majesty's name. For, like as the long war between the two houses of York and Lancaster then ended when Elizabeth daughter to Edward the Fourth matched in marriage with Henry the Seventh, heir to the house of Lancaster, so sith that the queen's majesty's name was Elizabeth, and for so much as she is the only heir of Henry the Eight, which came of both the houses as the knitting up of concord, it was devised that as Elizabeth was the first occasion of concord, so she, another Elizabeth, might maintain the same among her subjects, so that unity was the end whereat the whole device shot, as the queen's majesty's name moved the first ground.

The pageant now against the queen's majesty's coming was addressed with children, representing the forenamed personages, with all furniture due unto the . . . matter . . . costly and sumptuously set forth. . . . [The queen] required to have the matter opened unto her, and what they signified, with the end of unity and ground of her name. . . . But after that her grace had understood the meaning thereof, she thanked the City, praised the fairness of the work, and promised that she would do her whole endeavor for the continual preservation of concord, as the pageant did import.

From the beginning of her reign, Elizabeth was in no doubt as to what her people expected of her.

THE KING IN THE CHRONICLE PLAYS

To the Tudor chronicler—and of course to the historical playwright—the well-being of the state depended in large measure upon the king. He was God's anointed substitute,

His captain, steward, deputy-elect,

to whom all subjects owed allegiance but who, in turn, was responsible to High Heaven for his stewardship. The king ruled as well as reigned. If he followed wise counsel and was strong, peace was preserved and his people prospered; if he was weak or evil, then he and his land suffered.

Bid kings, bid kaisers, bid all states beware . . .
Who reckless rules, right soon may hap to rue,

warned the author of "The Complaint of the Duke of Buckingham" in *The Mirror for Magistrates*. Shakespeare was no sycophant of kings as such; instead he found them extraordinary subjects for studies in human nature. "For, though I speak it to you," argues King Hal,

I think the king is but a man, as I am. The violet smells to him as it doth to me; the element shows to him as it doth to me; all his senses have but human conditions . . . though his affections are higher mounted than ours, yet, when they stoop, they stoop with the like wing. (*Henry V*, IV, i, 103 ff.)

But Shakespeare knew that princes were placed by circumstance in positions of exceptional opportunity and temptation. The decisions they were compelled to make before the world were often fateful, not merely to themselves, but also to many people and to unborn posterities. Shakespeare's plays are full of allusions to the cares and responsibilities "twin-born with greatness" as well as to the "divinity that doth hedge a king."

This doctrine of monarchy, it will be seen, was, at bottom, a mild Elizabethan variety of the theory of Divine Right, but it was far from the extreme form which the *Jus Divinum* assumed under the early Stuarts. The theory, which was a logical heritage from feudalism and could be supported by Scripture, was one which Queen Elizabeth and most of her subjects accepted, but Elizabeth valued the good will of her people too highly, and was too sagacious a politician to insist upon a theory. Her "Golden Speech" to her last Parliament (November 20, 1601) contains but one expression of royal doctrine that saw her through many a difficulty:

> I know the title of a king is a glorious title. But assure yourself, that the shining glory of princely authority hath not so dazzled the eyes of our understanding, but that we well know and remember that we also are to yield an account of our actions before the Great Judge. To be a king and wear a crown is a thing more glorious to them that see it than it is pleasing to them that bear it: for myself, I was never so much enticed with the . . . royal authority of a queen, as delighted that God had made me his instrument to maintain his truth and glory and to defend his kingdom . . . from peril, dishonour, tyranny, and oppression.

King Henry V, as Shakespeare portrayed him, had far more in common with Elizabeth than with James I and his son Charles.

Nevertheless, Bolingbroke and other rebels in Shakespeare make a serious mistake which every loyal member of the Elizabethan audience would be quick to recognize—that of assuming the right of judging and correcting a sovereign.

> What subject can give sentence on his king?
> And who sits here that is not Richard's subject?

demands the Bishop of Carlisle as Bolingbroke presumes to mount the regal throne (*Richard II*, IV, i, 121 ff.). Even Parliament might go too far, and Richard's favorite, Bagot, has little faith in

> the wavering commons, for their love
> Lies in their purses; and whoso empties them
> By so much fills their hearts with deadly hate. (*Ibid.*, II, ii, 129–31.)

Earlier in the same play, "time-honoured" Lancaster resists a widow's plea for vengeance of Gloucester's death with these words:

> God's is the quarrel; for God's substitute,
> His deputy anointed in His sight,
> Hath caused his death; the which if wrongfully,
> Let heaven revenge; for I may never lift
> An angry arm against His minister. (*Ibid.*, I, ii, 37 ff.)

By special request of the conspirators, a play on Richard II was acted by the Chamberlain's Company on the eve of Essex's rebellion. If the play was Shakespeare's, nothing could have given less encouragement to personal vengeance of a subject on a king.

To be sure, absolutism was not the monarchial doctrine of all Englishmen of the sixteenth century. The extreme Puritans and other readers of Calvin's *Institutes* certainly questioned it, and so did the Catholics.[1] It was left to later generations, however, to challenge the theory. Shakespeare's acceptance of current political thought was much broader than mere political conservatism. His reasons, if he formulated them, were patriotic. Nowhere are Shakespeare's deep-rooted love of his country and his affectionate confidence in its people more clearly seen than in his treatment of his English kings and their relations with their subjects. Seldom is the monarch of the title the hero of the piece. Instead, the role of hero is taken by someone like Talbot or "the good Duke Humphrey" or the Bastard Faulconbridge—bluff, valorous, "trueborn Englishmen," as British as beef and beer, who are able in their loyalty to their land to put aside every lesser consideration and to overlook human error, even crime, in the king. Compared with the tragedies, Shakespeare's histories have few outstanding heroes, but they all have the same heroine— England. Love of England was in Shakespeare's blood; her past was his past, and his kings are all judged by just one standard—their success or failure to do their duty to their country.

Most of Shakespeare's monarchs are failures, and their reigns the woeful consequences of weakness, incapacity, and even crime. John is a malign compromiser; Richard II, a sentimental unfortunate misled by evil counsel, incapable of meeting realities, and given to self-dramatization. Henry IV is a man of blood and iron, but a politician and a reformed fox who failed to inspire confidence, though he tried hard to be a good king. His grandson Henry VI is a pure and saintly man, whose hand was "made to grasp a palmer's staff, and not to grace an awful princely sceptre,"

> His champions are the prophets and apostles,
> His weapons holy saws of sacred writ,
> His study is his tiltyard, and his loves
> Are brazen images of canonized saints. (*2 Henry VI*, I, iii, 60 ff.)

Richard III is a scheming Machiavel and a "foul defacer of God's handiwork," while Henry VIII, though a proud and gracious sovereign, is endowed with unkingly human frailties. Only Henry V wins unqualified approval. "This Henry," wrote Holinshed,

> was a king, of life without spot, a prince whom all men loved, and of none disdained . . . his virtues notable, his qualities most praiseworthy . . . a pattern in princehood, a lode-star in honour and mirror of magnificence.

[1] An expression of the belief that the king should be subject to those whom he governs and may be deposed by them when he fails to govern justly, according to the laws of the land, may be found in Thomas Starkey's *Dialogue between Cardinal Pole and Thomas Lupset* (c. 1538). The belief that the king is God's deputy is expressed by Robert Crowley in *The Way to Wealth* (1550).

Shakespeare accepted this estimate, and, in his portrait of a great national hero, he emphasized understanding of the common man and acceptance of the responsibilities as well as the privileges of office. If few modern critics have admired Shakespeare's Henry, it is merely that modern standards of kingship and manhood differ from those of the sixteenth century.

Every age has its political codes, and the chronicle plays of Shakespeare and his fellows are exemplifications of the accepted political philosophy of their time. The Elizabethan chronicler and the historical playwright, seeking for what constitutes a good society, found the answers plain to see—a strong centralized monarchy; national independence; social harmony, loyalty, order, good governance, and prosperity in the realm. Ulysses's discourse on degree (*Troilus and Cressida*, I, iii, 75 ff.), already quoted in part above (p. 45); Menenius's parable of the Belly and the Members (*Coriolanus*, I, i, 99 ff.), which Shakespeare found in Plutarch and which turns up in book after book in the sixteenth century; as well as the parable of the honey-bees (*Henry V*, I, ii, 183 ff.), which derives apparently from Sir Thomas Elyot's *The Gouvernour* (1531)—all make clear that the ideal state to the Tudors was a stratified society in which all the parts functioned smoothly for the good of the whole under the administration of a single sovereign:

> They [the bees] have a king and officers of sorts,
> Where some, like magistrates, correct at home,
> Others, like merchants, venture trade abroad,
> Others, like soldiers, armed in their stings,
> Make boot upon the summer's velvet buds,
> Which pillage they with merry march bring home
> To the tent royal of their emperor,
> Who, busied with his majesty, surveys
> The singing masons building roofs of gold,
> The civil citizens kneading up the honey,
> The poor mechanic porters crowding in
> Their heavy burdens at his narrow gate,
> The sad-eyed justice, with his surly hum,
> Delivering o'er to executors pale
> The lazy yawning drone. I this infer,
> That many things, having full reference
> To one consent, may work contrariously.

If we may judge from the way he expressed it, Shakespeare could see little but anarchy in democracy,

> where gentry, title, wisdom,
> Cannot conclude but by the yea and no
> Of general ignorance. (*Coriolanus*, III, i, 144 ff.)

Living when he did, Shakespeare would surprise us if he thought differently.

The history Shakespeare had to read was no doubt colored by Protestant and Tudor sympathies. But, at this late date, it is absurd to brand it as propaganda or to be impatient with Shakespeare for not advocating the social theories we hold dear today. He saw that "civil dissension is a viperous worm that gnaws the bowels of the commonwealth" (*1 Henry VI*, III, i, 72–3), that a house divided against itself shall fall, that the political sins of the fathers shall be visited upon the children, that a native king, however bad, is better than a foreign usurper, and that the enemy at the gate need evoke no fear if the king can speak for a determined and a united people. These are political axioms so universal that they can never become obsolete.

> O England, model to thy inward greatness,
> Like little body with a mighty heart,
> What mightst thou do that honour would thee do,
> Were all thy children kind and natural!
> (*Henry V*, Prologue to Act II, 16–19.)

VARIETY OF TECHNIQUE IN SHAKESPEARE'S HISTORY PLAYS

With no dramatic form did Shakespeare experiment more than with the historical play, in which, in all probability, both his earliest and his most mature work was done. Hence, Shakespeare's histories exhibit a variety of dramatic methods and, at the same time, his development as a playwright.

King John and the trilogy based upon the reign of *Henry VI* are chronicle plays of the primitive type, successions of episodes linked together with little structural unity. *Richard III* retains the old chronicle structure, but, in this play, Shakespeare imitated Marlowe by building his drama around a strong central figure that dominates the play through his unbridled singleness of purpose. *Richard II* is of still another type, a tragic story of the fall of a misfit prince, in which the interest lies, as in Marlowe's *Edward II*, in the character of the hero and in his conflict with the forces that eventually overwhelm him. The two parts of *Henry IV* represent a variety omitted in Polonius's catalogue—the comical-historical. Like the older chronicle plays, these dramas are episodic, and they are both unified within themselves and linked with their sequel, *Henry V*, by the personality of Prince Hal. But, in the underplot of low comedy which introduces Hal's roistering tavern companions, Shakespeare employed more unhistorical matter than elsewhere. *Henry V* is a dramatic epic, glorifying not only a great national hero, but also the dauntless spirit of the English, in a series of spectacular impressions connected by choric prologues. *Macbeth* and *King Lear* are tragedies of character, and *Cymbeline* a romance. Finally, in *Henry VIII*, probably written in collaboration with John Fletcher at the end of his career, Shakespeare followed another fashion. The vogue of the spectacular chronicle had been revived, but the audience had acquired a taste for civic pageants, "entertainments," and grandiloquent plays of court intrigue from Webster, Marston, Chapman, and Beaumont and Fletcher.

It is too much to expect the same technical excellences in the history plays which are to be found in comedy and tragedy. Yet, in spite of their unevenness, Shakespeare's histories exhibit remarkable structural unity. The eight plays from *Richard II* to *Richard III* are, in effect, a single eight-part drama in forty acts, a kind of Wagnerian *Ring* on the theme of Lancaster and York. The plays from *Richard II* through *Henry V* constitute a Lancastrian tetralogy, tracing the rise of that dynasty and the exploits of its most glorious member. The three parts of *Henry VI* and *Richard III* form a Yorkist tetralogy, tracing the inevitable decline of Lancaster before the rival house, and the civil wars resulting.

Both tetralogies have their roots in *Richard II*, which reveals the indirect crook'd ways by which the first Lancastrian came into power. The two parts of *Henry IV* show the crown resting uneasily upon the brow of the usurper, and, before Henry can embark upon the Crusade which would wash from his hands the guilty stain of Richard's murder, they reveal the fulfillment of Richard II's prophecy of bickering among the kingmakers:

> Thou shalt think,
> Though he divide the realm and give thee half,
> It is too little, helping him to all;
> And he shall think that thou, which know'st the way
> To plant unrightful kings, wilt know again,
> Being ne'er so little urged, another way
> To pluck him headlong from the usurped throne. (V, i, 59 ff.)

Henry V shows how all stain is washed away by the unselfish patriotism of the conqueror king. But even he implores the God of Battles

> Not today, O Lord,
> O, not today, think not upon the fault
> My father made in compassing the crown!
> I Richard's body have interred new,
> And on it have bestow'd more contrite tears
> Than from it issued forced drops of blood. (IV, i, 309 ff.)

Henry's victory at Agincourt was the answer to his prayer.

The three parts of *Henry VI* and *Richard III* treat of the more remote consequences of Richard's deposition, as prophesied by the Bishop of Carlisle in *Richard II:*

> O, if you raise this house against this house,
> It will the woefullest division prove
> That ever fell upon this cursed earth. (IV, i, 145 ff.)

The House of Lancaster bowed to a movement which was, in many ways, parallel to that which had placed it on the throne. Richard II had his fifteenth-century counterpart in monklike Henry VI, deposed by the ruthless Yorkists, and peace was restored only when the claims of the rival houses were united in the marriage of Henry of Richmond and Elizabeth of York at the accession of the Tudors. *King John* and *Henry VIII* lie outside the realm of this great epic and have no relation to it.

Individually, too, Shakespeare's histories have many technical excellences. *King John* has no truly dramatic conflict and no central character, but, beside the unsympathetic king, Shakespeare ironically developed the bluff Bastard Faulconbridge into a better Plantagenet than the tyrant head of the house. Like the old *Troublesome Reign of King John*, a two-part play which Shakespeare followed closely, *King John* is concerned with three main lines of interest: John's quarrel with the pope, the claims of Arthur of Brittainy to the English throne, and the wars with France. The emphasis, however, is not the same in the two works; Shakespeare converted a Protestant polemic into a study in human nature and a stirring patriotic play.

Richard II is constructed around the duel between the emotional king, reckless in prosperity, abject in adversity, and his foil Bolingbroke, who is realistic, silent, watchful, and willing that his friends shall work for him. *1 Henry IV* shifts its attention to the limitations of the new king and concentrates upon the insubordinations which cost him nine out of the fourteen years of his reign. Based, like its immediate sequels, partly upon Holinshed and partly upon a crude old rouser called *The Famous Victories of Henry V*, *1 Henry IV* remains the best of Shakespeare's histories. For variety the play has no equals. Scenes revealing the relations between "that vile politician" confronted by the cooling enthusiasm of those who had made him king, are balanced by the rollicking scenes in the Boar's Head Tavern where the bohemian Prince of Wales holds a very different court. There are rich contrasts of character—the foxlike king beside his refreshingly sincere son; the gallant, headstrong Hotspur beside the men of guile who use him as their unsuspecting tool and then desert him; this "Mars in swaddling clothes" and the soft unpromising prince; and Falstaff, that irresponsible mountain of incongruities. In the end, *1 Henry IV* reaches an incomparable climax when Hal wins his spurs at Shrewsbury in the defeat of his father's enemies by "breaking from the foul and ugly mists of vapours that did seem to strangle him."

Part II suffers the fate of most sequels. Although it ends in a coronation, it lacks the effective climax of the earlier play. There is no Hotspur. The madcap prince is more frequently at court allaying his father's fears than in the tavern provoking them. Falstaff, too, is in his Majesty's service, a grafter doing recruiting duty, an incorrigible metropolitan enduring in the sticks the disillusionment of looking up the acquaintances of his youth. *Henry V*, in its turn, is the most imaginative and stirring of these plays. To it everything serious in *Henry IV* had been tending, and around the new king everything revolves. To the modern reader, Henry's foreign wars may seem an overprompt response to his father's death-bed counsel and the jockeying of ecclesiastical politicians; to the Elizabethans, they were the most brilliant in English history. Shakespeare symbolized the national unity that war sometimes achieves by placing in Henry's army Fluellen the Welshman, Mac-Morris the Irishman, and Jamy the Scot. Obviously, Falstaff would have been out of place in their company.

The lesser histories may lack coherence and dramatic force, but they are not without good technical qualities. The first part of *Henry VI* develops two themes: the results of an overambitious policy abroad and of bitter rivalry among the factions at home. The play is the tragedy of Talbot, which Shakespeare conceived of as an unhistorical duel between him and Joan of Arc against a background of conflicting ambitions. In Part II, Richard of York, profiting by chaos, gets his chance at the crown. Part III shows the Yorkists triumphant, but only after father has lifted hand against son, and son against father. Technically, *3 Henry VI* is notable for the emergence of Richard of Gloucester, who, from the moment when he urges his father to repudiate his oath (I, ii), becomes the prime mover of his family's claims. In *Richard III*, Shakespeare filled in the outlines of this incredibly sardonic villain with broad strokes as Richard removes all obstacles between him and the crown and falls at last before "God's captain" on the field of Bosworth. *Henry VIII* is a thing of patches without a central character or a central theme. The conflict between Buckingham and Wolsey offered few possibilities. Such as there were are smothered as the conflict between the queen and the cardinal gains momentum. Wolsey's fall is over early; the conspiracy against Cranmer seems almost an afterthought, and what climax the play has lies in the birth of Elizabeth and the prophecy the archbishop utters at her baptism. Its chief attractions for the early audience existed in this and in the play's pomp and circumstance of sceptred pall.

SHAKESPEARE'S TREATMENT OF HISTORY

That Shakespeare was always an artist rather than a scholar cannot be too frequently emphasized; nowhere is that fact more clearly to be observed than in his treatment of history. Measured by modern scholarship, Holinshed had grievous shortcomings, but his book was magnificent material for a poet seeking stories that were capable of dramatic treatment. To the chronicler of Shakespeare's day, history was a pageant of wars and diplomacies, of intrigue and the pomp of courts, of vaulting ambition and pitiful ruin, a recital of the good deeds and the bad of kings and queens, great warriors and eminent statesmen, haughty nobles and high ecclesiastics—what John Richard Green contemptuously called "drum and trumpet history." The compilers showed little discrimination. Gossip, rumor, and anecdote are given the same prominence as documents. The appearance of a strange fish, a dragon, a fiery comet, or some other omen, is as fully and as seriously narrated as a murder or a battle or a change of dynasty. Shakespeare accepted these annals as he found them, and it is well that he did.

The student concerned with how Shakespeare dramatized Holinshed should be cautious. English history has been rewritten since Shakespeare's day, but it helps us little to see how the old chroniclers misled Shakespeare. The modern historian, for example, considers more authentic the belief that Macbeth was the leader of a conservative Celtic nationalist movement opposed to the Anglicizing policy of King Duncan (1034-1040). He even knows Lady Macbeth—Gruoch by name—to have been renowned for her piety and good works. Neither of these facts, however, has any bearing on Shakespeare's great play. The modern historian may have "historic doubts" about Richard III and pronounce the sixteenth-century biographies that Shakespeare knew sheer "invention and romance." These facts have significance for a student of Tudor myth-making; they tell us little about Shakespeare. Today, Joan of Arc is the hallowed symbol of the undying courage of a great people; Shakespeare must not be blamed for following Holinshed in representing her as a promiscuous wanton and a witch possessed by fiends. What is significant is that in the earlier scenes—the meeting with the Dauphin, for example—Joan is treated more reverently, and that, on his own responsibility, Shakespeare made the Dauphin prophesy: "Joan la Pucelle shall be France's saint" (*1 Henry VI*, I, vi, 29). Shakespeare's departures from Holinshed tell us a great deal.

In adapting factual material to the requirements of the stage, Shakespeare frequently made changes. History is not drama; events do not shape themselves in the best order. They must be reshaped to be theatrically effective and significant. Shakespeare's purpose was, through his imagination, to quicken into life the dry bones of history, and to interpret, in the events he found recorded there, the great constants of human nature and conduct. He chose a point of view, he selected details, he compressed events, "in little room confining mighty men." From the dry narrative, he had to recreate living people and make them speak. Occasionally, he invented a scene or gave it new emphasis and, when historical time interfered with his purposes, he did not hesitate to alter it. After all, it was only an outline which Shakespeare found in the chronicle. He may have subordinated history to drama, but seldom, in these plays, did he give his invention free rein, and he never consciously falsified essential truth. A few illustrations of what he did will make his method clear.

(1) First of all, in the chronicles, Shakespeare found a great deal more than he could possibly fit to the "two hours' traffic of the stage." With the exceptions of *Richard II* and *1 Henry IV*, which cover only a few months

apiece, Shakespeare's histories are all full-scope. Yet they have an apparent rapidity of action which the chronicles lack. Thus, five years of war between the Battle of Agincourt and the Treaty of Troyes are passed over in *Henry V;* the funeral of that conqueror is interrupted by news of the loss of one of his French provinces after another, though some of these misfortunes did not occur for thirty years. Two separate attempts of Henry of Richmond to invade England (1483 and 1485) are combined into one. Years of history are sometimes compressed into mere days or hours for the stage. One has but to turn through the three thick folio volumes of Holinshed's *Chronicles* to appreciate the dramatist's task of sifting from this mass of narration the dramatic wheat from the chaff and of arranging this selected material into a play.

(2) To the modern reader, some of Shakespeare's omissions may be startling. *King John,* like *The Troublesome Reign,* does not so much as mention Magna Charta, and *Henry VIII* is not concerned with the English Reformation and its theological problems. Only superficially are these events suitable material for popular drama. What today has become the foundation of English liberties probably had little interest for the Elizabethans. Holinshed barely alluded to the granting of the Great Charter, though he did mention its confirmation by king after king, and he did not quote it. Shakespeare's audiences had not yet heard it interpreted by zealous seventeenth-century Parliamentarians seeking a precedent for their political reforms, and meanings had not yet been discovered in it that would have astonished the original drafters of the document. Anyway, Magna Charta and the method by which it was obtained would not fit the theme of *King John.* Hence, in Shakespeare's play, the revolt of the barons has its uncomplicated cause in the imprisonment and death of Prince Arthur. Similarly, a discussion of the issues at stake in Henry VIII's break with Rome would have stifled drama. For Shakespeare's purposes the fact sufficed; a popular playwright does no wrong to let controversial sleeping dogs lie.

Sometimes, too, Shakespeare's omissions are puzzling for another reason. The reign of Richard II had been the subject of several Elizabethan plays, and its outlines were familiar to the auditors. In his *Richard II,* Shakespeare, therefore, left untold the long conflict between the king and the "lords appellant" to focus his attention upon the climax of that struggle in the closing months of Richard's reign. The modern reader cannot fully understand Shakespeare's play without some knowledge of the events that occurred before.

(3) Shakespeare's interest in history, like every true dramatist's, was personal rather than philosophical. Abstract causes may suffice for the historian or the social scientist, but on the stage a clash of principles must be embodied in the rivalries of complex human beings. The chronicles described the

situations; Shakespeare's task was to dramatize them—to create characters, to let them reveal themselves in word and deed so that we, his readers and spectators, can form our own opinions about them and the events through which they lived. For instance, Holinshed reports with some detail the charges and counter-charges of Bolingbroke and Mowbray—largely in direct discourse. Yet no reader of this account feels that he has been present at a deadly quarrel, the causes of which are far beneath the surface. But no reader of the opening of Shakespeare's *Richard II* doubts what he has seen, nor does the mocking exultation of the king escape him. Richard had waited ten years for this moment.

So far as possible, Shakespeare let his people speak what the chronicle set down for them—Katherine's defense and Wolsey's farewell to all his greatness are examples—but often he had very little to build on. Shakespeare accepted Holinshed's legend of the wild youth of Prince Hal and filled in the picture with Hostess Quickly's tavern in Eastcheap. The Jack Cade scenes in *2 Henry VI*—which are often held to Shakespeare's political discredit—are merely a record of what he found in the chronicle, except that Shakespeare touched them with humor. Cade is a lively rounded impression of the crafty, loud-mouthed demagogue—the professional agitator full of promises of something for nothing—drawn to the life. The account in the chronicle is flat. Owen Glendower was treated seriously by Holinshed. How quickly Shakespeare let Hotspur transform him into the eternal bore:

> O, he is as tedious
> As is a tired horse, a railing wife;
> Worse than a smoky house. (*1 Henry IV*, III, i, 159-61.)

Shakespeare's history plays are full of such brilliant portraits.

(4) Occasionally, of course, Shakespeare found the dramatic lead he needed in a mere allusion in Holinshed; some of his best characters and scenes are developed from brief passages in the chronicles. The whole character of Lady Macbeth, for example, is expanded from a single sentence:

> but specially [Macbeth's] wife lay sore upon him to attempt the thing, as she that was very ambitious, burning in unquenchable desire to bear the name of a queen.

Richard II's eloquent confidence in the power of Heaven to keep him king (III, ii, 36-62) has its origin in no more than a remark by the chronicler:

> the king knew his title true, just, and infallible, and his conscience clear, pure, and without spot of envy or malice.

The French, said Holinshed, on the night before Agincourt,

> as though they had been sure of victory made great triumph, for the captains had determined before how to divide the spoil, and the soldiers . . . had played the Englishmen at dice.

Shakespeare showed all this on the stage (*Henry V*, III, vii). The famous scene in *3 Henry VI* (II, v) in which poor King Henry meets a son who has killed his father and a father who has killed his son—an instance of the "heavy times, begetting such events"—is developed from but a sentence in Hall. The vision of his victims which Richard III sees on the eve of Bosworth has its basis in a rumor spread in the chronicle:

> The fame went, that he had the same night a dreadful and terrible dream, for it seemed to him being asleep that he did see diverse images like terrible devils which pulled and hailed him, not suffering him to take any quiet or rest.

There is no mention of a vision to Richmond, and the symbolic fitness of the scene in Shakespeare's play is evidence of what he could make of a mere suggestion. Shakespeare did much the same thing when, in *Julius Cæsar*, he transformed what, in Plutarch's *Lives*, was Brutus's vision of a "wonderful strange and monstrous shape of a body coming toward him" into the ghost of Cæsar.

(5) Sometimes, too, Shakespeare found it convenient to modify chronology for dramatic effect. For example, as we have seen (above, p. 230), he altered the ages of his characters whenever he liked. Historically, King Duncan in *Macbeth* was a young man at the time of his murder; Arthur of Brittainy, who is one of the most appealing of Shakespeare's boys, was actually about fifteen at the time of the story, a knight who had seen service in battle, and by no means so helpless and unambitious as Shakespeare implied. His mother Constance is represented as a sorrowing young widow fighting for her child, whereas, in Holinshed, at this time she was already divorced from her second husband and married to a third. Isabella of France, Richard II's queen, was only a child of eleven at his deposition; John of Gaunt speaks patriarchal wisdom, although he was only fifty-nine when he died. King Henry IV, represented as shaken and wan with care, was only thirty-two when he deposed Richard, while Hotspur and Prince Hal, of the same age in the play, were thirty-nine and sixteen respectively, at the Battle of Shrewsbury. Dramatically, Shakespeare was justified in making these changes, just as he was justified in showing Antony and Cleopatra on the stage caught in a mesh of passion, when they were really in unromantic middle life and old enough to know better.

(6) Frequently, Shakespeare's liberties with time occur because he was impelled to rearrange events for greater dramatic effect. In the play, John's excommunication by the pope occurs immediately after he has patched up a compromise with Philip of France; historically, the excommunication did not occur until twelve years later. Hal's reconciliation with his father took place, not before the Battle of Shrewsbury, as in Shakespeare's drama, but nearly ten years after. Because Shakespeare needed a dramatic opponent for

Talbot, he kept Joan of Arc alive for twenty-two years, until after Talbot's death, and attributed to her a master-stroke four years after her execution in the severance of the Burgundian alliance upon which the English position in France depended. As he read farther in the reign of Henry VI, Shakespeare saw Margaret, Henry's dear-bought French queen, not only as a strong-minded, courageous woman, but also as the evil genius of the House of Lancaster, the symbol of an inglorious peace with the loss of Henry V's conquests, and an ambitious factionary. Hence, she is shown engaged in a mortal woman's war with "that proud dame, the Protector's wife," Eleanor of Gloucester, who had died years before Margaret came to England. She is seen as "Captain Margaret," fighting against the murderous scions of the House of York. She is revealed competing with Warwick for a French alliance, although the two embassies were years apart. When news of King Edward's marriage arrives, Warwick makes an immediate alliance with her, although, historically, the kingmaker nursed his insult for six years before turning against the king he had made. Finally, in *Richard III*, though Shakespeare knew that Margaret had returned to France in 1475 and died there in 1482, she is kept alive at the English court, a pitiful shadow of herself, uttering tragic prophecies. Thus, in a single symbolic character, Shakespeare clarified history. He deduced the woes of York from its crimes against Lancaster, and asserted the justice of Fate upon both houses.

Similarly, Shakespeare gave emphasis to the career of Richard of Gloucester by making him the symbol of York. Although born in 1452, Shakespeare's Richard takes part in the first campaign of the Wars of the Roses and fights valiantly at St. Albans in 1455 (*2 Henry VI*, V, i–iii). It is Richard's dream that is responsible for both his father's and his brother's struggle to possess the crown. In *3 Henry VI*, Richard's passion for power is studied in detail; in *Richard III*, he ceases to be the servant of his house and thinks only of himself. The chronicles are not so clear cut.

(7) Finally, when his needs required, Shakespeare did not hesitate to interpolate unhistorical episodes into the narrative he found in the chronicle, or even to invent scenes. Sometimes the added material has another source. *King Lear* not only has a tragic ending which is unhistorical, but it is also equipped with a parallel plot taken from Sidney's *Arcadia*. *Cymbeline* combines history from Holinshed with a *novella* from Boccaccio and an episode from the fairy tale of Snow White. *Macbeth* combines details from two murders, King Duncan's and King Duff's, both related within a few pages of one another in Holinshed. In Holinshed, Shakespeare found the description of Wolsey's banquet which the king attended in disguise. But it was his own idea to have Henry VIII meet Anne Bullen there. Dramatic fitness, not history, warrants Prince Hal's challenge to Hotspur and their meeting on the field of Shrewsbury, as well as the death of Richard III at the hands of Harry Richmond.

The historian may be content to know that both Hotspur and Richard fell to unnamed adversaries, but not the playwright.

Some of Shakespeare's most striking scenes are only pseudo-historical: the interview between Richard II and John of Gaunt, the formal abdication of Richard, Talbot's assignation with the Countess of Auvergne, the factionary plucking of the roses in the Temple Gardens, Richard III's wooing of the Lady Anne. They are too numerous even to catalogue.

Not the least interesting of these imaginary scenes are those which concern ordinary workaday life. The protagonists of history were the mighty of the land, but Shakespeare never forgot to dramatize the gossip of the common folk in the streets. There is "the exquisite symbolic idyll" (*Richard II*, III, iv) of the honest gardeners who liken Richard's kingdom to a neglected plot which

> Is full of weeds, her fairest flowers choked up,
> Her fruit-trees all unpruned, her hedges ruin'd,
> Her knots disorder'd, and her wholesome herbs
> Swarming with caterpillars.

There are the puzzled citizens in *Richard III*, full of wise saws but taken in by nothing (II, iii and vi); the grousing common soldiers in *Henry V* (III, ii and IV, i); the porter and his assistant holding back the crowds at Elizabeth's baptism (*Henry VIII*, V, iv); and, in the same play, the old woman's resentment at the royal tip she receives when she brings the king word of the birth of a girl-child instead of a prince:

> An ordinary groom is for such payment.
> I will have more, or scold it out of him. (V, i, 172-3.)

Of like nature are the scenes of domestic relationship: Richard II's parting with his queen (V, i); the Roman justice of York, when he discovers Aumerle's treason, and the anxiety of his duchess for her "transgressing boy" (V, ii and iii); the teasing, undemonstrative understanding of Hotspur and his Kate (known to history as Elizabeth), who nevertheless dwells but in the suburbs of his good pleasure and hardly gets civil attention from her lord (*1 Henry IV*, II, iii and III, i); the heartbroken, feminine reasonableness of Northumberland's wife and daughter-in-law (*2 Henry IV*, II, iii). For these scenes, full of universal human feeling, Shakespeare had no warrant from the chronicles.

In Shakespeare's histories, then, there is stirring drama, rich imagination, some poetry, a lesson to ponder, but taught as experience teaches. No better summary of what is best in them can be found than the Prologue to *Henry VIII*:

> Those that can pity, here
> May, if they think it well, let fall a tear;
> The subject will deserve it. Such as give

Their money out of hope they may believe,
May here find truth too. Those that come to see
Only a show or two, and so agree
The play may pass, if they be still and willing,
I'll undertake may see away their shilling
Richly in two short hours.

AN OUTLINE OF SHAKESPEARE'S ENGLISH HISTORY PLAYS[2]

THE LIFE AND DEATH OF KING JOHN

Dates of the reign: 1199–1216
Period covered by the play: Summer, 1199–October, 1216
Historical events treated or alluded to in the play: ENGLISH NATIONALISM *vs.*
ENTANGLING FOREIGN ALLIANCES

(I) Embassage of Chatillon from Philip of France (unhistorical); claim of Arthur Plantagenet not only to the throne of Poitou, Anjou, Maine, and Touraine (historical), but also of England and Ireland (unhistorical); quarrel between the Faulconbridge brothers over their inheritance (unhistorical, but developed from similar stories of Morgan of Beverly, brother of King John [told by Stow], and of Jean du Dunois, son of Lewis, Duke of Orleans in the fifteenth century [told by Hall]).

(II) Jealous enmity between Queen Elinor and Constance, mother of Arthur; John's compromise with Philip of France; betrothal of Blanche of Castile to Lewis the Dauphin (1200).

(III) Embassage of Pandulph from Innocent III (1211); John's defiance of the papacy over the appointment of Stephen Langton as Archbishop of Canterbury (1207–11); excommunication and deposition of John by papal decree (1212); war between England and France (1202, 1212); death of Limoges at the hands of Philip, bastard son of Richard Cœur de Lion (1199); capture of Arthur (1202); claim to the English throne by Lewis the Dauphin through Blanche of Castile (1216).

(IV) Purposed blinding of Arthur (1202); second coronation of John (1202); rumored death of Arthur (1202); invasion of Kent by the French (1216); death of Queen Elinor (1204); prophecy of Peter of Pomfret (1212); appearance of five moons (1200); death of Arthur (1203); defection of the barons (1213).

(V) John's submission to the pope, resignation of the crown and its return as a papal fief, fulfillment of the prophecy of Peter of Pomfret (1213); homage of the English barons to the Dauphin (1213–16); withdrawal of the papal support to the French claim (1216); battle with the French (1217); exposure of French treachery by Melune; death of King John; return of the English barons (1216).
(There is no mention in Shakespeare's play of Runnymede and Magna Charta.)

[2] The order of events recorded in this outline is that of the plays, which does not always follow that of history.

THE TRAGEDY OF KING RICHARD THE SECOND

Dates of the reign: 1377–1399
Period covered by the play: April, 1398–February, 1400
Historical events treated or alluded to in the play: THE LANCASTRIAN REVOLU-
TION OF 1399

(I) Accusations of embezzlement, the treasons of the past eighteen years, and responsibility for the death of Thomas of Woodstock made by Henry Bolingbroke against Thomas Mowbray, Duke of Norfolk (1398); their meeting in the lists at Coventry, banishment of both (1398); farming out of the realm by Richard to William Scroop, Earl of Wiltshire and Lord Treasurer, Sir John Bushy, Sir William Bagot, and Sir Henry Green, and issue of blank charters as sources of revenue (1398).

(II) Death of John of Gaunt (1399); rebellion in Ireland; confiscation of Henry of Bolingbroke's inheritance; appointment of the Duke of York as Lord Governor during King Richard's absence in Ireland; defection of the barons by Richard's misrule; return of Henry of Bolingbroke; resignation of the Earl of Worcester as Lord High Steward; flight of the king's favorites, Wiltshire, Bushy, Bagot, and Green; Bolingbroke's oath that he returned only to claim his inheritance; meeting of York and Bolingbroke; rumors of Richard's death; disbanding of the Welsh troops (1399).

(III) Capture and execution of Wiltshire, Bushy, and Green (1399); return of Richard; meeting with Bolingbroke at Flint Castle (1399); the queen's reception of news of Richard's troubles (unhistorical).

(IV) Accusation by Bagot, Fitzwater, and others of the complicity of Aumerle in Woodstock's death; death at Venice of Thomas Mowbray, Duke of Norfolk; denunciations of Bolingbroke's acts by the Bishop of Carlisle (antedated by about a month; Carlisle's prophecy of civil war is unhistorical); abdication of King Richard and his imprisonment in the Tower; plot of the Abbot of Westminster and others against Bolingbroke (the Oxford Plot) (1399).

(V) Parting of Richard and his queen (unhistorical); prophecy of Richard concerning the Percy rebellion (unhistorical); imprisonment of Richard in Pomfret Castle (1399); Bolingbroke's reception by the Londoners (1399); Aumerle's complicity in the Oxford Plot (1400); murder of King Richard by Pierce of Exton (1400).

THE FIRST PART OF KING HENRY THE FOURTH

Dates of the reign: 1399–1413
Period covered by the play: September, 1402–July, 1403
Historical events treated or alluded to in the play: CIVIL WAR: THE PERCY REBEL-
LION

(Except for the legend of the wild youth of Prince Hal, the Falstaff scenes of both *1* and *2 Henry IV* are wholly unhistorical.)

(I) Rising in Wales; capture of Edmund Mortimer by Owen Glendower and marriage of Mortimer with Glendower's daughter (1402); defeat of the Scots at Holmedon (1402); King Henry's demand of the Scot-

tish prisoners and refusal to ransom Mortimer; defection of Northumberland, Hotspur, and Worcester (1402).

(II) Harry Hotspur's disregard of a temporizing letter (unhistorical).

(III) Meeting of the conspirators at Bangor to divide the kingdom (1405,
after Hotspur's death, but reported by Holinshed as occurring in
1403); lack of success of King Henry's expedition against the Welsh
(1402); reproach of Prince Hal by King Henry for his ignoble life,
and reconciliation between father and son (1412); preparation for
civil war (1403).

(IV) Mobilization of the rebel forces at Shrewsbury and illness of Northumberland (1403); King Henry's offer of pardon to the Percies
(1403).

(V) Deception of Hotspur by the double-dealing of Worcester; battle of
Shrewsbury; death of Henry Hotspur (but by hands unknown); cap-
ture and execution of Worcester and Vernon; capture and release of
Douglas (1403).

THE SECOND PART OF KING HENRY THE FOURTH

Dates of the reign: 1399–1413
Period covered by the play: July, 1403–April, 1413
Historical events treated or alluded to in the play: CIVIL WAR: COMPLETE SUP-
PRESSION OF FACTION

(I) Rumors and news of Shrewsbury (1403); rebellion of Archbishop
Scroop of York (1405).

(II) Flight of Northumberland to Scotland (1405).

(III) Death of Owen Glendower (1409, according to Holinshed).

(IV) Meeting of the rival forces at Shipton Moor in Gaultree Forest;
politic dealing of Westmoreland; arrest and execution of Archbishop
Scroop, Mowbray, and Hastings (1405); illness of King Henry
(1412); defeat and death of Northumberland and Lord Bardolph
(1408); episode of the crown (1413); death of King Henry IV (1413).

(V) Accession of King Henry V; dismissal of his unworthy associates;
coronation of Henry V (1413).

THE LIFE OF KING HENRY THE FIFTH

Dates of the reign: 1413–1422
Period covered by the play: Spring, 1414–May, 1420
Historical events treated or alluded to in the play: CONQUEST OF FRANCE

(I) Parliament bill for disendowing the church (1414); claim of Henry
to the French throne, encouraged by the Archbishop of Canterbury;
embassage from France, insult of the tennis balls (1414).

(II) Preparation for the war (1415); treason of Cambridge, Scroop, and
Grey, and their execution (1415); embassy of Exeter from King
Henry to the French (1415).

(III) Siege and surrender of Harfleur (1415); French council of war
(1415); Henry's just and charitable conduct of the war; episode of
the theft of a pyx by a soldier [Bardolph]; defiance of the French;
their overconfidence and play at dice for the English prisoners and
spoil (1415).

(IV) Sobriety of the English and the sickness and hardship they endured; suggestion by the French that Henry agree upon a ransom; its refusal; battle of Agincourt; rally of the French, plunder of the English camp by the French prisoners, and the order for their execution; victory of the English; return of Henry to Calais (1415).

(V) Treaty of Troyes; betrothal of King Henry and Katharine of Valois; Henry named heir of France (1420).

THE FIRST PART OF KING HENRY THE SIXTH

Dates of the reign: 1422–1461; 1470–1471
Period covered by the play: November, 1422–July, 1453
Historical events treated or alluded to in the play: ENGLAND'S LOSS OF FRANCE AND GROWTH OF CIVIL FACTIONS

(I) Funeral of King Henry V (1422); revolt of the French (1422); loss of Guienne (1451), Champagne (1429), Rheims (1429), Orleans (fictitious, not in English possession in Henry V's time), Paris (1436), Guisors (1449), Poitiers (fictitious, not in English possession), Rouen (1449); coronation of Charles VII at Rheims (1429, but proclaimed at Poitiers, 1422); capture of Talbot (1429); cowardice of Sir John Fastolfe (1429); Winchester's intention to kidnap the young king from Eltham (charged, 1426); siege of Orleans (1428–9); meeting of Charles VII and Joan of Arc (1429); dissension between Humphrey of Gloucester and Henry Beaufort, Bishop of Winchester (1425); ransom of Talbot (1433; according to Holinshed, 1431); death of Salisbury and Gargrave at Orleans (1428), in the presence of Talbot (unhistorical); relief of Orleans by Joan of Arc and Charles (1429).

(II) Recapture of Orleans by Talbot (fictitious, but based upon the account of the recapture of Le Mans, 1428); burial of Salisbury (1428); interview of Talbot and the Countess of Auvergne (fictitious); dissension between Richard Plantagenet and the Earl of Somerset; the plucking of red roses and white in the Temple Gardens (unhistorical); meeting of Edmund Mortimer and Richard Plantagenet (unhistorical); death of Mortimer, Plantagenet proclaimed his heir (1425).

(III) Renewed dissension between Gloucester and Winchester, their outward reconciliation (1426); Richard Plantagenet created duke of York (1426); proposed coronation of Henry VI in France (1431); loss and recovery of Rouen (unhistorical); cowardice of Sir John Fastolfe (repeated); death of Bedford, regent of France (1435); Burgundy's desertion of his English allies (1435), at Joan of Arc's persuasion (unhistorical); Talbot created Earl of Shrewsbury (1442).

(IV) Coronation of King Henry VI at Paris (1431); Fastolfe deprived of the Garter (1429), by Talbot (historically by Bedford); strife between the factions of the roses; York made regent of France, Somerset military commander (1443?); imbroglio between York and Somerset over relief of Talbot (unhistorical); siege of Bordeaux, death of Talbot and his son (1453).

(V) Overtures of peace between England and France (1435); betrothal of Henry VI to the daughter of the Count of Armagnac (1442); loss of Paris (1436); capture and execution of Joan of Arc (1430–1); truce between the English and the French (1444); arrangement by Suffolk of a marriage between Margaret of Anjou and Henry VI (1444); Humphrey of Gloucester opposed (the infatuation of Suffolk with Margaret is unhistorical).

THE SECOND PART OF KING HENRY THE SIXTH

Dates of the reign: 1422–1461; 1470–1471
Period covered by the play: May, 1445–May, 1455
Historical events treated or alluded to in the play: GROWTH OF CIVIL FACTION: BEGINNING OF THE WARS OF THE ROSES

(I) Arrival of Margaret, England's "dear bought" queen (1445); continued rivalry of Gloucester and Winchester; impatience of Queen Margaret at King Henry's submissiveness to Gloucester; conspiracy against Humphrey of Gloucester (1446-7); appeachment of an armorer [Thomas Horner] by his servant [Peter Thump] (1446); love of Queen Margaret for Suffolk (unhistorical); appointment of Somerset as regent of France, replacing York (1446); arrest of Eleanor Cobham, Duchess of Gloucester, on charges of sorcery (1441).

(II) Sham miracle at St. Albans [from Sir Thomas More's *Dialogue . . . of Images and Reliques,* 1530]; support of York's claim by the Earls of Warwick and Salisbury (1447-8?); sentence of Eleanor Cobham (1441); dismissal of Gloucester as Protector (1446); judicial duel between the armorer and his servant (1446); penance of Eleanor Cobham (1441).

(III) Further losses in France (1450); arrest of Humphrey of Gloucester (1447); rebellion in Ireland, York made regent of Ireland (1448); murder of Humphrey of Gloucester (1447); suspicion of Suffolk by the Commons (1449-50); banishment of Suffolk (1450); death of Cardinal Beaufort, Bishop of Winchester (1447).

(IV) Death of Suffolk (1450); Jack Cade's rebellion (1450); return of York from Ireland (1450), to raise an army to claim the crown (1452); death of Cade (1450); Somerset committed to the Tower at York's demand (1452).

(V) Meeting of York and an embassy from the king near Dartford, resulting at first in submission of York, then, at the release of Somerset, in mutual accusations of treason (1452), and the outbreak of civil war (1455); Yorkist victory at the first battle of St. Albans and death of Somerset (1455).

THE THIRD PART OF KING HENRY THE SIXTH

Dates of the reign: 1422–1461; 1470–1471
Period covered by the play: May, 1455–May, 1471
Historical events treated or alluded to in the play: THE WARS OF THE ROSES

(I) Flight of King Henry from the battle of St. Albans (fictitious); assembly of Parliament (1455, 1460, combined); York sits in the chair of state (1460); York declared heir to the throne and protector of the realm (1460); outbreak of hostilities; Lancastrian victory at Wake-

field; capture, humiliation, and death of York and his son Rutland
(1460).

(II) Appearance of three suns on the morning of the Yorkish victory at
Mortimer's Cross (1461); Lancastrian victory at the second battle of
St. Albans (1461); knighting of Edward, Prince of Wales (1461);
Yorkist victory at Towton, death of Clifford, and flight of King
Henry and Queen Margaret to Scotland; coronation of Edward IV
(1461); proposed marriage of King Edward with Bona of France
(1464); Richard created Duke of Gloucester and George Duke of
Clarence (1461).

(III) Capture and imprisonment of King Henry VI (1465); marriage of
King Edward and the widow Grey [Elizabeth Woodville] (1464);
Queen Margaret in France (1462, 1464–70); Warwick in France
(1464); defection of Warwick (1468); defection of Clarence (1468);
league with Margaret (1470); marriage of Edward, Prince of Wales,
to Warwick's younger daughter [Anne] (1470); marriage of Clarence to Warwick's eldest daughter (1469).

(IV) Capture of King Edward (1469); restoration of King Henry VI
(1470); Warwick and Clarence joint protectors of the realm (1470);
escape of King Edward (1470); proclamation of Edward IV (1471);
reimprisonment of Henry VI (1471).

(V) Meeting of the hosts at Coventry, reconciliation of Clarence and Edward (1471); defeat and death of Warwick the Kingmaker at Barnet
(1471); defeat of Queen Margaret at Tewkesbury, death of Prince
Edward (1471); murder of Henry VI (1471); restoration of Edward
IV (1471).

THE LIFE AND DEATH OF KING RICHARD THE THIRD

Dates of the reign: Edward IV: 1471–1483; Edward V: 1483; Richard III:
1483–1485
Period covered by the play: May, 1471–August, 1485
Historical events treated or alluded to in the play: UNION OF THE RED ROSE AND
THE WHITE

(I) Arrest of George, Duke of Clarence (1477); funeral of King Henry
VI (1471); wooing of the Lady Anne (fictitious); marriage of Richard and Anne (1472); enmity between the queen's kindred and the
king's fostered by Richard; execution of Clarence, episode of the
malmsey-butt (1478).

(II) Attempted reconciliation of court factions by King Edward (1483);
death of Edward IV (1483); Richard made Protector (1483); public
fear of political change (1483); capture of Prince Edward, arrest of
Rivers, Grey, and Vaughan (1483); Queen Elizabeth takes sanc-
tuary with the Duke of York (1483).

(III) Entrance into London of King Edward V; York brought from sanc-
tuary; both lodged in the Tower; sounding out of Hastings by
Catesby; promise of reward to Buckingham; execution of Rivers,
Grey, and Vaughan; assembly of the lords in the Tower, episode of
the strawberries; execution of Hastings; attainder of the princes;
Richard offered the crown (1483).

(IV) Coronation of King Richard III (1483); rumor of the illness of Queen Anne (1485); murder of the princes in the Tower (1483); defection of Buckingham (1483); death of Queen Anne (1485); Richard's offer of marriage to his niece Elizabeth of York, through her mother (1485); capture of Buckingham (1483).

(V) Execution of Buckingham (1483); expedition of Henry of Richmond (1483, 1485); defeat and death of King Richard at Bosworth Field (1485); proclamation of Henry of Richmond as King Henry VII and his marriage to Elizabeth of York (1485).

THE FAMOUS HISTORY OF THE LIFE OF KING HENRY THE EIGHT

Dates of the reign: 1509–1547
Period covered by the play: June, 1520–July, 1544
Historical events treated or alluded to in the play: INTRIGUE AT THE TUDOR COURT

(I) Meeting of King Henry VIII and Francis I at the Field of the Cloth of Gold (1520); enmity between the Duke of Buckingham and Cardinal Wolsey (1520); breach of peace, attachment of English goods by the French at Bordeaux (1522); visit of the Emperor Charles V to England, his bribery of Wolsey (1520); arrest of Buckingham (1521); opposition to Wolsey's tax commissions to finance the French wars (1525); intercession of Queen Katherine (unhistorical); accusation of treason against Buckingham (1521); criticism of gallicized Englishmen (1519); revels at the Cardinal's palace in York Place (1527); meeting there of Henry VIII and Anne Bullen (unhistorical).

(II) Trial and execution of Buckingham (1521); beginning of divorce proceedings against Katherine of Aragon (1527); Cardinal Campeius in England (1528); Anne Bullen created marchioness of Pembroke (1532); trial of Queen Katherine, her appeal to the pope (1529).

(III) Interview of Wolsey and Campeius with Katherine (1529); dissimulation of Wolsey, displeasure of the king (1529); return of Campeius to Rome (1529); marriage of Henry and Anne (1532, according to Holinshed); Katherine named Princess Dowager as the widow of Prince Arthur (1533); Wolsey's aspirations to the papacy (1529); interception of Wolsey's papers by the king (unhistorical, but based upon a mischance that befell Thomas Ruthal, Bishop of Durham, in which Wolsey had a hand); fall of Wolsey (1529); Sir Thomas More made Lord Chancellor (1529); Cranmer made Archbishop of Canterbury (1533).

(IV) Coronation of Queen Anne (1533); death of Wolsey (1530); death of Queen Katherine (1536).

(V) Conspiracy against Cranmer (1544); birth of Princess Elizabeth (1533); Cranmer's appearance before the Council (1544); baptism of Princess Elizabeth (1533).

SUGGESTED REFERENCES

CAMPBELL, LILY B. *Shakespeare's Histories: Mirrors of Elizabethan Policy.* San Marino, Huntington Library, 1947.

COURTENAY, T. P. *Commentaries on the Historical Plays of Shakespeare* (2 vols.). London, H. Colburn, 1840.

DAVY, S. "The Relation of Poetry to History, with Special Reference to Shakespeare's History Plays," *Transactions of the Royal Society of Literature*, Second Series, XXIV (1903), pp. 163–99.

HEARNSHAW, F. J. C. "Shakespeare as Historian," *The Contemporary Review*, CXXIV (1923), pp. 729–38.

KINGSFORD, C. L. "Fifteenth Century History in Shakespeare's Plays," in *Prejudice and Promise in Fifteenth Century England*. London, 1925.

MARRIOTT, J. A. R. *English History in Shakespeare*. New York, Dutton, 1918.

PALMER, JOHN. *Political Characters of Shakespeare*. London, Macmillan, 1946.

A series of essays on Brutus, Richard III, Richard II, Henry V, and Coriolanus.

PHILLIPS, JAMES E. *The State in Shakespeare's Greek and Roman Plays*. New York, Columbia University Press, 1940.

With an introductory chapter on Tudor political thought.

SCHELLING, FELIX E. *The English Chronicle Play: A Study in the Popular Historical Literature Environing Shakespeare*. New York, Macmillan, 1902.

SMITH, ROBERT M. *Froissart and the English Chronicle Play*. New York, Columbia University Press, 1915.

TILLYARD, E. M. W. *Shakespeare's History Plays*. New York, Macmillan, 1946.

A study of the background—philosophical, historical, and literary—of Shakespeare's chronicle plays, and an analysis of them in relation to Elizabethan thinking about an ordered commonwealth.

WARNER, BEVERLY E. *English History in Shakespeare*. New York, Longman's, Green, 1894.

I3

SHAKESPEAREAN TRAGEDY

> Think ye see
> The very persons of our noble story
> As they were living. Think you see them great,
> And follow'd with the general throng and sweat
> Of thousand friends. Then, in a moment, see
> How soon this mightiness meets misery.
>
> —*Henry VIII*, Prologue, 25–30.

IN HIS "DEFENSE OF POETRY" (1579), THOMAS LODGE described the chief themes of tragedy as "the sour fortune of many exiles, the miserable fall of hapless princes, the ruinous decay of many countries." His contemporary Richard (?) Puttenham added that the purposes of such writings were "to show the mutability of fortune and the just punishment of God in revenge of a vicious and evil life" (*The Art of English Poesie*, 1589). However unsatisfactory these statements may be, even if taken together, as a description of Elizabethan tragedy, they are as near as the age came to a formal definition. The ideas emphasized in these statements are fundamental to an understanding of the serious drama produced by Shakespeare and his fellow-playwrights. Hence, it may be helpful to digress for a moment to see how this philosophy came into being.

THE ELIZABETHAN CONCEPTION OF TRAGEDY

We must again refer to tradition and the medieval and classical heritage of the Elizabethan drama. The miracle play, as we have observed, was bent upon vivifying a scriptural story and developing the happy theme of God's redeeming mercy on sinning mankind. Therefore, it contributed little to the problems which must be faced in tragedy. But the morality play, by a shift of emphasis, perceived in the Fall of Man the origin of "the heartaches and the thousand natural shocks that flesh is heir to," and so the inevitable cause of the falls of lesser men. It conceived of life as a contest between Virtue and

·[322]·

Vice for the possession of Man's soul; it concentrated upon the Four Last Things—Death, Judgment, the pains of Purgatory or Hell, and, alternately, the joys of Heaven, which were to be had if a man remembered the first three and refrained from sin or repented in time. By thus facing the presence of evil in the world, the moral play concerned itself with an essentially tragic conception. The road to ruin, the way of all flesh, the wages of sin, are in one form or another universal tragic themes.

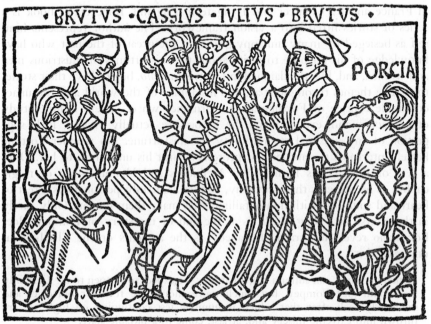

Julius Cæsar
(From Boccaccio's *De Claris Mulieribus*, Johan Zainer, Ulm, 1473)

A more significant medieval contribution to the later drama, however, has been mentioned only casually before, because it was a literary form quite apart from the stage—the tragic narratives of the falls of princes from felicity to wretchedness. The themes of these stories were not unlike those of the morality plays, and, as the quotation from Dante's letter to Can Grande della Scala made clear (see above, p. 250), it was this type of non-dramatic literature that the Middle Ages thought of as tragedy. "Tragedie is to seyn a certeyn storie," says Chaucer's Monk,

> As olde bookes maken us memorie,
> Of hym that stood in greet prosperitee,
> And is y-fallen out of heigh degree
> Into myserie, and endeth wrecchedly. . . .

> For certein, whan that Fortune list to flee,
> Ther may no man the cours of hire withholde.
> Lat no man truste on blynd prosperitee;
> Be war by thise ensamples trewe and olde.
> (*The Monk's Tale*, B. 3163 ff.)

The vogue of these tales had its origin in Boccaccio's *De Casibus Virorum Illustrium*, written about the middle of the fourteenth century, and frequently translated or imitated in later generations, notably by Laurent de Premierfait in France and by Chaucer and Lydgate in England. Boccaccio's book is a series of stories fitted into a vision framework. The author represents himself as besieged by many unhappy ghosts of the great of the past who have knowledge of his purpose to write about the misfortunes of illustrious men and women, and, like the damned in Dante's *Inferno*, beg to have their stories told. The themes throughout are the instability of the world and the unaccountable caprice of Fortune as she turns her wheel. There is little study of character, and, except when the heroes are actually vicious, little suggestion of any personal responsibility for misfortune. No wonder Fortune herself interrupts the author and protests against his unfairness to her. Only a few of Boccaccio's figures—like Alcibiades and Hannibal—are of tragic calibre as he presents them—worthy, admirable, manly personalities, great of heart and soul, but with minor failings that make them human. Only rarely in the course of a long work, as at the end of the story of Pompey, does Boccaccio reveal his grasp of tragedy as the ancients or the Elizabethans understood it:

> If such greatness can suffer a fall, what may we expect to happen to us? Certainly we should pity Pompey, but much more should we fear for ourselves and sedulously seek after that which is humble, lest continuing on high we are thrown into extreme misery and, at last, come to a pitiable state.

The brief sketches related by the Monk in Chaucer's *Canterbury Tales* are but dull imitations in miniature of Boccaccio, and it may be significant that the Knight and the Host of the Tabard Inn join in cutting the narrator off with the time-worn popular preference for the happy ending:

> for litel hevynesse
> Is right ynough to muche folke, I gesse. . . .
> Swich talkyng is nat worth a boterflye,
> For therinne is ther no desport ne game. (B. 3959 ff.)

Later, Chaucer returned to tragedy in *Troilus and Criseyde* to trace without boredom the adventures of a hero

> Fro wo to wele and after out of joye.

The story of these Trojan lovers became one of the most popular in the sixteenth century. Shakespeare himself dramatized it, but, by the time he wrote his play, the character of the heroine in the hands of popular moralistic authors had become so unsympathetic—degraded, some critics have thought —that Shakespeare's *Troilus and Cressida* is more ironic and satirical than tragic. It became, in Thersites's phrase, simply the story of a "scurvy foolish doting . . . young Trojan ass that loves a whore" (V, iv, 4 ff.), told against the background of dreary strife over another light of love, Helen of Troy.

It was John Lydgate, however, rather than Chaucer, who served as a link between these medieval narrative "tragedies" and the Elizabethan drama. As *The Falls of Princes* (*c*. 1430–8), Lydgate translated Laurent de Premierfait's version of Boccaccio's book. A stern moralist, Lydgate regarded these stories

Fortune and Her Wheel
(From Lydgate's *The Falls of Princes*, Pynson, 1494)

·[325]·

in his commentary as examples of divine justice rather than as arguments for contempt of the world. All this execration of Fortune which one heard was to Lydgate merely that "which foolis vsen in ther aduersite for excusacioun" (Prologue to Book VI, 282–3):

> Vertu is cause off long prosperite;
> And whan pryncis fro vertu down declyne
> Ther fame is shrouded vndir the cliptic lyne.

> For fals Fortune, which turneth as a ball,
> Off vnwar chaunges thouh men her wheel atwite,
> It is nat she that pryncis gaff the fall,
> But vicious lyuyng, pleynli to endite.
> (Prologue to Book II, 40–6.)

Lydgate's purpose, therefore, was to tell of

> The fal of many that sat on hihe stages,
> How thei for vicis stood ay in noun certeyn,
> Cam to myscheef for ther gret outrages.
> (Prologue to Book IV, 176–8.)

What had begun as a means of impressing men with the mutability of Fortune and of earthly happiness, became in Lydgate's hands merely illustrations, in the morality manner, of God's punishment of sinners here rather than hereafter.

The subsequent steps were easy. Lydgate's translation proved popular; some thirty manuscripts of it have survived. Pynson printed it in 1494 and again in 1527, Tottel in 1554, and Wayland in 1555. It begot offspring and became the progenitor of numerous expansions and imitations, the most important of which was *The Mirror for Magistrates* (1559).

Conceived originally as an appendix to a new edition of Lydgate, *The Mirror for Magistrates* discovered in the fields of British history and legend "such as Fortune had dallied with here in this island" and became an inexhaustible quarry of historical tragedy. The book rapidly grew by accretion. The nineteen legends which are contained in the first edition of 1559 begin where Lydgate left off and concern misfortunes from the reign of Richard II, including, among others, Thomas of Woodstock, Duke of Gloucester; Lord Mowbray; King Richard II; Jack Cade; Richard Plantagenet, Duke of York; Richard Neville, Earl of Warwick; King Henry VI; George Plantagenet, Duke of Clarence; and King Edward IV. All of these persons became subjects of Shakespearean drama. Later editions added more figures, mainly from the reign of Richard III, among them Anthony Woodville, Earl of Rivers; Lord Hastings; Henry, Duke of Buckingham; Richard Plantagenet, Duke of Gloucester; Eleanor Cobham, Duchess of Gloucester; Humphrey, Duke of Gloucester; and Cardinal Wolsey. In 1574, *The First Part of the Mirror for Magistrates*, covering the period from the landing of Brut to the coming of the Romans, was published. In 1578, *The Second Part* was issued. This edition dealt with the tragedies from the conquest of Cæsar to the invasion by William the Conqueror. By 1610, the legends were gathered together and the collection was completed. In addition, there were several imitations of this popular book of verse, like Richard Robinson's *The Reward of Wickedness* (1574) or Anthony Munday's *The Mirror of Mutability* (1579), the latter drawn from the Bible and illustrating the Seven Deadly Sins. In prose there were Thomas Beard's *The Theatre of God's Judgments* (1597) and John Reynolds's *The Triumphs of God's Revenge* (1621). Their titles indicate clearly where the emphasis of these books lay; it is a strange theory that looking-glasses were first invented to show men and women their imperfections. But, unpromising as this philosophy was for great art, the "mirrors" pointed the way to material for the historical and the tragic playwright.

Moreover, at least the method of *The Mirror for Magistrates*, if not its literary form, approached drama. In *De Casibus*, Boccaccio had raised a pageant of shades begging to have their stories told and generally permitting the author to do so unaided, without interruptions. Lydgate followed the same method. But the authors of *The Mirror for Magistrates* permitted the ghosts, somewhat lugubriously, to narrate their own misfortunes, make their own complaints, regretfully confess their faults, and moralize about their own downfalls. The book is a collection of soliloquies. It is significant that *Gorboduc*, the first English dramatic tragedy, was based, like *The Mirror*, upon a legend in the national chronicles, and that one of its authors was Sir Thomas Sackville, who contributed some of the best poetry to *The Mirror*.

The discovery of dramatic material, however, was not in itself enough to produce stage drama. As we have seen, the early tragedians turned for models to the plays of the Latin philosopher-dramatist, Seneca the Younger. Seneca had selected as his subjects some of the traditional heroes of *De Casibus* story—notably Agamemnon, Œdipus, Thyestes, Medea, and Hercules—and was recognized by such medieval writers as Dante and Lydgate as among the great writers of "tragedy." His plays of ambition and revenge, with their emphasis upon retributive justice, could not fail to appeal to audiences accustomed to the "salarye of synne" as it was displayed by *The Mirror for Magistrates* and its forerunners. Classical decorum permitted Seneca to report crimes only by messenger or some similar device; the Elizabethan playwrights, however, did not deny their theatre the thrills of horror any more than does the modern movie-producer. In Plutarch's *Lives*, in the "tragical discourses" of the Italian *novelle,* written by Bandello and Cinthio and translated by Painter and Fenton and Pettie, the Elizabethan tragedian found whatever else he needed. Some dramatic types which were good "theatre," like the Senecan tragedy of blood and revenge, became stereotyped with stock ingredients: ghosts who superintend the revenge or incite it; tricky intrigue and counter-intrigue; stock motives and devices, like feigned madness and amateur dramatics; crimes of adultery, incest, and murder; rant; and complaining, moralizing heroes who reproach themselves for their incapacities or their inaction. Only rarely does a playwright, like Shakespeare, accept an old threadbare plot without giving it new significance. In theme and type, Shakespeare's tragedies are, superficially at least, like other Elizabethan tragedies.

Some account of the development and refinement of Elizabethan tragedy has already been given (see above, pp. 76 ff.) and need not be repeated here. Of course, had it not burst its Senecan and medieval shackles to substitute a hearty affirmation of life for the Stoic spirit of negation and contempt of the world, it should never have produced Shakespeare. The drama of the late 1580's and 1590's with greater spiritual insight focused attention upon human character fearlessly outfacing death and horror, shaping its own destiny in defiance of Fortune, and manifesting a gallant faith in this life, even if it must be lived in a world in which there is ugliness and sin. Like the last fight of the *Revenge*, like the tragedy of Dunkerque, the best Elizabethan drama reflects the view of life of a people "free, stout, hault, prodigal of life and blood." Had it not been so, Hamlet could hardly have exclaimed:

What a piece of work is a man! How noble in reason! How infinite in faculty!
In action how like an angel! In apprehension how like a god!

Man delighted the Elizabethans—and Woman, too—when they penned their greatest tragedies.

It is now time to return to Shakespeare to see how he poured his new wine into the old bottles. Although there is no such thing as a typical Shakespearean tragedy, yet, when allowances are made for the demands of his individual subjects, experiment, and varying emphasis, there are some characteristics which are general to all or to a majority of Shakespeare's serious plays. The following is no Procrustean bed of rules which tolerates no exception; it allows for tall and short.

THE REVERSAL OF FORTUNE

All of Shakespeare's tragedies, in the last analysis, concern themselves either with a reversal of fortune or with a fall from happiness to misery, from high estate to low. Some, like *Antony and Cleopatra, Richard II, Coriolanus,* and *Richard III,* are stories in the tradition of the medieval *Falls of Princes* or *The Mirror for Magistrates.* Richard II even recognizes his plight as a fit subject for *De Casibus* tragedy and himself as King in the Dance of Death, confronted by the mocking Reaper:

for within the hollow crown
That rounds the mortal temples of a king
Keeps Death his court and there the antic sits,
Scoffing his state and grinning at his pomp,
Allowing him a breath, a little scene,
To monarchize, be fear'd, and kill with looks,
Infusing him with self and vain conceit,
As if this flesh which walls about our life
Were brass impregnable; and humour'd thus
Comes at the last and with a little pin
Bores through his castle wall, and—farewell king!
(III, ii, 160–72.)

It is of no avail for the Bishop of Carlisle to observe

My lord, wise men ne'er sit and wail their woes,
But presently prevent the ways to wail. (*Ibid.*, 178–9.)

Tragedy, in Richard's view of things, would seem to be the natural portion of men in high place, and this idea finds expression elsewhere in Shakespeare's work:

O place and greatness! Millions of false eyes
Are struck upon thee. Volumes of report
Run with these false and most contrarious quests
Upon thy doings; thousand escapes of wit
Make thee the father of their idle dream
And rack thee in their fancies.
(*Measure for Measure*, IV, ii, 60 ff.)

The correlative idea that safety lies in lowly position and in scorn of worldly ambition also finds expression on occasion. Poor saintly Henry VI, chid from the battle by the virago who is his queen, wishes he were dead or permitted to live like a homely country swain, scorning the ambitious life of the world which produces nothing but grief and woe and tragic falls (*3 Henry VI*, II, v).

Other of Shakespeare's plays, like *Titus Andronicus, Macbeth, Hamlet*, and *Julius Cæsar*, relate the accompaniments and the consequences of crime. Even *Othello* and *Romeo and Juliet*, which concern a more personal overthrow because of human weakness or tragic chance, conform to the general pattern. There are frequent allusions to Fate, the "divinity that shapes our ends" (*Hamlet*, V, ii, 8–11), "Destiny that hath to instrument this lower world and what is in 't" (*The Tempest*, III, iii, 53–4), "giddy Fortune's furious fickle wheel" (*Henry V*, III, vi, 28), and "malignant and ill-boding stars" (*1 Henry VI*, IV, v, 6). There are occasional renunciations of the world, like Gloucester's (*King Lear*, IV, vi, 34 ff.), and many a *memento mori*, like Hamlet's musings over Yorick's skull or "imperious Cæsar, dead and turned to clay" (V, i, 199 ff.).

Antony and Cleopatra
(From Boccaccio's *De Claris Mulieribus*, Johan Zainer, Ulm, 1473)

TRAGEDY AND MELODRAMA

The themes of Shakespeare's tragedies are all essentially stirring and selected for their theatrical effectiveness:

> unnaturalness between the child and the parent; death, dearth, dissolutions of ancient amities; divisions in state, menaces and maledictions against king and nobles; needless diffidences, banishment of friends, dissipation of cohorts, nuptial breaches, and I know not what. (*King Lear*, I, ii, 155 ff.)

All are sensational to a great degree, and even the best are full of deeds of violence that are melodramatic:

> Of carnal, bloody, and unnatural acts,
> Of accidental judgments, casual slaughters,
> Of deaths put on by cunning and forced cause,
> And . . . purposes mistook
> Fall'n on the inventors' heads. (*Hamlet*, V, ii, 392 ff.)

In this fashion, *Titus Andronicus* is stuffed with atrocities; in *Romeo and Juliet* there are street brawls and the opening of a tomb by moonlight; in *Hamlet* an avenging ghost that walks, a girl who goes mad, and young hotheads who fight in a churchyard. *Macbeth* has its weird sisters and other apparitions, its murder in the dark, and a mad queen who walks in her sleep. Othello stifles his lady in bed; Lear goes mad during a storm on the heath, and Gloucester's eyes are plucked out. A bald, unvarnished catalogue of such scenes reads like the attractions of a first-class chamber of horrors.

These ingredients provide thrills for the groundling—Elizabethan and modern—and there has been no lack of critics who have found it easy to total up the crimes that occur in Shakespeare's tragedies and raise a superior eyebrow. *Titus Andronicus* is admittedly crude, but Shakespeare was young when he wrote it or collaborated with another playwright on it, and he gained in experience. *Hamlet* is the same kind of play, but here the old revenge plot has a new kind of introspective hero and, hence, a new significance. Only superficially are the melodramatic plots important to what is best in Shakespeare's tragedies. The romantic stories are only a framework; beyond them and within them, Shakespeare perceived something much more subtle, more poetic, more lastingly deep and moving. In portraying human character, Shakespeare was always a realist. One has but to conceive of these stories as they might be told on the police-court blotter or in the tabloids to appreciate the sublimity of Shakespeare's genius.

THE TRAGIC HERO

The heroes of Shakespearean tragedy are all persons of high degree or at least members of great houses with respectable connections—emperors and princes, like Antony and Hamlet; great generals, like Othello and Coriolanus; leaders of the state, like Brutus; or persons of social prominence, like Romeo. That only the great of the earth could be suitable subjects for tragedy was a theory as old as the Greeks. Tragedies of middle-class domestic life—like *Arden of Feversham*, *A Yorkshire Tragedy*, or *A Woman Killed With Kindness*, which are the obscure ancestors of modern tragedy—were comparatively few in number in Shakespeare's day. Only two of Shakespeare's tragedies, *Othello* and *King Lear*, treat family relationships, and only two others, *Romeo and Juliet* and *Antony and Cleopatra*, are love tragedies. None of these plays, however, is an exception to the general rule that serious drama must be about conspicuous people. Even the Moor fetches his life and being from men of royal siege. Tragedy of the Ibsen variety is not Elizabethan.

On the whole, this conception of the hero conferred an intensity upon Shakespearean tragedy which many a modern play lacks. To be sure, "the slings and arrows of outrageous fortune," "the pangs of disprized love," remorse of conscience, jealousy, and hate are much the same in peasant and prince. But the greater the dignity of a man, the greater is his responsibility, the greater is his fault, and the more difficult is it for him to face adversity. "Dionysius the Tyrant of Sicily felt greater pain when he was expelled his kingdom than Milo did, being banished from Rome," wrote William Painter in the story of "The Duchess of Malfi," upon which Webster based his tragedy:

> for so much as the one was a sovereign lord, the son of a king, a justiciary on earth, and the other but a simple citizen of a city. . . . So likewise the fall of a high and lofty tree maketh greater noise than that which is low and little. High towers and stately palaces of princes be seen farther off than the poor cabins and homely shepherds' sheepcotes; the walls of lofty cities more aloof do salute the viewers of the same than the simple caves which the poor do dig below the mountain rocks. (*The Palace of Pleasure*, 1566.)

Furthermore, upon the choice of the prince depends "the safety and the health of the whole state" (*Hamlet*, I, iii, 20–1), and in his fall from greatness one sees the weakness of man and the omnipotence of Fate as no tale of private misfortune could reveal it. So, in Shakespeare,

> the death of Antony
> Is not a single doom; in the name lay
> A moiety of the world. (*Antony and Cleopatra*, V, i, 18–19.)

Lear's madness is

> A sight most pitiful in the meanest wretch,
> Past speaking of in a king (IV, vi, 208–09),

and the fates of rulers are almost always foreshadowed by terrifying portents:

> When beggars die, there are no comets seen;
> The heavens themselves blaze forth the death of princes.
> (*Julius Cæsar*, II, ii, 30–1.)

Shakespearean tragedy has no concern with the falls of sparrows; its interest is in eagles.

A Shakespearean tragedy is usually the story of one person who gives his name to the play, or who, like Brutus in *Julius Cæsar*, is obviously its protagonist. Some of Shakespeare's tragedies, like *Richard II, Richard III*, and *Coriolanus*, are one-man plays, but even in the others, during his most trying hour, the hero must act his dismal scene alone. Unity is seldom disturbed by the playwright's development of rival spheres of interest at the expense of the hero. For all his attractiveness, Mercutio has a definite dramatic function which only he can perform, and he never threatens to run away with the play; only momentarily does Antony steal the spotlight from Brutus to deliver Cæsar's funeral oration; and Lady Macbeth, who is a driving force during the early scenes of the drama, drops out after Act III and returns only as she is about to die. Indeed, in Shakespeare's tragedies, the women characters are largely subordinate as compared with the men or with their sisters in comedy. Neither Tamora nor Lavinia in *Titus Andronicus* has an interest comparable to that of Titus and his sons; Brutus's Portia, for all her wifely devotion, is but a shadow; Queen Gertrude, Ophelia, Desdemona, Volumnia, and Virgilia are significant only in relation to the heroes, and Cordelia, more prominent than her wicked sisters, is of minor importance when compared with Lear. Only in the love tragedies do the heroines occupy positions of interest comparable to the men, and then the fact is recognized in the titles of the plays. Moreover, each is granted her own scene in which to die. Unlike Gounod's opera, Shakespeare's play shows Romeo dead before the lady stirs and permits no pathetic double aria at death. In *Antony and Cleopatra*, Antony dies at the end of Act IV; the entire fifth act is Cleopatra's. Only then, when all of her tricks have failed her, is she worthy of Antony:

> We'll bury him; and then, what's brave, what's noble,
> Let's do it after the high Roman fashion,
> And make Death proud to take us. (IV, xv, 86–8.)

THE EXTERNAL CONFLICT

The action of a Shakespearean tragedy is a conflict of opposing forces or a complication of such contests involving the hero. This conflict may be *external*, i. e., outside the hero himself, his engagement with forces that seek to dominate him; or it may be *internal*, i. e., a struggle of opposing desires contending for mastery within his own mind and heart. Usually, in the better tragedies, the conflict is quite complex. In its simplest form, the tragic conflict is represented merely by two persons or two groups of persons in one of which the hero is a principal. Or, more properly, by the ideologies, the emotions, or the motives that animate these groups. Thus, Richard II and Bolingbroke are opposed, or Antony and Octavius. So, too, the love of Romeo and Juliet is in conflict with the feud between their houses, and in the same play youth runs counter to crabbed age. In *Julius Cæsar*, the old republican order, represented by Brutus, is opposed to the new totalitarian order, represented by Cæsar, Antony, and Octavius. In the sequel to this play, Antony's efforts to break his strong Egyptian fetters represent not merely a conflict between love and honor, or the claims of empire over the hero's private life, but also all that Roman discipline and the dalliance of the East popularly stand for. In *King Lear*, the characters range themselves into two clearly opposed groups of Right and Wrong, Good and Evil, reminiscent of the morality plays. In some cases, notably *Macbeth*, the external conflict includes that of the hero against Fate.

Occasionally, the contentions between opposing groups are complicated by minor conflicts within the groups themselves. Thus, Macbeth and Lady Macbeth stand together, but they do not at first see eye to eye on catching the nearest way to attain their end. So, too, Brutus must be wooed to join the conspiracy; he and Cassius quarrel about the ways and means of maintaining their armies and on the conduct of the war. There are similar disagreements between Antony and Octavius, but, characteristically, they bury their differences until a later time. Sometimes the conflict is very uneven or one-sided. The opposition which lies between Richard III or Macbeth and the crowns they covet is easily and quickly brushed aside; then other forces gather strength to remove the usurpers. Othello and Desdemona, opposed by Iago, must of necessity contend in the dark with an adversary they cannot recognize, and so they both seem helplessly passive as a result.

We may, for a moment, pause to consider the external conflict in *Hamlet* in this connection, because this play, too, is often spoken of as having a delaying protagonist pitted against a villain who is more active than he. Claudius's counter-intrigue does involve the use of numerous tools—Polonius, Ophelia, Rosencrantz and Guildenstern, Queen Gertrude, Laertes, and even that water-fly Osric. The king wraps everyone, except Hamlet, around his finger. Yet Hamlet does not fight merely a defensive war, and the way in which stroke parries stroke is illustrative of Shakespeare's method at its best. Claudius may be "a mildew'd ear" and "a cutpurse of the empire and the rule," but he is also an oily, shrewd contriver who coveted his brother's throne and his brother's wife and succeeded in committing both murder and incest without arousing comment or suspicion (cf. I, ii, 1 ff.). His nerve breaks only once.

The first act of *Hamlet* is taken up with preliminary exposition and the revelations of the ghost, ending with the son's resolve to avenge the "foul and most unnatural murder" of his father. Act II begins Hamlet's campaign. He puts his "antic disposition" on, frightens Ophelia, and convinces her and Polonius that he is mad because of love (II, i, ii)—score for Hamlet. Claudius, who is uneasy about Hamlet's strange behavior of late, sends Rosencrantz and Guildenstern to visit him (II, ii). Ironically, it is Hamlet's sham which arouses Claudius's suspicions—score for the king. Instantly on guard, Hamlet baffles his old school-fellows, greets the players, and resolves upon a play, which he doctors up and later whimsically calls *The Mousetrap, or The Murder of Gonzago,* to test the ghost's word and to "catch the conscience of the king" (II, ii). Rosencrantz and Guildenstern report their failure to the king; Claudius and Polonius, in hiding, watch the encounter between Hamlet and Ophelia, with the result that Claudius is convinced that love is no cause of Hamlet's melancholy. He even doubts that it is madness at all, scents danger to himself, and resolves that "madness in great ones must not unwatch'd go" (III, i). Hamlet's play is most successful in unnerving the king, who gives himself completely away (III, ii). But immediately after, while he is still celebrating, Hamlet must undergo another interview with Rosencrantz and Guildenstern (the episode of the recorder), bandy words with Polonius about the shape of a cloud, and be summoned to his mother's chamber (III, ii). So far, if either has an advantage, it is Hamlet.

On his way to see Gertrude, however, Hamlet makes his tragic error. He has his first opportunity to act, and he rejects it. Deceived into believing that the murderer whose conscience he has just possibly aroused is really penitent as he kneels at prayer, Hamlet passes up his present opportunity for one in the future. He must have a perfect revenge and destroy both the body and the soul of his victim. This failure—however it may be interpreted—is the fatal turning point in the duel between the two opponents. *The Murder of Gonzago* gave away Hamlet's secret as well as the king's, and Claudius has now been spared only that he may plot Hamlet's death.

Hamlet's interview with his mother, who is also an unsuspecting agent of the king, begins his downfall. He kills the eavesdropping Polonius, whom he mistakes for Claudius. Self-righteously, he rebukes his mother; and, by turning her eyes into her very soul, he goes too far. The ghost's original injunction had contained a double caution:

> Taint not thy mind, nor let thy soul contrive
> Against thy mother aught.

One may well wonder if for a Hamlet these are not impossible conditions; whatever the case, he had accepted them. Now the ghost finds it necessary to intervene and to whet the avenger's almost blunted purpose. Gertrude cannot see the spectre to which the prince speaks, but, after Hamlet's rash act and the frenzied words he has already uttered to her, she would have been convinced of his madness, had he not reassured her and confessed that he was but mad in craft. Hamlet leaves Gertrude his penitent but helpless ally; all she can report is what she has seen (III, iv). But the death of Polonius makes Hamlet's intentions unmistakable to his adversary:

> It had been so had we been there.

In Act IV the prince is removed to England. During his absence Ophelia goes mad, and Laertes returns to demand satisfaction for his father's death (IV, iii, v). Just as Claudius has calmed Laertes down sufficiently to lead up to a revelation of how, for everyone's good, he had shipped the dangerous, popular prince to his death, they are interrupted by news of Hamlet's return (IV, vi, vii). Claudius and Laertes now concoct the fencing match with poisoned foils and a poisoned cup—the Italian manner—their alliance being confirmed by the death of Ophelia (IV, vii) and the fight in her grave (V, i). At the fencing, Hamlet, already mortally wounded, must make the opportunity he had waited for. He has succeeded, but so has Claudius. As in war, anything can happen until the end; the critic, like the historian, can in retrospect evaluate the tide of oscillating fortune for the opponents.

THE INTERNAL CONFLICT

Yet, important as is the external conflict in this play, most readers—as distinguished from spectators in the theatre—are more engrossed by the greater battle which is waged within the soul of Hamlet between his desire for revenge and those puzzling inner forces—the subjects of his soliloquies—which keep him from it. Internal conflicts are likewise to be found in other plays. In *Julius Cæsar*, there is "poor Brutus, with himself at war," as he weighs the claims of patriotism and friendship; in *Macbeth*, the conflict between duty and ambition is succeeded by that between ambition and remorse of conscience; in *Antony and Cleopatra*, the debauchee that Antony has become often falls

> too short of that great property
> Which still should go with Antony. (I, i, 57–8.)

In *Othello* and *King Lear* and *Timon*, the mental and emotional stresses and strains provide the deeper tragedy. In *Romeo and Juliet*, there is almost no internal conflict at all. Generally speaking, Shakespeare's early tragedies concentrate upon contending external forces, his more mature works upon some form of spiritual civil war.

The internal conflict frequently is very complex. Most Hamlet character study has been made in the attempt to pluck out the heart of his mystery. We listen to Hamlet's own soul-searching, but we are still as puzzled as were Rosencrantz and Guildenstern. All we can be certain of is that Hamlet should never have undertaken his task at all. That is all we need to know. Apparently it did not occur to Shakespeare to have Horatio analyze his friend as Aufidius did Coriolanus:

> Whether 'twas pride,
> Which out of daily fortune ever taints
> The happy man; whether defect of judgment,
> To fail in the disposing of those chances
> Which he was lord of; or whether nature,
> Not to be other than one thing, not moving
> From the casque to the cushion, but commanding peace
> Even with the same austerity and garb
> As he controll'd the war. But one of these—
> As he hath spices of them all—not all—
> For I dare so far free him—made him fear'd;
> So, hated; and so, banish'd. But he has a merit
> To choke it in the utterance. So our virtues
> Lie in the construction of the time. (IV, vii, 37 ff.)

THE "TRAGIC FLAW"

Each of Shakespeare's tragic heroes is dominated in one way or another by some ruling passion. It is the essence of his serious plays that in the last analysis the hero is to a large degree the author of his proper woe. The "slings and arrows of outrageous fortune" and other external forces against which the hero contends are not alone responsible for the catastrophe; the citadel is somehow always betrayed from within. Shakespeare's tragic heroes are usually their own worst enemies, and in a very real, if not a complete sense, "character is destiny" in his plays:

> The fault, dear Brutus, is not in our stars,
> But in ourselves, that we are underlings.
> *(Julius Cæsar, I, ii, 140–1.)*

> Nay, if I turn mine eyes upon myself,
> I find myself a traitor with the rest.
> *(Richard II, IV, i, 247–8.)*

Virtue! A fig! 'Tis in ourselves that we are thus and thus. *(Othello, I, iii, 322 ff.)*

This is the excellent foppery of the world, that, when we are sick in fortune . . . we make guilty of our disasters the sun, the moon, and the stars, as if we were villains by necessity. *(King Lear, I, ii, 128 ff.)*

> I see men's judgments are
> A parcel of their fortunes, and things outward
> Do draw the inward quality after them
> To suffer all alike. *(Antony and Cleopatra, III, xiii, 31 ff.)*

There are many expressions of this inexorable doctrine of personal responsibility in Shakespeare's tragedies, and it is significant that his villains understand it better than the good men. Hamlet explains this idea most fully:

> So, oft it chances in particular men,
> That for some vicious mole of nature in them,
> As, in their birth—wherein they are not guilty . . .
> By the o'ergrowth of some complexion,
> Oft breaking down the pales and forts of reason,
> Or by some habit that too much o'er-leavens
> The form of plausive manners, that these men,
> Carrying, I say, the stamp of one defect,
> Being nature's livery, or fortune's star—
> Their virtues else—be they as pure as grace,
> As infinite as man may undergo—
> Shall in the general censure take corruption
> From that particular fault. The dram of eale
> Doth all the noble substance of a doubt
> To his own scandal. *(I, iv, 23 ff.)*

It should be clear that in Shakespearean drama the "tragic flaw" is not necessarily a vicious blot or even unworthiness. It is less often wickedness than weakness which breaks hearts in Shakespeare's tragedies. Usually, it is merely the slight sullies which the gods lay on us to make us men:

> the taints of liberty,
> The flash and outbreak of a fiery mind,
> A savageness in unreclaimed blood,
> Of general assault. *(Hamlet, II, i, 32 ff.)*

As in life, so in Shakespeare, incapacity, blindness, "the heyday in the blood," an error in judgment, good intentions, the inability to face fact, a sense of false security, all are visited as sharply as willful disobedience of some universal law. The tragic failing, however, is never originally an abnormality; it may even grow out of misapplied strength or excess virtue. Thus, Othello's free and open nature may "as tenderly be led by the nose as asses are" (*Othello*, I, iii, 407–08), Brutus's "honourable metal may be wrought from that it is disposed" (*Julius Cæsar*, I, ii, 313–4), and Edgar's honesty is such that he is "so far from doing harms that he suspects none" (*King Lear*, I, ii, 196–7). Lear is but an irascible old man

> That still would manage those authorities
> That he hath given away,
>
> (I, iii, 17–18.)

and Cordelia suffers

> even for want of that for which I am the richer,
> A still-soliciting eye, and such a tongue
> As I am glad I have not.
>
> (I, i, 233 ff.)

Rarely is the tragic hero in Shakespeare's plays merely "Fortune's fool," although the worst that can be said about Romeo and Juliet is that they are children of impulse. Only Macbeth and Richard III are villains. Some of the others are far from being good; all, however—even Macbeth and Richard—are men of great potentialities who readily inspire admiration. But all of Shakespeare's gods have feet of clay.

> In tragic life, God wot,
> No villain need be; passions spin the plot,
> We are betray'd by what is false within.
> (George Meredith, *Modern Love*.)

Nor does the "tragic flaw" serve to render the fates of these men their just deserts; few of the characters of Shakespeare's plays who manage to survive —like Octavius, Bolingbroke, or Aufidius—have natures that are as fine as those of the men they throw down. Shakespeare's play-world is just like ours. He understood what a man had to be and do to succeed politically, and he portrayed that in Octavius Cæsar, Henry IV, and the Tribunes in *Coriolanus;* but he was more interested in men like Brutus and Hotspur and Hamlet, who have no such aptitude.

THE MISFIT CHARACTER

As a corollary to what has been said above, it will be seen that Shakespeare's tragic heroes are generally misfits who have been placed by Fate or circumstance in precisely the environment to which they are temperamentally unsuited. Some are hard men of war called upon to play a role in the piping times of peace—like Othello, who was bred in the tented field and understands the direct logic of battle, but is unversed in the subtle ways of the domestic world. Or, like Coriolanus, a matchless officer called upon to compromise, to play the politician, and to beg votes from those he scorns for having shirked the duty he is all too conscious of having done for them. Some are soft men of peace called upon to play the roles of hard men of

Coriolanus (From Boccaccio's *De Claris Mulieribus*, Johan Zainer, Ulm, 1473)

action—like Brutus the idealist who provides a respectable front for a group of pragmatic politicians and is even put in actual command, although he lacks the unscrupulousness demanded by such leadership. Or, like Hamlet, the perfect Renaissance prince, possessed of "the courtier's, soldier's, scholar's eye, tongue, sword," a grief-stricken introvert confronted by times that are out of joint and a task in which even if he wins he must lose. Some are great men with an incapacity for resisting that before which they should be most strong—like Antony, whose "taints and honours wage equal in him," or Macbeth, who lacks the balance of his colleague Banquo. Some, like Lear and Coriolanus, are giant oaks that will break rather than bend. Some, like Othello, are men of the heart, tricked into trusting their heads. Others, like Romeo and Antony again, reveal a fatal infatuation with some interest or

·[339]·

ungovernable frame of mind. All lack the qualities which their situations demand.

The easiest way to appreciate how closely character and plot are dependent upon one another in Shakespeare's plays is, in imagination, to shift these heroes from one play to another. Romeo is not Hamlet in love, nor is Cleopatra Juliet in middle life. Put Othello in Hamlet's place, or Hamlet in Othello's, and there simply is no play.

THE TRAGIC MOOD

Finally, there is exaltation rather than depression at the end of a Shakespearean tragedy, and no Götterdämmerung. Axes chopping down the cherry orchard do not ring through darkened desolation (as in Chekhov's *The Cherry Orchard*), and there is no drunken Paycock reminding a Joxer that "th' whole worl's . . . in a terr . . . ible state o' . . . chassis!" (as in O'Casey's *Juno and the Paycock*). What we have witnessed in Shakespeare's play is the wasteful ruin of a great personality, but we are not crushed.

> The stroke of Death is as a lover's pinch,
> Which hurts, and is desired. (*Antony and Cleopatra*, V, ii, 298–9.)

> When we are born, we cry that we are come
> To this great stage of fools. . . .
>   Men must endure
> Their going hence, even as their coming hither;
> Ripeness is all. (*King Lear*, IV, vi, 186–7 and V, ii, 9–11.)

After the sunset there always appear the faint rosy tints of a new dawn. Behind the overcast skies the sun is rising, and the children of darkness are gone. The senseless feud between Montague and Capulet has cost a terrific price, but, as the heads of the rival houses shake hands over their dead, there are better days in store for fair Verona. Fortinbras will rule in Denmark, and Horatio lives to report Hamlet and his cause aright to the unsatisfied. Malcolm has his rightful heritage in Scotland, and Kent, Albany, and Edgar will clear away the rubble of Lear's kingdom. Crime has been punished;

> The gods are just, and of our pleasant vices
> Make instruments to plague us. (*King Lear*, V, iii, 170–1.)

Good may have been defeated, but it is not changed; it is still Good.

Moreover, throughout the tragedy, we are made akin to magnificence and nobility of life, even when we cannot believe that the gods are on our side. We are awakened to the capacity of humankind to endure what it must and to win what it can before submitting to the defeat which is the ultimate lot of man. Romeo shaking "the yoke of inauspicious stars from this world-wearied flesh"; plume-plucked Richard resignedly likening the prison where he lives unto the world, but seizing an axe from his assailants; Lear stretched on the rack of this tough world until he knows not what he says; Macbeth tired and musing on what might have been, but resolving to die with harness on his back; Othello realizing that, like the base Indian, he has thrown a pearl away richer than all his tribe; Coriolanus remembering how

> like an eagle in a dove cote, I
> Flutter'd your Volscians in Corioli;
> Alone I did it

—all die well.
At its best, the peculiar calm at the close of a Shakespearean tragedy is akin to the exaltation described by Wordsworth:

> In which the burthen of the mystery,
> In which the heavy and the weary weight
> Of all this unintelligible world,
> Is lightened:—that serene and blessed mood,
> In which the affections gently lead us on,—
> Until, the breath of this corporeal frame
> And even the motion of our human blood
> Almost suspended, we are laid asleep
> In body, and become a living soul.
> (*Lines, Composed a Few Miles above Tintern Abbey*, 1798.)

SUGGESTED REFERENCES

BRADBROOK, M. C. *Themes and Conventions of Elizabethan Tragedy*. Cambridge University Press, 1935.

BRADLEY, A. C. *Shakespearean Tragedy. Lectures on Hamlet, Othello, King Lear, Macbeth*. London, Macmillan, 1904.
   One of the great classics of Shakespeare criticism.

BOWERS, FREDSON THAYER. *Elizabethan Revenge Tragedy, 1587–1642*. Princeton University Press, 1940.

CAMPBELL, LILY B. *Shakespeare's Tragic Heroes, Slaves of Passion*. Cambridge University Press, 1930.
   A study of Shakespeare's tragedies in relation to the philosophy of his day concerning the nature of the emotions.

CHARLTON, H. B. *Shakespearian Tragedy*. Cambridge University Press, 1949.
   A series of lectures on Shakespeare's major tragedies in a companion volume to the same author's *Shakespearian Comedy*.

FARNHAM, WILLARD. *The Medieval Heritage of Elizabethan Tragedy*. Berkeley, University of California Press, 1936.
   The dramatic and non-dramatic background of tragedy as Shakespeare's contemporaries conceived of it.

LUCAS, F. L. *Seneca and Elizabethan Tragedy*. Cambridge University Press, 1922.

MACCALLUM, M. W. *Shakespeare's Roman Plays and Their Background.* London, Macmillan, 1910.

NICOLL, ALLARDYCE. *Studies in Shakespeare.* Hogarth Lectures on Literature Series. London, The Hogarth Press, 1927.
On Shakespeare's great tragedies.

SCHÜCKING, LEVIN LUDWIG. *The Baroque Character of the Elizabethan Tragic Hero.* British Academy Lecture. Oxford, 1933.

——. *Shakespeare und der Tragödienstil seiner Zeit.* Bern, A. Franke Ag. Verlag, 1947.
A study of the conception of tragedy by Shakespeare and his contemporaries.

SIMPSON, PERCY. *The Theme of Revenge in Elizabethan Tragedy.* British Academy Lecture. Oxford, 1935.

THORNDIKE, ASHLEY H. "The Relations of *Hamlet* to Contemporary Revenge Plays," *Publications of the Modern Language Association,* XVII (1902), pp. 125–220.

14

SHAKESPEARE IN PRINT

His mind and hand went together, and what he thought he uttered with that easiness that we have scarce received from him a blot in his papers.
—"To the Great Variety of Readers," First Folio, 1623.

CHANGES IN THEATRICAL CONVENTIONS SINCE SHAKE-speare's day have, on the whole, modified rather than diminished the appeal of his plays in the theatre. The platform stage has given way to the picture-frame stage, the several arts of the producer, the scene-painter, and the actor have each had their creative claims allowed, and the audience has come to expect of the theatre what the Elizabethans hardly dreamed of. Yet *Hamlet, Romeo and Juliet,* and *Twelfth Night* still evoke emotion or delight in the theatre, but they are no longer the Elizabethan plays which bore these names. Likewise, Shakespeare's plays may today be read with pleasure in almost any modern text; but even the barest unannotated edition is the work of generations of scholars who have patiently studied the materials which the seventeenth century bequeathed to posterity. Why did not Shakespeare himself set forth a satisfactory edition of his own works? How can a faithful rendering of what he wrote be arrived at? Was he the sole author of what has come down as his work? Is Shakespeare's style sufficiently distinct to enable his work to be distinguished from that of his contemporaries? Is it possible to arrange his plays in chronological order and so supplement the colorless facts of biography with some knowledge of his development as an artist? These are some of the questions that have fascinated students of Shakespeare for centuries, and to which they are still attempting to find answers.

PLAYS WRITTEN FOR THE PUBLIC THEATRE

One of the fundamental reasons for the existence of these scholarly questions concerning Shakespeare and his work is the attitude which his age adopted, not only toward the theatre, but also toward literature as a profession. Fashionable poetizing was expected of every well-bred Elizabethan gentleman, but in Shakespeare's day trying to "live by verses" was considered degrading. Even so eminent a man of letters as Ben Jonson was made to feel the ignominy attached to his calling. In *Timber*, he speaks of being "upbraidingly call'd a Poet, as if it were a most contemptible nickname," and in *Epicœne* (II, ii), he permits Sir John Daw to draw a neat distinction: "Every man who writes is not a poet. They are poets that live by it, the poor fellows that live by it." Gentlemen, like Sir Philip Sidney or John Donne, might write, but they were expected to affect, at least, a disinclination to anything so undignified as publishing. Authors of no social standing, like Chapman or Shakespeare, who were dependent upon their literary labors for a living, sent their products forth, like bread upon the waters, hopefully equipped with dedications to a patron. As in the Middle Ages, so in Shakespeare's day, literature was still regarded as a cultural avocation.

Toward authorship for the public stage, of course, the attitude was much more severe. "And must the basest trade yield us relief?" sigh the destitute scholars in *The Return from Parnassus* when nothing but the theatre is left to them. Plays imitating Greek and Latin models, to be sure, were legitimate literary exercises, but those written for professional actors were in a class by themselves—"baggage books," Sir Thomas Bodley called them when he expressed the pious wish that none should ever be admitted to the great library he was founding at Oxford. Samuel Daniel, who did not hesitate to publish drama written according to classical models, took care that they should not be regarded as acting plays:

> God forbid I should my papers blot
> With mercenary lines. . . .
> No, no! My verse respects not Thames nor Theatres.
> *(Delia, Sonnet 53.)*

Even Shakespeare wrote about being

> Shamed by that which I bring forth
> And so should you, to love things nothing worth.
> (Sonnet 72.)

Profitable as they often were in the theatre, plays could add nothing to a man's literary reputation.

It is not surprising, therefore, to learn that, of the hundreds of plays written and produced on the Elizabethan stage, only a small fraction got into print. Exact statistics, of course, are not available, but a fair ratio of production to publication may perhaps be determined from figures derived from Philip Henslowe's *Diary*. Of over two hundred and eighty plays mentioned as having been commissioned or produced by the companies for which Henslowe served as banker between 1592 and 1603, only forty odd have come down to us.[1] When they were put into print, plays were frequently set forth without the author's name, and usually without the customary dedication. It was not until the beginning of the seventeenth century that dramatists began to oversee the publication of their plays, and even then there is some dubiety. Dedicating *The Widow's Tears* (1612), George Chapman wondered "if any work of this nature be worth the presenting," and the few plays which do bear dedications almost always express the conventional apology that the "greatest of the Cæsars," or the "great princes of Italy," had deemed it "no diminution of their greatness" to accept such trifles. Even Shakespeare's fellow-actors referred to plays we like to regard as immortal as "the meanest of things" which will be "made more precious when they are dedicated to Temples." "We cannot but know [your] dignity greater," they wrote to the Earls of Pembroke and Montgomery, "than to descend to the reading of these trifles."

THE RELUCTANCE TO PUBLISH PLAYS

There are several understandable reasons for the indifference—or the reluctance—which dramatists who valued their literary reputations felt about publishing. Plays were often hurriedly or carelessly written under pressure or in installments; while such work might do for the stage, it would need more than a little furbishing before it could be submitted to a critical reading audience. It is too much to expect that Thomas Heywood should have pride in seeing in print all of the two hundred and twenty plays in which he said he had a main finger, many of them "loosely written in taverns" on odd sheets of paper. Again, the Elizabethan custom of collaboration tended to destroy all feeling of individual ownership in a product. Even the best writers frequently worked with others in composing plays, and almost all freely adapted or appropriated old materials. The manuscript of *Sir Thomas More*, for example, is in five different hands. Shakespeare himself seems to have begun his career as a "play-doctor," as it would be called today; and some of the methods of Elizabethan playmaking suggest the co-operative collaborative efforts that Hollywood employs in manufacturing the modern movie. The desire to see such work in print must have been slight. Furthermore, according to Thomas Heywood, honest authors scorned "a double sale of their labours, first to the stage and after to the press" (*The Rape of Lucrece*, 1608), and appear to have been content with the single publication afforded by the stage. But a more important reason was the general belief that plays, unlike other written matter, depended for their effect upon actual stage representation. "Comedies are writ to be spoken, not read," wrote John Marston in the Preface to his *Parasitaster, or The Fawn* (1606); "remember the life of these

[1] E. K. Chambers, *The Elizabethan Stage*, III, 182.

things consists in action." In 1604, when he had printed his *Malcontent* to vindicate himself from charges of personal satire, he did so regretfully. "Only one thing afflicts me, to think that scenes, invented merely to be spoken, should be enforcively published to be read." Throughout Shakespeare's career, therefore, works meant to be read were literature; those designed for the mouths of actors were art of another kind, ephemeral products of no permanent literary value which required "the soul of lively action" to be fully effective. One need not conclude from these facts that all Elizabethan playwrights were careless workmen; they merely regarded themselves as artists of the theatre instead of men of letters.

Yet, throughout Shakespeare's lifetime and in the years following, interest in dramas as reading matter was growing. Plays were never an important commodity to the book-trade, but the new interest is reflected in the lengths —legitimate or not—to which publishers went to supply the demand. Quite probably, the authors and the players themselves were the last to perceive it. Thomas Middleton unquestionably expected a reading audience for *The Roaring Girl* (*c.* 1611) when he addressed an epistle to "the comic play readers" and described the piece as "good to keep you in an afternoon from dice at home in your chambers." But, according to Sir John Suckling,

> The first that broke silence was good old Ben,
> Prepar'd before with Canary wine,
> And he told them plainly he deserved the bays,
> For his were call'd Works, where others' were but Plays.
> ("A Sessions of the Poets" [*c.* 1637], in *Fragmenta Aurea*, 1646.)

As a scholar who took pains to observe the laws of dramatic composition exemplified by the ancients, Jonson regarded his dramatic efforts much more seriously than most. His labor was a notorious joke with his contemporaries. When he gathered his plays together in 1616, dignified the collection by the title *The Works of Ben Jonson*, and offered it to a reading public, there was an outburst of merriment that lasted a generation. "Pray, tell me, Ben," asked one of the wits,

> where does the mystery lurk,
> What others call a play you call a work? . . .
> The author's friend thus for the author says
> Ben's plays are works, when others' works are plays.
> (*Wit's Recreations, Selected from the
> Finest Fancies of Modern Muses*, 1640.)

Some writers were even indignant. Thomas Heywood wrote with scorn: "My plays are not exposed unto the world in volumes to bear the title of *works*, as others" (*The English Traveller*, 1633). Shakespeare's plays were looked upon in the same way.

One asked another what Shakespeare's works were worth, all being bound to-gether. He answered, not a farthing. "Not worth a farthing!" said he; "why so?" He answered that his plays were worth a great deal of money, but he never heard that his works were worth anything at all. (R. C., *Conceits, Clinches, Flashes and Whimsies,* 1639.)

The explanation is easily supplied: "Shakespeare's works? Why Shakespeare's works? . . . They are plays" (*Captain Underwit, c.* 1640).

However, the appearance of collected editions of Jonson (1616), Shake-speare (1623), Lyly (1632), Marston (1633), and Beaumont and Fletcher (1647), shows clearly that plays were beginning to have a double character, as productions to be seen and heard on the stage, and as dramatic poems to be enjoyed in reading. As early as 1610, in some verses commending "this sec-ond publication" of *The Faithful Shepherdess,* Beaumont warned his friend Fletcher that

> Your censurers now must have the quality
> Of reading, which I am afraid is more
> Than half your shrewdest judges had before.

When productions were prohibited on the stage altogether, the opinion naturally became more common. Commending the 1647 Folio of Beaumont and Fletcher, "John Web." wrote:

> What though distempers of the present age
> Have banish'd your smooth numbers from the stage?
> You shall be gainers by 't; it shall confer
> To th' making the vast world your theatre.
> The press shall give to ev'ry man his part,
> And we will all be actors, learn by heart
> Those tragic scenes and comic strains you writ.

But in Shakespeare's day, the critical judgment of a reader was hardly ex-pected.

ELIZABETHAN DRAMATIC MANUSCRIPTS

For students in even the elementary problems of Shakespeare's text, these conditions are of the greatest importance. It will be clear that only the un-usual Elizabethan play was originally designed for a reading audience, that most playwrights were indifferent about seeing their work in print, and that, having once disposed of the stage rights of a play, in most cases the author relinquished all claim to it. The theatrical company, in such cases, became the owner of the copyright. Shakespeare's plays, like the rest, were written primarily for the playhouse. It is now the belief of scholars that, when they were printed, the early editions were set up from his own autograph manu-script after it had seen service as prompt-copy. Further, it will also be clear that a hastily prepared manuscript, poorly written and imperfectly revised, might give a minimum of trouble to actors who used the author's work merely as a scenario, but it would be quite unsatisfactory if submitted to a printer as copy.

Unfortunately, though several of Shakespeare's signatures have been preserved, there is not one scrap of his autograph manuscript to give us an idea of how he wrote, unless, indeed, the three leaves of a manuscript play, *Sir Thomas More*, about which handwriting experts disagree, are in his hand. There is the testimony of Shakespeare's fellow-actors, however, that "his mind and hand went together, and what he thought he uttered with that easiness that we have scarce received from him a blot in his papers." This statement leads one to suppose that Shakespeare was a facile writer, but the plays themselves are ample evidence that he was far more painstaking than the average playwright. Shakespeare's papers must have been "writ fairer" than most. But whatever may have been the condition of the manuscripts Shakespeare submitted to the players, there must have been many a slip between what he originally wrote and what finally passed down to posterity in a printed text. What could happen will be clear if we describe the possible adventures of an Elizabethan dramatic manuscript between the time it left its author's hands and its appearance in print.

To be performed, a play had first to be "allowed" by the Master of the Revels or his deputy who served as censor and whose supervision must seem unreasonably severe to twentieth-century minds. Among the subjects which Elizabethan authorities considered dangerous were not only those likely to offend decency and good taste, like oaths and "unchaste, unseemly, and unshamefaced speeches," but also discussion of any subject likely to promote discontent or sedition, especially religion or politics. The Master of the Revels was originally a court officer—like Philostrate in *A Midsummer Night's Dream*—who planned and supervised royal entertainments and festivities. In 1581, when Elizabeth placed the control of the drama in the hands of this official, he assumed the right of censorship of all plays and required his license before any could be performed. During Shakespeare's lifetime, only two persons held the office: Sir Edmund Tilney, and his nephew Sir George Buc, who was appointed deputy in 1597 and allowed gradually to take over all of the duties of the office until Tilney's death in 1610, when he became Master. Buc was succeeded in 1622 by Sir Henry Herbert, who held office until the closing of the theatres in 1642 and assumed it again at the Restoration. All of Shakespeare's plays, therefore, were submitted to the perusal of either Tilney or Buc.

Their scrutiny of plays was more than casual. Realistic drama which inevitably held up a mirror to the age suffered most because the official mind usually cannot distinguish innocent humor from barbed satire. Romantic drama, on the other hand, was suspected of allegory. Complaints against misinterpretation and "mice-eyed decipherers" were frequent. "Now a man may not talk of a dog," wrote Thomas Nashe, "but it is surmised that he aims at him that giveth the dog in his crest [i. e., Shrewsbury]; he cannot name straw, but he must pluck a wheat-sheaf [i. e., Burghley] in pieces" (*Strange News*, 1592). "Let me but name bread, and they will interpret it to be the town of Bredan in the Low Countries" (*Christ's Tears*, 1594). Ben Jonson, too, girded at the ignorant "politic picklock" of his play:

> so solemnly ridiculous, as to search out who was meant by the gingerbread woman, who by the hobby-horse man, who by the costard-monger, nay, who by their wares. Or that will pretend to affirm in his own inspired ignorance what Mirror for Magistrates is meant by the justice, what great lady by the pig-woman, what concealed statesman by the seller of mousetraps. . . . As also such as shall . . . challenge the author of scurrility, because the language some-where savors of Smithfield. (*Bartholomew Fair*, 1614.)

In short, as Jonson wrote in the Preface to *Volpone* (1606), "Application is now grown a trade with many; and there are that profess to have a key for the deciphering of everything." Few officials were as sensibly liberal as Sir Francis Walsingham, who remarked about *A Play of Cards* (1582) which dealt with current abuses: "It is fit that they which do that they should not, should hear that they would not."

Censorial repression sometimes seriously affected a dramatist's conceptions. In the case of *Sir Thomas More*, mentioned above, Tilney insisted upon drastic revision.

> Leave out the insurrection wholly and the cause thereof and begin with Sir Thomas More at the Mayor's sessions, and a report afterwards of his good serv-ice done being Sheriff of London upon a mutiny against the Lombards, only by a short report and not otherwise at your own perils. E. TILNEY.

It is to be regretted that no such careful bookkeeper as Sir Henry Herbert held office during Shakespeare's time. His office-book is full of notes like the following:

> I took it ill and would have forbidden the play, but that Beeston [the company's manager] promised many things which I found fault withal should be left out, and that he would not suffer it to be done by the poet anymore, who deserves to be punished.

On one occasion, no less a person than King Charles curbed his severity, and Herbert stolidly recorded the event:

> The King is pleased to take *faith, death, slight* for asseverations and no oaths; to which I do humbly submit as my master's judgment—but, under favour, con-ceive them to be oaths, and enter them here to declare my opinion and sub-mission.

It is amusing to hear Shakespeare's characters evading the strict statute against oaths on the stage and swearing "By Janus" [the two-faced god] (*The Merchant of Venice*, I, i, 50, and *Othello*, I, ii, 53), and to hear some of Jonson's "swear upon the liturgy of Love, *Ovid de arte amandi*" (*The New Inn*, III, ii). But there is something like double injury in another of Sir Henry's entries:

> Received of Mr. Kirke, for a new play, which I burnt for the ribaldry and offense that was in it, £2.[2]

When he was satisfied, the censor wrote his license across the end of the manuscript in some such form as follows:

> This second Maiden's Tragedy (for it hath no name inscribed) may with the reformations be acted publicly. 31 October, 1611. G. BUC.

> This play, called The Seaman's Honest Wife, all the oaths left out in the action as they are crossed in the book and all other reformations strictly observed, may be acted, not otherwise. This 27 June, 1633. HENRY HERBERT.

Whether or not Shakespeare was obliged to revise any of his work because of the censor is not known, but his words in Sonnet 66 about "art made tongue-tied by authority," shows that he could not have forgotten official watchfulness. Plays for which there are parallel quarto and folio texts, however, reveal some interesting variations which may be traces of censorship. The deposition scene in *Richard II* (IV, i, 154–318), which was capable of misrepresentation, was not printed until after the death of Queen Elizabeth. There was some pruning of a few outspoken lines in *King Lear* (I, ii, 157–66; I, iv, 153–69; III, vi, 18–59); a jest on German and Spanish costume disappeared in the folio text of *Much Ado* (III, ii, 34–7), and another on the Scotch in *The Merchant of Venice* (I, ii, 83); and an unpatriotic sentiment was dropped from *2 Henry IV* (I, ii, 24 ff.). An effort, though a perfunctory one, was also made to excise the oaths before the First Folio was printed, or to substitute euphemisms for them. Some of these changes may represent ordinary revisions or cuts, but they may also represent the stricter surveillance over stage and press in the time of James I. Any serious suppression of what Shakespeare may have written, however, would not appear in any printed edition.

After a manuscript had been approved by the Office of the Revels, it was returned to the theatre's bookkeeper or prompter, whose business it was to prepare it for performance. If the author was a seasoned man of the theatre, like Shakespeare, there was probably less touching up necessary than in the case of an inexperienced writer. In any event, the bookkeeper looked over the script, correcting careless omissions, such as speech prefixes, revising

---

[2] See *The Dramatic Records of Sir Henry Herbert, Master of the Revels, 1623–73*, ed. Joseph Quincy Adams, New Haven (1917), pp. 23 and 39.

what he considered oversights in the text, clearing up obscure handwriting, and marking passages that might be cut. He called for music during the rest periods, if the performance was not to be continuous. He was especially concerned with stage directions, augmenting or revising those supplied by the author, and making them practicable for the stage. He called for stage noises at the proper places, made sure that necessary properties would not be overlooked, and sometimes gave directions for "business." In short, he made clear the way in which he thought the play ought to be staged.

Only a few Elizabethan prompt-copies have survived, but, in those which have, like Munday's *John a Kent and John a Cumber*, Massinger's *Believe as You List*, *The Second Maiden's Tragedy*, and *Sir Thomas More*, for example, the bookkeeper's annotations are easily recognizable by the difference in handwriting. A few examples from the manuscript of *Believe as You List* (1631), which is in Massinger's autograph, will make the bookkeeper's activities more clear. Generally, he revised directions freely, making them more specific and removing from them the author's explanations of his play. Notes about costume, such as "Stoics in philosophers' habits" or "Antiochus, habited like a king," were usually allowed to stand, but the national, social, or occupational status of characters held little interest for him. For the author's "Metellus, a proconsul of Lusitania, Sempronius a Centurion," he wrote simply, "Enter Metellus and Sempronius"; for "Berecinthius, a flamen, three Asian merchants," "Enter Berecinthius with three papers, and three merchants"; and for "Enter Cornelia and a Moor waiting woman," "Enter Cornelia and a Moor woman." Occasionally, if the author seemed needlessly literary, he simplified his direction, thus: "Enter Antiochus and guard," for "Enter Officers leading in Antiochus, his head shaved in the habit of a slave"; or "Enter Jailer with bread and water" for the author's "Enter Jailer, with brown bread and a wooden dish of water." He was more specific about supernumeraries than the author, often mentioning by name the actor assigned to the role. For the author's "Enter Prusias, Queen Philoxenes, Attendants," he wrote, "Enter Prusias, Queen Philoxenes: Rowland, William Mago, Mr. Balls, Nick, and Lady"; and for "Enter Servant with many swords," "Enter R. Baxter with Sword." He made notes about properties, to the author's "Enter Chrysalus," for example, adding "with a writing and pen." Frequently, he anticipated his needs, calling for entries a few lines earlier than the author, to give his actors time to walk to the front of the stage, and he made sure that his properties would be handy: "Table ready, and six chairs to set out" (75 lines early); "the great book of accounts ready" (135 lines early); "all the swords ready" (340 lines early). He also arranged to have his actors in readiness: "Mr. Hobs called up," "Gascoigne and Hubert below ready to open the trap door for Mr. Taylor," "Antiochus ready, under the stage," "Harry Wilson and boy ready for the song in the arras," the latter note appearing 55 lines before the direction, "The lute strikes and then the song." Sometimes he wrote his notes in the imperative: "Be ready, ye two merchants: William Pen, Curtis, and guard."[3] The document affords a very interesting glimpse behind scenes at an Elizabethan performance.

Other adventures of a playhouse manuscript may be more briefly summarized. When the bookkeeper was ready, he gave the revised manuscript to the company scrivener who copied out the parts for the individual actors. One such actor's part which has survived from the Elizabethan theatres was used by the famous Edward Alleyn of the Admiral's Men in the title role of Robert Greene's *Orlando Furioso*. Originally in the form of a long roll about six inches wide, it contains only the lines of Orlando with the cues from the preceding actor, and bears corrections, evidently in Alleyn's hand.[4] In addition, the prompter made a "plot" or brief summary of the action, characters, and properties required, and had it tacked up back-stage for reference. If, by any chance, the original prompt-book was lost, and no transcript was available, the players might find it necessary, with the aid of the "plot" to assemble as many of the players' parts as they could, and, with scissors and paste, reconstruct a continuous text, filling in from memory. From a note in Herbert's office-book, it is known that the "allowed book" of *The Winter's Tale* was missing in 1623 when the Folio was printed. Some scholars have sought in the theory of assembly from actors' parts explanations to textual problems in other plays as well.

Whatever may be true in such special cases, the effect of the use of the author's manuscript as a prompt-book in the theatre upon a play that found its way into print can be readily surmised. If such a script were first carefully edited, the prompter's notes would either be crossed out or translated into descriptive phrases. Frequently, however, the bookkeeper's annotations seem to have passed over untouched into the printed text. A few remnants of this sort of alteration have been distinguished in Shakespeare's plays, but there are doubtless more that cannot now be recognized. A seasoned playwright, thinking in terms of the theatre, would probably use stage language as naturally as the prompter and visualize his scenes on the stage as he penned them. But imperative directions, like "Away Tybalt," "Play music," and "Whistle boy" (Q2, *Romeo and Juliet*, III, i, 93; IV, iv, 20; V, iii, 18); "Lie down," "Sleep," "Wind horn" (Q1, *A Midsummer Night's Dream*, III, ii, 86; III, ii, 450; IV, i, 101); "Tear the supplication," "Sound trumpets," "Sound a parley" (*2 Henry VI*, I, iii, 42; III, ii, 14; IV, viii, 3)—to mention only a few—are characteristic prompter's notes. Sometimes the prompter's directions duplicate the author's, even in a printed text, as in *The Comedy*

---

[3] Ed. C. J. Sisson, Malone Society Reprints (1927).
[4] See W. W. Greg, *Dramatic Documents from the Elizabethan Playhouses*, 2 volumes, Oxford (1931).

of Errors (IV, iv, 149), where "Run all out" is followed in the next line by
"*Exeunt omnes*, as fast as may be, frighted." Occasionally, they even creep
into the dialogue itself. In *Coriolanus* (I, iv, 41 ff.), Marcius harangues the
Roman army before Corioli, ending with:

> If you'll stand fast, we'll beat them to their wives,
> As they us to our trenches follows.
> > *Another alarum and Marcius follows them to*
> > *the gates and is shut in.*
> So, now the gates are ope; now prove good seconds.
> 'Tis for the followers Fortune widens them,
> Not for the fliers. Mark me, and do the like.
> > *Enter the gate.*
> *1. Sol.* Fool-hardiness; not I.
> *2. Sol.*   Nor I.
> *3. Sol.* See, they have shut him in.

Both the word *follows* and the imperative direction *Enter the gate* may be
theatrical excrescences, supplied by the bookkeeper, either to clarify the
author's directions, or inserted to supply a deficiency and not removed when
the anticipatory description of the action was added by a reviser. Similarly,
in *A Midsummer Night's Dream* (I, i), two imperatives, "Stand forth Demetrius" and "Stand forth Lysander," which are printed in italics as stage
directions in both the quarto and the folios, have now been incorporated into
Ægeus's speech. "The competitors enter" (*Twelfth Night*, IV, ii, 11) or
"Ring the bell" (*Macbeth*, II, iii, 85) may be other instances of the sort.

Likewise, the occasional substitutions of actors' names for the roles they
played may have been made by the prompter rather than the author, particularly in the case of minor parts. Shakespeare himself may have been
responsible for the appearance of "Kemp" and "Cowley" instead of Dogberry
and Verges in both the quarto and the folio *Much Ado* (IV, ii), and for
"Will Kemp" instead of Peter in Q₂ of *Romeo and Juliet* (IV, v); (see above,
p. 159), but it may have been a prompter who wrote "Enter . . . Jack Wilson," instead of Balthazar, who sings a song in *Much Ado*, II, iii (folio).
"Bevis" and "John Holland" appear among the followers of Jack Cade in
2 Henry VI; "Gabriel" comes in for a messenger, and "Sinklo" and "Humphrey" for keepers in *3 Henry VI*; "Sinklo" appears again for a player in the
Induction to *The Taming of the Shrew* and for a beadle in *2 Henry IV*
(quarto); and "Tawyer with a trumpet before them" brings in the amateur
actors in *A Midsummer Night's Dream*. When a play was printed, the clumsy
manuscript might be discarded for a convenient type-copy, and into the
margins of this book the prompter might make his notes. If the play were
reprinted later from playhouse copy, like some of Shakespeare's in 1623,
these additions might also find their way into the new text. Hence, it will be

clear that many of the problems in Shakespeare's text may have originated in the adventures that befell his manuscripts in the playhouse.

"GOOD" AND "BAD" QUARTOS

By 1623, when the First Folio of Shakespeare was published, seventeen of his plays had already appeared in print in quarto,[5] thirteen of them in from two to six editions. Since, as we have seen, it is unlikely that the author himself would publish them, we may very well ask how it happened. The Preface to the First Folio mentions the abuse of earlier readers "with diverse stolen and surreptitious copies, maimed and deformed by the frauds of injurious impostors that expos'd them," and assures the purchaser of the volume that there he shall find the author's plays, "cur'd, and perfect of their limbs, and all the rest, absolute in their numbers as he conceived them." For a long time, the claims there advanced led to the belief that the Folio alone was authoritative, and that all of the Shakespearean quartos were poor texts, dishonestly obtained without the consent of the company for which Shakespeare was writing. It was assumed, therefore, that all of the quartos were fraudulently printed. Since most of the editions were regularly registered for publication with the proper authorities, the stationers seemed always on the side of the thief. Such unauthorized publications were called "pirated" editions. Early nineteenth-century scholarship is full of acrimony against these grizzled outlaws who so frequently made the greatest of playwrights their victim.

Modern scholars, however, lean to a more optimistic view of the quartos. Led by the late A. W. Pollard, whose *Shakespeare Folios and Quartos* (1909) and *Shakespeare's Fight with the Pirates and the Problems of the Transmission of His Text* (1917, revised 1920) are fundamental studies, they began an investigation of publishing conditions in Shakespeare's day and a more thorough examination of the quartos and folios themselves. As a result, the modern belief is that, far from being the ruling practice in the Elizabethan book-mart, piracy was exceptional, and that Elizabethan printers, taken as a whole, were neither exceptionally stupid nor exceptionally dishonest. Moreover, crediting printers and stationers with "a moderate degree of honesty

---

[5] *Quarto* and *folio* are printer's terms designating the size of books and referring to the manner of folding the sheets of printer's paper in their manufacture. In a *quarto*, eight pages are printed on a single sheet which is then folded twice to form a unit of *four* leaves, the volume being made by stitching together these "signatures" and trimming the top edge to release the pages. An average quarto edition of a play consists of about a hundred pages, approximately 6¾ x 8½ inches in size. Collected plays, however, require a larger type-page; hence, the printing forms are so arranged that the printer's paper is folded once through the middle, forming two leaves, or four pages. This is a *folio*. For strength in binding, however, three of these folded sheets are slipped inside of one another. The First Folio of Shakespeare consists of 454 leaves (908 pages) approximately 8½ x 13⅛ inches in size. Applied specifically to Elizabethan plays, the terms *quarto* and *folio* denote, respectively, simply editions of single plays or of collections.

which succeeds in maintaining itself when times are not too hard," and granting the owners of plays, in their turn, a moderate degree of common sense, "which, when one horse has been stolen from a stable in which others are still kept, sets about getting a new lock for the stable door," Mr. Pollard believed that piracy was combated with considerable success, and that pirated editions are few and readily distinguishable. It is too much to believe that a prominent company, like the Lord Chamberlain's-King's company, should within a few years have been victimized seventeen times in the case of one popular playwright. The general belief of scholars now is that only five Shakespeare quartos were unauthorized or "bad": *Romeo and Juliet* (1597), *Henry V* (1600), *The Merry Wives of Windsor* (1602), *Hamlet* (1603), and *Pericles* (1609). Recently, *The Taming of A Shrew* (1594), *The First Part of the Contention Betwixt the Two Famous Houses of York and Lancaster* (1594), and *The True Tragedy of Richard Duke of York* (1595), formerly looked upon as source plays, have been added to the list, but there is as yet no unanimity of agreement about them.[6] It is to these poor texts that the editors of the First Folio referred as "maimed and deformed."

The claims of the First Folio editors are not alone responsible for the exaggerated belief in piracy; there is other evidence as well. The publisher of *Troilus and Cressida* (1609), for example, commending the play to the reading audience as "never stal'd with the stage, never clapper-clawed with the palms of the vulgar," bids that audience "thank fortune for the scape it hath made amongst you. Since by the grand possesser's wills I believe you should have prayed for them rather than been prayed." This sounds very much like the public exultation of a successful pirate, and lends considerable color to a remark by Thomas Heywood in *The English Traveller* (1633) to the effect that the actors thought it "against their peculiar profit" to have plays come into print. Why? The theory has been that, if people could read a play for sixpence, they would not pay admission to the playhouse to see it. Such logic, however, could have appealed to the Elizabethans no more than it does to us today. Another suggestion is that, if plays were printed, rival companies might buy copies and act them on the stage. Yet, granting both the indifference of authors and the reluctance of some actors to put a play in print until its usefulness on the stage was over, it is too much to believe that all plays which came to the press did so in opposition to their owners' wishes, or that there were not many occasions when a company might authorize publication. Some editions, no doubt, were unauthorized, but it is inconceivable that all or even most of them could have been.

---

[6] See Peter Alexander, *"The Taming of A Shrew,"* *Times Literary Supplement* (September 16, 1926), and *Shakespeare's Henry VI and Richard III*, Cambridge (1929); and Madeleine Doran, *Henry VI, Parts II and III, Their Relation to The Contention and The True Tragedy*, University of Iowa Studies, Humanistic Series (1928).

AUTHORIZED PUBLICATION

Some of the occasions for authorized publication may be briefly described. (1) If a company disbanded, and an accounting was necessary, everything belonging to the troupe—playbooks, as well as costumes and properties— came into the market. Some of the most popular plays would interest other companies; some could be disposed of to a publisher. (2) When hard times or other adversity overtook a company, the actors might make ends meet by selling a few manuscripts to the printers, without relinquishing their stage- rights in them. (3) If a play fell foul of the authorities, or failed on the stage, the author might be permitted to publish his work to clear himself and his associates of serious charges, or to demonstrate to his readers how good a play it was. (4) If piracy had been committed, the company might authorize an edition to counteract it, or (5) as a special courtesy, return to a popular author the publishing rights to plays he had written. Instances of play publi- cation for all of the above reasons are plentiful in Elizabethan times.

In the case of the Shakespearean quartos, we can only surmise the reasons for publication. (1) If, as some scholars believe, Shakespeare first belonged to the Pembroke company, its bankruptcy in 1593 may account for the publication of the first of Shakespeare's quartos, *Titus Andronicus* (1594) and *The Taming of A Shrew* (1594), which bear on their title-pages the statement that they were acted by that company. At the same time, Lord Strange's Men acquired the stage-rights. (2) The building of the Globe in 1599 and the consequent need for ready money may help to account for the publication of five of Shakespeare's most popular plays in 1600: *The Mer- chant of Venice, Much Ado about Nothing, 2 Henry IV, A Midsummer Night's Dream*, and *Henry V*, the latter, however, in an imperfect text. (3) The unintentional offense to Lord Cobham through the misrepresentation of his heroic ancestor as Sir John Oldcastle, may account, not only for the change of the name to Falstaff, but also for the publication of *1 Henry IV* (1598), the harmless play in which he appears. (4) Authentic texts of *Romeo and Juliet* (1599) and *Hamlet* (1604–05) were issued to counteract the im- perfect ones published previously; it is possible that the description of *Love's Labor's Lost* (1598) as "newly corrected and augmented" may refer to a similar correction of a "bad" quarto which has not come down to us. (5) Finally, although as a member of the company, Shakespeare must have given his con- sent in these cases, and perhaps even have overseen the printing, it cannot be said that the publication of any of his plays was permitted for the honor of the author. The publication of the First Folio is significant in this connec- tion. "It had been a thing, we confess, worthy to have been wished," wrote Shakespeare's fellows, "that the author himself had liv'd to have set forth and overseen his own writings. But since it hath been ordain'd otherwise, and he by death departed from that right," his friends made it "the office of their care." Thus, what would have been a courtesy to the living became an honor to the dead.

PIRATICAL PUBLICATION

But what about piratical publishing and the causes and practice of piracy in Shakespeare's day? Obviously, piracy was fostered by the age's indefinite, medieval ideas concerning literary property, except as it involved a commercial bookseller. To us moderns, copyright means protection for the author, the publisher being only his agent. In Shakespeare's day, the only recognized property rights in a book were those of the publisher who received from the Honourable Company of Stationers regulating the booktrade protection against any infringement by a trade competitor. No questions seem to have been asked as to how the manuscript was obtained. In practice, piracy seems to have been conducted in numerous ways, some of which may be described.

(1) A pirate might procure a copy of a desired book which, in medieval fashion, was circulating privately in manuscript. Gentlemen might disdain publication, but they frequently permitted copies of their writings to be made for friends who, in turn, might have copies made. It is possible that one of these copies might fall into a printer's hands. Sidney's work first found its way into print by this course, and Nashe, Lodge, Daniel, Bacon, and others complain of the theft or illicit sale of their work. Shakespeare's "sugar'd sonnets" also circulated among his private friends as early as 1598 and were piratically published from a private transcript in 1609. A few of them had previously been picked up and printed in *The Passionate Pilgrim* "by W Shakespeare" (1599), and Thomas Heywood stated that Shakespeare "was much offended with M. Jaggard that altogether unknown to him presumed to make so bold with his name." Plays, too, were sometimes copied, according to the Preface to the Beaumont and Fletcher Folio (1647); indeed, some of the dramatic manuscripts which have been preserved may have been private, and not playhouse, copies. But plays, no doubt, were less frequently transcribed than writings of other kinds. Whether any of the Shakespearean quartos were published from private transcripts is not known, but *Troilus and Cressida* (1609) may represent such a text. Copy so obtained, however, would not of necessity be "bad."

(2) A hireling of the company might turn pirate and, to obtain extra pocket money, supply a printer with copy. Years before Shakespeare's time, a printer issued *Gorboduc* "exceedingly corrupted," having succeeded in "getting a copy thereof at some young man's hand that lacked a little money and much discretion." The young man may very well have been one of the actors in the play. The pirate-actor might not, of course, have access to

the authoritative prompt-copy, but he would have his own part, a minor one, perhaps, and he might be able to obtain the parts of one or more of his fellows. He would have been present at rehearsals and at performances; with his actors' parts as a basis, he would be able by his memory and invention to patch up a text that would satisfy the printer. The text might be spotty as to correctness, best in the pirate's own part and in those interwoven with his own. Dr. W. W. Greg has made it seem probable that the 1602 *Merry Wives of Windsor*, formerly thought to have been a rude sketch of a play later revised, was obtained in this way, the pirate being the actor who played Mine Host of the Garter.[7] More recently, the *First Part of the Contention* and *The True Tragedy*, formerly thought of as a two-part play revised by Shakespeare as *2* and *3 Henry VI*, have been explained as "bad" quartos obtained from pirate actors.[8] A similar suggestion has been made with regard to the 1603 *Hamlet*.[9]

(3) The pirate might obtain his copy by sending a stenographer or a memorizer to the theatre to take down the play. Thomas Heywood complained that, by this method, some of his dramas reached his readers in mangled form. His *If You Know Not Me* was so popular, he said, that the audiences

> Did throng the seats, the boxes, and the stage
> So much, that some by stenography drew
> The plot, put it in print, scarce one word true.

Other plays of his, he wrote in the Preface to *The Rape of Lucrece* (1608), came into the printer's hands in corrupt versions "copied only by the ear." To take down an entire play by shorthand and escape detection could not have been easy. Elizabethan gentlemen, to be sure, were accustomed to filling their notebooks with brilliant sayings from plays, but anyone constantly writing during a performance would have attracted attention. Yet some of the "bad" Shakespeare quartos, like *Romeo* (1597), *Hamlet* (1603), and *Pericles* (1609), give support to the theory that they were pirated by stenography.

The stigmata of a stenographic text may be surmised:

(a) The stage directions would not be those of the author or the prompter, but those of an eye-witness who described what he saw on the stage. Thus, in the 1597 *Romeo and Juliet*, there is inserted into a conversation between

---

[7] *Shakespeare's Merry Wives of Windsor 1602*, ed. W. W. Greg, Oxford (1910) (Tudor and Stuart Library).

[8] Peter Alexander, *Shakespeare's Henry VI and Richard III*, Cambridge (1929).

[9] J. Dover Wilson, "The Copy for *Hamlet* 1603" and "The *Hamlet* Transcript," *The Library*, 3rd Series, July and October (1918); and R. Crompton Rhodes, *Shakespeare's First Folio*, Oxford (1923). The pirate is believed to have been the actor who played the role of Marcellus.

Old Capulet and Paris the direction: "Paris offers to go in, and Capulet calls him again." When Juliet pleads with her parents, there is a note: "She kneels down"; when the nurse leaves after advising Juliet to forget Romeo and marry Paris, "She looks after Nurse"; and when Juliet finally drinks the potion, "She falls upon the bed within the curtains." In the 1603 *Hamlet*, there are these descriptive stage directions: "Enter the ghost in his night gown," "Enter Ophelia playing on a lute, with her hair down singing," "They catch one another's rapiers, and both are wounded. Laertes falls down, the Queen falls down and dies," and instead of "Enter Osric," "Enter a Braggart Gentleman." None of these directions appears in later editions.

(b) The strain of note-taking also leaves its marks on the text. The writer, being fresh at the beginning, commences well, but toward the end tends to flag.

(c) Conditions of the theatre might also leave their mark. Not all actors speak with a distinctness sufficient for note-taking; laughter or commotion might drown out the words. Thus, phrases might be misheard, passages omitted, and points lost. Bits of actor's "gag," not supplied by the author, might creep in. In *Romeo and Juliet* (1597), the little word "Catso" has intruded (II, ii, 21), and in *Hamlet* (1603), "O I have it" is introduced just before the prince remembers the rugged Pyrrhus speech (II, ii). There is also some feeble clowning attached to the advice to the players (III, ii) and in the grave-diggers scene, which is very poorly rendered, such phrases appear as "Y'are gone, go, y'are gone, sir."[10]

No one theory, however, quite satisfactorily explains how plays were pirated. The condition of some texts even suggests that a combination of methods was employed.

But had theatrical companies no means of protecting themselves against the Jolly Rogers of the book-trade or of redress if their property had been stolen? The general belief is that they could expect little from the authorities controlling printing. If the company had reason to fear the piracy of a popular play, it could do little except forestall the thief by selling the play to a printer. Such apprehension may explain the publication of *Richard II* (1597), *Richard III* (1597), and several others. If a play had already been pirated, little could be done to salve the honor of the troupe except issue an authoritative edition. A letter from the Lord Chamberlain, Philip, Earl of Pembroke and Montgomery, to the Stationers' Company, dated June 18, 1637, suggests, however, that in Caroline times the players could rely upon some protection. The note concerns some play-books belonging to the King's and Queen's Men which "having been lately stolen or gotten from them by indirect means, are now attempted to be printed." It recalls an earlier letter

---

[10] See *The Tragicall Historie of Hamlet Prince of Denmarke 1603*, ed. G. B. Harrison, Bodley Head Quartos, London (1923).

written by his brother and predecessor concerning the theft of the players' books,

> by means whereof, not only they themselves had much prejudice, but the books much corruption, to the injury and disgrace of the authors,

and directs the Master and the Wardens to permit no plays to be published without a written certificate from the managers of the companies. Such a course "can be hurtful unto none but such as are about unjustly to prevail themselves of others' goods." Whether it was possible earlier to call in such aid is not known. It is not likely, however, that the players could have troubled a busy court officer about every single piracy.

In Shakespeare's day, the players probably had to be content with indirect official protection by having a printer they could trust act as their agent and obtain the copyright to a play they wished especially to protect without actually publishing the play. The printer who acted for the Shakespearean company was James Roberts, who enjoyed the monopoly of printing play-bills, and who would not deliberately endanger a friendly and profitable relationship by a little piracy on the side. In the Stationers' Register there are a number of provisional entries like the following:

> 1598. xxij Julij. James Roberts. Entered for his copy under the hands of both the wardens a book of the *Merchant of Venice*, or otherwise called the *Jew of Venice*, provided, that it be not printed by the said James Roberts or any other whatsoever without license first had from the right honorable the Lord Chamberlain.

> [1600]   4 Augusti   *As You Like It*, a Book [i. e., a playbook]; *Henry the Fifth*, a Book; *Every Man in His Humour*, a Book; *The Comedy of Much Ado about Nothing*, a Book: to be staied.

> 1603. 7 February. Master Roberts. Entered for his copy in full court holden this day to print when he hath gotten sufficient authority for it, the book of *Troilus and Cressida* as it is acted by my Lord Chamberlain's Men.

Other companies apparently did the same. In 1600, the Admiral's Men borrowed the unusually large sum of forty shillings from Henslowe "to give unto the printer to stay the printing of *Patient Grissell.*"

Mere entry, however, does not seem to have afforded very effective protection. Of the Shakespearean plays so stayed, *The Merchant of Venice* and *Much Ado about Nothing* were later issued in authentic texts; *As You Like It* remained unprinted until 1623; but *Troilus and Cressida* was issued by another printer in spite of the "grand possessors" in 1609, and *Henry V* appeared in a mangled text printed in the very year in which it was stayed. *Hamlet*, entered to Roberts without condition in 1602, was pirated by another in 1603, and *Pericles*, entered unconditionally to Edward Blount in 1608, was pirated by another in 1609. And what could happen, once a printed play became derelict by its owner's going out of business without disposing of his copyrights, was various.

AN ATTEMPTED SHAKESPEAREAN COLLECTION IN 1619

One interesting example of what could occur concerns an attempted collection of Shakespearean or pseudo-Shakespearean work in quarto size by the stationer Thomas Pavier in 1619. The enterprise appears to have been discreditable from both a literary and a commercial point of view. As a beginning, Pavier owned the copyright of five plays:

1. *A Yorkshire Tragedy*, issued by him in 1608 as "by William Shakespeare."

2. *Sir John Oldcastle*, issued by him in 1600 as acted by the Admiral's Men. This play, for the writing of which Henslowe advanced money to Munday, Drayton, Wilson, and Hathway, was an answer to *Henry IV* in which Falstaff was originally called Oldcastle.

3 and 4. *The First Part of the Contention Betwixt the Two Famous Houses of York and Lancaster*, and its sequel, *The True Tragedy of Richard Duke of York*, originally published in "bad" texts in 1594 and 1595, and now issued by Pavier, who acquired the copyright in 1602, as *The Whole Contention between the Two Famous Houses, Lancaster and York . . . Divided into Two Parts: And Newly Corrected and Enlarged*. Written by William Shakespeare, Gent.

5. *Henry V*, originally issued in a "bad" text in 1600 and now reprinted by Pavier, who had acquired the copyright in 1600 and issued a reprint in 1602.

To these texts which Pavier owned he added several others. From Nathaniel Butter he apparently got permission to appropriate *King Lear*, originally published in 1608, and from Arthur Johnson *The Merry Wives of Windsor*, issued in a "bad" text in 1602. In addition, he picked up *Pericles*, which had been published in 1609 without license from the Stationers' Company, and *The Merchant of Venice* and *A Midsummer Night's Dream*, which he seized as derelicts of the trade, since their original publishers were dead and the plays had not been reprinted since 1600. These ten plays constituted Pavier's assembly of material, for the printing of which he engaged William Jaggard. It was, of course, nothing to either of them that they were reprinting poor texts and ascribing to Shakespeare plays that were not his.

The subsequent history of the venture and its final abandonment may be briefly told. Less than half way through, when only the *Contention* and *Pericles* had been put through the press, Pavier, for some reason, changed his plans. Perhaps the King's Men somehow learned of the scheme and appealed to the Lord Chamberlain in behalf of themselves and of the dead poet. Whatever the reason, Pavier either was forced to give up his venture or convinced of the prudence of such a step. But, being a frugal man who did not wish to lose his outlay, he determined not to issue a collected volume, but to dispose of the plays quietly as single quartos. Some risk was apparently involved, because Pavier made careful efforts to cover his tracks by using false dates and fraudulent imprints, even on the plays to which he had a legal right. On all but *Henry V* he conspicuously displayed the name of Shakespeare as the author; to the *Whole Contention* he gave no date at all; to *Sir John Oldcastle, The Merchant of Venice, A Midsummer Night's Dream* and *King Lear*, he gave the dates of their original publication, 1600 and 1608; and to *Henry V* he gave a purely fictitious date, 1608. Only *A Yorkshire Tragedy, The Merry Wives,* and *Pericles,* are correctly dated 1619. *The Merchant of Venice* and *A Midsummer Night's Dream* he issued as from the press of James Roberts, who had printed at least one of them and who was now dead. To *King Lear* and *The Merry Wives* he assigned the imprints of their rightful owners. On the rest there is merely "Printed for T. P." without the customary full address where the volumes could be purchased.

So successful was Pavier's concealment of his misdemeanors that the facts were not discovered until 1906–10, and then only after the most amazing piece of literary detective work on record. An account of this bibliographical problem would be too detailed and technical here, but the clues involve (1) evidence that these plays were frequently bound together in the seventeenth century to make a single volume; (2) continuity of the printer's signatures in the *Contention* and *Pericles;* (3) identical watermarks in the paper upon which the quartos bearing different dates were printed; (4) identification of the decorative devices and of the type as belonging to the printer William Jaggard and in use around 1619; and, most important of all, (5) the similarity in style of the various title-pages and the identity of common parts of certain title-pages bearing differing dates, as shown by recurrent flaws in the letters, by accurate measurements, and by composite photography. Pavier's editions, however, did sufficient damage. On his authority apparently, *A Yorkshire Tragedy* and *Sir John Oldcastle* were admitted to the Third Folio (1664), when several plays ascribed to Shakespeare were added, and because of him generations of scholars puzzled over problems falsely raised by apparently duplicate editions of *A Midsummer Night's Dream* and *The Merchant of Venice* in 1600, and of *King Lear* in 1608. Only one collection of the ten plays in seventeenth-century binding is still in existence. Just three hundred years after Pavier's projected collection, in 1919, it was sold for $100,000 to the late Henry Clay Folger, and is now in the Shakespeare Library in Washington.

THE FIRST FOLIO OF 1623

The Pavier venture of 1619 must have made clear, if nothing had before, that a reading public was ready for a collected edition of Shakespeare's plays.

In 1623, John Heminge and Henry Condell, the only survivors of the little band of players Shakespeare had joined thirty years before, gathered his plays together and published them in one volume. They did not claim to be editors of the plays in the ordinary modern sense of the word. "We have but collected them," they wrote, "and done an office to the dead . . . without ambition either of self-profit or fame, only to keep the memory of so worthy a friend and fellow alive as was our Shakespeare." Their ideal, as it appears from the Preface, was to present *all* of the plays of the author so far as it was humanly possible for them to succeed. The thirty-six plays which they selected for inclusion in the volume form the basis of the Shakespeare "canon," or body of his authoritative work, and the texts selected, even if they sometimes leave something to be desired, were the best that could be obtained.

Consideration of their editorial task will make clear some of their problems. The materials they had at their disposal could roughly be divided into two classes: (a) plays which had never been in print before, and (b) plays which had been issued in quarto. In the case of the first class their duty was comparatively simple, and the bulk of the material makes evident the debt posterity owes these editors. For twenty of Shakespeare's plays, the First Folio is the only text that has come down to us: nine comedies—*The Tempest, The Two Gentlemen of Verona, Measure for Measure, The Comedy of Errors, As You Like It, The Taming of the Shrew,*[11] *All's Well that Ends Well, Twelfth Night,* and *The Winter's Tale;* five histories—*King John, 1, 2, 3 Henry VI,* and *Henry VIII,* and six tragedies—*Coriolanus, Timon of Athens, Julius Cæsar, Macbeth, Antony and Cleopatra,* and *Cymbeline.* Copy for these plays was doubtless supplied by the prompt-books of the Globe. Many were probably Shakespeare's original manuscripts; others, notably *Macbeth,* may have been cut-down acting versions, or, like *The Winter's Tale,* where the allowed book was missing, some other substitute for the "first original." Taken together, this probably was not very clean copy for the printers, but it represented the most authentic, perhaps the only, text available.

The second body of material presented more difficulties. Here were sixteen plays, *Pericles* being omitted, in forty-five different editions, the texts ranging from the authoritative form of *Romeo and Juliet* (1599) and *Hamlet* (1604-05) to corrupted, mangled things like *Henry V* (1600) and *The Merry Wives* (1602). For all of the really "bad" quartos, except the last two named, there had been published a reasonably accurate text. The simplest

[11] Unless, indeed, *The Taming of A Shrew* and *The Contention Betwixt the Two Famous Houses of York and Lancaster* and its sequel *The True Tragedy of Richard Duke of York,* issued previously, represent "bad" texts of *The Shrew* and *2* and *3 Henry VI.*

procedure for the Folio editors would have been to purchase a carefully selected set of quartos and reprint them. In some cases, of course, the compact, legible quartos had long since replaced Shakespeare's manuscripts for use in the theatre, and, hence, represented the best substitute that could be found for the original versions. Yet in only a very few instances can it be shown that they followed this simple expedient. *Love's Labor's Lost* and *The Merchant of Venice* were apparently reprinted without significant change from the good quartos of 1598 and 1600; *Romeo and Juliet* from the last quarto (1609), itself but one step removed from an authentic text printed from prompt-copy. *A Midsummer Night's Dream*, strangely enough, seems to have been reprinted from Pavier's falsely dated issue of 1619, which was a reprint, however, of a "good" quarto. Perhaps no other was readily available. In all other cases, the editors either printed from an independent source, corrected their quartos by more accurate copy, or reprinted quartos that had been used as prompt-copy. Hence, while in strictness it cannot be said that Heminge and Condell justified their claim of presenting Shakespeare's plays according to "the true original copies," or "absolute in their numbers as he conceived them," their text probably comes as near to that ideal as was possible.

Having assembled the copy, the editors classified the plays as *Comedies, Histories,* and *Tragedies,* and arranged the texts in these groups in what seemed to them a suitable order. They supplied an epistle dedicatory addressed "To the Most Incomparable Pair of Brethren, William, Earl of Pembroke, &c., Lord Chamberlain to the King's most Excellent Majesty, and Philip, Earl of Montgomery, &c., Gentleman of his Majesty's Bed-Chamber," and their "singular good lords," as well as an address "To the great Variety of Readers," both signed by John Heminge and Henry Condell. Ben Jonson contributed his lines "To the Memory of my Beloved, the Author, Mr. William Shakespeare, and What he hath Left Us," and Hugh Holland, L. Digges, and I. M. also submitted commendatory verses. For the title-page, Martin Droeshout, a young Flemish engraver, was engaged to prepare a portrait, while opposite to it, B. I[onson], in a graceful epigram, bade the reader seeking the real Shakespeare "look not on his picture, but his book." How much other editorial work was expended upon the copy must be a matter of conjecture. To manage the business side of the project and the distribution of the book, the actors formed a syndicate composed of William Jaggard and Edward Blount, prominent printer and bookseller, respectively, and the principal controllers of the copyrights of those plays that had already been printed in quarto. It was "at the charges of W. Jaggard, Ed. Blount, I. Smithweek, and W. Aspley" that the book was printed.

The First Folio of Shakespeare is not a notable specimen of book-making; the age knew volumes that were handsomer and more correctly printed, even

Mr. WILLIAM
SHAKESPEARES
COMEDIES,
HISTORIES, &
TRAGEDIES.
Publiſhed according to the True Originall Copies.

LONDON
Printed by Iſaac Iaggard, and Ed. Blount. 1623.

Title-page of the First Folio, 1623

if the Puritan William Prynne did grumble that "Shakespeare's plays are printed in the best crown paper, far better than most Bibles." It has been estimated that there are no less than 3500 palpable errors in the book and 2000 minor ones. Whatever else is true, however, the First Folio of Shakespeare represents the greatest contribution in a single volume to secular literature, and next to the Gutenberg Bible the most sought after by collectors. How large the original edition was can only be estimated; 500 to 1000 copies is the figure usually accepted by scholars. The latest census accounts for around two hundred existing exemplars, most of them in England and America; seventy-nine copies are in the Folger Library alone. Some years ago a copy brought £17,000. The original price was about £1.

Textual criticism may be said to have begun almost immediately. By 1632, the time was ripe for a second edition. The Second Folio was a reprint of the First, column for column, but some correction and emendation of what seemed to the editor the most glaring blunders were attempted. And, in compensation, the Second Folio contributed its own quota of printer's errors. So, in turn, the Third Folio (in two issues of 1663 and 1664, the latter adding seven plays formerly attributed to Shakespeare), reproduced the Second, and the Fourth (1685) the Third. Each successive printer, motivated by a real desire to improve the text and working by his best lights, corrected the spelling, the punctuation, and occasionally the wording of the original, and each added a few more errors to the accumulation that had been growing.[12] It is too much to expect collation of texts in the seventeenth century or any scientific textual criticism, though the editors meant well. But at each stage Shakespeare's text receded farther from the original, and the authority of the First Folio was gradually lost sight of. Even the Bodleian Library, which received a copy in sheets direct from the publishers, sold its worn copy of the First Folio as soon as it received a fresh copy of the Third.

At the beginning of the eighteenth century, when a new edition was called for, the vogue of the portly folio had passed, and Shakespeare appeared in handy library editions of several calf-bound volumes with biographical introductions and notes. Shakespeare's earliest editors include: Nicholas Rowe (1709–10), Alexander Pope (1723–5), Lewis Theobald (1733), Sir Thomas Hanmer (1743–4), William Warburton (1747), Samuel Johnson (1765), George Steevens (1766), Edward Capell (1768), and Edmund Malone (1790). Most of these editions were reprinted several times before being outmoded. But today this early scholarship leaves much to be desired. As Dr. R. B. McKerrow has remarked, "It simply never occurred to men like Pope, Theobald, and Capell that the Shakespeare quartos were not in the same position with respect to the author's original text as the classical manuscripts

[12] See Matthew W. Black and Matthias A. Shaaber, *Shakespeare's Seventeenth Century Editors, 1632–1685*, New York, Modern Language Association (1937).

were, in that they did not represent ends of separate lines of descent from it, but in most cases successive members of a single line."[13] Gradually, however, an editorial method was evolved, and scholars depended less upon conjecture and more upon collation of texts. Gradually, also, the Shakespeare quartos were seen to bear another relation to what the author wrote than variant manuscripts of a classical author.

MODERN EDITIONS OF SHAKESPEARE

Modern editions of Shakespeare differ from the quartos and folios in five essential ways: (1) by the modernization of spelling and punctuation, (2) by the correction or emendation of typographical and other errors, (3) by the provision of lists of *dramatis personæ*, (4) by the division of the plays into acts and scenes, and (5) by the insertion or alteration of the stage directions for the convenience of the reader. Except in the cases of (1) and (2), the labor involved was largely that of bringing all of the plays into conformity with the peculiarities of some. Actor lists, complete divisions into acts and scenes, and fairly elaborate stage directions do exist in the First Folio, but they are the exception rather than the rule. Counterparts to the lists of characters found in all modern editions are present in only seven of the thirty-six plays which make up the First Folio, and in each case they appear at the end of the play, not at the beginning where they would be most useful to readers. It is possible that "The Actors' Names" may have a playhouse origin, for the brief descriptions placed opposite the characters, such as "Gonzalo, an honest old Councellor," "Speed, a clownish servant," "Lucio, a fantastic," or "Roderigo, a gull'd gentleman," read like brief reminders to the producer of the type of player required for each part. Division into acts and scenes also appears in the First Folio, although not one of the quartos issued during Shakespeare's lifetime had any formal division. However, only seventeen plays in the First Folio are completely divided into acts and scenes, twelve are divided only into acts, and seven are left either altogether undivided or only partially divided.

With regard to stage directions, there is even more variation. The range is from the elaborate masque- or pageant-like directions of *The Tempest* and *Henry VIII* to plays where little besides bare entrances and exits are noted. Modern stage directions to Shakespeare's plays usually do little more than supply the formal direction for the action implied in the dialogue. In only two plays in the Folio is anything said of setting. That of *The Tempest* is briefly described as "an uninhabited island," and that of *Measure for Measure*, "Vienna." All modern editions since Nicholas Rowe's (1709) have indicated the setting, not only for each play, but also for each scene. In each case it has

[13] *The Treatment of Shakespeare's Text by His Earlier Editors*, British Academy lecture (1933), p. 21.

been derived from the text. The same is true of the modern elaboration of directions for the action. It takes no great ingenuity to express what the dialogue implies. Unfortunately, however, all of these alterations, made in the eighteenth century, have become traditional, in spite of the fact that they are the result of regarding plays written for the Elizabethan platform stage as if they had been written for the scenic stage of fifty years after the Restoration.

THE CHRONOLOGY OF SHAKESPEARE'S PLAYS

Few modern students of Shakespeare are content to read his plays as single works; they wish to see them in relation to one another and to possible external events, so that they may observe the development of the author's style, the growth of his artistic powers, and the influences that helped to mould his mind and art. Hence, numerous attempts have been made to arrange the plays in the order in which they were composed. Yet, important as it is, Shakespeare chronology is one of the most difficult of scholarly problems. In many cases, lack of sufficient data makes it impossible to determine the order of succession; most of the dates usually assigned to individual dramas are conjectural, and few scholars have dared to be dogmatic in their opinions. For the works of modern authors, information to answer a question of this kind is usually both accessible and exact; in the case of Shakespeare and his fellow-Elizabethans, it is almost wholly lacking. The traditional order of the First Folio which classifies the plays according to type and places *The Tempest* first and *Cymbeline* last, while adhered to in many modern editions, is now universally abandoned as of no chronological significance. But, at the same time, any rearrangement must rest upon uncertain and casually recorded data, much of which is subject to individual interpretation.

A description of the sources of information from which students must make deductions will make clear both the nature of the evidence and the perplexities it presents.

(1) *Records of performance* are but few in number and, at best, usually furnish only a date before which a play was composed without any information as to how long before. Thus, the account-book or *Diary* of Philip Henslowe records the performance of "hary the vj" on March 3, 1592, and "titus and ondronicus" on January 23, 1594—perhaps Shakespeare's *1 Henry VI* and *Titus Andronicus*. The *Gesta Grayorum* (1594), an account of the revels of the law students at Gray's Inn on December 28, 1594, mentions a performance of *The Comedy of Errors;* John Manningham, a student in the Middle Temple describes in his *Diary* a production of *Twelfth Night* there on February 2, 1602; Thomas Platter, a Swiss visitor to London, records in his diary seeing a play on *Julius Cæsar* on September 21, 1599; the first edition of *Love's Labor's Lost* (1598) mentions a performance at court the previous

Christmas; and an account of the burning of the Globe Theatre, June 29, 1613, refers to *Henry VIII* as a new play. The subject is complicated by the fact that the Revels Accounts of court performances, which record productions of *Othello* and *Measure for Measure* in 1604 and *The Tempest* in 1611, as well as the *Diary* of Dr. Simon Forman, which describes performances of *Macbeth* in 1610, *The Winter's Tale* in 1611, and *Cymbeline* at some indeterminate date, have been seriously suspected of forgery.

(2) *Literary allusions* constitute another body of evidence. Of these the most important is Francis Meres's eulogy of Shakespeare in *Palladis Tamia* (1598) in which there is specific mention of twelve plays: *The Two Gentlemen of Verona*, *The Comedy of Errors*, *Love's Labor's Lost*, *Love's Labor's Won* (unidentified), *A Midsummer Night's Dream*, *The Merchant of Venice*, *Richard II*, *Richard III*, *Henry IV*, *King John*, *Titus Andronicus*, and *Romeo and Juliet*—all of which must have been in existence before that date. There is also an allusion to Talbot, a character Shakespeare introduced into *1 Henry VI*, in Thomas Nashe's *Pierce Penniless* (1592); a quotation from *Julius Cæsar* in Ben Jonson's *Every Man out of His Humour* (1599); and a note about *Hamlet* made by Gabriel Harvey some time between 1598 and 1601. Like the notices of performances, these allusions and numerous others are uncertainly Shakespearean and, at best, furnish only a terminal date.

(3) *References in the plays to datable historical events* may also assist in establishing the dates of the plays. Shakespeare, however, was sparing in topical allusions, and passages thought to refer to current happenings or controversies must be interpreted cautiously. There is no subject about which there is less agreement among scholars. Yet the chorus which introduces the last act of *Henry V* alludes clearly to the campaign of the Earl of Essex in Ireland, and thus fixes the date, if not of the entire play, at least of the performance at which that prologue was used between March 27 and September 28, 1599. In *Hamlet*, also, there is an allusion to the revival of the child actors (1599); in *Macbeth*, to the house of Stuart; and, perhaps, in *A Midsummer Night's Dream*, to the baptism ceremonies of Prince Henry of Scotland (1594). The statement on the title-page of the first edition of *Romeo and Juliet* (1597) that the play was acted "by the right honourable the Lord Hunsdon his servants" dates, not the play, but its publication. Shakespeare's company was known as Lord Hunsdon's Men from July 23, 1596 to March 17, 1597.

(4) *Links between the plays themselves* furnish a few clues. The most marked, of course, are those in plays that constitute a series, like the histories, especially the continuity of *Richard II*, *1* and *2 Henry IV*, and the author's promise at the end of the last-named play to continue the story in *Henry V*. Thus, the chronological sequence for four plays is established. Robin Good-

fellow's pointed assurance in *A Midsummer Night's Dream* that "naught shall go ill, Jack shall have Jill," likewise seems to link the play with *Love's Labor's Lost*, which "doth not end like an old play, Jack hath not Jill." If so, only the order of composition is determined, not definite dates for either play.

(5) *Dates of publication* on title-pages or dates of registration in the books of the Stationers' Company are less valuable for the study of Shakespearean chronology than might at first be supposed, because, as we have seen, Elizabethan plays were almost never written for publication and those which "escaped into print" usually did so after their popularity on the stage had declined. Yet, for several of Shakespeare's dramas, no more reliable information exists, among them *Richard III* (1597), *Romeo and Juliet* (1597), *Richard II* (1597), *1 Henry IV* (1598), *Much Ado* (1600), and *The Merry Wives of Windsor* (1602). *As You Like It* was entered for publication in 1600 and *Antony and Cleopatra* in 1608, but neither appeared in print before 1623. *Troilus and Cressida* was registered in 1603, but no edition earlier than 1609 is known. The date of licensing or of publication, therefore, though exact in itself, fixes little more than a downward limit, but it is sometimes helpful.

(6) *Variations of style and versification,* as well as other forms of "internal evidence," are the least reliable types of evidence for dating plays. Great caution must be exercised in drawing inferences from them. As Shakespeare grew in experience as an author, it is logical to assume that his style of writing reflected his intellectual development, that his taste improved, that his knowledge of life, and, hence, his ability to study character, deepened, and his technique generally became increasingly individual. Especial attention has been given to the variations that can be noticed in Shakespeare's blank verse, and its growth from a stereotyped to a flexible medium. Certain broad characteristics of Shakespeare's development as an artist can, of course, be recognized, but, obviously, a detailed literary and psychological analysis of his work is possible only *after* the proper order of his plays has been established, and not *before.* Much has been made of the comparative frequency of rhyme and of prose as an indication, respectively, of early or late work. But subject matter and mood to a large extent determine style of writing, and allowance must be made for experiment, for revision, or for passing influences. Yet, taken as a whole, "internal evidence," when tactfully and objectively used, is valuable, if only as corroborative data or as a check upon other evidence. In the cases of several plays, notably *The Taming of the Shrew, All's Well that Ends Well, Coriolanus, Cymbeline,* and *Timon of Athens,* little or no other reliable information exists as to the date of composition.

Thus, the chronology of Shakespeare's plays is far from certain, but students have found it necessary to establish at least a working sequence. The following table represents a consensus of opinion of the leading modern scholars and should serve as a guide to the reader.

DATE	COMEDIES	HISTORIES	TRAGEDIES
1590–2	Love's Labor's Lost	1, 2, 3 Henry VI	
1592–4	The Comedy of Errors		
	The Two Gentlemen of Verona		
1593–4		Richard III	Titus Andronicus
1594–6	A Midsummer Night's Dream	King John	
	The Merchant of Venice	Richard II	
1594–7	The Taming of the Shrew		Romeo and Juliet
1597–8		1, 2 Henry IV	
1598–9		Henry V	Julius Cæsar
1597–1600	The Merry Wives of Windsor		
1598–1600	Much Ado about Nothing		
1599–1600	As You Like It		
1599–1601	Twelfth Night		
1600–01			Hamlet
1600–04	All's Well that Ends Well		
1601–03			Troilus and Cressida
1603–04	Measure for Measure		
1604–05			Othello
1605–06			King Lear
			Macbeth
1607–08	Pericles		Antony and Cleopatra
			Timon of Athens
1608–10			Coriolanus
1609–10	Cymbeline		
1610–11	The Winter's Tale		
1611–12	The Tempest		
1612–13		Henry VIII	

SUGGESTED REFERENCES

ALBRIGHT, EVELYN MAY. *Dramatic Publication in England, 1580–1640: A Study of Conditions Affecting Content and Form of Drama.* MLA Monograph. New York, Heath, 1927.

BLACK, MATTHEW W. *and* SHAABER, MATTHIAS A. *Shakespeare's Seventeenth Century Editors, 1632–1685.* MLA Monograph. New York, Heath, 1937.

BROOKE, C. F. TUCKER (ed.). *The Shakespeare Apocrypha, Being a Collection of Fourteen Plays which Have Been Ascribed to Shakespeare.* Oxford, Clarendon Press, 1918.

GREG, W. W. *Dramatic Documents from the Elizabethan Playhouses: Stage Plots, Actors' Parts, Prompt Books* (2 vols.). Oxford, Clarendon Press, 1931.

Volume I is commentary; Volume II, reproductions and transcripts.

——. *The Editorial Problem in Shakespeare: A Survey of the Foundations of the Text.* Oxford, Clarendon Press, 1942.

JUDGE, CYRIL BATHURST. *Elizabethan Book-Pirates.* Cambridge, Harvard University Press, 1934.

KELLNER, LEON. *Restoring Shakespeare: A Critical Analysis of the Misreadings in Shakespeare's Works.* London, George Allen and Unwin, 1925.

MCKERROW, RONALD B. *The Treatment of Shakespeare's Text by His Earlier Editors, 1709–1768.* British Academy Lecture. Oxford, 1933.

——. *Prolegomena for the Oxford Shakespeare: A Study in Editorial Method.* Oxford, Clarendon Press, 1939.

Mr. William Shakespeare's Comedies, Histories, and Tragedies. Faithfully Reproduced in Facsimile from the Editions of 1623, 1632, 1664–5, 1685 (4 vols.). London, Methuen, 1904–10.

NEIDIG, W. J. "The Shakespeare Quartos of 1619," *Modern Philology,* VIII (1910), pp. 145–63.

Conclusive proof by composite photography that the title-pages of Thomas Pavier's reprints bear fraudulent dates and imprints.

POLLARD, ALFRED W. *Shakespeare's Folios and Quartos. A Study in the Bibliography of Shakespeare's Plays.* London, Methuen, 1909.

——. *Shakespeare's Fight with the Pirates and the Problems of the Transmission of His Text* (2nd edition). Cambridge University Press, 1920.

RHODES, R. CROMPTON. *Shakespeare's First Folio: A Study.* Oxford, Blackwell, 1923.

The Shakespere Quarto Facsimiles (43 vols.). Issued under the superintendence of F. J. Furnivall by William Griggs and Charles Praetorius. London, W. Griggs and C. Praetorius, 1885–91.

SHIPHERD, H. ROBINSON. "Play Publishing in Elizabethan Times," *Publications of the Modern Language Association,* XXXIV (1919), pp. 580–600.

Studies in the First Folio. Written for the Shakespeare Association in Celebration of the First Folio Tercentenary, 1623–1923. London, Humphrey Milford, Oxford University Press, 1924. Contents include:
W. W. Greg, "The First Folio and Its Publishers."
Sir Sidney Lee, "A Survey of First Folios."
Allardyce Nicoll, "The Editors of Shakespeare from First Folio to Malone."
R. Crompton Rhodes, "The First Folio and the Elizabethan Stage."
M. H. Spielmann, "Shakespeare's Portraiture."
J. Dover Wilson, "The Task of Heminge and Condell."

TANNENBAUM, SAMUEL A. *The Handwriting of the Renaissance, Being the Development and Characteristics of the Script of Shakespere's Time.* New York, Columbia University Press, 1930.

The New Variorum Shakespeare, edited by H. H. Furness and H. H. Furness, Jr., Philadelphia, Lippincott, 1871 ff.

A reference edition with exhaustive notes, variant readings, and extensive quotation from Shakespeare literature, in which about half of the plays have appeared. Since the death of H. H. Furness, Jr., the work is being carried forward by a committee of the Modern Language Association.

SHAKESPEARE'S REPUTATION

If we wish to know the force of human genius, we should read Shakespeare. If we wish to see the insignificance of human learning, we may study his commentators.
—William Hazlitt, *Table Talk* (1821).

The words of Mercury are harsh after the songs of Apollo.
—*Love's Labor's Lost*, V, ii, 940.

THERE IS A COMPLAINT ATTRIBUTED TO CATO THE ELDER, who when past eighty was compelled to defend himself before the Senate, that "it is hard to have lived with one generation, and to be tried by another." To the student of Shakespeare's after-fame, there are many times when this truism of the Roman statesman comes vividly to mind. It is not that Shakespeare's writings have ever suffered serious neglect, or that each generation, measuring its heritage with its own characteristic standards, has found them wanting. It is rather largely because, both in English-speaking nations and abroad, Shakespeare has always been placed upon a pinnacle and his name bracketed with those of Homer, Virgil, and Dante, that the generations which came after have not always been able to see him steadily and see him whole. "A veneration of Shakespeare," wrote Lord Lyttelton in 1765, "seems a part of your national religion, and the only part in which even your men of sense are fanatics."[1] Each age, to be sure, has differed in its attitude toward the plays and what it found attractive in them, and each has belittled its predecessors' appreciation of them. Much of the praise bestowed upon Shakespeare, too, has been empty and conventional, merely making louder the common cry. But it is one of the highest tributes to Shakespeare's universality that, in spite of shifting values, each age has rediscovered the greatest of the Elizabethans as a contemporary and judged his work by its

[1] *Dialogues of the Dead.* Compare Edward Gibbon's statement: "Idolatry of Shakespeare is inculcated from our infancy as the first duty of an Englishman."

own ideals. The results have not always been the best. In the words of the late Sir Walter Raleigh:

There is no book, except the Bible, which has been so misread, so misapplied, or made the subject of so many idle paradoxes and ingenuities. The most careless and casual lines in his plays have been twisted and squeezed in the hope that they will yield some medicinal secret. His poetry has been cut into minute indigestible fragments, and used like wedding-cake, not to eat, but to dream upon. The greatest poet of the modern world is at this day widely believed to have been also the most irrelevant, and to have valued the golden casket of his verse chiefly as a hiding-place for the odds and ends of personal gossip. These are the penalties to be paid by great poets when their works become fashionable. . . . To love and to be wise is not given to man. (*Shakespeare*, 1907.)

SHAKESPEARE'S CONTEMPORARY FAME

It is sometimes assumed that Shakespeare was not properly appreciated in his own day. Nothing could be further from the truth. From the very first reference to him by Robert Greene as the "upstart crow, beautified with our feathers" (see above, p. 6), he appears to have made his mark upon London, and there is ample, if not voluminous, evidence that his work was popular. Between 1591 and 1616, there are more than two hundred allusions to Shakespeare and his writings, more than a hundred different authors quoting or parodying lines from the plays and poems, and occasionally mentioning the author by name. In *Palladis Tamia* (1598), Francis Meres described Shakespeare as the most excellent in both comedy and tragedy for the stage, and listed him among the "most passionate among us to bewail and bemoan the perplexities of love," while the antiquary William Camden, in his *Remains Concerning Britain* (1605), included him among the "most pregnant wits of these our times."

As might be expected, most of the allusions to Shakespeare are to his plays on the stage. But before the publication of the First Folio in 1623, sixteen of the plays had appeared in print in forty-five editions, thirty-two of which bore the author's name on the title-page. Of the Poems and Sonnets, before their collection in 1640, there had appeared twenty-five editions, one of which (*Venus and Adonis*, 1637) was printed as far from London as Edinburgh. Moreover, William Drummond of Hawthornden was reading and buying Shakespeare's books in Scotland in 1606. In addition, the appearance during Shakespeare's lifetime of no fewer than six works now not believed to be his, bearing either his name or his initials on the title-page, corroborates the statement of Thomas Walkley, the publisher of *Othello* (1622), that "the author's name is sufficient to vent his work." The publishers of *Troilus and Cressida* (1609) went even further. After pointing out that "the most displeased with plays are pleased with his comedies," they became prophetic:

"And believe this, that when he is gone, and his comedies out of sale, you will scramble for them and set up a new English inquisition." It was even possible for a Mr. Richardson of Magdalen College, Oxford, to insert a passage of Juliet's love-making (II, ii, 177–82) into a sermon and preach it "twice at St. Mary's 1620, 1621, applying it too to God's love to his Saints either hurt with sin or adversity, never forsaking them." The idolatry of Shakespeare thus began early.

The nature of this contemporary appreciation, warm as it generally is, is a little disappointing, even when one remembers that literary criticism was slow in developing in England. On the literary side, the opinion is summed up by Francis Meres who describes Shakespeare as "mellifluous and honey-tongued" and alludes to his "sweet witty soul," and "fine filed phrase." Others call him "sweet," or "gentle," or "friendly," or "brave" (i. e., splendid), or "ingenious," or "silver-tongued," and speak of his "smooth comic vein," his "right happy and copious industry," or "that nimble Mercury," his brain. Still others compare him with various classical poets—Catullus, Martial, Ovid, Plautus, or Terence. And though there was not the outburst of elegies at his death as there was at Ben Jonson's in 1637, several of Shakespeare's contemporaries—John Weever (1595), R. Barnefield (1598), John Davies of Hereford (c. 1611), Thomas Freeman (1614), and William Basse (1622)—did write short poems or epigrams in his praise. All of these eulogies, however, are filled with the usual clichés and point out only obvious things.

An examination of the basis of Shakespeare's contemporary reputation suggests again the need for distinguishing between literary eminence and popularity on the stage. As a literary man, Shakespeare was less famous for his plays than for his *Venus and Adonis* and *Lucrece*, the works which we have come to regard as more Elizabethan than for all time. In 1598, R. Barnefield addressed him as

> Shakespeare, thou, whose honey-flowing vein,
> Pleasing the world, thy praises doth obtain,
> Whose *Venus*, and whose *Lucrece*, sweet and chaste,
> Thy name in fame's immortal book have plac'd.

Venus and Adonis is alluded to much more frequently than any other work, and *Lucrece* is surpassed in the number of mentions by only *Hamlet* and *Henry IV*. But popular as the poems were for the average Elizabethan, "grave moral Spenser" unquestionably stood higher as a poet than Shakespeare; so probably did Daniel, Drayton, and Warner. Shakespeare, however, was among the more excellent, a rather remarkable fact when one considers that the reputation was built upon the poetry of his youth. In the public theatres, as we shall see, his popularity was high.

When, in 1623, the publication of the First Folio made all of Shakespeare's plays available to the reader, there was opportunity for something like criticism. Prefixed to the book, in an address "To the great Variety of Readers," there was something between a charge and an invitation:

> From the most able, to him that can but spell: there you are number'd. We had rather you were weigh'd. . . . It is not our province, who only gather his works, and give them you, to praise him. It is yours that read him. And there we hope, to your divers capacities, you will find enough, both to draw, and hold you: for his wit can no more lie hid, than it could be lost. Read him, therefore; and again and again. And if then you do not like him, surely you are in some manifest danger not to understand him.

The response to this invitation through the centuries must be eminently satisfying to the shades of those who penned it. The work of Shakespeare's earliest editors, it is pleasant to record, was not without contemporary recognition. In a manuscript miscellany, which once belonged to the Salisbury family and is now in the National Library of Wales, there are these verses:

To My Good Friends Mr. John Heminge and Henry Condell

> To you that jointly, with undaunted pains,
> Vouchsafed to chant to us these noble strains,
> How much you merit by it is not said,
> But you have pleased the living, loved the dead;
> Raised from the womb of earth a richer mine
> Than Cortes could with all his Casteline
> Associates; they did but dig for gold,
> But you for treasure much more manifold.[2]

The first critic of Shakespeare was none other than his fellow-dramatist Ben Jonson, who supplied the First Folio with the greatest eulogy ever written of a contemporary: "To the Memory of my Beloved, the Author, Mr. William Shakespeare, and What he hath Left Us." Opening his poem with the frank admission that Shakespeare's writings are so excellent that "neither man nor muse can praise too much," Jonson affirms that he is merely stating the general opinion: " 'tis true, and all men's suffrage." Then he launches into his own eulogy:

> Soul of the age!
> The applause! delight! the wonder of our stage!

As he looks for names with which to compare Shakespeare, Jonson rejects Chaucer and Spenser, as "great, but disproportion'd muses," and though Shakespeare had "small Latin and less Greek," he unhesitatingly calls forth his own masters, the Greek and Latin dramatists—Æschylus, Euripides, Sophocles—

> All that insolent Greece or haughty Rome
> Sent forth, or since did from their ashes come. . . .

[2] (Printed by Sir Israel Gollancz in *Studies in the First Folio*, by Members of the Shakespeare Association [1924], p. xxx.)

> The merry Greek, tart Aristophanes,
>   Neat Terence, witty Plautus, now not please;
> But antiquated, and deserted lie
>   As they were not of Nature's family.

But Shakespeare, unlike the others,

> was not of an age, but for all time.

Jonson's praise, however, was not unseasoned with blame. A fellow-crafts-man, it is to be expected, would have a keen eye for shortcomings. Unlike Jonson, Shakespeare had been a facile worker, and what he had written for immediate effect in the theatre was not quite always proof against cold scrutiny in the study. When the players praised Shakespeare for having "never blotted out line," Jonson had replied, "would he had blotted a thousand." In his common-place book, afterward published as *Timber, or Discoveries upon Men and Matter* (1641), he wrote his justification of what Shakespeare's fellows thought a malevolent speech. Moreover, in conversation with Drummond of Hawthornden, he had called attention to the absurdity of a shipwreck in Bohemia, and had gone so far as to say that Shakespeare "wanted art." But he tempered his mild censure with the greatest praise:

> for I lov'd the man, and do honour his memory (on this side idolatry) as much as any. He was, indeed, honest, and of an open and free nature: had an excellent phantasy, brave notions, and gentle expressions: wherein he flow'd with that facility that sometime it was necessary he should be stopp'd. . . . His wit was in his own power; would the rule of it had been so too. . . . But he redeemed his vices with his virtues. There was ever more in him to be praised than to be pardoned. (*Timber.*)

And now, in his elegy, Jonson had long ceased to be the envious critic looking for spots in the sun. He praises with a whole heart:

> Yet must I not give Nature all. Thy art,
>   My gentle Shakespeare, must enjoy a part.
> For though a poet's matter Nature be,
>   His art doth give the fashion. And, that he
> Who casts to write a living line, must sweat,
>   (Such as thine are) and strike a second heat
> Upon the Muses' anvil; turn the same,
>   (And himself with it) that he thinks to frame;
> Or for the laurel he may gain a scorn,
>   For a good poet's made as well as born.
> And such wert thou.

For more than a generation, no critic went beyond Jonson's strictures upon Shakespeare—his lack of learning and his facility that was often carelessness. Indeed, the lines thus laid out reach down to our own time. What is all the critical condescension of Pope and Warburton and the eighteenth-century talk about Nature and Art if not an elaboration of Jonson's principles? And Voltaire's "natural born savage, drunk with the wine of genius" is only a step removed from John Milton's "sweetest Shakespeare, Fancy's child" warbling his "native wood-notes wild." The difference is one of degree rather than of kind. The Jonsonian eulogy was also continued. Poet after poet called Shakespeare the age's wonder and promised honor to his name through all posterity. There are substantial testimonies to his continued popularity. By 1639, his book had become the study of ladies in the country,[2a] and John Johnson wrote in the *Academy of Love, describing the folly of young men and the fallacy of women* (1641): "If it were not for some of the old out-of-date grandames . . . the young sparkish girls would read in Shakespeare day and night." About the same time, Anthony Van Dyck was painting a portrait of Sir John Suckling in the classical garb of a poet, but holding Shakespeare's Folio open at *Hamlet* (Frick Gallery, see illustration p. 441). According to Milton, Shakespeare and Jonson became the closest companions of King Charles's solitudes, and, if *The Northern Nuntio* (August 8, 1643), a Royalist newspaper, can be believed, there were even some who set "Shakespeare's plays at a better pitch of authority than the Gospel of Christ."

A comparison, too, of

> The sweat of learned Jonson's brain
> And gentle Shakespeare's easier strain[3]

was inevitable. Shakespeare excelled in the natural vein; Jonson was grave, ponderous, erudite. "Comparing him with Shakespeare you shall see the difference betwixt Nature and Art."[4] Those who sought to lessen Shakespeare's worth when they placed him beside Jonson were confronted by the question: What "other Master . . . could better teach a man to write a good play,"[5] or by the sad but confident shaking of the head:

> And if thy learning had been like thy wit,
> Ben would have blusht, and Jonson never writ.
> (Robert Wild, *The Benefice, c.* 1646.)

THE PERIOD OF THE RESTORATION

After the Restoration, the critical mantle of Ben Jonson fell upon the shoulders of John Dryden, and, to a large degree, the spirit of Jonson's criticism may be found in the judgments of Dryden. A great deal had happened in the interval of years between them. There had been civil war; the theatres had been closed for nearly eighteen years; the older traditions of the drama, if

---

[2a] Letter from Mrs. Ann Merricke to Mrs. Lydall, January 21, 1639.

[3] Sir John Suckling, *Fragmenta Aurea* (1646).

[4] Richard Flecknoe, *Short Discourse on the English Stage* (1664).

[5] "To the Readers," *Five New Plays* (1658), by Richard Brome.

not actually broken, had at least been diluted with another kind of drama that had entertained the exiles in France. Taste had changed, and it was impossible for the Restoration drama to begin where the Jacobean drama had left off. Even before the closing of the theatres, a change of taste had become noticeable.

> When Shakespeare, Beaumont, Fletcher, rul'd the stage,
> There scarce were ten good palates in the age,

wrote Sir John Suckling in *The Goblins* (1646), and William Cartwright, commending the plays of Fletcher in the folio edition of 1647, made this comparison:

> Shakespeare to thee was dull, whose best jest lies
> I' the Lady's questions and the Fool's replies,
> Old fashioned wit, which walkt from town to town
> In turn'd hose, which our fathers call'd the Clown;
> And which made bawdry pass for comical.
> Nature was all his art! Thy vein was free
> As his, but without his scurrility.

Dryden's criticism of Shakespeare concerned three points: his style, his language, and his wit. Poetry, in Shakespeare's age, was but in its infancy, the plots of plays were lame, and the stories ridiculous and incoherent, grounded on impossibilities. "Shakespeare, who many times has written better than any poet in any language," nevertheless in many places wrote "below the dullest writers in our or any precedent age" ("An Essay on the Dramatic Poetry of the Last Age," *The Conquest of Granada*, Part II, 1672). In short, to Dryden Shakespeare's misfortune was that he was one of the "giant race before the flood,"

> When men were dull, and conversation low.

He even brought the actor Thomas Betterton upon the stage as Shakespeare's ghost and had him publicly confess:

> Untaught, unpractis'd in a barbarous age,
> I found not, but created first the stage.
> (Prologue to *Troilus and Cressida*, 1679.)

This lack of information about dramatic history is disarming. Yet it was also Dryden who wrote:

To begin with Shakespeare; he was the man who of all modern, and perhaps ancient poets, had the largest and most comprehensive soul. All the images of Nature were still present in him, and he drew them not laboriously, but luckily. . . . Those who accuse him to have wanted learning, give him the greater commendation: he was naturally learn'd; he needed not the spectacles of books to read Nature; he look'd inwards and found her there. I cannot say he is everywhere alike. . . . He is many times flat, insipid; his comic wit degenerating into clenches, his serious swelling into bombast. But he is always great, when some great occasion is presented to him. (*Of Dramatic Poesie*, 1668.)

In another place he added:

> If Shakespeare were stripped of all the bombast in his passions, and dress'd in the most vulgar words, we should find the beauties of his thoughts remaining; if his embroideries were burnt down, there would still be silver at the bottom of the melting-pot: but I fear . . . that we who ape his sounding words, have nothing of his thought, but are all out-side. . . . Therefore, let not Shakespeare suffer for our sakes, 'tis our fault who succeed him in an age which is more refin'd, if we imitate him so ill. (Preface to *Troilus and Cressida*, 1679.)

Reminiscent as some of this is of what Ben Jonson had said earlier, here is the essence of what the critics were to say for the next hundred years.

Dryden's contemporary Thomas Rymer, on the other hand, had nothing of condescension in him and no sympathy for any drama except Greek and Latin. Rymer was an antiquary, historiographer royal, and one of the most learned men of his time. But it is hard to take seriously his ventures into literary criticism which bear these opinionated titles: *The Tragedies of the Last Age Consider'd and Examin'd by the Practice of the Ancients, and by the Common Sense of All Ages* (1678) and *A Short View of Tragedy, Its Original, Excellency, and Corruption* (1693). It is in the latter volume that Shakespeare's works, particularly his *Othello* and *Julius Cæsar*, receive boisterous treatment. Rymer's method is sufficiently illustrated in his chapter on *Othello*. "From all the tragedies," he began,

> acted on our English stage, *Othello* is said to bear the bell away. The subject is more of a piece, and there is indeed something like, there is, as it were, some phantom of a fable. . . .

He then reduced the plot of the play to a short paragraph, with proper emphasis upon the elopement, Desdemona's handkerchief, and Iago's villainy, and came quickly to these conclusions:

> What ever rubs or difficulty may stick on the bark, the moral, sure, of this fable is very instructive.
> First. This may be a caution to all maidens of quality how, without their parents' consent, they run away with Blackamoors. . . .
> Secondly. This may be a warning to all good wives, that they look well to their linen.
> Thirdly. This may be a lesson to husbands, that before their jealousy be tragical, the proofs may be mathematical.

In the rest of his criticism Rymer concerned himself with the characters, the thoughts, and the language of the play. "In the neighing of an horse, or in the growling of a mastiff, there is a meaning, there is as lively expression, and, may I say, more humanity, than many times in the tragical flights of Shakespeare." In Desdemona he found nothing "that is not below any country chambermaid with us," and at last in despair he took refuge in this re-flection:

> The Italian painters are noted for drawing the madonnas by their own wives or mistresses; one might wonder what sort of Betty Mackerel Shakespeare found in his days to fit for his Portia and Desdemona.

Rymer, of course, is the representative, not so much of the age as of an ex-treme point of view. Unfortunately for him, he had composed a play en-titled *Edgar, or The English Monarch* (1678), in illustration of how a tragedy should be written, and "by his own example damned his rules."[6] *Edgar* was never acted. The deliberate attack upon Shakespeare turned many against him, and the considered attitude of the age is expressed in one of Dryden's letters to another critic, John Dennis, in 1694:

> You see what success this learned critic has found in the world after his blas-pheming Shakespeare. Almost all the faults which he has discover'd are truly there; yet who will read Mr. Rymer or not read Shakespeare? For my own part I reverence Mr. Rymer's learning, but I detest his ill-nature and his arrogance. I, indeed, and such as I, have reason to be afraid of him, but Shakespeare has not.

The new age, it is clear, was conscious of its superiority in all things, in-cluding the theatre. In the period which produced Rymer it is not surprising to read in John Evelyn's *Diary:* "I saw *Hamlet, Prince of Denmark* played; but now the old plays began to disgust this refined age, since his Majesty's being so long abroad" (November 26, 1661). Or to hear in a new Prologue to James Shirley's *Love's Tricks* (1667):

> In our old plays the humour Love and Passion
> Like doublet, hose, and cloak, are out of fashion:
> That which the world call'd wit in Shakespeare's age,
> Is laught at, as improper for our stage.

It is refreshing to learn that Margaret Cavendish, the Marchioness of New-castle, defended Shakespeare's plays against such as say "they were made up only with clowns, fools, watchmen, and the like," and suggested the study of Shakespeare's characters (*Sociable Letters*, 1664).

The diarist Samuel Pepys, while perhaps not a typical Restoration play-goer, was nevertheless articulate of some of the age's opinions about the old dramatic fare. He thought *Romeo and Juliet* a play "of itself the worst that ever I saw in my life, the worst acted." *A Midsummer Night's Dream* he called the "most insipid ridiculous play that I ever saw in my life"; *Twelfth Night* was at one time "but a silly play," and at another time "one of the weakest plays that ever I saw on the stage"; *Henry VIII*, which he had heard others praise, was "so simple a thing made up of a great many patches, that, besides the shows and processions in it, there is nothing in the world good or

---

[6] Dryden, Prologue to *Love Triumphant* (1694).

well done." And *Othello* seemed "a mean thing" when read beside *The Adventures of Five Hours*. In fact, the only Shakespearean plays Pepys seems to have liked were *Hamlet, Macbeth*, and *The Tempest*. In the case of *Hamlet*, it was probably Betterton's acting rather than the play that gave him pleasure. At various times he thought *Macbeth* "a pretty good play," "a most excellent play for variety," and "a most excellent play in all respects, but especially for divertisement." He called *The Tempest* "the most innocent play that ever I saw . . . the play has no great wit, but yet good, above ordinary plays." Seeing it again a week later, he found it "full of so good variety that I cannot be more pleased almost in a comedy." But the plays Pepys liked, one must hasten to explain, were not Shakespeare's but adaptations of them. If Shakespeare had begun to disgust this refined age, he was by no means dropped from the stage. Instead, he was "reformed and made fit" (see below, pp. 412ff.).

THE EIGHTEENTH CENTURY

If the seventeenth century had been content simply to praise or to blame Shakespeare, the eighteenth continued the tradition and more. But it also saw the birth of Shakespearean scholarship, and in this field its main contributions were two. After many blunderings, beginning with the work of Nicholas Rowe (1709), an editorial method was evolved and the foundations were laid for a sound study of Shakespeare's text. Gradually, Shakespeare was recognized as having become an English classic; his text was eventually approached in the spirit of exact scholarship and edited in the same way as ancient classics were edited. Then, as the century wore on, scholars awoke to the fact that, since Shakespeare was an Elizabethan, his plays could best be understood by a study of the life of his age, especially of Elizabethan stage history and of the conditions under which Shakespeare and his fellow-dramatists had worked. Thus, the foundations of the modern historical study of Shakespeare were laid in the work of Edmund Malone (1741–1812) and of George Steevens (1736–1800), who, as early as 1766, had pointed out that "a perfect edition of the Plays of Shakespeare requires at once the assistance of the antiquary, the historian, the grammarian, and the poet."

In addition to this general Shakespearean scholarship, eighteenth-century students also made contributions to special phases of study. In 1753–4, for example, Charlotte Lennox made a collection in three volumes of Shakespeare's sources entitled *Shakespear Illustrated, or The Novels and Histories on which the Plays of Shakespear Are Founded*, which was the result of a study that had begun with Gerard Langbaine in 1691. Far more substantial was Edward Capell's *The School of Shakespeare; or Authentic Extracts from Divers English Books . . . Shewing Whence His Several Fables Were*

Taken (1779). These volumes mark the beginnings of the study of Shakespeare's debt to his predecessors. The first important general treatise upon the reading which went into the making of the plays was Richard Farmer's *Essay on the Learning of Shakespeare* (1767). Other scholars, notably William Oldys (1696–1761), added considerably to the known facts and traditions of Shakespeare's biography. The multiplication of editions of his works went steadily on, between thirty and forty different editions, and many reprints, appearing during the century. "Were Shakespeare to revisit this globe," wrote an author in *The Universal Magazine* in 1793, "the first thing that would surprise him would be to learn that above one hundred and fifty thousand pounds have lately been devoted toward splendid editions of his works."

To the eighteenth-century critics, also, Shakespeare was irresistibly attractive. As early as 1725, the reputation of the dramatist had become such that it was possible for Alexander Pope to say in the Preface to his edition of Shakespeare's plays that an effectual and not a superficial criticism

> would be the best occasion that any just writer could take to form the judgment and taste of our nation. For of all English poets Shakespeare must be confessed to be the fairest and fullest subject for criticism, and to afford the most numerous as well as most conspicuous instances, both of beauties and faults of all sorts.

The early eighteenth century, through Dr. Johnson's time, was content with this "encomiastic criticism." Admirers continued to praise the agreeableness of Shakespeare's wit, the sprightliness of his conversation, the beauty of his thought and imagery, the felicity of his language, his axiomatic wisdom, his lively imagination, his ability to delineate the passions, the consistency and propriety of his characters—in short, his skill in holding the mirror up to Nature and in representing life. There were some condescensions about Shakespeare's loose plotting, his carelessness of detail, his pompous language, and his verbal quibbling. But these faults were usually attributed to the barbarity of the age in which he lived or to the fact that he wrote to please an audience. Indeed, Pope attributed most of Shakespeare's faults to his "being a player and forming himself first upon the judgments of that body of men whereof he was a member," and he summed up what was apparently a common point of view:

> Shakespeare (whom you and every playhouse bill
> Style the divine, the matchless, what you will)
> For gain, not glory, wing'd his roving flight,
> And grew immortal in his own despite.
> (*Imitations of Horace*, 1737.)

In general, this criticism was an examination of beauties and blemishes, the better part being, according to Pope, the pointing out of excellences. In his edition, Rowe frequently called attention to especially striking passages, and both Pope and Bishop Warburton continued the practice. In his text, Pope even distinguished brilliant passages by inverted commas or by starring a whole scene. He also provided an elaborate index to Characters, Manners and Passions, Thoughts or Sentiments, Speeches, Descriptions, and Similes and Allusions. The practice was continued throughout the century, giving rise to periodical essays, like those of Joseph Warton on *The Tempest* and *King Lear* in *The Adventurer* (1753), which are little more than a running commentary upon the particular play chosen, or to such elaborate anthologies as Dr. William Dodd's *Beauties of Shakespeare* (1752), which is still occasionally reprinted. This tradition has continued, producing *The Shakespeare Key* (1879) by Charles and Mary Cowden-Clarke and, recently, *Stevenson's Book of Shakespeare Quotations*, arranged and edited by Burton Stevenson (1938).

Before the eighteenth century was far advanced, however, several general topics stood out in the discussion and were treated by almost all who wrote. One of these was the old Jonsonian subject of Art and Nature that had already been the basis of Dryden's criticism. Most critics cherished the tradition of Shakespeare's lack of learning and professed admiration for the fact that "art had so little, and nature so large a share in what he did." *The Spectator* (1711) distinguished two kinds of geniuses, those disciplined by rules of art, and the more admirable who

> stand up as the prodigies of mankind . . . by the mere strength of natural parts, and without any assistance of art or learning, have produced works that were the delight of their own times and the wonder of posterity. There appears something wild and extravagant in these great natural geniuses that is infinitely more beautiful than all the turn and polishing of what the French call a *bel esprit*, by which they would express a genius refined by conversation, reflection, and the reading of the most polite authors. (Number 160.)

Shakespeare was a remarkable example of this type of natural, unspoiled genius. In another essay, *The Spectator* (1714) went so far as to say:

> Shakespeare was indeed born with all the seeds of poetry, and may be compared to the stone in Pyrrhus's ring, which as Pliny tells us, had the figure of Apollo and the Nine Muses in the veins of it, produced by the spontaneous hand of Nature, without any help from art. (Number 592.)

The early eighteenth century sought to explain Shakespeare as the "pure voice of Nature," and his book as the "true picture of Nature." "If ever any author deserved the name of an original," wrote Alexander Pope, who was well aware that Shakespeare had used earlier sources for his works,

> it was Shakespeare. Homer himself drew not his art so immediately from the fountains of Nature; it proceeded thro' Ægyptian strainers and channels, and came to him not without some tincture of the learning, or some cast of the

models, of those before him. The poetry of Shakespeare was inspiration indeed: he is not so much an imitator, as an instrument, of Nature; and 'tis not so just to say that he speaks from her, as that she speaks thro' him. His characters are so much Nature herself that 'tis a sort of injury to call them by so distant a name as copies of her.

Dr. Johnson said much the same thing:

> This therefore is the praise of Shakespeare, that his drama is the mirrour of life; that he who has mazed his imagination, in following the phantoms which other writers raise up before him, may here be cured of his delirious ecstasies, by reading human sentiments in human language; by scenes from which a hermit may estimate the transactions of the world, and a confessor predict the progress of the passions.

Other critics supplied the exposition of the theme. As the century wore on one heard more and more about "original genius" as a mysterious, unaccountable, supernatural gift—"that divine emanation, which in its nature is inexplicable." By the end of the century the Romantic deification of Shakespeare as the greatest example of the natural genius was practically complete.

A more important and substantial subject of interest, however, was the justification of this "darling of Nature" as a dramatic artist before a world brought up on the pseudo-classical rules. Critic after critic was obliged to admit that in his plots Shakespeare did not adhere to the unities; he cared nothing for time; he mixed comedy and tragedy; his construction was loose; and a few even called attention to breaches of decorum. *The Spectator* disposed of the first objection in a characteristic fashion which left nothing to say:

> Who would not rather read one of his plays, where there is not a single rule of the stage observed, than any production of a modern critic, where there is not one of them violated? (Number 592.)

It remained for the nineteenth century to discover in Shakespeare the higher unity of tone and impression. Pope even dared to suggest that Shakespeare should be judged by an entirely different set of laws:

> I will conclude by saying of Shakespeare, that with all his faults, and with all the irregularity of his drama, one may look upon his works, in comparison of those that are more finish'd and regular, as upon an ancient majestic piece of Gothic architecture, compar'd with a neat modern building: the latter is more elegant and glaring, but the former is more strong and more solemn. It must be allow'd, that in one of these there are materials to make many of the other. It has much the greater variety, and much the nobler apartments, tho' we are often conducted to them by dark, odd, and uncouth passages. Nor does the whole fail to strike us with greater reverence, tho' many of the parts are childish, ill-placed, and unequal to its grandeur.

This passage is almost an anticipation of Bishop Hurd's *Letters on Chivalry and Romance*. As the century advanced, the early idea that Shakespeare grew immortal in his own despite was gradually replaced by the insistence that he was a conscious artist possessed of good sense and judgment. Thus, the way was prepared for Coleridge. The matter of decorum was ably handled by Dr. Johnson's common sense:

> Dennis is offended that Menenius, a senator of Rome, should play the buffoon; and Voltaire perhaps thinks decency violated when the Danish usurper is represented as a drunkard. But Shakespeare always makes nature predominate over accident. . . . His story requires Romans or kings, but he thinks only on men. He knew that Rome, like every other city, had men of all dispositions; and wanting a buffoon, he went into the senate-house for that which the senate-house would certainly have afforded him. . . . These are the petty cavils of petty minds.

These peculiar questions were made especially pressing for the eighteenth century by the strictures of Voltaire. During his sojourn in England (1726–9), Voltaire had become an ardent Shakespearean, and, as he worded it, had "first showed the French a few pearls which I found in his enormous dunghill." But when his countrymen also grew enthusiastic about the Englishman, he became alarmed for Corneille and Racine. A characteristic Voltaire utterance is his notorious summary of *Hamlet:*

> I am certainly very far from justifying the tragedy of *Hamlet* as a whole; it is a coarse and barbarous piece which would not be endured by the lowest rabble of France or Italy. Hamlet becomes mad in the second act, and his mistress becomes mad in the third; the prince, pretending to kill a rat, kills the father of his mistress, and the heroine throws herself into the river. Her grave is dug on the stage; grave-diggers make puns worthy of them, holding death's heads in their hands; and Prince Hamlet replies to their abominable coarseness by no less disgusting extravagances. Meanwhile, one of the actors conquers Poland. Hamlet, his mother, and his stepfather drink together on the stage; at table, there is singing and quarreling, fighting and killing. It would seem that such a work is the fruit of the imagination of a drunken savage. ("Dissertation sur la tragédie ancienne et moderne," prefixed to *Sémiramis,* 1748.)

Unfair as this is as criticism, or even as a summary of the story, Voltaire was not blind to the excellences in Shakespeare. He admitted that Shakespeare was a genius:

> The Italians, the French, and men of letters of all countries who have not passed some time in England, take him for a mere mountebank of the fair, a droll far below Harlequin, the sorriest buffoon who ever amused the mob. And yet in this same man there are passages which exalt the imagination and penetrate the heart. Truth and Nature themselves speak their own language without any mixture of art. He reaches sublimity without having searched for it. ("Art dramatique," in *Dictionnaire philosophique,* 1765.)

It will at once be apparent that Voltaire's was but an extreme statement of what English critics had said before, and that, at worst, he was little more than a French Rymer or Gildon. However, the English would permit no foreigner to speak so slightingly of a national idol, and the controversy across the channel soon became fierce. Shakespeare's most ardent defender was Mrs. Elizabeth Montagu, the famous "blue-stocking," whose *Essay on the Writings and Genius of Shakespeare, Compared with the Greek and French Dramatic Poets. With Some Remarks upon the Misrepresentations of Mons. de Voltaire* appeared in 1769 and ran through at least seven editions. Though the controversy produced no unusual criticism, it made Shakespeare's position even more secure than it had been before.

After Johnson's time, the interest was narrowed to Shakespeare's characters. All the early critics, of course, had admired them and spoken of their truth to nature and of the propriety of the language they used. Before 1765, however, there were few extended studies; from then on Shakespeare was considered in detail. The first character analysis, interestingly enough, was of Falstaff, in a supplement to Corbyn Morris's *Essay towards Fixing the True Standards of Wit, Humour, Raillery, Satire, and Ridicule* (1744). It was Dr. Johnson, however, more than any other single man who was responsible for the new character study. Embedded in the notes to his edition of Shakespeare are little masterpieces of analysis, like this study of Falstaff which deserves quotation because of the attraction the character had for the new students:

But Falstaff unimitated, unimitable Falstaff, how shall I describe thee? Thou compound of sense and vice; of sense which may be admired but not esteemed, of vice which may be despised, but hardly detested. Falstaff is a character loaded with faults, and with those faults which naturally produce contempt. He is a thief, and a glutton, a coward, and a boaster, always ready to cheat the weak, and prey upon the poor; to terrify the timorous and insult the defenceless. At once obsequious and malignant, he satirizes in their absence those whom he lives by flattering. He is familiar with the prince only as an agent of vice, but of this familiarity he is so proud as not only to be supercilious and haughty with common men, but to think his interest of importance to the Duke of Lancaster. Yet the man thus corrupt, thus despicable, makes himself necessary to the prince that despises him, by the most pleasing of all qualities, perpetual gaiety, by an unfailing power of exciting laughter, which is the more freely indulged, as his wit is not of the splendid or ambitious kind, but consists in easy escapes and sallies of levity, which make sport but raise no envy. It must be observed that he is stained with no enormous or sanguinary crimes, so that his licentiousness is not so offensive but that it may be borne for his mirth.

The new character analysis is represented by three books published about the same time and written by students who worked independently. They are *Remarks on Some of the Characters of Shakespeare*, published in 1785, but written about 1770 by Thomas Whately, an Under-Secretary of State for Lord North; *A Philosophical Analysis and Illustration of Some of Shakespeare's Remarkable Characters* (1774), by William Richardson, Professor of Latin in the University of Glasgow; and *An Essay on the Dramatic Char-*

acter of Sir John Falstaff, published in 1777, but written in 1774, by Maurice Morgann, also a statesman, and later secretary to the embassy for peace with America.

Whately's opening remarks are a clear statement of the new method of approach. Older critics, he pointed out, had, for the most part, confined themselves to plot, and the so-called rules of the drama, which are by no means the first requisite in dramatic composition. More worthy of attention are "the distinction and preservation of Character, without which the piece is at best a tale, not an action; for the actors in it are not produced upon the scene." Shakespeare was "excellent beyond comparison" in the art of characterization:

> No other dramatic writer could ever pretend to so deep and so extensive a knowledge of the human heart; and he had a genius to express all that his penetration could discover. The characters, therefore, which he has drawn, are masterly copies from nature; differing each from the other, and animated as the originals, though correct to a scrupulous precision.

The rest of his book is devoted to a comparative study of Richard III and Macbeth. The method may, on the whole, appear as little more than an amplification of that of Dr. Johnson and earlier writers, but there were some essential differences. Criticism was becoming less judicial and detached, and more interpretative and philosophical; and dramatic creations were treated not as beings in a play, but as actual historic men and women. Richardson, for example, was not concerned with dramatic values or mere esthetic appreciation. He was frankly the moral philosopher, whose "intention is to make poetry subservient to philosophy, and to employ it in tracing the principles of human conduct." His first book treated Macbeth, Hamlet, Jaques, and Imogen; later works dealt in the same way with Richard II, King Lear, Timon of Athens, Falstaff, and the female characters.

The most influential of this group, Maurice Morgann, went even further. His purpose was the vindication of Falstaff's courage, for he could "not conceive Shakespeare ever meant to make cowardice an essential part of his constitution. . . . Cowardice is not the impression which the whole character of Falstaff is calculated to make on the minds of an unprejudiced audience." Even Falstaff's flight at Gadshill was but the great humorist's preparation for a jest. Morgann's distinction between mental impressions and the Understanding made him the first impressionistic critic of Shakespeare. Dr. Johnson's reaction to the book was amusingly sensible:

> Why, Sir, we shall have the man come forth again, and as he has proved Falstaff to be no coward, he may prove Iago to be a very good character.

Yet Morgann's book, or its method, has colored almost all subsequent character criticism. The real subject of the study, however, was not Falstaff alone, but "the arts and genius of his Poet-Maker Shakespeare; and thro' him sometimes, with ambitious aim, even to the principles of human nature itself." Here was the beginning of the study of Shakespeare—and human life— through his characters, which was to occupy the attention of most of the critics of the next century.

Eighteenth-century criticism, then, may be said to have anticipated a great deal that was to be more fully treated later. Quite early, Shakespeare's reputation had become a matter of national pride which developed into little less than idolatry as the century drew to its close. It is clear, too, that from Rowe on, Shakespeare's book was treated as literature to be read and studied rather than as practical drama meant to be acted. The ground was ready for the Romantics.

THE ROMANTIC PERIOD

Taken by and large, the Romantic critics of the early nineteenth century are the greatest—at least the most enthusiastic—that Shakespeare has ever had. The age in which they lived looked upon all great men with reverence and sought to make a miracle of their existence. Shakespeare, more than all other authors, it idealized and completely exalted above the world of common men. "O mighty poet," exclaimed Thomas De Quincey,

> thy works are not as those of other men, simply and merely great works of art; but are also like the phenomena of nature, like the sun and the sea, the stars and the flowers; like frost and snow, rain and dew, hail-storm and thunder, which are to be studied with entire submission of our own faculties, and in the perfect faith that in them there can be no too much or too little, nothing useless or inert—but that, the farther we press in our discoveries, the more we shall see proofs of design, and self-supporting arrangement where the careless eye had seen nothing but accident! (*On the Knocking at the Gate in Macbeth*, 1823.)

"A rib of Shakespeare would have made a Milton," wrote Walter Savage Landor in his *Imaginary Conversations* (1846), "the same portion of Milton all poets born ever since." For Thomas Carlyle, Shakespeare's was the greatest of intellects, the man himself was a prophet, and the grandest thing the English had yet done.

> Consider now, if they asked us, "Will you give up your Indian Empire or your Shakespeare, you English; never have had any Indian Empire, or never have had any Shakespeare?" . . . Should not we be forced to answer: "Indian Empire, or no Indian Empire; we cannot do without Shakespeare!" ("The Hero as Poet," from *On Heroes, Hero-Worship and the Heroic in History*, 1840.)

Hence, Shakespeare's book must be read and judged quite differently from those of other men. "Shakespeare is as much out of the category of eminent authors [Bacon, Milton, Tasso, Cervantes] as he is out of the crowd. He is inconceivably wise, the others conceivably" (R. W. Emerson, "Shakespeare, or The Poet," *Representative Men*, 1844).

> Others abide our question. Thou art free.
> We ask and ask—thou smilest and art still,
> Out-topping knowledge.
> (Matthew Arnold, *Shakespeare*, 1849.)

The passages just quoted will at least make clear that the new criticism was unrestrained by any rational fear of "superstitious veneration," and that it was unchecked by a desire to attain a justly balanced evaluation of the poet. For Dr. Johnson's explanation: "We must confess the faults of our favourite to gain credit to our praise of his excellencies," the Romantic critics had no need; they openly flaunted their idolatry. Moreover, in the pride of their discovery, they wrote about the dramatist as if they alone understood him, and made no effort to conceal their contempt for earlier critics who were less carried away than themselves. "It may be said of Shakespeare," wrote William Hazlitt,

> that those who are not for him are against him: for indifference is here the height of injustice. . . . An overstrained enthusiasm is more pardonable with respect to Shakespeare than the want of it.

Hazlitt had no sympathy for Dr. Johnson's common-sense analysis of the beauties and faults of the dramatist. Johnson had no poetry in his soul, "the shifting shapes of fancy, the rainbow hues of things, made no impression on him," he was pedestrian and unperceptive, "he reduced everything to the common standard of conventional propriety,"

> making criticism a kind of Procrustes' bed of genius, where he might cut down imagination to matter-of-fact, regulate the whole into logical diagrams and rhetorical declamation. (*Characters of Shakespeare's Plays*, 1817.)

Whether or not this is a fair estimate of Dr. Johnson's Shakespearean criticism is immaterial; all of the essential characteristics of the Romantic mind, however, appear in Hazlitt's impatience. They make clear that the difference is not so much that between two ages as that between two temperaments or two philosophies that might be found at any time. The new criticism was of the heart and not the head; it was intuitively sympathetic and interpretative, emotional rather than intellectual, impressionistic, subjective, and imaginatively free. "A genuine criticism," wrote Hazlitt, "should reflect the colours, the light and shade, the soul and body of a work." "Assuredly," said Coleridge,

> that criticism of Shakespeare will alone be genial which is reverential. The Englishman, who without reverence, a proud and affectionate reverence, can

utter the name of William Shakespeare, stands disqualified for the office of critic. (*Lectures on Shakespeare*, 1818.)[7]

Hazlitt's book, wrote Francis Jeffrey in *The Edinburgh Review* (August, 1817),

> is written less to tell the reader what Mr. H. *knows* about Shakespeare or his writings, than to explain to them how he *feels* about them—and why he feels so —and thinks that all who profess to love poetry should feel so likewise.

The same might be said of much Shakespearean criticism that is written in the purely romantic vein.

Coleridge, Lamb, Hazlitt, and their contemporaries also differed from most of their predecessors in regarding Shakespeare's plays not merely as works of art, but as embodiments of real life as well. "His plays alone are properly expressions of the passions," said Hazlitt,

> not descriptions of them. His characters are real beings of flesh and blood. (*Lectures on the English Poets*, 1818.)
>
> Hamlet is a name, his speeches and sayings but the idle coinage of the poet's brain. What then, are they not real? They are as real as our own thoughts. Their reality is in the reader's mind. It is *we* who are Hamlet. (*Characters*, 1817.)

The tribute here implied to the vitality which Shakespeare gave his characters is of the highest. It was the easiest sort of illusion to think of them as so many fellow-creatures of whose existence the plays preserve our only record (see p. 394). It was Maurice Morgann who had first said that Shakespeare's characters may be considered as historic rather than dramatic beings, but the nineteenth-century critics supplied the exposition of this theme. Some of the most penetrating—as well as some of the most irrelevant—character analysis these critics produced was the result of forgetting that these figures were, after all, only the creatures of art, their lives limited by the plays in which they appear. Frequently, in their romantic analyses, these critics lost all contact with Shakespeare's text.

Another idea from Morgann developed in the early nineteenth century was that of the impression, which became the basis of judgment in a character or in a play. In appreciative or interpretative criticism, the critic, endeavoring to subject himself to his author, cannot get much beyond the general impression left by a work as a whole. But he can check the impression against the text, and he can make sure that he is not merely underscoring

---

[7] The *Lectures* are not preserved as they were delivered. Coleridge spoke extempore, but his practice was to make copious notes beforehand. The fragments of such notes which remain, together with stenographic reports of the lectures, have been collected in T. Ashe's *Lectures and Notes on Shakspere . . . by Samuel Taylor Coleridge* (1883), and, more recently, by Professor T. M. Raysor, *Coleridge's Shakespearean Criticism*, 2 volumes (1931).

the passages that are most appealing to him. This danger the Romantic critic, in his enthusiasm, did not always avoid. Led by Goethe and Coleridge, he sought to establish contact with Shakespeare's mind and to test everything by his own experience of life. Hence, he often read himself into his appreciation of Shakespeare. Indeed, both Coleridge and Lamb emphasized the "powers which [Shakespeare] positively creates in us," and our frequently mistaking them

> for nothing more than indigenous faculties of our own minds, which only waited the application of corresponding virtues in him to return a full and clear echo of the same. (Charles Lamb, *On the Tragedies of Shakespeare*, 1818.)

Such methods allowed the Romantic critic free scope for his own personality. All were either poets themselves, or brilliant essayists.

As illustration of how even a great critic might, in his interpretation, take only a selected passage as a text and spin from it something that might be quite unsatisfactory to another reader, we may quote two of the sentimental theories about *Hamlet*. In *Wilhelm Meister* (1796), Goethe tells how his hero found the key to the prince's character in the couplet:

> The time is out of joint. O cursed spite,
> That ever I was born to set it right!

With apparently some assistance from the self-reproaching soliloquies, he goes on:

> In these words, I imagine is the key to Hamlet's whole procedure, and to me it is clear that Shakespeare sought to depict a great deed laid upon a soul unequal to the performance of it. In this view I find the piece composed throughout. Here is an oak tree planted in a costly vase, which should have received into its bosom only lovely flowers; the roots spread out, the vase is shivered to pieces.
> A beautiful, pure, and most moral nature, without strength of nerve which makes the hero, sinks beneath a burden which it can neither bear nor throw off; every duty is holy to him—this too hard.

Similarly, Coleridge identified himself with the prince:

> Hamlet's character is the prevalence of the abstracting and generalizing habit over the practical. He does not want courage, skill, will, or opportunity; but every incident sets him thinking, and it is curious, and, at the same time, strictly natural, that Hamlet, who all the play seems reason itself, should be impelled, at last, by mere accident to effect his object. I have a smack of Hamlet myself, if I may say so. (*Table Talk*, 1827.)

These famous idealizations of Shakespeare's most puzzling character have been quoted here because from one or the other sprang much subsequent interpretation of the character, both in criticism and on the stage. Yet how shockingly unreal and incomplete are these portraits, both in the virtues they assign the character and in the blame they imply. In both cases, the method was essentially subjective. One result was ludicrously like both Wilhelm Meister and his creator; the other, as Coleridge himself knew, resembled no one so much as S. T. C.

Obviously, the virtues and the faults of Romantic criticism of Shakespeare were those of Romantic literature generally; it had a strong personal accent, which, however, was often given a universal significance. At its best, as in Coleridge and Hazlitt, its excellence depended not so much upon the method employed as upon the taste and capacities of the critic. With the more gifted, the reader feels that his sympathy with Shakespeare is being stimulated and his understanding of the plays and of life is being promoted. At its worst, it becomes mere sentimental rhapsodizing, as in Mrs. Anna Brownell Jameson's *Characteristics of Women: Shakespeare's Heroines* (1832), or purely imaginative as in Mrs. Mary Cowden-Clarke's *The Girlhood of Shakespeare's Heroines* (1864). The tradition has been carried on in Ludwig Lewisohn's *The Last Days of Shylock* (1931) and in Percy Mackaye's recent tetralogy of plays, *The Mystery of Hamlet, Prince of Denmark, or What We Will* (1949) (see below, p. 437).

Occasionally, too, as a result of their interest in the processes of the imagination, the Romantic critics denied Shakespeare any dramatic merit at all. At least they preferred to treat his plays as poetic rather than theatrical art. As early as 1754, David Hume had alluded to Shakespeare's "total ignorance of all theatrical art and conduct" (*History of England*), and the central idea of Charles Lamb's criticism was that "the plays of Shakespeare are less calculated for performance on a stage, than those of almost any other dramatist whatever" (*On the Tragedies of Shakespeare*, 1818). Acting, Lamb argued, deals only with the superficial aspects of the emotions, and all of Shakespeare's characters have

> something in them which appeals too exclusively to the imagination to admit of their being made objects to the senses without suffering a change and a diminution. . . . Whereas the reading of a tragedy is a fine abstraction. It presents to the fancy just so much of external appearances as to make us feel that we are among flesh and blood, while by far the greater and better part of our imagination is employed upon the thoughts and internal machinery of the character. But in acting, scenery, dress, the most contemptible things, call upon us to judge of their naturalness.

The library, instead of the theatre, had now definitely become Shakespeare's abode.

To the Romantic Period, also, belongs the most ambitious enterprise for illustrating Shakespeare pictorially. The Boydell Shakespeare Gallery, originated by the print-makers John Boydell and his nephew Josiah, opened in Pall Mall in 1789, and to it contributed the most eminent artists of the day:

Sir Joshua Reynolds, Henry Fuseli, George Romney, Benjamin West, John Hoppner, Richard Westall, Francis Wheatley, James Northcote, Robert Smirke, Angelica Kaufman, and Thomas Stothard, to name only a few. It mattered little that not all even of the artists named had talents which were suited to the undertaking; the Boydells were liberal commissioners, and most of the popular painters of the day contributed several canvases to the collection. The Shakespeare Gallery eventually cost over a hundred thousand pounds.

The ideal behind the project was partly patriotic, but mainly artistic. Foreigners maintained that England could produce only portrait painters and lacked talent for what the age considered the noblest branch of pictorial art, historical painting. The Boydell Gallery was intended to prove the contrary; with a fit subject to inspire them, English artists could remove this foreign reproach. Yet characteristically there was the pretense at least of Romantic misgiving. "Though I believe it will be readily admitted," wrote John Boydell in the first catalogue to his collection,

> that no subjects seem so proper to form an English school of Historical Painting, as the scenes of the immortal Shakespeare; yet it must be always remembered that he possessed powers which no pencil can reach; for such was the force of his creative imagination, that though he frequently goes beyond nature, he still continues to be natural, and seems only to do that which nature would have done, had she o'erstep'd her usual limits. It must not, then, be expected that the art of the Painter can ever equal the sublimity of our Poet. . . . For what pencil can give to his airy beings "a local habitation and a name"?

Unfortunately the Shakespeare Gallery proved the ruin of its founders. They paid their artists well, the French Revolution, by interrupting continental trade, ruined their print business, and their efforts to recoup their losses by publishing in 1802 a handsome portfolio of engravings of their Shakespeare paintings proved a failure. Finally in 1804 John Boydell petitioned Parliament for permission to dispose of the collection by lottery. The prize was drawn early in 1805, but the new owner could not maintain the collection intact. A few months later the paintings were sold at Christie's in separate lots, and today the pictures—some of them enormous canvases—are scattered in public galleries and private collections all over the world. The sum realized at the sale amounted to only approximately six thousand pounds. (See illustrations, pp. 451-2.)

THE LATER NINETEENTH CENTURY

In method and in point of view, the Romantic spirit has colored all Shakespearean criticism to the present day. The later nineteenth-century critics in many ways merely supplied a more sober exposition of the themes of the Romantics. Coleridge, for example, had spoken much about the man Shakespeare, and the variety of Shakespearean study which is most typical of the Victorian period is that which refused to be content with the works alone, but sought to augment the scanty details of biography by reconstructing the personality of the author. "Shakespeare is the only biographer of Shakespeare," wrote Emerson, with a characteristic subjective appeal, "and even he can tell nothing except to the Shakespeare in us; that is to our most apprehensive and sympathetic hour." "Shakespeare," according to John Keats, "led a life of allegory. His works are the comments on it" (Letter to George and Georgiana Keats, February 18, 1819).

Hence, book after book tried to pass from the creation to the mind of the creator, and, thence, to the heart of his mystery. Critics studied Shakespeare's life in relation to his books, searching for passages that could be interpreted as self-revelatory, and treating the plays, not as separate dramatic entities, but as parts of a harmonious unity and design. Naturally, the Sonnets, which seemed most probably autobiographical, received much attention, for, as Wordsworth had written, "with this key Shakespeare unlocked his heart." Others tried to reconstruct his conception of life and the world, his attitude toward religion, the state, society, nature, science, art, education, love, women, marriage, family life. They attempted to arrange his works in chronological order in the hope that this would reveal the true history of the growth and progress of his soul. The nineteenth-century critic did not easily miss what he desired to find.

The number of these interpretative studies is huge, and it will be possible here to mention only a few examples. It may at once be said that the product is not of uniform excellence. But some such desire to reconstruct imaginatively the man Shakespeare animates alike the books of the German critic Hermann Ulrici,[8] H. N. Hudson,[9] G. G. Gervinus,[10] Hippolyte Taine,[11] Walter Bagehot,[12] Edward Dowden,[13] Karl Elze,[14] A. C. Swinburne,[15] the Dutch scholar Bernhard ten Brink,[16] Barrett Wendell,[17] and the Danish scholar George Brandes.[18] Most of these volumes may still be read with profit or interest today. In our time, the following authors have in many ways con-

[8] *Shakespeare's Dramatic Art* (1847).
[9] *Shakespeare: His Life, Art and Characters* (1848).
[10] *Shakespeare's Commentaries* (1849–50).
[11] *History of English Literature* (1863).
[12] *Shakespeare the Man* (1853).
[13] *Shakespeare: His Mind and Art* (1875).
[14] *William Shakespeare* (1876).
[15] *A Study of Shakespeare* (1880).
[16] *Five Lectures on Shakespeare* (1893).
[17] *William Shakespeare: A Study in Elizabethan Literature* (1894).
[18] *William Shakespeare: A Critical Study* (1895–6).

tinued the tradition: Sir Walter Raleigh,[19] Frank Harris,[20] John Masefield,[21] Lytton Strachey,[22] Helene Richter,[23] Friederich Gundolf,[24] Sir J. Dover Wilson,[25] J. Middleton Murry,[26] and Kenneth Muir and Sean O'Loughlin.[27] True, the portrait which emerges in many of these books is more often a self-portrait of the critic. The reader comes sadly to the realization that it is possible to believe almost anything about Shakespeare. A misapplication of methods, to be sure, does not of necessity invalidate a theory. Yet, it might be added, the basic question of whether or not Shakespeare is revealed in his work was hotly debated in the nineteenth century and, on the whole, left unanswered. Some held, with Walter Pater, that "as happens with every true dramatist, Shakespeare is for the most part hidden behind the persons of his creation" (*Appreciations*, 1889).[28]

Commenting upon the lack of agreement among some of the recent interpreters of Shakespeare the man, T. S. Eliot has written:

> If the only way to prove that Shakespeare did not feel and think exactly as people felt and thought in 1815, or in 1860, or in 1880, is to show that he felt and thought as we felt and thought in 1927, then we must accept gratefully the alternative. . . .
>
> My own frivolous opinion is that Shakespeare may have held in private life very different views from what we extract from his extremely varied published works; that there is no clue in his writings to the way in which he would have voted in the last or would vote in the next election; and that we are completely in the dark as to his attitude about prayer-book revision. I admit that my own experience, as a minor poet, may have jaundiced my outlook; that I am used to having cosmic significances, which I never suspected, extracted from my work (such as it is) by enthusiastic persons at a distance; and of being informed that something which I meant seriously is *vers de société;* and to having my personal biography reconstructed from passages which I got out of books, or which I invented out of something because they sounded well; and to having my biography invariably ignored in what I *did* write from personal experience; so that in consequence I am inclined to believe that people are mistaken about

[19] *Shakespeare* (1907).

[20] *The Man Shakespeare and His Tragic Life Story* (1909); *The Women of Shakespeare* (1911). The four women referred to in Harris's book as having influenced Shakespeare are his mother, wife, mistress, and daughter.

[21] *William Shakespeare* (1911).

[22] "Shakespeare's Final Period," in *Books and Characters* (1922).

[23] *Shakespeare der Mensch* (1923).

[24] *Shakespeare Sein Wesen und Werk* (1928).

[25] *The Essential Shakespeare* (1932).

[26] *Shakespeare* (1936).

[27] *The Voyage to Illyria* (1937).

[28] See W. T. Brewster, "The Reconstruction of Shakespeare's Personality," in *Shakesperian Studies by Members of the Department of English and Comparative Literature in Columbia University* (1916).

Shakespeare just in proportion to the relative superiority of Shakespeare to my-self. (*Shakespeare and the Stoicism of Seneca*, a Shakespeare Association lecture, 1927.)

Mr. Eliot makes sound sense.

Another of the tenets of Coleridge's criticism which was developed in detail in the nineteenth century was that "the judgment of Shakespeare is commensurate with his genius" (*Lectures*, 1802). Thus, the greater Roman-tics had completely rejected the idea of the uncultivated natural genius, beloved of their immediate predecessors, and substituted for it that of a clear and deep thinker. No man, Coleridge argued, had ever yet been a great poet without being, at the same time, a profound philosopher—a logical con-clusion from the Romantic conception of poetry as "the blossom and the fragrancy of all human knowledge, human thoughts, human passions, emo-tions, language." He spoke of "our myriad minded Shakespeare," who was "the morning star, the guide, and the pioneer, of true philosophy."

> Shakespeare, no mere child of nature; no automaton of genius; no passive vehicle of inspiration possessed by the spirit, not possessing it; first studied patiently, meditated deeply, understood minutely, till knowledge, become habitual and intuitive, wedded itself to his habitual feelings, and at length gave birth to that stupendous power, by which he stands alone, with no equal or second in his own class. (*Biographia Literaria* [1817], Chapter XV.)

In Shakespeare's works, the nineteenth-century critics found a marvelously accurate picture of human life and character, and they came to think of the great Elizabethan as a seer and the possessor of a power greater than life. For them it was not sufficient to represent Shakespeare as a master poet and dramatist; he must also be shown to have been a great teacher, whose book contained the key to all human problems and the quintessence of human wisdom. "What point of morals," asked Emerson,

> of manners, of economy, of philosophy, or religion, or taste, of the conduct of life, has he not settled? What mystery has he not signified his knowledge of? What office, or function, or district of man's work, has he not remembered? What king has he not taught state, as Talma taught Napoleon? What maiden has not found him finer than her delicacy? What lover has he not outloved? What sage has he not outseen? What gentleman has he not instructed in the rudeness of his behaviour? ("Shakespeare, or The Poet," in *Representative Men*, 1844.)

Whether or not the German critics, Schlegel or Lessing or Goethe, had anticipated the English in their discovery of Shakespeare the philosopher need concern us little here; such study was but a logical development of English thought about the master dramatist. In his famous Preface (1765), Dr. Johnson had remarked casually that from Shakespeare's works "a system of civil and œconomical prudence" might be collected, and, as early as 1775, Elizabeth Griffith had conducted a persistent search for ethical teachings in

The Morality of Shakespeare's Drama Illustrated. It was left for the nine-teenth-century critics, however, to complete the discovery. One heard more and more about what Shakespeare was rather than what he did; more of Shakespeare the prophet and the moralist, and less of Shakespeare the artist. Hence, Shakespeare's plays became the hunting ground for the philosophers. They culled mottoes and aphorisms from them, and moral sentences for the guidance of human life.[29] Half seriously, they compiled *Shakespeare Alma-nacs*, fitting each historical day in the calendar with a suitable quotation from the writings of "the immortal Shakespeare."[30] Still others tended to fit the plays into a continuous esthetic, ethical, philosophical system, which, like the reconstructions of the poet's personality, often revealed much more about the critic than about Shakespeare.[31] As J. W. Mackail has remarked, "To read a philosophy into Shakespeare is hurtful, because it stands between us and him and vitiates our view" (*Shakespeare after Three Hundred Years*, a British Academy lecture, 1916).

Likewise in the nineteenth century, instead of being merely an inspired prodigy, Shakespeare was seen to have had special learning of all kinds. From about 1850 on, the number of treatises upon Shakespeare's knowledge of the law, of medicine, of farming, of botany, of music, of zoology, of geography, of ethnology, is truly astounding. The authors usually were themselves specialists in the fields of knowledge to which they welcomed Shakespeare. The method is familiar even today—that of collecting allusions and technical terms from the mass of his writings. Few were content that "mere prattle without practice" should be the extent of his knowledge; that Shakespeare was a "bookish theoric" was unthinkable.[32] His allusions must throw light

[29] Only a few typical examples need be cited: Michael Henry Rankin, *The Philosophy of Shakespeare Extracted from his Plays and Interspersed with Remarks* (1841); Sir F. B. Watson, *Religious and Moral Sentences Culled from the Writings of Shakespeare, Compared with Passages Drawn from Holy Writ* (1843); Anon., *Bible Truths with Shake-spearean Parallels* (1862). Some are just harmlessly sentimental, like *The Sweet Silvery Sayings of Shakespeare on the Softer Sex*, compiled by an Old Soldier (1877), 328 pages! In the possession of the writer is an entertaining example, much less serious than the average, entitled *The Oracles of Shakespeare; with a Selection of Aphorisms from the Same Author* (1845). The *Oracles* is really a game in which such questions as "Am I Beloved?" "Is My Love Constant?" "Shall I Ever Be Married?" "What Kind of Wife Shall I Have?" are answered by lottery assisted by Shakespeare.

[30] *The Shakspere Almanack* for 1849 and following years. American compilations were a *Shakespearian Annual Almanac*, by O. Phelps Brown (1870); a *Calendar of American Chronology Illustrated by Quotations from Shakespeare* (1872); and *Events in the History of New York City with Illustrations from Shakspeare*, by a New Yorker [John B. Moreau] (1880 on).

[31] Extreme examples may be found in the books of Charles Downing, who, under the name of "Clelia," wrote on *God in Shakspeare* (1890), *The Messiahship of Shakspeare* (1901), and *Shakspeare as Pan-Judge of the World* (1913).

[32] The views expressed by Dr. A. O. Kellogg, assistant physician in the State Lunatic Asylum at Utica, New York, are typical, even if today they sound extravagant: "Shake-

upon the dark years of his biography before he became an actor. Does he notice glowworms, dragon-flies, moths, gnats, and spiders—truly he was a born entomologist; does he mention nocturnal cats and neighing stallions—he was a student of zoology; can he discourse of military matters—he must have been a soldier; does he quote legal technicalities—he must have been apprenticed to a lawyer; does he mention faraway places—surely Shakespeare was a traveler.

One of these little treatises, however, must at least be given honorable mention, because it was a refreshing burlesque of the methods and the conclusions to which they led. Written by William Blades, the great bibliographer, it is entitled: *Shakspere and Typography; Being an Attempt to Show Shakspere's Personal Connection with, and Technical Knowledge of, the Art of Printing.* . . . (1872). But it was taken quite seriously by some of Blades's contemporaries—a circumstance that delighted him immensely—and is today occasionally included in Shakespeare bibliographies along with other books having similar titles without comment as to its real purpose. No one, at least so far as the present writer is aware, has applied the method to answering the question, "Was Shakespeare a Murderer?" though the evidence is voluminous, and the deductions are inescapable.

If there was little change in the spirit or the standards of criticism in the nineteenth century, there was considerable development in scholarship, which, in turn, left its mark upon criticism. The Shakespeare scholars of the early nineteenth century carried on the traditions of Edmund Malone and sought to explain Shakespeare by a knowledge of his age. Antiquarian scholars, like Francis Douce (1757–1834), Nathan Drake (1766–1836), and Joseph Hunter (1783–1861), began more especially a study of ancient manners and customs as well as early literature for the light they could shed on Shakespeare. Other scholars, like John Payne Collier (1789–1883), who unfortunately was not always trustworthy, and James Orchard Halliwell (1820–89), searched public records and similar archives and added considerably, not only to the knowledge of Shakespeare, but also of the theatrical conditions in which he worked. With Collier and others, Halliwell founded the Shakespeare Society (1841–53), the purpose of which was to make accessible to students Elizabethan materials illustrative of Shakespeare. And

---

speare's knowledge extended far beyond the range of ordinary observation and comprehended subjects, such, as in our day . . . were regarded as strictly professional and special. . . . The knowledge displayed was far in advance of the age in which he lived, and, as we shall have occasion to show, was not possessed by any one in his time, however eminent in any special department of science to which he might be devoting himself; and many facts not known or recognized by men of his age appear to have been grasped by the inspired mind of the poet, to whose acute mental vision it would seem from his writings, they were as clear and certain as they have been rendered by the positive deductions of . . . the scientific research and experience of the last two centuries." (*Shakespeare's Delineations of Insanity, Imbecility, and Suicide,* 1866.)

the study of Shakespeare's text was continued with a scientific method. At least some of the significant results of these scholarly labors were made use of by many of the critics to whose opinions we have already referred. The foundations of criticism, from the historical point of view adopted by the moderns, were laid early.

The principal development in Shakespearean scholarship in the second half of the nineteenth century was scientific criticism. The older investigations continued, but, under the influence of the new scientific movements, the younger scholars applied to Shakespeare the theories of evolution and development, and turned their attention to the chronology of his plays and tests for determining date and authorship. The leaders in these studies were F. G. Fleay (1831–1909), F. J. Furnivall (1825–1910), and the members of the New Shakespeare Society, founded in 1873. The influence of these investigations can be observed in many of the studies of Shakespeare's life and works already mentioned, notably in that of Professor Dowden, who adopted the division of Shakespeare's career into the four periods evolved by the scholars, though his designations of them—"In the Workshop," "On the Heights," "In the Depths," "In the World"—were fanciful. His principal concern was with the development of Shakespeare's taste, his mind, and his art. In the nineteenth century, the scholar and the critic, while remaining strictly separate, became, so far as Shakespeare was concerned, increasingly dependent upon one another.

THE TWENTIETH CENTURY

Modern criticism of Shakespeare represents, as a whole, a reaction against the Romanticism of the nineteenth century. The younger critics regard with misgivings, if not distrust, what they call the "mere connoisseurship" of their elders. They desire once more to do justice to Shakespeare as a man of the theatre and prefer to think of him as a popular actor-dramatist, living in an age when drama was none too reputable, and writing Elizabethan plays for production in an Elizabethan theatre as entertainment for an Elizabethan audience. His plays, they argue, were written not merely to be read, but to be heard and seen in a theatre, and, hence, cannot be judged esthetically simply as poetry, nor even as we judge drama today. Granted that Shakespeare's works deserve all the panegyrics that have been bestowed upon them, do we today understand his plays, they ask, as Shakespeare intended them to be understood? The drama, the stage, the audience, all have changed greatly since the sixteenth century. Far from being an isolated, aloof philosopher, Shakespeare, they believe, was technically and psychologically conditioned by the playhouse in which he worked, by the traditions of the drama he had learned to write, and by the audience to which he was appealing. The Elizabethans, they maintain, brought to popular plays, like *Hamlet*, conceptions and expectations that we do not share with them, just as the playgoer of today brings to the theatre a whole body of ideas the Elizabethan did not have.

Hence, the twentieth-century historical critic prefers to approach Shakespeare through an understanding of the conditions which Shakespeare understood, accepted, and turned to dramatic advantage. In *The Elizabethan Hamlet* (1895), John Corbin rejected the gentle, sweet youth of the nineteenth-century commentators, and attempted to reconstruct the Elizabethan backgrounds of the play, as did Professor C. M. Lewis in *The Genesis of Hamlet* (1907). In *Shakspere and His Predecessors* (1896), Professor F. S. Boas laid especial stress upon the indebtedness of Shakespeare to the work of the earlier Elizabethans; Professor G. P. Baker's *The Development of Shakespeare as a Dramatist* (1907) and Professor Brander Matthews' *Shakspere as a Playwright* (1913) focused attention upon Shakespeare's dramatic craftsmanship and his compliance with the expectations of his audiences. In *Prefaces to Shakespeare* (five series, 1927–47) and various lectures, Granville-Barker, himself a man of the theatre, has illuminated the subject of Shakespeare as an Elizabethan playwright, as have the various members of the Shakespeare Association in England. Others, like Sir M. W. MacCallum in *Shakespeare's Roman Plays and Their Background* (1910), Professor W. W. Lawrence in *Shakespeare's Problem Comedies* (1930), or Professor Lily B. Campbell in *Shakespeare's Tragic Heroes* (1930), have studied Shakespeare's methods of composition, the restraining traditions of classical and medieval story, or the dramatist's relation to the philosophy of his day concerning the nature of the emotions. Professor L. L. Schücking in *Character Problems in Shakespeare's Plays* (1919) and Professor E. E. Stoll in *Shakespeare Studies: Historical and Comparative in Method* (1927) and *Art and Artifice in Shakespeare* (1933), as well as other shorter studies, have found their subjects precisely in that aspect of Shakespeare's technique that the Romantics held secure from question—the characters. Shakespeare, they argue, aimed at being dramatically effective and not psychologically consistent.

It is possible here to name only a few of the modern critics of Shakespeare and their works; others will be found in the bibliographies to the various chapters of this book. The modern critic, it is clear, is much more willing than his forebears to admit that Shakespeare shared, to a large extent, the thought and opinion and prejudices of his Elizabethan audience, that there are many vestiges of primitive dramatic art in his plays, and that, Elizabethan conditions of authorship being what they were, there may even be a great deal of writing in the plays that is not Shakespeare's. Historical criticism, it should be noted, was not absent in the nineteenth century, and the works of some of the better appreciative critics, like Professor A. C. Bradley (*Shakespearean Tragedy*, 1904) and Sir Walter Raleigh (*Shakespeare*, 1907) are distinctly affected by it. The moderns have merely given fresh emphasis to the distinction in Shakespeare of those elements which are of an age from those of all time. L. C. Knights's *How Many Children Had Lady Macbeth? An Essay on the Theory and Practice of Shakespearean Criticism* (1933) is an amusing, wholesome satire on the barrenness of some Shakespearean "scholarship."

At the same time, there are other students who, in their search for hidden allusions and allegorical or mythological symbols in Shakespeare's plays, approach a kind of neo-Romanticism. Notable among them, on the one hand, is Miss Lillian Winstanley, whose *Hamlet and the Scottish Succession* (1921), *Macbeth, King Lear, and Contemporary History* (1922), and *Othello as the Tragedy of Italy* (1924), examine the plays named in relation to contemporaneous events and find in them topical allusions to the Darnley murder, the Essex conspiracy, the personal history of James I, the St. Bartholomew Massacre, and the dominance of Spain. Shakespeare's works are no mere plays; they are political propaganda as well. On the other hand another kind of longing animates the metaphysical criticism of G. Wilson Knight, whose *Myth and Miracle, An Essay on the Mystic Symbolism of Shakespeare* (1929) is the first of a series of supersubtle volumes including *The Wheel of Fire, An Essay in Interpretation of Shakespeare's Sombre Tragedies* (1930), *The Imperial Theme* (1931), and *The Shakespearean Tempest* (1932). Knight's method is the search for a general philosophical concept in a drama, "that burning core of mental or spiritual reality from which each play derives its nature and meaning"—usually some kind of tension between two abstractions. He has been followed by others who attach philosophic rather than merely dramatic significance to Shakespeare's imagery.

Obviously, it is difficult to estimate accurately the strength and the weakness of the newest criticism of Shakespeare, and it is impossible to predict the future. But the ablest of the moderns, like Granville-Barker, for example, characterized by essential realism and imagination at the same time, are advancing the understanding of Shakespeare's art. A return to the text of Shakespeare, a distrust of generalizations, a closer examination of what the poet wrote, and a re-evaluation of this writing in the light of known fact are sure to produce lasting results. There is, of course, the obvious danger of assuming that when one has accounted for the conditions under which an artist worked, he has accounted completely for the artist himself. Similarly, because of the simple difficulty of *knowing*, not merely surmising, what a play meant to the Elizabethans or what the author's *intentions* really were, the historical critic may merely be substituting another kind of subjectivity for that which he rejects.[33] Finally, the timid reader, confronted by innumer-

[33] See Lascelles Abercrombie, *A Plea for the Liberty of Interpreting*, a British Academy lecture (1930).

able perplexities—which he might never have noticed for himself—may, with Logan Pearsall Smith, come to the conclusion that no one can appreciate Shakespeare, much less write about him, without a special license.[34]

"And so," with the words of the Preface to the First Folio,

> we leave you to other of his friends, whom if you need, can be your guides; if you need them not, you can lead yourselves and others. And such readers we wish him.

SUGGESTED REFERENCES

BABCOCK, ROBERT WITBECK. *The Genesis of Shakespeare Idolatry, 1766–1799. A Study in English Criticism of the Late Eighteenth Century.* Chapel Hill, University of North Carolina Press, 1931.

BENTLEY, GERALD E. *Shakespeare and Jonson: Their Reputations in the Seventeenth Century Compared* (2 vols.). University of Chicago Press, 1945.

A demonstration that during their lifetimes and for the remainder of the seventeenth century, Ben Jonson's reputation was far superior to Shakespeare's.

BRADBY, ANNE (ed.). *Shakespeare Criticism, 1919–35.* With an Introduction by the editor. London, Humphrey Milford, Oxford University Press, 1936.

A selection of some of the most significant modern criticism, mainly English.

BROWN, IVOR *and* FEARON, GEORGE. *Amazing Monument: A Short History of the Shakespeare Industry.* London, Heinemann, 1939.

An amusing account of Shakespeare as a national and international industry, a paying concern which is part worship, part racket. Published in America as *This Shakespeare Industry,* Harper and Brothers.

DUNN, ESTHER CLOUDMAN. *Shakespeare in America.* New York, Macmillan, 1939.

ELSON, L. C. *Shakespeare in Music.* Boston, L. C. Page, 1901.

Shakespeare in opera.

HAINES, C. M. *Shakespeare in France, Criticism Voltaire to Victor Hugo.* London, Humphrey Milford, Oxford University Press, 1925.

HALLIDAY, F. E. *Shakespeare and His Critics.* London, Duckworth, 1949.

HUGHES, C. E. (ed.). *The Praise of Shakespeare, an English Anthology.* London, Methuen, 1904.

JOHNSON, CHARLES F. *Shakespeare and His Critics.* Boston and New York, Houghton, 1909.

A sketch of Shakespeare's reputation.

[34] *On Reading Shakespeare* (1933).

JONES, F. L. "Echoes of Shakespeare in Later Elizabethan Drama," *Publications of the Modern Language Association*, XLV (1930), pp. 791–803.

JUSSERAND, J. J. *Shakespeare in France under the Ancien Régime*. London, T. Fisher Unwin, 1899.

LOVETT, DAVID. "Shakespeare's Characters in Eighteenth Century Criticism," *English Literary History*, II (1935), pp. 267–89.

MCGINN, DONALD J. *Shakespeare's Influence on the Drama of His Age*. New Brunswick, Rutgers University Press, 1938.

MCKEITHAN, D. M. *The Debt to Shakespeare in the Beaumont and Fletcher Plays*. Austin, University of Texas Press, 1938.

NICOLL, ALLARDYCE (ed.). *Shakespeare Survey: A New Annual Survey of Shakespearian Study and Production* (Vol. 1 and 2). Cambridge University Press, 1948, 1949.

RALLI, AUGUSTUS. *A History of Shakespearian Criticism* (2 vols.). Oxford, Clarendon Press, 1932.

A summary of esthetic opinion on Shakespeare from 1616 to 1925 in England, America, France, and Germany.

RAYSOR, T. M. "The Study of Shakespeare's Characters in the Eighteenth Century," *Modern Language Notes*, XLII (1927), p. 495.

ROBINSON, HERBERT SPENCER. *English Shakespearian Criticism in the Eighteenth Century*. New York, H. W. Wilson Company, 1932.

SALAMAN, MALCOLM C. *Shakespeare in Pictorial Art*. London, The Studio, 1916.

Shakespeare Criticism in Germany, 1740–1815. A Selection of German Texts, including Outstanding Criticisms and Translations of the Plays. With an Introduction in English by R. Pascal. Cambridge University Press, 1937.

The Shakspere Allusion Book: A Collection of Allusions to Shakspere from 1591 to 1700 (2 vols.). Originally Compiled by C. M. Ingleby, Miss L. Toulmin Smith, and by Dr. F. J. Furnivall, with the Assistance of the New Shakspere Society: Re-edited, Revised, and Re-arranged, with an Introduction, by John Munro (1909), and Now Re-issued with a Preface by Sir Edmund Chambers. Oxford, Clarendon Press, 1932.

SHÜCKING, LEVIN LUDWIG. *Shakespeare im Literarischen Urteil seiner Zeit*. Heidelberg, Carl Winters, 1908.

Shakespeare's reputation in his own day.

SMITH, D. NICHOL (ed.). *Eighteenth Century Essays on Shakespeare*. Glasgow, J. MacLehose and Sons, 1903.

———(ed.). *Shakespeare Criticism, 1623–1840*. London, Humphrey Milford, Oxford University Press, 1916.

An anthology of critical opinion in English from Heminge and Condell to Carlyle.

————. *Shakespeare in the Eighteenth Century.* Oxford, Clarendon Press, 1928.

Three lectures: Shakespeare's reputation before the eighteenth century, eighteenth-century Shakespearean scholarship, eighteenth-century criticism.

WARNER, B. E. (ed.). *Famous Introductions to Shakespeare's Plays by the Notable Editors of the Eighteenth Century.* New York, Dodd, Mead, 1906.

From Heminge and Condell to Malone.

WESTFALL, ALFRED VAN RENSSELAER. *American Shakespearean Criticism, 1607–1865.* New York, H. W. Wilson Company, 1939.

SHAKESPEARE ON THE

STAGE

How many ages hence
Shall this our lofty scene be acted over
In states unborn and accents yet unknown!
—*Julius Cæsar*, III, i, 111–13.

I F , AS WE HAVE SEEN , SHAKESPEARE HAS BEEN REDISCOV-ered by successive generations of critics and reinterpreted according to the characteristic standards of the age that produced them, the same is true of the plays upon the stage. Shakespeare's roles have always had an irresistible at-traction for actors. It is the purpose of this final chapter to give a brief ac-count of the fortunes of his plays on the stage, their adaptation to changing theatrical conditions, and the presentation of these Elizabethan survivals be-fore audiences that had come to expect in the theatre what Shakespeare's con-temporaries hardly dreamed. Seldom since his own time, however, has any play of Shakespeare's been acted exactly as it was written. In the compromise with varying theatrical ideals and public taste, it has always been Shakespeare who has given way—never the theatre. At best, to fit the two hours' traffic of the modern stage, his dramas have been pruned of characters and episodes "least prejudicial to the plot or sense," with the remaining scenes transposed and redistributed at the discretion of the producer. At worst, Shakespeare has simply been rewritten, his plots and characters reconstructed, his store in-creased by new roles and episodes, and his verse polished to suit contemporary taste. Not until the nineteenth century did the tendency to produce Shake-speare "according to the original text"—as the playbills put it—become steadily progressive. That has usually meant merely acting as much or as little as the producer saw fit or felt he had time for.

BEFORE THE RESTORATION

In the public theatres of his own day, Shakespeare's popularity was high; he was considered, as we have seen, among "the most excellent in both comedy and tragedy for the stage." Some of his plays, of course, were more attractive than others. *Hamlet* and *Henry IV* share the honor of being most frequently alluded to, and *Richard III* and *Romeo and Juliet* were also appealing. In general, Leonard Digges was probably not unreasonably eulogistic of Shakespeare's creations when he wrote:

> So have I seen, when Cæsar would appear,
> And on the stage at half-sword parley were
> Brutus and Cassius, oh, how the audience
> Were ravish'd; with what wonder they went thence,
> When some new day they would not brook a line
> Of tedious, though well-labour'd, *Catiline*.
> *Sejanus*[1] too was irksome. They priz'd more
> Honest Iago or the jealous Moor. . . .
>   when let but Falstaff come,
> Hal, Poins, the rest, you scarce shall have a room,
> All is so pester'd. Let but Beatrice
> And Benedick be seen, lo, in a trice,
> The cockpit, galleries, boxes, all are full
> To hear Malvolio, that cross-garter'd gull.
>   (Commendatory Verses Prefixed to *Shakespeare's Poems*, 1640.)

Yet an allusion in *The Return from Parnassus* (*c.* 1600–02), one of a series of satirical academic plays written at Cambridge, seems to imply that Shakespeare was the favorite only of the uncultivated and not of gentlemen of breeding and taste. A character, significantly named Gullio, quotes *Romeo* and *Venus* and vows to have the author's picture in his study, and the boorish actors, Kempe and Burbage, representatives of the "basest trade," are introduced putting the scholars Philomusus and Studioso through a try-out for the stage, speaking contemptuously of the abilities of university men, and praising their fellow Shakespeare, who "puts them all down." But, according to the title-page of the first edition of *Hamlet* (1603), that play had the unusual honor of being acted "in the two Universities of Cambridge and Oxford."

Of the original actors in Shakespeare's plays, unfortunately, we know little. The greatest, however, was Richard Burbage (1567?–1619), a son of that James Burbage who built the Theatre (1576). He excelled in tragedy, and for him, apparently, Shakespeare created his tragic heroes—Richard III, Romeo, Henry V, Hamlet, Macbeth, Othello, and Lear. Allusions to "the English Roscius," as he was called, are frequent. At his death in 1619, several elegies

---

[1] Both *Catiline* and *Sejanus* were plays written by Ben Jonson.

were composed on him, ranging from the simple "Exit Burbage" to one of considerable length containing these lines:

> He's gone, and with him what a world are dead
> Which he revived, to be revived so.
> No more young Hamlet, old Hieronymo,[2]
> Kind Lear, the grieved Moor, and more beside
> That lived in him have now forever died.
> Oft have I seen him leap into the grave
> Suiting the person which he seemed to have
> Of a sad lover with so true an eye
> That there I would have sworn he meant to die.
> Oft have I seen him play his part in jest
> So lively that spectators and the rest
> Of his sad crew, whilst he but seemed to bleed,
> Amazed, thought even then he died indeed.
> (*On the Death of the Famous Actor, R. Burbage.*)

Another writer described being taken over Bosworth Field by an innkeeper who was "full of ale and history," and who supplemented from Shakespeare's plays his knowledge of the battle which had been fought there,

> For when he would have said "King Richard died
> And call'd 'A horse! A horse!' " he "Burbage" cried.
> (Richard Corbet, *Iter Boreale*, c. 1620.)

In the comic ranks of Shakespeare's company stood Will Kempe (dates uncertain) who is known to have acted Peter in *Romeo and Juliet* and Dogberry in *Much Ado.* He was best in low-comedy roles, in jigs and comic songs, and for him Shakespeare created the clowns in his early comedies. Kempe left the Chamberlain's Men about 1598 or 1599, however, to perform a Morris dance marathon from London to Norwich, traveled abroad, returned to act in a rival company, and disappeared. His successor in the Shakespeare troupe was Robert Armin (dates unknown) who was best at court jesters, and for him such roles as Touchstone, Feste, Trinculo, and the Fool in *Lear* were probably written. Other members of Shakespeare's company who are known by name, if not by their roles, were John Heminge, the company's manager; Henry Condell; Thomas Pope; Augustine Phillips; Richard Cowley, who acted Verges in *Much Ado;* John Lowin; and William Sly.[3] Of the early seventeenth-century successors to these men and their Shakespearean roles still less is known.

Acting in the public theatres of London was prohibited by the Puritan Parliament in September of 1642, and the production of plays may be said

[2] The hero of *The Spanish Tragedy.*

[3] For an interesting attempt to assign roles in Shakespeare's plays to known members of his company, see T. W. Baldwin, *The Organization and Personnel of the Shakespearean Company* (1927), pp. 394 ff.

to have ceased until the Restoration of Charles II in 1660. The restrictions, however, were only partially effective; the players, deprived of their occupation, did not tamely submit to the laws passed against them, and sporadic attempts were made to revive plays in London or in the country. In spite of severe penalties, such as flogging, fines, and the confiscation of costumes, the players occasionally gathered, either privately in noblemen's houses, or secretly at one of the dismantled theatres, some barn, or other hiding place, where they performed before an audience eager to snatch even a momentary pleasure in the theatrical world of make-believe. No new plays, of course, could be written for such performances, but the Elizabethan and Jacobean drama had had infinite variety, and it was a simple matter to cut down a popular play to a length that would not detain a crowd conspicuously long. Such abridged versions were called *drolls*, and several from Shakespeare have survived: "The Bouncing Knight, or The Robbers Robbed" (from *1 Henry IV*), "The Grave-makers" (from *Hamlet*), "The Merry Conceited Humours of Bottom the Weaver" (from *A Midsummer Night's Dream*),[4] "The Mad Wooing, or A Way to Win and Tame a Shrew" (from *The Taming of the Shrew*), and "The Boaster, or Bully Huff Catch'd in a Trap" (from *1 Henry IV*).[5] Nothing is known about the performance of any of these skits, but their survival shows that Shakespeare was not neglected on the stage even during the Interregnum. The drolls are the earliest adaptations of Shakespeare to current theatrical conditions.

THE RESTORATION

When it was clear that the Stuarts would return, the players gathered again, acting at first in the old theatres. The Red Bull was opened as early as 1659, the Phoenix or Cockpit in Drury Lane, as well as Salisbury Court in Whitefriars, in the next year. Acting under these makeshift conditions must have been similar to what it had been before the closing of the theatres. But in July, 1660, Charles II granted patents or monopolies to Thomas Killigrew (1612–83) and Sir William Davenant (1606–68), giving them power to form two companies of players and to build two new theatres. Thus were established the two major playhouses in London, which were to endure, with occasional rivalry from lesser unauthorized houses, until 1843. By November, 1660, both companies were organized. The Killigrew, or King's Company, composed in the main of the older actors, first acted in a converted tennis court in Vere Street, then moved to the Theatre Royal in Bridges Street, Covent Garden, in May, 1663, and later, after this playhouse was destroyed

---

[4] Printed by Francis Kirkman in *The Wits, or Sport upon Sport*, Part I (1662, 1672); Part II (1673); reprinted by John James Elson, Ithaca (1932).

[5] Printed in *The Theatre of Ingenuity* (c. 1698); reprinted by J. O. Halliwell as *Shakespearean Drolls* (1859).

by fire, to a new Theatre Royal in Drury Lane, built by Sir Christopher Wren in 1674. Davenant's troupe, known as the Duke of York's Company, was composed mainly of young men. It opened in Salisbury Court, moved to a new playhouse in Lincoln's Inn Fields in June, 1661, and settled finally in a large new theatre in Dorset Garden in November, 1671. From 1682 to 1695, during the union of the two companies, acting took place at the Theatre Royal, Drury Lane.

This is not the place to relate the complicated theatrical history of the Restoration. So far as Shakespeare's plays were concerned, these were divided between the two companies. On December 12, 1660, Davenant, taking first pick, was granted a royal warrant for the exclusive performance of plays he thought would be most popular, among them Shakespeare's *The Tempest, Measure for Measure, Much Ado about Nothing, Romeo and Juliet, Twelfth Night, Henry VIII, King Lear, Macbeth,* and *Hamlet,* together with a two months' right to *Pericles.* The warrant alludes to Davenant's proposition for "reforming" the plays he sought, and "making them fit" for his company; what he meant will soon be clear. On August 20, 1668, he was granted more plays, including Shakespeare's *Timon of Athens, Troilus and Cressida,* and the three parts of *Henry VI.* On January 12, 1669, Killigrew was granted most of Jonson and Beaumont and Fletcher, but also Shakespeare's *The Winter's Tale, King John, Richard II, The Two Gentlemen of Verona, The Merry Wives of Windsor, The Comedy of Errors, Love's Labor's Lost, A Midsummer Night's Dream, The Merchant of Venice, As You Like It, The Taming of the Shrew, All's Well that Ends Well, Henry IV* (both parts), *Richard III, Coriolanus, Titus Andronicus, Julius Cæsar, Othello, Antony and Cleopatra,* and *Cymbeline.* Killigrew's was a longer list than Davenant's, but it probably offered less immediate opportunity for adaptation to new conditions.

To the England of Charles II, the England of Elizabeth, though it was little more than half a century removed, seemed crude and barbarous. As we have seen, taste had changed. The old plays had "begun to disgust this refined age"; to Pepys and his contemporaries, Shakespeare seemed "silly" and "ridiculous." Yet most of the Restoration critics vaguely recognized in the old drama a grandeur to which their own "correct" art could not aspire. As Dryden wrote:

> Our builders were with want of genius curst;
> The second temple was not like the first.

The pseudo-classical criticism was established, and, in the new theatres, other influences as well had begun to operate. In France, the Royalist exiles had become accustomed to scenery, spectacle, mechanical ingenuity, and actresses. Even before the Interregnum, the public playhouses had been learning of the advantages of spectacle and music from the court masques—even if they meant a sacrifice of drama. At Rutland House in 1656, Davenant, finding an opportunity to experiment, gave the English their first taste of opera in his *Siege of Rhodes*, "made a representation by the art of perspective in scenes, and the story sung in recitative music." The new English theatres, which catered to the limited audience of the world of fashion, were up-to-date. However much the Restoration theatre may have owed to Elizabethan example, it took no pride in that relationship. "Now for the difference betwixt our theatres and those of former times," wrote Richard Flecknoe,

> they were but plain and simple, with no other scenes nor decorations of the stage but only old tapestry and the stage strewed with rushes, with their habits accordingly, whereas ours now for cost and ornament are arrived to the height of magnificence. ("A Discourse on the English Stage," in his *Love's Kingdom*, 1664.)[6]

However, he added significantly:

> but that which makes our stage the better makes our plays the worse perhaps, they striving now to make them more for sight than hearing; whence that solid joy of the interior is lost and that benefit which men formerly received from plays, from which they seldom or never went away but far better and wiser than they came.

Under such circumstances, Shakespeare, far from being neglected, was "reformed and made fit." And it was Sir William Davenant—Shakespeare's godson—who led the way. The new age was interested primarily in three things: elaborate scenery, machines, costume, and spectacle; music and opera; and a super-refinement of honor into heroics. Nothing was easier. *Macbeth* (D. G. 1673),[7] wrote John Downes,

> altered by Mr. Davenant, being dressed in all its finery, as new clothes, new scenes, machines, as flyings for the witches, with all the singing and dancing in it . . . it being all excellently performed, being in the nature of an opera . . . it recompensed double the expense. (*Roscius Anglicanus*, 1708.)

The opening scene of *The Tempest* (L. I. F. 1667), altered by Dryden and Davenant, had a background representing

> a thick cloudy sky, a very rocky coast, and a tempestuous sea in perpetual agitation. This tempest . . . has many dreadful objects in it, as several spirits in horrid shapes flying down amongst the sailors, then rising and crossing in the air. And when the ship is sinking,[8] the whole house is darkened, and a shower of

[6] Compare Killigrew's remarks to Samuel Pepys, *Diary*, February 12, 1667.

[7] The abbreviations of the names of London theatres, used here and in the following pages, are the conventional ones: T. R., the Theatre Royal in Vere Street or Bridges Street; D. L., the Theatre Royal in Drury Lane; L. I. F., the Duke's Theatre in Lincoln's Inn Fields; D. G., the Duke's Theatre in Dorset Garden; and C. G., the Theatre Royal in Covent Garden.

[8] In Shakespeare's play, of course, the ship does not sink.

fire falls upon them. This is accompanied with lightning, and several claps of thunder, to the end of the storm.

In the Restoration theatres, Shakespeare's comedies were, for the most part, neglected as being too romantic or too chaotic in plot. But as early as 1662, Davenant mixed up *Measure for Measure* with Benedick and Beatrice into something resembling a balanced Restoration comedy called *The Law against Lovers* (L. I. F. 1662). John Lacy, the actor, transformed *The Taming of the Shrew* into *Sauny the Scot* (T. R. 1667), giving the play an English setting and offering greater opportunities to a coarse Scottish servant of Petruchio. Thomas D'Urfey rendered *Cymbeline* pathetic in *The Injured Princess, or The Fatal Wager* (D. L. 1682). Charles Gildon, the critic, produced a Restoration play with operatic elements in *Measure for Measure, or Beauty the Best Advocate* (L. I. F. c. 1699). *The Merchant of Venice* was replaced by George Granville's *The Jew of Venice* (L. I. F. 1701), which emphasized the comic possibilities of Shylock—the role was acted by Thomas Dogget, a low comedian—and lasted on the stage until Charles Macklin, in 1741, presented what his age at least regarded as "the Jew that Shakespeare drew," an almost tragic villain. *The Merry Wives* became thoroughly vulgar as *The Comical Gallant, or The Amours of Sir Falstaff* (D. L. 1702) at the hands of John Dennis. *Twelfth Night* became *Love Betray'd, or The Agreeable Disappointment* (L. I. F. 1703) by Charles Burnaby, with new characters and episodes added in the manner of the time.

Two of these adapted comedies have been reserved for special notice because they illustrate most clearly the taste of the age and its attitude toward Shakespeare. One is *The Tempest, or The Enchanted Island* (L. I. F. 1667) by John Dryden and Sir William Davenant, who merely added to Shakespeare's play what, in the words of the adapters, was designed as "the counterpart to Shakespeare's plot, namely that of a man who had never seen a woman; that by this means the two characters of innocence and love might the more illustrate and commend each other." The pious purpose of this structural balance today seems but a thin blind for some inexcusable pandering to Restoration taste. The magician Prospero is the guardian, not of one, but of two guileless daughters, Miranda and Dorinda, and also of an equally innocent youth, Hippolyto (a role always played by an actress), who is the rightful heir to the dukedom of Mantua and has been brought up in a cave on the far side of the island without ever having seen a woman. The possibilities for salty comedy were thus infinitely multiplied. Hippolyto catches a glimpse of Dorinda and admires her, meets the shipwrecked Ferdinand and learns from him that there are many beautiful women in the world. Thereupon Hippolyto resolves to have them all for himself. Hence, merely to curb this ambitious youngster and preserve Miranda as his own, Ferdinand is at last forced to fight him in a duel and so to fulfill a prophecy which said that

Hippolyto should die if ever he saw a woman. He is, however, easily brought back to life by magic. In addition, there are other "reformations." Shakespeare's jester becomes a boatswain and his drunken butler the master of a ship; Caliban has an unpleasant sister named Sycorax, who makes amorous advances to Trinculo, and Ariel has a "gentle spirit for his love" named Milcha, who dances a saraband with him at the end of the play. The whole is set out with music and much theatrical frippery to the utter ruin of Shakespeare's delicate comedy. All the while there is ringing in the audience's ears the Prologue's protest that "Shakespeare's magic could not copied be" and that his "power is sacred as a king's." This adapted *Tempest*, in its turn, suffered a further sea-change into an opera within a year, and one is obliged to record that Hippolyto and Dorinda did not finally disappear from the stage until 1838, when William Charles Macready at last—and with some misgivings—produced *The Tempest* from Shakespeare's text.

The other adapted comedy is a paradise of dainty devices, probably by Elkanah Settle, called *The Fairy Queen, an Opera*, "sent to cure your incredulity" with music by Henry Purcell (D. G. 1692). Shakespeare's fairy play became a spectacle with elaborate sets of cypress trees, grottoes, cascades, and marble pedestals; with masques and dances involving Night, Mystery, Secrecy, Sleep, and their attendants, troupes of fawns, dryads, naiades, savages, haymakers, and the Four Seasons. Bottom is entertained by a fairy masque, Juno appears in a machine drawn by peacocks, and Phœbus in a chariot with four horses. While a symphony plays, two swans, gliding on a river, turn into fairies and execute a dance, and, in a Chinese garden, decorated with porcelain vases and orange trees, a Chinaman sings a song in praise of primitive simplicity and dances with a Chinese woman, after which "six monkeys come from between the trees and dance" also. This confection was too expensive to be profitable, but, in the following century, it begot a progeny of operatized versions of Shakespeare's daintiest play. Hollywood is apparently nothing new; it is just a state of mind.

Shakespeare's tragedies, in their turn, were likewise "improved" according to the best contemporary taste. *Romeo and Juliet* was given a happy ending by James Howard (L. I. F. 1662) through the simple expedient of keeping the lovers alive, "so that when the tragedy was reviv'd again 'twas play'd alternately, tragical one day and tragicomical another, for several days together." Davenant added Duncan's ghost to the cast of *Macbeth*, expanded the parts of Lady Macduff and Seyton, and turned the witches into the song-and-dance team they remained almost to this day. Dryden rewrote *Antony and Cleopatra* as an original heroic play called *All for Love, or The World Well Lost* (D. L. 1677), and refined Shakespeare in *Troilus and Cressida, or Truth Found Out Too Late* (D. G. 1679), transforming both heroines from complex feminine characters into more simple women dominated by a ruling passion. Thomas Shadwell added a love interest to *Timon of Athens, the Man Hater* (D. G. 1678), and in his Preface remarked modestly, "I can truly say I have made it into a play." His version seems at least to have outlasted Shakespeare's on the stage. In his *History and Fall of Caius Marius* (D. G. 1679), Thomas Otway rifled Shakespeare of half a play by removing the passionate lovers Romeo and Juliet to Rome and employing the feud between Marius and Sylla as background—a strange transformation that banished Shakespeare's play from the stage until 1744. Even so, Otway's denouement—that of having the heroine awake before her lover's death—was retained by both Colley Cibber and David Garrick, survived well into the nineteenth century, and is still to be seen in Gounod's opera.

The most notorious of all the Restoration adaptations, however, was the *King Lear* (D. G. 1681) of Nahum Tate, who became King William's poet-laureate and was the friend of Dryden. Perceiving Shakespeare's play "a heap of jewels, unstrung, and unpolish'd," Tate found the "one expedient to rectify what was wanting in the regularity and probability of the tale . . . as love betwixt Edgar and Cordelia that never chang'd word with each other in the original." Having supplied the love interest dear to the Anglo-Saxon heart, the author progressed to a happy ending, excluding the Fool en route as destructive of unity of tone. Tate's *Lear* completely banished Shakespeare's play from the theatre until well into the nineteenth century. Garrick restored the tragic ending, but it was not until Macready produced the play in 1838 that the love scenes were finally dropped and the Fool returned to the stage. *Hamlet, Othello*, and *Julius Cæsar* alone among Shakespeare's great tragedies seem to have been treated with some respect, but all, especially *Hamlet*, were cut and some of the scenes transposed in the interests of greater unity and theatrical effectiveness.

Shakespeare's histories, in their turn, were either transformed into spectacle as was *Henry VIII*, or fitted with contemporary political parallels. Tate's *The Sicilian Usurper* (D. L. 1680) was a redaction of *Richard II* inspired by the Popish Plot and suppressed after two days on the stage. The same author's *The Ingratitude of a Commonwealth, or The Fall of Caius Martius Coriolanus* (D. L. 1681) was a similar venture:

> to make gold from ore
> And turn to money what lay dead before.

John Crowne's *The Misery of Civil War* (D. G. 1680) and *Henry the Sixt, the First Part* (D. G. 1681) were reworkings of 2 and 3 *Henry VI*, "old gather'd herbs," which in "sweet Shakespeare's garden grew," but into which were sprinkled both some "oily words" and "a little vinegar against the Pope." Colley Cibber's *Richard III* (D. L. 1699), although feared as likely to "put weak people too much in mind of King James then living in France," was nevertheless, with the omission of its first act, permitted to survive, and has had a remarkably long life on the stage. Composed largely of shreds and patches from Shakespeare's *1 Henry IV, Richard II, 3 Henry VI*, and *Richard III*, with some additional writing, it has been acted even in the twentieth century by Shakespeare repertory companies. Shakespeare's original version has seldom been revived.

Even if today these "improvements" of Shakespeare appear to have been wanton tinkerings with an art that the adapters did not comprehend, they need not be looked upon as reflecting any lack of appreciation of Shakespeare. Far from it. Davenant was second to none in his reverence for his godfather. Neglect is the result of indifference, but, to his Restoration adapters, Shakespeare was still the "divine" or—amusing irony—the "inimitable." Their versions were in reality a tribute, and evidence of what Tate called "my zeal for all the remains of Shakespeare."

> If then this heap of flowers shall chance to wear
> Fresh beauty in the order they now bear,
> Even this is Shakespeare's praise. Each rustic knows
> 'Mongst plenteous flowers a garland to compose,
> Which strung by this coarse hand may fairer show,
> But 'twas a power divine that made 'em grow.

Nor will theatrical necessity, alone, fully explain their manhandling of Shakespeare's lines. The Restoration apron stage, even with scenes, could still produce a fluid, loosely constructed drama. It was left for the eighteenth and nineteenth centuries to fit Shakespeare to a stage technique for which his plays were never written. To the Restoration mind, Shakespeare was often obscure and indecorous. The "reformers" merely felt called upon to make his plays conform to contemporary critical taste; they smoothed the rough work of this artless genius, omitted what they thought was low or destructive of unity, and added what they thought would please. Space does not permit extensive illustration, but two passages from a single scene in Davenant's *Macbeth* will make this chastening process clear. For the fierce contumely of Shakespeare's Macbeth:

> The Devil damn thee black, thou cream-fac'd loon;
> Where got'st thou that goose look?

Davenant substituted the insipid

> Now Friend, what means thy change of countenance?

And the magnificent lines which Shakespeare's broken hero speaks upon hearing the news of his wife's death were displaced by Davenant with

She should have died hereafter.
I brought her here to see my victines [victims?, victories?], not to die.
Tomorrow, tomorrow, and tomorrow,
Creeps in a stealing pace from day to day,
To the last minute of recorded time:
And all our yesterdays have lighted fools
To their eternal homes. Out, out that candle. . . .

This was the man, it will be remembered, who believed that he wrote "with the very spirit that Shakespeare" (see above, p. 28).

Still, the Restoration versions are much more reprehensible for what they encouraged than for what they actually were. Once the text had been tampered with, adaptation became traditional, and Shakespeare, even in our own day, has all too frequently been treated as raw material to be shaped by the creative faculties of actor or producer. Worse, the adaptations drove the originals from the stage; until well into the nineteenth century in the case of several great plays, like *King Lear*, *The Tempest*, and *Richard III*, the playgoer *saw* one version on the stage and *read* another—if he read Shakespeare. Why did they survive? Often, one suspects, because they were actor-made and actor-proof, providing parts that were more showy for the star and easier to convey over the footlights than pure Shakespeare.

Like the Shakespearean period, the Restoration seems to have been an age of great actors. By far the most famous was Thomas Betterton (1635?–1710), who was the leading player in the Duke's Company at Lincoln's Inn Fields and Dorset Garden. Pepys the diarist saw Betterton's *Hamlet* and praised it highly. If tradition may be believed, Betterton's acting of the role, as well as that of Henry VIII, was in the pure Shakespearean tradition (see above, p. 26). He was a versatile actor, playing not only tragic roles, like Hamlet, Othello, Troilus, and Lear, but also comic ones, like Mercutio, Falstaff, Sir Toby Belch. In the King's Company at the Theatre Royal, the leading actor was Charles Hart (?–1683), Shakespeare's grandnephew, who was described by a contemporary as being to the theatre of his time what Burbage had been nearly a century before. His best roles were Othello and Brutus.

However, it is the actresses, new to the stage of the Restoration, that are of the greatest interest. Unfortunately, too little is known of the earlier actresses and their Shakespearean roles, and it will be possible to name only a few: Margaret Hughes (?–1719), mistress of Prince Rupert, and almost certainly the actress who played Desdemona on December 8, 1660, when a woman first appeared on the English stage; Elizabeth Barry (1658–1713), most famous as Dryden's and Otway's heroines, and known to have played Cordelia in Tate's *King Lear;* Mrs. Saunderson (?–1711), Betterton's wife, whose Lady Macbeth was admired by Colley Cibber; and Anne Bracegirdle (1663–1748), who also acted with Betterton after 1695 and played Isabella,

Portia, Desdemona, Ophelia, Cordelia, and Mrs. Ford, either in Shakespeare's originals or in adaptations of them. Eclipsed in fame by Nance Oldfield in 1707, she retired from the stage.

THE EIGHTEENTH CENTURY

Throughout the eighteenth century, the two patent theatres created in the days of Killigrew and Davenant maintained their position of complete or partial monopoly of all theatrical productions. The companies had long before cast off their royal designations; new playhouses replaced the old, and numerous rivals grew up. The Licensing Act of 1737 renewed the old monopoly by theoretically closing every playhouse except those at Drury Lane and Covent Garden (opened in 1732 as the successor to Lincoln's Inn Fields), but in various ways the managers of the minor theatres succeeded either in evading the law or in obtaining special privileges. London was adequately supplied with houses of entertainment, and provincial theatres, especially at fashionable watering places, like Bath and Cheltenham, when these developed, increased in number and importance. The theatre still retained its air of fashion, but the middle classes came more and more to the playhouses and brought a new taste into the theatre. The comedy of manners and the heroic play soon gave way to sentimental comedy, bourgeois tragedy, the pantomime, comic opera, and melodrama. It was to these new tastes that the minor theatres frequently catered.

On the whole, the eighteenth century may be said to have been a good age for Shakespeare on the stage. The Italian opera, always a spectacular production, and in the 1720's the pantomimes of John Rich, relieved the legitimate drama of the need of being both eye- and ear-filling. It speaks well for the age that, even before the Garrick fever settled upon the town, so many of Shakespeare's plays were in favor. The standard tragedies, such as *Hamlet*, *Macbeth*, *Lear*, *Othello*, *Julius Cæsar*, *Richard III*, and *Henry VIII*—probably because of the opportunities for processions and theatrical splendor—early became stock productions. The comedies, with the exception of the adapted *Tempest*, were still neglected. The Restoration versions, for the most part, still prevailed. However, except for certain stalwarts, like Tate's *King Lear* and *The Tempest*, the plays seem to have been acted in reasonably good versions, and the alterations to Restoration taste disappeared. Moreover, the early years of the eighteenth century also saw the production of such unusual pieces as *Cymbeline*, *Much Ado*, *Richard II*, *King John*, *Henry V*, *Henry VI*, *The Merry Wives*, *As You Like It*, *Twelfth Night*, *The Merchant of Venice*, *The Winter's Tale*, and *All's Well*.

Fresh alterations of Shakespeare, however, were by no means lacking on the eighteenth-century stage. In 1716, Christopher Bullock elaborated the Sly episodes from *The Taming of the Shrew* in *The Cobbler of Preston* (L. I. F.), with a hero named Toby Guzzle. Shortly after, there was produced at the rival Drury Lane another farce with the same title by Charles Johnson, but with some political raillery directed at the Jacobites and the Pretender. In 1735 at Drury Lane, when the rage of the ballad opera was at its height, Shakespeare's farce became *A Cure for a Scold* at the hands of J. Worsdale, and was offered as an afterpiece to *Richard III* (D. L.). *Coriolanus* was given political significance by John Dennis as *The Invader of His Country, or The Fatal Resentment* (D. L. 1719), and, in 1749 at Covent Garden, the same play became a stately rhetorical tragedy at the hands of James Thomson, author of *The Seasons*, a version often fused with Shakespeare's *Coriolanus* by later actors, at least until the time of Kemble. Lewis Theobald, Shakespeare's editor, made *Richard II* (L. I. F. 1719) conform to the unities and added a love interest between Aumerle and a daughter of Northumberland. In 1722, John Sheffield, Duke of Buckingham, made *Julius Cæsar* over into two regular tragedies with choruses, but they were never acted. Aaron Hill built his *Henry V* (1724) upon Shakespeare's foundation; Colley Cibber transformed *King John* into a she-tragedy called *Papal Tyranny in the Reign of King John* (c. 1736, performed at C. G. 1745), by virtually removing Faulconbridge and emphasizing Constance. James Miller's *The Universal Passion* (D. L. 1737) was a strange amalgamation of *Much Ado* and Molière's *Princesse d'Elide*. *Love's Labor's Lost* became *The Students* (1762) with love's labor no longer wasted, but this play was probably not acted.

Even *As You Like It*, which was entirely unknown on the stage until 1740, became *Love in a Forest* (D. L. 1723) by Charles Johnson. Johnson "weeded Shakespeare's beautiful parterre" of Touchstone, Audrey, William, Corin, and Phebe altogether, substituted a duel with rapiers for the wrestling bout with dialogue taken from the quarrel of Bolingbroke and Mowbray in *Richard II*, had Jaques woo Celia[9] with words that Touchstone had once used to Audrey and Benedick had spoken to Beatrice, and removed the conversion of the villain by having Oliver commit suicide and by inventing another brother, Robert, to take his place in the forest. As if this were not enough, Johnson "tuned the sacred bard's immortal lyre" by introducing into a scene between Rosalind and Orlando, Viola's sentimental speech from *Twelfth Night*, "She never told her love," a great favorite in the eighteenth century. Finally, from *A Midsummer Night's Dream*, the burlesque of Pyramus and Thisbe was presented before the duke in the last act to give the disguised Rosalind an opportunity to change her dress and reappear in her own character. But here, in the very worst of the eighteenth-century adaptations, the words at least are generally Shakespeare's own, even if they were selected from various plays without regard to character or context, and the author at least saw possibilities in one of Shakespeare's most pleasing come-

[9] Compare George Sand's version of this play, *Comme il vous plaira* (1856).

dies. *The Modern Receipt, or A Cure for Love,* by J. C. (1739), also an adaptation of *As You Like It,* seems not to have been acted.

Even David Garrick, for all his vaunted worship of Shakespeare, laid tampering fingers upon several plays. He turned both *The Tempest* and *A Midsummer Night's Dream* into operas, the latter renamed *The Fairies* (D. L. 1755), with the rude mechanicals omitted, with Puck appropriating Ariel's "Where the bee sucks" and Oberon singing "Sigh no more, ladies" from *Much Ado.* In addition, there were other songs from Shakespeare, Milton (parts of *L'Allegro*), Waller, Dryden, and others. Garrick added a scene to *Romeo and Juliet* (D. L. 1748), composed a dying speech for Macbeth (D. L. 1743), and adapted *Cymbeline* (D. L. 1761) and *Hamlet* (D. L. 1772). He turned *The Taming of the Shrew* into an afterpiece called *Catherine and Petruchio* (D. L. 1756), and *The Winter's Tale* into a dramatic pastoral called *Florizel and Perdita* (D. L. 1756), protesting all the while:

> 'Tis my chief wish, my joy, my only plan,
> To spill no drop of that immortal man.

But a reaction set in quite early in the century against an unholy meddling with Shakespeare's text with an eye to "improving" it. In his *Historical Register for the Year 1736,* Henry Fielding made sport of Colley Cibber's *King John* and had his character Medley say:

> Shakespeare is already good enough for people of taste; he must be alter'd to the palates of those who have none. . . . I have too great an honour for Shakespeare to think of burlesquing him, and to be sure of not burlesquing him, I will never attempt to alter him for fear of burlesquing him by accident.

These words are a breath of fresh air. By the middle of the century, as the Romantic undercurrent gathered force and the idolatry of Shakespeare became complete, there was growing disapproval, and Garrick's "restorations from Shakespeare" to several of the versions he acted are a healthy sign. None of the eighteenth-century adaptations had the life of those of the Restoration, and no permanent additions were made to the collection. After the eighteenth century, "improvements" of Shakespeare tend to disappear altogether, but it still remained the proper thing for famous actors to publish their versions of the plays, their alterations consisting, for the most part, only of the transposition of scenes and the omission of passages that "wound the patience," usually poetry. Bell's edition of *Shakespeare's Plays, as They Are Now Performed at the Theatres Royal in London* (1774) is an interesting collection of acting versions that had become standardized. But in Bell's edition, there is still a good deal of non-Shakespearean matter.

It will be possible here to name only a few of the great actors of the eighteenth century who appeared in Shakespeare's roles. Robert Wilks (1665?–1732), manager at various times of both the patent houses, was best in Farquhar's plays, but also played Othello, Hamlet, Macduff, and Prince Hal. Colley Cibber (1671–1757), the famous actor-manager of Drury Lane, poet-laureate and hero of Pope's *Dunciad*, played such characters as Iago, Wolsey, Jaques, Shallow, and Richard III, though his particular bent was for fops. Barton Booth (1681–1733), once the associate of Betterton, played Brutus, Lear, Hotspur, and Henry VIII. James Quin (1693–1766), the immediate predecessor and early rival of Garrick, acted at both the patent houses in tragic as well as comic roles, his best parts being Coriolanus and Falstaff. Charles Macklin (1697?–1797), after trying Iago, Malvolio, and Mercutio, at last made a reputation as Shylock (1741) (see illustration, p. 448), and later produced *Macbeth* with Scottish kilts and a Highland setting. He was one of the first actors to give thought to appropriate historical costume and background for Shakespeare's plays. Theophilus Cibber (1703–58), the son of Colley Cibber, was famous as Ancient Pistol, who, in his hands, became a swaggering trooper of George II's armies. Henry Woodward (1714–77), who created Sheridan's Captain Absolute in *The Rivals* (1775), was the greatest Mercutio of his day, his other roles being Pistol, Sir Andrew Aguecheek, Stephano, Polonius, Falstaff, and Justice Shallow.

By far the greatest and the most versatile of the eighteenth-century players was David Garrick (1717–79), the friend of Dr. Johnson, who played no less than seventeen of Shakespeare's characters, with Hamlet, Lear, Richard III, and Benedick as his best (see illustration, p. 445). He burst into fame in 1741 at Goodman's Fields, an unlicensed, unfashionable theatre, played for a time at Drury Lane, the Smock Alley Theatre, Dublin, and Covent Garden, and, from 1747 until his retirement in 1776, was manager of Drury Lane, where he produced no less than twenty-four of Shakespeare's plays. In many respects a typical child of his age, Garrick represents in the theatre the return to nature which heralded the Romantic movement. Even if his head was a little turned by the adulation of his contemporaries, he was to a large extent personally responsible for an enormous popular vogue of Shakespeare. He adopted a more natural style of acting than had prevailed before, he improved the staging, and, though he accomplished much less than he professed, he did much to restore Shakespeare's text to the stage. At least he omitted some of the added matter and restored some of Shakspeare's language, if not all of his plots, to *Macbeth* (1743), *Romeo and Juliet* (1748), *Coriolanus* (1754), *King Lear* (1756), *The Tempest* (1756), *Antony and Cleopatra* (1759), *Cymbeline* (1761), *A Midsummer Night's Dream* (1763), and *Timon* (1771).

Perhaps Garrick's most characteristic Shakespearean venture was the imposing Jubilee spectacle he organized at Stratford in September of 1769 to do honor to the poet. (See illustration, p. 450.) Carefully as this master showman laid his plans, there seems to have been some doubt that a country jubilee

would in itself be attractive, but the date was set to coincide with the Warwickshire racing season, and the project caught the fancy of the world of
fashion and the world of letters. In November, 1768, Garrick was elected an
honorary burgess of Stratford, in return for which distinction he undertook
to supply the new town hall with a statue of Shakespeare. The Jubilee ceremonies of 1769 were opened by a serenade to the ladies, followed by a song,
written by Garrick, entitled "The Warwickshire Lad." Then followed ceremonies of veneration in the town hall, during which Garrick presented to the
Corporation the statue of Shakespeare which still stands in the niche in the
north gable, together with a portrait of himself, and, in turn, received suitable
relics made from the wood of the famous mulberry tree which Shakespeare
is supposed to have planted. Afterward, the company, with Garrick at its
head, went to the church where Shakespeare was buried to hear an oratorio
composed by Dr. Thomas Arne. On the second day came the great event—
the recitation in an especially constructed rotunda of an ode, also composed
by Garrick and modestly delivered by him to music by Dr. Arne—after
which there was a masquerade. On the third day the Jubilee Handicap was
run in a downpour of rain, which some thought was the judgment of Heaven
upon such carryings on. The final event was to have been the Shakespeare
pageant, a procession of characters from the plays starting at Shakespeare's
tomb and ending with the coronation of a bust of the dramatist erected
before his birthplace in Henley Street, which was decorated, after the manner of the time, with "a curious emblematical transparency depicting the sun
struggling through the clouds to enlighten the world and inscribed with the
motto: 'Thus dying clouds contend with growing light.' " (See illustration,
pp. 446–7.) But the sun refused to shine, the procession was postponed, and Garrick moved the whole thing to Drury Lane where he could control the
weather. There he acted his Jubilee more than ninety times. The wits of the
day made merry at Garrick's expense, but his Jubilee was the first of the
celebrations which, to this day, have made Stratford "the Mecca of the
English-speaking world."

Garrick's closest rival was "the silver-tongued" Spranger Barry (1719–77),
a Dublin silversmith who turned to the theatre after bankruptcy in business,
and succeeded well as Hamlet, Macbeth, Lear, Romeo, and Othello. One of
the handsomest men of his time and the most accomplished lover on the stage,
Barry was the greatest Romeo of the century (see illustration, p. 444). Edward Shuter (1728?–76), the creator of Hardcastle in Goldsmith's She Stoops
to Conquer (1773) and Sir Anthony Absolute in Sheridan's The Rivals
(1775), acted at Covent Garden such roles as Falstaff, Mercutio, and Polonius. John Henderson (1747–85), "the Bath Roscius," was considered by
many second only to Garrick, whose jealousy he excited. His best parts were
Shylock, Hamlet, and Falstaff.

Among the actresses of the century, first mention must be given to Hannah Pritchard (1711–68), the greatest Lady Macbeth of her day. She played with Garrick for twenty years and succeeded in comedy as well as in tragedy in such roles as Rosalind, Imogen, Beatrice, Volumnia, and Hermione. Peg Woffington (1714?–60), another of Garrick's leading ladies, was unsurpassed in "breeches parts," like Rosalind, Portia, or Viola, but was successful also as Mrs. Ford, Cordelia, Ophelia, and Desdemona (see illustration, p. 444). Still another was Susannah Cibber (1714–66), the divorced wife of Theophilus Cibber, who played Juliet to Barry's Romeo and Cordelia to Garrick's Lear, and was especially famous as Constance in *King John*. Garrick's Juliet was George Anne Bellamy (1731?–88). Others worthy of note were Mary Ann Yates (1728–87), one of the greatest tragic actresses of her day, her best Shakespearean roles being Cleopatra, Desdemona, and Cordelia; Frances Abingdon (1737–1815), who also played with Garrick, was the creator of Lady Teazle in Sheridan's *The School for Scandal* (1777), and was best as the accomplished lady of fashion, playing such roles as Beatrice, Desdemona, Olivia, and Rosalind; Mrs. Elizabeth Pope (1744?–97) (see illustration, p. 449); Mrs. Elizabeth Hartley (1751–1824); and Elizabeth Farren (1759–1829).

The last quarter of the eighteenth century saw the rise of the Kemble family and their productions of Shakespeare on the grand scale that was considered a just tribute to his genius. The greatest was John Philip Kemble (1767–1823), who essayed no less than twenty-seven Shakespearean roles—ten more than Garrick—and was supreme as Coriolanus and Macbeth. His acting was admired by Lamb, Hazlitt, Scott, and the other Romantic critics. His younger brother Charles (1775–1854) was best in comedy in such roles as Falstaff, Mercutio, or Benedick, though he also played Hamlet and Romeo. Still another brother, Stephan (1758–1822), played secondary roles. But it was their sister Sarah Siddons (1755–1831) who remains the greatest English actress (see illustration, p. 449). She was unsurpassed as Lady Macbeth and Queen Katherine, and seldom rivaled as Volumnia, Desdemona, Ophelia, and Rosalind. Upon the hem of her robe in Reynolds's portrait of her as the Tragic Muse, Dr. Johnson inscribed his name, saying, "I would not lose the honour this opportunity afforded to me for my name going down to posterity on the hem of your garment."

No more serious actor-manager ever lived than John Philip Kemble. His romantic productions were attempts to make Shakespeare impressive and, at the same time, palatable to his audience. Perhaps the key to his success in his age lay in his discovery in the plays of "the picturesque, by which Shakespeare himself quite as much as any other quality, transcended all other writers for the stage" (James Boaden, *Memoirs of the Life of John Philip Kemble* [1825], I, 423). During his successive managements of Drury Lane (1788–1802) and Covent Garden (1802–17), important physical changes took place in the theatres which were altered and renovated; Drury Lane was rebuilt in 1794, and, after the fires of 1808 and 1809, both were rebuilt on a grand and imposing scale. One of the great disadvantages of the monopoly system which limited the theatres to two was that it encouraged unmanageably huge playhouses. Drury Lane (1794) had a proscenium opening 43 x 38 feet, and a stage depth of 92 feet. Covent Garden (1809) had a proscenium opening of 42 x 36 feet and a stage 68 x 82 feet. Both had seating capacities of well over three thousand. Acoustics were bad, and the distance from the stage made it impossible for many of the spectators—particularly the rowdiest element who haunted the cheaper galleries—either to see or to hear. Moreover, the public taste had been excited by all kinds of sensational importations from Germany and France, and had grown accustomed to music, spectacle, and melodrama. If, therefore, at this day the Shakespearean productions of Kemble seem somewhat reactionary and cold, just when acting was beginning to be subtle and intimate, it must be remembered that he was adapting the fluid unscenic Shakespearean technique to conditions of stage and audience that made anything but an elaborate, lavish setting impossible.

According to his friend and biographer James Boaden, Kemble's notion of producing Shakespeare was

> not to order the prompter to write out the parts from some mutilated promptcopy lingering on his shelves; but himself to consider it attentively in the author's genuine book; then to examine what corrections could be properly admitted into his text; and, finally, what could be cut out in the representation, not as disputing the judgment of the author, but as suiting the time of the representation to the habits of his audience, or a little favoring the powers of his actors in order that the performance might be as uniformly good as it was practicable to make it. (*Ibid.*, II, 2.)

Yet he put back into *The Tempest* (D. L. 1789) the Dorinda-Hippolyto plot that had been omitted by Garrick; his *Richard III* (1783) was still Cibber's; his *King Lear* (D. L. 1788) restored many of the Tate "improvements" which had also been dropped by Garrick; his *Macbeth* (D. L. 1794) retained the singing and dancing witches and Garrick's dying speech for Macbeth; his *Winter's Tale* (1801) did restore some pure Shakespeare, but it retained some of Garrick's lines; his *Measure for Measure* (1794) restored much of the background of low life in Vienna, but it also contained some writing of his own; the *Coriolanus* (D. L. 1789, C. G. 1806, 1811) in which he made his greatest name was not only cut and rearranged, but liberally seasoned at the end by scenes from Thomson; and the *Midsummer Night's Dream* which was produced under his auspices in 1816 was a virtual pantomime, concocted by Frederick Reynolds with additional songs from eighteenth-century versions and including "the Cretans, the Amazons, the Minotaur, Ariadne in the Labyrinth, the Mysterious Peplum or Veil of Minerva, the Ship Argo, and the Golden Fleece." By now the reader has surely come to take the reverent protestations of the Shakespearean producer in a somewhat Pickwickian sense.

It was perhaps in the matter of costume and setting that Kemble's ideals had more significance, at least to his successors. Up to the end of the eighteenth century, as the illustrations in these pages make clear, practically no attempt was made to secure historical accuracy in these matters. Such an ideal was unknown to Shakespeare, and it was equally unknown to the actors and producers of the seventeenth and eighteenth centuries. But the theatrical prints of the time make it easy to distinguish several conventional types of attire: (1) fashionable contemporary dress (with court dress for kings and princes), used for all plays without special exoticism; (2) Roman costume, used for classical plays; (3) Oriental dress, and (4) special costumes for certain Shakespearean characters, like Falstaff, Richard III, Henry VIII, or Hamlet. Actresses, however, wore the silken or satin magnificence of court ladies of the time, with panniers or hoops, trains or towering headdresses, whether they were representing Cleopatra or Mrs. Ford. Even the witches in *Macbeth*, as produced by Garrick's company, wore powdered wigs, rouge, red stomachers, point lace aprons, and mittens. The backgrounds for acting were the stock sets of the playhouse which saw service in all kinds of plays.

Kemble was the first actor seriously to be moved by Romantic antiquarianism. According to Boaden, he studied

the antiquities of his own and other countries, to be acquainted with the architecture, their dress, their weapons, their manners; and he by degrees assembled about him artists who could best carry his designs into effect. To be critically exact was the great ambition of his life. (*Ibid.*, I, 157-8.)

Mrs. Siddons, meanwhile, seems to have busied herself with similar matters. Not only did she alter her style of acting to suit the new theatres, but, inspired by the simplicity and severity of antique sculpture,

she now saw that tragedy was debased by the flutter of light materials, and that the head, and all its powerful action from the shoulder, should never be encumbered by the monstrous inventions of the hair-dresser and the milliner. (Boaden, *Memoirs of Mrs. Siddons* [1827], II, 291.)

Accordingly, when *The Winter's Tale* was revived during Kemble's last season at Drury Lane (1801–02),

in Paulina's chapel, she now stood one of the noblest statues that even Grecian taste ever invented. The figure composed something like one of the muses in profile. The drapery was ample in its folds, and seemingly stony in its texture. Upon the magical words, pronounced by Paulina, "Music, awake her: strike"; the sudden action of her head absolutely *startled*, as though such a miracle had really vivified the marble. (Boaden, *Memoirs of the Life of John Philip Kemble*, II, 314.)

Yet reform continued tardy. Kemble himself played Hamlet in a court dress of rich black velvet, adorned with the star of the Garter; as Richard III on Bosworth Field he wore silk stockings and long quartered dancing shoes; his Lear and Macbeth appeared in a flowered-satin lounging robe; and Benedick, in his production of *Much Ado,* in the full uniform of a British infantry officer. The ballroom witches, however, disappeared from *Macbeth* (D. L. 1794):

> in the cauldron scene, new groups were introduced to personify the black spirits and white, blue spirits and grey. The evil spirits had serpents writhing round them, which had a striking effect. [O Romanticism!] (W. C. Oulton, *Continuation to Victor's Theatres of London,* II, 139.)

By 1825, producers were citing their authorities for details of costume and setting. The way had been paved for Charles Kean and Henry Irving.

THE NINETEENTH CENTURY

When Kemble retired in 1817, no successor appeared to replace him. Edmund Kean (1787–1833), the only possibility, was a great Romantic actor —Coleridge said that to see him act was like reading Shakespeare by flashes of lightning—but he was too unstable and even more inclined than his predecessors to treat Shakespeare as a means of self-exhibition. Neither Charles Kemble nor Charles Mayne Young (1777–1856) had the managerial ability to carry on. Shakespeare continued to be performed, but he tended to recede into the background of public estimation. The period from 1817 to 1837 is characterized by the persistent efforts of Frederick Reynolds and Henry R. Bishop to operatize Shakespeare's comedies: *The Comedy of Errors* (1819), *Twelfth Night* (1820), *The Two Gentlemen of Verona* (1821), *The Merry Wives* (1824), *As You Like It* (1824), *The Taming of the Shrew* (1828), and *All's Well* (1832)—all filled with whatever incredible plunder could be gathered from the plays, sonnets, and poems, and set to music.

The next important, if not great, actor of Shakespeare was William Charles Macready (1793–1873), who made his first appearance in Birmingham as Romeo in 1810 and won the approval of audiences in England, France, and America in a career that lasted for over forty years (see illustration, p. 459). He was manager of Covent Garden from 1837 to 1839, and of Drury Lane from 1841 to 1843, but was temperamentally unsuited to the task and lacked the judgment to make the most of his successes. His productions of Shakespeare had a magnificence of scene and costume till then unparalleled upon the English stage. He constructed Druid circles to lend a spectral loneliness to the heath in *King Lear;* he constructed a huge moving diorama for *Henry V,* showing the English fleet leaving Southampton and gradually arriving at Harfleur, the English and the French camps before Agincourt, and the king's entry into London; and he made *King John* a magnificent spectacle.

Macready's greatest service to Shakespeare, however, was his complete—if sometimes faint-hearted—restoration of Shakespeare's text to the stage. This reform may perhaps be traced—if one is not too optimistic—to a growing public acquaintance with what Shakespeare actually wrote. *King Lear*, *Coriolanus*, and *The Tempest* were produced in authentic, if somewhat abridged, versions in 1838. The only serious addition to the script was the time-consuming spectacle. Macready's principal associates were his supporting feminine stars: Mary Amelia Warner (1804–54), who was most successful in serious roles; Helena Faucit (1817–98), who was best as Shakespeare's younger heroines; and Priscilla Horton (1818–95), who played such roles as Ariel, the Fool in *Lear*, and one of the singing witches in *Macbeth*. For a time, Macready's principal rivals were Charles James Mathews (1803–78) and his popular wife, Madame Lucia Vestris (1797–1856), who succeeded Macready as managers of Covent Garden (1839–42). Their most distinguished production was *A Midsummer Night's Dream* (1840), an authentic version for the first time since 1642.

In 1843, at last, the patents granting a monopoly of theatrical production to Drury Lane and Covent Garden were abolished, and the principle of a free theatre was for the first time legally established in London. No longer was it necessary, as in the eighteenth century, to obtain special license, to sandwich a play between the two parts of a concert, or to seek to avoid the official eye by some similar subterfuge. Even before 1843, minor playhouses, like Sadler's Wells (built 1740), the Royalty (1787), Astley's Amphitheatre (1804), the Adelphi (1806), the Lyceum (1816), the Royal Coburg (1818), had managed to maintain themselves with popular shows of various kinds; after 1843, the number of theatres rapidly increased. As a result, the two royal houses at once lost prestige; in 1847, Covent Garden became permanently an opera house, while Drury Lane has continued to produce opera, pantomime, and circus spectacles, as well as drama.

From 1843 to 1862, Sadler's Wells Theatre was the most important house for Shakespeare. Here, away from the fashionable centre of London, under the leadership of Samuel Phelps (1804–78), Shakespeare's plays became popular entertainment once more. The associations of the place were all against any such success. Sadler's Wells had been a cheap and disreputable resort; Grimaldi the clown had appeared there, aquatic spectacles, terrific melodramas, ballets, and pantomimes had succeeded one another, and the clientele was rough and disorderly. To Sadler's Wells, Phelps brought Shakespeare, Webster, Beaumont and Fletcher, Massinger, and Otway. With frequent changes of bill and comparatively simple staging, Phelps produced thirty-four of Shakespeare's plays, including a restored *Richard III* (1845), *King Lear* without cuts (1845), *Macbeth* without the expanded witch scenes (1847), and even *Pericles* (1854)—and he made them pay.

The Princess' Theatre is chiefly remembered for the splendid Shakespearean productions, 1850–9, of Charles Kean (1811–68), son of Edmund Kean (see illustration, p. 454). Like Phelps, Kean was hardly a great actor. He had a bad voice and an unprepossessing figure. Moreover, in his productions, poetry was always sacrificed to accommodate gorgeous scenery, and everything else to enhance the leading role for Kean himself as star performer. What he played was unalloyed Shakespeare; but what he omitted was Shakespeare, too. He was fitting Shakespeare to scenery instead of scenery to Shakespeare. His audiences, however, did not expect too much in the theatre.

In Kean's productions, strict historical accuracy as to scenery, costumes, and accessories reached its climax—if not something more appalling. Every one of his representations was the result of the most minute search for originals of styles in costume, armor, architecture, and consultation with the most learned experts, antiquarian and artistic. His programs and his printed texts literally bristle with scholarly and "Historical Notes." The account of the problems presented by *The Winter's Tale* (1856) has already been quoted (see above, p. 155), and for the same play the notes on costume read as follows:

> Leontes (first dress)—From a Figure of the Lycian King, Jobates, on a Vase in the Hamilton Collection. Engraved in Tischbein's Hamilton Vases, vol. 1., pl. 1.
>
> Mamillius, the King's Son, from a Vase in the Collection of Mr. Rogers. The Toy from an actual Greek one in terra-cotta, preserved in the British Museum.

The costumes and customs represented in *The Merchant of Venice* (1850) belonged to the year 1600, when Shakespeare wrote the play.

> The dresses are chiefly selected from a work by Cesare Vecellio, entitled *Degli Habiti Antichi e Moderni di diversi Parti del Mondo*. In Venetia, 1590,

and even the procession which opens the comedy "is copied from a print in the British Museum, by Josse Amman, who died in 1591." Kean's contemporaries, of course, ridiculed and burlesqued his program notes, but such things had their impressive value, as Hollywood knows today. In this manner, Kean produced thirteen of Shakespeare's plays. His principal supporting actress was his wife Ellen Tree (1805–80).

The mantle of Charles Kean fell squarely upon the shoulders of Henry Irving (1838–1905), who began his career in provincial troupes, joined the company of Hezekiah Bateman at the Lyceum Theatre in London in 1871, and was its manager from 1878 to 1902. As to Kean, so to Irving, a Shakespearean production was a special production. But to Irving, also, any play was a great unified effort with all its parts of equal strength. Like Kean, he mounted Shakespeare elaborately, but, like the artist Kean never was, Irving composed his scenic effects like a painter. His method, of course, like Kean's, necessitated a drastically abridged text, but whatever scenery he adopted he employed sincerely, as he said

> to meet the requirements of the stage, without sacrificing the purpose or the poetry of the author . . . and I trust that any change which I have ventured to introduce . . . in the ordinary scenic arrangements has been made in the spirit of true reverence for the works of our greatest dramatist. (From Irving's advertisement of *Macbeth* [1888], in *The Times*, quoted by Professor G. C. D. Odell, *Shakespeare from Betterton to Irving*, II, 440.)

His greatest productions were his *Hamlet* (1878); *The Merchant of Venice* (1879), in which Shylock became a sentimentalized tragic figure; *Much Ado about Nothing* (1882); *Henry VIII* (1892); and *King Lear* (1892). Irving's leading lady for nearly a quarter of a century was Ellen Terry (1848–1928), who had made her debut as a child of eight with Charles Kean as Mamillius in *The Winter's Tale* in 1856, and as Puck in *A Midsummer Night's Dream* (1857), when she rose through a trap-door sitting on a mushroom. Excellent in both comedy and tragedy, Ellen Terry made a vivacious Beatrice and Portia (see illustration, p. 461), a lovely Queen Katherine, Imogen, and Cordelia, and a wholly satisfactory Ophelia.

The Irving traditions were carried on by Johnston Forbes-Robertson (1853–1937) (see illustration, p. 462), and Herbert Beerbohm Tree (1853–1917) (see illustration, p. 464). Forbes-Robertson studied under Samuel Phelps and acted at different times with Henry Irving, playing Claudio to Irving's Benedick and Ellen Terry's Beatrice in *Much Ado* (1882), and playing Romeo to the Juliet of Helena Modjeska (1881) and Mary Anderson (1885). In 1895, with Mrs. Patrick Campbell (1865–1940), he began producing Shakespeare at Irving's old theatre, the Lyceum—*Romeo and Juliet* (1895), *Hamlet* (1897), *Macbeth* (1898), and *Othello* (Lyric, 1902). His greatest roles were Romeo and Hamlet. Herbert Beerbohm Tree's productions were even more lavish than Irving's. A versatile actor himself, he secured a good supporting cast, producing at Her Majesty's Theatre *Julius Cæsar* (1898), *King John* (1899), *The Winter's Tale* (1906, with Ellen Terry as Hermione), *Antony and Cleopatra* (1907), *The Merchant of Venice* (1908), *Henry VIII* (1910), *Macbeth* (1911), *Othello* (1912), and *Henry VIII* (1916). It was Tree, more than anyone else, who fitted a three-act division upon Shakespeare.

SHAKESPEARE ABROAD

Shakespeare's plays first reached the Continent, not as literature, but in the repertories of itinerant English actors, who, during the Elizabethan and early Stuart periods, wandered through Dutch, German, and Scandinavian towns and were almost universally popular. Among the Shakespearean dramas known to have been performed by them on these tours are *Titus Andronicus,*

Hamlet, King Lear, Romeo and Juliet, The Merchant of Venice, The Taming of the Shrew, Julius Cæsar, and at least the comic interlude of *A Midsummer Night's Dream.* Because few of the spectators could understand English, the versions in which these plays were acted were probably crude adaptations emphasizing action rather than poetry. Even so, the influence of this imported Elizabethan drama upon both the Dutch and the German drama was fundamental and formative. In France and southern Europe, English actors were less popular and less influential. Nowhere was Shakespeare's name mentioned as author; indeed, the earliest Continental allusion to him was French, and, to say the least, unenthusiastic. "This English poet possesses a fine imagination," wrote Nicolas Clement, librarian to Louis XIV, on a copy of the Folio of 1632 in a catalogue of the royal library some time between 1675 and 1684, "he thinks naturally, he expresses himself with finesse, but these good qualities are obscured by the filth he introduces into his comedies." Thus, the tone of French opinion of Shakespeare for the next hundred and fifty years was set early. Later, though an occasional French visitor to England, like the Abbé Prévost, showed a momentary interest in Shakespeare, it was not until the time of Voltaire that Shakespeare was popularly introduced to the French, and, thence, to southern and eastern Europe. As we have seen, however, Voltaire repented of his youthful romantic enthusiasm, but curiosity about the English playwright was aroused. Before the end of the eighteenth century, translations of the plays had appeared not only in French and German, but in Dutch, Italian, Spanish, Danish, Hungarian, Polish, and Russian as well. Today, even in the Orient, Shakespeare is acted in the native theatres (see illustration, p. 463).

By the end of the eighteenth century, also, Shakespeare may be said to have become international on the stage. The German actor Friedrich Schroeder (1744–1816) produced *Hamlet* and *Othello* for the first time in Hamburg in 1776, *The Merchant of Venice* and *Measure for Measure* in 1777, *King Lear, Richard III,* and *Henry IV* in 1778, *Macbeth* in 1779, and *Much Ado* in 1792. The "Sturm und Drang" dramatists, of course, worshipped Shakespeare, and adaptations of *Macbeth* by Schiller and *Romeo and Juliet* by Goethe were produced at the Weimar Theatre in 1800 and 1812, respectively. Since that time the better known plays have been in the repertories of the greatest German actors, some of whom, like the troupe of the Meiningen court theatre, traveled in England. By far the most distinguished of the German producers was Max Reinhardt (1873–1943). During his incumbency as director of the Neues Theatre in Berlin beginning in 1905, he produced, with the aid of much modern stage mechanism, some three thousand performances of twenty-two of Shakespeare's plays, of which the most famous was *A Midsummer Night's Dream.* Summoned to Hollywood, Reinhardt supervised the production of this play as a moving picture in 1935.

On the French stage, that stronghold of classical regularity and decorum, Shakespeare was slower of acceptance. His tragedies appeared first in the form of adaptations, pruned of "barbarities," with revised plots and happy endings. Of the early French versions, the most important were those of Jean François Ducis (1733–1816), who knew no English, but worked from the modified translations of Antoine de la Place (1745) and Pierre Letourneur (1776–82): *Hamlet* (1769), *Romeo and Juliet* (1772), *King Lear* (1783), *Macbeth* (1784), *King John* (1791), and *Othello* (1792). In *Othello*, the actor François Joseph Talma achieved one of his greatest triumphs. Today, Ducis's adaptations of Shakespeare seem mere perversions, but had he done less, Shakespeare would perhaps never have been acted on the French stage. From his versions, as well as from the criticism of Voltaire, a knowledge of Shakespeare—such as it was—spread to Italy and eastern Europe. English actors performing Shakespeare were hissed on the Parisian stage in 1822, but, after a visit to France of Charles Kemble, Edmund Kean, and William Charles Macready in 1827-8, the standard plays found their way even into the repertory of the Théâtre Français, Sarah Bernhardt playing Lady Macbeth and Hamlet, and Monnet Sully playing Hamlet. Shakespeare, however, is not congenial to the French, and even the version of *Hamlet*, made in 1847 by Alexandre Dumas and Paul Meurice and long standard on the French stage, originally had a happy ending. In Italy, such players as Madame Ristori, Eleanora Duse, Tommasso Salvini, and Ernesto Rossi have acted Shakespearean roles. For the French and the Italians, however, the Shakespearean drama has been a fruitful source of operas or symphonic music.

SHAKESPEARE IN AMERICA

In America, the first recorded performance of Shakespeare was Cibber's *Richard III*, produced by a company of actors headed by Thomas Kean and Walter Murray in Nassau Street, New York City, on March 5, 1750. Thirteen plays of Shakespeare were in the repertory of the American Company headed by the English actor Lewis Hallam, which acted at various times in such centres as Williamsburg, Charleston, Annapolis, Philadelphia, and New York, from 1752 to 1775. Occasionally, as many as nine of the better known dramas were produced in a single season. Occasionally, too, because of moral objections, the players, familiar with subterfuge in the minor theatres of London, had to disguise their offerings. In Puritan New England (1761), *Othello* became "A Moral Dialogue in Five Parts, Depicting the Evil Effects of Jealousy and Other Bad Passions," while in Quaker Philadelphia, between the parts of a concert, there was delivered (gratis) "A Serious Historical Lecture, in Five Parts, on the Fate of Tyranny, Exemplified in the Life and Character of King Richard III" (1788). After the Revolution—during which Shakespeare's plays were occasionally performed by both the British and the

American troops—Shakespeare was again produced with frequency. For a time, at the beginning of the new century, his plays constituted as much as a quarter of the entire repertory. Moreover, Shakespeare accompanied the young nation on its pioneering, and performances of his plays in the frontier settlements were numerous. Quite early, also, English stars visited America, always with a repertory that was largely Shakespearean. George Frederick Cooke, Edmund Kean, Junius Brutus Booth, Charles and Fanny Kemble, William Charles Macready, Charles Kean, Henry Irving, Johnston Forbes-Robertson—all visited the United States and Canada, frequently on tour. As a result, particularly toward the end of the nineteenth century, when travel became a pleasure rather than a risk, English stars, like Henry Irving, Ellen Terry, Forbes-Robertson, and Mrs. Patrick Campbell, were as well known in America as at home. In turn, American actors, like John Drew II, Ada Rehan, and Mary Anderson, were as famous in London as in New York.

It will be possible here to name only a few of the more distinguished American players who have achieved fame as interpreters of Shakespeare. One of the earliest was the impassioned, muscular Edwin Forrest (1806–72) (see illustration, p. 459), who first played subordinate roles with Edmund Kean and is best known for his impersonation of Spartacus in Robert Montgomery Bird's *The Gladiator*. Forrest encouraged American playwrights, but he was also seen in Shakespeare's more turbulent roles—Richard III, Lear, Macbeth. In 1836, he visited England, playing at Covent Garden and touring the provinces. Charlotte Cushman (1816–76), also a melodramatic player, began as a singer, but turned to the drama as Lady Macbeth at the Bowery Theatre, New York, in 1836. (See illustration, p. 458.) She has the distinction of being one of the few actresses who have essayed the roles of Shakespeare's heroes. With her sister Susan, she played *Romeo and Juliet* (1845); later she played *Hamlet* (1842–52) and Cardinal Wolsey in *Henry VIII* (1857). E. L. Davenport (1816–77) also began acting in 1836. In 1846, he played Romeo to the Juliet of Anna Cora Mowatt (1819–70) and accompanied her to England in 1847.

The greatest American actor, however, was Edwin Booth (1833–93), the son of the gifted, but erratic, Junius Brutus Booth. While still in his teens, he began playing Richard III in 1849, became famous as Hamlet, traveled in England (where he was not popular), and returned to New York, where, beginning in 1863, he produced Shakespeare with magnificence at the Winter Garden Theatre. In *Julius Cæsar* (1864), the roles of Cassius, Mark Antony, and Brutus were taken by three brothers—Junius Brutus Jr., John Wilkes, and Edwin. In 1865, after the mad act of John Wilkes Booth, Edwin withdrew from the stage and returned only on the insistence of his public. In 1867, the Winter Garden Theatre was destroyed by fire, and Booth built his own playhouse, which he opened with *Romeo and Juliet* in 1869 and devoted to Shakespearean productions of so splendid a nature that he became bankrupt in 1874. As an actor, Booth had the limitations of his age, but his Hamlet and Iago are believed to be unsurpassed.

The most magnificent American productions of Shakespeare's comedies, though often at the expense of the text, were those of Augustin Daly (1838–99). A dramatist, but not an actor, Daly was manager first of the Fifth Avenue Theatre (1869) and then of Daly's in New York (1879) and Daly's in London (1893). A conscientious producer of high artistic standards, he gathered one of the ablest companies of actors ever assembled, including Fanny Davenport (1850–98), who was distinguished as a light comedienne; Adelaide Neilson (1846–80), who was a favorite as Viola, Imogen, Rosalind, and Juliet; Ada Rehan (1860–1916), still considered the greatest Katharine the Shrew (see illustration, p. 460); John Drew II (1853–1927), an excellent Benedick; and Viola Allen (1869–1948), attractive as Viola in *Twelfth Night*, other comedy roles, like that of Mistress Ford in *The Merry Wives*, and as Lady Macbeth in the company of J. K. Hackett.

Other actors who produced Shakespeare in America and who deserve mention are Lawrence Barrett (1838–91), Booth's manager, who toured with him as co-star in Shakespearean repertory; Robert Mantell (1854–1928), the last of the old school of vigorous Shakespearean actors, but for many years the only one who toured the country in Shakespeare's plays; E. H. Sothern (1859–1933) and Julia Marlowe (1866–   ), noted for their romantic interpretations of the better known plays; Richard Mansfield (1857–1907), and Walter Hampden (1879–   ), who, from 1916 on, was the most active exponent of Shakespearean repertory in the twentieth century.

THE TWENTIETH CENTURY

Since 1900, Shakespearean producers have tried in various ways to break with the traditions of the past under which, all too frequently, Shakespeare spelled ruin in a costly production dominated by a single star performer. Hence, there grew up, in England particularly, companies of actors, like that led by Sir F. R. Benson (1858–1939), that at the "Old Vic" in London, and that at the Memorial Theatre in Stratford, trained to perform Shakespeare adequately with a maximum of text and a minimum of scenery and with the emphasis upon the whole production rather than upon the individual star.

Another movement, represented by the Elizabethan Stage Society (1895), William Poel (1852–1934), and Sir Philip Ben Greet (1857–1936) has been in the direction of even greater simplicity. The ideal of these producers is to reconstruct in a hall or some other kind of auditorium so far as possible an actual replica of the Elizabethan stage, and to produce Shakespeare on a platform with no scenery except a curtain, and with texts that are uncut.[10] Several of Shakespeare's plays, including *Henry V*, *Twelfth Night*, and *Hamlet*, were so produced either by the Elizabethan Stage Society or another. A favorite with the Ben Greet Players was a production in this manner of the First Quarto of *Hamlet* (1603). For the average theatre audience, the plan is somewhat academic and precious, but it has enabled the minority interested in the history of the stage to understand at least approximately the spirit of Elizabethan performance and the pleasure of a rapid, continuous play. In 1912, the Earl's Court Theatre in London was reconstructed for a performance of *The Merchant of Venice*, and, about the same time, the Maddermarket Theatre in Norwich was built with a platform stage. In America, the experiment has been tried in a few of the universities, notably at Harvard.

A third movement is that of the "new" symbolic staging with its simplification of scene and its application to Shakespeare. Suggestion rather than complete realization is its ideal. By the pictorial use of light and shade, simple block sets, symbolic forms, and differing planes for differing dramatic actions, the "new" scene designers have sought to create or to assist in creating a suitable mood for the play. Its principal advocates have been Gordon Craig in England and Norman Bel Geddes and Robert Edmond Jones in America.

If these various new movements have resulted in no notable productions of the plays, the principal advantage has been to provide the theatre with a modern approximation to the simplicity and freedom of the Elizabethan stage and to familiarize both producers and audiences with a rapid, loosely localized performance. Experiments have likewise led to the production of plays not often acted. On the other hand, they have led to a search for a way of producing Shakespeare that will be unconventional, even if it is nothing else, such as the productions in "modern dress" of the late 1920's and early 1930's. With the justification that Shakespeare and his producers for two centuries had paid no attention to historical accuracy in dress, audiences who did not share the convention were treated to the incongruity of hearing Elizabethan blank verse spoken by a Hamlet in plus-fours, smoking a cigarette; a Petruchio in the outfit of a Western cowboy, transporting his bride in a motorcycle sidecar; a Macbeth in khaki and a trench helmet; or a Falstaff who suggested a barroom rounder (see illustration, p. 467). It is one of the highest tributes to Shakespeare's verse that audiences at such productions occasionally forgot the absurdity and listened to the poetry. In their ideal form, the modern-dress productions did throw the emphasis upon Shakespeare's lines

---

[10] In 1844 and again in 1846, Benjamin Webster produced *The Taming of the Shrew*, uncut, before a simple curtain, without scenery and everything that was then thought essential to the proper presentation of Shakespeare. But these productions were merely ineffective experiments.

and not upon an eye-filling costume, but that was not their purpose. Anyway, Shakespeare's universality cannot be proved by treating his Elizabethan plays as if they were modern.

In general, it may be said that the twentieth-century actor prefers a single special production of Shakespeare, or at most a few productions, to a whole repertory. John Barrymore (1882–1942) appeared in *Richard III*, Cibber's version (1920), and *Hamlet* (1922), the latter a somewhat Goethean interpretation; David Warfield in *The Merchant of Venice* (1922) (see illustration, p. 465); Jane Cowl in *Romeo and Juliet* (1923), *Antony and Cleopatra* (1924), and *Twelfth Night* (1930), the latter an unusually effective experiment in simplified staging; Otis Skinner in *The Merry Wives of Windsor* with Minnie Maddern Fiske and Henrietta Crosman (1925); Lyn Harding and Florence Reed in *Macbeth* (1928), with settings by Gordon Craig; Raymond Massey in *Hamlet* (1931), a production more notable for its Norman Bel Geddes settings than in its interpretation of the play, the ghost being subjective; Katharine Cornell in *Romeo and Juliet* (1935); Alfred Lunt and Lynn Fontanne in *The Taming of the Shrew* (1935); and John Gielgud, Laurence Olivier, and Peggy Ashcroft in *Romeo and Juliet* (1935). During the winter of 1936, New York was treated to contrasting Hamlets in the productions of Leslie Howard and John Gielgud, while, in 1937, Maurice Evans's New York production of *Richard II*, directed by Margaret Webster (see illustration, p. 468), was rivaled by that of John Gielgud in London. More recently, the stage has seen a Cæsar and a Cassius in the uniforms of a modern Fascist state (New York, Mercury Theatre, 1937), a Cressida in a luxury flat (London, Westminster Theatre, 1938), and a musical version of *The Comedy of Errors*, entitled *The Boys from Syracuse* (New York, 1938, and on the screen, 1940). Then, late in 1939, New York was regaled for a short time by *Swingin' the Dream*, not a motion picture but a musical variation of *A Midsummer Night's Dream*, reset in nineteenth-century New Orleans. The book was by Gilbert Seldes and Erik Charell, with reorchestration of the traditional incidental score by Felix Mendelssohn, plus additional music by Jimmy Van Heusen and others. There were two orchestras, led by Benny Goodman and Bud Freeman, with Don Voorhees as general director, and a cast which included Louis Armstrong as Bottom (in a fireman's outfit), Maxine Sullivan as Titania, Butterfly McQueen as the Puck, Billy Bailey the dancer, and a whole corps of jitterbugging Harlem Rhythmettes. Thus Shakespeare provided mirth for a Mardi gras carnival. There had been no adaptation like this since the seventeenth century. Other recent versions in the movies have been *A Midsummer Night's Dream*, a lavish, but badly cast and generally unsuccessful, production by Max Reinhardt (1935); *Romeo and Juliet*, with Leslie Howard and Norma Shearer (1936); *As You Like It*, with Laurence Olivier and Elisabeth Bergner (1937), *Henry V* (1943) and *Hamlet* (1948), the last two starring Laurence Olivier, who, since 1946, has been Sir Laurence Olivier (see illustration, p. 469).

The most notable productions on the New York stage in recent years have been those directed by Margaret Webster and starring various actors: an uncut *Hamlet* with Maurice Evans as the prince and Mady Christians as Queen Gertrude (1938); *1 Henry IV*, with Maurice Evans as Falstaff (1939); *Twelfth Night*, with Maurice Evans as Malvolio and Helen Hayes as Viola (1940); *Macbeth*, with Maurice Evans and Judith Anderson (1941); *Othello*, with the Negro actor Paul Robeson as the Moor, José Ferrer as Iago, and Uta Hagen as Desdemona (1943); and *The Tempest*, with the ballet dancer Vera Zorina as Ariel, Arnold Moss as Prospero, and the Negro actor Canada Lee as Caliban (1945). During 1946–7, the same director was the moving spirit of the American Repertory Company, founded by Eva Le Gallienne, Walter Hampden, Ernest Truex, Victor Jory, and Richard Waring, in a series of classics, among them *Henry VIII*, a play seldom seen on the modern stage.

In 1946, *The Winter's Tale* was produced by the Theatre Guild Shakespearean Company, with Henry Daniell, Florence Reed, and Jessie Royce Landis under the direction of B. Iden Payne and Romney Brent. In Paris, also in 1946, the distinguished French actor, Jean Louis Barrault, appeared as Hamlet in a new translation of the play by André Gide. In 1948, *Antony and Cleopatra* was produced by Guthrie McClintic with Katharine Cornell as the queen and Godfrey Tearle as Antony. In the same season, *Macbeth* was produced with Michael Redgrave and Flora Robson, on leave from the movies. With much rearrangement, cutting, and rewriting, the same play went Hollywood in the hands of Orson Welles (1948). In 1949, there was Richard Whorf's short-lived *Richard III*, with Shakespeare's text instead of the more usual Cibber adaptation. In the same year, Shakespeare also succumbed to the vogue of the musical in *Kiss Me Kate* (an adaptation of *The Taming of the Shrew* with tunes by Cole Porter).

During the war, Shakespeare held his own as entertainment both in the British and the American fields of operation. Most notable of the productions given his plays was the "G. I. *Hamlet*" presented with G. I. actors by Maurice Evans, a major in the Army Special Services in charge of entertainment in the Central Pacific area. Compared to more traditional conceptions, this *Hamlet*, costumed in whatever was handy, had an air of romantic melodrama and portrayed the prince as a rough and ready extrovert capable of holding the attention of audiences of men, a considerable number of whom had never seen a play on the stage before. In the same category, one should mention again the spectacular and moving technicolor version of *Henry V*, alluded to above, with Laurence Olivier as Henry and Renée Asherson as Princess Katharine. Produced during the war, this film was first shown to troops in all of the theatres of operation and released for exhibition in the United States in 1946.

An interesting experiment, akin to the unsatisfied longings of the Romantic critics to know more about Shakespeare's creatures and their stories than the dramatist had seen fit to tell, prompted a tetralogy of plays on the background of *Hamlet*. The whole was entitled *The Mystery of Hamlet, King of Denmark; or What We Will*, written by Percy Mackaye and produced at the Pasadena Playhouse on four successive nights in April and May of 1949. "What may this mean," asks Shakespeare's Hamlet of his father's ghost,

> That thou, pale corse, again in complete steel
> Revisit'st thus the glimpses of the moon,
> Making night hideous, and we fools of nature
> So horridly to shake our disposition
> With thoughts beyond the reaches of our souls?
> Say, why is this? Wherefore? What should we do?
>   (I, iv, 51–57.)

Mackaye's plays offer an answer to these questions in terms of the theatre by setting forth events and conflicts supposedly shared by the chief persons of Shakespeare's tragedy in the thirty years preceding the death of the King and his reappearance as a ghost on the ramparts of Elsinore. Part I, entitled *The Ghost of Elsinore*, presents events thirty years before Shakespeare's *Hamlet*; Part II, *The Fool in Eden Garden*, treats happenings seven years later; Part III, *Odin Against Christus*, is set twenty-two years later than Part II; and Part IV, *The Serpent in the Orchard*, follows immediately upon Part III.

Meanwhile, at the "Old Vic" in London, in the Open Air Theatre in Regent's Park, at the Memorial Theatre in Stratford, war or no war, Shakespeare's plays continued in popular repertory. Bombed out of the Victoria Theatre in 1941, the "Old Vic" Company was reorganized in 1944, and toured the United States in 1946. Under the leadership of Donald Wolfitt, another company of English actors also visited the United States in the same season. No other author in the world's literature is so much alive on the modern stage.

SUGGESTED REFERENCES

COHN, ALBERT. *Shakespeare in Germany in the Sixteenth and Seventeenth Centuries: An Account of English Actors in Germany and the Netherlands, and of the Plays Produced by Them during that Period.* London, Asher and Company, 1865.
    Contains the texts of several adaptations of Shakespeare's plays.
KILBOURNE, FREDERICK W. *Alterations and Adaptations of Shakespeare.* Boston, The Poet Lore Press, 1906.

ODELL, GEORGE C. D. *Shakespeare from Betterton to Irving* (2 vols.). New York, Scribner, 1920.

Shakespeare on the English stage since the Restoration.

Shakespeare Adaptations: The Tempest, The Mock Tempest, and King Lear. With an Introduction and Notes by Montague Summers. London, Jonathan Cape, 1922.

SPENCER, HAZELTON. *Shakespeare Improved: The Restoration Versions in Quarto and on the Stage.* Cambridge, Harvard University Press, 1927.

SPRAGUE, ARTHUR COLBY. *Shakespeare and the Actors: The Stage Business in His Plays, 1660–1905.* Cambridge, Harvard University Press, 1945.

WEBSTER, MARGARET. *Shakespeare without Tears.* New York, Whittlesey House, 1941.

WINTER, WILLIAM. *Shakespeare on the Stage.* Three Series, New York, Moffat, Yard, 1911–16.

Interesting as reminiscence.

GENERAL BIBLIOGRAPHICAL NOTE

In addition to the titles listed by chapter, the reader will find the following volumes of interest:

BATESON, F. W. (ed.). *The Cambridge Bibliography of English Literature* (4 vols.). Cambridge University Press, 1941.

"The Drama," I, 487 ff.; "William Shakespeare," I, 539–608.

EBISCH, WALTHER *and* SCHÜCKING, LEVIN L. *A Shakespeare Bibliography.* Oxford, Clarendon Press, 1931.

A classified selected list, heavily foreign.

——. *Supplement for the Years 1930–1935.* Oxford, Clarendon Press, 1937.

JAGGARD, WILLIAM. *Shakespeare Bibliography. A Dictionary of Every Known Issue of the Writings of Our National Poet and of Recorded Opinion thereon in the English Language.* Stratford-on-Avon, The Shakespeare Press, 1911.

729 double-columned pages; 36,000 distinct entries arranged in an author, subject, title index. Difficult to use.

SHAKESPEAREAN SCENES

AND CHARACTERS

It is a pretty mocking of the life.
Here is a touch. Is't good. . . .
                  I will say of it,
It tutors nature. Artificial strife
Lives in these touches, livelier than life.
                  —Timon of Athens, i, i, 35 ff.

THERE IS NO BETTER WAY OF CONVEYING COM-
pletely both the substance and the spirit of much that has been described in
the foregoing pages without the aid of pictures. The illustrations which follow constitute a carefully selected supplement to the text. In these scenes
from Shakespeare's plays as they have been conceived by engravers and
painters, in the portraits of popular actors and actresses, and in the glimpses
of notable stage productions the reader can perceive how each generation has
interpreted its favorite playwright and given his work its characteristic stamp
of approval. Shakespeare in modern dress is nothing new, nor has a plea ever
been necessary for the liberty of interpreting.

Some of these illustrations are well-known; most are being reproduced here
for the first time. Supplementing the scenes and portraits are several, like the
photographs of the Globe Theatre model, which are placed here rather than
elsewhere in the volume, because of the requirements of half-tone reproduction. Full bibliographical and other details as to the sources of these pictures will be found in the List of Illustrations on p. vii.

A Model of the Globe Theatre

Anthony Van Dyck: Sir John Suckling as a Poet (see p. 379). *Copyright, The Frick Collection, New York*

TOP: Scenes from *The Taming of the Shrew* and *Othello*. Rowe's edition, 1709
BOTTOM: Scenes from *Antony and Cleopatra* and *The Tempest*. Theobald's edition, 1733

Sir John Falstaff and His Companions at Gad's Hill, 1736

·[443]·

TOP: Scenes from *Twelfth Night* and *The Merchant of Venice*. Hanmer's edition, 1743–44
BOTTOM: Edward Shuter, Peg Woffington, and George Anne Bellamy in *The Merry Wives*, 1756
Spranger Barry and Miss Nossiter in *Romeo and Juliet*, 1759

David Garrick in Four of His Principal Tragic Characters

Characters represented are: Mistress Ford, Bardolph, Falstaff *(Merry Wives);* Ancient Pistol *(Henry V);* Hecate and the Witches *(Macbeth);* Slender *(Merry Wives);* Poor Tom *(King Lear);* Richard III; The Ghost *(Hamlet);*

The Procession of Shakespeare's Characters at the Jubilee at Stratford-upon-Avon, 1769

Miss P. Hopkins as Lavinia *(Titus Andronicus)* and Mrs. Yates as Isabella *(Measure for Measure).* Bell's edition, 1774

The Gravedigger (*Hamlet*); Friar Laurence and Romeo (*Romeo and Juliet*); Orlando and Rosalind? (*As You Like It*); The Apothecary (*Romeo and Juliet*); Shylock and Antonio (*Merchant of Venice*); Katherine of Arragon, Henry VIII, and Cardinal Wolsey (*Henry VIII*)

The Procession of Shakespeare's Characters at the Jubilee at Stratford-upon-Avon, 1769

BOTTOM: Mr. Dod as Mercutio and Mr. Bensley as Iago. Bell's edition, 1774

TOP: Mr. Kemble as Hamlet and Mr. Macklin as Shylock. Bell's edition, 1793
BOTTOM: Mr. Lewis as Prince Hal and Mr. Holmes as Faulconbridge. Bell's edition, 1793

TOP: Miss Stuart as Joan la Pucelle (*1 Henry VI*) and Mrs. Siddons as Lady Macbeth. Bell's edition, 1793

BOTTOM: Mrs. Pope as Cleopatra and Mrs. Abington as Rosalind. Bell's edition, 1793

TOP: Scenes from *Macbeth* and *Much Ado*. A Dutch translation, 1776–82
BOTTOM: Herr Brockmann and Mlle. Doebbelin as Hamlet and Ophelia, c. 1776
"O'erstep not the Modesty of Nature": David Garrick and Shakespeare's
Characters

TOP: Robert Smirke: Scene from *Much Ado*
BOTTOM: William Hamilton: Scene from *The Winter's Tale*
(THE BOYDELL GALLERY)

Juliet and Nurse

TOP: Matthew William Peters: Scene from *The Merry Wives*
George Romney: Cassandra: Scene from *Troilus and Cressida*
(THE BOYDELL GALLERY)
BOTTOM: *Romeo and Juliet* in the Juvenile Theatre, 1823

Tinsel Portraits of Popular Actors, c. 1850: Mr. Mead as Hotspur, Mr. Anderson as Macbeth, Mr. Phelps as Sir John Falstaff, and Mr. Marston as Prince Henry

Edmund Kean as Richard III, c. 1820

Scenes from Charles Kean's Production of *The Winter's Tale*, Princess Theatre, 1856

·[455]·

TOP: George Cruikshank: Falstaff Enacting the Part of the King (*1 Henry IV*), 1857
BOTTOM: Scene from *Antony and Cleopatra*, Drury Lane, 1873

John Gilbert: The Trial of Katherine of Arragon, 1859

TOP: Charlotte Cushman as *Lady Macbeth*
BOTTOM: Edward Grützner: Selective Service in Gloucestershire: Falstaff and His Recruits, 1876

TOP: Edwin Forrest as King Lear and Macbeth
BOTTOM: Mr. Fleming as Edgar and W. C. MacCready as Shylock

John Drew and Ada Rehan as Petruchio and Katherina in Augustin Daly's Production, 1887. *Courtesy of the New York Public Library*

Ellen Terry as Portia, 1887

Sir Johnston Forbes-Robertson as Hamlet, 1907. *Courtesy New York Public Library*

TOP: Scene from *Macbeth* as Presented in Bombay, c. 1910. *Courtesy New York Public Library*

BOTTOM: Edwin Austin Abbey: King Lear. *Courtesy Metropolitan Museum of Art, N. Y.*

H. Beerbohm Tree and Phyllis Neilson-Terry in *Othello*, 1912

David Warfield as Shylock in David Belasco's Production, 1922

Romeo and Juliet at the Kamerny Theatre, Moscow, c. 1925

Shakespeare in Modern Dress: Oscar Asche as Falstaff in *The Merry Wives*, 1929

TOP: Scene from *Cymbeline* in B. Iden Payne's Production, 1937. *Courtesy B. Iden Payne*
BOTTOM: Maurice Evans and Ian Keith in *Richard II* in the Margaret Webster Production, 1937

Scenes from the Laurence Olivier
Productions of *Henry V* released
through *United Artists* (1945) and
Hamlet released through *Universal
Pictures* (1948)

Shakespeare on Television: Scene from *Julius Caesar* at the Folger Library, 1949. *Courtesy the Socony-Vacuum Oil Co.*

INDEX